BUSINESS AND SOCIETY

McGRAW-HILL SERIES IN MANAGEMENT

Keith Davis, Consulting Editor

BUSINESS AND SOCIETY: ENVIRONMENT AND RESPONSIBILITY

KEITH DAVIS, Ph.D
Arizona State University

ROBERT L. BLOMSTROM, Ph.D.
Michigan State University

THIRD EDITION

McGRAW-HILL BOOK COMPANY

New York St. Louis San Francisco Düsseldorf
Johannesburg Kuala Lumpur London Mexico
Montreal New Delhi Panama Paris
São Paulo Singapore Sydney Tokyo Toronto

To
Sue
and
Marge

BUSINESS AND SOCIETY:
Environment and Responsibility

890 DODO 79

This book was set in Times Roman by Creative Book Services, division of
McGregor & Werner, Inc. The editors were Thomas H. Kothman and
Joseph F. Murphy; the designer was Joseph Gillians; the production super-
visor was Thomas J. LoPinto.

Library of Congress Cataloging in Publication Data

Davis, Keith, date
    Business and society.

  First ed. (1966) published under title: Business and its environment; 2d
ed. (1971) under title: Business, society, and environment.
    Bibliography: p.
    1. Industry—Social aspects. I. Blomstrom, Robert L., joint
author. II. Title.
HD60.D3   1975   658.4'08   74-14713
ISBN 0-07-015524-0

CONTENTS

PREFACE

The earth is traveling through space at a high rate of speed, and changes within the whole social system on the earth seem to be moving about as fast. If business wishes to remain viable and potent in its role as a major social institution, it needs to be flexible and relate to these new conditions. That is what this book is all about. It seeks to relate business to its external culture, that is, to the whole social system. It takes a system point of view, relating business to ecology, pluralism, and social power. Hopefully, the discussion also is challenging and constructive, showing how mankind's institutions work together to achieve a better *quality of life* for all of us.

It is a myth to think that we understand business just because we see business in operation every day. Experience shows that many people know about its *practices,* but too few know and understand its *social role* and *relationships*. In this book we hope to challenge the reader to give more thought to these latter items.

We have designed this book for college students, business managers, and others interested in institutions in our society. In universities and colleges the book is suitable for courses in Business Policy, Business and Society, Social Responsibility of Business, Social Issues in Business, and related courses. We have sought to present illustrations, problems, and cases to make ideas more meaningful and practical. We have also tried to achieve a readable style, avoiding the technical language of specialized volumes written for one particular discipline. Another objective has been to include a discussion of multinational business in order to show how the concepts we are developing apply to global business sytems.

We are grateful to many people who have helped with this book. Without them we could not have completed it. We especially thank several of our colleagues who have discussed these ideas with us and provided critical comment for different chapters of the book. The administrative support of Deans Glenn D. Overman and Kullervo Louhi and Dr. Harold E. Fearon has been encouraging. We also appreciate the typing assistance of Mrs. Patricia Welch. Finally, we are grateful to our wives for their encouragement and assistance.

We hope the result will be worthwhile to you, the reader.

Keith Davis
Robert L. Blomstrom

PART 1

THE INTERFACE
OF BUSINESS
AND SOCIETY

BUSINESS IN A SOCIAL WORLD

Business leadership does not end at the plant gate, and business leaders cannot insulate themselves from those responsibilities that do not bear directly on profit.

Charles B. McCoy[1]

What we seek is not a problem-free society but a problem-solving society. . . .

Herbert D. Doan[2]

As twilight settled over a suburban Maryland community, the president of a small wholesaling firm talked in quiet tones with his sales vice-president. They were trying to decide what to do next with an alcoholic salesman. On earlier occasions they had warned him and referred him to a community agency, which he refused to see, but his problem had persisted until it was seriously affecting sales in his district. Was his work a precipitate cause of his problem? Should more corrective action be tried? What action?

Not many miles away in a high-ceilinged government office, three administrators with the National Aeronautics and Space Administration were implementing a program change that required a private contractor to lay off or transfer some three hundred men. They knew that the change was unexpected and would materially affect the economy of a community near the work site. What standards of action should be expected of the contractor in this situation? What standards would he actually apply? Would he cause political repercussions for this sensitive government activity? Was this situation a joint contractor-NASA responsibility?

Across the Atlantic in Africa the general manager of a British subsidiary tossed restlessly in his bed, wondering whether to reduce prices of a retail product in an overpriced, semicartelized market. With his new production facilities he was sure he had the lowest costs in the country and could win any price war that

---

[1]Charles B. McCoy, quoted in *Company and Community,* Wilmington, Del.: E. I. du Pont de Nemours & Company, n.d., p. 33.

[2]Herbert D. Doan, "Controlling Society's Weeds," *Chemical Engineering Progress,* May 1969, p. 30.

developed. Competitive economics dictated a price cut, but from the *total view* would this decision be wise? How would the community and government react to a price war? How would his labor union react if he caused layoffs of its members in competitors' plants? What about effects on investors in native plants of this capital-poor country if he bankrupted a few native businesses in this price war?

The three incidents just discussed represent only a moment in time in a day involving thousands of similar decisions concerning business and society. Each new day brings thousands more new decisions, and so does the next—and the next. Businessmen throughout the world are busily trying to make socioeconomic systems function effectively, and they continually face decisions involving the social system outside the firm.

This "world beyond the company gate" is the subject of this book. This subject is generally called *business and society,* and it is defined as *the relationship of business with the social system outside its own formal organization.* This book is, in short, a study of social relationships from the reference point of business: How does business affect society, and how does society affect business in our modern, complex world? How can each live with the other so that the potential benefits of each may be received? Although this discussion will focus on business's relation with society, the ideas presented apply also to other institutions in their relationships with society. All institutions need to relate responsibly with the world beyond themselves.

A MOVE TOWARD SOCIAL CONCERN

Modern society presents business with immensely complicated problems that it did not have formerly. One hundred years ago the three incidents mentioned at the beginning of this chapter would hardly have been relevant to a business discussion. Societal relationships in those days were simpler than they are today, and even the meager complexities that did exist were usually overlooked. Decisions were clear-cut. If a man could not perform his work (the alcoholic incident), dismiss him; if a contract was canceled, lay off the men; and if you can do so, price your competitor out of the market. Each action was considered "in the public interest" because of its favorable effect on costs and prices according to the invisible hand of economic competition originally described by Adam Smith in 1776.[3] If matters of social concern were raised, a suitable answer was the "Bah! Humbug!" of Ebenezer Scrooge in Charles Dickens's *A Christmas Carol.*

Beginning in the 1950s there was a sharp shift in public mood toward more social concern, and this mood was reflected in extensive social demands the public made on its institutions. Since business interacts with much of society, perhaps more of these demands were made on business than any other institution. Historically business has seen its mission as an economic one, and by sticking strictly to

[3]Adam Smith, *An Inquiry into the Nature and Causes of the Wealth of Nations* (1776), New York: Modern Library, Inc., 1937, p. 423.

its economic role it had left the social side of its activities largely untended. The result was that it was vulnerable to this new area of demand.

There are many reasons for the new social conscience which the public developed, but certainly one of the fundamental ones was that society had solved most of its economic problems arising from the Depression of the 1930s, so it was ready to move on to new ground. With economic problems minimally out of the way, social problems became more visible. In essence the abounding success of the economic machine had created an affluence which released society from economic bondage and allowed it to turn to other challenges. The most visible challenges were the social issues such as urban blight, disadvantaged people, ecology, and equality of opportunity. This reason and other reasons for the change in mood will be discussed in later chapters, but at this point the important idea is that there were valid reasons for the public shift in attitudes. It was more than a fickle swing of emotions or a chance happening.

An Age of Discontinuity

The demands made on business are part of a larger series of changes occurring throughout the social system. Many difficult problems are arising because of very rapid change which is upsetting the delicate equilibrium in our complex society. It is clearly a system relationship in which social, educational, technological, and other types of change are closely interwoven. Change increases the disequilibrium among various elements of society, thereby increasing the friction among them. This condition, in turn, requires much larger inputs of effort, resources, and knowledge in order to restore effective harmony in the system.

Our modern civilization, according to Peter Drucker, is experiencing more than an age of routine change. It is passing through an *age of discontinuity* in which change is so severe that it will create whole new institutions and significantly alter existing institutions. The four most significant discontinuities are:[4]

1. Technological innovations such as the computer and television, which are having major effects not only on business but on the whole society

2. Development of a world economy of one market but without suitable institutions for handling it, with the one exception of the multinational corporation

3. A pluralistic social system in which social tasks are mostly entrusted to large institutions

4. Most important of all, a knowledge revolution which has made knowledge the crucial resource of society

Each of these ideas will be discussed further in our book to show how they are affecting the relationship of business and society.

[4]Peter F. Drucker, *The Age of Discontinuity: Guidelines to Our Changing Society,* New York: Harper & Row, Publishers, Incorporated, 1968.

An Example: Jet Air Travel

Consider the changes wrought by one small part of the technological revolution—jet air travel. With jet air transportation, people from around the world have been brought into frequent contact. They begin to see the strengths and weaknesses of their own communities and nations and to increase pressures for change therein. At the same time the simple fact of their travel gives cause for new international business to service them with rental cars, hotels, transportation, airports, and similar facilities. Whole new areas have been opened to large numbers of tourists, such as Hawaii, the South Pacific, and the Caribbean. In turn, these areas experience a new economic outlook, changes in real estate values, higher capital and educational needs, and other developments.

In some cities jet aircraft have significantly altered the demography and business practices of a city. Formerly the downtown area was the business center, having developed around a railroad or port because it was the hub of commerce in earlier days. Now the downtown area is decaying, and often the hub of activity is centering near the airport and near freeways which are conveniently located to it. An example is the substantial expansion of hotels, business offices, and manufacturing on both sides of the Los Angeles International Airport.

We have been considering only a few of the "ripples" in the lake of civilization made by one development—jet air travel. When the world's many other changes are combined with this one, we begin to see the massiveness of forces tending toward disequilibrium. Each of these changes is interfacing with most or all of the others, making new demands upon old institutions, upsetting the relationships among institutions, and even creating needs for new institutions. How in this immensely complex situation can society maintain and enlarge the desirable values of life, such as justice, equality, freedom, and virtue? The task is a massive one.

A Call for Greater Social Responsibility

Insofar as the changing public mood applies to business, it is insisting upon a greater social conscience, social concern, and social responsibility. The idea of *social responsibility* is that decision makers are obligated to take actions which protect and improve the welfare of society as a whole along with their own interests. The net effect is to enhance the quality of life in the broadest possible way, however the quality of life is defined by society. In this way harmony is achieved between business's actions and society's wants. The businessman acts in a manner that will accomplish social benefits along with the traditional economic gains which the firm seeks. He becomes concerned with social outputs as well as

Business Concern for Social Issues Is Developing Too Slowly

A number of critics feel that business is not moving fast enough into social concern and social responsibility. Following is one of these critics' comments.

> Business, in its daily conduct, reflects a disconcerting insensitivity to changing public demands and expectations. The lethargic response of the auto companies and of the oil companies to matters of pollution and safety are leading examples. As contrasted to its leadership in technology, business's habits and conservatism dictate that it merely be responsive, and be dragged, heels dug in, into the new social values, rather than providing innovative leadership.
>
> Business responds in a piecemeal fashion and only to the critics who have enough power or enough nuisance value to enforce their demands. To put it differently, our institutions are impacted only by well-organized complaints by people who have clout. We are not yet grappling with the great issues now facing man, but are only involved in quieting the loud mouths. We are not thinking about the total way of life that is being reshaped, but rather are involved in making concessions and modifications to our status quo. Our managerial conscience is not yet adequately challenged or disturbed.

From Harold M. Williams, "The Challenge to Business," in George A. Steiner (ed.), *Selected Major Issues in Business' Role in Modern Society*, Los Angeles: Graduate School of Management, University of California at Los Angeles, 1973, pp. 7–8. Reprinted with permission.

economic outputs, and with the total effect of his economic and institutional actions on society.

The difference between social responsibility and traditional business decision making is that traditional decision makers confine themselves primarily to narrow economic and technical values, but social responsibility extends thinking to social values as well. It also requires thinking in terms of the whole social system, rather than the narrow interests of a single organization, group, or person. It is clearly a system way of thinking. In Chapters 2 and 3 we will discuss extensively the implications of this definition.

Areas of Social Responsibility Are Expanding

The widening circle of social responsibility is illustrated by Figure 1-1. The inner circle represents the traditional responsibility of business for its basic economic functions. This traditional responsibility has some social implications, such as the need to provide employment and to refrain from restraint of trade, but it is primarily an economic activity. The intermediate circle represents the widening area of responsibility that arises directly from performance of the basic economic functions. These responsibilities have quickly become significant and are represented by such issues as equal employment opportunity and prevention of pollution from business operations. The outer circle represents an area that is still

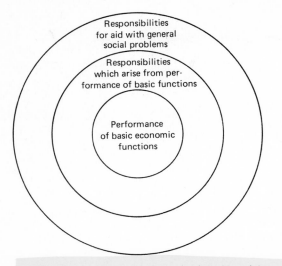

Figure 1-1 A widening circle for business's social responsibilities.

not well defined, but there is a rising public expectation for business to modify its singular pursuit of economic goals and help society with some of its unsolved general social problems. Business operations may not directly cause these problems, but they are indirectly involved in some instances; so the feeling is that since business is a major institution controlling major social resources, it should work as a corporate citizen to help society with its general social problems. Business will not have primary responsibility for solving these problems, but it should provide significant assistance. Examples are prevention of urban decay and training hard-core unemployed.

The extent of the intermediate and outer circles is represented by the following summary of areas of social involvement that have been proposed. It is clear from this list that society is proposing a significant change in the social contract between business and society. Society is asking business to engage in a broader range of social activities that serve a wider area of social needs. Emphasis is shifting from the economic quality of life to a more nebulous social quality of life.

Proposed areas of social involvement include the following:

Ecology and Environmental Quality
- Cleanup of existing pollution
- Design of processes to prevent pollution
- Aesthetic improvements
- Noise control
- Dispersion of industry
- Control of land use
- Required recycling

Consumerism
- Truth in lending, in advertising, and in all business activities
- Product warranty and service
- Control of harmful products

Community Needs
- Use of business expertise with community problems
- Reduction of business's role in community power structure
- Aid with health care facilities
- Aid with urban renewal

Governmental Relations
- Restrictions on lobbying
- Control of business political action
- Extensive new regulation of business
- Restrictions on international operations

Business Giving
- Financial support for artistic activities
- Gifts to education
- Financial support for assorted charities

Minorities and Disadvantaged Persons
- Training of hard-core unemployed
- Equal employment opportunity and quotas for minority employment
- Operation of programs for alcoholics and drug addicts
- Employment of persons with prison records
- Building of plants and offices in minority areas
- Purchasing from minority businessmen
- Retraining of workers displaced by technology

Labor Relations
- Improvement of occupational health and safety
- Prohibition of "export of jobs" through operations in nations with low labor costs
- Provision of day-care centers for children of working mothers
- Expansion of employee rights
- Control of pensions, especially vesting of pension rights
- Impatience with authoritarian structures; demand for participation

Stockholder Relations
- Opening of boards of directors to public members representing various interest groups
- Prohibition of operations in nations with "racist" or "colonial" governments
- Improvement of financial disclosure
- Disclosure of activities affecting the environment and social issues

Formulation of Corporate Social Policy Is a Major Activity

As a result of rising public expectations for business social responsibility, formulation of corporate social policy has become an activity of major importance. Following are the comments of one analyst.

The formulation of specific corporate social policy is as much a function of strategic planning as the choice of product and market combinations, the establishment of profit and growth objectives, or the choice of organization structure and systems for accomplishing corporate purposes.

Rather than wholly personal or idiosyncratic contributions (like supporting the museum one's wife is devoted to) or safe and sound contributions like the standard charities, or faddist entry into fashionable areas, corporate strategic response to societal needs and expectations makes sense when it is closely related to the economic functions of the company or to the peculiar problems of the community in which it operates.

From Kenneth R. Andrews, "Can the Best Corporations Be Made Moral?" *Harvard Business Review*, May–June 1973, p. 59. Reproduced with permission.

Economic Activities
- Control of conglomerates
- Breakup of giant industry
- Restriction of patent use

The broadened expectations of business represent a significant change in public attitudes toward business. Public attitudes are only one criterion for formulating social policy, but in a democratic society public attitudes tend to dominate in the long run; so business needs to respond to these expectations in some effective way. The response may be to argue that some of these proposals are not appropriate for business, but at least business needs to respond.

Origins of the Modern Social Responsibility Debate

Prior to the 1950s analysts wrote about business power and abuses as we shall discuss in Chapters 8 and 9, but the first definitive work on business social responsibility was published by Howard R. Bowen in 1953. This book represents the origin of the modern social responsibility debate. The book, titled *Social Responsibilities of the Businessman,* was devoted completely to the idea of social responsibility and how it might apply to business.[5] Bowen discussed the general social and economic benefits that might result from recognition of broader social goals in business decisions. The book provided remarkably good coverage of a subject that was rather undeveloped at that time. Part of its completeness resulted

[5]Howard R. Bowen, *Social Responsibilities of the Businessman,* New York: Harper & Brothers, 1953.

from the fact that it developed from a study group established by the Federal (now National) Council of Churches in 1949.

Following publication of the Bowen book, a number of other authors gave major attention to social responsibility, and the subject area gradually began to be defined.[6] In an early work Benjamin M. Selekman commented as follows:[7]

> The crisis which has led to concern about social responsibility is . . . complex. It stems from nothing less than the age-old problem of power—with its dangerous as well as its beneficent aspects. Not until businessmen recognize that they are the administrators of power systems can they face realistically the task of how to discharge morally the power they wield.

In 1961 a significant contribution to the theory of social responsibility was made by Eells and Walton in the *Conceputal Foundations of Business*. They described social responsibility as follows:[8]

> When people talk about corporate social responsibility they are thinking in terms of the problems that arise when corporate enterprise casts its shadow on the social scene, and of the ethical principles that ought to govern the relationships between the corporation and society. They are concerned with the impact of the corporation on the individual and the possibilities of reconciling big business, big labor, and big government with the values deeply rooted in our form of government. . . .

Meanwhile business's need for social concern became a popular topic in board rooms, study groups, and business meetings. Major universities added the topic to their executive programs. One of your authors taught the topic in one of the earliest courses in the University of California (Los Angeles) executive program at Lake Arrowhead in 1958. At first businessmen looked on the subject mostly as a curiosity, but gradually they began to recognize its significance. The first semipopular book on the subject, the kind of book read by businessmen, was published as *Business and Society* by Joseph W. McGuire in 1963.[9] The book developed from a series of popular television programs on the subject offered in the Pacific Northwest in 1962. Social responsibility issues were finally reaching the group that would have to implement them, the businessmen.

[6]For early examples see Adolph A. Berle, Jr., *Power Without Property*, New York: Harcourt, Brace & World, Inc., 1959; Edward S. Mason, *The Corporation in Modern Society*, Cambridge, Mass.: Harvard University Press, 1959; Earl F. Cheit (ed.), *The Business Establishment*, New York: John Wiley & Sons, Inc., 1964; William T. Greenwood (ed.), *Issues in Business and Society*, Boston: Houghton Mifflin Company, 1964; and the books mentioned in the next three footnotes.

[7]Benjamin M. Selekman in "Preface" to Sylvia K. Selekman and Benjamin M. Selekman, *Power and Morality in a Business Society*, New York: McGraw-Hill Book Company, 1956, p. vii. See also Benjamin M. Selekman, *A Moral Philosophy for Management*, New York: McGraw-Hill Book Company, 1959.

[8]Richard Eells and Clarence Walton, *Conceptual Foundations of Business*, Homewood, Ill.: Richard D. Irwin, Inc., 1961, pp. 457–458.

[9]Joseph W. McGuire, *Business and Society*, New York: McGraw-Hill Book Company, 1963.

BUSINESS IS PART OF A LARGER SOCIAL SYSTEM
A System Concept

The complex relationship of business to society becomes evident when expressed in terms of a system concept. The idea of system provides a means of understanding the dynamic variability of business's interactions with other parts of society. In an ultimate sense every action which business takes is related to the external world around it; and, in turn, everything which occurs in the external world is related to business. If we can identify the significant relationships business has with its external world, we can relate business effectively to that larger framework we call the social system. In this manner we can better understand the contributions which business and society make to each other. This knowledge should provide managers with better inputs for making socially effective decisions. It should also give society a better understanding of the mission business has in the social system, as well as better criteria for determining how well business achieves its mission.

What Is a Social System?

All systems are not social systems. There are mechanical, biological, and chemical systems, and other types. A *system* is a combination of interrelated parts operating as a whole. It becomes a *social system* when it relates to people. It follows that a *social system* involves people and/or their organizations in relationships consisting of some observable whole. Normally the system is seeking certain human objectives. A corporation or a local parent-teacher association is a social system seeking objectives. At a different level so is a national association of corporations or parent-teacher organizations.

The basic operation of a system is that it receives inputs from its environment, processes these in some way, and then releases outputs to the environment. Although this is a simple relationship, it can become immensely complex when there are a multitude of inputs and outputs of many types. Such is the case of General Motors Corporation or International Business Machines. Their system inputs and outputs are worldwide.

In considering the social system nature of business, certain system characteristics merit discussion, such as subsystems, dynamic and stabilizing tendencies, interface with environment, and value systems.

Subsystems That Make an Interrelated Whole

The important point about a system concept is that it allows us to see something as a *whole*. This gives us more understanding of the role played by the different parts and of the workings of cause and effect in the system. Each part has its own function. It is "doing its own thing," which may be entirely different from what other parts are doing, but it is in some way affecting the whole. An example is the biological system known as the human body in which the eyes perform one function and the hands another. An additional point, already evident, is that the parts in the system are *interrelated,* affecting each other in various ways through their inputs and outputs among themselves.

A system such as an individual business is also part of a larger system, which is part of an even larger system—and so on, until all interrelated parts have been joined in terms of the largest known system. When one refers to a smaller system in relation to a larger one, the smaller system is called a subsystem. Thus, something is a whole system from one point of view, but a subsystem from a larger point of view. The subsystem is also called a lower-order system, compared with the larger one which is a higher-order system. In this manner, systems exist in hierarchies from lower order to higher order.

A local laundry illustrates the relation of systems and subsystems. This one business is a subsystem of an association of local laundries. The local laundries are part of a larger system called the laundry industry, which is a part of the service industry (as distinguished from the mining industry, for example). The service industry itself is a subsystem of the larger system we call business. In turn, business is a subsystem of the larger system we call society.

The laundry is also a subsystem of other system hierarchies, such as a community named Rockford or all local business as represented by the Rockford Chamber of Commerce. Likewise, the laundry has its own social subsystems, such as the managerial group or the truck drivers.

To be sure, the laundry is not alone in an isolated world. It is tied to other social systems in a multitude of ways.

The system concept suggests that the most productive analytical approach for understanding systems is to begin one's analysis from the view of as large a system as possible, because this view gives a clearer understanding of the role and contribution of all the subsystems involved. This is one of the reasons why business is giving more attention to relations with its broad social environment.

Dynamic and Stabilizing Tendencies

A social system is understood to be *dynamic.* This is one of its important characteristics. People contribute to this dynamism because they are living, thinking, acting beings. They add the variability and uncertainty of human behavior to systems, making social systems a difficult challenge for administrators who must manage them. Life does not hold still for organizations or persons.

In spite of its dynamic nature a social system tends to operate in some degree of *equilibrium,* which means a degree of accommodation and working harmony both among its parts and with its external environment. Equilibrium is interpreted as a dynamic, continuously floating balance of interacting forces rather than a static state of complete harmony. It is like a quiet ocean filled with moving sea life and waves, all operating in a balanced system. However, when a typhoon builds towering waves that are destructive or the water becomes so polluted that sea life is dying, we would at some point conclude that disequilibrium is occurring. In the same manner a business needs to maintain satisfactory equilibrium, both internally and externally, in order to survive and make reasonable progress toward its objectives. If its internal parts are working against one another, they are dissipating their energies in friction among themselves, and the organization is weakened. Likewise, if an organization lacks working harmony with its external environment, its progress toward objectives is reduced or entirely stopped.

Normally an organization maintains effective equilibrium by continuously taking corrective action as minor imbalances occur. It can do this because the people within the system have the human capacity to make choices and partly determine the future for the system. This internal and external self-correcting tendency is called *homeostasis.* Social systems may live in perpetuity. Unlike man, they do not have to die. And unlike man, they do not necessarily age. A social system can be stronger at an age of 100 years than it was at an age of 25 years. It is capable of self-renewal indefinitely, provided its leadership and membership have the capabilities to keep it serving the broader society of which it is a part. As we shall see, the idea of homeostasis is important for business organizations as they try to maintain themselves in a constantly changing, sometimes hostile environment.

Viability: The Drive to Grow

Associated with the idea of homeostasis is a drive for *viability,* and it implies something more than the maintenance of harmony and continuity for the business. Viability means the drive to live *and grow,* to accomplish potential not yet reached, and to achieve all that a living system is capable of becoming.

People bring viability to the business system. They seek growth. Thus, the system which they operate can move beyond simple maintenance and achieve growth in the quality and quantity of services it renders. In a world of hunger and ignorance, growth has become a key focus for social development.

One author has developed the thesis of *counterpoint,* which means that in order to keep competitive and growing, a business must constantly strive to upset the same equilibrium it is trying to achieve. This creates a state of dynamic tension between the forces of change and stability. This tension exists both in headquarters and in operating areas. Although it is a seeming contradiction of effort, counterpoint is necessary in order to maintain the viability of the organization in a changing world.[10]

Business Viability

History shows that business is remarkably viable in response to change. It has operated as a substantially more open system than a number of other institutions, and this openness has stimulated its response to change. Generally it has responded faster than educational institutions, the military, the church, or the judiciary. Some areas in which it has been especially progressive are technology, migration to frontiers, improved working conditions, and international development. As far back as the Jamestown colony of Virginia, business was a prime mover in developing the New World.

Since modern society is experiencing unusually major social changes, business is diligently seeking a viable accommodation to these changes. To accommodate may be costly, in the same way that new technology has required expensive factory alterations, but failure to accommodate would be even more costly because business's significance as an institution would decline as a result of its inability to meet human expectations.

Accommodation does not imply direct conformity to existing culture, for business is always transmitting values *to* society as well as receiving values *from* society. In fact, if business is to be a viable, vigorous institution in society, it must initiate its share of forces on its environment, rather than merely adjust to outside forces as a bucket of quicksand does. Every business needs a drive and spirit all its own to make it a positive actor on the societal stage rather than a reactor or a reflector. To expect business to be otherwise is to deny it the opportunities available to other institutions.

In connection with adaptation, one of the shallowest criticisms that can be made of business is that 50 or 100 years ago it had some practices, long since changed, which by today's standards are considered "bad." For example, it is said that business used to employ workers twelve hours a day, which is "proof" that businessmen were heartless villains. To evaluate this situation rationally, we must ask whether this historical practice was out of line with needs and practices of that time in history. Did business "villains" and shopkeepers work less than their employees or less than farmers or government workers? And was productivity so low that longer hours were necessary in order to maintain reasonable subsistence? Historical events need to be evaluated in terms of historical conditions and standards. For example, businessmen 100 years ago did not use atomic energy,

[10]Neil W. Chamberlain, *Enterprise and Environment: The Firm in Time and Place,* New York: McGraw-Hill Book Company, 1968.

which "proves" how technologically backward they were—or does it? **Actually,** criticisms of this sort are merely evidence of business progress and adaptation.

Interface with an External Environment

A system such as an individual business relates to other businesses and social groups throughout society. This area of contact between one system and another is the system *interface*. Areas of interface are important because they are sources of inputs into the system. These inputs give it additional resources and provide it with information feedback which enables it to take corrective action to maintain equilibrium with its environment.

For example, the manager of a large manufacturing branch plant was asked to speak at a luncheon of a local ministerial association which consisted of ministers from most churches in the community. He was asked to discuss what his company was doing locally to improve employment and promotion of disadvantaged employees. This meeting and speech provided an interface between the branch plant and the ministerial association.

The trade-offs of information, power, and other values which occur at the point of interface are called *social transactions*. These transactions maintain a process of social exchange in the system in the same way that economic transactions provide economic exchange in the economic system. In the example just mentioned some of the social transactions probably included the following. From the company to the ministers came an explanation of the values it held and the actions it was taking, a redefinition of company image in the ministers' minds, an image of the quality of leadership of the manager himself, and a view that the company alone could not solve this broad social problem. From the ministers to the company came an image of their ability to view problems realistically, their capacity to understand business problems, their moral commitment, and the implied threat of their power for moral persuasion in the community. Assuming these social transactions, would you consider this to be a productive social exchange? Have both parties profited from the exchange, or has one profited at the expense of the other? These are the kinds of questions which can be asked about all social transactions.

In the luncheon transaction just mentioned, the manager was acting to maintain his organization as an open system. So was the ministerial association. Each was acting as an open social system by accepting influence from its environment and, in turn, exerting its own influence externally. The influences it receives are social inputs, and those which it gives are social outputs. It is evident from the definition that business organizations are open systems in interaction with such external groups as customers, labor unions, government, community agencies, and others. Research supports this view. After a thorough study of the changes of ten companies over a period of many years, one researcher concluded that "these data imply that forces external to the organization itself instigate and moderate many of the dominant structural changes."[11]

Public Visibility: The Glass House

In its interface with the environment business has prominent public visibility compared with other institutions. *Public visibility* refers to the extent that an organization's activities are known to persons outside the organization. The activities may be directly observed, such as polluting smoke seen coming from a smokestack or purchase of a product which is deficient. Activities also may be indirectly communicated by news media, neighbors, and other sources. The importance of public visibility is that it makes business activities subject to public examination, discussion, and judgment. If acts are not known, they cannot be judged.

Since business is an advertiser, a major employer, and a supplier to customers—to name just a few of its activities—its acts are widely visible much of the time. It lives in a glass house. In contrast, penal institutions are substantially closed systems which have much less public visibility. They are isolated spatially and socially, serve a limited membership, and restrict communication by means of minimum mobility. They have little contact with outside society, and they have changed very slowly over history.

Public visibility is different from the idea of public image often mentioned in public relations. Public image refers to what people think about an organization's acts, while public visibility refers to the extent to which its acts are known. A business may have high visibility and either high or low image. Similarly, it may heve low visibility and either high or low image.

A striking illustration of business visibility occurred in the winter of 1969 when a drilling accident caused crude oil to leak in the Santa Barbara Channel of California. It was a catastrophe because it despoiled some coastal areas and damaged property and wildlife. Newspapers around the nation discussed it week after week. There were severe criticisms of business, lawsuits against businesses, and political crises concerning the event.

At that time one of the authors was in Los Angeles, 60 miles south of Santa Barbara in the direction which ocean currents flow; so he went to beach areas near Huntington Beach to see if oil pollution had reached this far. As he approached the beach, an unpleasant odor was evident one to two blocks away, affecting homes and apartments near the beach. Upon reaching the beach on this warm, sunny day, he found it bare of people for over a mile

---

[11]William H. Starbuck, "Organizational Metamorphosis," in R. William Millman and Michael P. Hottenstein (eds.), *Promising Research Directions,* Bowling Green, Ohio: The Academy of Management (Bowling Green State University), 1968, p. 132.

in each direction, except for one man walking his dog. Sure enough, there were temporary signs every 100 feet saying "WARNING. Beach pollution. Do not enter." This beautiful place was desolate. There were not even any seagulls, and a resident stated the pollution had either killed them or driven them away. The pollution, however, was *not* oil pollution. It was *sewage pollution!* Because of heavy rains, some municipalities that had storm sewers and sanitary sewers interconnected in order to save money were dumping large amounts of raw sewage into the ocean because their systems were overloaded.

In Santa Barbara the pollution was caused by private business; in the Los Angeles area it was caused by municipal government. Since the oil companies were following federal standards for ocean drilling, the worst accusal that could be made was carelessness and poor planning. The same accusals could be applied to the municipalities. In both instances metropolitan areas were affected, but the Los Angeles pollution, especially the odor, seemed to affect a large number of homesites and people. In both cases the pollution was temporary, but in Los Angeles it was more of a health hazard.

The important point about these two events is that the business pollution received the adverse publicity because of the greater public visibility of business. Considering the whole situation, there seemed to be no reason to judge the Santa Barbara pollution as being more serious or more willful than the Los Angeles pollution; however, the national press gave the business pollution the adverse publicity. Regardless of arguments about what is and is not news, or what is fair or unfair reporting, the simple fact is that the business pollution received much publicity, while the municipal pollution did not. This is business's glass house.

Values: A Source of Business Drives

Overriding all business's system relationships is the fact that business operates in an environment of social values, both those of society and those which business has. For an individual business, values derive from a multitude of sources, such as the mission of business as a social institution, the nation in which a business is located, the type of industry in which it is active, and the nature of its employees. For example, the people in a steel mill might have entirely different views toward steel import quotas and labor unions than the people in an engineering research organization.

Over a period of time, values become institutionalized, meaning that they are accepted by a large number of people in the organization. Sometimes these values are an official policy, but more often they are merely an informal understanding among people in the organization. The values are, of course, held in different degrees by each person in the organization, and some persons do not support certain values at all; nevertheless some values become generally accepted as institutional ones. With regard to business and society these values perform two important functions. First, they become guides for employee decisions in the interface of business and its environment. Second, they become strong motivators for people in a business. Thus they become a key factor in the system relationship of business with society. They are discussed further in Part Two, "Business Ideology."

Definition of Business

Viewed in a broad way, the term *business* typically refers to the development and processing of economic values in society. Normally we use the term to apply to the private (nongovernment) portion of the economy whose primary purpose is to provide goods and services for society in an effective manner, but lines of distinction are getting hazy as business and government overlap their functions in organizations such as the Communications Satellite Corporation and the Tennessee Valley Authority. In addition, *business* is a term applied to economic and commercial activities of institutions having other purposes, such as the business office of an opera association. The Metropolitan Opera Association, for example, negotiates with labor, invests capital, and makes layoffs in ways similar to those of private business. So also does the Tennessee Valley Authority.

Let us consider further the Metropolitan Opera Association of New York City. Its primary social mission is artistic and cultural; however, in 1969 it failed to meet its September 15 opening date because of labor troubles.[12] Its executive committee determined that it could not open until labor contract settlements gave it some basis for predicting expenses and knowing that it could operate throughout the season in order to recoup its costs. The preceding year it had ended the season with a $3.5 million deficit.

The Opera Association is a social system composed of subsystems, one of which is a business system. Presumably the musicians were qualified and prepared to perform if business issues could be settled. Music was the Opera Association's primary mission; however, the mission was delayed because of a failure in one of its lower-order systems, the business function. In today's organized society even artistic activities—at least the major ones—require a successful business function.

VIEWING THE WHOLE BUSINESS SYSTEM

Chris Argyris states that all organizations have three essential core activities. These are (1) achieving objectives, (2) maintaining the internal system, and (3)

---

[12]"Discord Keeps Met Curtain Down," *Business Week,* Nov. 8, 1969, pp. 34–35.

adapting to the external environment.[13] Typical books on business tend to emphasize the first two core activities; however, our book is directed primarily toward the third: adapting to the external environment. We shall discuss the importance of this environment in management policy making and decision making.

Our objective in this book is to integrate a number of disciplines and value systems affecting business so that we can examine the business environment as a whole. The total system is generally something different from the sum of its parts. Consider an animal dissected and described in a laboratory. Even if the parts are sewn back together, they do not restore the living animal and show its living responses as a system. A similar situation exists with the business system. We recognize that this book cannot truly picture a living business system, but at least its emphasis will be integrative rather than functional.

This is not a book on business ethics, but rather an analysis of business in its social environment. One influence in that environment is ethics, but there are many other influential factors. When it is necessary to discuss ethical norms, we plan to cover different points of view wherever practical so that each reader can make his own decisions. This book, therefore, does not offer a normative ethic of what business *ought* to do to be right with the world. Rather, it offers a discussion of how business and society mutually interact in performing their functions.

In the remaining chapters of Part One we discuss some of the frameworks by which business relates to society, such as social responsibility, pluralism, technology, and social change. We also examine the business and managerial roles in the social system. In Part Two we discuss business ideology, including its historical development.

In Part Three we relate business to some of its major publics, such as government, owners, customers, and labor. Part Four, "Business and the Community," moves into some of society's most current and controversial issues which involve business. Some of the issues covered are urban problems, less-advantaged citizens, the interface with education, relationships with art and the professions, and pollution. Then, in Part Five we discuss the broader involvement of business in an international world. A concluding chapter offers some interpretations of what is happening and where trends may be leading.

SUMMARY

The subject of business and society covers relationships of business to the broader social system outside its own formal organization. In an age of discontinuity the public expects business to develop greater social conscience, social concern, and social responsibility relating to its actions. Social responsibility is defined as the obligation of decision makers to pursue actions which protect and

[13]Chris Argyris, *Integrating the Individual and the Organization,* New York: John Wiley & Sons, Inc., 1964, p. 120.

improve the welfare of society as a whole, rather than only their own interests. Society expects business to show much more concern for social effects which arise directly from performance of business's economic functions, and society also expects business to help solve a number of general social problems that only indirectly relate to business activities.

Business and society interact in a system framework; consequently, a social system approach may aid understanding of their relationship. Social system frameworks imply inputs from society and outputs to it, subsystems that make an interrelated whole, dynamic and stabilizing tendencies, interface with environment, and social values.

STUDY GUIDES FOR INTERPRETATION OF THIS CHAPTER

1. Is the relation of business with society worthy of serious thought and study? Explain.

2. What are the benefits to business and to society which can be achieved by using a system framework to analyze their relationships with each other?

3. In terms of business and society discuss the Santa Barbara and Los Angeles beach pollution mentioned in this chapter.

4. What is the difference between a social discontinuity and routine social change?

5. What decision would you make for each of the three cases introducing this chapter? Give reasons for your decisions.

PROBLEM
A Proposal for Self-Regulation

In a Midwestern city a mover of household goods made a proposal to members of his local movers' and warehousers' association. He observed that for years the movers had been wrangling with customers about claims for damage to household goods that had been moved. At times the disputes became bitter, with customers writing to local legislators, the chamber of commerce, and the Interstate Commerce Commission. Most claims were small, ranging from $25 to $300, but the amounts were large enough to cause both the customer and the mover not to want to make concessions. Much mover time was lost in these arguments, and there was substantial loss of customer goodwill.

The mover proposed that the movers' association should establish an office of impartial arbitrator to handle all unresolved claims of less than $1,000. The office was to be supported by mover fees based on the dollar volume of business done by each mover. Movers would agree to binding arbitration, and when the customer also agreed, the arbitration procedure would be invoked. In this state arbitration agreements of this type were legally binding. The mover claimed that arbitration by a third party would be better received by the customer than a mover-negotiated settlement, and this approach might also discourage government regulation as a result of consumer complaints. He referred to a successful program of this type in another city and said a recent report of the Ralph Nader consumer advocate organization had commented favorably about it.

Another member favored the proposal with the following comment: "It's generally a lot better for business to try to resolve its own problems than have them become political or regulatory problems. With fair-minded arbitration we could eliminate many unnecessary rules that increase our costs of operation."

One member objected: "We would lose control of our business. I already have a fair claims manager who handles consumer complaints, and I don't need any third party running my business. Furthermore, if a complaint cannot be resolved, the customer can always go to small claims court."

1. Discuss extensively the social issues raised by this case.

2. If you were one of the members of the movers' association, how would you vote on the proposed arbitration plan? Would you add another organization to the existing complexity of settlement organizations in the social system?

ARGUMENTS FOR AND AGAINST
SOCIAL RESPONSIBILITIES
FOR BUSINESS

*It is a fallacy that business can prosper—or, indeed, even
exist–without regard to broader social concerns.*

S. Prakash Sethi[1]

*Indeed, a businessman can hardly find a better measure of his
contribution to social welfare than his own profits.*

"Fortune's Wheel"[2]

Two business friends decided to have a drink together after work. As they sat discussing various ideas, the discussion somehow moved to the social responsibility of business. They were surprised to learn that although they worked in similar management jobs, they were strongly divided in their viewpoints about the social responsibility of business. One believed that business has substantial social responsibilities. The other was equally sure that "the only social responsibility" is to provide customer goods and services at the lowest price consistent with reasonable profit and that any other responsibilities are a threat to the business system. The argument became heated at times, and the short visit they had planned turned into a long and serious discussion.

The scene just described has been repeated many times during recent years. There are sound arguments for both sides of the issue, and there are honest differences of opinion. The issue is one of the most important that business has ever faced, and it is also a significant issue for society. Is all this social responsibility talk just a passing fad, or is it truly a fundamental change in the required direction of business?

Since there are valid differences of opinion, the arguments for and against social responsibility need to be examined early in this book so that they can be considered as the reader moves through the book. First we will discuss the

[1]S. Prakash Sethi, "Corporate Social Policy in a Dynamic Society: Options Available to Business," *California Management Review,* Winter 1972, p. 4A.
[2]"Fortune's Wheel," *Fortune*, June 1973, p. 2.

arguments favoring social responsibility, and then we will present arguments against social responsibilities for business. We will lump together the arguments used by both business leaders and the general public, because sometimes both parties support the same argument although their degree of support may differ. Many of these points of view are discussed in more depth later in the text. The purpose of this chapter is simply to introduce some of the main arguments.

ARGUMENTS FOR SOCIAL RESPONSIBILITY
Changed Public Expectations of Business

One of the most potent arguments for social responsibility is that public expectations for business have changed. It is reasoned that the institution of business exists only because it satisfies valuable needs of society. Society gave business its charter to exist, and that charter can be amended or revoked at any time that business fails to live up to society's expectations. Therefore, if business wishes to remain viable in the long run, it must respond to society's needs and give society what it wants.

The argument suggests that social responsibility issues are a sign of deep, far-reaching social change. There are certain basic forces at work which are changing social expectations in the long run in the direction of greater social payouts from business. The old idea of economic payouts for society—a job which business performed admirably—is no longer enough. In fact, one line of reasoning is that significant new expectations exist precisely *because* business was immensely successful in meeting the old expectations. The argument can be explained in terms of the familiar Maslow need hierarchy that is used in motivation theory.[3] Maslow proposed that human needs exist in some order of priority so that as basic needs are relatively satisfied, other needs move in to dominate human expectations. In the Maslow hierarchy basic physical and security needs are followed by *social* needs. If we assume that physical and security needs have been relatively satisfied in advanced nations, and there is ample evidence to support this conclusion, then it follows that social needs will tend gradually to dominate public expectations. This argument suggests that the changes in public expectations are fundamental, far-reaching, and significant. They are likely to last until they are reasonably satisfied, allowing the public to move to new priorities according to its hierarchy of needs.

Of course, people do not all move uniformly along a hierarchy of needs, and people have different ways of expressing their needs, so there will still be differences of opinion about social responsibility. All that the Maslow hierarchy defines is the basic direction of public expectations. If this line of reasoning is

[3]For an expanded discussion of the Maslow need hierarchy, see Keith Davis, *Human Behavior at Work*, 4th ed., New York: McGraw-Hill Book Company, 1972, pp. 42–52.

accepted, then ecological issues, racial unrest, and similar social issues are not *causes* of the social responsibility trend. Rather, they are *effects* of the much more fundamental causal factor, which is a far-reaching change in the expectations of the public. Since public expectations are changing, it follows that business activities need to move toward more social concern in order for business to remain viable.

This argument suggests that production of goods is no longer *the one* central focus of the social system. Public expectations are changing, and now production goals must share the spotlight with the elusive goal of quality of life. Since public expectations are more in the direction of quality of life, new relationships between business and society need to be defined which will bring business activities closer to social desires for a better quality of life.

Better Environment for Business

Another argument favoring social responsibility is that it creates a better environment for business. This concept rationalizes that a better society produces environmental conditions more favorable for business operation. The firm which is most responsive to improvement of community quality of life will as a result have a better community in which to conduct its business. Labor recruiting will be easier, and labor will be of a higher quality. Turnover and absenteeism will be reduced. As a result of social improvements, crime will decrease, with the consequence that less money will be spent to protect property, and less taxes have to be paid to support police forces. The arguments can be extended in all directions to show that a better society produces a better environment for business.

This argument is actually a sophisticated concept of long-run profit maximization. It seems a contradiction to suggest that spending money for social programs will provide more profit for the business, but this is the normal result of the better community and better society which these programs bring. Truly low-cost production in the long run depends on a better social environment; therefore, the firm which does not contribute to it will be inviting lower profits sometime in the future.

Public Image

Another argument is that social responsibility improves the public image of business. Each individual firm seeks an enhanced public image so that it may gain more customers, better employees, and other benefits. This type of behavior is traditional with business; therefore, it is easy to extend this public-image concept to the accomplishment of various types of social goals. According to this line of reasoning, social goals are now a top priority with members of the public; thus the firm which wishes to capture a favorable public image will have to show that it also supports social goals.

A favorable image is also important in a firm's money markets. For example, some banks have established policies that they will not make business loans for projects which cause substantial pollution. In other instances banks have set aside funds for special low-cost loans for projects which help solve social problems. From the investor point of view, a number of individual and institutional investors have said they will not buy stock in firms which support socially undesirable actions. They take this position for two reasons: (1) they object on ethical grounds, and (2) they maintain that the firm's practices may cause long-run problems which will jeopardize their investment.

Avoidance of Government Regulation

A related concept is that business engages in socially responsible behavior to avoid regulation by government. Regulation is costly to business and restricts its flexibility of decision making. From the businessman's point of view it is desirable to retain freedom in decision making so that he can maintain the initiative in meeting market and social forces. This view is also consistent with political philosophy which wishes to keep power as decentralized as possible in our democratic system. Government is already a massive institution whose centralized power and bureaucracy threaten the balance of power in the American system. Any action by business which encourages further growth of government could be a disservice to the public and possibly erode its freedoms.

Prevention of more governmental controls is also consistent with good organizational theory, which holds that decision making should be kept as near as possible to the point where an operating problem occurs. For various reasons, therefore, if the businessman by his own socially responsible behavior can prevent government from introducing new restrictions, it can be argued that he probably is accomplishing a public good, as well as his own private good.

Sociocultural Norms

Another argument for social responsibility is that of sociocultural norms. The businessman operates under a set of cultural constraints in the same way that any other person in society does. Research shows that these cultural norms are powerful determinants of behavior. They are as real as technical, legal, and market constraints. Consequently, as society's norms change, the businessman's behavior will change. If society moves toward norms of social responsibility as it is now doing, then the businessman is subtly and inevitably guided by these same norms. Society's norms gradually are internalized by the businessman. Though his decisions are not fully determined by these norms, his decisions are influenced toward a socially defined behavior which reflects some sense of social responsibility. In other words, profits are sought and achieved within whatever current social norms exist.

Stated in terms of utility theory, modern managers have a utility function in which they desire more than economic satisfactions. It is in the nature of most people to be guided by many stars rather than just one. It is hoped that one of these stars will be the well-being of other people and of society in general. In this manner the manager is guided to pursue profit in ways which are socially responsible.

One version of this theory, called *lexicographic utility theory*, holds that each person's utility function exists in some order of priority in the manner of Maslow's need hierarchy. Each businessman's multiple goals are ranked, and some sort of target of satisfactory accomplishment is set for each one. Then, as each goal is achieved, the businessman shifts to the next goal. For example, a businessman may have a primary goal of a certain percentage of profit and a secondary goal of low pollution. As long as he is making his profit target, his decision will be guided by the alternative which gives the lowest pollution. Or, stated in another way, when several alternative actions will give acceptable results, his final decision is triggered by his next-priority objectives. In this way the businessman appears to be acting in a socially responsible way even though his first priority is profit.[4]

Balance of Responsibility with Power

Another argument for social responsibility by business is that business's responsibility should be more related to its power. It is reasoned that businessmen have vast amounts of social power. They do affect ecology, minorities, and other social problems. In turn, an equal amount of social responsibility is required to match their social power. If each institution is to perform its social role in an orderly relationship with other institutions, then responsibility must be accepted wherever there is power. Any other arrangement invites irresponsible behavior. This idea is rather well accepted by businessmen, because historically they have strongly favored balanced power and responsibility among social institutions, particularly in their views on responsibilities of labor unions.

System Interdependence Requires Social Concern

Related to social power and responsibility is the idea that the modern social system is so complex and interdependent that almost any internal act of business has some influence on the external world. In ancient times the social system was a rather simple one in which institutions could follow their relatively independent ways without seriously encroaching on the quality of life of the whole society. The candlemaker could follow his trade without serious concern about its social effects. Modern society, however, is an interdependent world. The petroleum refinery which makes candle wax is so interwoven with society in terms of its

[4]For further details see Harold L. Johnson, *Business in Contemporary Society: Framework and Issues*, Belmont, Calif.: Wadsworth Publishing Company, Inc., 1971, pp. 71–76.

social effects that it must be concerned about ecology, minority employment, and a host of other social issues. Business and other institutions do affect the quality of life; thus the logic of the situation dictates that they must show concern about their external influences on the system.

Stockholder Interest

Another argument for social responsibility is that it is in the interest of the stockholder for business to engage in certain kinds of responsible behavior. Of course, this argument applies to such concepts as public image and avoidance of government regulation, but economist Henry C. Wallich also shows that it applies in a strict economic sense to stockholder interests.[5] Through sophisticated analytical procedures he shows how diversification of ownership portfolios radically alters the interest of the stockholder. Corporate activities which would not be worthwhile to a stockholder in a single firm definitely become worthwhile to a diversified stockholder. He shows that types of responsible behavior which bring returns to the corporate sector as a whole actually operate to the benefit of the holder of a diversified portfolio; therefore, failure to be responsible deprives stockholders of returns they might otherwise enjoy. An example of this kind of responsible behavior is training hard-core employees, because even if employees move to another company, the benefit of their training is not lost to the diversified investor. Businessmen seem to support this point of view, because in one survey of business involvement in urban problems 60 percent of business executives reported that they thought their urban activities would "open up new opportunities for profit."[6]

Let Business Try

One interesting argument for business social responsibility is sort of a backhanded one. It is that many other institutions have failed in handling social problems, so why not turn to business. Many people are frustrated with the failures of other institutions, and in their frustration they are turning to business. Viewpoints are along the following lines:

"Give business a try. Maybe it can come up with some new ideas."

"Let business have a role. It couldn't do any worse!"

"Who else is left? We've tried all the others!"

---

[5]Henry C. Wallich and John J. McGowan, "Stockholder Interest and the Corporation's Role in Social Policy," in William J. Baumol et al., *A New Rationale for Corporate Social Policy,* New York: Committee for Economic Development, 1970, pp. 39—59.
[6]Joseph W. McGuire and John B. Parrish, "Status Report on a Profound Revolution," *California Management Review,* Summer 1971, p. 80.

Many of these comments are exaggerated and not very flattering to business. They are made more out of desperation than reason. Many of the people who make them have exorbitant expectations of perfection in human institutions; thus business will probably fail in their eyes as other institutions have done. On the other hand, the issue which they raise remains a nagging question: Have we performed poorly with some social problems precisely because we have not used business's capabilities for solving them?

Business Has the Resources

A related argument is that business has valuable resources which could be applied to social problems; therefore, society should use these resources. In some cases this argument is based on the mistaken assumption that since business has all the money, all that society has to do is tap the till of business and then its social problems will fade away. In most cases, however, there is the reasoned assumption that business has a substantial pool of (1) management talent, (2) functional expertise, and (3) capital resources. Probably it is without peer among institutions in all three of these resources. For example, institutions that work in social areas seem to be especially deficient in management talent, and business is known worldwide for its investment in this resource; therefore, perhaps the two types of institutions could be mated in a way that would bring beneficial results.

As a further point, business is known for its innovative ability. Perhaps some of this could be applied to social problems where innovation is sorely needed. In addition, business values focus on productive increase of resources, while many other institutions give more emphasis to conserving and distributing existing resources. For certain social problems productive use of limited resources is greatly needed. Perhaps business's productivity orientation can make a contribution.

Another business resource is certain environmental conditions which are favorable to the solution of some kinds of social problems. The work is reality-oriented; therefore, the less-advantaged students who could not tolerate the abstractions of public school may find that business gives them a feeling of accomplishment. Those who are semiliterate may want to improve in reading, writing, and mathematics, since having a job gives them purpose in learning. Similarly, on the job minority employees may for the first time in their lives feel that they are equal members of a team. Business as an employer can provide a climate for action, reality, teamwork, and a feeling of doing something useful.

Problems Can Become Profits

Another argument is that if business's innovative ability can be turned to social problems, many problems could be handled profitably according to traditional business concepts. It is recognized that not all problems can be handled in this way, but the fact that some can be so handled should encourage business to become more active in social areas. For example, phosphate strip mining companies in Florida have found that after mining they can convert the land to homesites on lakes, resulting in better land than it was originally—all with a profit. Chemical companies have found that they can reclaim some wastes at a profit, and other firms are examining similar profit possibilities.

Prevention Is Better than Curing

One final point is that prevention is better than curing. If business delays dealing with social problems now, it may find itself constantly occupied with putting out social fires so that it has no time to accomplish its goal of producing goods and services. Since these social problems must be dealt with at some time, it is actually more economical to deal with them now before they develop into serious social breakdowns that consume most of management's time.

Some of the points that have been mentioned have a more rigorous theoretical framework than others, and several of them overlap; but taken as a whole, they are a powerful argument for business assumption of social responsibilities. On the other hand, there are also some strong arguments against business assumption of social responsibilities. These arguments also merit examination.

ARGUMENTS AGAINST SOCIAL RESPONSIBILITY
Profit Maximization

Perhaps the most powerful argument against business assumption of social responsibilities is the classical economic doctrine of profit maximization. This doctrine was presented by Adam Smith in 1776 and has influenced economic thinking since then. The doctrine explains that businessmen perform a social good when they improve efficiency and reduce costs in order to maximize profit. Even though they are driven by their own selfish desire for profits, the invisible hand of competition forces them to act in the public interest in the long run by reducing costs and prices. Thus the businessman is most socially responsible when he attends strictly to business interests and leaves other activities to other institutions.

Since business operates in a world of poverty and hunger, the economic efficiency of business is a matter of top priority and should be the sole mission of business. Business's function is economic not social, and economic values should be the only criteria used to measure success. In this kind of system managers are the agents of the stockholders, and all their decisions are controlled by their desire to maximize profits for the stockholders while reasonably complying with law and social custom.

Corporate Social Responsibility Is Inappropriate

Economist Milton Friedman has argued strongly for years that social responsibility is inappropriate corporate action. Following is one of his comments:

Have you ever heard anybody suggest that the "Mom and Pop" corner grocery store should sell food below cost to help the poor people who shop there? Well, that would obviously be absurd! Any corner grocery that operated that way would be out of business very soon. The same is true on the larger scale. The large enterprise can have money to exercise social responsibility only if it has a monopoly position: if it's able to hire its employees at lower wages than they are worth; if it's able to sell its product at a higher price than can otherwise be charged. If it is a monopoly, it ought to be prosecuted under the antitrust laws. Any businessman who boasts to the public that he has been using corporate funds to exercise a social responsibility should be regarded as asking for an investigation by the Antitrust Division of the Justice Department.

From Milton Friedman, "Milton Friedman Responds," *Business and Society Review*, Spring 1972, pp. 6–7. Reprinted with permission.

As explained by Milton Friedman, an economist and major proponent of this point of view:[7]

In a free enterprise, private property system, a corporate executive is an employee of the owners of the business. He has direct responsibility to his employers. That responsibility is to conduct the business in accordance with their desires, which generally will be to make as much money as possible while conforming to the basic rules of the society . . . . Insofar as his actions in accord with his "social responsibility" reduce returns to stockholders, he is spending their money. Insofar as his actions raise the price to customers, he is spending the customers' money. Insofar as his actions lower the wages of some employees, he is spending their money.

According to this line of reasoning, if executives do use resources for social responsibility, they are in effect imposing taxes and then deciding how the taxes shall be spent. This approach "involves the acceptance of the Socialist view that political mechanisms, not market mechanisms, are the appropriate way to determine the allocation of scarce resources to alternative uses,"[8] and it inevitably leads to decreased economic efficiency.

Business Costs of Social Involvement

Another argument is the excessive business costs of social involvement. Business has very substantial economic resources, but it must use them wisely

[7]Milton Friedman, "Does Business Have a Social Responsibility?" *Bank Administration*, April 1971, pp. 13–14.
[8]Ibid., p. 14.

because these resources will quickly dwindle into economic impotence unless they are self-renewing. Although business can invest small amounts of its resources in social obligations, as it has done in the past, it cannot really commit major economic resources for social responsibility unless the costs of these resources are paid by government or other institutions.

As a matter of fact, if business is pushed into social obligations, these additional costs will drive out marginal firms in various industries. This has already happened with marginal metal foundries and cement plants which could not meet the high cost of new pollution equipment. They have closed their doors permanently. Chemical firms and others have had similar problems.

Costs to Society for Social Responsibility

Another more fundamental issue is that society ultimately must pay the costs of social responsibility activities. As presently constituted, many social proposals do not pay their own way in an economic sense; therefore, someone must pay for them. Are the citizens of society willing to pay these costs, and would this be a wise use of their limited resources? Ultimately society pays all costs! Can it afford these costs?

The cost to society revolves around three points. One is cost/benefit analysis which compares potential benefits with potential costs. The argument is that many costs far outweigh the benefits. For example, it is argued that some consumer protection legislation provides meager consumer benefits compared with the economic costs of the large bureaucracy set up to enforce the legislation plus the loss of consumer freedoms because of overprotective legislation. It is not enough that some social action is desirable. The action must also be desirable *in relation to its social costs.*

Another cost issue is that limited resources require the setting of *social priorities.* All social needs cannot be accomplished at once. Some actions must precede other actions. Many social responsibility proposals are idle pipe dreams that may be possible some decades in the future but are unreasonable expectations for the present. In some cases they cost too much for society to afford. For example, the federal Clean Water Act proposes zero water pollution by 1985. It is estimated that the removal of the last 1 or 2 percent of pollution will cost from $250 billion to $1 trillion. No one knows for sure, but this is a cost which society hardly has the resources to bear. Perhaps it can be accomplished sometime, but not in the one decade that is proposed.

A third cost issue is that some persons claim the public is being misled about who will pay the costs. The public thinks that social responsibility for business means that business and stockholders will bear all costs so that the citizen will get these benefits "free." As a matter of reality, consumers and the general public will bear most of the costs of business social responsibility activities, because business will pass these costs on through the price structure. If the public knew that it would have to pay the costs, and if it knew how high the true costs were, it would not demand many of the social actions that it is now demanding. It would opt for more economic efficiency in order to protect and enhance its affluence.

Lack of Social Skills

An additional argument against business assumption of social respon-sibilities is that many businessmen may lack the perceptions and skills to work effectively with social issues. It is said that their outlook is primarily economic and that their skills are the same. They really do not feel at home in social matters. If society is going to depend on someone to work with social problems, why choose a group which is so poorly qualified? Does society really want economic and technical people meddling in social affairs? Will they broaden their outlook, and will their skills transfer? Can business really do the job? Is it better equipped than government and other institutions?

A more extreme interpretation of this view is held by some leftists who believe that businessmen are crass and ignoble people who grasp for every dollar they can and who single-mindedly engage in the pursuit of profit. In this view, businessmen would not hesitate to take advantage of their neighbors whenever a dollar is concerned. Obviously, men like this are not to be trusted with programs which primarily show concern for one's neighbors. They are philosophically and emotionally unfit for the job.

Dilution of Business's Primary Purpose

Another argument is that involvement in social goals might dilute business's emphasis on economic productivity, divide the interests of its leaders, and weaken business in the marketplace, with the result that it would accomplish poorly both its economic and its social roles. This means that society would get less productivity and that the economic role of business in society would become confused. Perhaps other institutions would step in to try to fill the economic gaps left by business, with the result that too many cooks would spoil the economic broth by accomplish-ing less and less productivity. Similarly, social goals also would be inadequately achieved, leaving society the poorer both socially and economically.

A related issue from business's point of view is that failure in either economic or social areas will reduce business's public image. As seen by some businessmen, it might be better not to risk the chance of lowered public image. They feel they have enough to do in meeting the economic expectations of society. There is, additionally, an uneasy feeling that many of the problems people wish to assign to business are not really solvable and would make business the scapegoat in this social exchange.

Weakened International Balance of Payments

Arguments against business assumption of social responsibility often omit the international balance of payments, but this appears to be a real issue. If social programs add to business costs, then these costs must be recovered, and generally they will be added to the price of the product. Similarly, if social activities dilute business's capacity for high productivity, then this lower efficiency is likely to lead to higher product costs. If these firms compete in international markets with other firms which do not have these social costs added to their product, then firms from the United States will be at a competitive disadvantage. They will have fewer sales internationally, leading to a weakened international balance of payments for the United States. Since the international balance of payments is often in poor condition, this may further weaken it and lead to undesirable international monetary problems. In addition, fewer sales mean fewer jobs for United States workers.

For example, Arizona produces more than half the copper in the United States. If the people of Arizona require the mines and smelters to use expensive pollution control equipment which increases copper costs 2 or 3 cents a pound, then buyers may turn elsewhere for cheaper copper. Since copper is a standardized metal internationally, they might turn to African mines rather than United States mines. The result would be declining copper employment in the United States and a less favorable balance of trade because of copper imports. Furthermore, from the point of view of national defense this would make the United States more deficient in meeting its copper needs, perhaps endangering the security of the nation in time of war.

Business Has Enough Power

Another argument is that business already has enough social power; therefore, society should not take any steps which give it more power. According to this line of reasoning, business is one of the two or three most powerful institutions in society at the present time. Business influence is felt throughout society. It is felt in education, in government, in the home, and in the marketplace. It molds many social values. The process of combining social activities with the established economic activities of business would give business an excessive concentration of power. This concentration of power would threaten the pluralistic division of powers which we now have among institutions, probably reducing the viability of our free society. This is too great a risk to take as long as there are other institutions available which might solve our social problems. In short, society does not want business to be the giant social institution which towers over all other private institutions. Business already has all the power society can wisely allow it to have.

A more extreme version of this view is held particularly by leftists. They believe that private business is an institution which is absolutely no good. It follows that society certainly does not wish to give more power to an institution which is already considered undesirable.

Lack of Accountability

Another point of view is that businessmen have no direct lines of accountability to the people; therefore, it is unwise to give businessmen responsibility for areas where they are not accountable. Accountability should always go with responsibility, and it is poor social control to allow any other kind of arrangement. Until society can develop mechanisms which establish direct lines of social accountability from business to the public, business must stand clear of social activities and pursue only its goal of profit where it is directly accountable through the market system. The social needs of the people certainly should not depend on the occasional helping hand of businessmen. In their well-meaning naïveté in deciding what is good for society, businessmen might become benevolent, paternalistic rulers.

Lack of Broad Support

One final point is that business social involvement lacks a broad base of support among all groups in society. If business does become socially involved, it will create so much friction among dissident parties that business cannot perform its social assignment. Although many persons desire business to become more socially involved, others oppose the idea. There is lack of agreement among the general public, among intellectuals, in government, and even among businessmen themselves. Various reasons have been mentioned earlier for this opposition. It is both rational and emotional, but it is real. Regardless of the reasons, the fact that there is divided support for business social involvement means that it will operate somewhat in a hostile environment which could cause it to fail in its social mission and also cause disastrous side effects.

CONCLUSION

Business already has assumed a certain minimal role of social responsibility, but it certainly has not solved social problems. The question that remains is: Shall business assume a more significant social role, or shall it not? The preceding discussion shows that there are many sound reasons for both points of view. Each person needs to decide in his or her own mind how much weight to give these arguments based on his or her values and aspirations for society. Then collectively

Social Responsibility Applies to All Types of Organizations

> Under any circumstances, we are moving in the direction of demanding that
> our institutions take responsibility beyond their own performance and beyond their
> own contribution. We will demand this not only of business enterprise but of all other
> institutions as well—the university and the hospital, the government agency and the
> school. [11]

From Peter F. Drucker, "The Concept of the Corporation," *Business and Society Review*, Autumn
1972, p. 16.

these opinions will determine social priorities and public policy toward social
responsibility for business. For example, are economic efficiency, productivity,
and profit maximization valued highly? If so, perhaps it would be better if business
stayed out of social issues. On the other hand, does society wish to call upon
business's plentiful resources for dealing with social issues and also place social
responsibility where considerable social power lies? If so, this is a signal for
business to move more into social responsibility.

A move toward social responsibility would be a fundamental change for
business. In the last two decades, goaded by pollution and other developments,
society has been considering this issue. It appears that the direction of change has
already been decided. Society wants business *as well as all other major institutions*
to assume significant social responsibility. Social responsibility has become the
hallmark of a mature, global civilization. It is necessary in an interdependent
world. Henry Ford II has expressed a businessman's view of this development as
follows: "As I see it, there is no longer anything to reconcile, if there ever was,
between the social conscience and the profit motive."[9]

Certainly in affluent nations such as the United States a reordering of
priorities has occurred which places more emphasis on business social responsibility, and even less-developed nations gradually may fall in line as they face social
pressures and realize the interdependence of the global system. Consequently, in
subsequent chapters we will be examining the changing role of business and
discussing how business may implement some of the social decisions that it faces.

SUMMARY

Business assumption of significant social responsibility will require a fundamental change in the business sytem. There exist many sound reasons both for
and against this change. The decision is not an easy one, and it depends on the
values people hold and the way they want their world organized. It appears that
society is opting for substantially increased social responsibility from all its major
institutions; consequently, the idea of social responsibility will be discussed
further in Chapter 3.

[9]Henry Ford II, quoted in *Company and Community,* Wilmington, Del.: E. I. du Pont de Nemours &
Company, n.d., p. 3.

STUDY GUIDES FOR
INTERPRETATION OF THIS CHAPTER

1. What do you consider the two strongest arguments for business assumption of social responsibilities? Explain why.

2. What do you consider the two strongest arguments against business assumption of social responsibilities? Explain why.

3. What arguments additional to those in the text can you present both for and against business assumption of social responsibilities?

4. Explain how the Maslow need hierarchy may relate to current demands for more social responsibility from institutions.

5. Discuss how the concept of economic efficiency and profit maximization applies to social responsibility issues.

PROBLEM
The Cans of Mixed Nuts

A member of a statewide consumer organization wrote the organization complaining that some cans of mixed nuts which he bought misrepresented their contents. He said that the picture on the front of the can showed a rather even proportion of five varieties of nuts; however, the contents showed an uneven mixture favoring the cheaper varieties. The consumer organization investigated the complaint and found that none of the cans specified proportions of nut varieties therein and that some cans of different companies did have pictures which misrepresented the mix. For example, one can showed a relatively even mixture of nuts in the picture, but a count of contents showed 221 peanuts, 9 almonds, 5 cashew nuts, 1 Brazil nut, and ½ of a pecan!

Based upon the results of the investigation, a member of the board of governors of the consumer organization proposed that it sponsor federal legislation to require mixed nuts to be sold only in clear glass jars so that any consumer could judge the contents for himself. Another member suggested that mixed nuts offered for sale be required to have equal proportions of each nut by weight.

1. Discuss the proposed legislation in terms of a cost/benefit analysis.

2. As a businessman how would you react to each of the proposed items of legislation? Could you offer any reasonable alternative proposals?

3. In this instance what is the extent of the social responsibility of the nut packer toward consumers and owners of the business?

CHAPTER 3

SOCIAL POWER AND SOCIAL RESPONSIBILITY

Business is a citizen, too, and in that sense it has proportionate responsibilities to go well beyond the letter of the law.

Walter P. Cartun[1]

Each business has responsibilities in some way commensurate with its powers.

George A. Steiner[2]

There is a rising public clamor for something called "social responsibility" on the part of business as well as other social institutions. In the face of all this clamor how do businessmen know what to do to meet the demands of various claimants for responsibility? What do they expect? How do they define responsibility? And what particular responsibilities should be given priority? One observer says: "The main responsibility of business is to serve its customers at a fair price." Another says: "Business's main responsibility is to its stockholders to maximize their profits." At another extreme a local activist charges: "Business materialism and unemployment are substantial causes of juvenile delinquency; therefore, business should provide jobs for teenagers who want them." Another citizen insists that business substantially underwrite a new hospital because "business has the money, and we can't afford to raise our hospital charges or pay higher taxes for the hospital."

In the face of all these claims, what guides do managers have to assist them in making judgments about social responsibility? Should they avoid social involvement beyond their community? Should they pay attention only to the loudest claimant or to each squeaky wheel? Should they support only those activities in which they have a personal interest? Certainly they know that, regardless of the claims made upon them, they cannot solve all society's problems. If they tried to

[1]Walter P. Cartun, "Fact and Fiction of Social Responsibility," *S.A.M. Advanced Management Journal*, January 1973, p. 36.
[2]George A. Steiner, "Social Policies for Business," *California Management Review*, Winter 1972, p. 22.

do so, they would preempt the work of other institutions that deal with social problems. Furthermore, their resources are limited; they must use them carefully and put them to the best long-run use. But how should they respond to these different claims on their organization?

In this chapter we explore the idea of social responsibility. Then we discuss how constitutionalism becomes a major instrument for crystallizing social responsibility practice.

DECISION MAKING AND SOCIAL RESPONSIBILITY

During the last 100 years, business thinking and action have changed dramatically. Business practices of a century ago would not be accepted even by a backward firm today. It is academic whether business initiated these changes or whether society pushed business into them. In actuality, progress was mutual; each initiated changes on the other, assisted by other institutions in the total social system. Business could not have come as far as it has without the help of society, nor could society have developed to its present state without corresponding business progress. As the years have passed, business gradually has broadened its activities beyond its own gates into the general community, until today business shares power for economic growth, social stability, community improvements, education, and a host of other public needs.

These expanded social powers are probably greater than the narrow property rights which business had a century ago and which gave control only over property. Business holds these social powers not by legal right, but by reason of responsible and competent performance. Out of these expanded relationships the idea of social responsibility is developing as a reciprocal of evident social power.

What Is Social Responsibility?

Social responsibility is concerned with the public interest. As explained earlier, social responsibility is the obligation of decision makers to take actions which protect and improve the welfare of society as a whole along with their own interests. It builds a better quality of life, thus harmonizing organizational actions with society's wants.

The substance of social responsibility arises from concern for the consequences of one's acts as they might affect the interests of others. This idea exists in most religions and philosophies of the world, but often there is a tendency to limit its application to person-to-person contacts. Social responsibility moves one large step further by including institutional actions and their effect on the whole social system. Without this additional step, personal and institutional acts tend to be divorced. A businessman can lead a model personal life but continue to rationalize his organization's pollution of a river because no direct personal consequence is involved. He can consider river pollution a "public problem" to be solved by public action. The idea of social responsibility, however, requires him to consider his acts in terms of a whole social system and holds him responsible for the effects of his acts anywhere in that system.

Social responsibility, therefore, broadens a person's view to the total social system. When people's primary frame of reference is themselves, they may be counted upon for antisocial behavior whenever their values conflict with those of society. If their values are limited primarily to a certain group or organization, they tend to become partisans acting for that group. But, if they think in terms of a whole system, they begin to build societal values into their actions, even when they are for a certain organization. This is the essence of social responsibility.

The idea of social responsibility recognizes that each person is attached to an extended social system on which he or she is partly dependent; consequently, certain obligations or social responsibilities arise from this attachment. The same reasoning applies to groups and institutions. Businessmen apply social responsibility when they consider the needs and interests of others who may be affected by business actions. In so doing, they look beyond their own personal interests and also beyond their firm's narrow economic and technical interests.

While it is true that only businessmen (rather than businesses per se) make socially responsible decisions, they decide in terms of the objectives and policies of their business institution. Thus each business institution and the entire business system eventually come to stand for certain socially responsible beliefs and actions. But in the last analysis it is always the businessman who makes the decision. The business institution can only give him a cultural framework and policy guidance.

Suboptimization and Social Responsibility

When a group's values are predominantly partisan without a socially responsible concern for the public interest, then from the view of the larger social system the partisan group is *suboptimizing* general social benefits. This means that the group is optimizing benefits to itself but that benefits to others are being largely neglected by its narrow view. The result is that benefits to the larger system are poorly served. The partisan group gains at the expense of others. In extreme cases, the social disequilibrium may become so intense that *all groups lose,* even the group which is seeking gain for itself alone.

An example of the costs and dangers that can result from social suboptimization is the experience of a British factory closed by a pay conflict with ten attendants of women's lavatories. The situation moved a government official to comment wryly: "One of the lavatories is working, but the factory is stopped."

When the attendants refused to clean certain women's lavatories, the company asked women employees to use other facilities available during the dispute. The women refused. They said this would be strikebreaking, so they stopped work and went home. Their absence from their work stations forced the factory to be closed, putting men off the job. In a day, the strike of attendants was settled. All employees then returned to work, but they demanded a day's pay for the day they were off the job. The company refused to pay for no work, so the employees walked out leaving the lavatory housekeepers working but a closed factory.

At this point the following organizations and interest groups had already been involved: the British government at different levels, the National Trade Union Congress, the Transport and General Workers Union at various levels, women lavatory attendants, women employees, men employees, other trade unions, management, and others. Somehow in this partisan bickering among different pluralistic groups the public need of productivity was bypassed. Britain became poorer because groups suboptimized their own interest without social responsibility toward the larger interests of all employees and customers, and the general public interest. Hence, "One of the lavatories is working, but the factory is stopped."[3]

Both Intended and Actual Outcomes Are Important

For a decision to be socially responsible it needs to be made with an *intended outcome* of serving the general welfare. Thus the decision must *in its origin* be socially responsible. In other instances it is quite possible that a decision made for selfish and partisan reasons may by chance serve the public welfare, but since the decision makers were not acting with the public interest in mind when they made their decision, it cannot be said that they were acting responsibly toward the broader society. Their socially desirable result was purely a matter of chance, and a chance result does not define a responsible act.

On the other hand, a socially responsible intention does not guarantee results in the public interest. A decision may, because of poor judgment or unforeseen events, actually cause results against the public interest; consequently, intent alone is not enough for determining responsible action. The *actual outcome* also needs to serve public welfare. Society cannot long accept well-intentioned decision makers that are so incompetent that they cause unfavorable results. Since both intentions and outcomes are important to society, the truly socially responsible decision is one that serves the public interest both in its intended outcome and in its actual results.

In summary, an intended outcome of serving public welfare always must be present for a decision to be considered socially responsible, and normally (i.e.,

---

[3]"Not Even Good Enough for the Lavatory," *The Economist*, June 28, 1969, p. 19.

most of the time) the actual outcome needs to serve the public interest. If actual outcomes normally are unfavorable, it will be judged that the decision maker is trying to act responsibly but is so incompetent that he is unable to do so.

It is certain that criteria of both intention and outcome will be applied in the future to judge the social responsibility performance of business. Society needs to know that businessmen responsibly consider social outcomes when they make a decision, and it also needs to know that their intentions are producing worthwhile results. Consistently poor results might indicate poor judgment, inadequate education in social values, lack of sufficient power to bring about intended outcomes, or something else; but in any case society needs to evaluate results as well as intentions in order to take the necessary corrective action. It is said that the road to social chaos is paved with good intentions and bad decisions.

Degrees of Social Responsibility

There are degrees of social responsibility depending on their intended outcome in comparison with other decision alternatives. Decisions are maximally socially responsible when decision makers develop the largest possible number of alternatives and choose the one which they believe will result in the highest benefit for society. Normally decision makers do not go this far. They merely develop a satisfactory number of alternatives and choose one of the better ones. In this instance the decision advances social welfare less than the maximum possible, but it is still a socially responsible decision because public benefit is intended and achieved. Society wants actions which serve public welfare, but it also allows those actions to serve other interests at the same time.

If we require all acts to be exclusively in the public interest, we deny the psychological fact that all persons act in their own interest. Social responsibility does not try to remake people; rather it asks of them only that they consider the broader social system and try to act in a way which benefits others as well as themselves. In this manner they serve their *self-interest* but not a *selfish interest,* because this is a social exchange in which both they and their neighbors benefit.

In a similar manner actions for the benefit of a single organization may be socially responsible if they serve the broader public interest. To require that organizational acts be only in the public interest is to deny the diversity of interests in a free society. Centers of initiative are many, and, in order to maintain these centers, their goals must be served as well as the general welfare. But the price which public society exacts for this social freedom is that private organizational acts shall be taken with due concern for public responsibility. There is concurrent private freedom and public responsibility.

For example, John Doe Corporation decided to open a chain of franchised hamburger restaurants, each to be owned locally by its operators. It planned to serve a standardized menu (with some local exceptions) of good quality pure foods and to meet or exceed grade A sanitation standards in each community. Buildings would have much more attractive design and landscaping than typical "mom-and-pop" hamburger stands. Management services, financial aids, centralized purchasing of nonperishable items, and other services would be provided to franchisees.

John Doe Corporation entered the hamburger business in order to employ its capital profitably; however, it also attempted to operate in a socially responsible manner in a number of ways. It attempted to upgrade mom-and-pop standards of food quality and service, thus making it possible for locally owned business to remain competitive. It gave attention to upgrading underprivileged neighborhoods, providing locations that were aesthetically attractive, upgrading sanitation, and providing franchisee participation in control. Though it acted in its own interest, it also believed it acted in the public interest in a socially responsible manner.

In the real world an individual decision usually starts a series of consequences some of which are favorable while others are unfavorable. For example, when a business discharges an employee, the discharge by itself can hardly be considered in the public interest. The decision as a whole, however, could be in the public interest because it protected other employees, encouraged the discharged employee to reassess his own capabilities, and caused him to seek other employment which proved in the long run to be more appropriate to his talents. This example suggests that a single effect of a decision cannot be considered by itself. The only rational approach is to consider the entire system and evaluate the *net effect* on the public interest of the total results of any decision, evaluating both positive and negative results. Any decision whose intended and net results are positive is minimally socially responsible, but some decisions may produce a larger amount of net positive outcomes than others.

Moving toward More Responsible Behavior

If a business merely complies with the law, is it being socially responsible? Some persons say that this is not social responsibility, because anyone is required to do the same. On the other hand, a firm could choose not to follow the law and, instead, take the consequences, as many businesses have done in the past. Compliance with social law such as a fair employment law is a conscious act. When it has intended favorable consequences, it can be called socially responsible behavior; however, mere compliance with law is a rather minimal social action. The obviously more responsible firm is one which seeks to respond to social needs beyond the minimum requirements of law. It is the kind of firm which most persons have in mind when they talk about the social responsibility of business.

In making a socially responsible decision, a firm needs to consider long-range effects on society along with short-range effects. For example, a firm which builds row upon row of look-alike houses may be saving $500 on each house and passing along $400 of the saving to each buyer, thus serving consumer price interests. In the long run, however, the look-alike construction may create conditions for rapid development of a city slum. In this instance the lack of a long-range outlook may result in serious social costs. Both short-range and long-range social costs and benefits need to be evaluated in an effective decision.

Further, a business is more effective when it develops a wide variety of decision alternatives, rather than merely picking the first positive alternative that becomes evident. Within limits, as the number of alternatives increases, there is greater possibility for an improved decision. Too often firms are weak in decision planning, and society is the loser.

Forecasting is also important in a socially responsible decision. A firm needs to try to understand what the environment will be like during the entire time that a decision will be implemented. It is especially important for a business or any other organization to try to predict the long-run system implications of its decisions. For example, the automobile industry is faulted for the myopic vision which prevented it from perceiving the serious environmental problems that developed from automobile emissions. Even though it was a transportation expert on which the public depended, the automobile industry was unable to foresee and prevent the environmental degradation that resulted from its actions. It failed in its social responsibility for environmental protection.

Social Responsibility Applies to All Organizations and Life Roles

Although this book emphasizes *business* social responsibility, business is not alone in having social responsibilities. All organizations, public and private, have social responsibilities to protect and enhance public quality of life. A labor union or a government office is no more excused from social responsibility than a business is. Each needs to act in a way which protects and serves public interests.

In a similar manner social responsibility applies to all persons in all their life roles, such as employee, camper, renter, and automobile driver. Individuals who toss their rubbish along a roadside are just as irresponsible as a business which pours pollutants into a river. They may argue that their offense is less in magnitude, but when added cumulatively, individual offenses are the result of a massive offense against the public interest. As a matter of fact, quality of life will be improved less than people expect if only business is socially responsible. Substantial improvement in quality of life will be achieved only when most organizations and persons act in socially responsible ways.

Public Interest Cannot Be Determined Exactly

Although the public interest is a useful guide for responsible decision making, there is no exact way to determine what the ''public interest'' is, how to

The Corporation Is More than an Economic Institution

When one uses the phrase the "social responsibility" of the corporation, one is not indulging in rhetoric (though many corporate officials are), or thinking of *noblesse oblige* (which fewer corporate officials do), or assuming that some subversive doctrine is being smuggled into society (as some laissez-faire economists suggest), but simply accepting a cardinal socio-psychological fact about human attachments. Unless one assumes that loyalty and identification are simply momentary transactions, or that employment is simply a limited relation of service-for-payment, then the corporation is a social world, with social obligations to its members, as well as an economizing instrument competitively providing goods at least cost to an economic world of consumers.

From Daniel Bell, "The Coming of Post-Industrial Society," *Business and Society Review/Innovation,* Spring 1973, p. 17. Reprinted with permission.

measure it, or how to serve it. For these reasons socially responsible decisions will always be made in a state of imperfection and uncertainty. Consider the following situation.

In a Midwestern metropolitan area of 1 million persons a local grocery chain withdrew from its shelves all copies of one issue of a popular national magazine because they were alleged to have obscene photographs. The decision was made by the company president after store managers had notified him of substantial customer complaints as soon as the magazine was placed on sale. According to the president, each store was primarily a grocery store, and magazines were strictly a supplementary business. Store policy was to maintain a family image and environment to which women could freely bring their children while shopping. Since this magazine's content for this particular week was judged not fit for family consumption according to general community standards, it was withdrawn from magazine racks. The president said the store was not on an antismut campaign and would display the next issue of the magazine for sale if it met community standards for family use.

When a local news reporter contacted the magazine's director of promotion in New York City, the director said the store action was censorship and added that people should be allowed to make their own judgments of what to buy. On the other hand, both the local mayor and the chain's majority stockholder told the reporter they agreed with the chain's action. When the state director of the Civil Liberties Union was contacted, he agreed, stating that the store had a right to sell what it pleased, especially since the magazine could be purchased elsewhere in the community.

It is evident from this case that the public interest is difficult to define. In addition, conflicts among basic values are the most difficult to resolve. Should a free press be preserved or should community standards be preserved? What were the real community standards? Was the president using the situation to justify censorship according to his own standards? Was his decision truly socially responsible, or was he allowing himself to be influenced by a few prudish dissidents in the community? As president of the chain store, what would you have done?

Social Responsibility and Social Response

The concept of social responsibility is merely a preliminary step toward social effectiveness of business. It is the underlying value which gives businessmen a sound basis for social action. It is the philosophy which justifies business involvement in its social community, but philosophy by itself is incomplete. It must be followed by effective social action. In the words of one observer, "Philosophy without program is shadow without substance. Perhaps one should talk, therefore, less of corporate social *responsibilities* and more of corporate social *responses*. The former is too redolent with legalisms and the notion of fixed obligations; the latter, more open, permits voluntary and creative undertakings by business on behalf of society's larger needs."[4]

If business and society get stuck on the legalisms of social responsibility, they will drift into inaction. The ultimate need is a business *response* which provides progress toward the desirable end of a more effective society. As shown in Figure 3-1, the desirable end is achieved through a sequence of philosophy, process, and function. In the area of business and society, the philosophy is social responsibility, and the process is creative decision making by business. Creative decisions lead to the function of social action by business, which produces the desirable end of a better society. Social responsibility is only the beginning of the sequence.

One fact is certain: Businessmen cannot withdraw into isolation and avoid the issues of social responsibility and social response. Neither can they claim that business is amoral and exempt from considerations of responsibility. The simple fact is that business is a major social institution, and as such it is importantly involved in social values. This is to its credit—a mark of its status. If business were not importantly involved in societal value systems, this fact would be evidence that it is detached from the mainstream of society and is of little significance. But business is in the mainstream of life and, hence, in the mainstream of building a better quality of life.

The quality of life, as distinguished from traditional economic needs, has become the dominant theme of need in the United States. This means that the next great opportunity for business service is the meeting of social needs. This opportunity is comparable to the economic one which prevailed 200 years ago. Business,

---

[4]Clarence C. Walton, "Recreating the City of Man," in *A Call to Social Action,* St. Louis, Mo.: Beta Gamma Sigma, 1968, p. 17. Italics in original. See also Dow Votaw and S. Prakash Sethi, "Do We Need a New Corporate Response to a Changing Social Environment?" *California Management Review,* Fall 1969, pp. 3–31.

PHILOSOPHY ⟶ PROCESS ⟶ FUNCTION ⟶ END (GOAL)

| Social responsibility | Creative social decisions by business | Social action (social response) | More effective society |

Figure 3-1 A philosophy of social responsibility provides a basis for an effective social response by business.

if it is to remain vigorous, increasingly will turn its creative efforts toward serving social needs in a profitable manner. In the long run, provision of many traditionally "social" needs such as education and resource conservation may be a primary or line function of many businesses in the same way that manufacturing is today.

THE POWER-RESPONSIBILITY EQUATION
Social Power

Most persons agree that businessmen today have much social power. Their counsel is sought by government, and what they say and do influences their community. This type of influence is *social power*. It comes to businessmen because they are leaders, intelligent men of affairs, people with a record of accomplishing projects successfully, and managers of vast economic resources.

In the same way that physical assets are an economic resource, power is a social resource. It may be used for good or evil, and for social gain or social loss. It is subject to abuse and corruption, but it also is an agent for responsible social improvement. In a complex social system it is highly dynamic, moving back and forth across the interfaces of organizations as it is redistributed by means of their social exchanges.

An example of business abuse of power, using government as an ally in this instance, is the plumbing contractor licensing board in a small community. Most of the appointees to this board are plumbing contractors. As a result of contractor dominance on the board, it rejected seven of the last eight applicants for the license required to set up a plumbing business. These rejections helped maintain favorable competitive conditions for the contractors already in business.

Most power exercised by business is functional power; that is, the power granted to business by society is roughly sufficient for business to perform the functions which society expects of it. It is power "to do," rather than power "over." The businessman deals with other persons in functional roles such as employee, customer, and vendor, not as subjects of his monolithic power. There is, consequently, much pressure from claimants to keep his power within reasonable bounds. In this instance, reasonable power is defined as that power which is necessary to perform an appropriate function.

The power of businessmen relates to their role as businessmen. Like other persons, they are also citizens, and in their citizen role they may take a position on public issues. When they speak and act as citizens only, and those involved recognize this fact, the social power applied is that of citizens and is not directly attributable to business. In practice, however, it is often difficult to distinguish between these two roles, thereby further complicating the power-responsibility relationships of businessmen.

Social Responsibility Goes with Social Power

To the extent that businessmen and other groups have social power, the lessons of history suggest that social responsibility should be equated with it. Stated in the form of a general relationship, *social responsibilities of businessmen arise from the amount of social power they have.*

The idea that responsibility and power go hand in hand appears to be as old as civilization itself. Wherever one looks in ancient and medieval history—Palestine, Rome, Britain—men were concerned with balancing power and responsibility in their political systems and other institutions. Men, being somewhat less than perfect, have often failed to achieve this balance, but they have generally sought it as a necessary antecedent to justice. This idea has its origins in reason and logic. It is essentially a matter of balancing the two sides of an equation. As stated by one philosopher, ''The demand of the law in a well-ordered society is that responsibility shall lie where the power of decision lies. Where that demand is met, men have a legal order; where it is not, they have only the illusion of one.''[5]

The idea of balanced power and responsibility is a value supported by Protestant, Catholic, and Jewish faiths,[6] and it is also a part of business philosophy. For example, one of the rules of scientific management is that authority and responsibility should be balanced in such a way that each employee and manager is made responsible to the extent of his authority, and vice versa. Although this rule refers only to relationships within the firm, it should apply as well to the larger society outside the firm. As a matter of fact, businessmen have been strong proponents of balanced social power and responsibility in external society, particularly in their views on responsibilities of labor leaders.

Objections to a Balance of Power and Responsibility

The logic of reasonably balanced power and responsibility is often overlooked by those who object to social responsibilities for business. The fallacy of their objections is that usually they are based on an economic model of pure

[5]John F. A. Taylor, ''Is the Corporation above the Law?'' *Harvard Business Review, March*–April 1965, p. 126.
[6]John W. Clark, *Religion and Moral Standards of American Businessmen,* Cincinnati: South-Western Publishing Company, Incorporated, 1966, especially p. 172.

Social Responsibility Reflects Major Social Change

If the leaders of business continue to conceive of social responsibility as a mere euphemism for charity, a surrogate for the corporate image, a concern only for the public relations department, or simply a passing fad, they will fail to meet what may be one of mankind's great challenges, and will, as a price for their failure, lose their own leadership roles in society and bring about the fall of the very organizations with which they are identified. They will make the wrong decisions, using irrelevant data, inappropriate criteria and anachronistic goals, and will find inadequate solutions to the wrong problems; they will take actions which can only aggravate the real problems while producing misleading feedback for their decision-making systems.

Growing both in size and persuasiveness is a body of evidence which compels the businessman to consider seriously the possibility that social responsibility is more than an expedient response to temporary conditions. If, as now seems very likely to be the case, social responsibility appears in the eyes of future historians to have been one of the important manifestations of profound social change, leaders of business must immediately begin to see it as such and to orient their words and actions around a better view of reality.

From Dow Votaw, "Genius Becomes Rare: A Comment on the Doctrine of Social Responsibility, Pt. II," *California Management Review,* Spring 1973, pp. 16–17. Reprinted with permission.

competition in which market forces leave business theoretically without any social power and, hence, no social responsibility (a balanced zero equation). This zero equation of no power and no responsibility is a proper theoretical model for pure competition, but it is theory only and is inconsistent with the power realities of modern organizations. They possess such great initiative, economic assets, and power that their actions do have social effects. In reality, therefore, the "no responsibility" doctrine assumes that business will keep some of its social power but will not worry about social responsibility.

At the other extreme, some persons would have business assume responsibilities as a sort of social godfather, looking after the less-advantaged, public health, juvenile delinquency, or any other social need, simply because business has large economic resources. This position overlooks the fact that business operates in a complex society, which has other institutions available to serve people in these areas. Business is one of many centers of initiative in the social system; hence, no need exists to make it a monolithic dispenser of welfare, overshadowing the state as it cares for everyone's problems. The "total responsibility" doctrine also confuses business's function of *service* to society with *servitude* to society. Workers, investors, and others participate in a business as free persons—not as slaves of society. They have their own lives to live, and business is their cooperative venture for fulfilling their own private needs while serving public needs.

The "no responsibility" and the "total responsibility" doctrines are equally false. According to the first doctrine, business keeps its power but accepts no responsibility, thereby unbalancing the power-responsibility equation. According to the second doctrine, responsibility far exceeds power, again unbalancing the equation.

The Iron Law of Responsibility

If business social responsibilities could be avoided or reduced to insignificance, business decisions would certainly be easier. Social responsibilities are difficult to determine and apply. But what are the consequences of responsibility avoidance? If responsibility arises from power, then the two conditions tend to stay in balance over the long run, and the avoidance of social responsibility leads to gradual erosion of social power. This is the Iron Law of Responsibility: *In the long run, those who do not use power in a manner which society considers responsible will tend to lose it.* The law's application to man's institutions certainly stands confirmed by history. Though the "long run" may require decades or even centuries in some instances, society ultimately acts to reduce power when it is not used responsibly.

As it applies to business, the Iron Law of Responsibility insists that to the extent businessmen do not accept social responsibility obligations as they arise, other groups eventually will step in to assume those responsibilities. This prediction of diluted social power is not a normative statement of what we think *should* happen. Rather, it is a prediction of what will tend to happen whenever businessmen do not keep their social responsibilities approximately equal to their social power. Bowen's original study of business social responsibilities presented this idea as follows: "And it is becoming increasingly obvious that a freedom of choice and delegation of power such as businessmen exercise would hardly be permitted to continue without some assumption of social responsibility."[7]

History supports the mutuality of power and responsibility in business. Consider the example of unemployment. Business in the first quarter of this century remained callous about technological and market layoff. As a result, business lost some of its power to government, which administers unemployment compensation, and to unions, which restrict business by means of tight seniority clauses, supplemental unemployment benefits, and other means. Now business finds itself in the position of paying unemployment costs that it originally denied responsibility for but having less control than when it did not pay! Business power has drained away to bring the power-responsibility equation back into balance.

Balancing Power and Responsibility

In line with the foregoing analysis, proposals for a strictly economic function of business with no social responsibility lose some of their glamour because they

[7]Howard R. Bowen, *Social Responsibilities of the Businessman,* New York: Harper & Brothers, 1953, p. 4.

mean substantial loss of business power. It is unlikely that businessmen will concede their social power so easily because they are men of action who will not sit quietly on the sidelines of society. They want to be in the midst of progress, offering innovations in their areas of expertise.

It is even unlikely that society will permit businessmen to concede their power, because it is coming to recognize its need for them. The more probable outcome is that society will persuade businessmen to accept more social responsibility in order to balance the power-responsibility equation. Much "persuasion" will take the form of legal force on policy matters, but much operating initiative may be left to business. The paramount point is operating initiative. If business conduct is so irresponsible that operating initiative is assumed by government, then business will lose substantial social power.

It appears that both business leaders and the general public are coming to accept the idea of balanced power and responsibility. When businessmen accept the logic of this idea, their next step is learning to apply it when making decisions. Granted that there are no pat answers, they still need some guides, or else each will take off in a different direction according to his own views. At this point, the ideas already stated begin to offer operating help. If social responsibilities of businessmen need to reflect their social power, then, in a general way, *in the specific operating areas where there is power, responsibility will also reside. And the amount of responsibility will approximate the amount of power.* Consider the situation of two companies, each closing its plant in a different city. Company A is a major employer in a small town. It is moving its entire plant out of the community. Company B is moving its plant of the same size out of a large city, where it is one of many employers. Other things being equal, it appears that Company A needs to give more thought to social responsibilities in connection with its move because of its greater effect on its community.

Even accepting the greater responsibility of Company A, and some would not go this far, there is no measure of exactly how much more responsibility it has or of how it should adjust to its greater responsibility. Thus the equation of balanced power and responsibility serves only as a rough guide, but a real one. For example, do businessmen by their industrial engineering decisions have the power to affect workers' feelings of accomplishment and self-fulfillment on the job? If so, there is a balancing need for social responsibility. Do businessmen have power to determine the honesty of advertising? To the degree that they do, does not social responsibility also arise?

One matter of significance is that the conditions causing power are both internal and external to the firm. In the example of advertising honesty, power is primarily internal, being derived from the authority structure of the firm and management's knowledge of product characteristics. In the case of Company A, much of its social power is derived from the external fact that it is the only employer in a small town. Each case is contingent upon the situation, requiring operating appraisal of power-responsibility relationships each time a decision is made. There is no across-the-board set of instructions that can be given in advance to a company telling it what its social responsibilities are. Thus, social responsibility decisions are a part of modern contingency management, which says that optimum decisions vary according to the different conditions in each situation.

External power may even arise involuntarily through no overt decision or action on the part of business. In a small town, for example, a major flood on a small river endangered one side of town. A construction company which was building a freeway nearby had the only equipment available for quick construction of levees to protect the town.

Corporate Constitutionalism

Typically, when citizens think of getting business to be more socially responsible, they think of legislation to require certain actions of business, but another way is by pressures from other organizations and groups in a free society. When these pressures are resolved in an agreement, either oral or written, that limits the power of an organization to affect others, this agreement may be called *corporate constitutionalism,* because it restricts organizational power in the same way that a governmental constitution does. When defined in an organizational context, corporate constitutionalism means an agreement on policies and standards which protect society from arbitrary and unreasonable use of organizational power and establish due process for all parties involved. The words "arbitrary" and "unreasonable" are significant because any organization must have power in order to attain its objectives.

Constitutionalism does not destroy power, but rather it defines conditions for responsible use of power. Its dual purpose is to channel organizational power in supportive ways and to protect other interests against unreasonable organizational power. Constitutionalism is used to balance the power-responsibility equation. Its emphasis is upon the responsibility side of the equation, primarily limiting whatever power exists. This relationship with power suggests that as more power is acquired by organizations, more attention must be given to constitutional channeling of that power.

Near the beginning of the social responsibility movement Selekman pressed for more constitutionalism to limit business power. He spoke of the "urgency of a framework of constitutionalism for the modern corporation" in order to enhance its compatibility with modern society. He recognized the difficulties involved: "Indeed, the carrying out of social and moral responsibility in complex situations is hardly ever a tidy, roseate affair except in utopian narratives."[8]

Constitutional standards may be generated internally in response to social needs, as in the case of company codes of ethical practice. In this area, for example, one author has called for more corporate constitutionalism to protect

[8]Benjamin M. Selekman, *A Moral Philosophy for Management,* New York: McGraw-Hill Book Company, 1959, pp. 206, 219. For a study of political constitutionalism in the general context of social responsibility, see Richard Eells and Clarence Walton, *Conceptual Foundations of Business,* Homewood, Ill.: Richard D. Irwin, Inc., 1961, pp. 380–407.

subordinate managers from arbitrary decisions by their superiors. Since managers at present do not have the kind of job protection normally provided for labor, they need constitutional provisions for due process in resolving disputes.[9]

Standards more often are generated through agreement with external pressure groups, such as minority groups, community organizations, professional groups, government, and labor. The labor agreement is a constitutional document defining rights and duties of both parties. An example in another area is a manufacturing concern's informal agreement with city officials that it would use a fume-producing work process only during midday hours, when rising air currents would dissipate the offensive odors. If the process were used at night, odors might settle in the neighborhood for hours. In another city, domestic airlines agreed that jets taking off would pass a certain landmark before turning in order not to pass over the downtown area of the complaining suburb. In another city, airlines agreed with airport neighbors to tow airplanes in certain situations between 11 P.M. and 7 A.M. in order to eliminate noise from running engines.

An important corollary of corporate constitutionalism is *due process,* which defines the conditions for use of power and the conditions for appeal of its excessive use. In employee relations, for example, a foreman may be unable to discharge a man directly. He can only suspend the man and recommend discharge to a higher office or a board. This procedure notifies others who may check his action, and it delays action to prevent decisions based on emotion in the heat of an argument. If an employee wishes to challenge his foreman's action, due process may permit him to have a hearing if he requests it, before discharge can be finalized. Corporate constitutionalism thus provides procedural checks and balances on power.

SUMMARY

Social responsibility refers to the obligation of decision makers to take actions which protect and improve the welfare of society as a whole along with their own interests. It broadens viewpoints to the entire social system and thus reduces the tendency of partisan groups to suboptimize general social benefits. Social responsibility is the first step in a sequence of philosophy, decisions, and actions (social response) to create a more effective society.

Business has social power. Though objections are voiced, there are valid reasons for approximately matching social responsibility with social power. In the long run, those who do not use power in a manner which society considers responsible will tend to lose it. This is the Iron Law of Responsibility. Power is especially contained by constitutional agreements among organizations. Corporate constitutionalism provides standards to protect society from arbitrary and unreasonable use of organizational power.

[9]Robert Granford Wright, "Managing Management Resources through Corporate Constitutionalism," *Human Resource Management,* Summer 1973, pp. 15–23.

STUDY GUIDES FOR INTERPRETATION OF THIS CHAPTER

1. An electric utility operates in a labor market which has an adequate supply of labor to meet its needs; however, a local community group has asked the utility to add about 50 percent to its training budget for two years in order to train members of less-advantaged groups in the community. What factors should it consider in determining its decision?

2. A manufacturer of heavy durable goods is building a $90-million factory in a remote area off a country road 1 mile from the edge of a city of 500,000 persons. Should it spend $1 million additional to beautify and landscape its plant? What factors should it consider in deciding this issue?

3. Select an example of business social action from your local newspaper and appraise it in terms of the power-responsibility equation.

4. Interview five businessmen to learn their understanding of the term "business social responsibility," and then interpret their explanations in terms of the ideas presented in this chapter.

5. Discuss an example of corporate constitutionalism from your community or from some other source.

PROBLEMS
The LSD Affair

a. A nationally distributed magazine in one of its issues published instructions for making LSD, a dangerous drug with which juveniles tended to experiment. At the time the issue was published it was a felony in a large number of states to make, possess, or sell this drug. The magazine's management knew of these statutes but distributed the magazine in all states.

1. Was the magazine's management socially responsible in this action? Explain.

b. A local bookseller received the magazine in a state having felony laws regarding LSD. He knew of the laws and saw the instructions in the magazine. He placed the magazine on sale and sold it without warning to either juvenile or adult buyers.

1. Was the bookseller acting in a socially responsible manner? Explain.

c. In one state which had felony laws concerning LSD the governor of the state requested booksellers to withdraw the magazine from their sales racks.

1. If you were a bookseller who received this request, what would you do? Why?

2. A representative of the American Civil Liberties Union criticized the governor for interfering with freedom of the press. Appraise his actions in terms of social responsibility.

The Expensive Park

In a city of about 20,000 persons a regional manufacturer is spending over $2.5 million to convert 260 acres which it owns into a public park, including golf, swimming, and tennis. The manufacturer estimates that during the park's fifth year of operation it will reach its peak planned profit of $50,000 annually. The manufacturer's only plant is in this city, and it employs about 1,000 persons. It is the town's major taxpayer; and there is already a city park, but it is smaller and of lower quality than the one the manufacturer is building.

1. Appraise management's actions in terms of social responsibility to all claimants of the organization.

A PLURALISTIC SOCIETY

*A society capable of continuous renewal would be characterized
first of all by pluralism—by variety, alternatives, choices and
multiple focuses of power and initiative. We have just such
pluralism in this society.*

John W. Gardner[1]

Today's society and polity are pluralistic.

Peter F. Drucker[2]

A subsidiary of one of the largest 500 companies in the United States bought
several thousand acres of ranch land in order to develop it. The plan was to develop
a seaside resort with hotels, a leisure-living community among rolling hills, golf
courses, an airstrip for light airplanes, some new farm land, and a large "green
belt" of land permanently dedicated to the county government to be kept in its
natural state. The plan for land use was carefully devised and reasonable. No
industrial zoning was proposed.

The land purchase was easy compared with the hornets' nest of controversy
which surrounded the land's development. Conservation groups protested that the
land should not be developed at all, but should be reserved for public use. The
conservationists and a group of sports fishermen joined in opposing the seaside
resort, because they felt it would mar the rugged beauty of the coastline and
perhaps pollute a popular fishing area. Farmers who had property within 2 miles of
the airstrip claimed that noise from airplanes would disturb them and frighten their
cattle. Another group of farmers insisted that the added farm land and population
would increase water use so much that the underground water table on which they
depended might be depleted. A historical group insisted that agreements be made
to protect certain old homesites and other points significant to the history of the
state. A group of hotel managers in the nearest resort community insisted that a
new resort was not needed, because there were not enough tourists for two resorts.

[1]John W. Gardner, "Toward a Self-renewing Society," *Time,* Apr. 11, 1969, p. 40.
[2]Peter F. Drucker, *The Age of Discontinuity: Guidelines to Our Changing Society,* New York: Harper
& Row, Publishers, Incorporated, 1968, p. x.

A labor group argued that zoning must provide adequate low-income homes and apartments near the expensive hotels and leisure-living homes so that workers in the hotels and shops would not have to travel long distances to work.

There were also various government groups to negotiate with, such as the state water resources board and the county zoning board which had to give final approval for the project. Several lengthy zoning controversies developed, such as whether streets in residential areas should have expensive concrete curbs and gutters with sidewalks. After nearly a year of delays, one company executive observed: "In spite of our experience in this field, we didn't know what we were getting into."

What the company was "getting into" was a pluralistic community in which organized groups were representing the special interests of groups of citizens. This chapter discusses some of the interest groups interacting with business and then examines the elements and modes of operation of a pluralistic society. Pluralism is the basic social framework within which business operates in the United States.

INTEREST GROUPS INTERACTING WITH BUSINESS
Increasing Social Complexity

Centuries ago business was a rather uncomplicated relationship involving only a few interest groups, and it had been that way throughout history. There were owners who supplied the small amount of capital needed, employees who performed the work, and customers who purchased the products, as shown in Figure 4-1a. Government and religion stood weakly on the side performing their political and moral regulatory rules, and their influence was relatively minor. In small businesses such as a "mom-and-pop" grocery store, the employee supplied his own capital, and he and his family operated the store, so even the separate ownership role was bypassed. There was a direct relationship only between the

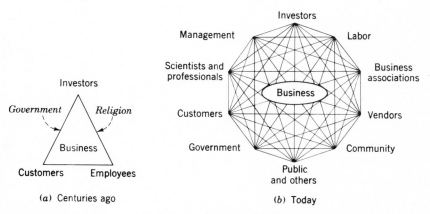

(a) Centuries ago   (b) Today

Figure 4-1 Business complexity centuries ago and today.

owner-employee and his customers. There are even today many shops of this type, but in advanced nations most commerce is achieved by larger organizations with entirely different and more complex modes of action.

During the last two centuries, revolutions in science, education, productivity, and culture developed in a way that expanded institutions and interest groups until the social system became significantly more complicated. Each group in the system developed its own specialized activity, which then had to be integrated with other activities to make the system function effectively. Many of these groups are active participants in the business environment as shown in Figure 4-1b, which is more complex than Figure 4-1a.

The purpose of Figure 4-1b is to portray most of the groups directly involved with business, and the words "Public and others" at the bottom of the chart are intended to represent the idealized norm which we call the public interest and all other groups which relate to business. Some of these other groups are agriculture, minority groups, conservationists, journalists, news media, educators, nonprofit foundations, churches, and medical services. In the example reported at the beginning of this chapter, most of the groups fit the classification "Public and others," since the business was not yet operating in the community.

A Community of Competing Groups

The president's suite in today's business is less a place for autocratic decisions than a place for reconciliation of the multitude of competing groups pressuring business in terms of their own interests. Although the number of competing interests demanding reconciliation has expanded greatly, cultural guides to help an executive make the right decision have hardly expanded at all. In addition to the expanded *number* of interests pressing on business, the *kinds* of decisions needed and the cultural conditions for them have changed drastically but without corresponding changes in guidelines for business. The result is that modern managers develop a *social vertigo* trying to balance all interest groups because they cannot relate to enough familiar points of reference. Like a pilot flying blind, they become disoriented and confused because the familiar horizon is gone; consequently, they are quietly searching for more guides such as professionalism and the idea of social responsibility.

Likewise, the passengers in the airplane—who in this instance are the publics of business—rise in confused disharmony because they have lost the horizon also. What is the social purpose of business? Upon what pillars does its legitimacy of power rest? What functions should it perform? How can society judge the effectiveness of its performance? In modern society we expect a business to be many things to many people, such as:

A better place for investment

A better place to work

A better supporter of ethical ideals

A better company to buy from

A better company to sell to

A better taxpayer and supporter of government

A better neighbor in the community

A better contributor to social goals, public interest, and human progress

The unique development of modern business life is competition among institutional interest groups, as shown in Figure 4-1b. Economic competition in the marketplace has been diluted by *social competition* among various business claimants seeking higher economic payouts, more prestige, power, and other benefits. Competition has moved partly from the marketplace to committee rooms, business offices, and legislative halls. The old competition was judged by precise, impersonal economic standards of conduct, but the new competition is based upon social standards which are vague, nebulous, and overrun with personal views and emotions. The old competition was primarily among persons acting individually, but the new competition is among interest groups and institutions which act for people as a collective community. They may act as much for power and institutional survival as they do for people.

The Changing Role of Business Clients

The interest groups which deal directly with business and, therefore, have a direct claim to certain outputs from it are the *clients* of business. Examples are customers, stockholders, and employees. The role of these clients has been changing in a dramatic fashion during the last century.

Owners Even the traditional ownership role has changed to an investor role. As large organizations have increased their dominance of business, one or a few persons can no longer supply the capital needed. The result is that ownership has been dispersed through stock markets to millions of persons who think more like investors than owners, as will be discussed in the chapter concerning ownership claims on business. Of equal importance is the fact that business investors in modern society are changing from individuals to institutions. Individuals place their money in mutual funds, insurance plans, pension plans, trust funds, and other institutions, which then invest the funds as representatives of millions of small investors. These institutions have tens of billions of dollars invested in corporate stocks, and each year they increase their investments. Indeed, changes in the ownership role have been significant, as will be discussed in a later chapter.

Management The relationship of ownership to management has also changed. One or two centuries ago the principal owners of business were also its managers. Ownership vested people with symbolic powers of leadership which were substantially related to their property rights. They knew best how to manage their resources. Even when their leadership faltered, this turn of events was considered an exception to the rule, rather than a denial of the unity of owner and manager. If any conflict arose between owner and manager roles, it was internal, to be resolved within the person and never exposed to public consideration.

Today, as shown in Figure 4-1*b,* management is more a differentiated role, semiprofessional in nature, with accession by competence rather than ownership. In many large enterprises the entire top-management group owns less than 5 percent of the company's assets—sometimes less than 1 percent. Management has become a distinct type of work with its own educational programs, literature, and criteria for achievement.

Labor   As management changed, so did labor. In early times employees acted primarily as individuals in their relationships with owner-managers. Increasingly, however, employment became governed by group contracts negotiated by labor unions. The union arose as a separate institution with its own power groups and institutional interests. As an example of these evolving institutional relationships, a common term in personnel management today is *labor-management* relations, not employee-owner relations. Employees today find their employment conduct bound by management's rules, management-union contracts, and union rules, all of which are surrounded by a firm canopy of government intervention. In the crush of institutional claimants upon business, individual needs of employees are apt to be bypassed, as will be discussed in a later chapter.

Scientists and Professionals   Historically, labor unions have represented mostly manual skills; and as civilization became more advanced, the burgeoning scientific-professional-intellectual groups tended to develop separate institutional interests. In the 1960s labor-union membership stabilized and actually declined as a proportion of the labor force (less than 25 percent), while membership in scientific and professional occupational groups expanded dramatically. In the same manner that owners and managers differentiated their roles, it appears that manual workers and intellectual workers are developing separate institutional claims on business, as shown in Figure 4-1*b.* This growth of professional groups has been one of the most striking business developments in recent years.

Business Associations   In the same way that employees have joined together for their own interests, businesses have formed a multitude of business associations to serve the interests which they have. The result is a more complex web of customs and relationships. The extent of involvement of even small businesses is illustrated by a local automobile agency in an urban community.

Ruskin Automobile Agency joined the local chamber of commerce in order to cooperate with other businessmen in community affairs. It was a member of a local credit bureau which served businessmen by providing customer credit ratings. With other businesses it had helped organize a

Better Business Bureau to investigate and expose shady business practices because it was especially concerned about their effect on the used car market. Each of the three associations mentioned was also affiliated with a similar national association.

At the national level Ruskin Agency was a member of the National Automobile Dealers Association in order to represent its industry group to manufacturers and others. It also belonged to the National Federation of Independent Business, which sought to protect small business interests. Recently it joined the American Management Association, a nonprofit group concerned with training and development, in order to encourage growth of several of its managers. There were also other business-related associations to which it belonged.

Customers   At first glance it might seem that customers are the same as always, but their role also is changing, as will be discussed in a later chapter. They are more sophisticated and they have more choice, but at the same time they need more protection because technological complexity reduces their power to judge product quality at the time of purchase. In general, there is a tendency for their sovereign power to be lost to the producer as products become more complicated; consequently, through the consumerism movement they are exerting powerful countervailing pressures on business.

Vendors   Modern business also gives vendors a more significant role than they once had. Increasing scientific complexity requires business buyers to work closely with their vendors to develop better schedules, methods, and product reliability. Major buyer-vendor relationships are long run rather than consisting of a single commercial transaction. Sometimes deliveries are rescheduled or a part redesigned to fit a vendor's capabilities better. Vendors frequently have service representatives in buyers' plants, and buyers have their technical representatives in vendors' plants. When there is a powerful buyer purchasing a major part of a vendor's output, the buyer often acts responsibly to help the vendor maintain competitive efficiency and stable schedules to avoid layoff and bankruptcy. Large mail-order houses and automobile manufacturers, for example, actually have served as management consultants to improve vendor business practice.

Government and the Community   The increased role of government in modern business is well known and is discussed in a later chapter. The community, shown separately from government in Figure 4-1b, represents all *local* interests—including local government—in a business's employment community, and is discussed in Part Four of this book. The community is definitely one of the growth areas in business's relationship with its environment.

The Public Interest   It may appear strange that the public interest is separated from government and community in Figure 4-1b; however, neither government nor community—nor any other group—is sure to represent interests of all the public at all times. The "public interest" is an abstract, general term used to describe the greatest good for the greatest number. Where government is involved, powerful dictators, inept bureaucrats, or power-hungry politicians may work against the public interest rather than for it. We cannot say that Hitler represented the public interest merely because he represented government. Similarly, a community may serve its own interests to the detriment of other communities; hence it cannot always act in the public interest. The public interest is actually an idealized norm which all people use to judge the acts of others. Most institutions claim to represent the public interest most of the time. The problem is that their views of public interest may differ.

ELEMENTS OF A PLURALISTIC SOCIAL SYSTEM

The relationships described in connection with Figure 4-1b represent a *pluralistic society,* in which diverse groups maintain autonomous participation and influence in the social system. Business is influenced by these groups in its interface with them in the system. In turn, again at the points of interface, business exerts a countervailing influence on them. As indicated in both quotations introducing this chapter, pluralism is a basic reality of the modern business culture. The significance of this reality for business is that pluralism defines the fundamental framework within which business must live and grow. Unless businessmen understand the "rules of the game" by which pluralism operates, they are handicapped in their efforts to make business a responsible social institution. This is their environment. They must know it in order to perform their roles as leaders. Whether they prefer pluralism is not the issue. It, like the weather, is here. For this reason much of this book relates to how business deals with relationships, power, and responsibility in a pluralistic society.

Some of the major elements of pluralism are discussed in the following paragraphs. Emphasis is on pluralism in the social system (social pluralism), because pluralism within a system of government (political pluralism) provides a slightly different context, although the basic ideas still apply.

Diversity of Interests

In pluralism there are numerous economic, political, educational, social, artistic, and other groups developed by people to promote their welfare. There are, therefore, many different points of view represented in the interface of these groups. As shown in Figure 4-2, pluralism occupies a broad middle ground on a social continuum from monism at one extreme to anarchy at the other. Monism requires that all men's affairs be operated by one absolute social institution which satisfies all of their needs. It is a social system with a monolithic, centralized power structure. The other extreme, anarchy, implies an unorganized society in which

Figure 4-2 Pluralism occupies a middle ground on a continuum from one to an infinite number of social units.

each person pursues his own interests without regard for others. Pluralism, operating between the extremes, decentralizes social power by dispersing it to a variety of institutions performing different social functions.

Institutional Specialization

Pluralism is an institutional concept. It recognizes that although people act individually in their interests, they also form institutions which act as agents to represent these interests. Since there is a diversity of interests among people, they tend to form many different specialized institutions to serve their different needs. One reason for this is that institutional specialization appears to be more efficient socially in the same way that labor specialization has proved itself more productive economically.

In modern society large institutions have arisen to dominate nearly every field of activity. Peter Drucker observes, "Historians two hundred years hence may see as central to the twentieth century what we ourselves have been paying almost no attention to: the emergence of a society of organizations in which every single social task of importance is entrusted to a large institution."[3]

Multiallegiant Individuals

In connection with institutional specialization, each person specializes his own interests and contributions, so he relates to many institutions in order to fulfill all his needs. In other words, he divides his needs and assigns different need fulfillments to different institutions. The result is that no business, labor union, or other pluralistic organization can claim a person's full loyalty to the exclusion of all other organizations. Writers in labor relations refer to a worker's "dual allegiance" to management and union; however, in terms of the total business environment a better term to apply is *the multiallegiant individual,* because he allocates his allegiance among many institutions.

[3]Drucker, op. cit., p. 171.

Pluralism Has a Rich Historical Heritage

One item of considerable importance, which should rank high as a factor contributing to the uniqueness of American life, is pluralism. This concept . . . refers to the diffusion of power among a multiplicity of organizations and groups. A pluristic society is one in which there is a wide decentralization and diversity of power concentrations. A pluristic society, furthermore, is marked by frequent conflict between power centers. Such conflicts, however, are usually considered healthy, since out of controversy new associations and nexuses of power may spring.

The notion of pluralism has historically been considered basic to our sort of democratic society, for so long as power is diffused and allegiances to groups and organizations dispersed, individuals will find that they possess freedom of action and expression. This was recognized by James Madison, who, writing in *The Federalist*, expounded upon the virtues of pluralism and forecast the rise of a multiplicity of organizations in America.

From Joseph W. McGuire, *Business and Society*, New York: McGraw-Hill Book Company, 1963, p. 130. Used with permission.

In a drug firm, for example, one chemist may be a member of management, a chemical-society member, an investor in business, a consumer, a Boy Scout leader, a member of the local community, and so on. He does not depend on only one institution representing his social class to supply most of his needs. Whatever conflict exists is not primarily a class conflict, but is a result of institutions trying to resolve different role needs which have been assigned to them by a common population. The chemist may have different expectations as a consumer, investor, and manager; however, this conflict is not among three classes of different people.[4] Rather, it is a conflict *among his own diverse expectations* as represented by various institutions to which he is allegiant.

When a person relates directly to an organization, he is making a *role investment* in it. This investment may consist of time, tangible goods, status, security, or other values useful to him. For example, a business owner may risk his prestige and reputation in a shaky venture. The venture's economic risk is minor to him compared with possible loss of prestige and self-esteem in the event of failure. Similarly, a customer invests his time, economic resources, and judgment. If his purchase does not meet his expectations, he may be more angered by his mistake in judgment than by his economic loss. Thus men sometimes will fight about a dollar

[4]According to Eells and Walton, this is one element of pluralism which Karl Marx could not understand. He perceived only class conflict. See the chapter on pluralism in Richard Eells and Clarence Walton, *Conceptual Foundation of Business*, Homewood, Ill.: Richard D. Irwin, Inc., 1961, pp. 360–379.

or a word, but on another occasion they will lose $1,000 with a smile because their social investments in each situation are different.

In making his investment in an organization, a person trades off some of his values in expectation of reciprocal benefits. Thus, he makes a *social transaction* in which he gives something and gets (or expects to get) something in return. The return which he expects from his investment is a *role benefit,* gain, reward, or payoff. It comes to him because of his performance in one or more roles. It, like his investment, may consist of any kind of value which the organization provides him. It may vary in amount, certainty, and other ways. If the organization's payoff of benefits is less than he expects in relation to his total investments, he will bring pressure on it to increase benefits. Or he may reduce his investments to bring them more in balance with his benefits. He may even withdraw from any further involvement with the organization.

The sequence of a person's investments, benefits, and possible actions is shown in Figure 4-3. Although a person's role investments and benefits are not fully quantifiable, for purposes of illustration it is assumed that they are. In Organization A the individual's benefits were inadequate, and he eventually withdrew from the organization. Organization B returned him higher benefits than he expected; therefore, he was satisfied and considered increasing his investment in it. Organization C, the one in which he had the largest investment, returned a fair benefit, but one that was not proportionately as high as Organization B. In Organization D his benefits were not adequate, and he brought pressures to increase them.

A Relatively Open System

The elements of pluralism imply a relatively open system in which there is substantial social exchange among organizations at their points of interface. Some

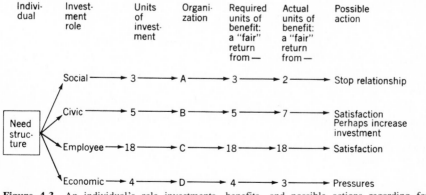

Figure 4-3 An individual's role investments, benefits, and possible actions regarding four organizations.

of the modes of interface are cooperation, bargaining, and competition. Both cooperation and conflict are built into the system by the fact that each organization has a specialized interest and constituency to serve. One company president comments, ''Coping with pluralistic objectives, most of which are conflicting, has indeed become the *sine qua non* of industrial management.'' He adds that, although managers will never be able to satisfy all the claimants on business, their constant striving to do so may be their greatest contribution to society.[5]

Diffusion of Power

A major operating mode of pluralism is power, but since there are many institutions applying it, power is diffused among a large number of decision makers. By means of diffused power, pluralism is ''as much opposed to the ambitious pretences of a James Stuart (the king can do no wrong), as it is to the Rousseauian version of democracy (the collectivity can do no wrong).''[6] No power center is completely independent to do exactly as it wishes, but each has some autonomy. This condition suggests that progress is made through politics, communication, innovation, negotiation, compromise, and consensus rather than by monolithic decision making.

Joint Venture

Since there is diffusion of power, major social institutions such as business are able to secure sufficient resources to perform their function only by developing a joint venture among a number of groups. That is, groups pool their capabilities and resources to accomplish an objective. The spirit of joint venture is developed by focusing on mutual interests and superordinate goals. Business, for example, is a joint venture of investors, managers, workers, communities, and others. Although these groups offer diverse inputs and expect diverse outputs from the venture, they join together in order to gain additional rewards from organized group effort. For example, investors seek more return on investment, greater security of investment, and pride of ownership. Managers seek status, a feeling of contribution, and self-esteem from a job well done. Without capital and workers they could not manage. Workers seek an opportunity to use their skills, social satisfactions, and higher pay. Working as individuals without associates, management, and extra capital, they might derive less of these desired benefits. Observe that the rewards expected in joint ventures are not only economic; they usually are also social and psychological. No person—even a poor one—lives by bread alone.

[5]Raymond H. Mulford, ''Pluralism Redefined,'' *Saturday Review,* Jan. 13, 1968, p. 33.
[6]Eells and Walton, op. cit., 1961, p. 363.

Limited research indicates that it is, indeed, difficult for business to meet the different expectations of those involved with it. A study of ninety-seven small businesses examined their ability to fulfill the needs of the following groups: community, government, customer, supplier, creditor, and owner.[7] There were only small correlations of satisfaction among the groups, and some correlations were negative. Customer satisfaction did correlate positively with supplier and owner satisfactions. Owner and community satisfactions also were positively correlated. The study shows that business cannot maximize for any group; thus it adopts a policy of reasonably satisfying several system components.

In summary of this section, pluralism is a complex social system not easily understood; however, some of its major elements are diversity of interests, institutional specialization, multiallegiant individuals, a relatively open system, diffusion of power, and joint venture.

OPERATION OF A PLURALISTIC SYSTEM
Claimants on Business

In the operation of a pluralistic system, those directly involved are not the only ones who can make claims on a business—or any other organization. Since pluralism is a system relationship, all social units are interconnected, and any unit which believes that its interests are even indirectly affected by business can become a claimant on it. The system relationship gives the unit an indirect social investment in the business which justifies a claim. Claims are made by such means as publicity, appeal to government, use of power, and trade-offs with other institutions that are in a more favorable position to bring pressures. An illustration follows.

A lumber company decided to cut certain redwood timber that it had owned for years. Conservationists who were opposed to this action felt that they could exert very little direct pressure on the company, and so they chose to work indirectly. They enlisted the support of businessmen in two nearby towns by convincing them that the forest was an important tourist attraction which would become more significant in future years as affluent people spent more money on recreation. They worked with county and state governments to try to have part of the land dedicated as a public recreational area. They also issued news releases about the situation and set up a speaker's bureau to furnish speakers on the subject to any available group.

[7]Frank Friedlander and Hal Pickle, "Components of Effectiveness in Small Organizations," *Administrative Science Quarterly,* September 1968, pp. 289–304; and Hal Pickle and Frank Friedlander, "Seven Societal Criteria of Organizational Success," *Personnel Psychology,* Summer 1967, pp. 165–178.

Claimants may also arise more or less involuntarily, not as a result of organization in advance, but from a series of events which begin to close in on their interests.

George Sykes's home adjoined a farm in a modest subdivision on the edge of a Midwestern city. He assumed that further subdivisions eventually would be developed on the farm. Three years after he bought his property he and his neighbors learned that a national manufacturer had taken a purchase option on the farm and was seeking industrial zoning in order to build a large foundry and forging shop on part of the property. Quickly he and his neighbors organized to prevent the industrial zoning, or as a minimum to get a buffer area of intermediate zoning established on that portion of the farm which was nearest their homes.

Discussions of business issues in the past have tended to focus on business members (such as employees) and other direct claimants (such as vendors). Now, however, the indirect claimants on business are getting a larger share of attention. One reason is that society is becoming more urbanized and crowded so that pollution, industrial noise, and similar matters are suddenly becoming critical; in a rural society they were a minimum concern. Another reason is that individuals and institutions have become more specialized and interdependent than they used to be; thus more people are affected by business in more ways and more often. A third reason is that our systems way of thinking is providing more evidence of the intricate ways in which business is related with all parts of society.

Social Constraints on Institutions

Since pluralistic institutions have autonomy, social constraints are required to integrate them into the system and check unbridled power. The most evident constraint is law, both legislative and administrative. Business is especially affected by administrative law, which consists of decisions and rules made by regulatory commissions and administrators, such as the Interstate Commerce Commission, Federal Communications Commission, Internal Revenue Service, and National Labor Relations Board.

Another constraint is the countervailing power of other institutions which respond to excesses by increasing opposing pressures. This means that the institutions partly regulate each other as a result of their diffused power. Countervailing powers eventually may reach constitutional agreements, as discussed earlier.

The cultural values and norms established by society also are powerful constraints. Even though most are unwritten, they become known and accepted ways of relating to one another and doing business. Sometimes these norms are formalized, such as ethical standards of professional groups and guides for social responsibility.

A constraint sometimes overlooked is the freedom of participants to withdraw their support of an institution. This potential action always stands in the background as a social control in a free society. For example, if customers go elsewhere and better workers take other jobs, a business cannot function effectively.

One point is certain. Good intentions of leaders are not a sufficient constraint on institutional power. Some of society's most undesirable results have developed out of high purposes. Noble objectives sometimes deteriorate into obsessions about the interests of one group, ignoring the interests of others. Leaders occasionally believe so strongly in their noble purposes that they adopt a *two-valued orientation* which assumes others are all wrong and they are all right, thus neglecting intermediate areas of social compromise between the two extremes. Their obsession with one approach leads to ignoble results in the manner of George Orwell's *Animal Farm:* "All men are equal, but some are more equal than others." Further, even though the motives of an individual or group are indisputably exalted, this does not assure that they have good judgment in their interpretations of business and society. Business relationships with society are intricate, complex systems in which two-valued orientations rarely apply.

Pluralism's Strengths and Weaknesses

Our discussion has treated pluralism as a fact of life for business in the United States, and it exists to some degree in many other advanced free nations of the world. Assuming that pluralism is a significant social framework in which business operates, what are its major strengths and weaknesses compared with more monolithic social systems?

Strengths of Pluralism

Support for Social Freedom   Many persons fear excessive power by business or any other institutions, because their freedoms will decline in this type of situation. They prefer to have power diffused broadly so that there is less chance for domination by any one institution. In this manner, tyranny and monolithic control are discouraged and people remain relatively free to conduct their own affairs. This approach places social control where it should be, because individuals and small groups are closest to daily affairs so they should know best how to conduct them. Further, by creating a widely dispersed set of loyalties, pluralism minimizes the danger that any leader will be able to rise to uncontrolled power.

With regard to business, pluralism both restricts businessmen and gives them freedom. They are restricted by the multitude of organizations that apply pressures to business, but at the same time they are left relatively free to conduct business subject to restrictions of law and custom.

Many Opportunities for Leadership   Since there are a multitude of organizations in a pluralistic society, there are also many opportunities for leadership. Many people can rise to the top of organizations in a pluralistic society; but in a monolithic society there are only a few opportunities for persons to secure top-leadership seasoning while others with leadership potential are held in the subordinate bureaucracy carrying out orders of the central leadership. Since there are so many leadership avenues open, persons with leadership potential need not feel suppressed in their efforts to gain leadership. In effect, pluralistic social organization is a training ground for leadership, and a progressive society needs a large supply of leaders.

Tolerance of Other Ideas   When people belong to a number of organizations, they become more understanding of the variety of people and ideas in a social system. They become aware that different ideas and approaches to problems are necessary to serve different needs. Since their own loyalties are diversified, they are tolerant of the loyalties of others likewise diversified. On the other hand, if people's social investments are in one monolithic organization, the total nature of their investment psychologically requires them to be partisan in order to protect their own interests. Their organization must be defended, because if it is lost, they lose all—psychologically, socially, and economically.

Improved Social Decisions   Since pluralism brings many organizations clamoring to present their different points of view, it provides a large variety of inputs into the social decision-making process. These inputs should shed more light on social issues than monolithic social designs are able to do, and the normal result should be an improved decision. In the philosophy of social science, truth is most nearly reached by examining an issue from as many points of view as possible, whereas physical science has truth only when there is one unerring, proven view of reality.[8] This means that pluralism is an effective vehicle for seeking social truth.

Pluralistic systems tend to be creative and innovative because their multiple areas of power and initiative provide alternative choices to society. There is capability for continuous social renewal, as mentioned in the first quotation introducing this chapter; consequently, society is better able to avoid aging and deterioration.

Satisfaction of Different Human Needs   The field of psychology indicates that people are individually different; consequently, they have different need and want patterns. It follows that the social system which should be most satisfying is one that serves different individual needs to the extent possible. Through its many centers of initiative and open interface between them, pluralism is an effective system for serving widely different needs while still maintaining social organiza-

[8]C. West Churchman, *Challenge to Reason,* New York: McGraw-Hill Book Company, 1968.

Alternatives to Pluralism

Pluralism is not the only answer. There are other ways to run a railroad—and a society. All of them involve concepts of government that make government the principal initiator and controller of organizational activity. Society, in effect, becomes a corporation, organized in good hierarchical form; and government takes over as manager. In ideal forms of socialism or communism, the resources of society and the returns achieved by government belong to the people. The people are owners and stockholders. In fact, however, in the socialized economies of Eastern Europe, government, like the management of many private corporations, develops a momentum of its own. While decisions are taken in the name of the people, the people's voice in planning and decision making may be very faint.

In these societies pluralism is suppressed in favor of order and hierarchy. Government leaders talk of coordinating efforts so that everyone can work together. They orchestrate the society. They operate the organizations of society as units of government. They frown on competition and conflict. Not content to act as referees, they stage and staff the whole shooting match.

From Harold J. Leavitt, William R. Dill, and Henry B. Eyring, *The Organizational World*, New York: Harcourt Brace Jovanovich, Inc., 1973, p. 277. Used with permission.

tion. It avoids both the extremes of anarchy and those of monolithic social control. It is a satisfying compromise between too much social organization and too little.

Weaknesses of Pluralism

Lack of Central Direction Diverse institutions tend to pursue their own interests unless there are superordinate goals to pull them together; therefore, a pluralistic system tends to depend on government to provide social goals, long-range plans, and policies to guide institutions toward the long-run public interest. Provided that government assumes this guiding role, then the free initiative which pluralism permits can become an innovative source of action for accomplishing public policy. If government does not accept its guiding role, then pluralistic organizations may become preoccupied with their own pet projects and short-range goals.

Emphasis on Institutional Power instead of Service In a system in which institutions have some freedom of action, there is always the possibility that institutional *power* will be overemphasized instead of institutional *service*. Institutions normally justify their existence by showing how they contribute to public needs. This is a positive, worthwhile measure of institutional performance. It is a valid social basis for granting power to perform designated institutional functions. However, in the absence of suitable checks and balances, this valid functional power can be diverted to power for its own sake; that is, "power to do" is diverted to "power over" others in the system. This kind of diversion makes organizations greedy for power and leads to power blocs and private wars among institutions for power supremacy. Power becomes the measure of success rather than the instrument by which service is rendered, and energies are diverted from more constructive public responsibilities.

As institutions become larger, there is the danger that they will lose sight of their service functions and rely on power to keep viable, unless constitutional provisions are established to limit power. Both the individual and total society need to be protected. The Labor-Management Relations Act, for example, has one set of provisions to protect the individual union member and another set to protect the public interest from union power.

Social Fragmentation Another weakness of pluralism is the possibility that so many different groups will arise that their objectives will overlap and they will dissipate their energies trying to maintain coordination and keeping off each other's toes. Just as too many cooks spoil the broth, too many pluralistic organizations could reduce progress to a quagmire of confusion and red tape. Each new institution further complicates the business environment. Since each institution is related to all others, the addition of one results in a geometric increase in complexity, rather than an arithmetic increase.

The fact that some pluralism is wise does not prove that more pluralism is wiser. At some point groups can be so splintered that each lacks the power to hold responsible leadership. Political parties in some European countries, for example, are so fractionated that none is strong enough to provide much-needed leadership. Divided responsibility and compromise become ends in themselves, while genuine political needs go unheeded for lack of leadership. In the business environment, government first moved in strongly. Then the unions came, followed by trade associations, professional and scientific societies, nonprofit organizations such as the Committee for Economic Development, and others. Recently we have added the institutional investor and social action groups. We must be cautious not to become so enamored of pluralism that we let complexity outstrip our capacity to coordinate society.

The point of diminishing returns in pluralism is the point where the increment from one more institutional finger in the pie is offset by the loss arising from additional complexity. Comparing pluralism with democracy, we recognize that an optimally free society is not one in which every citizen votes on every public issue regardless of its importance. Similarly, an optimally pluralistic society is not one in which every conceivable interest is represented by a separate institution competing for power.

Social fragmentation also has its effects on the individual. We can picture a situation in which a person finds his interests represented by so many hundreds of organizations that he feels close to none of them. Consequently, he can drift into a feeling of powerlessness, loneliness, and social alienation. He is like a person alone in New York's Times Square on New Year's Eve. Though he is surrounded by 100,000 people, he feels that none of them really care about him. He is alone in a crowd.

Elitism Technology and social systems are becoming increasingly complex, and it is inevitable that some persons should know more than others about these complex matters. These more knowledgeable persons are likely to rise within each organization. As they become more involved in abstract computer models, social planning, and decision making, they are likely to develop an elitist detachment from the persons they represent "who just don't understand the system." They come to the conclusion that they know what is best, because they alone can see the whole picture. If their group does not agree, it should be manipulated or coerced into agreement. Thus, the democratic basis of the organization becomes reversed. No longer are the leaders serving specific needs of individuals who constitute the group. This tendency can be observed in labor unions, minority groups, social action groups, and business trade associations. Controls are necessary to maintain democratic responsiveness to individual member needs.

In fact, individuality is the one "institution" not represented at the social-exchange table of pluralism. It stands to lose most if the institutional aspects of pluralism are overemphasized. Therefore, if individualism is a value which society cherishes (and we believe it does, within limits), then social controls and customs need to be established to obligate institutions to accept, respect, and even cultivate individualism (again, within reasonable limits).

Focus on Conflict It is sometimes said that pluralism focuses on conflict, since there are many autonomous organizations seeking their own goals. Certainly conflict does occur in pluralism, but it is not a special characteristic of pluralism compared with other social forms. In a pluralistic social system different groups can cooperate toward goals if they desire to do so.

> If, for example, five groups on a hill want water from a well in a valley, they can argue about who will bring it up the hill or each can get its own or they can *cooperate* to combine this task with other tasks to bring more need satisfactions to all. We can even assume that there is not enough water in the well for all of them. In this case they can still cooperate to dig another well, dam a stream, or seek some other water source. Or, each group can try to keep the water for itself. This is a human choice, not a creation of pluralism.

An additional point regarding conflict is that it cannot always be considered undesirable. Some conflict is probably necessary and desirable in order to stimulate creative ideas and encourage people to change. Without some conflict society would tend to be in social equilibrium, and the status quo would persist. Conflict becomes undesirable only when it dominates a social relationship.

In summary of this section, it is evident that pluralism has some ever-present weaknesses, particularly if they are carried to extremes; but it also provides several benefits which are key social values in the minds of many people. In any case, it is the social environment in which business operates in the United States and many other parts of the world.

SUMMARY

Pluralism is a social system in which diverse groups maintain autonomous participation and influence. In the operation of pluralism many groups influence business, and, in turn, business influences them. Major elements of pluralism are diversity of interests, institutional specialization, multiallegiant individuals with role investments in many institutions, a relatively open system, diffusion of power, and joint venture. Strengths of pluralism include support for social freedom, many opportunities for leadership, tolerance of other ideas, improved social decisions, and satisfaction of different human needs. Weaknesses include lack of central direction, emphasis on institutional power instead of service, social fragmentation, elitism, and an alleged focus on conflict. Although pluralism has its weaknesses, it displays viability as an open, flexible system with a capability for self-renewal. Businessmen need to understand pluralism because it is the social framework that governs their relationships with their external environment.

STUDY GUIDES FOR INTERPRETATION OF THIS CHAPTER

1. The beginning of this chapter described a corporation's efforts to develop certain ranch land. As the corporation's local manager on the site of this development, how would you respond to each of the groups mentioned? Why?

2. How has the business owner role changed during the last one or two centuries?

3. Define pluralism, business claimant, role investment, and multiallegiant individual.

4. Explain each of the major elements of a pluralistic social system.

5. Discuss the strengths and weaknesses of a pluralistic social system compared with more monolithic systems.

PROBLEMS
"An Open Letter to the Farmers"

In a Midwestern state the farmers typically burned field stubble after harvest of a certain crop. The crop was a major economic contributor to communities in some parts of the state. During one summer, unfavorable weather combined with heavy burning to produce a pall of thick smoke which hung over half of the state for two weeks. It irritated eyes and lungs and at times was so thick that it interfered with highway traffic. Complaints mounted from highway users, medical groups, city persons, and others. Legislators became alarmed and introduced a bill banning field burning. Although the legislation failed, it created animosity between city dwellers and farmers.

In a rural town of less than 5,000 population, a group of businessmen became concerned because they felt this animosity had harmed business relations with farmers. Working through a chamber of commerce committee they arranged to place an advertisement in the local newspaper. It read in part as follows:

AN OPEN LETTER TO THE FARMERS

From our conversations with other citizens of the community, we know that those of us listed below represent only a fraction of the people who share our feelings on the recent field-burning legislation.

We sympathize with you. . . . We not only sympathize—we stand ready to help in any way we can to bring about a workable solution to your dilemma. Granted: Air pollution must be eliminated. But we feel that lightning-fast legislation, singling out and virtually closing an entire industry, is not the answer. Especially when no alternate solution is offered.

Our silence in these past weeks has not meant that your city neighbors were not aware of your problem. Or that we "don't care" about its solution. Perish the thought! You are our neighbors—our friends—our relatives! Our destinies are intertied by bonds of understanding that go back many generations. We cannot and WILL NOT forget that agriculture has been the foundation-stone and backbone of this community.

Names of many of the town's major businesses appeared at the bottom of the advertisement. One of the names was that of a statewide bank which had a branch in the town. No person at the bank had prior knowledge of the advertisement, but its name was included routinely by a clerk because it was a member of the town's chamber of commerce, even though the name "chamber of commerce" did not appear in the advertisement.

When the advertisement appeared, many local citizens protested to the branch manager that the bank was "taking sides," and some threatened to withdraw their accounts. Other protests were made to executives in the home office. Some protests came from influential bank clients who represented interests favoring the legislation. Others complained about the bank's lack of neutrality.

1. Appraise the objectives and methods used by the advertisers and relate them to pluralism.

2. Discuss the manner in which pluralism operated as a part of the bank's environment in this episode. Who were the interest groups involved? Was public interest served?

The Ban on Imported Automobiles

During the 1960s imported automobiles gained an increasing proportion of the market in the United States. The United Steelworkers union estimated that 20,000 steelworkers lost their jobs because of imported steel and steel products. The steel industry as a whole experienced relatively hard times and low profit margins. There was a feeling in the industry and the union that more should be done to encourage use of steel products made in the United States.

On January 1, 1970, a large branch works of one of the nation's top steel producers announced on bulletin boards and in widely circulated memos that no imported automobiles would be allowed inside the plant gates. The company said that visitors, vendors, and others who drove imported automobiles to the plant would be provided with transportation inside the plant if necessary. A company spokesman said the action was taken because the plant had "a considerable stake in the continued success of domestic auto companies, which are its best customers."

Production workers were not affected by the ban, because they parked their cars in a company lot outside the main plant area; however, a local official of the United Steelworkers said he agreed with the company's action. He added: "We'd like to see all foreign-made cars banned from the United States."

An observer added that the idea was not new, because manufacturers and unions in the ailing hat industry had insisted for years that those doing business with them must arrive wearing hats.[9]

1. Appraise the company decision—and union agreement—in terms of pluralism. Select the major investment groups in this decision and identify the role investments of each.

2. Was the public interest served in this decision? Explain.

Mary Scroggins

Mary Scroggins graduated from Northwestern University in accounting. Immediately after graduation she was employed effective July 1 by the local office of a national accounting firm. During the employment process Mary was told that her normal hours of work would be 8:30 A.M. to 5 P.M., Monday through Friday, but that overtime work might sometimes be required, particularly in the months immediately preceding the income tax deadline of April 15. Mary is a member of a Christian religion whose Sabbath is on Saturday, and she is an active and devout member of her church. At the time of employment the accounting firm did not inquire about her religion, because it wished to comply fully with the Civil Rights Act concerning race, religion, creed, and national origin. Mary likewise did not mention her religion at this time.

[9]"Foreign Cars Get Bumped in Birmingham," *Business Week,* Jan. 10, 1970, p. 29.

During the following six months Mary proved to be a capable and loyal employee. Her performance was above average for her team, and her supervisor had remarked to his manager how pleased he was to have Mary in his group. He felt that, assuming she continued to grow, she had potential for promotions within the firm.

As the income tax period approached, Mary's supervisor began preparing overtime schedules for his group. Based upon past practice and consensus within the group, all overtime was scheduled on Saturdays. When Mary's supervisor discussed the tentative schedule with her, she said she would not work on Saturday because of her religious belief. In fact, her religious belief required her to stop work before sundown Friday.

1. What social issues are raised in this case?

2. What pluralistic interest groups are involved, and what is the nature of their interest?

3. As Mary's supervisor what would you do now?

CHAPTER 5

THE BUSINESS ROLE
AND SOCIAL ISSUES

Corporations exist because society wishes them to fulfill a purpose and when the social purpose changes, so will the activities of the corporations.

George A. Steiner[1]

Corporate legitimacy ultimately depends on how society evaluates the total impact of the firm, not just its economic impact.

Richard N. Farmer and W. Dickerson Hogue[2]

A ragged group of student activists was pressing hard against the police barricades across the street from a San Francisco hotel. A trained tactical police force separated them from the hotel itself. The students were chanting revolutionary slogans and shouting accusations at businessmen inside the hotel who were attending a meeting of the Fourth International Industrial Conference sponsored by Stanford Research Institute and the National Industrial Conference Board. Those attending included presidents or chairmen of over 150 major United States corporations and heads of over 50 of the largest companies of other nations such as Italy, Mexico, Belgium, Germany, and Sweden. They talked about their past mistakes and their long-run obligations to society.

Outside the hotel the activists wanted to change the world. "You are the enemy," one of them shouted at the businessmen. Inside the hotel the businessmen also spoke of changing the world, and their focus was the same as that of the students—meeting human and social needs. "The reformist fervor permeated the meeting," a reporter observed. Although no businessman was heard to return the accusation: "You are the enemy," one of them did comment: "I find this particularly ironic at a time when business and the general run of college students have moved closer together than ever before in their desire to satisfy the wants and needs of people the world over."[3] Were the top businessmen and students really

[1]George A. Steiner, "Social Policies for Business," *California Management Review*, Winter 1972, p. 18.
[2]Richard N. Farmer and W. Dickerson Hogue, *Corporate Social Responsibility*, Chicago: Science Research Associates, Inc., 1973, p. 21.
[3]"San Francisco 1969," *Forbes*, Oct. 15, 1969.

enemies? Or were they allies whose common ground was not yet recognized by the students? The students wanted action. The business leaders were men of action on an international basis.

Meanwhile, in another city (although probably something similar was happening in San Francisco), a laborer received a postcard saying that he could win some valuable prizes by calling at the office of a high-pressure sales firm. He and his wife and two young children arrived at the office about 7 P.M. and were told that they would have to submit to a sales presentation on housewares before they could receive their prizes. Then for the next 4½ hours they were bombarded with high-pressure sales pitches by two men. Sometimes during the marathon sales session they were given steak knives and promised other inducements if they would sign an installment contract for nearly $500 worth of merchandise, much of which they did not need. As the hour approached midnight, their resistance was so low they finally signed. The salesman placed the goods in the car trunk, and they were still there a few days later when the husband called the firm to ask it to take back the merchandise. The company refused; it had already assigned the contract to a finance company.

The two incidents illustrate many factors concerning business's role in the social system: a wide variety of business practice, differences between large international corporations and small businesses, conflict and misunderstanding concerning business's role, evolving viewpoints of this role, and difficulties in getting high-level ideals translated into lower-level business operations. This chapter compares the traditional economic role of business with the new social role which seems to be emerging. There is also discussion of the organizational adaptations business is developing to respond to social issues. Finally, functional analysis is presented as a way to evaluate which social actions can be performed better by business than by other institutions in a pluralistic social system.

The incident of high-pressure salesmanship is not a pleasant one.[4] Certainly business has its share of shady characters operating on the fringes of acceptable behavior or even in violation of law, but the same observations apply to other institutions. All human institutions are subject to the frailties of human nature; however, a description of these frailties does not explain the basic role of any institution in society.

THE TRADITIONAL BUSINESS ROLE
Institutions Serve Social Purposes

All institutions are tools of society. They are established by society, and in the long run they continue to exist with the consent of society. Each institution is viewed as a social asset for performing some purposeful, constructive role. These

---

[4]The final results were not as negative as they appear, because a pluralistic society provided other alternatives for the laborer. He appealed to a legal-aid society, which threatened legal action. This caused the sales firm to cancel his contract and take back the merchandise before any money had been paid. However, his long-run attitudes toward business deteriorated as a result of this experience.

facts do not prevent unethical behavior, poor quality, or straying from goals (even with the best of intentions); nevertheless, the social role remains to guide the institution's actions.

An institution's social role is not forever rigid. It will gradually evolve over a period of time in response to human needs. It may change its way of working with people, its manner of relating to other organizations, the activities it performs, and other characteristics. All these changes relate to its attempt to meet human needs and remain viable in the system. As it operates, people in society are evaluating it according to the social criteria that exist at that time. These criteria may change as time passes, initiating strong pressures on the institution to amend its activities to conform more successfully to the new criteria. In this dynamic manner, traditional practices give way to new practices, which in turn eventually become traditional and give way to even newer practices. These conditions describe the evolution of business's role, as well as the role of other institutions.

A Traditional Focus on Economic Productivity and Profit

The traditional focus of business has been almost exclusively economic. All other activities were strictly sidelines to be dabbled with when they became urgent through indirect effects on profit. This role has been strongly supported, by the doctrines of classical economics, which argued that through strict emphasis on economic values in a free market, maximum human benefits would result because goods and services would be produced efficiently. These goods and services were desperately needed by a poor and hungry society.

Both theory and practice concentrated on economic profit as the ultimate measure of a firm's success in its role. In this model, economic values were the only ones accounted for and owners primarily provided the capital to produce these values; thus emphasis was mostly upon obligations to ownership, rather than to other business claimants. This heavy emphasis on one client group and on one measure of performance caused questions to be raised about business performance as people began to think more in terms of a systems concept.

In reality, few people in society would deny that business should be "profitable," provided this term is interpreted to mean net gains of all types in relation to inputs of all types. Obviously business or any other institution wastes social resources unless it can provide outputs greater than inputs; and the greater the net gain, the better it is for society. The principal issue in modern industrial society, and the key to the evolving role of business, is differing expectations of what kinds of outputs should be emphasized and what groups should receive them. People want the outputs, but they want them in the form of broad social benefits along with economic profits.

The new broader demand for general benefits poses a new role for business. The result is that business managers, as the responsible agents of business, find themselves answering to many types of investors having both economic and noneconomic expectations. The idea of pure competition and maximizing economic profit appears workable primarily on college blackboards! As soon as the systems concept is made a part of the business environment, economic profit becomes only one of many values produced by the system. The question is: Does business have the leadership and flexibility to respond successfully to these new expectations?

On the other hand, economic profit cannot be rationalized out of the system, because this opposite extreme would equally ignore the systems concept. Economic deprivation and want in much of the world are evidence that economic profit is a social need. It is needed as a valid measure of productive use of capital, a criterion for allocating resources, and a just benefit for economic investors whether they are state citizens or private investors. For example, a significant international development has been Russian experimentation with the Liberman Plan starting in the 1960s. Russian economist Yevsei Liberman argued that industry should be judged at least partially by its return on capital, and a few factories have been freed from central planning to pursue this "novel" measure of efficiency. Apparently the Russian economy was deficient in this type of social measure and needed to give it more recognition in order to serve public needs.

The systems concept implies that what is needed is a balanced view which recognizes the need for economic profits along with social benefits (in a sense, social "profits") for those affected by business. Thus, it is appropriate to refer to a *balanced profit concept,* a *socially profitable business,* or a *socially beneficial business.* All of these phrases mean that a business is providing both social and economic outputs greater than inputs in a manner which reasonably serves the expectations of claimants on business.

AN EVOLVING BUSINESS ROLE

As society changed, it was inevitable that business's role within it would need to be reconsidered. In advanced nations, for example, business's enormous success in producing goods and services led to widespread material affluence. Precisely because of business's success, economic output took a lower priority on the scale of social needs. People began to ask: "Since business has been so successful in meeting our economic needs, could we expect similar success if we gave it a major role in solving some of our pressing social problems, such as urban blight?" They also asked: "Has business's concentrated drive for economic results contributed, either knowingly or unknowingly, to the social problems which have top priority today, such as environmental pollution?"

Some Insights from Systems Thinking

A systems framework has been particularly helpful to businessmen in perceiving their broader socioeconomic role. Businessmen feel more comfortable working in a rational analytical framework, and systems concepts provide this type

A Middle Ground of Business Social Involvement Offers the Most Promise

We hear Cassandra cries from some quarters. In a recently published article,* the author concluded that there can be no significant chance of social responsibility or other nonprofit oriented activity in a competitive product market and that the market treats nonprofit maximizing expenditures the same, whether they result from inefficiency, embezzlement or charity. If that conclusion is accurate, we *are* doomed, because, as we are only just now coming to realize, the market is rigged against the environment. But we have already seen that economics is too narrow a base from which to carry out decision analysis, even in the single firm. The doomsayers on one side are matched by equally extreme views in the opposite direction which hold that only the greed of the capitalist prevents us from achieving a state of economic and environmental bliss or that private business can easily absorb the costs of cleaning up the environment and solving our social problems. Both extreme positions are based on a very narrow and largely inaccurate idea of what social responsibility is all about.

From Dow Votaw, "Genius Becomes Rare: A Comment on the Doctrine of Social Responsibility, Pt. II," *California Management Review,* Spring 1973, p. 6.
*Henry G. Manne, "The Myth of Corporate Responsibility," *The Business Lawyer,* November 1970, pp. 533–539.

of framework. Businessmen are beginning to see that they cannot isolate their business in an economic cocoon because they have a systems interface with society. They realize that a healthy society is necessary for healthy business. If there is social decay, business will tend to decay also; therefore, poor home environments and crime in the streets are likely to be reflected in employee performance and crime in business.

Systems insights also help businessmen see the extended social effects of regular business activities. For example, when businesses move into new communities, they now cooperate more with other agencies to assure that facilities such as roads, private housing, schools, and cultural centers are available. They want to be sure that their arrival does not overload community facilities and that their employees will have a desirable community in which to live.

An example of systems thinking, in this instance without operating cost to the firm, is an isolated mining company which built a hydroelectric dam to supply its mines with power. It owned all the adjoining property and water rights, so it could have closed the property to public use. Looking beyond its own needs to those of its community, it saw that the lake was needed as a recreational area. Working with government, it built roads, picnic areas, and boat ramps and opened the area to the public for recreation. Private businesses were given leases to establish boat docks, snack bars, and related service facilities. Income from the leases paid for maintenance of the entire property.

The Role of Business Regarding Social Issues Needs Clear Definition

The changes under way in the corporate institution and managerial outlook are significant. They are tending to bring about a constructive response to growing public insistence that business take on more social responsibilities while continuing to improve the performance of its basic economic functions. *This process of adaptation of business structure and performance to the changing requirements of society can be facilitated greatly by the development of a clearer corporate rationale of the role business must play in the national community—a role as a responsible participant determined to resolve any conflict with humane values or the social environment.*

From *Social Responsibilities of Business Corporations,* New York: Committee for Economic Development, 1971, p. 25. Italics in original.

Business is essentially a partnership among investors, labor, customers, and the community, and some of these partners, particularly the community, have a strong interest in social outputs. The assignment which these partners have given business is to process economic and social resources productively for all the partners. To carry out its assignment, business is required to interface constructively with the social system. That is, *business is a system of systems within a larger system;* therefore, it must be concerned about its outputs to the larger system along with its inputs from that system.

Profit Making and Social Involvement

The preceding discussion suggests that modern business's role is evolving into a combination of profit making and social involvement. If this is happening, it is a major change in business's role. This is an age of discontinuity, not routine change, and it may see a reallocation of activities which are appropriate to business enterprise. If so, the changes which are occurring will be of a major social and political significance. There will be both opportunities and dangers for business. New organization structures and new reward criteria may be required by business in order to recognize social contributions along with economic ones.

As a minimum there is some recognition of the influence of social goals on business decision making. The real question is not *whether* social goals will influence business decisions and cost. Instead, the question is *how much* will this influence be? One author gives social and economic goals equal rank in decision making. He states: *"To realize its full promise in the world of tomorrow, American business and industry—or, at least, the vast portion of it—will have to make social goals as central to its decisions as economic goals; and leadership in our corporations will increasingly recognize this responsibility and accept it."* [5]

[5]Sol M. Linowitz, "Public Affairs: The Demanding Seventies," *Looking Ahead* (National Planning Association), May 1966, p. 2. Italics in original.

If social goals are going to be considered along with economic goals in decision making, then new models of thinking about business will need to be developed. One observer comments:[6]

> For a long time, business has operated on the notion that the mainspring of all its activity was the profit motive. This oversimplification, this notion that business always acted as if it were maximizing profits and had nothing else in mind, was an extremely useful fiction for organizing the total activity of business. We now reach a point where it has become quite impossible to go on pretending that business does nothing except maximize its profits. We are going to have to invent new concepts and find ways of expressing what business is doing when it is not maximizing profits.

Two Areas for Social Action

In the expanding social role of business two areas for social responsibility and action are developing. One of these is social responsibility for business degradation of both the social and physical environments. With regard to social environment, for example, there has been employment discrimination by business, so business is obligated to take affirmative action to correct this practice in order to restore some harmony to the environment. With regard to physical environment, business processes pollute the environment and business makes machines which pollute; therefore, business is required to take corrective action to the extent that action is technically and socially feasible. Again, this affirmative action helps restore harmony to the environment. In this manner, business products and services are required to bear the costs of maintaining harmony in the environment. Formerly these costs were passed on to society in the form of social costs which society had to bear.

A second area for action is social responsibility for adding to the general quality of life. That is, society is assigning to business a responsibility to build the quality of life in other than economic ways for the entire society. An example of this type of action is aid to education. Business did not directly cause educational problems, but it does stand to gain some benefit from their solution; thus it has some responsibility to help develop solutions.

Public attitudes are much more in agreement concerning the first area of social responsibility than the second. Surveys show that most persons expect business to prevent environmental degradation. They believe that pollution and other undesirable practices should be stopped at their source, rather than being passed on to society to try to clean up after their occurrence. With regard to the second area of responsibility, although there are differences of opinion, there are general feelings that as a citizen of society, business has responsibilities, as all other citizens do, to build a better quality of life in general, not just economic life.

[6]Max Ways, *Business Leadership in Social Change,* New York: The Conference Board, Inc., 1971, pp. 65–66.

Defining the Quality of Life

Although the phrase "quality of life" is frequently offered as a social goal, it is rarely defined. It is a nebulous concept which means different things to different people. We define *quality of life* as the social goals sought by people. Accordingly, it can vary from nation to nation and person to person, depending on who is using the term. On the other hand, there is some agreement because certain themes tend to recur. Considering these recurrent themes, we can say that quality of life means a social system which has freedom, high purpose, relative affluence, and people living in harmony with their inner spirit, their fellow man, and nature's physical environment.

The implications of this definition are that there is an open social system which provides freedom and participation for all persons. There is a wide diversity of choice so that persons may pursue life-styles of their own individual choosing. The high purposes of society seek to provide openness and trust in all relationships, both interpersonal and organizational. The system seeks to protect the dignity of individuals and to help them grow in psychological and social maturity. It also seeks through affluence to provide health care and the economic necessities of life. Economic hardship is no longer accepted as it was in the days of laissez faire. Harmony is expected within a person, among persons, and among organizations.

Although quality of life speaks of harmony, it is not a static concept that seeks to preserve a utopian status quo. Rather, it is a dynamic concept in which people live harmoniously with the changes occurring in nature and in themselves. It is, however, a utopian concept in the sense that most people use it as an ultimate goal that they realize probably will not ever be obtained absolutely. It is essentially a set of criteria by which judgments may be made about social progress.

Alternative Responses Available to Business

There are a number of ways in which business may respond to the social demands that are being made on it. One approach is *withdrawal,* by which business recedes further into its own shell, reducing its interface with society and trying to mind its own business. It passes its social costs on to society and generally leaves the problems for society to solve. This approach is similar to that of an individual who withdraws from society. It generally reflects some type of alienation from the system and tends to reduce the withdrawing party's influence in the system. In thinking about withdrawal as an option, one is reminded of what happened to prehistoric dinosaurs. They became extinct because they failed to change in response to their ever-changing environment. Withdrawal could produce a similar result for business.

Business could also use a *public relations approach*. This is a standby procedure which has been used generously in crises in the past. Business offers the public through the press and public speeches a multitude of stories about its accomplishments in social areas. All the while it is making negligible change in existing practices. In other words, business increases communication but does not increase its response to change.

Another alternative is a *legal approach*. Business depends on the law to protect it from change, because it knows that laws are amended very slowly in a large social system. Meanwhile, business does only the minimum required by law. Finally, when the law is changed, business fights it through long and expensive court battles. These battles delay action, discourage enforcement, and eventually result in some weakening of the law. Both society and business may be the loser in this battle, because needed social progress is delayed or prevented. Some legal battles may be necessary to define properly business's role in society, but too many of them are delaying tactics for changes that are rather certain to occur in the long run.

An additional approach is *bargaining,* by which business negotiates with pressure groups which make claims upon it. In this manner it attempts to resolve disputes with negotiated settlements which often produce some change. As business has learned in the past, settlements can be elusive because the interests of pressure groups change rather rapidly. Furthermore, a settlement with one group may not be satisfactory to other groups, so business needs always to keep system relationships in view as it bargains. Bargaining is not a desirable total solution, because in the long run it leads to a situation in which the strongest party wins.

Another alternative is *problem solving*. In this approach business makes a genuine study of society's and business's values and needs, and then it attempts to reconcile them in constructive ways. Effort is directed toward finding optimum ways for social progress, considering the interests of all parties in the situation. Business recognizes the full system impact of its decisions on the interdependent global community, and it acts with this global view in mind. In this manner business becomes an instrument of progress rather than its opponent or its passive acceptor.

Even in the desirable problem-solving mode there are poorer and better ways to respond. For example, a minimum type of problem solving is to seek solutions only in areas where public pressures, demands, and expectations are high. A more advanced type of response is to anticipate public pressures and expectations, responding to them in a preventive way before they become major irritants. Perhaps the most mature approach, although few firms will go this far, is to determine which social problems are affected by business power and to step in to try to help solve them as an obligation of power without waiting for public pressures or expectations. If business wishes to take the mature approach, it will need to clarify its social responsibility models, develop effective social inputs, and build sound policies and machinery for social response.

The problem-solving role is an ideal one for business. Business is known as an efficient problem solver, and people look to business for leadership in this area. Problem solving also will help business retain its position as a major social institution. If it can by its own merits contribute to social solutions, it will improve goodwill and acceptance of its role.

The machinery of pluralism also dictates that business will do some bargaining on social issues. Pressure groups will make claims on business, and it can hardly refuse to respond to them. With regard to the public relations and legal approaches, they may be used in a minimum way, but they are not effective as a dominant approach to social issues. The response of withdrawal is an inappropriate response for a major institution such as business is.

A word of caution is in order. Society should not expect too much of business. Pressures are very strong because society needs all the resources and skills that are available. There is grave danger that business will be persuaded to overcommit itself. In spite of business's capabilities, there is abundant evidence that far too much is expected and even demanded of business. In the system "everything is related to everything else"; thus there are no simple problems, and few of them yield to low-cost solutions. Business's toughest job in social areas may be convincing the public of its limitations.

BUSINESS'S RESPONSE TO SOCIAL CLAIMS
A Plan for Corporate Response

Assuming that a business wants to improve its social response, how does it go about achieving this goal? Who should do this, and how should it be implemented? Figure 5-1 outlines the necessary elements for improved social response by a firm. In order to make social action operational, the entire firm is involved. Social action generally starts at the top, but it is not completed until it permeates operating units of the organization. Three organizational groups are involved: top management, staff organizations, and operating departments.

The assignment of an action to a certain group in Figure 5-1 means only that the named group has primary responsibility for that action. All groups share some responsibility for most actions, but usually one group has the primary responsibility for a particular type of action. For example, top management primarily is responsible for decisions to commit resources to social action, but both staff and operating departments also make lesser decisions internally for using their resources.

Top Management's Role

In developing a suitable corporate social response, first and foremost top management needs to improve its interface with the environment in order to gain more social inputs from it. Management needs to learn what is happening in the social world in the same manner that it has historically sought to know what is occurring in the economic world. Unless it can develop social inputs, whatever

Organizational Group	Required Action
Top management	Improve interface with the environment and social inputs from it
	Develop organizational philosophy, commitment, and strategy
	Develop and communicate policies for social action
	Establish necessary staff organization in the area of social issues
	Commit resources to social action
	Revise performance expectations and rewards
Staff organizations	Improve interface with the environment and social inputs from it
	Evaluate inputs and recommend responses
	Communicate social information to entire organization
	Develop social audits for organizational appraisal and feedback
Operating departments	Improve interface with the environment and social inputs from it
	Revise operating procedures to conform to new philosophy and policy
	Apply resources to social action
	Evaluate and report results to management

Note that improved interface with the environment is a necessity common to all three organizational groups.

Figure 5-1 Actions required by different organizational groups when an organization initiates greater social involvement.

social decisions it makes will be ill-chosen, because decision outputs cannot be better than inputs except by chance. If management does not know what is happening in the social system, then it cannot respond to those unknowns. Plentiful and accurate inputs are essential; therefore, top management will depend on staff and operating departments for aid in gathering inputs.

Based on the inputs which it receives, top management will develop an organizational philosophy, commitment, and strategy for social action. These decisions are fundamental ones which give a sense of purpose and continuity to the firm; therefore, management needs all the counsel it can get in formulating them. Management needs to be sure that its responses serve the needs of most of society, rather than only the few claimants who are making the loudest noise.

In formulating philosophy a central issue is whether social involvement will be peripheral to the firm or an integral part of all that the firm does. In the first instance social involvement is a side interest, a hobby, a sometime thing, and a luxury to be toyed with only in prosperous times. In the second instance social involvement is a commitment, a necessary part of the whole, and a life-style to be applied day by day in all the firm's activities.

In examining the difference between the peripheral luxury and the committed life-style, it can be seen that in the 1960s much of business's involvement was of the peripheral type. It was often a limited response to a specific pressure, such as minority problems. Occasionally it was assigned to a specific department with a sigh of relief that it was now their problem and the other departments were released to proceed with their regular business. Philosophically it was a social luxury unrelated to the central objectives of the business. Perhaps top management had a broader vision, but at least this was the way most of the operating departments conducted their business.

In the 1970s a new concept of social involvement gradually began to be forged. Businessmen began to see an expanded purpose for the firm based on its system involvement in the whole of society. They began to recognize that a more complex system and changed values may require a new business life-style.

As a result of their new perceptions, businessmen are moving their firms gradually toward a more socially involved life-style. The change is not a quick shift from one extreme to another, but as shown in Figure 5-2, a gradual shift along a continuum. Based on its perceptions and experiences, each firm finds its place along the continuum. Some will move further than others, and some may not move at all. Movement is generally confined to the broad middle ground between the two extremes, because neither extreme provides payouts that are balanced enough to serve a wide range of business claimants.

Whatever philosophy a firm adopts, when it is finally chosen, top management needs to implement it with appropriate policies and resources. Top management's commitment must become reality in the firm's day-to-day activities. Policies are not easy to communicate; and even when they are understood, there is a tendency to bypass them because the reward system at operating levels may still be based only on economic criteria. This means that one of management's most important responsibilities is to change the reward structure so that social performance is judged along with economic performance. Admittedly this change is difficult, because social criteria are not as easily quantified as economic criteria.

The Staff Role

Organizations large enough to have staff units will depend on them for a number of support functions related to social involvement. The staff particularly

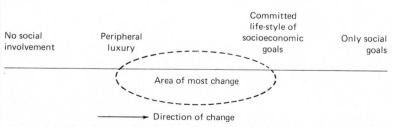

Figure 5-2   Continuum of social involvement for business showing area of most business activity.

will seek to improve social inputs from the environment through development of its *scanning function*. The staff is the firm's specialized organ for reaching out into the community and the world and learning the direction of social change so that the firm may respond to it. Its scanning responsibility in no way relieves line management from responsibility for interface with the environment, but it does provide a specialized talent to bring inputs, insights, and recommendations to management. Scanning is concerned with understanding society as a whole along with all its parts so that the full implications of change may be interpreted. It appraises current issues, but it also anticipates future issues so that the firm is prepared for the future as well as the present. A firm is limited primarily to *reactive* behavior when it responds only to current problems, but when it anticipates the future and moves to join in shaping coming events, it is a *purposive* organization. A purposive role gives an organization much more influence in a social system.

Staff activities are of two types. One type is represented by the regular activities of traditional staff departments such as personnel and public relations. The personnel department, for example, is significantly involved through equal-employment programs, and public relations interfaces with news media. Each of these activities is an important part of the firm's total involvement in social issues.

A second type of staff activity is carried on by a department set up specifically to monitor and coordinate all areas of a firm's social involvement. This department often is called a public affairs department. It may include certain traditional functions such as public relations, but on other occasions it is an entirely separate function so that it may more easily monitor all activities as a company tries to move toward more responsible social involvement. Its staff is highly visible and vulnerable, because it represents a new department not yet integrated into the firm's power structure and it works with a nebulous activity not easily defined or measured. The public affairs department normally reports to top management.

One study of public affairs departments revealed that all of them reported to higher management, and 75 percent of them reported to the chief executive officer, president, or chairman of the board.[7] A separate department for corporate responsibility was rather new, because 53 percent of the departments were established in the three years from 1969 to the end of 1971, when the survey was made.

Companies appeared to want older, more mature, educated persons for the role of corporate responsibility officer. Eighty-one percent were over forty years of age, and all except one had a college degree. Thirty-seven percent had advanced degrees. The background of the corporate responsibility officer usually was marketing and public relations (53 percent), but a number of others came from personnel and general management.

[7]Henry Eilbirt and I. Robert Parket, "The Corporate Responsibility Officer," *Business Horizons*, February 1973, pp. 45–51.

A major responsibility of staff is to develop effective procedures for appraising how well operating departments are meeting social performance goals. For example, has the affirmative action program for equal employment been successful? Are the salesmen's high-pressure methods leading to complaints and customer dissatisfaction? Is the company's advertising misleading? In developing appraisals of social performance, both qualitative and quantitative data can be used, but departments may respond better to quantitative data because they appear more objective. A comprehensive appraisal program is often called a social audit, and it is discussed in a later chapter.

An example of how the specialized staff role works is the business environment studies group in the public affairs department of a large American firm. This group has the role of monitoring the environment to identify and evaluate developing social issues for management consideration. The studies group essentially provides an early warning system to inform management of social developments. In turn, management develops plans for both bargaining and problem-solving approaches toward these issues.

When the studies group first began operating, it developed a list of nearly 100 potential demands that might be made on business, plus a list of about ten major social trends that were developing, such as more affluence and increasing emphasis on individualism. It then ranked the 100 demands in accordance with their convergence with the trends. It also weighed each demand in terms of the number of pressure groups pushing it and the strength of their pressures, and it evaluated the potential impact of each demand on the corporation. These quantitative and qualitative data then were used to guide management in determining social priorities for the firm.

Role of Operating Departments

Change eventually falls on operating departments, and usually its impact is greatest there. Since traditional ways of work must be revised to conform with new programs, change always brings some operating costs regardless of the benefits that may eventually accrue. In the case of social involvement there are often high beginning costs, while the benefits are long range, often indirect, and sometimes not very evident to an individual department. The result is that a cost/benefit analysis from a department's perceptions may be rather negative; therefore, management faces an additional task of helping departments see both a system view and a long-run view. Further, the departments need to be convinced that appraisals of departmental performance will include social measures as well as economic measures.

In one firm, for example, top management established a public affairs department and issued elaborate pronouncements about a need for social involvement by the firm. Detailed staff guidelines were developed and circulated to all departments. It seemed that the firm was going all out for social involvement. However, in the firm's quarterly departmental appraisals no mention was made of social involvement. At the end of the year departmental managers who made their economic targets but failed to perform in the social area were rewarded as usual. All the departmental managers got the message and subsequently devoted little attention to social issues.

FUNCTIONAL ANALYSIS TO DETERMINE AREAS OF SOCIAL INVOLVEMENT

One reason for social involvement is simply that, compared with other institutions, business has resources and capabilities which make it a better institution for certain social purposes. For the same reason, in some other areas business will be less involved or relatively uninvolved. In job training, housing, and minority employment, for example, it is capable of taking a leading role. In education its role may be substantial in areas such as vocational education, but on the whole its role probably will remain secondary to government's.

Functional Analysis

Since business will have variable involvement in different social needs, how will the extent of its involvement be determined? One helpful approach is *functional analysis,* which compares social priorities with institutional capabilities for serving them and then assigns the most important priorities to those institutions most capable of performing them. In this manner society should be able to make the best use of its resources by using the specialized capabilities of different institutions. This process supports pluralism by dividing social tasks among institutions. It also means that no single institution "owns" any function for all time. Situations may change, making other institutions more capable within the framework of the new conditions. Following is an example.

In 1968 Congress made the Federal National Mortgage Association (nicknamed "Fannie Mae") into a private corporation after it had been a government agency for thirty years. Fannie Mae was founded during depression years to feed money into the mortgage market at a time when business was weak and unable to do so. Eventually financial business became stronger and government processes became more cumbersome, so Fannie Mae was transferred to private ownership with some government ties.

The transfer proved quite satisfactory for all concerned. Fannie Mae streamlined operations, improved efficiency, and increased profitability so much that its stock price rose vigorously. It went through its first functional test successfully; in the credit pinch of 1969, it was able to feed more money into the mortgage market than it had been able to do in a similar pinch in 1966 when it was a government agency. In summary, "The career of the one-time government girl, Fannie Mae, now that she has turned to private enterprise, is proving an eye-popping success."[8]

A movement in the opposite direction occurred early in United States history when there were many private toll roads. Gradually it became evident that the need for personal transportation could be better served by tax-supported free public roads, and so they became the predominant form of highway. Private industry, however, continued to build most of the roads because it appeared to be functionally more efficient and free of political encumbrances.

The Long-Run View of History

When history is viewed in terms of centuries rather than years, the transfer of functions among institutions appears to be normal instead of revolutionary. It is the means by which society relates new conditions to institutional capabilities. Medical services originally were provided by spiritualists and witch doctors. Gradually they became a concern of religious orders, charitable institutions, government, and the physician operating as an individual professional person. In recent years government and large business are assuming more dominant roles. Hospitals are being managed by business-oriented administrators, rather than physicians. Large business is establishing franchised nursing homes. (Compare these with the alternatives of a county poor farm or public mental institution for senile persons fifty years ago. Which is likely to be more effective today?) And even individual physicians are now organizing into medical corporations with their associates.

Another example of changed conditions which respond to functional analysis is postal service. Centuries ago government was clearly the proper institution to operate postal service, although there were exceptions, such as the famed Pony Express of the American West which existed for eighteen months. The power of the state was necessary to maintain privacy of personal communication and to protect mail from highwaymen and pillage. The service was also a necessary activity of government in order to maintain control and coordination among its separated branches. Official documents had to be transported securely. Today, however, the postal service is a vast business activity in competition with a variety of other communication businesses. As a result the postal service has become a public corporation so that it may operate more like a business.

Even in its traditional function of handling packages, catalogs, and similar material, the U.S. Postal Service is being severely challenged. For example, in

[8]"Privacy Becomes Fannie Mae," *Business Week,* Aug. 30, 1969, p. 44.

1971 the private United Parcel Service delivered about 800 million parcels while the U.S. Postal Service delivered only about 480 million.[9] In the same year the Independent Postal Service and over 150 similar firms delivered additional millions of pieces of mail. These are private firms which pay the costs of doing business, including taxes, and still compete with the U.S. Postal Service. Clearly a new set of conditions has arisen that no longer requires a government monopoly on postal service.

Criteria for Functional Analysis

In assessing which institutions are the better ones for performing functions in a pluralistic social system, a number of criteria may be used. Following are several important ones.

1. Social effectiveness—predicted satisfactions of claimants concerning benefits

2. Economic efficiency—predicted performance of an activity without waste of resources

3. Resources—depth of resources available, alternative uses for those resources, and need for new resources if new functions are performed

4. Innovative and creative capacity; flexibility

5. Capacity to move with deliberate speed, without delay

6. Predicted negative by-products—
   a. Community, economic, and other dislocations caused by the institution's taking a function
   b. Risks to the institution's survival and viability caused by its new activity

These criteria may be illustrated by a brief comparison of small business and large corporations to determine the probable extent of their social involvement. Large business has a capacity to move with deliberate speed in terms of carefully reasoned plans, long-run cash flow, and professional management. It also has a depth of resources probably unparalleled in modern history. Although these resources have alternative economic uses, they are flexible enough for partial diversion if social priorities dictate this and if ways are devised to renew these resources as social functions are performed. Further, the economic role of large business particularly qualifies it to work with large and economically related social priorities, such as urban housing and job training.

Small business, on the other hand, has limited resources which are more likely to confine it to local projects and those of smaller dimensions (although not

[9]Timothy D. Schellhardt, "The U.S. Postal System Begins to Take Notice of Speedy Competitors," *Wall Street Journal* (Pacific Coast edition), Dec. 20, 1972, p.1.

necessarily of lesser importance). Its acceptance of social involvement will be more variable, because it will be substantially influenced by the personal attitudes of its owner-managers. It probably will be more innovative in taking fresh approaches to social problems because it affords a means of entry for persons with new ideas.

John Wilson is one of three investor-organizers of a small business devoted to literacy training of adults. He is an educator who has worked all his life with government rather than business, and, in fact, he has been somewhat disdainful of business. In this instance, however, Wilson feels that public schools provide inadequate environment and methods for literacy training of adults. He feels a deep need to take action now, using new methods and greater flexibility than public education seems able to provide. The main benefit or reward which he seeks in this situation is the feeling that he is using his skills more fully to provide a public service. He knows this area is crowded with others performing similar services, so he expects to compete. He has competed in the realm of ideas all his life, and in this instance he believes his ideas are better. He perceives business as the best social organization to achieve his purpose, and he is willing to risk his capital and other values to achieve his goals.

Wilson's choices reflect functional analysis to determine which institution is most appropriate to perform a particular social function. He chose business because he felt it was the best institution to do the job. He does not believe that business is the *only* institution which can provide literacy training for adults, but he does feel it is the desirable one in this situation. In the same way that Wilson used functional analysis, businessmen may use it to help them determine which areas of social involvement they are best qualified to serve.

SUMMARY

The business role traditionally has focused on economic performance in the production of goods and services, but this role gradually is evolving toward a more social orientation. Business is realizing that it is part of a system in which society desires both economic and social benefits in its interface with business. Society wants business to clean up its environmental degradation and generally to provide a better quality of life, which is defined as a social system which has freedom, high purpose, relative affluence, and people living in harmony with their inner spirit, their fellow man, and nature's physical environment.

In responding to social needs, business may use one or several of the following approaches: withdrawal, public relations, legal action, bargaining, and problem solving. Top management, staff, and operating departments are involved in social responses, but the activities of each differ somewhat. Functional analysis is frequently applied to determine areas in which business is best qualified for social involvement.

STUDY GUIDES FOR INTERPRETATION OF THIS CHAPTER

1. Discuss with two other persons whether they view business as the enemy of social change, as the student did in the incident at the beginning of this chapter. Try to analyze their ways of thinking, and report to class the results of your experience.

2. Compare the traditional role of business with the modern social role which seems to be evolving.

3. Discuss differences in the response alternatives available to business in areas of social involvement.

4. Explain the different actions required of top management, staff organizations, and operating departments when a firm initiates social involvement.

5. Explain how functional analysis can help determine the areas for most effective business involvement in social affairs.

PROBLEMS
Industrial Products Company

The purchasing manager of Industrial Products Company is Mr. Hale Drury. Industrial Products Company is located in a metropolitan seaport having over 1 million population. The company processes certain imported raw materials for sale to other manufacturers.

Recently a metropolitan crime commission which was appointed by the mayor to study crime in the community issued a report which emphatically and directly linked a local trucking contractor with the Mafia and with crime and corruption on waterfront docks. The report shows in detail how this firm seems to operate more efficiently (i.e., with lower costs) by paying bribes to give its trucks preference at the docks while other trucks wait, by collecting protection money from ship lines to prevent pilferage and damage on the docks, by collecting similar protection money from competing truckers to prevent pilferage and accidents, and by other practices.

For the last seven years Mr. Drury has purchased all contract trucking through the alleged Mafia-linked trucker because his bid price for services is about 2 percent lower than that of other truckers. Annual contract trucking purchases exceed $200,000. The trucker's services have been consistently of high quality, clearly equal to the services Mr. Drury could expect from other truckers.

The company policy manual for Mr. Drury's department includes the following statement: "The mission of the procurement department is to ensure that all products, materials, and services are purchased at the lowest cost and best terms possible. To accomplish this mission, all appropriate steps may be taken, including renegotiation, value analysis, and changing vendors.''

Mr. Drury believes the crime commission report is accurate, and he personally is much opposed to the Mafia and other organized crime. Although Drury is concerned, he is not sure what to do. He believes that if he awarded next year's contract to any other trucker which bid higher, his company would suffer some unfortunate trucking accidents, delays in delivery, pilferage, and other difficulties, in addition to paying more for trucking services. He is not sure management would support an award to a higher bidder solely on the basis of the crime commission's allegations.

1. If you were Mr. Drury, what would you do, why would you do it, and how would you go about it? (For some useful analysis, see Charles Grutzner, ''How to Lock Out the Mafia,'' *Harvard Business Review,* March–April 1970, pp. 45–58.)

Continental State Bank

Continental State Bank is located in a large Eastern city of over 1 million persons. Fifteen years ago the neighborhood where the bank is located was one of the city's more affluent sections, and the bank prospered. Since that time the neighborhood has deteriorated rapidly and fallen into disrepair. Now it is populated by low-skilled wage earners and the urban poor. The majority of residents are members of minority groups. During this time deposits have declined from $38 million to $27 million in spite of inflation, and bank profits have declined accordingly.

The state in which the bank is located does not allow branch banking; thus bank management feels that in order to restore the bank's former level of operations it must move to another location in a more affluent neighborhood. Major stockholders strongly support this view, because they have seen their investment decline in value. The bank's management has secured an option on a location 3 miles distant, and it is seriously considering a move.

The bank was forced to release its plans for a move when it routinely applied to the state banking commission for approval of a bank at the new location. When neighborhood people learned of the move, they rose in protest. A store owner stated that the bank was the last bastion of stability in the neighborhood and that if the bank left, the neighborhood would deteriorate further. Others claimed that the neighborhood would be without necessary banking facilities, because the closest other bank was over 1½ miles away. A local activist demanded: ''Reach out to the little people who need you.'' An owner of a cafe claimed that the bank deliberately discouraged customers so that it would have an excuse to move. He claimed that half the businesses in the neighborhood banked elsewhere because the bank had been unresponsive to their needs.

Bank spokesmen replied that the bank had spent large sums of money for market development without results. They claimed that other banks were close enough to serve the neighborhood. One bank spokesman explained the bank's position as follows: "We have a right to grow like any other business, and we are not a public agency established to solve community problems at the expense of stockholders." He added that Continental Bank would be glad to lease or sell its bank property to another bank if the residents could secure one or organize one.

An outside observer familiar with the situation said that it could be summarized in one fundamental question: Is the bank's major responsibility to its shareholders or to the neighborhood it serves?

1. With regard to Continental Bank, discuss the question presented in the last sentence of the case.

2. Assume you are a public member of the state banking commission. How would you vote on the petition of Continental State Bank? Why?

CHAPTER 6

THE MANAGERIAL ROLE
AND SOCIAL ISSUES

The managerial role, in contrast to many other professional roles, tends to be defined in terms of a system of multiple clients.

Edgar H. Schein[1]

It is through the vigilance of boundary agents that the organization is able to monitor and screen important happenings in the environment.

Dennis W. Organ[2]

Consider the situation of John Jones, a chemist promoted to laboratory manager. As a chemist, he usually knows when he is right, but as a manager he cannot be so sure. His decisions are restricted by social norms such as profit, justice, and human relations, none provable by laws of physical science. His new managerial role requires him to think beyond his narrow specialty of chemistry and even beyond the firm itself. When he is asked to decide whether a dangerous drug is ready for market tests, he needs to weigh new value systems before making his recommendation. What about danger to human life and the effect on the company's reputation and profits? Although he uses scientific facts in his decision, they are of less influence than when he acts as a chemist only.

The case of John Jones is a typical one. Managers are the main linking pins between business and society; therefore, their decisions need to be related to the values and expectations of the claimants in the social system. For this reason we can reach a better understanding of the business-society interface by discussing how managers perceive their roles in different parts of the world and how that role is evolving to improve business's response to social needs.

[1]Edgar H. Schein, "The Problem of Moral Education for the Business Manager," *Industrial Management Review,* Fall 1966, p. 9. Italics in original.
[2]Dennis W. Organ, "Linking Pins between Organizations and Environment," *Business Horizons,* December 1971, p. 74.

MANAGERIAL-ROLE BEHAVIOR

Role is a fundamental idea in understanding social systems because all persons therein act in role relationships to each other. William Shakespeare described role, in his famous passage from *As You Like It,* as follows:

> *All the world's a stage,*
> *And all the men and women merely players:*
> *They have their exits and their entrances;*
> *And one man in his time plays many parts.*

Role is the pattern of actions expected of persons in their activities involving others. Managers perceive themselves in a certain job which establishes a set of relationships with others; thus they act partly on the basis of what they think is expected of them. In other words, society's expectations influence their behavior. They become socially conditioned to act in a way which is consistent with the job of "manager."

The managerial role requires different conduct with different people rather than uniform conduct. One pattern of conduct is required with a subordinate, another with a fellow manager, and another with the local mayor; yet all three are managerial-role actions. Since these role variations are expected, managers need to develop role sensitivity for appraising each situation and do role thinking to select the most appropriate action.

Managers Have Similar Perceptions of Their Role

The most significant fact about the managerial role is that managers' perceptions of it appear fairly uniform throughout the world. There are cultural differences in role, but they are much less than might be expected. One reason for the relative agreement in role perceptions is that advancing technology presses people to adapt in uniform ways in order to reap its benefits. Thus, technology becomes a type of unifying agent in the work culture. Original studies by Kerr and others in the 1950s developed evidence that industrialization tends to cause a uniform work culture, including the managerial role. This tendency toward a uniform work culture exists even when social cultures are substantially different. Generally speaking, as industrialization advances, there is a move toward more democratization of employee and managerial roles.[3]

Subsequent studies comparing nations in different stages of industrial development have shown that they also have relatively similar perceptions of the managerial role. Since both technology and culture are somewhat different in these nations, it follows that there is something other than these two items that encour-

---

[3]Clark Kerr, John T. Dunlop, Frederick H. Harbison, and Charles A. Myers, *Industrialism and Industrial Man: The Problems of Labor and Management in Industrial Growth,* Cambridge, Mass.: Harvard University Press, 1960.

ages similar role perceptions. This additional factor appears to be the activities which managers perform to accomplish their jobs. Whatever the culture, managers need to perform rather similar activities, such as planning and organizing, and eventually these similar activities encourage them to perceive their roles in ways which are rather consistent with those of other managers, although still partly culturally conditioned.

One comprehensive study covered written responses of 3,641 managers in fourteen countries.[4] Research showed general uniformity in role perceptions regardless of country, although there were moderate cultural variations. Differences tended to group around clusters of nations having a common cultural background. Separate clusters existed for northern European, southern European, Anglo-American, and developing nations, while Japan stood by itself. Another study related 1,339 Australian managers to those from the fourteen countries and found general similarities, although they were most similar to British and United States managers.[5]

Further evidence of managerial similarities in developing and advanced nations is revealed in a survey of 215 Indian managers in Bombay and 230 United States managers in Philadelphia.[6] It was thought that since the Indian managers were reared in a strongly authoritarian culture with wide class differences and were supervising a different quality of labor in a less technological environment, they would be much more authoritarian than their counterparts in the United States. Although there was a tendency in this direction, the difference was not significant. The researcher concluded that the managerial perceptions of the two groups were substantially congruent.

The significance of these research projects is to show that managers' perceptions of their jobs are governed by both external cultural forces and internal job conditions. If society wishes to alter managerial role perceptions to produce a different response to social issues, one or both causal variables will need to be changed. Managers are products of their environment. They respond to conditions around them. To the degree that those conditions can be changed, their responses will also change as they perceive different roles for themselves. For example, if more social data inputs can be fed into a firm's information system, this information will be constantly intruding on the managers' consciousness as they perform their daily duties and should influence them to want to use it in relating their firm to

[4]Mason Haire, Edwin E. Ghiselli, and Lyman W. Porter, *Managerial Thinking: An International Study,* New York: John Wiley & Sons, Inc., 1966.

[5]Alfred W. Clark and Sue McCabe, "Leadership Beliefs of Australian Managers," *Journal of Applied Psychology,* February 1970, pp. 1–6. For a study emphasizing cultural differences between French and English managers, see Desmond Graves, "Cultural Determinism and Management Behavior," *Organizational Dynamics,* Autumn 1972, pp. 46–59.

[6]Arvind Phatak, "Managerial Attitudes in the United States and India," *The Economic and Business Bulletin,* Philadelphia: Temple University School of Business Administration, Summer 1969, pp. 15–21.

society. As another example, if more forces from pressure groups are brought to bear on managers, they will be culturally pressed to develop effective response patterns. Exactly these kinds of forces are affecting managers today, causing an evolution of the managerial role toward a more socially responsive manager.

A SOCIALLY RESPONSIVE MANAGERIAL ROLE

As society increasingly requires business to address itself to new priorities, the character of the managerial role is changing. Originally the managerial role was substantially similar to the role of ruler, deriving its powers through rights of monarchy, military control, church rank, or capital ownership. Gradually it evolved in response to social values and needs until now it is more of a differentiated occupation, semiprofessional, and frequently involved in social issues.

Although modern managers may have some ownership interest in their firms by means of stock options and profit sharing plans, they do not hold their management positions on the basis of ownership. They legitimize their power by competently performing a function which is needed and valued by owners, employees, and society alike. This condition is actually an *acceptance model of legitimacy,* meaning that managers maintain the legitimacy of their roles only as long as they are able to serve claimants in a satisfactory way. This relationship puts them under constant pressure to perform for a variety of claimants.

The manager of a large apartment complex was unable to satisfy the expectations of his tenants. His failure appeared to arise primarily from his inability to work with maintenance groups which kept the facilities clean, painted, and in good repair. Maintenance was so unreliable that some tenants charged discrimination. Although no discrimination existed, the complaints eventually involved public antidiscrimination groups. Finally all these pressures forced him out of his job.

The kind of managers we are discussing can be called *socially responsive managers.* In their decision making they give substantial weight to social inputs along with economic and technical inputs, and they seek to provide social outputs for a wide variety of claimants. The change toward this type of role will take years, but the trend is clear.

In the evolution to a more socially responsive managerial role two relatively dormant subroles have emerged. These are the roles of trustee and boundary mediator. They will be discussed in the following paragraphs along with four other roles that have undergone substantial changes as business has become more socially involved. These roles are system regulator, productivity catalyst, change agent, and leader. The following discussion emphasizes a social system interpretation of role, rather than the more traditional functional emphasis on management activities such as planning, organizing, directing, and controlling. Emphasis is upon certain social roles which society has assigned to management to perform.

A Manager as a Social Trustee

The modern professional manager also regards himself, not as an owner disposing of personal property as he sees fit, but as a trustee balancing the interests of many diverse participants and constituents in the enterprise, whose interests sometimes conflict with those of others. The chief executive of a large corporation has the problem of reconciling the demands of employees for more wages and improved benefit plans, customers for lower prices and greater values, vendors for higher prices, government for more taxes, stockholders for higher dividends and greater capital appreciation—all within a framework that will be constructive and acceptable to society.

From *Social Responsibilities of Business Corporations,* New York: Committee for Economic Development, 1971, p. 22.

The Role of Trustee

Management historically has acted as a trustee for owner interests, but the interests of others have been somewhat dormant. Social awareness has caused these dormant interests to emerge, requiring management to give much more emphasis to a wide variety of claimants that formerly received very little attention. The philosophy of these claimants is that society commits to management its social and economic resources with the expectation that management will employ them wisely to produce more outputs than inputs. As with legal trustees, management is expected not to dissipate the resources under its care but to enhance them if at all possible. Although management may in the short run hold these resources by means of legal forms such as ownership and rights of contract, in the long run it legitimizes its custody of these social resources by being an effective trustee.

The trusteeship role was recognized early in business literature. In 1925 Robert Brookings wrote: "Management is thus coming to occupy the position of trustee. . . . This change is not yet complete. It is a trend rather than an accomplished fact, but it is a very promising trend."[7] Chester Barnard, a distinguished figure in management, further clarified this role by pointing out that managerial actions are *representative behavior*. That which is representative is performed on behalf of others. It is done in terms of the goals and ethics of others rather than according to the performer's personal goals and ethics. For example, in a legal situation such as a trust or will, the trustee has wide latitude to apply judgment, but his judgment must be entirely divorced from his personal interest. As indicated by Barnard, the ethics of personal behavior are not identical with those of representative behavior except by chance.[8]

Regardless of how well personal ethics are defined by society, representative behavior requires a whole new set of ethical norms. A manager's decisional

[7]Robert S. Brookings, *Industrial Ownership: Its Economic and Social Significance,* New York: The Macmillan Company, 1925, p. 23.
[8]Chester I. Barnard, "Elementary Conditions of Business Morals," *California Management Review,* Fall 1958, pp. 1–13.

environment is so complex that it would be impossible to prescribe all his decisions by law. Even if this were possible, it would be undesirable because it would tie him in a straitjacket that would keep him from applying the talents which society wants from him. The result is that managers retain wide latitude to apply judgment, but they experience increasing pressures to act in a responsible manner as trustees of social investments. Since trustees act on behalf of others, many of whom are more concerned with the quality of life than its material productivity, managers are becoming more accountable to society for the quality of life created by their trusteeship actions.

One study reported that large corporations with sales of over $1 billion annually are substantially more active in performing their trusteeship function for all society than smaller firms with less than $250 million sales.[9] When the large companies were compared with the smaller companies, the large companies had a greater participation rate in fourteen of fifteen areas of social response. For example, in minority training 91 percent of large companies were active compared with 54 percent of the smaller companies. With regard to product defect responsibility and control, 50 percent of the large companies had programs compared with 8 percent of the smaller firms. It appears that large corporations with their greater economic resources and staff assistance have been able to respond more quickly to this new social trend.

The Role of Boundary Mediator

The growing emphasis on social issues has created a new significance for the role of boundary mediator. Just as a fluid system in physical science has boundary conditions, so does a dynamic organization have them. These are its points of interface with its environment, and management's job is to mediate or resolve these boundary interfaces in order to keep its organization effective. Its role is to achieve organizational objectives while supporting claimant objectives also. As shown in Figure 6-1, managers direct an open system, not a closed one. They

[9]Henry Eilbirt and I. Robert Parket, "The Current Status of Corporate Social Responsibility," *Business Horizons*, August 1973, pp. 5–14.

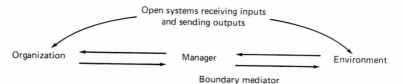

Figure 6-1 System relationship of the boundary mediation role of a manager.

A Boundary Agent Is Concerned with Conflict Resolution

In short, the boundary agent has to grapple with at least two different —sometimes contradictory—sets of goals, values, and beliefs. Therefore, the performance of the boundary agent is likely to be a key variable in the prevention, mitigation, and resolution of interorganizational conflict. If he is skillful in the judicious bending to pressures, compromising between conflicting demands, and balancing off some issues against others, he may be able to ward off serious conflict between organizations. On the other hand, if he is impulsive, rigid, or insensitive to others' beliefs and values, he may engender conflict even where it is not inherent in relationships between organizations.

From Dennis W. Organ, "Linking Pins between Organizations and Environment," *Business Horizons,* December 1971, p. 75. Reprinted with permission.

operate on the boundary between an organization and its external environment, receiving inputs from the environment as well as the organization and, in turn, transmitting outputs to both. Management should expect external pressures of all types and be prepared to mediate them. Similarly it receives *organizational* pressures that will affect the external environment and needs to resolve these to the satisfaction of both the internal and external systems. It uses a problem-solving approach to integrate the organization with the social system. There is strong evidence that competent, receptive boundary personnel of this type are an important element in any organization's capacity to absorb change from society.[10]

Managers are *mediators* rather than controllers, because they have no formal authority which they can apply to the external social system. They cannot tell society what to do, no matter how great the needs of their organization, because the external system owes no direct allegiance to their organization. Since they cannot *tell,* their next best choice is to *sell;* but as any salesperson knows, salesmanship is not successful in the long run unless the product sold is a desirable one. This means that managers as boundary mediators are required to conduct their organization's business in a way which meets social needs along with the firm's internal needs.

A distinguishing feature of the boundary mediation role is that role conflict develops. Different groups expect different actions by managers, and they are caught in a crossfire between them. Those inside the organization naturally are seeking to serve organizational objectives, while those outside the organization have different objectives in mind. The situation is often further confused by the fact that both those inside and those outside the organization are not in agreement among themselves. On a particular issue there may be five outside organizations pushing five different points of view and two internal groups (such as production and sales) pushing their different views. With seven different role senders pressing them with different expectations, managers are naturally in role conflict.

[10]Ronald G. Corwin, "Strategies for Organizational Innovation: An Empirical Comparison," *American Sociological Review,* August 1972, pp. 441–454.

Early research by Kahn and others provided evidence of role conflict in the boundary mediation role.[11] In a national study the researchers classified persons according to the frequency of their job contacts outside the organization. They found that as job-required outside contacts increased, there was an increase in feeling of role conflict. Persons with negligible outside contacts had the least role conflict, and those with frequent contacts had the most conflict. In between were those with occasional outside contacts. The differences among the groups were significant to the 0.001 degree.

The Kahn study also reported that persons with outside contacts experienced more job tension than those who had negligible contacts. As the frequency of contacts increased, however, there was not a corresponding increase in tension. The researchers suggested that one explanation is that persons who regularly dealt outside the organization may have developed better coping mechanisms from their frequent experience; thus they were able to handle more contacts without a corresponding rise in tension.

In the same manner that boundary mediation creates role conflict and tension, it also causes value conflicts within a manager's personal value system. Managers have many loyalties and interests other than those of their employer, and sometimes these interests come into conflict. Consider the following situation.

In a large city a plant produced considerable fumes and dust. Thirty years ago the plant was located on the edge of town, but the city grew, and the plant found itself near the edge of the downtown commercial area. Pressures built up for the plant to improve its control of fumes and dust. Figure 6-2 shows some of the value conflicts which the plant manager faced in this situation. Community citizens wanted a cleaner city in which to live and shop. (The manager and his family were citizens of the community.) The chamber of commerce wanted a cleaner downtown. (The manager was an active member of the chamber of commerce.) The fumes and dust could be prevented, but this would require over $1 million of capital that might otherwise be used for stockholder benefit. (The manager and his children owned stock in the firm.) The cost of pollution control equipment would probably raise the cost of the firm's products about 1 percent. (The manager had personal friends who were regular purchasers of the firm's products, and he had strong feelings about inflation.) This is only a partial listing of the conflicts involved, so it is easy to see why he felt stress and conflict in trying to decide this issue. (What would you do?)

Assuming that a manager in his boundary mediator role perceives an external claim, his next step is to screen it on the basis of its validity and strength. Does it

---

[11]Robert L. Kahn et al., *Organizational Stress: Studies in Role Conflict and Ambiguity,* New York: John Wiley & Sons, Inc., 1964, pp. 99–124.

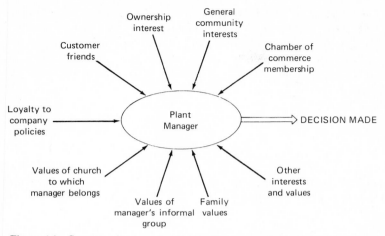

Figure 6-2 Sources of personal value conflicts generated in a plant manager concerning an air pollution problem.

come from a group which has a genuine investment in the situation? Is the claim consistent with socially accepted customs? What is the strength of the claimants? Let us take an extreme example. If a group comes to a manager and insists that he hire no person more than 10 pounds overweight because excessive weight is dangerous to health, he may sympathize with their cause and agree with their conclusion about danger to health, but he will pay little heed to their demand because it has weak rationality and is beyond the bounds of social custom. On the other hand, he may respond to a plea for hiring more handicapped persons, which would probably include a number of overweight and underweight persons.

After screening, many valid claims remain; therefore, a manager must further resolve them through working with claimant groups both inside and outside his organization. In the long run managers seek role action which brings net outputs greater than inputs.

The boundary mediation role is extremely important because it is largely through the behavior of boundary mediators that the organization adapts, or fails to adapt, to developments in the environment. Their vigilance is necessary to keep the organization on an even keel with the social system. If boundary mediators, both managerial and employee, fail in their responsibilities, the organization is sure to be the loser in the long run, because it will not adequately respond to changes in its environment.

The Role of System Regulator (Operating Management)

System regulation is concerned with effective internal operations of an organization. It is a traditional management role, but it has been amended greatly by the intrusion of social issues. Managers must now assure that their firm's operations are in harmony with the environment and with public expectations. This relationship also is true for each subordinate manager down the line to the lowest operating employee in the organization. Throughout the organization employees need to become convinced that the old order of considering only economic and technical criteria no longer applies. A new ingredient of social expectations has been introduced.

In the engineering department of one firm, for example, the traditional way to design a new branch plant was to seek the lowest unit cost having the required technical result. Now the designs are restricted by additional conditions with which the engineering manager needs to assure compliance. Some of these are building architecture and landscaping that are pleasing to the public, internal design pleasing to employees, control of pollution and noise, and work design which provides enriched jobs that are challenging to employees.

In getting its employees to conduct the business in harmony with its environment, management operates as a decision maker at key junction points in the intricate social system that forms an organization. In fact, an organization may be defined as a cluster of roles having a common objective. As part of the system, management is both independent and dependent, initiating action on others and having action initiated on it. Some earlier views of management made it exclusively an independent force initiating on others, but this view lacked realism in terms of actual operating conditions. Management performs in a dynamic system relationship rather than being the static authority structure pictured on an organization chart.

An essential contradiction of decision making is that the desirable consequences of a decision are likely to be partly offset by undesirable side effects. For example, the desirable consequences of fume and dust control in the city discussed earlier could be accomplished only with the undesirable consequences of costs to owners and customers, plus perhaps an additional push toward inflation. Few decisions produce only desirable consequences for all concerned. When a manager functions in roles such as trustee, boundary mediator, and system regulator, he has to make trade-offs among the consequences in order to produce some desirable combination of them.

This trade-off of consequences is usually perceived as a satisfactory decision, rather than one which is maximal. A maximal decision wholly favors one objective or group without regard for others. For example, a manager may maximize profits. An optimal decision considers all alternatives and selects the one which is definitely best. Satisfactory decisions, on the other hand, consider a number of alternatives and select one which at least meets minimum criteria. The difference is similar to looking for the sharpest needle in a haystack and looking for a needle only sharp enough for sewing.

The Role of Productivity Catalyst

A social role of central significance to management is that of productivity catalyst, which is to produce the largest possible flow of desirable outputs in relation to inputs. In this manner society receives the most from resources it has entrusted to those who manage organizations. Management is a catalyst in this situation rather than a producer, because management accomplishes work through others. Like a physical catalyst that encourages better results from a chemical reaction, management motivates employees toward a more effective result.

Since this role always has been performed, how has it changed? Is not productivity still a significant managerial role? Yes, it is, but the major change is that managers are now more responsible for social inputs (costs) and the social outputs (benefits) that result from these costs. It is a matter of social results along with economic results. Society wants its social resources to be used as wisely as its economic resources have been in the past, and even more so.

Some firms believe that they have been socially responsible if they merely keep from harming the environment or the social system as they go about their business. The productivity catalyst role suggests, however, that the truly socially responsible firm is one which enhances the environment. That is, the responsible firm acts in a way that produces social gains rather than mere absence from harm.

The Role of Change Agent

Management always has had responsibility for introducing change, but normally the change has been economic and technical change. The new dimension is introduction of social change. Business has become a vehicle for implementing social policy. For example, it has been required to implement social mandates with regard to minority employment, training of hard-core unemployed, price controls, limitations on export of funds in order to aid the international balance of payments, and a host of other policies. Particularly with regard to initiation of such matters as minority employment, it has been required to reorient the attitudes and habit patterns of its employees. Supervisors have been trained to be more sensitive to needs of minorities and hard-core unemployed, and policies have been revised. Management has become a social change agent.

In introducing change, management's role is more that of innovation than creativity. Normally creativity deals with the generation of ideas, but innovation deals with making them work. Compared with research scientists, who emphasize creativity, managers are more concerned with innovating to bring ideas to fruition. Since creative ideas are of no usefulness until implemented, the innovative role of management becomes more important as more and better ideas are generated in modern society.

Ideas without implementers simply increase the burden of conscience on society because people know that there are better ways and are frustrated by their deficient implementation. Modern society, having generated ideas beyond our capacity to absorb them, needs help in implementing change. It is turning to management, which is fast becoming a central resource needed by all the nations of the world because of its excellent ability to introduce change in ongoing systems. Social change will require of management the same kind of daring innovative ability that in the past it has applied to products.

The Role of Leader

Leadership is defined as behavior which induces energetic, emotionally committed, cooperative followers. People follow a leader because they see reasons, both emotional and rational, for following. Leadership finds those reasons and makes them more appealing. It encourages average people to achieve above-average results. If better people can be attracted and motivated, then better results should be reached, other things being equal. Some of history's great business leaders recognized this role, leaders like Andrew Carnegie, whose epitaph reads:

> *Here lies a man*
> *Who knew how to enlist*
> *In his service*
> *Better men than himself.*

The expansion of social responsibility issues has changed the leadership role in two significant ways. One change is that leadership has an increasing responsibility to treat employees with more concern, dignity, and support—in short, to treat them as human beings. Formerly employees were considered as an economic resource or as a large group of people called labor. Now business is expected to treat them as individual persons worthy of human concern. Business is seen as having an obligation to help people grow to the highest realization of their self-actualization needs. These developments have caused the leadership role to be redefined as less autocratic and more participative and supportive of employee needs. Leadership has become less a matter of personality and more a matter of competent role behavior. Modern leaders are moving away from detailed task prescription toward goal setting which allows participants more latitude in task performance. Ideas such as management by objectives, job enrichment, and organizational development are helping implement this change.[12]

A second change in the leadership role is that leadership is expected to be effective in social-system relationships external to the organization as well as in its traditional internal role. Its area of operation has become the macrosocial system

---

[12]For an extensive development of these ideas, see Keith Davis, *Human Behavior at Work: Human Relations and Organizational Behavior*, 4th ed., New York: McGraw-Hill Book Company, 1972.

along with the microsocial system. In the microsocial system, leadership deals with others from a hierarchical position of authority and status, but in the macrosocial system, it operates as an equal that must depend primarily on its problem-solving competence. People will be accepted as leaders only if they can sense the needs of society and offer problem solutions which help meet those needs. The true leaders in the macrosocial sense are those who work for social improvement rather than merely trying to pacify society regarding the external effects of their organization. The macrosocial system provides a whole new dimension for the leadership role. It requires new and different role behavior, and it offers both new problems and opportunities.

An Evolving Managerial Role

The managerial role is continually being redefined to gear it to new developments. The newest and largest redefinition relates to the external environment and social goals. Social needs and goals are turning the attention of people to the social obligations of managers to work toward a high quality of life as well as toward high economic productivity. This focus requires a modern manager to use socially desirable methods of operation toward socially desirable ends.

Since socially desirable methods and ends are not easy to achieve, the modern managerial role requires men and women who are intellectually capable, thoughtful, broadly trained, and professional in attitude. There is decreasing opportunity for those who think only of the internal system, who are unprepared, who fail to grow, or who work mainly from their emotions, even when their emotions favor desirable social ends. The practice of management is becoming increasingly professional.

SUMMARY

Management is a distinct occupational role, and managers throughout the world are substantially in agreement concerning their perception of this role. The effects of different cultures are evident but not large. As society moves toward more socially responsive organizations, the character of the managerial role is being redefined. Two relatively dormant subroles, trustee and boundary mediator, have emerged. The trustee is responsible for constructive use of social resources, and the boundary mediator works on the interface of an organization and its environment. Research shows that boundary mediation causes more role conflict and tension for a manager than most other roles.

Four additional roles that have changed significantly are system regulator, productivity catalyst, change agent, and leader. As a system regulator a manager is responsible for keeping operations in harmony with the environment. The role of productivity catalyst is changed to require more concern for social costs and outputs. The change agent increasingly is required to implement social mandates within the organization, and the leader now deals with human dignity and macrosocial issues. For each subrole there has been major change as the managerial role evolves to serve more socially responsive organizations.

STUDY GUIDES FOR INTERPRETATION OF THIS CHAPTER

1. Discuss why managerial role perceptions are substantially similar in spite of different cultural backgrounds.

2. A quotation introducing this chapter states: "The managerial role, in contrast to many other professional roles, tends to be defined in terms of a system of *multiple clients*." Discuss this statement.

3. Assume that a law is proposed—primarily because of the trusteeship role of managers—requiring persons to be fingerprinted, screened for felony convictions, and licensed in order to serve as officers or middle managers of corporations (government-incorporated organizations, profit and nonprofit). As a citizen, how would you react? Why?

4. Discuss how the roles of productivity catalyst and leader have changed as society moves toward more socially responsive organizations.

5. Discuss how the move toward social responsiveness may be changing other managerial roles, such as that of trainer and communicator.

PROBLEMS
Two Proposals for Reorganizing Business[13]

The following proposals have been made in France for reorganizing business in order to redistribute power.

One proposal has been made by a group of Christian businessmen in Lyons. They propose that the workers establish a workers' company that is legally comparable to the regular company set up by the owners. The two companies would then enter into a contractual agreement which would be the source of all power to manage the joint assets of the two companies. The top manager would be selected by the two companies and designated in their contract. He would have full freedom to manage, but he would be ultimately responsible to both companies.

A second proposal suggests that there should be a regular board of directors whose chairman would be the top executive of the business. In addition, the top executive's activities would be reviewed by a public court consisting of members of government as well as representatives of employers, employees, shareholders,

---

[13] Adapted from P. Heymann and J. Schmidt, "French Business Probes Its *Raison d' Être*," *Columbia Journal of World Business*, July–August 1967, pp. 75–76.

and consumers. The court would provide advice concerning the distribution of power in the business when cases of this type could not be resolved at lower levels. For example, a proper case for the court would be a complaint about the incompetence of a director.

1. If the first proposal were adopted in your nation, in what ways would it change the role of (a) the top manager and (b) other managers?

2. If the second proposal were adopted in your nation, in what ways would it change the role of (a) the top manager and (b) other managers?

3. Discuss the benefits and disadvantages of both proposals.

The Lear Jet

When William P. Lear, using mostly his own money, was engaged in a crash program to develop his highly successful business aircraft, the Lear Jet, the following events occurred.[14]

> Lear, a short-tempered perfectionist who has frequently fired the same employee three times in one week for minor miscalculations, was breathing down everyone's neck all the time—checking, criticizing, guiding, goading, demanding—and he was finally threatened with mutiny. A delegation of employees, ready to quit, stormed into Lear's office one day and complained bitterly that he never let them do anything by themselves. "You make all the decisions," one of them said. "We can't do a thing."
>
> "That's right," Lear snapped, "but I'll make a deal with you. You guys put up half the money, and from now on I'll let you make half the decisions." End of mutiny.

1. Do you agree with William Lear? In general, when the owner of a large business is also its top manager, in what ways, if any, is his managerial role changed from that of the corporate managers emphasized in this chapter?

---

[14]David Shaw, "What Bill Lear Wants, Bill Lear Invents," *Esquire,* September 1969, p. 188. Used with permission.

7

TECHNOLOGY AND SOCIAL CHANGE

Modern power is based on the capacity for innovation, which is research, and the capacity to transform inventions into finished products, which is technology.

J.-J. Servan-Schreiber[1]

Neither villain nor savior, technology is one practical means to an enlightened end.

Business Week[2]

On July 20, 1969, civilization made perhaps its greatest technological breakthrough when it placed two men on the moon and later safely brought them back to earth. This was a daring and exciting adventure which quickened men's minds to the wonders of technology and the universe. It was an impressive example of business's cooperation with other pluralistic groups to build and operate an effective system of people and equipment. It also illustrated how fast technology is advancing, because twenty years earlier most persons would have viewed this event as wild science fiction.

There is no doubt about it. Mankind is living in its greatest age of technological breakthrough, and business is intricately involved in it. Experts have estimated that 80 to 90 percent of all the scientists who ever lived are still alive today. This figure suggests in an approximate way that society is now in the process of absorbing 80 to 90 percent of the total technological change it has had. The result is that business is in the midst of a massive task of absorbing technology on a scale never before experienced. Technological change has become the *norm* instead of the exception. Because business has successfully applied new technology in the past, we expect that it will do so again, but this expectation should not blind us to the magnitude of the job. The statement from *Alice in Wonderland* is almost a

[1]J.-J. Servan-Schreiber, *The American Challenge,* New York: Avon, 1969, p. 240. Translated from the original French, *Le Défi américain:* Paris, Editions Deneol, 1967.
[2]"Technology Isn't the Villain—After All," *Business Week,* Feb. 3, 1973, p. 38.

truism for organizations in a technological society: "You have to run as fast as you can to stay where you are."

This chapter discusses some of the characteristics and effects of technological change and business's involvement with it. Modern technology has given businessmen new powers, but it also has given them new responsibilities, such as managing a more complex system and using technology in a way that enhances the quality of life.

ABUNDANT TECHNOLOGY

Throughout history technology has pressed onward like a glacier, overturning everything in its way and grinding all opposition into dust. Its unrelenting power has overcome all who tried to stand in its way. In eighteenth-century England, for example, a band of unhappy workers known as Luddites challenged the Industrial Revolution by roaming the countryside, smashing machinery and burning factories. From their narrow viewpoint, machines were enemies taking away jobs and freedom and harming mankind. But the Luddites were soon overcome by the benefits brought by the same machinery they opposed. They sank into oblivion, just as their more modern successors have done. And we know now that they were largely mistaken. Though the Industrial Revolution created new problems, it was a great advance in the history of man.

The glacier of technology grinds on toward progress because of man himself. Man, having tasted the fruit of knowledge, cannot suppress his desire for it. He forever seeks to expand knowledge of his environment.

Business Applies Technology

As soon as new knowledge exists, man wants to apply it in order to reap its benefits. At this point business becomes important because *business is the principal institution that translates discovery into application for public use.* Printing, housing, education, and television are all dependent on business activities to make them work productively. Society depends on business to keep the stream of discovery flowing into useful goods and services for all mankind. Less-developed countries have learned that scientific discoveries mean very little to them unless they have competent business organizers and managers to produce for their people what science has discovered. Developed countries have learned that their progress stops unless they operate a business system which contributes to discovery and uses discovery to produce for their people.

In further support of the role of business in technological development, a university study of 900 key inventions in this century reports that in most cases

Business Is the Principal Institution That Translates Discovery into Application for Public Use

Still a little enterprise, employing only 125 people in its central operations, Zoecon is another of those pioneering companies started by businessmen-scientists who hope to cash in on new technologies. Its products are chemical mimics, or analogues, of a hormone—known as the juvenile hormone—that retards an insect's development. Sprayed on insects at the right time, these synthetic imitators of natural secretions can disrupt the insect's growth, making some of them unable to survive and reducing the pestiness of others. These analogues do their job without creating any known hazards for animal life, including man. They can be made fairly selective in their action against bugs, and they do not persist in the environment.

From Gene Bylinsky, "Zoecon Turns Bugs against Themselves," *Fortune,* August 1973, pp. 94–95.

growing markets stimulated invention, rather than invention coming first and creating a market. In all but a few cases "market was the mother of invention."[3]

A Service Economy

In an agrarian economy the majority of the labor force is employed in farm work in order to produce food to sustain life. With the arrival of the Industrial Revolution, many nations gradually advanced from an agrarian society to an industrial one in which the labor force was employed predominantly in factory production and related work. Business was so successful in applying technology in factories that by the 1960s the United States became the world's first *service economy.*[4] This means that the majority of the labor force became for the first time employed in retailing, banking, insurance, and related service occupations, rather than in direct production work such as industry, farming, and construction. Production is no longer the primary user of manpower or the central economic and social problem.

The service economy is an event of great significance which should at least be equivalent to the Industrial Revolution in its effects throughout society. It will affect the distribution of occupations, educational patterns, leisure time, and other areas of society. For example, the size of service units tends to be small compared with factory units, even though corporate size may remain the same. The striking growth of the franchise movement in the 1960s is a reflection of the development of service industry. Service industries have also shown themselves to be resistant to unemployment during recessions; therefore, their dominance in the economy should help reduce employment fluctuations during economic swings.[5]

[3]What Is the Key to Progress?" *Business Week,* May 16, 1964, p. 132.
[4]Victor R. Fuchs, *The Service Economy,* National Bureau of Economic Research General Series, no. 87, New York: Columbia University Press, 1968; and Gilbert Burck, "The Still-Bright Promise of Productivity," *Fortune,* October 1968, pp. 134ff.
[5]U.S. Department of Labor, Manpower Administration, *Assessing the Economic Scene,* 1969, p. 6.

Concurrent with the service economy an "electronic revolution" began to dominate technological change. The focus of technology in the Industrial Revolution was on forming and making material products. In the electronic revolution the focus has changed to storage, processing, and transmission of images and information. This new era of technological breakthrough and social influence is represented by television and the computer. It is producing massive changes in service areas such as education, entertainment, medicine, and banking. Electronic technology may keep you alive in a hospital. Or, it can catch you if you try to forge a check!

Barbara walked into a branch bank and tried to open an account by depositing a check. She had what she thought was a foolproof system, because she was going to open small accounts in several banks on the same day, write overdrafts against them, and then leave town at once before she was caught. Unfortunately she was not aware of some of the bank's operations.

The bank was a subscriber to a private business which operates a check verification service. The business stores information about 11 million persons in its computer, filing the information according to each person's driver's license number. When Barbara tried to make her deposit, the bank clerk checked with the verification service, and its computer reported that Barbara was a felony suspect wanted for trying a similar scheme in another part of the state. A surprised Barbara was arrested by two patrolmen before she could leave the bank.[6]

SOME GENERAL EFFECTS OF TECHNOLOGY
Effects of Technology Are Pervasive

When technology is applied by business or any other institution, its effects are frequently widespread. They reach far beyond the point of immediate impact of the technology, and they have both desirable and undesirable results. The dominant climate becomes one of change and then more change. In a dynamic society technology operates as a multiplier, not as an additive, because it acts in a system relationship with other parts of society. Thus, invention of the wheel led to perhaps a dozen or more applications rather quickly. These applications, in turn, may have affected fifty other parts of the system and led to several additional inventions which similarly influenced society as multipliers.

The automobile serves as an example. It could not have been invented much earlier because hundreds of inventions had to precede it, such as

[6]"Los Angeles Company Helps Catch Crooks with Wary Computer," *Wall Street Journal* (Pacific Coast edition), May 12, 1969, p. 1.

improvements in metallurgy, vulcanization of rubber, electrical generation for sparkplugs, and refining of crude oil. Once these inventions existed, the automobile almost had to be invented, because there was a market for faster transportation than horses and bicycles and more individualized transportation than the faster trains offered.

When the technological breakthrough of the automobile did occur, its effects were pervasive throughout society. It had a profound effect on the whole ecological system. It changed the living habits of people, including their buying habits, the location of their homes, their independence, and their patterns of courtship. It increased the number of supermarkets and helped create drive-in movies. It expanded land areas allocated to roads, increased traffic to wilderness areas, and added pollution to the air. By means of the automobile truck, it altered shipping patterns and manufacturing locations. Hardly any area of society remained untouched by the automobile.

Higher Productivity

Perhaps the most fundamental effect of technology is greater productivity in terms of both quality and quantity. This is the main reason that most technology is adopted. In a hospital the objective may be qualitative, such as maintaining life with electronic monitoring equipment regardless of costs. In a factory the objective may be quantitative in terms of more production for less cost.

Some of the changes in technology have been striking. Nylon filament is extruded at 4,000 feet a minute, which is one-half million times faster than a silkworm produces silk. A good glassblower with a helper could make some 1,500 light bulbs a day, but a single machine can produce 132,000 bulbs *an hour*. Another dramatic example of productivity increase is the telephone system. It is estimated that if today's telephone system depended on manual operation as used in the 1930s, every woman in the United States over eighteen years of age would need to be employed in telephone work to handle the volume of calls now being made.

As a result of productivity improvements, real wages of employees tend to rise and prices of some products decline, which spreads the beneficial economic effects of technology throughout the whole social system. The result is that employees and citizens are motivated to want more technological advancement, thereby placing on business major responsibilities to introduce it with due concern for its social and environmental effects.

In advanced industrial nations perhaps the greatest effect of technology and the higher productivity it brings has been to satisfy the material needs of most of the people. With material needs satisfied in a minimum way, social needs are assuming priority, and people are giving more attention to the obligations of business to respond to social needs. In this manner business as a result of its own success has thrust itself into a new era and acquired a new set of problems to solve.

Although technology *in general* has been successful in bringing a better quality and quantity of output, in specific instances it often does not do so. Sometimes management is swayed by the enthusiasm of a functional specialist and adopts a change without adequate evaluation. It discovers later that the projected savings did not materialize because the specialist overlooked costs outside his field. When extended economic costs are included, savings dwindle or disappear; and when social costs are added, the change may be clearly unwise in its totality.

A petroleum company made an analysis of one of its regional offices handling credit card accounts. This office employed 500 persons and handled $25 million annually. An accounting study showed that the office could be abolished and all accounting done by a computer in the national office of the company at a saving of $75,000 out of an annual regional office cost of $500,000.

This saving appeared to justify centralization; however, investigation disclosed other factors affecting the decision. If the change were made, mail contact with customers would be slowed three days by regular mail or one day if air mail was used at an additional cost. Since no other jobs were available at the regional office, it was estimated that 325 employees would need to be moved to other offices including the central office. These costs were not computed in estimating the saving. Some other employees would be laid off or retired, which would incur additional costs of dismissal or early retirement benefits. As a matter of fact, the central office was in a large city in expensive office space, and no further space was available. Space would have to be leased or new facilities built.

Furthermore, fixed costs resulting from equipment lease cancellations at the regional office were not counted. Also omitted was the necessity for simultaneous operation of both offices during the changeover period. The company personnel director also observed that salary costs were generally higher in the national office, and he predicted that persons who transferred would soon get sizable increases in order to bring their salaries into line with those of other employees and to allow for living costs in their new community.

Considering the total picture, management decided that the saving would be less than $10,000 and that in terms of total economic and social costs to the company, the change would be unwise. It was not made.

System Complexity

An evident effect of technology is complexity. The modern washing machine does a better job than the old washboard and tub, but when it breaks down, it requires a specialist for repairs. And it may break down more often because of its complexity. The same reasoning applies to a complex production system. In November 1965, for example, an equipment failure on a power network in the Northeastern United States caused a power overload and opened circuit breakers nearby. In turn, a larger system became overloaded because of interties with other power systems. At once almost the entire Northeastern United States and part of Canada were gripped in a giant power failure which lasted throughout the night and into the next day. About 20 million people were affected. Gasoline stations could not pump gas, traffic lights stopped, elevators hung between floors, and so on. A localized problem on one circuit ballooned into a regional problem affecting other areas because of the intertie. Under conditions of this type, management is under great pressure to keep the whole system working all the time.

Also because of complexity, failure of one part in a system such as an airplane or a space ship can abort the whole operation for the long run. Moon rocket systems have over 1 million parts, and they must function properly in order to achieve a successful mission. Reliability of performance, therefore, assumes new significance. It is possible that technology eventually will lead to simplicity and small independent operational units, but that condition is far into the future. Meanwhile, more complexity in work and product systems is expected.

Unless the more complex system can be maintained reliably, it is not better than the system it replaces. Hans Christian Andersen in "The Nightingale" tells of an emperor who depended on a mechanized nightingale to sing its beautiful song. Its clockwork was so good that he banished the real nightingale. But eventually the clockwork failed and was discovered to be so complex that it could not be repaired. Again he came to depend on the real nightingale. Though technology is complex like the mechanical nightingale, we expect business to keep it "singing" for human benefit without having to return to old production systems.

Upgraded Job Skills

With the advance of technology, jobs tend to become more intellectual and otherwise upgraded. The job that once required a day laborer now requires a skilled craneman, and the job that formerly required a clerk now requires a computer expert. A generation ago the typical factory had a range of skills approaching curve *A* shown in Figure 7-1. This curve was shaped like the normal curve of intelligence among people. Being matched to people, it suggested that an adequate supply of labor would be available at all levels of business in the long run.

The System Complexity of Some Technology Makes It Difficult to Introduce

The scenario is simple and attractive: You walk into a downtown station and press a button, just as you would for an elevator; in no more time than it would take an elevator to arrive at your floor in a large building, a small, driverless vehicle glides silently up along its own exclusive guideway; you enter and, having chosen your destination when you pressed the button, are carried nonstop to another part of the city.

This not entirely hypothetical style of transportation is generally called "personal rapid transit"—even though you may well be sharing that small vehicle with one or two dozen other passengers. Abbreviated to PRT, it is currently the principal new mode of urban transit being developed for the immediate future by the federal Department of Transportation (DOT) and American private industry. The concept of PRT tends to blur at the edges, sometimes embracing everything from small subways to individual capsules to moving sidewalks. But most of the current attention is focused on small, fully automated, electric-powered vehicles, each carrying roughly one to two dozen passengers and running on an exclusive right-of-way, probably some form of aerial guideway.

From Daniel Jack Chasan, "An Answer to City Traffic May Be a Horizontal Elevator," *Smithsonian,* July 1973, p. 47.

In modern business the curve has moved toward the right, higher in skill, as shown in curve *B*. And in many organizations the skill distribution has become bimodal, as shown by the second top on the curve. Many scientific and professional people are required in research, development, planning, and other specialized work, creating the secondary bulge toward the skilled end of the scale.

Curve *C* represents the skill distribution which is developing in firms oriented toward research and development. Even though these firms manufacture products for sale, much of their effort is devoted to development and to building

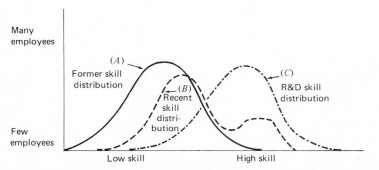

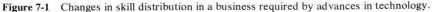

Figure 7-1 Changes in skill distribution in a business required by advances in technology.

prototypes. In some of these the number of engineers, scientists, and college-graduate specialists exceeds the total number of other employees.

The nature of technology is that it creates jobs that people are not yet prepared to fill. The bargain which technology strikes with a person is to take one job and offer him in return another one, usually requiring higher ability, for which he may not be qualified. It places a burden of training and education on the employee, the firm, and the nation. The poorly educated, the aged, and other marginal employees are the first to be dislocated, but they are often the ones least able to adjust. In economic terms, by requiring workers to be better prepared in order to contribute fully, technology increases the marginal productivity of skilled and intellectual work, while decreasing the marginal productivity of unskilled and manual work.

An individual organization can usually retrain employees who are ready and able to respond, and large firms usually have done this, but employees who are unable to respond flexibly constitute a larger social problem that requires assistance from other pluralistic groups. Society faces the immense task of motivating these persons, for without help they become the hard-core unemployed and the "untrainables." Without realizing it, high school dropouts have set their own job ceilings before ever starting to work!

After workers have endured the personal costs of upgrading their skills, the effects of technology are usually beneficial. Their pay tends to increase because of upgraded skills and increased productivity, and usually the new work is more challenging, giving more opportunity for personal growth and promotion. Research on alienation supports this view. It clearly shows that advanced technology reduces the level of alienation among both factory and office workers. Technologically advanced jobs are better jobs on the average.[7]

More Scientific and Professional Workers

The increased number of intellectual workers represented by curves B and C has placed new responsibilities on business for managing the creative spirit, sometimes called "maverick management." Historically, scientists worked in a small laboratory at their own pace, usually in an academic setting, but more and more they are working for big organizations, both private and public. Most certainly they perform best in a work culture different from that of the assembly line.

Creative and intellectual workers expect relatively high job freedom. They are motivated by opportunities which offer a challenge for growth and achievement. They are less motivated by the expectations of higher formal authority than by their own professional interests and perceptions of opportunities. Their

[7]Jon M. Shepard, *Automation and Alienation: A Study of Office and Factory Workers,* Cambridge, Mass.: The M.I.T. Press, 1971.

orientation is *cosmopolitan,* toward their profession and the world outside their organization, rather than *local,* depending primarily on the reward structure of the firm itself. Although they are a part of the company work culture, they are just as much a part of a separate scientific culture operating beyond their organization's boundaries. Under these conditions they have an organizational rootlessness which increases job mobility.

Business is adjusting its supervisory practices to meet needs of intellectual workers. Some companies have established dual promotion ladders so that distinguished technical people can rise to ranks and receive salaries that are equivalent to those of managers. Flexible work schedules are allowed. Profit sharing is provided to give creative persons a financial stake in the ideas they create and to discourage their rootlessness. Attendance at professional meetings and writing professional articles are supported. In further response to intellectual workers' cosmopolitan interests, they are allowed to teach part time or are given special assignments.

Scientific and other specialized workers make up the *technostructure* of modern organizations and more or less govern them through control of their decision-making processes. This condition exists regardless of what pattern of authority is shown on the organization chart. According to John Kenneth Galbraith the technostructure "embraces all who bring specialized knowledge, talent, or experience to group decision-making. This, not the management, is the guiding intelligence—the brain—of the enterprise."[8] "Technostructure" is a convenient term, although a broad one, for emphasizing the pervasive influence of technology and specialization in organizations.

Since the majority within the technostructure of most organizations are likely to be technically trained persons, care must be taken to assure that they do not become a *technical elite* dominating business and social decisions. They are the experts concerning the technical feasibility of their proposals. Their expertise in this area cannot be questioned, so they may become impatient with people who stand in the way of a technically feasible project. However, their expertise may be the factor which limits their broader view of social effects. Business managers, therefore, have a responsibility to assess pluralistic views *within* the firm, as well as viewpoints from pluralistic groups outside the firm, when making decisions about the use of technology. Decisions concerning technological changes are social decisions rather than narrow technological decisions. This requires socially responsible decision making by socially conscious managers.

Fortunately technical groups are beginning to recognize their own responsibilities for social effects of their recommendations. An illustration is the engineering professional group called the Institute of Electrical and Electronics Engineers. It has the following paragraph about quality of life in its statement of purpose.[9]

[8]John Kenneth Galbraith, *The New Industrial State,* Boston: Houghton Mifflin Company, 1967, p. 71.
[9]Article I, Constitution of the Institute of Electrical and Electronics Engineers, 1973.

The IEEE shall strive to enhance the quality of life for all people throughout the world through the constructive application of technology in its fields of competence. It shall endeavor to promote understanding of the influence of such technology on the public welfare.

More Emphasis on Research and Development

As technology has advanced, research and development (R&D) has become a giant new function in business. Research concerns the creation of new ideas, and development concerns their useful application. Direct research and development expenditures in industry in 1960 were over $10 billion, and these expenditures increased to about $30 billion by 1970. These figures do not include billions of indirect expenditures such as those required for planning and introducing new products.

Effective management of R&D is an important business responsibility because R&D brings social benefits through increased productivity. With the world's exploding population and the material needs of less-developed nations, society requires the material gains which R&D can provide. Society also depends on R&D to find ways to reduce pollution and otherwise improve the quality of life.

R&D has become so important in some companies that it is ranked along with production and sales as a primary function, or "line function," of their business. No longer do they only produce goods and sell them. With accelerated technology, many companies now develop goods, produce them, and sell them. In some instances R&D becomes the primary emphasis of an organization, with production secondary. Research and development becomes the largest department, having more employees than either production or sales. Its salary budget is larger, and it assumes an active voice in the councils of top management. The traditional industrial order of priorities shifts from production to R&D. The assumption is that new products must be developed in order to keep abreast of competition and that if something useful can be developed, production and sales will follow normally. R&D, therefore, becomes the key to market leadership in many situations. A number of companies can show that 25 to 50 percent of their revenues today are from products not even produced ten years ago.

Changes in Management

Technological advances seem to be increasing the proportion of managers in the labor force. The labor saving of technology primarily displaces lower-level workers, while the cadre of managers remains the same or even increases. Assume, for example, that a department before technological change has ten managers and ninety workers. Its ratio of managers to workers is 1 to 9. As a result of technological improvement ten workers are laid off, but the management cadre is not reduced. The ratio of managers is now 1 to 8. If one specialized manager is added, the ratio of managers to workers increases to 1 to 7.3. Meanwhile, the new firms that are developing also need managers. The result is that the proportion of managers in industrial society is inching upward, increasing business's difficulty in developing a large proportion of socially aware and responsive managers.

The manager shortage is likely to get worse before supply is able to catch up with demand. The business investment in training and education above the worker level is high and will continue to grow. Likewise the community investment will grow. Since management is a key factor in making other resources productive, it is beginning to receive priority in economic and social development. It, along with high-level technical manpower, constitutes a "takeoff" investment which less-developed nations require in order to escape their bonds of poverty.

Advancing technology requires more *biprofessional and multiprofessional managers*. These are people who are professionally trained in management and also in one or more other intellectual specialties which they need in order to understand the environment they manage. Examples are physics and management, and biochemistry and management.

An unusual illustration of the need for a multiprofessional manager is the pharmaceutical firm which spent several months seeking a man who had degrees in both biology and advertising, professional training in management, and a Ph.D. They wanted this man to manage their advertising department. They found him and paid the price required to move him from his present employer.

The trend toward multiprofessionalism places more responsibility on business to support education and training because preparation of this kind of person is expensive. Fortunately, technology's greater productivity eases the burden of the costly education which it requires.

New Expectations from Customers

Affluent citizens with new wants are another result of advancing technology. Now supplied with the necessities of life, affluent customers spend more money on semiluxuries such as boats and country homes. Having the power to buy more things, they are not going to buy more of the same things. They want something different. Many of them are becoming independent, demanding adaptation of products to their unique needs. Already there are hundreds more models of cars and combinations of accessories than in the days of the Model T Ford. Demand is expanding even for custom semihandcrafted automobiles, and this market is being served by customizing shops, custom parts wholesalers, and specialized magazines. Society has come almost full circle from handicraft production to standardized mass production items and back to semicustom production of some products, even though these custom items are constructed largely from standardized parts.

The new customer expectations place responsibilities on business to manage technology in such a way that needs of individual customers are served along with the needs of a mass consumption society. The complex factory of the future may be somewhat like an organ console, having an elaborate system from which a few operators produce many varieties of products in the manner that an organist produces a variety of sounds.

Capital Requirements

Another effect of technology is its insatiable demand for capital. At the turn of the century, an investment of $1,000 for each worker was adequate in a factory, but today investments in pipelines and chemical operations exceed $100,000 for each worker. Capital needs become staggering when considered in terms of new jobs. Assuming a moderate investment of only $10,000 for each worker and using forecasts of 20 million new jobs needed in the United States in fifteen years, $200 *billion* of new capital is needed. This figure does not include expenditures for capital replacement to keep the existing labor force employed. These developments require business to generate large amounts of capital and engage in more long-range planning and budgeting for capital use.

Further, the magnitude of investment units is increasing. An old factory could increase production by adding units of one machine at $1,000 and one man at a time. A modern factory having an integrated production system may discover that expansion is possible only in system units having twenty machines and much supporting equipment costing $3 million. The output potential of the system unit is likewise much greater than that of the one machine in the old factory. These conditions mean that expansion which permits idle capacity over an intermediate term is often technologically correct and in the public interest from a cost viewpoint. Expansion at the rate of consumer use, allowing no idle capacity, would be costly or not feasible technologically. Idle capacity, therefore, is not necessarily a social ill. During periods of business growth and technological change, wise use of resources requires investment in system units which will have idle capacity.

The changes that are occurring place new responsibilities on management to keep abreast of technology in order to be sure it is using investor funds in the best way. Further, management needs to reconsider organizational objectives to be certain they are broad enough. The wagon firm which looked upon itself as only making wagons has gone out of business, but the wagon firm which saw its objective as providing consumer transportation equipment could move into automobile and aircraft manufacturing. The attrition of technology is evident from a comparison of lists of the 100 largest manufacturers in 1909 and 1959. Less than one-third of the 1909 firms are on the 1959 list. In other words, advancing technology initiates action on management requiring adjustment, just as much as it does in the more publicized cases requiring workers to adjust.

Social Change Has Its Human Costs for Management

There are hopeful signs that large corporations in this country are developing processes for converting the rhetoric of corporate responsibility into meaningful action. The burden for implementing corporate policy on social issues is ultimately placed on middle-level managers, the same managers who are primarily responsible for planning and directing the operations of the business. Through the creative and persistent leadership of top management, the barriers to incorporating social change in the decentralized company can be overcome.

The response to social demands is not without human cost. Managers' careers have been tarnished by the bad luck of getting caught up in conspicuous incidents that may be learning experiences for the organization, but at their expense. Does somebody have to get hurt? Unfortunately, the answer all too often is *yes*. An urgent challenge for the top managements of large corporations is to make their organizations more understanding of the human costs of change as well as the demands of society.

From Robert W. Ackerman, "How Companies Respond to Social Demands," *Harvard Business Review*, July–August 1973, p. 98. Italics in original. Reprinted with permission.

Social Costs

In the same way that a lifesaving antibiotic may have side effects, technology also has system side effects. When they are negative, they become social costs, as will be discussed in later chapters. From society's point of view these social costs need to be calculated in the cost/benefit analysis of every proposed technological change. Very often some of these social costs are overlooked because the persons who work with technology do not think broadly enough of its system effects. However, even among the broadest thinkers, system effects frequently are not predictable. There is not even agreement concerning whether a particular technological change will result in net social costs or social benefits.

For example, how will television affect types of political leadership, morality of youth, mass propaganda, and cohesion of the family? No one is sure. Looking even more broadly, will teaching machines psychologically condition students in a way which causes them as adults to respond like robots to political propaganda, thus losing their democracy to a dictator? Will medical diagnostic and monitoring machines so dehumanize medicine that they will cause more ills than they cure? There is no way to know; hence, as we use these devices, we need to be continuously alert to feedback about negative side effects so that corrective action can be initiated.

A fact frequently overlooked is that technology can be used to correct side effects which exist. It is not unidirectional; it can be corrective as well as causative. For example, technology does cause pollution; however, technology can also be used to reduce pollution from both machine and human wastes. Technology does contribute to urban blight, but it can be used to increase beauty and make it easier for people to live in cities. It has already done so. For example, the smoke from one electric generating plant serving 100,000 homes is much less than the smoke from fireplaces in a similar number of homes in earlier days—and it can be better controlled. Further, the waste from one city sewage plant is much less than waste, stench, and disease in cities without sewage facilities.

Indeed, technology is creating all sorts of new situations to which people are reacting in unique ways. The technological revolution causes an associated social revolution. The problem with technology is that it moves so fast that it creates problems before society is able to work out solutions. For these reasons business firms associated with technological change are supporting research on its social effects.

One future-looking study was made by the Hudson Institute and reported by Herman Kahn, futurist and director of the institute.[10] He reported that in spite of the doomsayers about the social costs of technology, within the next 100 years it will provide solutions to all mankind's major problems, such as hunger, disease, and pollution. Thus it is a long-run benefactor of civilization. He estimates that by the end of the twenty-first century most of the world will be wealthy, having a world gross product of $400 trillion and a per capita income of $10,000. However, Kahn does recognize that on a number of fronts the situation may deteriorate in the short run.

SUMMARY

When we begin to see the intricate relationships of technological developments to each other and to many institutions, we realize that technological change is not a simple creation of business alone. Business responds merely as a system component. However, business is perhaps the primary agent for technological change, so it has major responsibilities for proper introduction of change. The system in the United States is now a service economy in an electronic age.

The effects of technology are pervasive throughout the system, producing both favorable and unfavorable results. Managers operating within the technostructure delicately balance specialized points of view in order to make broad decisions which are socially responsible. This need for breadth increases the demand for multiprofessional, socially conscious managers.

[10]"Good News Department," *Forbes,* Feb. 15, 1973, p. 86.

STUDY GUIDES FOR
INTERPRETATION OF THIS CHAPTER

1. Assuming that the swing to a service economy will continue, discuss its potential effects during the next twenty years. Present current manpower data or other information to support your discussion.

2. What do you consider to be the three most favorable effects of technology (a) in the whole society and (b) in your local community? Explain why you chose each. Do likewise for the three most unfavorable effects.

3. Discuss and chart the shift in job skills as technology advances.

4. It has been suggested that a law be passed prohibiting any business from making a technological improvement which results in the layoff of an employee (i.e., the laborer must be retrained and transferred within the business). Appraise the merits of this proposal as it applies to a pluralistic society.

5. Discuss management's responsibility for introducing technology into society.

PROBLEM
Peabody Electronics Associates, Inc.

Peabody Electronics Associates, Inc., is an electronics firm which markets a number of consumer and industrial items. One of its industrial products plants which employs 1,700 persons is located in a town of 50,000 persons about 50 miles from any large metropolitan area or major university. This location was chosen seven years ago because the plant uses mostly semiskilled labor, which was plentiful in the community, and the factory building of a bankrupt firm was available for a ten-year lease.

Recently the home-office research department made a technological breakthrough in design of the principal product produced in this branch plant. The new design will have much greater reliability and cost about one-half of what it does now; however, the labor force will be reduced 72 percent and will consist mostly of skilled workers and scientific personnel. Capital costs will increase fourfold, and the existing building is unsatisfactory because expensive, especially designed equipment and buildings will be required. During preliminary planning for the new facilities one scientist explained that the existing location would be unsuitable for a permanent plant, because scientific personnel would feel that a location this distance from a major university would hinder their opportunity for personal growth through education.

1. Evaluate from a social system point of view the alternatives available to this firm, and recommend the appropriate course of action with reasons supporting your choice of action.

PART 2

BUSINESS IDEOLOGY

CHAPTER 8

THE DEVELOPMENT
OF BUSINESS AS A
SOCIAL INSTITUTION

*An adequate theory of business responsibility will recognize that
the present business system is an outgrowth of history and past
cultural traditions. It will recognize that what we are today is, to
a very large extent, a function of what we were yesterday.*

William C. Frederick[1]

*In America the wisdom and not the man is attended to; and
America is peculiarly a poor man's country. . . . They find
themselves at liberty to follow what mode they like; they feel that
they can venture to try experiments, and that the advantages of
their discoveries are their own.*

Thomas Pownall[2]

Social systems are products of the value systems of society. They are the
summation of the individual beliefs of members of society concerning functions
and relationships of political, social, religious, and economic institutions which
make up that society. Social systems are never stable. They change over time
because social values of people change; and as social values change, the roles of
social institutions also change. In spite of what sometimes appears to be radical
change, change in social systems is usually a continuous process with one stage
building upon previous stages. Each stage usually retains something of older social
values and adds new ones. The first quotation at the beginning of this chapter
suggests that a look at history often can tell us something of the present. The
important thing about understanding history is that it provides a background
against which to understand, compare, and judge present trends and events.
Someone once said that people who do not understand history are bound to repeat
its mistakes.

In this chapter and the one following we will discuss the development of
business as a social institution and consider social ideologies concerning the proper
role and functions of business and businessmen. We shall not be concerned with

[1] William C. Frederick, "The Growing Concern over Business Responsibility," *California Management Review*, Summer 1960, p. 60.
[2] Thomas Pownall, *A Memorial, Most Humbly Addressed to the Sovereigns of Europe, on the Present State of Affairs between the Old and New World* (1780), quoted in Albert Bushnell Hart (ed.), *American History Told by Contemporaries*, New York: The Macmillan Company, 1929, vol. III, p. 76.

business history per se, nor with specific dates or incidents (except perhaps a few that mark major points of change). Rather, we will focus on the evolution of business to its position of major importance in today's complex American society and the different environments in which this evolution took place.

A FRAMEWORK FOR DISCUSSION

From meager beginnings, business has matured through a series of stages until today, in America, we have a highly complex free enterprise system called capitalism. Each stage has been characterized not only by changes in ways of doing things, but by changes in ways of thinking about how things should be done and about proper relationships which should exist among various institutions in society. Business has nearly always been recognized as a necessary institution of society, but it has not always played the same role or been accorded the same place in the social system. Sometimes business has played a passive role, adapting to social change as it occurred. At other times it has taken the lead in shaping social change.

Over time the shape of capitalism changes. There are different kinds of capitalism, depending on the way basic elements are modified. Our modern capitalism is the result of a series of modifications which can be identified as separate stages of development.[3] These stages can be distinguished from one another by examining the degree to which elements of capitalism are present or absent. Thus, *precapitalism*, while recognizing private property, did not philosophically accept profit and, in many cases, imposed severe restrictions on individual business freedom. *Mercantile capitalism* was characterized by the use of private property primarily for merchant and commercial activities set within a framework of strict control by strong central government. Conversely, *industrial capitalism* emphasized freedom of individual initiative in business, little or no interference by the state, and the predominant use of private property in industrial production. *Finance capitalism* implies control of private property and means of production by financial interests and absentee ownership rather than by owner-managers. And finally, *state capitalism* denotes regulation of business practice in the national interest and state determination of broad social policy.

BUSINESS IN ANTIQUITY
Business Emerges

No one can say at what point in history business activity first occurred. The Old Testament describes a relatively complex society based firmly upon private

---

[3]Further details of business heritage may be found in Meriam Beard, *A History of Business from Babylon to the Monopolists,* Ann Arbor, Mich.: The University of Michigan Press, 1962.

property, division of labor, and exchange. Manufacturing and trade were widely practiced and merchants were skilled in the use of contracts as early as 3000 B.C.

Rules and codes of conduct were formulated to govern relations between merchants and traders and also relations between merchants and governments. An excellent example of these codes is the Code of Hammurabi. Hammurabi, one of the great rulers of Babylon around 2000 B.C., promulgated a code consisting of over 300 laws. Many of these laws were in direct support of business and not only encouraged mercantile enterprise, but also actually provided government protection in a simple form of business insurance (at no cost to the merchant). These laws also contained elements not too far different from some of our own concepts of social insurance. For example:[4]

> If the brigand has not been caught, the man who has been despoiled shall recount before God what he has lost, and the city and governor in whose land and district the brigandage took place shall render back to him whatever of his was lost.
> If it was a life, the city and governor shall pay one mina of silver to his people.

Ancient Mediterranean Trading Cities

Prior to the Punic Wars (246 to 146 B.C.), most business activity occurred around the Mediterranean Sea. Philosophies concerning proper relationships among various social institutions were such that they provided a positive and favorable environment for business development in cities such as Carthage, Tyre, and Rhodes.

In these great trading cities business was accorded a high place in the scheme of things. While agriculture was recognized as an important foundation upon which cities must rest, business was generally looked upon as being more productive. Agriculture provided the necessary items for life, but business provided luxuries and items which raised standards of living. In short, business generated wealth, and wealth was desirable. Business was regarded as one of the most honorable professions, and businessmen enjoyed the highest social status.

There were three important reasons why business enjoyed a leading role in the social system of the times. First, there was no artificial class structure. Whether a man was rich or poor depended largely upon his own initiative, and it was important that the *opportunity* for wealth was open to everyone. Second, because no ruling class existed, anyone could hold public office. In reality, these offices were nearly always held by rich merchants who had time to devote to public duties. Therefore, it is reasonable to expect that public policy would favor business. Third, pre-Christian religious and business philosophies were surprisingly compatible. Temples often served as centers for local business transactions, and

---

[4]The Code of Hammurabi (2000 B.C.). See Edward C. Bursk, Donald T. Clark, and Ralph W. Hidy, *The World of Business,* New York: Simon & Schuster, Inc., 1962, p. 9.

religious leaders often became the chief money lenders in the community (at high rates of interest).

Greek Business Environment

Influenced by the teachings of social philosophers such as Plato and Aristotle, the Grecian environment within which business operated was generally hostile toward business. Both Plato[5] and Aristotle[6] were idealists and while both admitted the necessity of commerce in the ideal state, neither seemed willing to admit it to reality. Plato, in his *Laws* recommended such strict regulation of all commercial activities as to virtually stifle trade.[7] Aristotle, through his analysis of profit and interest, was not only instrumental in limiting commercial activity but contributed, perhaps more than any other man, to lasting negative social attitudes toward business activity. The following quotation summarizes his philosophies concerning business.[8]

> Of the two sorts of money-making one, as I have just said, is a part of household management, the other is retail trade: the former necessary and honourable, the latter a kind of exchange which is justly censured; for it is unnatural, and a mode by which men gain from one another. The most hated sort, and with the greatest reason, is usury, which makes a gain out of money itself, and not from the natural use of it.

In Greek society, the ruling class along with the military class and land owners occupied the elite positions in the social structure. Business activities were considered degrading, and anyone engaged in commerce was considered to be an inferior citizen. Merchants were not allowed to own property in the Greek city-states, nor could they hold public office, and in times of war they were pressed into military service in the lowest infantry ranks. But in spite of the hostile environment, business prospered simply because society could find no other way to solve the problem of providing for the needs and wants of citizens.

Roman Business Environment

The Roman scene was not greatly different from the Greek scene. Roman ruling classes shared Greek disdain for businessmen, and, theoretically, the highly compartmentalized social system allowed only a very low place for business as an

---

[5]Plato, *The Republic*, trans. by B. Jowett, Oxford: Clarendon Press, 1881, pp. 47–53.
[6]Aristotle, *Politics*, in Philip C. Newman, Arthur D. Gayer, and Milton H. Spencer (eds.), *Source Readings in Economic Thought*, New York: W. W. Norton & Company, Inc., 1954, pp. 6–14.
[7]Plato, *The Laws of Plato*, trans. by E. A. Taylor, London: J. M. Dent & Sons, Ltd., Publishers, 1934, pp. 309–313.
[8]Aristotle, op. cit., p. 11.

institution. But, as was the case in Greece, social theory and the reality of social needs were not compatible. In spite of its agricultural foundation, Roman society, dedicated as it was to militarism, found it difficult to provide the necessities of life for the populace, let alone any luxury items. Roman agriculture simply could not produce enough food. But as in all societies there was a large social class willing to supply items wanted by others—for a price. Without business, the Roman Empire could not have survived. Merchants provided food for the masses, luxuries for the elite, and money for military conquests.

Besides a well-developed commercial and financial mechanism, the Roman Empire left two legacies which were to play important parts in later development of business as an institution. First was a body of law which served as a basis for later systems of law. According to Roll:[9]

> During the height of its [the Roman Empire's] power when, for a time, patricians, the new land owners, and the commercial classes lived in comparative peace, there was evolved a body of laws which has had the most profound influence on later legal institutions. . . . Of more direct economic importance were the doctrines which Roman Jurists evolved for the regulation of economic relations.

Second was the Roman Catholic Church which became a major influence in shaping the social, economic, and political institutions in Europe for the next several centuries.

BUSINESS ENVIRONMENT OF THE MIDDLE AGES

The time span covered by the Middle Ages is generally agreed to be roughly from the fall of the Roman Empire in the fifth century to the middle of the fifteenth century. Certainly, the Middle Ages produced one of the most stable systems of all times, but it was a period of stagnation. The feudal system, with its nonmobile population divided into a rigid class structure, its agrarian base of large independent political units, and a powerful church which dominated not only religious but economic activities as well, did not produce an environment favorable to social change or to development of business as a social institution.

Class Structure

Well-defined class divisions were inherited from the Roman system. Division between the classes was sharp. Inequality of men on earth was recognized and accepted without question. Rights and obligations of each class were clearly defined, and every man knew what his position was in relation to that of everyone

[9]Eric Roll, *A History of Economic Thought,* 3d ed., Englewood Cliffs, N.J.: Prentice-Hall, Inc., 1956, pp. 37–38.

else. He knew exactly how to behave, what was expected of him, and what he could expect life to provide in the future. His world was in equilibrium. The self-sufficiency of the large land unit (the manor) along with the sedentary nature of the population produced little need for commercial activities. Traveling merchants who occasionally visited a manor were viewed with distrust.

Political Disunity

The early medieval political system was also a logical transition from the Roman system. As the empire declined, more administrative duties fell into the landlords' hands, thus forming the basis of the manorial system. Many of the large estates became political entities unto themselves. As towns developed and became independent of landlords, they soon became self-governing. Left without a central governing body, each manor and town passed its own laws and controlled its own activities as it saw fit. The result was a political patchwork which in itself was an important deterrent to the development of commerce. A traveling merchant moving across the countryside was often subjected to tolls and taxes by every landlord whose land he crossed. Towns also extracted heavy tolls and taxes and imposed laws which favored local exchange and penalized the foreign trader.

Universality of the Church

Probably the most powerful and important institution in all medieval society was the Roman Catholic Church. More than any other force the Church shaped social philosophy toward business and defined the role of business as an institution within the social system of the times. Not only was the Church universal in the sense that it was "the one" church, but it also attempted to take responsibility for all men's actions, both spiritual and temporal. In such a role of power the Church dictated beliefs, philosophies, and actions. There were several reasons for this power.[10]

First, by the end of the eighth century, the Church was the greatest landowner in Christendom. Much of the income received from these vast landholdings was in the form of produce. While a portion of this produce was consumed in everyday operation of the estate, much had to be disposed of in commerce, thus forcing on the Church a business function.

Second, the autonomous nature of feudal political units did not provide any ties of national unity. Canon law provided the only uniform codes governing social behavior, and the Church became a great administrative body possessing widespread judicial powers in secular as well as spiritual matters.

[10]For a detailed discussion of reasons for the strength of the Church, see H. Pirenne, *Economic and Social History of Medieval Europe,* trans. by I. E. Clegg, New York: Harcourt, Brace & World, Inc., 1956, pp. 13ff.

Third, the Church obtained strength by offering a spiritual doctrine which gave meaning to men's lives. Christianity offered to thousands a framework within which they could judge their relationship with others and justify their daily activities.

Church Philosophy versus Business

Ecclesiastical hostility toward business was not an attack on trade and commerce per se. Indeed the Church itself was deeply involved in many commercial activities. One historian comments that the Church acted as "a governor, a landed proprietor, a rent collector, an imposer of taxes, a material producer, an employer of labor on an enormous scale, a merchantman, a tradesman, a banker and mortgage broker, a custodian of morals, a maker of sumptuary laws, a schoolmaster, a compeller of conscience—all in one."[11] Rather, hostility was based on the belief that commercial activity turned men from the search for God by fostering self-interest and the pursuit of gain. Therefore, it was reasoned, to eliminate trade was to eliminate a sin.

During the early centuries of the Middle Ages, Church dogma, which relied heavily on the philosophy of Aristotle, was generally appropriate to the static economic system of the times. But as the economic environment changed through increased trade, development of towns and trade routes, and expanding markets, Church dogma became not only unrealistic but unworkable. Neither Church nor businessmen could successfully engage in economic activity and at the same time conform to Church dogma with its prohibitions against exchange, profit, and interest. Social demands for increased economic activities required a change in religious and social philosophy which incorporated in its value system acceptance of commercial activity and the economic institutions necessary for commercial growth.

The Protestant Revolution

Religious fetters of social theory which hampered business during the Middle Ages were virtually abandoned by the sixteenth century. The Protestant revolution of the sixteenth century further swept away Church condemnation of commercial activity.[12] Where early canonists condemned business activities as base and distinct from godly pursuits, the teachings of Protestant reformers, particularly John Calvin, encouraged business. Catholicism preached that the key to heaven lay in man's actions while on earth. Protestantism and Calvinism saw the

[11]James Westfall Thompson, *Economic and Social History of the Middle Ages: 300–1300*, New York: Century Company, 1928, p. 648.

[12]For a discussion of the Protestant revolution, see Max Weber, *The Protestant Ethic and the Spirit of Capitalism* (1905), trans. by Talcott Parsons, New York: Charles Scribner's Sons, 1958.

key to heaven as being conversion as stated by Jesus Christ. That conversion led to obligations to use one's talents productively while on earth. Some measure of spiritual worth, then, was to be found in the successful pursuit of a temporal calling. Thus, Calvinism emphasized traits such as diligence, industry, thrift, and conservatism, equated spiritual worth with temporal success, and provided a religious climate which encouraged business activities based on the profit motive.

Herein lie the elements of the "individual ethic" that we, today, are prone to point to in our heritage—the belief that the individual, by diligence, thrift, wise investment, and prudent management of funds, can rise to a position of wealth. Many historians believe that one of the major underlying factors in the rise of capitalism was the change in social philosophy exemplified in the teachings of John Calvin. Heilbroner comments: "Calvinism fostered a new conception of economic life. In place of the old ideal of social and economic stability, of knowing and keeping one's 'place,' it brought respectability to an ideal of struggle, of material improvement, of economic growth."[13]

MERCANTILISM

The new conception of economic life which emerged from Calvinist philosophy paved the way for the development of business as an important institution of society. The strength of the mercantile system depended upon changing laws, customs, philosophies, and roles of social institutions. Based upon a wholly different set of underlying philosophies, mercantile policies were devoted to building strong nations through economic superiority. This was a system based upon mutual dependence between state and commercial interests. National good and merchant profit were considered to be two sides of the same coin. Among the more important aspects of mercantile ideology were (1) the identification of money with wealth, (2) political unification and strong government, (3) protectionism and state intervention, and (4) power. Each contributed toward a positive environment for business development.

Importance of Money

Accumulation of treasure in the form of hoards of precious metal and money was nothing new to the mercantile period. For centuries persons who had the largest hoards of money or precious metal were considered to be the wealthiest, and wealth gave the owner power—power to command goods and services.

Mercantile philosophy expanded the concept of wealth and power to the nation as a whole, and business was assigned the major role in accumulating a

[13]Robert L. Heilbroner, *The Making of Economic Society*, Englewood Cliffs, N.J.: Prentice-Hall, Inc., 1962, p. 55.

hoard of national treasure. National policy was designed to encourage and support business, but at the same time to regulate it. Early policy was designed to encourage business to generate an absolute flow of money into the country while preventing money from leaving the country. Because of the fallacies of storing wealth in nonproductive hoards, prohibitions against movement of gold and silver gave way to a balance-of-trade concept similar to that in effect today. The theory was simple: A country that exported more than it imported was bound to have a net inflow of money. According to mercantile philosophy, not only were exports supposed to exceed imports, but emphasis was placed on (1) importing those items of raw materials (relatively low in price) which were needed for home industry or consumption and (2) exporting finished goods (of relatively high value).

Importance of Central Government

National economic power depended upon unification of political power—a centralized political unit strong enough to impose and enforce a uniform set of commercial laws, uniform tariffs, and a uniform monetary system. To these ends merchant capitalists joined forces with rising central monarchies by financing their struggles against feudal lords and the authoritarian power of the Church. Strong central governments brought a variety of benefits to business: domestic markets were widened, movements of merchandise became safer, a uniform set of laws (based on Roman law) developed, internal communications were improved, currency was stabilized, and important commercial concessions and monopolies were often granted to merchants for political support.

Protection and State Intervention

In the early phases of the mercantile period the Crown did little more than replace the rigidities of feudalism with rigidities of nationalism. While government did encourage commercial and industrial enterprise, it did so by favoring a few at the expense of masses who were disenfranchised from economic opportunity through a rigid monopoly system. The state, theoretically, controlled all business, and one could engage in a particular economic activity only by receiving a monopoly from the Crown. Discontent with this system was manifested in the Puritan revolution of the mid-seventeenth century. The whole philosophy of the mercantile system was challenged, and emphasis shifted from state *intervention* to state *protection*. Emphasis also changed from monopoly to free trade.

After the Puritan revolution, policy was directed toward making the nation as nearly independent of other nations as possible. To accomplish this task, several basic concepts were stressed. First, the country was to produce all its own foodstuffs and manufactured articles. Second, the country was to control its own merchant shipping. Third, a colonial system was to be developed in a manner which produced raw materials and absorbed surpluses of manufactured goods.

Power

No longer was the state perceived as owning the rights to all business activity. Instead, the function of government was perceived to be one of support and control in which laws and economic policies were designed to produce national supremacy. The key to economic supremacy under mercantilism was power. Military power was necessary to obtain and hold foreign markets and to protect shipping. State power, in turn, depended upon economic activity to provide money necessary to protect commerce, enforce laws, and fight wars. Only by encouraging and at the same time regulating business activities could the nation achieve its goals.

BUSINESS ENVIRONMENT IN AMERICA

Although the American colonies were a direct product of English mercantile policy, American business was bound to develop its own unique brand of capitalism. From the start our institutions were born and matured in a capitalistic environment that was different from the mercantile capitalism of Europe. With few exceptions, the colonies themselves were founded squarely on the opportunity for private gain. Georgia was founded directly by the Crown as an experiment in growing mulberries, as well as a political effort to contain the Spanish in Florida. New York and Nova Scotia came directly under the Crown through war. All the other colonies were founded by groups of individuals stirred to action by the profit motive. Charter companies and individual proprietors were the chief agencies of settlement. The main contribution to actual colonization made by the English government was to transfer large tracts of land to private ownership for redistribution to individual farmers. These vast amounts of land, available for little effort or money, allowed the American farmer to start out as a capitalist farmer, owning his land and tools and producing for a market, as well as for himself and his family.

American craftsmen, too, started as capitalists. English industrial production remained under monopolistic authority of craft guilds which controlled production, set wages, and dictated the status of apprentices, journeymen, and masters. While the craft system of production followed immigrants to America, the guild system did not. Any craftsman possessing sufficient skill and capital could set up shop in America, free to employ his capital and take risks in any way he saw fit. Mercantile policy put severe restrictions on his ability to compete in foreign trade, but he enjoyed freedom of competition in local markets.

American merchants were also capitalists from the beginning. With the exception of those who acted as agents for large European trading companies, merchants were entrepreneurs in every sense of the word. Free from restraints of the European guild system, they traded in whatever commodities offered a profit, took title to merchandise as well as handling consignments, employed people for wages, and in many cases owned means of transportation.

Thus, whatever type of business endeavor colonists might choose in the new country, all the elements of a new kind of capitalism were present. They were free to own property and to employ that property according to individual initiative and toward any opportunity that was attractive. Of course, until the end of the Revolution, colonists were always subject to restrictions imposed by the English mercantile system, but within the system they were free to make entrepreneurial judgments, and often they moved outside the system as a matter of convenience or necessity.

Conflict of Two Systems

Colonial systems of mercantilism were based firmly upon two ideas. First was the idea that colonies should provide raw materials for industry at home and should also absorb surpluses of articles produced in the mother country. The second idea was that in order to make the colonial system work properly, government regulation of business activity was necessary.

In retrospect it appears inevitable that, from the mercantilistic point of view, the American colonial experiment was doomed to failure. The American Colonies did not fit well into the British mercantile scheme for two reasons. First, colonization to some extent was a protest movement. Many American settlers had fled their home countries to escape governmental tyranny in business, social, political, and religious activities and beliefs, and their belief in mercantile philosophy was already weakened by the time they arrived in America. Regulation imposed by an absentee government did little to strengthen colonists' beliefs in strong central government. Laissez faire philosophies and emphasis on the natural rights of the individual, as these ideas were reflected in the American Constitution and the Bill of Rights, were logical outgrowths of experience under British mercantile policy.

Second, British mercantilism did not work well in America because England refused to accept the Colonies as a separate economic unit, viewing them instead as an extension of British agriculture and extractive industries. Herein lay the contradictions that led to the breakdown of mercantilism. Colonies were expected to import more from England than they exported, thereby creating a balance of trade in favor of England. Moreover, balances were to be paid in gold and silver. But since the Colonies bought more than they sold, there was simply no way for them legally to obtain money necessary to pay these balances and still stay within the mercantile system.

For these reasons American business developed to a far greater extent outside the mercantile system than inside. Much of what could be produced, particularly in the Northern Colonies, was either not wanted by England or was in direct competition with British goods. Many items that were wanted by England were consumed by the Colonies themselves. Therefore, in order to survive, the Northern Colonies were forced outside the mercantile system by the very policies that were supposed to tie them closely to the mother country. The Southern Colonies produced tobacco, rice, indigo, and forest products, all of which enjoyed the protection and encouragement of the English mercantile system. But they, like their Northern neighbors, ran headlong into problems of paying their debts to England. Southern production depended heavily on availability of fresh land. When England closed Western lands to Southern plantation owners, bankruptcy or rebellion appeared to be the only alternatives.

Experiment in Freedom

The story of the American Revolution need not be recounted here. But perhaps it is appropriate to look at the economic philosophies under which the new nation started. When the Founding Fathers set about writing the Constitution, they were mindful of producing a document which would be the foundation of a strong nation and, at the same time, would provide protection against injustices inherent under types of government with which they were familiar. They had just fought a war to escape the economic tyranny of England. Armed with their own experiences and supported by the laissez faire ideology of such men as Adam Smith,[14] it was only natural for them to conceive of the government's relation to economic activity as being supportive rather than regulatory. But freedom also brought with it a responsibility to formulate national policy concerning economic development. Limited resources and mercantile tradition favored support of agriculture and commercial activities. In spite of urging by President Washington and Alexander Hamilton,[15] manufacturing remained a relatively unimportant economic activity until well into the first half of the nineteenth century.

Preparing for Industrialization

The period between the Revolutionary and Civil Wars was one of experimentation, adjustment, growth, and development. But above all, it was a period of transition which not only shifted business emphasis from mercantilism to industrialism, but also heralded sweeping social changes which were to alter the

[14]Adam Smith, *An Inquiry in the Nature and Causes of the Wealth of Nations* (1776), New York: Modern Library, Inc., 1937, Book IV, chap. 9.
[15]Alexander Hamilton, *Report on Manufacturers* (1791), extracts in William McDonald (ed.), *Selected Documents Illustrative of the United States, 1776–1861,* New York: The Macmillan Company, 1898, pp. 111–112.

whole environment of business after the Civil War and raise serious questions concerning relationships between business and other institutions within the social system. Industrialism brought with it a concentration of economic power that threatened to move the whole social system out of equilibrium and required a rethinking of the proper roles for various social institutions.

Between 1800 and the Civil War, strong forces were at work which removed the important barriers to industrial expansion. Population increases, along with growth of cities and expanded agriculture, consolidated some markets and created new ones. Expanded transportation meant new access to raw materials and ability to deliver finished products to distant places. Improved communications meant that business could be transacted faster and easier than ever before. And the wave of inventions that appeared during these fifty years added to the base of European technology and provided the technological structure necessary for industrialization.

Political Environment

In spite of substantial increases in industrial activities during the 1840s and 1850s, political environment posed severe restrictions on full development. Depressions of 1819–1821, 1837–1843, and 1857–1858 had demonstrated to business the need for protective tariffs, a sound banking system, a cheap and nonmilitant supply of labor, and sympathetic courts. But the Southern agrarian aristocracy remained in firm control of the executive, legislative, and judicial branches of the federal government, and they strongly opposed those things needed by business. They opposed protective tariffs, were against federal support of railroads, turnpikes, or canals, favored state banking and cheap money, fought chartering of a Pacific railroad, opposed homesteading, and would not support a favorable immigration plan.

The election of 1860 provided the wedge. Quick to take advantage of the split in the Democratic ranks, the Republican party offered sanctuary to the abolitionists and included economic planks in the platform which offered to industrialists reforms needed for expansion. Unfortunately, Republican success in this election pushed the Southern leaders into an untenable position, one which seemingly could be resolved only by secession.

Corporate Form of Business

Perhaps more important to industrial expansion than any other single factor was the development of the corporate form of business and the general laws under which corporations were organized. Cooperative business ventures of one kind or another had been used for many years. Joint stock ventures of the seventeenth and eighteenth centuries are examples. But the total capital fund available for such ventures was limited to the private fortunes of a few individuals. However, inventions and expansion of markets stimulated the growth of business enterprise. Large amounts of capital were necessary, and these could best be raised by distributing risk and potential profit among individuals of limited financial means, as well as those with substantial resources. In addition to providing large capital funds, the corporation had the effect of making large numbers of people owners of business. Ownership in business caused thousands of people to adopt the businessman's point of view and to encourage business decisions which would yield a profit. Partly because of the recognition of economies of scale, partly as a result of changing business environment, and partly because of changes in public attitude, the corporate form of business was quite popular by midcentury. By 1850, security exchanges had been established in New York, Boston, and Philadelphia.

SUMMARY

No one knows when business activity began, but from its humble beginnings somewhere in antiquity, the development of business as a social institution can be traced with a reasonable degree of certainty. Phases in business maturity can be established, and environmental characteristics that either encouraged or discouraged business development can be recognized.

This chapter has summarized the role and functions assigned to business in various social systems that have existed over time. It is important to note that in every social system discussed (except colonial America) there was one social institution that held a predominant position of power. In each of these cases the dominant institution was unable fully to meet social expectations for a prolonged period of time, and, as a result, that institution was either replaced or modified. This chapter also discussed the combination of elements which together produced the environmental foundations necessary for the development of business as a major American social institution.

STUDY GUIDES FOR INTERPRETATION OF THIS CHAPTER

1. Explain the relative insignificance of business as a social institution during the Middle Ages.

2. The Protestant revolution had a major effect on business. Study the revolution developing in the Church in the latter half of the twentieth century and explain what long-run effects you think it will have on business.

3. Mercantilism was essentially a system of government intervention and regulation of business in the interests of the state. What similarities do you see between mercantile policies and present-day government policies concerning business?

4. Explain the following statement: America, from its very inception, was bound to develop its own brand of capitalism. To what extent have environmental factors been important?

5. Contrast capitalism as it was perceived by the Founding Fathers of America with capitalism as it exists today.

CHAPTER 9

THE HERITAGE OF
BUSINESS IDEOLOGY

The chief business of the American people is business.

Calvin Coolidge[1]

*Many a once-powerful man has learned the hard way that it is
wiser to stay within the bounds of common morality than to give
the public an appetite for reform.*

Saul W. Gellerman[2]

Not long ago a medium-sized city in the Midwest underwent a property-tax reform program. All property within the city boundaries was reappraised, but there was no adjustment in the tax rate. Every property owner, both residential and business, experienced a sharp rise in taxes. Residential property had been reassessed two years earlier and valuations had been raised to 40 percent of the current market value, but many business properties, particularly manufacturing firms in the outskirts, had not been reassessed for five years and valuations of their properties remained at 25 percent of market value at the time of assessment. With completion of the tax reform program, assessed valuation on *all* property was raised to 50 percent of the current market value. This increase, along with inflationary increases in market value, resulted in many manufacturing firms having a much larger *percentage* increase in taxes than residential owners.

The president and principal stockholder of one manufacturing firm complained bitterly and attempted in every way he could to have the assessed valuation on his firm's property lowered. The assessor's office and the tax reform committee refused. Eventually the controversy reached the local newspapers. Arguments supporting both sides appeared in editorial form and in the "letters to the editor" section. Many of the letters and editorials supporting the manufacturing firm came

---

[1]Calvin Coolidge (speech before the Society of American Newspaper Editors, June 17, 1925), quoted in the *New York Times,* June 18, 1925.

[2]Saul W. Gellerman, *Motivation and Productivity,* New York: American Management Association, 1963, p. 16.

from the president himself. Those supporting the assessor's office came largely from members of the community.

Arguments supporting the president's demand for tax reductions fell generally into four categories:

My firm started here with practically nothing, and management, under my leadership, with hard work and personal sacrifice built it to what it is today.

My colleagues as well as myself were willing to take a chance by setting up our plants here. Only through good management have we survived.

Every member of this community has had an equal chance to build a successful business, but only a few have succeeded.

This tax reform program is not only inequitable, but it penalizes high performance.

Arguments supporting the tax assessor fell into three categories:

Big business takes everything out of the community and puts nothing back in.

All the businessman is interested in is high profits at everybody's expense.

Those guys that run the big plants are out for themselves and no one else.

Undoubtedly everyone in the above example who entered the controversy probably thought he was expressing a rational opinion concerning one localized incident. What is more likely is that they were expressing philosophies and ideas about business behavior in general that had grown up over long periods of time.

Recently, questions of proper relationships which should exist between business and other social subsystems have occupied increasing amounts of time of business executives, government officials, theologians, scholars, and others. These questions have revolved around the responsibilities of business in the social suprastructure. Answers to these questions do not come easily. Indeed, answers may be different at different times depending on existing contingency models. But, one step toward finding workable answers is to examine the foundation of values and ideologies upon which our social system is built.

In this chapter, we shall examine industrialism as it emerged and functioned during the period after the Civil War. We shall also discuss social philosophies which supported business actions during the period and those which contributed to government regulation. Finally, we shall discuss the changing relationships between business and government which have emerged during the twentieth century.

INGREDIENTS OF INDUSTRIALISM

By 1860 all the necessary elements were present to support the sweeping social and economic changes that occurred during and following the Civil War. In a number of ways the war itself stimulated combinations of social, political, and economic forces necessary for large-scale industrialism. The demands of war and the expansion and refinement of the industrial foundations already present combined to launch America into its amazing industrial development.

Armies required large and dependable supplies of standardized products which could not be obtained from small geographically dispersed firms. Military needs, therefore, favored consolidation and growth of firms that could use large-scale mechanized manufacturing processes. However, integration and mechanization were expensive and depended upon the availability of adequate capital and credit resources. To expand national credit resources, the government issued greenbacks and government bonds, thus providing money to pay for military goods. The high profits from government contracts and high protective tariffs which insulated business against foreign price competition made possible large independent capital accumulations needed for industrial expansion. Furthermore, a new National Bank system was established which eliminated unsound currency, absorbed a substantial part of the government bond issue, and provided the financial stability necessary to support war and postwar business expansion.

Other factors also contributed to the right combination for industrial expansion. Refinements of inventions and their application to large-scale manufacturing produced a technological base well suited to mass production of peacetime products. The growth in population, both from natural causes and from favorable immigration laws, assured a market large enough to absorb mass-produced articles and provided a large supply of labor to work in the factories. Finally, the intercontinental railroad system which was built after the war and the accompanying disposal of public domain provided further dimensions to industrial development. Settlement of the West provided a national market for manufactured goods. Simultaneously, Western farming provided surplus agricultural products which went into world markets, thus providing foreign balances with which to pay for machinery and other capital goods. Railroads provided means for rapidly moving manufactured goods to the West and returning raw materials and agricultural surpluses to the East.

Thus, many factors were at work during and immediately following the Civil War which, in combination, produced the dynamic environment necessary for American industrial and social change. By the time the Civil War ended, a sound financial base existed, the technology for mass producing goods had largely been developed, there were large markets hungry for cheap manufactured articles, and there was a large and willing labor force. Only one other ingredient was essential, and that one ingredient was someone to put it all together.

The Robber Barons

However fortuitous circumstances surrounding the Civil War might have been, it is doubtful that America would have experienced the rapid industrial development it did had there not emerged a group of men who had the vision, drive, ambition, and capabilities to recognize the potential and take advantage of the opportunities. Who were these men? For the most part, the industrial capitalists of the post–Civil War period were a different group from the merchant capitalists of earlier periods. Few merchants transferred their capital into industrial development. As the shipping trade became overextended, many old merchant families moved into public works promotions, insurance, and banking.

If merchants did not become industrialists, where did the class of industrial capitalists originate? They came largely from independent farmers, skilled craftsmen, and small storekeepers. Eli Whitney and Cyrus McCormick came from such backgrounds. Andrew Carnegie came from a family of country weavers, John D. Rockefeller's father was a peddler, and John Gates spent his early years on a farm.

There developed, then, a group of men who were different from the Eastern merchants. They had talents which were different, and their outlooks, interests, and visions differed also. A hardy breed, they understood the potentials of the changes taking place around them; they recognized the structure and strength of the new foundations of business; and they were willing to take up the challenge. This group of men who were sometimes condemned as "Robber Barons" and sometimes praised as "Captains of Industry" were the vital and indispensable ingredient required for America to become an industrialized and affluent society.

Questions sometimes arise concerning why the Robber Barons were such an important force in America's economic growth. What made America different from other countries? What made these men different from men in other parts of the world? Other men in other countries also have amassed fortunes, but their countries have not always experienced economic growth. Part of the answer seems to lie in the ability of the Robber Barons to organize and utilize the unique combination of circumstances that existed at the time. But perhaps more important were their philosophies concerning work and the use of money, philosophies which had roots in the Protestant ethic. While fortunes amassed in other countries were sometimes deposited in foreign banks and used for personal consumption by the owners, thereby making the money unavailable for productive uses, the Robber Barrons believed that wealth should not remain idle but should be used to create more wealth. Thus, emphasis on productivity and reinvestment of wealth made massive capital accumulations possible, and shrewd use of these capital accumulations created unprecedented economic growth for America.

BUSINESS IDEOLOGIES AND VALUE SYSTEMS

Central to America's development was a body of social and economic philosophy which was shared by business leaders and society and which provided both reason and justification for business activities. Several major philosophies which were popular during the nineteenth century will now be discussed.

Business systems are a product of beliefs, mores, and customs of the society in which they exist. Indeed, their very existence depends upon social philosophies which condone and support various kinds of business actions. Businessmen (whether they realize it or not) must have some basic set of philosophies to guide their actions. Beliefs and value systems concerning what is right and wrong are basic to all business activity and serve as a justification for doing or not doing something in a particular way. The society which business serves also develops philosophies and value systems by which actions of businessmen and other groups are judged. Usually these actions are judged by how well they contribute to net social well-being throughout the whole system.

As long as value systems and philosophies of businessmen are compatible with those of society, and as long as resulting business practices contribute positively to social goals, society will accept, support, and encourage contemporary business practices. On the other hand, if business values give rise to business practices which society believes are contrary to the common good, society will initiate and enforce curbs against those practices.

Judged by today's standards, many of the Captains of Industry engaged in highly unethical practices. However, these practices become quite understandable when judged against the background of business and social philosophies which were popular during the last half of the nineteenth century. Businessmen used these philosophies to justify, both privately and publicly, their business activities. And because, for the most part, society shared these same philosophies and values, businessmen enjoyed wide public support for their activities—at least in the period immediately following the Civil War.

Individualism, Work, and the Protestant Ethic

Several different terms have been used to describe social philosophies which stemmed from the Protestant revolution and the teachings of Martin Luther and John Calvin. Max Weber formalized the term "Protestant ethic" in the title of his book *The Protestant Ethic and the Spirit of Capitalism*. Others have affixed names to various parts of the Protestant ethic, thus creating terms such as "individual ethic," "work ethic," and "capitalistic ethic." While all are interrelated within the general framework of the Protestant ethic, they are often discussed separately. Whatever name is used, these philosophies had a profound influence on both business and individual behavior and upon society's beliefs about the propriety of business behavior. They are often at the heart of many of today's philosophical conflicts concerning what business ought to be and what it ought to do.

Generally stated, the *Protestant ethic* held that every man had both a spiritual and a temporal calling. While man's first responsibility was to worship God and live by His laws, an important measure of his service to God was how well he fulfilled his temporal calling.

An integral part of belief in the Protestant ethic was the concept of individualism.[3] As a philosophy it stressed man's relation to his environment. The philosophy taught that man was limited only by his own capabilities and initiative. Inherent in the philosophy were concepts of equal opportunity and individual freedom, i.e., man's freedom and obligation to pursue to the limit of his capabilities his own interests as he saw fit without interference from outside forces. In short, man was master of his own destiny.

A second integral part of the Protestant ethic was the belief in work. Hard work, diligence, initiative, and judgment were considered godly traits. Inherent in the work philosophy was the concept of natural talent. Every man, so the philosophy stated, was endowed by the Creator with a certain set of talents. Man not only had the right to develop and use his talents, but he had the moral obligation to use these God-given gifts to climb to the top. Conversely, laziness or failure to maximize the use of natural talents was considered to be a sin because it was a waste of what God had given for his use on earth. Christ's parable of the talents was considered an expression of this view.

A further part of the Protestant ethic was concerned with money. Thrift and frugality were considered God-given attributes, since contrary action would waste the resources God had provided. Not only did man have the moral obligation to use his talents in work, but also he was obligated to use them to preserve and increase the wealth God gave him. This was evidence of his stewardship; hence, his ability to amass wealth was a major criterion for judging success. According to the philosophy man had a further obligation to use his material wealth, not for his own aggrandizement, but for the good of his fellow man. He was supposed to use his fortunes to do God's work. In a way, the rich were considered to be trustees for the poor.

Because of the nearly universal belief in the Protestant ethic, businessmen operating after the Civil War were able to explain and justify their activities in terms of this ethic. The Protestant ethic was a philosophy of many businessmen of all faiths, not just Protestants. But more important was the fact that the Protestant ethic was a philosophy of society, so most nonbusiness people shared these beliefs with businessmen. While few men actually achieved great wealth, it was important for everyone to believe that opportunities for wealth were open to any individual *if only he chose to take advantage of them*. Thus, while businessmen used the Protestant ethic to justify their actions, society used the same philosophy as a basis for accepting these actions.

Laissez Faire and the Classical Tradition

America had, in the eighteenth century, fought a war with England over government and business relations. Difficulties resulting from government inter-

[3]For a discussion of individualism as a social philosophy, see John Willard Ward, "The Ideal of Individualism and the Reality of Organization," in Earl F. Cheit (ed.), *The Business Establishment,* New York: John Wiley & Sons, Inc., 1964.

ference with American business under British mercantilism were still fresh in the minds of businessmen. It was no wonder that the men who framed the Constitution were careful to define the role of the new government in terms of laissez faire, which to them meant, "Let business alone."

Adam Smith, whose widely read book appeared in 1776, was a staunch advocate of laissez faire and provided theoretical support for this philosophy. Government, it is true, played a part in Smith's economic system, but its role was supportive. It should provide defense and justice, construct and maintain public works, and provide other essential activities that would not be carried on by private business because they could not be made to yield a profit. But Smith felt that government should not in any way become involved in workings of the market system. The greatest public good could be achieved in the Smithian system by businessmen bidding freely among themselves and by supply and demand freely adjusting to each other. The key to the whole system was freedom of competition, which assured the greatest good for the greatest numbers. The system always produced full employment, lowest operating costs, lowest prices, and economic growth.

American political and economic philosophies of the nineteenth century warmly embraced Smithian theory as an ideal model. While the model did not describe the actual business system, it did provide a philosophical model against which to judge government and business relationships.

Social Darwinism

Approximately 100 years ago, Charles Darwin published a most provocative book entitled *The Origin of Species,* which indirectly provided the basis for one of the most popular nineteenth-century philosophies of business behavior. In its original biological context, Darwinian theory proposed that all forms of life evolved, over time, from a few basic types and that, through a process of natural selection, only the strongest and most fit survived.

When Herbert Spencer applied the theory to society and explained social development in terms of social evolution, he gave America a new business philosophy.[4] Applying Darwinian theory to society as a whole, Spencer reasoned that if environment were not tampered with, the most able men would rise to leadership through a process of "natural selection." Nature somehow endowed only a few persons with exactly the right combination of characteristics to master their environment fully. Noninterference with the natural selection process, according to social Darwinism, would produce the greatest good for the greatest numbers by placing the most fit in positions of leadership.

Here was a philosophy ready-made for the Captains of Industry. As the nineteenth century wore to a close and society became more intolerant of business

[4]Richard Hofstadter, *Social Darwinism in American Thought,* rev. ed., Boston: Beacon Press, 1955.

practices, business leaders championed social Darwinism as a rational justification for their position, their riches, their actions, and their power.

Philosophies of Machiavelli

Threads of Machiavellian philosophy also appeared in nineteenth-century business philosophy and continue to appear today. Niccolò Machiavelli (1469–1527) in his famous book, *The Prince*,[5] discussed the problems a prince faced in ruling his people. In his discussion, he not only identified with great clarity many problems in political administration, but also suggested what he considered appropriate solutions to the problems.

Relationships between means and ends are illustrative of Machiavellian philosophy. According to Machiavelli, means should be subordinate to ends (power of the prince); that is, a prince should take whatever measures are necessary to keep his subjects "united and obedient." Adapting this to business philosophy, it became popular to think of the businessman as feeling justified in resorting to any means to reach the end of profit. Strong arguments can be made to demonstrate that the Captains of Industry were guided by this philosophy.

The phrase "Do unto others before they do unto you" is also Machiavellian in origin. He referred to those who fared better by "overreaching men by their cunning" than did those who trusted to honest dealing, and he concluded that the prince should be prepared to deal with individuals at their own level and beat them at their own game. In short, one should be prepared to use unlawful means or be devious, if necessary.

While most businessmen today do not operate according to either of these philosophies, it is important to recognize that many people perceive business actions as being based on the above principles.

Pragmatism

William James[6] and John Dewey[7] added another facet to social philosophy. These philosophers viewed social progress as a process of change which could and should be controlled by men. Unlike social Darwinism, pragmatic thought viewed man's environment as a variable which could be controlled and manipulated. Experimentation with new ways of doing things would produce the greatest good for the greatest number, and the test of experimentation was: Does the new way work better than the old?

[5]Niccolò Machiavelli, *The Prince* (1513), Oxford: Clarendon Press, 1909.
[6]William James, *Essays in Pragmatism,* New York: Hafner Publishing Company, Inc., 1948.
[7]John Dewey, *Human Nature and Conduct* (1922), New York: Henry Holt and Company, Inc., 1935; and John Dewey, *The Public and Its Problems,* New York: Henry Holt and Company, Inc., 1927.

From the businessman's point of view, pragmatic thought was a mixed blessing. It encouraged industrial development and experimentation with the business system at large, and as long as results were socially profitable, businessmen received support from the rest of the social system. On the other hand, when results from business activity were viewed as socially unprofitable, the whole business system became suspect and subject to change.

INDUSTRIALISM: RESTRUCTURING THE SOCIAL SYSTEM

The post–Civil War years brought a whole new way of life for the American people. Because of industrialization, life became easier in many ways. But also with industrialization came an increase in business size and business power. While the first sixty years of the century had been the golden age of the small entrepreneur, the last forty were the golden age of big business, because during these years business became the most powerful group in the social system. Since most businesses were small before the war, business decisions had only limited social effects. Most businesses operated in very small closed markets, and effects of decisions were not felt outside their immediate environment. But as businesses became large after the war, effects of business decisions reached much further and had much greater social impact. Rate changes by railroads, for example, or price changes in farm machinery affected people from coast to coast.

At the same time that business was growing and gaining strength, other groups within the social system began to achieve identities of their own and become stronger. Set within the framework of the general social system, each group formed a subsystem with individual characteristics of its own and with its own culture and beliefs. Together they became the foundations of the complex pluralistic environment in which business exists today. Most of the social subsystems that rose to importance were not new. Each had stood weakly on the sidelines contributing in one way or another to business growth and power. And so long as business performance continued to satisfy the expectations of the various groups, each was content to remain passive. But when business, through misuse of power, failed to continue meeting the expectations of these groups, countervailing forces were brought to bear to modify business behavior. Among these groups were consumers, stockholders, government, and labor.

Growth of Business Power

As business size increased after the Civil War, old forms of business organizations became inadequate and unsuited to business needs. Consolidation and growth depended, in large measure, on increased use of the corporate form of business which provided large financial accumulations. With the increased economic activity that followed the war came a stiffening of competition, and because this competition was largely price competition, the winners in the struggle were invariably those firms which had sufficient financial strength to lower prices and either destroy or absorb competitors. Rate competition between railroads, for example, drove passenger fares and freight rates below costs in many cases, and in the sugar industry eighteen out of forty refineries were driven out of business by price cutting.[8] The net result of competitive warfare always seemed to be a worsening of the consumers' position. While consumers often benefited temporarily from price wars, etc., they invariably paid higher prices and accepted poorer service in the long run. As consolidations grew larger and power increased, business began to dictate what society should have, rather than responding to social values. In response to public discontent, price wars and business takeovers were usually rationalized by big business as being in the public interest. For example, when John D. Rockefeller combined his resources with several others to launch the Standard Oil Company, he gave the reason: "To stabilize the oil industry."

Finance Capitalism

As capital resources of the country became more highly concentrated in the hands of a few, a new kind of competition appeared. Rather than many small firms competing freely among themselves, the monopolists began to compete with one another, and this competitive struggle led to further consolidation of business. Size, it seemed, was the key to power, and power was the key to survival.

Most early industrial combinations were put together by men who were themselves industrialists. They were principal owners of large firms and were actively engaged in the operation of the firm. Although by modern standards they were often unscrupulous, a main objective of theirs was to produce goods and services. But, as competition became more severe and larger combinations were needed, control shifted to financial interests. For these men, production of goods and services was subordinated, in large measure, to the objective of maximizing personal fortunes. To accomplish their own personal ends, stocks were manipulated, government officials were bribed, public domain was misappropriated, and consumers were cheated and ignored. The corporate form of business was no longer adequate to support the new huge concentrations. Therefore, new forms had to be devised. Pools, trusts, and holding companies appeared, and it was against these combinations and the men who controlled them that much antitrust legislation was directed.

[8]Harold Underwood Faulkner, *American Economic History,* New York: Harper & Brothers, 1949, p. 432.

Misuse of Monopoly Power

Monopolies may be formed (and often are) which are not contrary to public interest and which in some cases are considered to be in the best public interest. We have, in our society today, many monopolies sanctioned by law and considered to perform certain economic functions in the best way. Public utilities are monopolies that are looked upon as being socially desirable.

Questions, then, concerning business concentrations during the latter part of the nineteenth century, and public reaction to them, did not revolve around the desirability of large-scale business per se. Society, as a result of industrialization, enjoyed a greater quantity and variety of goods and services than at any previous time. Rather, questions concerned the use of monopoly power. In actual practice consumers, suppliers, and competitors were all at the mercy of the monopolists. History abounds with evidence of misused monopoly power. Through economic dominance, monopolists crushed competitors by controlling prices, dictated to suppliers by the same means, and subjected consumers to high prices, poor quality, and undependable service.

With economic power came political power as well. Through bribery and coercion of public officials, business leaders exerted a tremendous influence on public policy and were usually able to manipulate it in their favor if the occasion arose, as it did frequently. Records concerning disposal of public domain to business, awarding of municipal contracts, legalizing monopoly practices, and protection from criminal acts of others all attest to the political power enjoyed by business.

THE AGE OF REFORM

Regardless of harsh criticisms which have been leveled at big business for its activities during the post–Civil War years, those few years were truly an age of innovations that carried American society to new high standards of living. New products appeared, old products were improved and refined, new services were offered and others modified, and all this was accompanied by a general lowering of prices. Articles which before the Civil War had been luxuries now became staples in many cases. Ready-made clothing and shoes, processed foods, iron and steel implements, and machinery, to mention only a few items, were generally within the economic reach of the masses. Transportation and communication were broadened and cheapened, and innovations such as electricity and natural gas were widely available. Writing in 1889, one reporter noted over forty-five inventions, discoveries, and applications which were in wide use.[9]

In spite of tremendous strides forward in material well-being, by 1890 public

[9]*The Literary Digest* (1905), quoted in Arthur C. Bining, *The Rise of American Economic Life,* New York: Charles Scribner's Sons, 1949, p. 389.

dissatisfaction with big business performance was enormous. This general dissatisfaction stemmed largely from business's disregard for social and economic rights of the "little man." When business began to strangle competition through huge corporations, pools, and trusts; when prices were artificially maintained; when products and services were not improved; when small stockholders lost their savings through watered stocks; when public property was freely appropriated to private use; and when labor was forcibly suppressed, a rising tide of protest appeared in spite of the predominant laissez faire philosophy. Beginning in 1870, and continuing through the early years of the twentieth century, the wave of public revolt against monopoly business practices resulted in a general reassessment of social institutions and their proper roles and functions within the social system.

Government Intervention

The first organized drive to limit and control business activity through government intervention came from consumers. Working in organized groups or through journalists, they made themselves heard at the national as well as the state level and exerted enough pressure to influence legislation against undesirable business practices. Probably the best organized action was the Granger movement. Working through state legislatures, these groups urged enactment of laws which would prohibit greater charges for short hauls than long ones, forbid consolidation of parallel rail lines, and establish maximum rates and fares. As a result of the agrarian movement, several state laws were passed to regulate railroads, and these laws were upheld by the U.S. Supreme Court until 1886. At that time, the Court reversed itself, saying the states had no right to interfere with interstate commerce.

Continued agrarian pressure along with general public dissent resulted in the first federal legislation to regulate business. In 1887, the Interstate Commerce Act was passed. Successful evasion of the law and court decisions favorable to the railroads made the law largely ineffective in the years immediately following. However, after the turn of the century, it was strengthened by remedial legislation such as the Elkins Act of 1903, the Hepburn Act of 1906, and the Mann-Elkins Act of 1910. By 1915, the political and economic power of railroads was firmly checked. Without question, the Interstate Commerce Act was important as a major piece of restrictive legislation. But much more important from a social system's point of view is that it marked a change in social definition of the role of government and government-business relationships. No longer was the proper role of government thought to be weak, passive, and supportive. The proper role of government was thought to be one of power and regulation.

By 1890, public revolt against all monopoly practice was widespread, and the clamor for antitrust legislation was loud and sharp. As a result, the first piece of general antitrust legislation—the Sherman Act—appeared in 1890. However, the vagueness of its wording and business influence in courts produced disappointing results. Administrations under Harrison, Cleveland, and McKinley exhibited little interest or talent in enforcing the act.

Interest in business regulation and business activity was revived after the turn of the century. A group of public-spirited writers led by Ida Tarbell, Lincoln Steffens, and Upton Sinclair, who became known as the "muckrakers," dissected American business for public view in various magazines of the times. This literary movement emphasized the worst facets of government and business and revived the crusade against business.

The antitrust movement reached its peak with the passage of the Clayton Act and the Federal Trade Commission Act in 1914. Since that time, however, there seems to have been a reversal in the roles of the public and government concerning the enforcement of antitrust laws. While government interest and activity in antitrust enforcement has steadily increased since 1915, it has been observed that public concern has lessened. Hofstadter[10] suggests that the reason for this reversal in government and public roles may be that the whole antitrust issue has become so complex that it is beyond the full comprehension of the average man, with the result that only an organization of specialists in case law and economic theory can cope with the problem.

Labor Emerges

While labor will be discussed in detail in a later chapter, a few comments are appropriate here because it was during the period between the Civil War and the turn of the century that labor emerged as a major social institution. With growth in size of firms, separation of management from ownership, and increased immigration, relations between business and labor changed. No longer were personal relationships and a sense of personal responsibility possible on the part of many employers. As greater numbers of persons filled cities and became wholly dependent upon wages for their livelihood, a labor movement which had been largely weak and ineffective began to gain strength.

Emergence of the labor movement changed the shape of society and complicated the environment of business. As the labor movement grew, it added to the social system another power group with which business had to relate. Serious and widespread strikes and even violence plagued business during this period. The most extreme and spectacular examples of labor violence were the activities of the Molly Maguires.[11] The Molly Maguires were a secret group (composed mostly of coal miners) who were organized to carry out a campaign of physical violence against mine owners and mine bosses. Beatings, sabotage, and murders, as well as the strike, were their weapons. However, with the conviction and execution of their leaders for criminal acts, the organization was disbanded.

While most organized labor activity was not as violent as the activities of the

[10]Richard Hofstadter, "What Happened to the Antitrust Movement?" in Cheit, op. cit., p. 151.
[11]Wayne G. Broehl, Jr., *The Molly Maguires,* Cambridge, Mass.: Harvard University Press, 1964.

Molly Maguires, labor emerged as an organized social group capable of exerting strong economic pressure against business.

STATE CAPITALISM EMERGES

During the 1930s a marked change in relationships among American social institutions became evident. Until 1930 the function of government had been primarily to support the business system in its role of economic leadership and to mediate between business and society through a growing body of regulatory legislation. After 1930, however, the role of government changed from passive judgment of business behavior to active economic leadership. Putting it another way, government's role changed from judging how well business performed its responsibilities to society to defining what those responsibilities ought to be.

The Great Depression

The stock market crash of 1929 and the subsequent national economic collapse put American free enterprise squarely on trial for its existence. Widespread unemployment, decline of purchasing power, collapse of markets, and declining standards of living all threatened American social stability and gave rise to serious questions about the validity of the classical self-adjusting economic model of Adam Smith. Because traditional economic theory and social philosophy looked to business for leadership in maintaining economic equilibrium and satisfying social expectations, all the problems surrounding the economic collapse were placed squarely in the lap of business. Business, however, was unable to respond, and when it became evident that business, by itself, could not generate enough momentum to stimulate economic recovery, Americans began to look to other social institutions for corrective action. Government quickly took the initiative.

Under the general rubric of the "New Deal" the government set about systematically injecting massive amounts of economic "help" which were, in large part, contrary to traditional Smithian economic philosophy. Two of the more notable and controversial government attempts to stimulate the economy were the NRA (National Recovery Administration) and the PWA (Public Works Administration). Although subsequently declared unconstitutional by the U.S. Supreme Court, the NRA was an attempt to override natural market forces by artificially maintaining prices. The PWA, on the other hand, was an attempt to expand employment and purchasing power through extensive public works programs which were planned, administered, and paid for by the government. Through these and a variety of similar programs, government interjected itself into virtually every corner of business activity. According to Cochran and Miller:[12]

[12]Thomas C. Cochran and William Miller, *The Age of Enterprise*, New York: The Macmillan Company, 1942, pp. 355–356.

Under the New Deal the federal government became a great employer of men, the greatest user of the nation's savings, the greatest underwriter of debt. The government assumed much of the risk-taking activity of private enterprise. It assumed leadership in finance and construction. Above all, it supplanted private business as the chief planner of the nation's economic life.

The Great Depression also brought about a reexamination of social as well as economic philosophies, thus further modifying the environment of business. Beginning in the 1930s government set about defining in legal terms many social responsibilities of business—particularly as they applied to employees and consumers. Wage and hour laws, safety codes, social security obligations, workman's compensation for injury on the job, and responsibility for product safety and performance are illustrations of this new environment. Concurrently, a redefinition of power relations among social institutions took place. For example, the Wagner Act established labor as a major power group. As a result labor was now in a position legally to impose social restrictions on business behavior. By 1940 business found that it was no longer *the major power group* in society, but only *one power group* whose decisions and actions were frequently challenged by other powerful groups—notably organized labor and government.

Keynesian Economics

Events of the early 1930s demonstrated that the classical economic model was no longer functioning adequately. Clearly, what was needed was a new economic model that would explain what was happening and also would prescribe corrective measures. In 1936 the English economist John Maynard Keynes provided that model in his *General Theory of Employment, Interest, and Money*.

Central to the new model was the assumption that the market mechanism and the price system would *not necessarily* adjust automatically to ensure full employment of resources. Furthermore, the model challenged the ideas of thrift and saving. Full utilization of resources, the model stated, depended upon investment and consumption and not upon savings which were set aside and hoarded. In other words, money should be put to work in productive activities—a concept the Robber Barons had followed in the previous century. Finally, the model struck directly at the philosophy of laissez faire. No longer should government be viewed as a weak and passive institution. Rather, it should be the central force responsible for directing and balancing the economic system. Since it was clear that the economic system was not self-adjusting, some force other than business should be responsible for economic performance. Government, through its powers to regulate and through its ability to formulate and impose monetary and fiscal policy, was uniquely suited to perform this function.

Even though the Keynesian model explained much of what was already happening in America, most businessmen and much of society rejected the model because it struck directly at the hearts of both traditional economic philosophy and the Protestant ethic. Nevertheless, it offered justification for forces that were already at work in the American social system and provided a basis for changing social philosophies and values.

Individualism versus the Social Ethic

Events of the 1930s also encouraged a reevaluation of the Protestant ethic. The values of hard work and thrift were seriously questioned, and for many the concept of individualism and self-determination no longer seemed to be effective or appropriate. The individual ethic, so popular in the last century and the early twentieth century, was largely being replaced by the social ethic. The term "social ethic," as used here, does not imply belief in socialism as a political system. Rather it is used to describe an ever-increasing belief that man no longer can control his environment or be master of his destiny. During the Depression when people saw their life's savings evaporate in bank failures, when many lost their homes or businesses through foreclosures and bankruptcy, when many who wanted to work could not secure employment over long periods of time, and when many depended upon welfare checks from the government for physical survival, it became evident that man is not always "an island unto himself." Implicit in the social ethic is the belief that individuals have become so interdependent and so subordinate to various power groups in society that they are dependent upon these groups for physical, social, and economic security. Thus members of society began to expect government, business, and organized labor to provide those things which they could not provide for themselves. Individual risk increasingly was transferred to social institutions.

EARLY BUSINESS ATTITUDES OF SOCIAL RESPONSIBILITY

Concepts of business social responsibility are not new in America. Indeed businessmen, in one way or another, have been involved in social issues ever since the American business system began. This section will discuss briefly the historical development of business thought and action regarding social responsibility.[13]

Early company involvement of American business in community affairs came with the development of company towns. As early as 1820 a group of New England businessmen known as the Boston Associates had developed towns around their textile mills in Lowell and Waltham, Massachusetts. Because of the isolated location of these and many other towns, businessmen frequently found

[13]Discussion in this section relies on Morrell Heald, *The Social Responsibilities of Business: Company and Community, 1900–1960,* Cleveland: The Press of Case Western Reserve University, 1970.

themselves, sometimes unwillingly, but inescapably, involved in and responsible for existing local social conditions. Although there was often a genuine concern for employees' living conditions, more practical business considerations of attracting and keeping labor also prompted businessmen's concern for social conditions in the towns. Whatever the reasons, services and facilities such as company housing, stores, libraries, and schools were often provided by employers. Unfortunately, these paternalistic endeavors often produced employee bitterness and ill will toward the company rather than promoting the spirit of well-being and contentment that was intended.

As company towns were replaced by urban industrial concentrations, the emphasis of business involvement in social welfare shifted from paternalism to philanthropy. To be sure, paternalism remained very much in the scheme of things, and practical reasons for business involvement continued to be important. But there also seemed to be an increasing belief that business and community had many things in common. For example, the Cleveland Hardware Company stated: "Although we believe that what we are doing [in plant and community improvement] is most practical and philanthropic, our company does not feel that it is a philanthropy, but a good business proposition."[14]

While corporate social concerns in the late nineteenth century centered largely around workers' living conditions in limited and well-defined communities, many business leaders viewed their individual social responsibility from a broader perspective. Trained as they were in tenets of the Protestant ethic, many prominent businessmen looked upon themselves as trustees who were responsible to the less fortunate public. From such a philosophical position they directed their personal wealth toward community welfare projects of a broader nature.

Andrew Carnegie was one of the leaders in personal philanthropy. His philanthropic philosophies and activities had a strong influence upon other wealthy men and, perhaps more important, were instrumental in establishing patterns of corporate social involvement in the first half of the twentieth century. Carnegie believed not only that it was his moral duty to amass a fortune but that it was also his moral duty to use his wealth in the public interest. Writing in 1889, he urged wealthy men:[15]

> . . . to consider all surplus revenues which come to him simply as trust funds, which he is called upon to administer . . . in the manner which, in his judgement, is best calculated to produce the most beneficial results for the community—the man of wealth thus [would become] the mere trustee and agent for his poorer brethren, bringing to their service his superior wisdom, experience, and ability to administer, doing for them better than they would or could do for themselves.

By the turn of the century many business leaders subscribed to the concept

[14]Ibid., p. 16.
[15]Andrew Carnegie, quoted in *The Gospel of Wealth,* Edward C. Kirkland (ed.), Cambridge, Mass.: The Belknap Press of Harvard University, 1962, p. 25.

that individual commitment to social problems was not enough. In increasing numbers they accepted the belief that social problems should be seen as a demand on corporate resources. To be sure, there was little or no concern about the extent to which business was responsible for creating social problems. The question rarely was who or what caused the problems and how they could be prevented in the future, but rather, how and to what extent business should be involved in alleviating existing problems.

The Age of Reform

The outpouring of public criticism of business which occurred around the turn of the century forced upon businessmen a new sensitivity to public opinion and a new sense of urgency to respond to that criticism. The nineteenth-century philosophy of individual trusteeship was expanded to a philosophy of corporate trusteeship, thus providing a rationale for twentieth-century corporate involvement in community affairs. Jane Addams, a prominent Chicago leader in social work, noted a changing relationship between society and big business. She observed a growing belief that "a large manufacturing concern has ceased to be a private matter; that not only a number of workmen and stockholders are concerned in its management, but that the interests of the public are so involved that the officers of the company are in a real sense administering a public trust."[16] Arthur Hadley, president of Yale University, also noted in 1906: "The president of a large corporation is in a place of public trust. In an obvious sense he is a trustee for the stockholders and creditors of his corporation. In a less obvious but equally important sense he is a trustee on behalf of the public."[17]

Business responded to the corporate trusteeship concept in a number of ways during the first two decades of the twentieth century and in so doing established enduring patterns of corporate involvement in community affairs. E. H. Gray, chairman of US Steel Corporation pioneered the idea of reporting company activities to the public by publishing the corporation's annual report. Many business leaders worked primarily through civic organizations such as chambers of commerce, Kiwanis, and Rotary. They also supported public agencies such as the Red Cross and YMCA. In addition, local crises and catastrophes sometimes provided opportunities for direct involvement in societal needs. For example, during the San Francisco earthquake Standard Oil provided help through donations of fuel, money, and other resources. Company barges were opened to house the homeless, and company-owned land was used for the same purpose. Also, large sums of money were donated by the company and by many individual company officers.

[16]Jane Addams, *Democracy and Social Ethics*, New York: The Macmillan Company, 1911, pp. 142–143.

[17]Arthur T. Hadley, *Standards of Public Morality*, New York: The Macmillan Company, 1912, p. 79.

Closer to home, businessmen began to focus on industrial relations, employee welfare, and working conditions. Some companies depended upon agencies such as the YMCA to look after employee welfare, but other companies developed their own programs of employee health and safety, work methods study, profit sharing plans, employee representation in management, gifts of community facilities, financial support of hospitals, and company recreation programs.

Concurrently, a concept of service was growing among business leaders. Cyrus McCormick attributed the prominent position of International Harvester Company in the farm machinery industry to its policy of customer service which was formalized in its agricultural extension department. During the years immediately following the end of World War I a few business leaders talked of the "Fair Deal" and *Forbes Magazine* concluded: "The business of modern business is service."[18] Service, to these men, meant something more than providing product service. It meant service to the subsystems of society wherever possible and in whatever ways were appropriate.

Thus the seeds of a rational system of response to corporate social responsibility were sowed between 1900 and the close of World War I. There was a growing conviction among many prominent business leaders that a close relationship existed between social and economic performance and that the health of the business system depended on both.

Social Responsibilities in the Twenties

Businessmen had learned only too well in the periods immediately preceding the turn of the century the power of public opinion. Arthur Hadley had observed: "Industrial corporations grew up into power because they met the needs of the past. To stay in power, they must meet the needs of the present, and arrange their ethics accordingly."[19] During the decade of the nineteen-twenties they set about reexamining their thoughts about their responsibilities to society and defining the needs of the "present." The recognition grew that business had in fact become a major social institution and as such could not ignore other segments of society such as employees, customers, stockholders, suppliers, and dealers.

One question which concerned thoughtful business leaders of the times was the question of the relation of business to the public. The unprecedented prosperity of the period which was commonly attributed to the miracles of mass production led to the idea that businessmen knew best what was necessary for the public's well-being. Well aware of the power of public opinion, many businessmen set about creating a favorable public opinion of business through massive public relations programs. Others, led by such men as Henry Ford and Edward A. Filene believed that actions spoke louder than words. They believed that business could

[18]*Forbes,* quoted in Morrell Heald, op. cit., p. 47.
[19]Hadley, op. cit., p. 96.

best serve society by concentrating on making business more efficient. The drive to increase profits through more efficient production methods would lead to more employment, higher wages, lower prices, and improved living conditions, thus working toward the betterment of society. The latter group believed that favorable public opinion would come from the positive evidence of business performance rather than from concerted efforts to mold public opinion through advertising and public relations programs.

Another continuing concern was the issue of management trusteeship. By 1920 professional managers were firmly established as a group separate and distinct from owners. In their role of corporate policy makers some leading managers publicly recognized their responsibility to a variety of social groups. Owen D. Young, chairman of General Electric, stated: "The old notion . . . that the heads of business are the paid attorneys for stockholders, to exploit labor and the public in the stockholder's interest is gone—I hope forever."[20] Thus, in ordering the groups to which management was responsible, Young not only advocated multiple responsibility but he placed both employees and the public ahead of stockholders. John D. Rockefeller, Jr., saw business as a partnership between labor, capital, management, and the community. Howard J. Heinz perceived his responsibilities to be to stockholders, employees, those who distributed his products, and consumers.

For most businessmen of the twenties, however, stockholders remained the central group to whom responsibility was owed. Even though there was a growing awareness on the part of most businessmen that business had both social and economic obligations, the vagueness of social guidelines made them hesitant to become involved in social issues except as they might relate to economic performance. Nevertheless, the framework of future philosophy of corporate social responsibility was evident.

A third area of social concern which received attention during the nineteen-twenties was the problem of business giving. Demands for business participation in solving social problems of the community had been increasing steadily since before the turn of the century. The flood of appeals for support from a multitude of social welfare agencies left business with a sense of genuine frustration. Often businessmen had little or no way of evaluating agencies making requests, and evaluating large volumes of individual requests for assistance took valuable time. The emerging Community Chest provided an orderly vehicle through which business could shape philanthropic policy and participate responsibly in solving community problems.

All businessmen did not agree that the Community Chest should be supported by business. Many continued to emphasize that the primary function of business was production and efficiency. Community welfare services, it was argued, should be supported by individuals. Furthermore, corporate philanthropy might not be good for the community, and there was a question of whether or not it

---

[20]Ida M. Tarbell, *Owen D. Young: A New Type of Industrial Leader,* quoted in Heald, op. cit., p. 97.

was legal to use corporate funds for such purposes. Other businessmen, arguing for the Community Chest, pointed out that welfare services financed by the chest improved living conditions, attracted better labor, reduced taxes to support municipal welfare agencies, and reduced welfare programs of the corporation itself.

Obviously, the Community Chest could not act as a vehicle for all business giving or all business involvement in community affairs, but it did provide a workable model for many relationships between business and community.

Depression and War

The wave of adverse opinion and public recriminations against business which occurred during the nineteen-thirties put business on the defensive. Concern with the public image of business and with what most businessmen perceived as government interference with the economic system occupied most of the thinking of businessmen during the Depression, and thus left little time for the broader aspects of social responsibility. To regain public favor, business turned to public relations campaigns to "make the public look upon business as a good servant rather than a selfish master."[21]

Preoccupation with the business image led to increased support of the Community Chest and other welfare agencies. Contributions to such organizations were visible evidence of social concern and therefore could be emphasized in public relations programs. But preoccupation with public image and welfare contributions seemed to lead business actions directly away from key issues of public concern such as social security and industrial relations. It was directly upon these and other major social issues that the New Deal focused. Nevertheless, some thoughtful observers of business continued to try to interpret the role of management. Events of the Depression seemed to emphasize as never before the managerial role of mediation between various and often competing social groups.

Business emerged from World War II enjoying a reaffirmed public confidence which stemmed from the "production miracles" of the war effort. To a large degree business found itself submerged in problems of moving from a wartime to a peacetime economy, and while business literature of the nineteen-fifties was full of discussions of social responsibility, little went beyond the established concept of corporate trusteeship. Most of business's social actions were extensions of already existing social interests. In addition to response to social welfare agencies, business was drawn into participation in broader social institutions such as education, the arts, and politics. Then in 1953 Howard R. Bowen published *Social Responsibilities of the Businessman*, which marked the beginning of the modern age of social responsibility discussed throughout this book.[22]

[21]Raymond Moley, "The Future of Corporate Prophets," *Vital Speeches of the Day*, II, July 15, 1936, quoted in Heald, op. cit., pp. 193–194.
[22]Howard R. Bowen, *Social Responsibilities of the Businessman*, New York: Harper & Brothers, 1953.

SUMMARY

The favorable environment which existed after the Civil War allowed business to emerge as the leading power group in American society. One result of the economic power of business was a tremendous increase in availability of products at ever-decreasing prices. A second and less desirable result was misuse of power by business. Use of power which produced undesirable social payouts generated widespread public dissatisfaction with the performance of business as a social institution. To justify their role and their performance, businessmen turned to a number of social ideologies. Because most Americans shared with business-men belief in these ideologies, business enjoyed general public support. But toward the close of the nineteenth century public belief in these ideologies began to diminish, and public support of business turned to outright hostility.

As public dissatisfaction with business increased in the first decade of the twentieth century, the role of government was enlarged to include a regulatory function, and a wave of legislation directed at controlling business followed. At the same time, there was a growing recognition on the part of some thoughtful business leaders that business must accept some share of the responsibility for social problems. The concept of individual trusteeship was extended to a concept of corporate trusteeship, and some companies experimented with company pro-grams directed specifically toward employee welfare.

During the nineteen-thirties a further redefinition of institutional roles occur-red. The economic collapse and the inability of business to generate recovery led to serious questioning of the Protestant ethic and Smithian economics. As a result government assumed many functions previously reserved for business and, by law, forced the attention of business to issues such as social security and employee health and safety. Although the "production miracles" of World War II and the postwar economic prosperity reestablished public confidence in the business system, business concern with issues of social responsibility continued to focus largely on already established concepts. In the mid-fifties, however, business thought and business literature began to focus on broader issues of business social responsibility.

STUDY GUIDES FOR
INTERPRETATION OF THIS CHAPTER

1. Looking back over the last 100 or so years, identify periods in which society redefined roles of social institutions. In each case give specific reasons for the redefinition and explain the new roles which were assigned.

2. From periodical literature, speeches, newspapers, etc., give as many ex-amples as you can that illustrate that some businessmen still subscribe to one or more of the ideologies mentioned in this chapter.

3. What is meant by the social ethic? Contrast, point by point, the social ethic with the Protestant ethic. Give modern examples of demands on business that reflect belief in the social ethic.

4. In his book *The American Challenge,* J.-J. Servan-Schreiber refers to the "post-industrial society." Characteristics of this new society are as follows: (1) industrial revenue may be fifty times greater than in the preindustrial period; (2) most economic activity may have shifted from primary (agriculture) and secondary (industrial production) areas to service industries, research institutes, and nonprofit organizations; (3) private enterprise may no longer be the major source of scientific and technological development; (4) the free market may take second place to the public sector and to social services; (5) most industries will be run by cybernetics; (6) the major impetus for progress will come from education and the technological innovations it utilizes; (7) time and space will no longer be a problem in communication; (8) the gap between high and low salaries in the postindustrial society may be considerably smaller than today. (A society starts reaching the postindustrial level when per capita income reaches $4,000 per year.) Using each of the above criteria, comment regarding how close American society is today to achieving the postindustrial level and what effect the achievement of each criterion will have on the relationship of business to the rest of the social system.

10

BUSINESS VALUES AND CODES OF CONDUCT

I never met a corporation that has a conscience.

George Meany[1]

Throughout society there is an intricate web of social patterns which defines how people deal with social situations. In government there are trade-offs among legislators to gain support for appropriations which benefit their particular districts; and at a wedding there is frequently a personal gift given to the church functionary who performs the ceremony. Are these practices socially "proper"?

Since business is a dominant social institution with high public visibility, its proper conduct is a matter of special social concern. Consider the following practices. Are they proper?

Regis Discount Furniture advertised in a metropolitan newspaper: "End of Month Sale: five-piece bedroom set, $399 value, special price $325." The facts were that the manufacturer's suggested retail price was $399, and Regis's advertising manager knew that the set sold for $399 in most nondiscount furniture stores. In the Regis store, however, this particular bedroom set had never sold for more than $325.

In another city a meat packer gave kickbacks to purchasing agents of clubs, hotels, and other buyers.[2] On its federal income tax return it claimed these kickbacks as a business expense, and the case finally was taken to

[1]George Meany (president, AFL-CIO), quoted in an announcement of a social responsibility conference, Chicago: Urban Research Corporation, 1973.

[2]"Kickbacks Paid," *Wall Street Journal* (pacific Coast edition), Nov. 5, 1969, p. 1.

federal court. In the court hearing, an agent of the Internal Revenue Service testified that this was such a common practice among packers that the Revenue Service had adopted a standard formula for compromising claims for deductions of this type.

Whether business values are consciously established or not, they exist in the cultural heritage of civilization. Whether written or not, they do guide actions of businessmen. The question, then, is not whether to have them; rather, it is how intelligently they are established and applied.

In this chapter we discuss business value systems and the managerial values that are related to them. We also examine guides to business conduct offered by others, such as professional associations. In later chapters we discuss specific applications of business values to various claimants, such as government, customers, labor, and less-advantaged persons.

AN INCREASING INTEREST IN BUSINESS VALUES

Society has a new social awareness which is encouraging it to reassess and improve its social conduct in major ways. Business will need to move with society and, it is hoped, even lead it in some instances. There are many reasons for society's general reassessment of its values, and business is a part of these; however, major business reassessment was triggered by the electrical conspiracy cases initiated in 1960. On June 22 of that year, a number of electrical manufacturers were indicted in the United States District Court, Eastern District of Pennsylvania, for alleged conspiracy to fix prices and restrict competition in the sale of electrical equipment. There were subsequent convictions in this case.

In the wake of the electrical conspiracy indictments, the United States Secretary of Commerce convened in 1961 a Business Ethics Advisory Council to encourage voluntary improvement of business conduct. Its stated purpose was to explore "some approaches to the development of ethical guidelines that might be useful to the business community" and to encourage businessmen toward self-regulation. Strictly speaking, this council was not a group of businessmen working for self-regulation, for over half the committee consisted of educators, clergymen, and journalists. Some businessmen were on the committee. This council issued a call for better self-regulation and pointed out six areas for self-evaluation: general understanding of ethical issues, compliance with law, conflicts of interest, entertainment and gift expenses, customers and suppliers, and social responsibilities.

Surveys of businessmen at this time showed that they were aware of social issues in the conduct of their businesses and that a number of them were concerned that business practices had not kept up with social standards of conduct.

One survey covered 1,531 readers of *Harvard Business Review,* 84 percent of them in management.[3] Sixty-eight percent of respondents felt there were "a few" or more unethical practices in their industry. When asked about the one practice they would most like to see eliminated, they stressed gifts and bribes, unfair pricing, and misleading advertising. When asked whether they favored a self-developed ethical code for their industry, 71 percent favored a code and only 10 percent opposed it. The benefits most expected from an ethical code were its usefulness as an aid in refusing unethical requests (87 percent) and its personal help as a clear definition of the limits of acceptable conduct (81 percent). On the negative side, 11 percent believed the code might protect inefficient firms and retard industry growth.

Other results of the survey showed that although businessmen were alert to social responsibilities, they disagreed on what was the proper conduct in specific situations. They recognized that there were no simple, clear-cut answers. Generally they rated themselves as higher in ethics than the "average businessman," and they looked to top management for leadership to improve practice.

Increasing interest in business values was shown to be worldwide when the thirteenth International Management Congress met in New York City in 1963. Several thousand delegates from more than half the nations of the world attended this triennial meeting, and one of the principal issues discussed at the congress was the ethical standards of business.

Shortly thereafter a survey of 323 United States managers showed that managerial concern about ethical practice persisted.[4] Seventy-one percent thought their competitors engaged in at least a few unethical practices. (The comparable response to a slightly different question in the Harvard survey mentioned earlier was 68 percent.) Marketing managers had the lowest opinion of competitors, with 23 percent saying "frequently." Personnel men had the highest opinion of competitors, with 35 percent saying "seldom" or "never." The entire group said marketing and purchasing had the most unethical practices, and they designated pricing as the main problem area. The majority of respondents felt the public image of business practices was "not too high," and the majority also felt that more could be done to raise ethical practices. They particularly favored active discussions of business ethics among business people.

The conspiracy cases, Business Ethics Advisory Council, 1963 International

[3]Raymond C. Baumhart, "How Ethical Are Businessmen?" *Harvard Business Review*, July–August 1961, pp. 6ff. See also the thorough analysis of this survey and others in Raymond Baumhart, *Ethics in Business*, New York: Holt, Rinehart and Winston, Inc., 1968.
[4]Thomas F. Schutte, "Executives' Perceptions of Business Ethics," *Journal of Purchasing*, May 1965, pp. 38–52.

Management Congress, surveys of business practice, and similar developments in the early 1960s spurred an increasing interest in business values and codes of conduct. Further interest was stimulated by social developments which related to business, such as concern for poverty, pollution, and urban deterioration. Businessmen around the world began to realize that business needs clear-cut social usefulness as well as economic usefulness. These events of the 1960s have set the stage for major social efforts by business and other institutions in the 1970s, which may become known as the "Decade of Social Concern."

MANAGERIAL VALUE SYSTEMS
Values Affect Behavior

An underlying feature of business conduct is the value system of its people. In the ultimate sense these values derive from the society in which people live; thus they are not likely to be of better ethical quality than the general population whence they came. However, the public trust placed in businessmen does place special obligations on them to uphold the highest possible ethical standards of their society and even to help lead society toward improved practices. Managerial values especially are important because of the power that managers wield in organizations.

A businessman's values affect all that he does in business, because they provide the social norms on which he depends for guidance. They determine what he thinks is right and wrong, what is desirable and undesirable, and what attitudes he has toward social issues. They determine the kinds of ideas that he can understand and accept. Whatever he does, they color his outlook toward the world. They are the ethical guidelines that he uses to rationalize decisions he makes, regardless of how realistic those decisions appear to others.

Values are different for each manager, because they depend on his perception of reality. When he looks across his desk into his office, his perception of what is there will be different from that of an associate alongside him with an almost identical physical view. He may see people wasting time, while his associate sees new furniture just purchased. Similarly, he will see something different from what his associate sees when both are looking at a balance sheet. The reality which is there is identical, but each person's perception of it is not likely to be fully correct or fully complete because each situation contains ambiguous factors and unknowns. Each selects by means of perception those factors which are meaningful to him in terms of his experience, values, and capabilities.

Each manager's values exist as a total system with each value rubbing against other values, amending and restraining them and, in turn, being amended and restrained. No one value independently determines behavior. An example of the relationship among values is the evidence that managers who are more religious tend to be more receptive to social concerns. They also are less interested in the single-minded pursuit of profit without recognition of social interests.[5] Further, managers are shown to have a relatively broad range of value interests compared with those of people in other occupations. Managers need this broadness, because their roles as trustee, boundary mediator, and change agent require them to deal with many conflicting values in their daily work.

Guides for Making Value Judgments

Some of the conflicting values which managers have to balance in making decisions are the following:

Technical—based on physical facts, science, and logic

Economic—based on market values determined by supply and demand

Social—based on group and institutional needs

Psychological—based on personal needs of individuals

Political—based on general welfare needs of the state

Aesthetic—based on beauty

Ethical—based on what is right

Spiritual—based on what God has revealed

Since managers do mediate among many claimants and value systems, there is no set of rules telling them exactly what to do in each situation. Managers are left with no choice other than to make judgments based upon whatever general ethical guides society can furnish. There is evidence of some social agreement concerning the seriousness of breaches of social conduct. In a theft, for example, research indicates that in order for one theft to be considered twice as serious as another, the amount stolen must be about sixty times as large. The act of theft is considered a breach of conduct, even if the amount is only $5; and since the breach has already been committed with the $5 theft, a person must steal much more (about $300) in order to make his deed twice as bad.[6]

With regard to business, many of our ethical guidelines arise from the following value considerations.

1. Is there unfair gain to the person doing it? An example is a conflict of interest in which a manager gains through a purchase contract he makes with a firm in which he has a secret interest.

2. Is there unfair harm to others? An example is private disclosure of unfa-

[5]John Senger, "The Religious Manager," *Academy of Management Journal*, June 1970, pp. 179–186.
[6]Clarence C. Walton, *Ethos and the Executives: Value in Managerial Decision Making*, Englewood Cliffs, N.J.: Prentice-Hall, Inc., 1969, pp. 31–33.

vorable financial information, which places stockholders not receiving the disclosure at a disadvantage.

3. How substantial is the unfair gain or the harm to others? For example, water pollution used to be minor. Now it is widespread and substantial; thus it is considered to be much more serious. Especially in evaluating harm, two additional criteria are useful.

    a. Are there offsetting gains? For example, urban renewal often harms those who must relocate their homes, but it is said that the larger community eventually will receive an offsetting gain.

    b. How irreversible is the harm? Traditional detergents, for example, are considered more harmful pollution than newer biodegradable ones which soon lose their polluting power.

4. Was the act a personal one, or was it representative behavior according to established practice? Discharge of an employee because of personal dislike is more serious than discharge for inadequate performance. Similarly, gain from manipulation of company stock is improper, compared with proper gain from exercising an established stock option.

5. Is there adequate due process, such as the right to appeal unjust decisions, to return faulty merchandise, and so on?

In general, it appears that society develops business conduct guidelines for two primary purposes. One purpose is to assure that knowledge and power are used in fair and responsible ways with others. Therefore, the balancing of responsibility with power becomes a major basis for setting ethical guidelines on business power. In a similar manner, when business is subject to the power of others, such as bad-check artists, ethical guidelines are set up to protect business from their power.

A second purpose for conduct guidelines is to make business more effective as a social institution. Society expects certain social benefits from business, and it is reasoned that business can provide more of these benefits if it operates efficiently. To accomplish these ends, conduct guidelines are prescribed.

Business Values of Managers

What values do managers hold concerning business? Managers are neither cut in the image of the early Robber Barons, nor are they professional people with rigid standards of conduct. Instead, they have a remarkably wide variety of viewpoints on issues, and these viewpoints become even more diverse when managers have to apply values in operating situations.

One survey presented twenty-six case situations to 103 California managers at all organizational levels.[7] Managers reported how they would

decide each case by selecting one of four choices. Two choices gave preference to profit or personal advantage, and the other two gave preference to
ethical values or social goals. Managers were substantially divided on such
issues as selling speculative land, layoff of older employees compared with
younger ones, and use of insider information for stock purchase.

Perhaps because the managers worked in a region with air pollution,
the case with the highest agreement involved installation of a costly air filter
which reduced net income of a refinery for several years. Even though no
ordinance compelled this installation, 96 percent of the managers favored it.
Other areas of more than 90 percent agreement were hiding plant shutdown
information from employees (91 percent rejected), use of inferior materials
in an underbid contract (93 percent rejected), padding an expense account
(93 percent rejected), and president performing time-consuming community
activities on company time (95 percent accepted).

In the survey just mentioned, even when there was nearly uniform agreement
on a social point of view, a few managers persisted with a view which tended to
maximize profits. Agreement of all business managers on their social responsibilities is as unlikely as agreement of all economists, politicians, or educators on
their social responsibilities. Diversity provides checks and balances.

Managerial value systems give strong support to market freedom. Even
though managers recognize the need for regulation and adapt to it once it is
established, they would prefer to have the flexibility that goes with freedom. Part
of this preference is the normal human desire of most persons to be free of
restrictive controls; however, there is also an important philosophical foundation
for placing a high value on market freedom. Managers, as well as others, believe
that by keeping economic decisions free and decentralized they are helping
maintain political democracy and other human freedoms. They believe that freedoms are mutually linked in a system relationship and that erosion anywhere in the
system increases the probability of erosion elsewhere in the system.

The quest for market freedom is not peculiar to managers but is a general
cultural phenomenon. Almost all groups seek autonomy, even though—like
business—they are subject to controls. Educators seek academic freedom for their
group so that ideas can be freely traded. Laborers want to be free to make whatever
demands they wish without wage and other governmental controls. Minorities
want freedom to operate their own interests. All are brothers in their search for
operating freedom, and all can philosophically justify it as a contribution to the
public interest.

[7]John W. Clark, *Religion and Moral Standards of American Businessmen,* Cincinnati: South-Western
Publishing Company, Incorporated, 1966, especially p. 98.

Four Primary Claimant Groups

Surveys, managerial speeches, and other data indicate that business managers essentially see themselves as serving many claimants, trying to provide each with some quality of output larger than inputs. Most typically they classify their claimants into four groups: investors, employees, customers, and society (including government). Values supporting benefits to these four groups usually apply to both private and public organizations, and many managers have shown the capacity to move from one to the other and perform effectively without modifying their value system about these areas of benefit. For example, a government office must satisfy its citizen customers by producing services just as much as a private factory must satisfy customers by producing goods. Personnel services of the two institutions are even more similar. Likewise, the government office must in the long run provide an output for citizen investors, or else it will not receive adequate operating appropriations, or capital for expansion. It is true that measurement of investor return is slower and more indirect in public organizations, but it is there. Government offices do close and charities do go out of business when they inadequately use the resources society has invested in them.

Management's tendency to classify claimants in terms of investors, employees, customers, and society was clearly shown by a survey of 152 chief executives and finance executives.[8] The executives were asked to rank their responsibilities to four claimants; and since the focus of the study was financial, creditors were on the list instead of customers. Many executives detected this "oversight" and gave such a hearty write-in vote for customers that they ranked third! Further, there was no difference in the average rank order given by the chief executives and the finance executives, even though it might be assumed that the finance managers would give more emphasis to creditors. The average rank order of the five groups was as follows: stockholders, employees, customers, creditors, and society. In ranking society last, a number of executives voluntarily added that, in their opinion, service to other claimants is effective service to society as a whole.

BUSINESS CODES OF CONDUCT

All businesses must meet certain standards of law and minimum cultural standards. All are further influenced by the general cultural milieu of their time. But in spite of these tendencies toward uniform conduct, there are important differences among businesses. Each has its own personality, as each human being

[8]Arthur W. Lorig, "Where Do Corporate Responsibilities Lie?" *Business Horizons,* Spring 1967, pp. 51–54.

does. These organizational differences are reflected in company codes of conduct, and they do produce different results.

Models of Business Conduct

As a guide to understanding different types of business conduct, Walton classifies six models of conduct.[9]

1. The austere model. It gives almost exclusive emphasis to ownership interests and profit objectives.

2. The household model. Following the concept of an extended family, this model emphasizes employee jobs, benefits, and paternalism.

3. The vendor model. In this model, consumer interests, tastes, and rights dominate the organization.

4. The investment model. This model focuses on the organization as an entity and thus on long-term profits and survival. In the name of enlightened self-interest it gives some recognition to social investments along with economic ones.

5. The civic model. Its slogan is corporate citizenship. It goes beyond imposed obligations, accepts social responsibility, and makes a positive commitment to social needs.

6. The artistic model. This model encourages the organization to become a creative instrument serving the cause of an advanced civilization with a better quality of life. The organization's people perform in the manner of artists, building some of their own creative ideas into the institution's actions, leading it toward new contributions not originally contemplated.

The six models may be thought of as points on a continuum from low to high social responsibility. Regardless of the model sought by an organization, one of its most important jobs is to establish and blend its values together so that they become a consistent, effective system that is known and accepted by claimants. The system must be strong enough to withstand challenges by partisan pressure groups, but flexible enough to move with a changing society. Establishing and maintaining an organizational value system is a difficult management task.

Written Codes of Conduct

Business conduct standards are expressed in meetings, bulletins, company magazines, employee statements, policy manuals, and countless other ways.

[9]Clarence C. Walton, *Corporate Social Responsibilities,* Belmont, Calif.: Wadsworth Publishing Company, Inc., 1967, pp. 122–141.

Many organizations also have a written code of conduct or creed which establishes the general value system that the firm tries to apply. Written creeds are developed in order to define organizational purpose, establish a uniform ethical climate within the organization, and provide guides for consistent decision making.

Written creeds are especially important for large organizations, branch units, and franchisers. These types of organizations tend to have complex structures, difficult lines of communication, and regional, national, or even international images which they are trying to project. Retail franchisers usually find that systemwide standards are necessary because clients expect a uniform quality of service. Consider, for example, the rapid growth of Kentucky Fried Chicken based on a uniform product and Holiday Inns based on a dependable standard of service.

Figure 10-1 presents a short code of conduct for an electronics firm. The code presents a generalized ideal that the firm seeks to attain, and this ideal is supplemented by policies which explain how the ideals will be achieved. Observe that the code recognizes obligations to each of the main claimant groups affecting the business—employees, owners, customers, and the community and general society. Codes of this type help people both within and without the firm realize that the firm is not serving any single interest, such as stockholders or employees alone, but is seeking to balance the interests of several claimants on the organization. These codes also give employees a sense of purpose, because they show employees that the firm is providing useful outputs needed and wanted by various segments of society.

The codes of some firms deal directly and specifically with abuses that tend to occur in their industry. An example is the code of an air-conditioning firm that says: "We will not extend hidden discounts or gratuities." With regard to customer complaints, this same code adds: "We will assume full responsibility for the satisfactory performance of installations designed and installed by us and will make prompt and cheerful corrections of our mistakes." In this instance the firm believed so strongly in its own efforts for integrity that it was willing to have an unbiased arbitrator adjudicate its disputes: "In the event of controversy with a customer, or his representative, which cannot be amicably settled, we agree to submit the matter to arbitration."

Large firms face ethical issues of conduct every day, but occasionally they face crises that test the integrity of management. For its 1973-model automobiles the Ford Motor Company faced a decision about whether to report a violation of automobile emission test standards. Top management discovered that certain lower management personnel in the engine division performed unauthorized maintenance during emission tests. If the unauthorized maintenance was reported to the Environmental Protection Administration, the tests would be voided and new tests would be required which would delay introduction of 1973 models. Ford officials did report the unauthorized maintenance. For a time it appeared that emergency action by Congress might be required to allow the company to keep producing automobiles, but finally the problems were solved with some delay in introduction of new models.

Considering company codes as a whole, one weakness is that they are sometimes stated for their public relations value and not really made an actuality within the company. One of the greatest limitations of codes is that those who prepare them assume that the meaning and feeling shared at the time they are written can be transferred to others by distributing a document for others to read. This is not so. Conduct codes are too complex and full of values to be conveyed in a few written words. For this reason, businesses use participation in planning a code in order to build more understanding and commitment to it. In addition, reevaluations in which there is wide participation will help maintain standards. Equal in importance with participation is the necessity for higher managers to support the code by example, because the standards they set will tend to be the ones others use, regardless of what the written statement says.

Specific areas of conduct are illustrated by the following discussion of conflict of interest and business gifts. Other areas are examined in subsequent chapters in connection with the subject to which they apply.

PRINCIPLES OF BUSINESS CONDUCT

Since its establishment our company has been, and continues to be, dedicated to the following Principles of Business Conduct.

ARTICLE I
TO MAINTAIN . . .
the human dignity and self-respect of the individual by supporting a sound and equitable program of human relations and by providing the opportunity for self-expression and personal growth.

ARTICLE II
TO EARN . . .
a fair profit to make possible the economic stability and growth of the company and to provide a just return on the investment of the stockholder.

ARTICLE III
TO MERIT . . .
the respect and confidence of our customers, suppliers, and competitors by maintaining the highest standards of product quality and service at fair prices.

ARTICLE IV
TO SUPPORT . . .
worthwhile community programs and to encourage employees to participate in important community affairs.

ARTICLE V
TO FULFILL . . .
our responsibility to society and government by conducting our business in a manner that will earn trust and confidence.

ARTICLE VI
TO REQUIRE . . .
that our employees refrain from actions which constitute a conflict of interest.

ARTICLE VII
TO PERPETUATE . . .
our priceless heritage of complete integrity in the conduct of all our operations.

Figure 10-1 Code of conduct of an electronics firm.

Conflict of Interest

A *conflict of interest,* such as mentioned in Figure 10-1, arises when an employee, either management or nonmanagement, has an interest in a transaction or is a party to a transaction that is so substantial that it reasonably might affect his independent judgment in his acts for the business. Both purchasing and sales are special areas of sensitivity, but the situation could exist anywhere.

One area of conflict of interest is substantial financial investment in a supplier, customer, or distributor. Usually it is acceptable to hold a small percentage of stock in a publicly owned supplier, especially when it is listed on a public stock exchange. The amount of ownership permitted varies. In one company it is 10 percent of outstanding stock; in another it is 0.1 percent. Another criterion is the percentage of the employee's total investment funds involved in this one investment. Some companies require key executives and purchasing agents to disclose outside business interests. One company's standard reads as follows: "Any member of management who has assumed, or is about to assume, a financial or other outside business relationship that might involve a conflict of interest must immediately inform his supervisor of the circumstances involved."

Another area of conflict of interest is the use of privileged information or one's official position to make transactions for personal gain. An example is the purchase or sale of real estate whose value might be affected by company activities.

In its totality, conflict of interest is difficult to control because of its many variations and dependence on personal interpretation. For these reasons, the most effective approach is self-discipline by ethically oriented individuals; however, management needs to provide a basic code to encourage uniform action and to provide follow-up to assure that a few unprincipled persons do not pull down the whole level of ethical practice. In the last analysis, a company's conduct can never be better than its people.

Business Gifts and Entertainment

Related to conflict of interest are business gifts, particularly those which are of more than nominal value and might influence a business decision of the person receiving it. Nominal value is, of course, difficult to define, and there are many situational and cultural variables which must be interpreted to determine appropriateness of a gift. Consider the following situation.

Walker Wright made a $70 business transaction with the Jones Company, using the services of a Jones employee named Baxter. Wright usually dealt with Baxter in his transactions with the Jones Company; so, when he completed his $70 transaction, he left Baxter a cash gift of $10 which he hoped would influence Baxter to continue his good service.

Conduct Guidelines on Sales Promotion and Gifts in a Manufacturing Firm

Sales Promotion

Our reputation for integrity is a priceless asset and the product of continuous effort by all of us. The truth, well told, must be the objective of all our promotional efforts.

A momentary advantage gained through even slight misrepresentation or exaggeration can jeopardize our future success. This applies equally to our personal discussions with others about our company and to our promotional efforts. Our company's reputation is completely in our hands, to be enhanced or damaged by the nature of our actions.

Gifts

It is official company policy that neither our company nor its employees may at any time give gifts to, or accept gifts from, any competitive company, supplier, or customer, or their representatives.

In this situation was Wright trying to influence Baxter? Yes, he was. Was the gift nominal? That depends on interpretation, but we still need more cultural and situational information before we can determine the ethical appropriateness of the gift. For example, if the Jones Company is an office supply company and Wright is the office manager of a small five-person office, what would be your answer? What would your answer be if Wright were a sales manager taking four clients to dinner at his favorite restaurant and leaving a tip for the waiter, Baxter? In this instance the tip is an established way of trying to influence good service, and it is even included by the employer in computing appropriate wages for his waiters.

In determining appropriateness of a gift, factors such as the following need to be evaluated: value of gift, purpose of gift, the circumstances in which it occurred (for example, more leniency at the Christmas season and for store openings), influence sensitivity of the recipient (such as a purchasing agent), and general cultural practices (i.e., accepted business practice). In application of these criteria, for example, an advertising item of nominal value with the donor's name imprinted thereon, such as a mechanical pencil or an appointment calendar, is usually an acceptable gift. It has low value, has a purpose which is an accepted business practice (advertising), and is given under open circumstances (name imprinted thereon).

In an effort to keep gifts within reasonable bounds most firms have guides restricting employee acceptance of gifts. Some are informally communicated, while others are quite specific, such as no gifts of more than $10 value, received not oftener than annually.

Entertainment of customers and suppliers is usually defined separately from gifts. Entertainment is an accepted business practice and is much more liberally interpreted because it is a social situation in which business affairs are conducted. One company informally distinguishes entertainment from gifts as follows: "If you can eat it or drink it on the spot, it's entertainment." Applying this definition and the $10 gift rule just mentioned, a business dinner costing $15 at an expensive club is permitted entertainment, but the gift of a $15 ham is prohibited. Entertainment is generally controlled through expense account policies and rules.

CONDUCT GUIDES OFFERED BY OTHERS

The conduct of a business is influenced strongly by external organizations which interact with it. These organizations may be classified as professional associations, business associations, and public advisory grousp.

Professional Associations

As occupational groups professionalize, they tend to develop codes of conduct which support fairness, full disclosure, independent decisions free of influence, and other actions in the public interest. These codes govern the conduct of their members in business and thereby determine minimum standards of conduct in their jobs. The codes also spill over into surrounding functions and eventually become adopted by the whole business. The standards for buying and selling sponsored by the National Association of Purchasing Management, for example, surely encouraged the growth of companywide policies on gift giving and acceptance.

Professional codes normally apply to professional conduct of a person both as an employee and as a businessman seeking consulting contracts or managing a firm providing professional services. Thus, an architectural firm and an engineering consulting firm are governed by codes of their profession. For example, the code of the American Society of Civil Engineers states that the civil engineer "shall not create obligation on prospective clients or employers through extravagant entertainment, gifts, or similar expenditures," and "He shall not engage in 'fee splitting' or other distribution of fees for other than services performed and in proportion to the value of such services." In this manner business conduct is governed directly, as well as indirectly, by codes of professional associations.

It appears that codes of ethics established by occupational groups, especially professional groups, are an excellent way to develop higher standards of business conduct. Even though the influence of these codes is mostly indirect, it is powerful because it brings the weight of professional opinion on business. Since professional codes are developed democratically by those who must live by them, they earn strong commitment from members. Their image is favorable because they are a means to achieve status and public recognition for an occupation. Originating with many groups, these codes offer avenues for experimentation and variety in the search for better standards of conduct. They can work their way piece by piece into organizational life, proving their value as they go.

A major advantage of professional codes is their democratic gradualism. Reformers would have businesses suddenly change into ethical models by edict from the president, but conversions of this type seldom stick. The democratic gradualism represented by professional codes tends to be more lasting. These codes are not substitutes for internal codes within each organization, but they are an important adjunct to them. In a number of cases they serve to stimulate a business to develop better internal codes.

Business Associations

There are hundreds of business associations representing specific groups such as florists, retail druggists, and soft drink bottlers. These groups are primarily operating to promote their own interests, but in doing this they often find it necessary to set ethical standards for dealing with consumers and others. A primary reason for these standards is to control unscrupulous members and to maintain a public image for services fairly and reasonably rendered.

Florists, for example, in order to join an association for telegraphic delivery of flowers from one city to another must agree to inspections to assure that flowers ordered from a distant city have been delivered. Without inspections it would be relatively easy and "safe" for a florist to substitute flowers of lesser quality in a funeral bouquet and pocket the difference. The inspection discourages potential dishonesty and maintains a public image of dependability by expelling offenders. Individual florists are under pressure to maintain high standards, because if they are expelled from the organization, they cannot participate in this additional source of business.

One business group which has achieved national prominence for its recommendations, especially regarding business policy for social action, is the Committee for Economic Development (CED). It is a select group of about 200 business leaders, including some educators. It is nonprofit, nonpartisan, and nonpolitical. Its reports and recommendations represent carefully developed, balanced viewpoints oriented toward general public benefit rather than partisan needs of business. The CED represents primarily a managerial ideology, the kind found among career managers in larger businesses.

Public Advisory Groups

Various claimant groups in the general society offer business proposed standards which they wish it to adopt. There are hundreds of these groups, including religious groups, foundations, minorities, and ecology groups; and they represent the greatest source of pressure for business change. One difficulty with these external pressure groups is that there are so many different views among them that a firm may find itself caught between opposing views. For example, some groups want United States multinational firms to refrain from imposing American culture on other nations. On the other hand, other groups want American culture imposed to provide equality for minorities and women because they feel these are "moral issues" which merit outside force.

There are significant differences between the approaches taken by professional associations, discussed earlier, and public advisory groups. The professional groups self-generate a code for their own self-control, both in business and out of it. They seek to raise their own standards for their own betterment and as an example to others. Advisory groups, on the other hand, seek to raise the standards of others. They say to business: "This is the way we think you ought to live if you want to live better." This kind of advice is useful, but it is of a different quality than professional codes. It lacks the reality that being on the inside can bring, and it lacks the personal commitment that self-generated standards for one's self can provide. Sometimes it has the taint of the ivory tower because it comes from the "sayers," not the "doers."

The most effective way that a business can distinguish helpful advice from unrealistic, poorly founded, or partisan advice is to open lines of communication with advisory groups and listen attentively to all that they have to say. They are a valid source of inputs into business. These inputs show the kinds of issues that are troubling society, and they give some feedback to business about how its social posture is being evaluated. While not all solutions offered will be useful, some solutions are likely to be; therefore it is worth screening all of them in order to gain the better ones. If business is to operate as an open system, it really has no other choice than to listen to the voice of claimants who feel that they have a valuable input for business. In a sense open communication is business's social obligation to the community in return for business's charter to operate as a leading social institution.

SUMMARY

There is a growing interest in business values because of business's dominant position in society. Surveys show that most businessmen are aware of value issues, believe that there are some unethical practices in business, and want to improve standards of conduct. Since businessmen mediate among many claimants and value systems, they must make frequent value judgments. Codes of conduct give them useful guides for making proper judgments. Two social purposes of business conduct guidelines are to assure a balance of responsibility with power and to help business become more effective as a social institution.

Professional associations, business associations, and public advisory groups help business establish and maintain effective codes. Professional codes of conduct are especially effective because they focus on the public interest, are self-generated, develop gradually, earn strong psychological commitment from members, and maintain indirect as well as direct influences on business.

STUDY GUIDES FOR INTERPRETATION OF THIS CHAPTER

1. Discuss arguments both for and against the conduct of Regis Discount Furniture and the meat packer mentioned at the beginning of this chapter.

2. Discuss the historical events and conditions which triggered greater attention to business values and codes of conduct in the 1960s.

3. You are president of a bank which is building a new branch in a middle-class neighborhood. Indicate ways in which the following value systems may apply to your decisions about this new branch: technical, economic, psychological, political, and aesthetic.

4. Discuss some of the value considerations, such as unfair gain or harm, which help define ethical guidelines for business.

5. It is said that professional codes are especially effective in improving business standards. Why? How many of the reasons given apply also to codes developed by business associations?

PROBLEMS
The Medical Gifts

For years it has been the practice of pharmaceutical companies to aid students in medical schools with medical gifts, such as plastic models of human organs and samples of company drug products. This practice occurred with the knowledge and implied approval of medical schools which sometimes cooperated in distributing the gifts. The practice originated with two purposes in mind: (1) to provide informational advertising of company products, and (2) to aid students in the arduous and expensive task of completing medical school.

Recently the Blazer Corporation sent samples of some of its popular drug products to seniors at Eastern Medical School. The wholesale value of each sample kit was about $50. Shortly thereafter an organized group of twenty-four students returned the samples, protesting that the donor was trying to buy their loyalty. The students released their letter to news media and received favorable national publicity for their action.

1. In the role of marketing manager, what response, if any, would you make to the students, and why?

2. In the same role, what response, if any, would you make within the firm, and why? Is it possible for conditions to change, making a formerly accepted practice now unacceptable? In this case what pertinent conditions have changed?

3. The Blazer Corporation also gives three student scholarships to Eastern Medical School. The scholarships bear the Blazer name. Their annual cost is nine times the cost of the drugs sent to Eastern seniors. Further, the cost of medical scholarships given by Blazer to all schools is five times the cost of drugs given to all schools and their students. Should the company reconsider its scholarship policy, and why?

The Advertising Episode

The advertisement of a food company showed an animated cartoon of a bandit making a holdup to secure the advertised food product because he craved it so greatly. The scene then shifted to regular photography of a household where a family member was enthusiastically sneaking a bite of the advertised food, and this person was also labeled a bandit. The entire theme was comical.

The cartoon bandit was a person who appeared to be Mexican-American, and the household bandit appeared to be an Anglo-American. In one state a representative of the Mexican-American Anti-defamation Committee approached the program director of a television station and asked him to discontinue showing the commercial because it portrayed Mexican-Americans as thieves.

The advertising code of this station contained the following statement: "Taste and Decency: Advertising shall be free of statements, illustrations, or implications which are offensive to good taste or public decency." The population proportion of Mexican-Americans living within the viewing area covered by this station was approximately 15 percent.

1. As program director, what factors would you consider in your response to the protest? What action would you finally take, and why?

The Prince Company

The Prince Company is a producer of cosmetics for men and women. Its products are sold throughout the United States, and for the last thirty years it has had a very favorable growth pattern. All the firm's manufacturing operations are in two plants, one each in the Eastern and Western United States. There are warehouses and district sales offices in a number of other locations.

Recently the president of a regional black militant organization approached the firm and secured an interview with the president. He produced evidence that the black community buys 15 percent of the firm's products, and he insisted that he would expose the company's irresponsibility toward minorities unless it gives blacks 15 percent of the company's jobs. He also demanded that the company give black business 15 percent of its business spending, including purchases, banking, advertising, insurance, and other services.

The evidence of 15 percent black consumers was not gathered scientifically by the militant, but the president's own internal sources indicate that the figure is approximately correct. Investigation by the president disclosed that black employment in the firm is 9 percent in a community in which 10 percent of the labor force is black. Three percent of the managerial group is black. Business conducted with black business is estimated to be about 4 percent of the company's business.

1. As the president, what will you do in this situation? Explain in detail.

2. What are the social responsibilities of the firm in this situation?

The Peabody Company

The Peabody Company is a major producer of chemicals in the United States. International sales are about 10 percent of the company's business. Top management's policy with regard to environmental pollution is to meet fully all legal requirements for its prevention, but to go no further than the minimum required by law. Management believes that any pollution control beyond the requirements of law will reduce the firm's competitiveness, because other firms which meet only minimum requirements will have lower costs.

Recently a group of dissident young managers in the firm have become disenchanted with management's policy. They believe that the firm has a social responsibility to go much further than the minimum required by law, and as an example they cite a successful competitor that is known for its outstanding pollution control efforts.

1. The men requested an appointment to present their case to the company president. As president how would you respond to them?

2. The men talked with the company president but were not satisfied with his uncompromising attitude. They asked his permission to present their case to the next meeting of the board of directors. As president how would you respond?

3. Assume that the dissidents, following an unsatisfactory response from the president, called newspapers and issued a formal news release condemning the firm's policy. As president what would you do? If you were the supervisor of one of the dissidents and you learned of his participation in the news release, what would you do?

4. Assume that following an unsatisfactory response from the president the dissidents took no further action; however, the following week one of the engineering dissidents made a speech before his professional engineering meeting in the community condemning the president and the company for its policy. You are the man's supervisor and have reliable evidence of his actions. What would you do?

PART 3

**BUSINESS AND
ITS PUBLICS**

THE BUSINESS INTERFACE WITH GOVERNMENT

We are in an economy which more and more is being politically directed and ordered.

Louis T. Rader[1]

Jack Smith grew up outside a small town in a forest country of the Northern United States. Like most of his friends, he attended public schools. At the outbreak of World War II, Jack entered the Army and served four years. Upon discharge, he enrolled in the state university and received his degree with support from the federal government's GI Bill of Rights.

After graduation, he moved to the Rocky Mountains and obtained a job with a lumber company. Shortly thereafter he married and bought a home with a federal Veterans Administration guaranteed mortgage. Jack was smart and capable. He advanced rapidly with his company and was able to save money. With the help of a federal Small Business Administration loan, he built a sawmill and entered business on his own. He was, at the same time, the successful bidder in a timber sale held by the United States Forest Service.

Because Jack was a veteran, he received priority in bidding on some land which the United States Bureau of Land Management was selling at public auction. He was successful in obtaining a small parcel of land and built a modest home on it. His retired parents soon moved into the house, where they lived comfortably with the aid of their Social Security checks.

As Jack became more firmly established in business, he became more interested in local and state development. Under a federal program, he was instrumental in having his town declared a recreation area, which made it eligible

[1]Louis T. Rader, "Will Management Be Automated by 1975?" *Management Science,* July 1968, p. 721.

to receive federal funds to develop recreation. A park and swimming pool were built. He was also active in getting the government to build a large dam and irrigation project close to town. He was appointed to the state planning commission and was elected to the state chamber of commerce.

One day Jack wrote to his congressman: "I urge you to do everything in your power to curb increasing governmental give-away programs. Government's willingness to enter virtually every phase of private and business life is rapidly destroying the American heritage of individualism. In addition, the high taxes which businessmen must pay to support these programs are rapidly destroying the profit motive and sapping the vitality of the business system. I demand that you exert all effort to preserve free competition and our laissez faire tradition."

To illustrate a different point of view toward government-business relationships, consider the case of Bill Jones. Bill was born and grew up in a medium-sized Eastern town in which there were two major employers. One of the major employers was a large privately owned manufacturing company. In addition to being a major source of employment for local townspeople, the company was also the major taxpayer in the community. The other major employer was a large government installation, and because it was a government installation, it paid no taxes at all.

Bill's father owned and operated a successful medium-sized business in the community. While he was by no means rich, Bill's father had ample financial resources to educate his son outside the public school system. Bill received his early education in a parochial school, and during his high school years, he attended a private boys' school.

Bill's father believed strongly in business involvement in community affairs. He not only gave generously of his own time but also encouraged employees at all levels in his company to become involved in important community projects. His company usually contributed relatively large sums of money to these projects.

After finishing high school, Bill entered the armed forces. During Bill's absence, his father retired and lived comfortably from investments and annuities which he had accumulated during his business career.

Bill applied for and received a four-year college scholarship from the Ford Foundation. He attended a private university where he majored in sociology.

After graduation Bill accepted a job with the government as a sociologist. He now often makes speeches on the immorality of business and the failure of the private sector to meet needs of society. He urges more involvement by the government in the operation of the economic system.

Both Jack Smith and Bill Jones follow idealistic concepts. Smith, although he has gained much from government, follows idealistic concepts of individualism and laissez faire which are far removed from modern reality. He wants the benefits of government without its interference. Jones, although he has gained much from private enterprise, follows an idealistic concept of the social ethic and of bureaucracy and monolithic central planning. Neither view is wrong. What is important is that both business and government, and their representatives, agree on what kind of socioeconomic system we should have.

THE LAISSEZ FAIRE TRADITION: A FICTION?

Like Jack Smith and Bill Jones, thousands of businessmen and government officials today are deeply concerned about government-business relationships. Also, like these two men, most of these same people enjoy a vast variety of benefits which stem directly from the free enterprise system and from government participation in the system.

A Dual Ideology

John R. Bunting has pointed out that most businessmen are victims of dual economic ideology.[2] They are, according to Bunting, happily inconsistent, arguing on the one hand for a pure form of free enterprise and decrying unrestrained competition on the other. To illustrate, he contrasts two speeches given before a convention of businessmen. In the first speech a businessman thoroughly denounced "price chiselers" and accused them of "leading us back to cutthroat competition." "The only way to ensure profits," the speaker continued, "is to stick together, keep prices high, and maybe push them higher." Bunting, then a Federal Reserve officer, followed with a speech entitled "Free Markets and the Federal Reserve System." In his speech, Bunting explained ". . . how the Federal Reserve, by its decision to stop pegging government bonds, had helped to start a trend back to free-market principles." Although the speeches contradicted each other, the audience made no distinction. They agreed with both speakers.

Businessmen do appear to have a schizophrenic philosophy toward the roles of business and government in the national economy. The reason businessmen seem to be inconsistent is that modern business philosophies are a blend of those portions of classical and modern economic models which best fit their needs. When a businessman says he believes in the free enterprise system and laissez faire, he does not mean that he accepts Adam Smith's laissez faire and pure competition. He is talking about something else. How a businessman feels about a particular act of government depends on how it affects him. For example, in a major Eastern city many businessmen who believe in free enterprise opposed the efforts of a large store to sell nationally labeled whiskeys at a price below that set by the state liquor control agency. Apparently their own financial interests and other values in the situation took precedence over the value of free competition.

[2]John R. Bunting, *The Hidden Face of Free Enterprise: The Strange Economics of the American Businessman,* New York: McGraw-Hill Book Company, 1964.

Modern Concepts of Competition and Laissez Faire

While businessmen, over time, have professed a belief in perfect competition and laissez faire, they have recognized, to an increasing degree, that these economic models simply do not fit the realities of today's economic system.

Businessmen today have modified these theories to fit their needs. For the modern businessman, pursuit of self-interest means securing and holding a competitive advantage. Laissez faire means to him minimum interference with *his* pursuit of self-interest and maximum support of his endeavors. The modern businessman often views the problem emotionally, so that when he advocates cuts in government spending, he often means in all areas or regions except his own. Or when he encourages free trade and cutting tariffs, he usually means in all areas except his own. For example, when a recent decision to close a number of military establishments in various parts of the country was announced, floods of letters poured into Washington from businessmen in the affected areas protesting the closing of *their* installation.

Business efforts of the type described are not necessarily wrong. On the contrary, they add strength and vitality to the economic system. What is important is that both business and government, as two major agents of society, agree upon what kind of system is best. Businessmen's thinking, reflected in their speeches and actions, appears to affirm their belief in monopolistic competition and their rejection of a pure laissez faire philosophy. On the other hand, government's actions often appear to emphasize a belief in a weakly modified form of pure competition. What is needed by each is an understanding of the other's basic philosophy. Failure to understand and respect the other's point of view will result in continued conflict.

The focus of this chapter is on the general roles of government and business in the American free enterprise system. More and more, business is becoming involved in what have traditionally been considered nonbusiness problems of society. In the following section we discuss the growing concern in the business community regarding the business image and the growing role of business in coping with social problems. Then we proceed to various relations between government and business. Finally we discuss the roles of business and businessmen in politics and the separate and joint responsibilities of each for a strong national economy.

THE BUSINESS IMAGE

Businessmen's concern over public views of business is nothing new. Indeed, businessmen have been fighting against an unfavorable public image for hundreds of years. People have distrusted the business system to one degree or another since the earliest forms of business emerged. But people throughout the world and over time seem simultaneously to have held two opposing views of business. Since business has been the prime mover in economic development over the centuries, people have looked favorably upon economic results generated by business. Job opportunities, investment opportunities, and a constant flow of new and improved products have led a majority of people to accept and encourage business growth. On the other hand, a deep and persisting fear remains that too much economic power has been concentrated in big business. This fear is reflected in periodic waves of restrictive public policy directed toward the business system.

A Socially Unstable Image

In America, the public attitude toward business has been remarkably inconsistent, vacillating between support and encouragement of business growth and attacks on concentrations of economic power. These attitudes are, in turn, reflected in ever-changing public policy toward business, which has left businessmen unsure of their economic behavior. Public attitudes toward business seem to be a function of national emergencies. Figure 11-1 shows the relationship, over time, between public confidence in and public suspicion of the American business system. During periods of national emergencies, such as war, when national security depended upon performance of America's productive powers, public confidence in business has always been high. National need for production has been accompanied by reductions in restrictive policies and emphasis on policies which favored business integration and increased capital accumulations.

On the other hand, during periods of national crisis resulting from internal economic and social disorders, when national well-being depended, as it did during the Depression of the 1930s, on something other than America's technological and production abilities, business seemed either unable or unwilling to respond. The result was a wave of legislation which restricted and modified business activities.

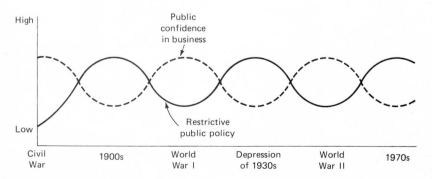

Figure 11-1 Historical relationships between public confidence in business and government restrictions on business.

Today's Challenge

In the 1970s the United States faces numerous serious social problems of major proportions. Urban congestion, ghetto poverty, education of disadvantaged citizens, transportation deficiencies, and air and water pollution are some of the major issues. In a variety of ways and from a variety of sources, business is under attack for either contributing to the problems or for failing to devote enough effort toward solutions.

Businessmen are keenly aware of the demands being made upon them by society and are struggling not only to enhance the image of business as a socially responsible institution, but also to find answers to the question of how best to accomplish the tasks ahead. In increasing numbers, business leaders are accepting the challenge of social problems. The question bothering most business leaders today is not whether business should participate in solutions to social problems, but how and to what extent.

Many business leaders have concluded that the problems are so large and so complex that no single social institution working alone can solve them. Instead, many are becoming increasingly convinced that only a partnership between the major institutions of American society—particularly government and business—can achieve national social and economic objectives.

HOW MUCH GOVERNMENT?

In the history of America there has never been a question (as many people would like to believe) of whether or not there would be government participation in the business system. The Constitution itself provided for certain government intervention, but it stressed minimum intervention. At the same time both the Declaration of Independence and the Constitution stressed individual rights and equality of individuals. These assertions, along with social philosophies of pragmatism, social Darwinism, and the Protestant ethic, combined to suggest that the best government is the least government. Nevertheless, throughout the development of the American social system the question has persisted: What kind and how much government intervention is appropriate? In light of today's complex social demands the roles and responsibilities of government and other major social institutions are again being reexamined.

Big Business and Big Government

Originally the rationale for increasing government involvement in the social system was to limit and control the growth and power of big business. But business has continued to grow. So has the size and power of government. Some American businesses have incomes that exceed the gross national product of some developing countries. At the same time the federal budget is over $200 billion, which is more than the combined spending of all Presidents from Washington through the first two terms of Franklin D. Roosevelt. The Chief Executive deals with twelve Cabinet departments, approximately fifty independent agencies, and some fifty interagency committees. And to make the whole organization function, the government employs over 2½ million people. The federal government is the biggest spender, the biggest employer, the biggest property owner, the biggest tenant, the biggest insurer, the biggest lender, the biggest borrower, and the biggest customer in the free world.

As government has grown, it has been subject to many of the same criticisms that have been directed toward big business—particularly the criticism that bigness breeds too much power. Government does exercise broad powers which many businessmen consider to be violations of individual liberties. They condemn increasing authoritarian control by government with its restrictions and regulations. They contend that excessive government involvement in the private sector of our economy has a demoralizing effect which invites evasions of laws, destroys the American innovative spirit, crushes the profit motive, and therefore dilutes the strength and vitality of the economy. Many among this group cry for a return to the good old days of laissez faire.

Both business and government have grown tremendously, and they will continue to grow. But, utopian pleas to return to the "good old days" will do little to develop strong business-government relationships. Those who make utopian pleas often view government as a powerful enemy bent on destroying what is left of the free enterprise system. They want less government. Conversely, some segments of society view business as a hostile and self-centered force which is completely insensitive to the needs of society and dedicated only to self-aggrandizement. These groups urge more government power and more government involvement in social and economic problems. A more enlightened point of view was expressed by Roger Blough when he said:[3]

> Blind opposition [by business] to governmental growth and to the enlargement of government power can, I believe, be as disastrous to the progress of this economic revolution as the failure to guard our freedoms with discerning vigilance. The idea that government must be the natural and irreconcilable enemy of the individual and his enterprises is—it seems to me—as anachronistic in this day and age as the outworn Marxist doctrine of eternal enmity between owner and employee.

The Concept of Functionalism

In a modern, complex society, there is plenty for everyone to do Obviously, some jobs which are necessary to society's well-being can best be done by

---

[3]Roger M. Blough, "The Real Revolutionaries" (address before the Whirlpool Corporation Management Club, Benton Harbor, Mich., Sept. 15, 1963), New York: United States Steel Corporation, 1963, p. 15.

government. Equally obvious is the fact that other jobs can best be performed by business. This is the concept of functionalism, which holds that social functions should be performed by the institutions which can do them most efficiently. National defense, reclamation, and policing activities appear to be functionally appropriate jobs for government. On the other hand, research and development, product planning, product decisions, actual production, and market innovation appear to be appropriate business functions.

In simple societies division and assignment of social functions usually appear to be uncomplicated matters, with functions relatively well defined and clearly delegated to one institution. But as societies advance economically and socially, they also become more complex, and the concept of functionalism becomes less easy to apply. Not only are social problems more difficult to define because they are more complex, but lines of responsibility become blurred as well, and questions of who can do things best are not always clear.

World War II is an excellent example of functionalism. If the war effort did nothing else, it unified competing social groups in a way seldom before possible. The national objective of victory was clearly defined and was accepted by each societal subgroup. Each group clearly understood and accepted what its inputs should be. Government set priorities and provided funds, business provided technical and managerial know-how, labor provided an uninterrupted supply of manpower to make the national defense machine work, consumers were willing to forgo consumer goods, investors were willing to accept lower returns, and so on. The point is, that for one of the few times in American history all the subgroups had a common objective toward which they could make positive contributions and receive satisfactory social payouts.

World War II also laid the foundations for extensive reexamination of the social and economic systems and raised serious questions about established concepts of functionalism. Social philosophies and value systems have undergone marked changes, and the social turbulence which has resulted from these changes has produced new and unfamiliar contingency models of social responsibility with which managers in both business and government must work. These changes have produced an environment which is radically different from anything business or government has heretofore experienced.

New social values and philosophies are often in direct conflict with traditional, well-established values of managers in business and government, and these managers often find themselves in a kind of social vertigo with no familiar horizons to guide them. However, within the new contingency models there is developing a reallocation of traditional functional responsibilities. Jobs which were once considered to be the domain of government are in certain instances being shifted to private business. Examples of responsibilities that have shifted from government to business are providing community services such as garbage disposal, financing high-risk minority businesses, training hard-core unemployed, and improving the quality of national waterways. Similarly, functions which were once considered to be solely business functions are now being shifted to, or at least shared by, government. Examples of functional responsibilities that have shifted from business to government are setting product standards such as automobile emission standards, enforcing product quality, and allocating productive resources. Courtney C. Brown summarized the changing functional relationships between business and government by commenting: "More of the methods of business are getting into government and more of the purposes of government are getting into business."[4]

The Vital Partnership

As our society becomes more complex and as social problems become more severe, there is an increasing business recognition of the need for joint action by business and government. Former Secretary of Commerce John T. Connor called this joint action "the vital partnership."[5]

Evidence of this emerging need for the vital partnership became apparent in late 1968 during a symposium in which ten members of the Committee for Economic Development (CED) were asked to present their views on how corporations can help solve some of the social and economic problems facing America today. All agreed that American business must become more involved in social problems. The consensus was "that the corporation as such should identify those social problems on which its particular resources and skills can be most effectively brought to bear, and make these virtually as much a part of its business objectives as traditional commercial activities."[6]

When a similar conference was held in 1971 by the Conference Board, business leaders again expressed the need for more cooperation between business and government.[7] The same theme also appears, from time to time, in public speeches by thoughtful business leaders. For example, H. Robert Sharbaugh, president of Sun Oil Company, expressed this view:[8]

> Government's role today is not essentially that of policeman or regulator or manager of the economy. Rather, in the area of its own expert knowledge, government's role is much more nearly that of a senior partner in a group of interrelated institutions, including business and education, which seek jointly to establish national priorities and develop public policies responsive to the needs of people.

[4]Courtney C. Brown, "The Fading of an Ideology," in Robert W. Miller (ed.), *The Creative Interface,* Washington: The American University, 1968, p. 39.
[5]John T. Connor, "The Vital Partnership," in ibid., p. 3.
[6]Emilio G. Collado, "Toward a More Productive Dialogue," *Saturday Review,* Jan. 13, 1968, p. 62.
[7]*Business Leadership in Social Change: Report on a Public Affairs Conference,* New York: The Conference Board, 1971.
[8]H. Robert Sharbaugh, "Meeting the Challenges of the 70's" (speech before the Petroleum and Petrochemical Division of the American Institute of Chemical Engineers, Houston, Tex., Mar. 1, 1971).

In the broadest sense the vital partnership should not be limited only to business and government. Other social institutions such as organized labor should also be included because they too have a stake in and contribute to social well-being. However, because this book is about business, we shall discuss only the roles of business and government. Like any other partnership, if it is to be successful, roles of the partners in the vital partnership need to be clearly defined and agreed upon. While there is increasing agreement that a partnership between business and government is desirable, few seem entirely sure of what the role of each partner should be.

The Public-Private Corporation

An example of the vital partnership at work is the public-private corporation. Public-private corporations are the result of attempts to identify a specific public purpose and fulfill those purposes by utilizing the resources and managerial capabilities of private business. An example of a public-private corporation is the Corporation for Public Broadcasting. Such enterprises are chartered by Congress, but incorporated as private corporations. The major part of the operating budget comes from federal government sources and the balance from private sources such as foundations, corporate gifts, and individual donations. Thus the stockholders are largely the American public, and the board of directors is selected by the President with the advice and consent of Congress. The major argument supporting establishment of public-private corporations is that it removes the activity from many restrictions imposed upon government managers and allows the expertise of private business to be applied to areas of public concern.

While the track record of public-private corporations is sometimes questionable, these institutions appear to provide a viable vehicle by which government can set objectives and provide funds without establishing another government agency.

THE ROLE OF GOVERNMENT

As social values and expectations change and as social and economic problems become broader and more complex, the roles and responsibilities of major social institutions are subject to continuing reexamination. Two persistent, broad, and critical questions remain unanswered. What is it exactly that we, as a society, want, and in what priority do we want these things? And who does what, and how do we direct our productive resources toward gaining the things we want? Society is trying harder than ever before to answer these questions and, through the concept of functionalism, to define the roles of institutions.

Setting Objectives

There is a growing belief among leaders, in both business and government, that government has assumed responsibilities which functionally are outside its areas of special expertise. There is also growing agreement that the special areas of government expertise are setting national objectives, providing political capacity to achieve objectives, providing funds, and accepting public accountability. Other functions may be more effectively performed by other institutions. Andrew Rouse observed: "Maybe we have come to expect more of government than it can deliver effectively. Maybe we need to get private, profit-making corporations more involved. I believe we need to invent new institutions of government. We need to mesh the skills of private management with the public need."[9]

Saying it another way, there appears to be a general feeling, especially among the business community, but shared by some in government, that the proper role of government is rule maker and referee and that it should not, at the same time, attempt also to be a player. According to Peter Drucker,[10] the proper role of government is to formulate social objectives so that they can become opportunities for other institutions to serve society. Except for a few instances, government's role is not "to do," because it is generally an inefficient performer. The reason why other institutions may accomplish many social functions better than government is that a government, by design, is a protective institution rather than a performing and creative institution. Active business executives also support the same idea. The chairman of the board of one company commented: "Government must lead. But it cannot be the sole problem solver. Its role is to define problems, articulate desired results, organize, directly and indirectly, the whole potential of the society, in a coordinated effort to remake the society and save it from destroying itself."[11]

Directing Resources

If one of the major roles of government is to establish national objectives, how are productive resources to be channeled toward achievement of these objectives? One alternative is voluntary action on the part of both consumers and producers. Voluntarism is based on the premise that in order to achieve a new order of social wants and expectations, all parties are willing to give up whatever is necessary to achieve the stated goals. This means, for example, that in order to have a clean environment or to enjoy a public transportation system at less than

[9]Andrew L. Rouse, quoted in "There Is a Threat of Losing Control," *Business Week,* Oct. 17, 1970, p. 100.

[10]Peter F. Drucker, *The Age of Discontinuity: Guidelines to Our Changing Society,* New York: Harper & Row, Publishers, Incorporated, 1968, pp. 225–242.

[11]Irwin Miller, "Business Has a War to Win," *Harvard Business Review,* March–April 1969, p. 8.

cost, people are willing to give up the intensive use of their automobiles. Voluntarism has been only modestly successful so far, and there is little evidence that the record will improve.

A second and more realistic alternative for directing productive resources toward desired social goals is through government actions, and this is the second major role of government. Roy L. Ash, while president of Litton Industries, suggested:[12]

> Government, at various levels, is the only means operating at a scale suitable for making most of the major transferences implicit in our developing new set of values. In itself it is, or can be, the market for some of our needs. More importantly, it is the only workable authority that can decide which exchanges we will make and the pace and order in which we will do so.

Government can direct productive resources through the use of several tools—taxing and spending, regulation, standards, incentives, and administrative action. These tools are already being used. Standards for acceptable automobile emission levels are a good illustration of government-imposed standards leading toward national objectives. Similarly the Water Pollution Control Act of 1972 set standards for water pollution and regulates industry's pollution practices.

While it seems clear that government should order national priorities, set objectives, and formulate rules, what is not so clear is that government has a responsibility to help business and other institutions comply with the rules. Compliance with new standards and rules often imposes heavy financial and other types of burdens on business. Therefore, government should and sometimes does come to the aid of businessmen by providing research and development funds, authorizing issues of tax-free bonds for pollution control purposes, and similar help.

THE ROLE OF BUSINESS

Changes in social values and expectations which have occurred since World War II have created for many business managers demands to which they often are poorly prepared to respond. Trained in the economics of the nineteenth and early twentieth centuries and indoctrinated with social philosophies of earlier times, businessmen have viewed themselves as being primarily responsible for high economic performance and profit. Businessmen have been accustomed to working in a predictable environment, i.e., an orderly system in which business objectives were formulated at the top of the organization and business activity was judged by economic performance. However, in recent years the public, through dramatic and

---

[12]Roy L. Ash, "Opportunities in Crisis—Realities vs. Rhetoric," in *Business Leadership in Social Change,* New York: The Conference Board, 1971, p. 16.

sometimes disruptive means, has demanded a voice in establishing business objectives. These bottom-up pressures have left business unsure of exactly what its role should be.

Most business leaders actively support community action programs in their own communities as a means of exercising social responsibility. They view involvement in community problems as good corporate citizenship. They believe that business should be involved just as other members are involved and should cooperate with other institutions in finding solutions to problems of the local community. For example, many companies have operated centers for the Job Corps; established and operated legal-aid offices for disadvantaged citizens; participated in Community Chest drives; participated in river or lake beautification projects; helped organize and finance minority businesses; and donated money, equipment, and executive talent to a variety of other community projects. In cooperation with government, business has trained hard-core unemployed and supported nondiscriminative hiring. While many of these activities have been successful in their own local areas, they have had only mimimal impact on the broad overall social problems because, in large part, they have been treating localized symptoms rather than addressing the central problems.

Profit

Many thoughtful leaders in society feel that the profit motive is the real key to bringing corporate resources to bear on the broad basic social problems. Few, if any, corporations could for long periods of time afford to channel large portions of their resources toward solutions of any problems, social or economic, without being paid for their expenditures. Many feel, to one degree or another, that business is making a social contribution by performing its economic functions effectively and efficiently. And this view is supported by at least one eminent social scientist. Theodore V. Purcell says: "I argue that management has a social responsibility to make a profit."[13]

Only by making profits, it is argued, can business maintain and increase the assets which are so necessary for solving the immense social problems facing America today. Experience has shown that direct expenditure of money, by itself, on problems such as urban decay, pollution, transportation, hard-core unemployment, and poverty has done little to produce lasting solutions. Most businessmen and many government leaders believe that these problems can be solved only by bringing to bear the research and development expertise of business along with its organizational and productive resources. These activities require a strong economic base and must be paid for from profits.

[13]Theodore V. Purcell, "Work Psychology and Business Values: A Triad Theory of Work Motivation," *Personnel Psychology,* Autumn 1967, p. 246.

Product Decisions

Closely related to producing profits is the business role of supplying society with goods and services which are consistent with changing social values. Traditionally the role of business has been to make product decisions on behalf of society, thereby allocating resources to the production of goods and services it believed society wanted. Product decisions were made on the basis of social value systems as they were perceived by business. How well products satisfied social wants was determined in the marketplace. However, as the economy has changed from one of scarcity to one of abundance, something more is being asked of business. It is being asked to provide products and services that not only satisfy consumer wants but that, at the same time, are consistent with new social values, such as ecological compatibility and consumer safety. Saying it another way, business is asked to make product decisions according to questions of not only will it sell, but is it good for the customer and society.

Assisting Government

It is becoming increasingly clear that before business can effectively work toward solutions to major social problems, there must be an adequate political and philosophical framework within which to work. For example, consider World War II or the space program, which are often cited as models of business performance. The reason that business was able to perform so well in these two situations is that explicit purposes and priorities were set forth by government and were endorsed by a large proportion of the population. But business cannot and should not try to establish that framework. George Cabot Lodge explains:[14]

> If we are speaking about a war to remake our domestic society in the U.S., then the initial prerequisite for successful conduct is the definition of the struggle, the establishment of goals and priorities, and criteria for measuring victory. When such a political and ideological framework is in place, business can work efficiently within it. For unelected businessmen, however, to suppose that they can erect such a framework is to suggest anarchy.

All this, then, suggests a new role for business—a role of strengthening government. Roy Ash suggests that ''an important role of business can be to help government develop its capabilities to function.''[15] George Cabot Lodge is more emphatic. ''Perhaps the most urgent and essential social responsibility of business

---

[14]George Cabot Lodge, ''Why an Outmoded Ideology Thwarts the New Business Conscience,'' *Fortune,* October 1970, p. 150.

[15]Ash, op. cit., p. 17.

is to contribute to the building of a more adequate political structure and authority based on a clearer, more explicit, and more realistic ideology."[16]

How business is to perform this role is the subject of the next section.

BUSINESS IN POLITICS

In recent years questions about the proper role of business in politics have been widely discussed, and many reasons both for and against corporate involvement in politics have been advanced. For example, in justifying corporate political involvement, Edwin M. Epstein comments: "Corporate political involvement enhances the quality of pluralism and provides an additional safeguard against the authoritarian potential of a mass society."[17]

Arnold Maremont, on the other hand, states:[18]

> It is my conviction that business ought, for its own good, to stay out of politics.
> I favor the widest possible participation in politics on an *individual* basis, for when it becomes the province of the elite few, our system is in danger. It is when corporations begin running political classes, conducting political schools, and urging that their executives enter the political arena to expound the corporation viewpoint that I become deeply fearful of the consequences.

Business has, to one degree or another, been involved in political activities since the founding of America, and there is every reason to believe that it will continue to be involved.

Need for Business Involvement

Most businessmen, at least those who direct large business units, feel that there is an increasing need for business involvement and that business can and should influence government wherever appropriate. David J. Galligan, in his post as director of the Citizenship Responsibility Program of the New Jersey State Chamber of Commerce, summarizes the feeling for increased involvement as follows. "What is happening in today's business-government relationship is not something new in our political process but rather an accelerated and genuine

---

[16]Lodge, op. cit., p. 152.

[17]Edwin M. Epstein, *The Corporation in American Politics,* Englewood Cliffs, N.J.: Prentice-Hall, Inc., 1969, p. 285.

[18]Arnold H. Maremont, "The Dangers of Corporate Activity in Politics," *Business Topics,* Winter 1960, p. 7. Italics in original.

interest on the part of business concerning developments that portend great changes in our free enterprise system."[19]

Many government leaders share the belief that business ought to participate in the political process to the fullest extent possible for the social benefit of all concerned. While addressing a group of businessmen, one government leader said: "As a member of government, I would urge corporate participation, through business connections, partnerships, institutions of assorted kinds, and as individuals. Politics needs you desperately, and there is no better place for business to participate in government than at the local level."[20]

The question most businessmen are grappling with is not whether business should be in politics, but rather *how and to what extent* it should be involved. Most responsible businessmen view political involvement as part of corporate citizenship; i.e., because business is one of the major social institutions, it has an obligation to become involved in the political process which directs and controls forces for social well-being. Others view political involvement as a necessary matter of self-interest. Still others think that business should be in politics to balance the power of other social institutions. For example, some feel that since labor is in politics *as labor,* business should also be in politics *as business* to balance the equation. Otherwise, labor's political power may become dominant, thereby destroying pluralism. All these views are valid. The important point is that business is a major social institution and its viewpoints are needed on major issues *where it is qualified,* just as its efforts are needed on social problems *where it is qualified.*

What Are Proper Political Activities for Business?

Businessmen need to become more concerned with governmental processes. Because of the growing complexity of government-business relationships, businessmen can ill afford to stand silent. Just as business needs the support of government to do its job, so also government needs participation by businessmen in formulating public policy. It needs advice and information from business leaders in making policy decisions, and this is true at local and state levels as well as at the federal level. But yet the nagging question remains: For the business firm, what kinds of political actions are proper?

When discussing what is or is not proper political action for business it is important to distinguish between activities a person may perform as an individual or private citizen and those he might perform as a representative or agent of his company. A good rule of thumb is that business, *as business,* should support

[19]David J. Galligan, *Politics and the Businessman,* New York: Pitman Publishing Corporation, 1964, p. 3.
[20]J. Eric Johnson, "Business and Community Goals," in *Business Leadership in Social Change,* op. cit., pp. 44–45.

The Washington Representative

Although his role has been forming for several decades it is only in the past decade that the mission of the Washington Representative has undergone drastic change in terms of emphasis and scope. This change has been caused by two significant and well known phenomena. The first of these is the growth, complexity, and involvement of government in the decision-making process of the corporation. The second is the growth of business itself. As business has grown, so has its need for information upon which to base its decisions relative to government. The sheer size and breadth of the American corporation has eliminated any semblance of isolation from government influence. Today, as never before, there is no successful American corporation that does not consider the factor of government in any major decision it makes.

From J. D. Johnson, "The Washington Representative," reprinted by permission from the May 1971 issue of the *Michigan Business Review*, p. 6, published by the Graduate School of Business Administration, The University of Michigan.

issues—not candidates. For example, no one would argue with the propriety of a company president endorsing a candidate for political office so long as it is clear that he is acting as an individual. Individuals can and should endorse any candidate they choose. But when a company president or any company officer uses his title or his company name in publicly endorsing a candidate in a paid political advertisement, this is a questionable use of company position and borders on violation of the Corrupt Practices Act, which will be discussed in the next section. It may give some persons the impression that the company—not the individual—has endorsed the candidate. While there is nothing illegal about such action, it appears inconsistent with the philosophy of corrupt practices legislation. The same reasoning applies also to union officers because the Corrupt Practices Act applies equally to them.

On the other hand, a variety of issues continually arise which affect business in diverse ways. As a good citizen in the community, business should make its viewpoints known and should support or oppose issues which it believes will be beneficial or detrimental to the community and to the business itself. Questions of business involvement in the political arena generally fall into three broad categories: financial support, providing information, and direct involvement of company personnel in the political process.

Financial Support and the Corrupt Practices Act

Financial involvement by business in political activity has been a matter of public concern since at least the beginning of this century. Early in the century legislation appeared which limited the financial participation by business in the federal election process.[21] The Tillman Act of 1907 prohibited contributions by business to campaign funds involving election to federal offices. The first objective of this law was to destroy business influence over elections; the second was to protect stockholders from use of corporate funds for political purposes to which they had not given their assent; and the third was to protect the freedom of the individual's vote. Later the Corrupt Practices Act of 1925 broadened this concept (this later became section 610 of the U.S. Criminal Code), and the Labor-Management Relations Act of 1947 (section 304) extended the prohibition to labor. Today both business and labor are by law prohibited from making donations to political campaigns from company or union funds.

In spite of the Corrupt Practices Act it appears that illegal corporate contributions to political campaigns have continued. Investigations indicate that there were violations during the 1968 presidential campaign although no formal charges were made. And in 1973 a number of businessmen were indicted for or admitted to making illegal gifts from corporate funds to both political parties during the presidential campaign of 1972.

Such illegal acts on the part of business have added to social dissatisfaction with methods of financing elections. In 1972 Congress further strengthened the rules on political giving through the Election Campaign Practices Act. This law requires that candidates for federal office and their political committees must make public the names and addresses of supporters who contribute more than $100 to a campaign fund.

While both the Corrupt Practices Act and the Election Campaign Practices Act have helped to control financial involvement in the election process by business, many people argue that this is not enough. They argue that federal elections should be publicly financed, thereby eliminating whatever influence business and other special interest groups might have on the outcome of elections. Thus, society, through the legislative process, is defining proper political action for business in at least the area of political giving.

Providing Information

The function of communicating the business point of view on issues of public concern is often considered to be one of the foremost social roles of business leaders. Because of their knowledge and experience, business leaders are qualified to make judgments about business-related issues in the same way a medical doctor is qualified to make judgments about issues concerning medicine. Dissemination of business views takes place in a number of ways and at a number of political levels (city, county, state, and federal), and each activity is a proper political function for business.

[21]For a discussion of legislation prohibiting business and labor contributions to political campaigns see Edwin M. Epstein, *Corporations, Contributions, and Political Campaigns: Federal Regulations in Perspective,* Berkeley, Calif.: University of California Institute of Government Studies, 1968.

Many businessmen feel that they can best make the business point of view known to legislators through direct correspondence. One survey of businessmen showed that 98 percent felt that business representatives should write to legislators explaining their company's position on pending legislation.[22] Other businessmen feel that company representatives should take advantage of every opportunity to explain the business point of view through speeches and public forums such as those sponsored by the Conference Board and the Committee for Economic Development. Still others feel that businessmen should belong to organizations such as the United States Chamber of Commerce that are designed to make the political climate more favorable to business. And some businessmen feel that they can be most effective politically by working through trade associations.

Lobbying

Discussions of political activities of businessmen often bring up the subject of lobbying and whether or not it is a responsible political activity for business to engage in, and if so, what kind of behavior is acceptable.

Lobbying has nothing to do with the Corrupt Practices Act. The Corrupt Practices Act is concerned with the election process itself. Lobbying refers to behavior *after* the election and is concerned with securing legislation favorable to a particular point of view. This is the normal working of a pluralistic society in which society wants the viewpoints of business as well as of other interest groups. Farmers, laborers, teachers, and conservationists, among others, are well represented in the capitals. Business should also be represented to provide a balanced point of view and to maintain an open pluralistic system. Also, with as large a population as we have, often the only way to get representation is through groups. Hence, many businesses that cannot afford individual representatives turn to organizations such as trade associations to make their points of view known. Lobbying has become, for many trade associations, one of their primary functions.

What is acceptable behavior for lobbyists? There are unscrupulous lobbyists just as there are unscrupulous people in other endeavors. Therefore, the actions of a few should not condemn the entire process. The fundamental roles of lobbying are communication and expression of viewpoints, and getting the ear of legislators for desired purposes. Obviously, graft, blackmail, and unreasonable pressure are as reprehensible in lobbying as they are in other endeavors. There is a real difference between buying dinner for a legislator while discussing issues of public concern and using compromising pictures of legislators (real or staged) to exert pressures for favored treatment.

Another question is: Toward what ends are lobbying activities directed? When applied to administrative decisions such as an antitrust settlement for a large corporation or an Agriculture Department decision to allow the dairy industry to

[22]Stephen A. Greyser, "Business and Politics, 1964," *Harvard Business Review,* September–October 1964, pp. 22ff.

raise milk prices, the question of propriety arises. In these illustrations lobbying tries to alter laws and regulations that are currently being enforced by government—not pending legislation. A good rule of thumb to follow is that lobbying activities are appropriate and desirable activities for business so long as they are directed toward influencing legislation which has not yet become law. Conversely, lobbying activity which seeks to secure favored treatment for one company or one industry under existing laws are questionable at best.

One government leader recounted what he considered to be responsible lobbying on the part of one company in trying to modify a product warranty bill.[23]

"John Wheeler of Sears came in with none of the ideological baggage of the Chamber of Commerce," says Pertschuk. "He had really read the bill carefully." Wheeler contacted one of Pertschuk's colleagues at the crucial moment—between hearings on the bill and the secret committee "markup" of the measure into final form. Wheeler then submitted a written brief on those provisions that Sears found "unworkable in the market place," and suggested changes. These included a provision for informal dispute settlement procedures before a claimant can sue. "They made a case for their amendments, we adopted them, and then they worked aggressively for the bill, even for the section strengthening the Federal Trade Commission," says Pertschuk.

Businessmen in Politics

Because of the special talents which business leaders have, they are often called upon to assume either political posts or leadership of a government project on a temporary basis. In addition to responsible positions at the national levels, businessmen often accept political jobs at local and state levels. The important point is that, by political involvement, businessmen are often in an excellent position to influence government policy in the same way that leaders of other pluralistic groups are able to do.

While some businessmen do attain public offices, companies often resist having their executives and/or employees become active participants in party politics for two main reasons. First, employees in a corporation who rise to high places in a political party or who campaign for political office while still in the employment of the company may generate public criticism of the company itself. Even though the individual and the company may be unselfishly motivated, skeptics are likely to consider such a person a "tool of business" with special interests and, therefore, a poor public servant.

Second, loss of a key individual from the organization may impose serious hardships on a company's operations. A policy of leaves of absence for political activity creates an even greater dilemma. Few businesses can operate effectively if

[23]Michael Pertschuk, quoted in "Why the Corporate Lobbyist Is Necessary," *Business Week,* Mar. 18, 1972, p. 63.

Businessmen in Government

It is obvious that success in the private sector is not automatically transferable to the public sector. In fact, to succeed in government the businessman must develop some qualities that are almost the opposite of those he needed to succeed in business. Where he was persistent, he must now also be resilient; where he was guarded, he must be open; where he was arbitrary, he must be sensitive; where he viewed problems with a narrow focus, he must deal comprehensively with them; and where he was informed, he must be at least a little intuitive.

From Frederic V. Malek, "Mr. Executive Goes to Washington," *Harvard Business Review*, September–October 1972, p. 67. Reprinted with permission.

they are unsure, from election to election, which employees will remain and how many will return.

Furthermore, from a personal standpoint, many individuals may not be willing to make the necessary sacrifices. Movement into public office from private employment often demands that the individual face a substantial financial loss.

Whatever the method used, both business and government need each other's help. The strength and growth of the national economy depend upon cooperation, and as society grows more complex, the need for cooperation and understanding will become more important and demanding.

SUMMARY

Several times in the history of America, society has redefined roles of social institutions and relationships among these institutions. Universality and growing intensity of social problems are causing another redefinition of roles and relations.

There is a growing belief that social problems cannot be solved by any single social institution. Rather, solutions will come only by institutions working together in partnership, each performing those functions which it is best equipped to perform. Government, by its very nature, should formulate social objectives. Business, on the other hand, should apply its management, technological, and research capabilities directly to achievement of social objectives and to helping government better perform its own functions. Also, business—as business——should be in the political arena because its viewpoints are needed to maintain the pluralistic balance.

As society becomes more complex, it seems clear that national economic performance depends on both a strong government sector and a strong business sector. If complex social and economic problems are to be met and solved, greater trust, understanding, and cooperation will be needed between business and government as well as other social institutions.

STUDY GUIDES FOR INTERPRETATION OF THIS CHAPTER

1. The U.S. Postal Service and the Corporation for Public Broadcasting are examples of public-private corporations. List other areas of public interest or social need that you think could be served by institutions of this type. Select one area and develop as many persuasive arguments as possible for and against establishing a public-private corporation to serve this need.

2. In 1964 the following summary of a study on business and political activity (Figures 11-2 and 11-3) appeared in the *Harvard Business Review*. Conduct a similar survey of businessmen in your community and compare your results with the published survey.

3. What is meant by the term "vital partnership"? What evidence can you present that such a partnership is being formed?

4. Compile arguments both pro and con on the question: Should businessmen be

	1959	1964	
In Which of the Following Activities Does/Should Your Company Engage?"*	**Does**	**Does**	**Should**
Urge employees to register and vote	70%	68%	73%
Belong to organizations designed to make the political climate more favorable to business	44	50	59
Participate actively in formulating trade association policy on government issues	25	48	55
Belong to organizations designed to improve the efficiency of government operations	36	40	64
Encourage employees to participate actively in campaigns	21	31	47
Urge executives to serve as elected officials in the city where plant is located	16	29	45
Take stands on specific political issues	22	24	39
Encourage campaign contributions by employees	15	21	31
Allow candidates to come into the plant and meet employees	14	21	29
Invite elected officials to meet with the management group	13	21	46
Have top managers make talks on important issues	14	20	38
Employ specialists to deal with elected officials	13	20	20
Carry articles on current public issues in the company paper	15	19	37
Give employees time off to work on campaigns	12	14	20
Perform services for politicians	12	12	9
Invite elected officials to talk to employee groups	6	12	35
Consider political activity in recommendations for promotions	3	5	7

Question did not include "should" in 1959.

Figure 11-2 Opinions on Company Political Activities. Source: Stephen A. Greyser, "Business and Politics, 1964," Harvard Business Review, September –October 1964, table 3, p. 177. Reproduced with permission.

	1964	1959
Company X offers cash to those politicians who will take it	7%	5%
Company X's representative writes a legislator to explain the firm's position on pending legislation	98	96
Company X invites campaigning politicians into the plant	56	54
Company X hires legislators as consultants	14	14
Company X gives executives time off to work on a campaign	64	71
Company X makes available a few jobs which selected legislator can give to constituents	3	5
Company X's president endorses a candidate in a newspaper advertisement	55	52
Company X provides legal and other specialized services to politicians	13	15
Company X's representatives take legislators to lunch on company funds	57	60
Company X gives presents or vacation trips to legislators	1	2
Company X contributes to candidate's political campaigns*	52	—

This statement was not included in 1959.

Figure 11-3 Percentage of Respondents Rating Selected Company Political Activities as ''Proper.'' Source: Stephen A. Greyser, ''Business and Politics, 1964,'' *Harvard Business Review,* September–October 1964, table 4, p. 177. Reproduced with permission.

active in politics: (a) as individual businessmen? (b) as representatives of business firms?

5. Select from newspapers or magazines an example of political action by business, and evaluate it in terms of propriety.

PROBLEMS
What's in a Name?

During a recent political campaign a newspaper advertisement appeared which endorsed certain candidates for the office of President and Vice President of the United States. The advertisement was placed and paid for by an organization of businessmen. It told why the organization felt that the two men were the best candidates and also solicited financial contributions to support the organization. Although the advertisement was signed by the executive director of the organization, there also appeared at the bottom of the advertisement a list of the names of approximately 100 business leaders. Nearly all of these men were presidents or board chairmen of the country's leading businesses. Each man was identified by his corporate title and his company's name. The following sentence appeared at the extreme bottom of the advertisement: ''Partial list of founding members. Corporate affiliations are for identification only.''

1. Discuss whether or not the inclusion of titles and company names, along with the names of individual founding members, constitutes endorsement of candidates for political office by the various companies.

2. Does the disclaimer statement at the bottom of the advertisement relieve the company from charges of endorsing candidates?

The Hammermill Paper Company

The accompanying advertisement (Figure 11-4) is one of a series from an advertising campaign by Hammermill Paper Company. Other advertisements which appeared during 1969 discuss issues such as poverty and welfare, voting age, citizen safety on the streets, and privacy for citizens. The format and text of all the advertisements are quite similar.

1. In what ways is/is not the company acting responsibly with these advertisements?

2. To what extent is the company politically involved by such a campaign?

3. Do you feel that the company is supporting one side or the other of this social issue? Why?

The Port Authority of New York and New Jersey

In 1921, the states of New York and New Jersey formed the Port of New York Authority. The original reason for establishing the organization was to permit states that used New York City harbor to participate in the planning and development of that port.

Over the years the Port Authority of New York and New Jersey, as it is now called, has become a major operator of transportation facilities in and around the city. It operates primarily as a public business, charging consumers mainly on the basis of services needed. It operates six interstate tunnels and bridges, four airports, two heliports, and ten marine and vehicular terminals. These operations began in 1930, when the Holland Tunnel was transferred, without cost, to the Authority. The Authority continues to charge a toll of 50 cents even though the facility has been paid for for several years. As a bistate agency, the Authority can ignore federal laws requiring that tolls be removed when cost of construction is paid.

In the 1960s, the Authority obtained approval to build huge twin 110-story skyscrapers in New York City as a World Trade Center. A 16-acre site in downtown Manhattan was obtained to accommodate the buildings. The center was completed in the early 1970s. Approximately 130,000 people can use these buildings daily.

At the same time, the Authority has avoided becoming involved in the problems of mass transit in Greater New York. This has resulted in a heated

Is a college education still a luxury, or has it become a necessity that should be tax deductible?

A prerequisite for employment? A "union" card? A modern-day work permit? Is this what a college degree has come to mean in today's complex and technically-oriented working world?

A great many people think so. And they feel obligated to provide their children with this "necessity." Yet with the cost of a college education soaring to nearly $4000 a year, most people need some kind of help to handle it. One proposal is to make college costs an income tax deduction, like any other professional expense.

But others argue that going to college is a luxury. An option for those who can afford it; unnecessary for those who can't. They feel that an income tax deduction certainly won't solve the college-cost problem; will be, at best, an after-the-fact alleviation of expense in favor of a small minority. Everybody's taxes help support public colleges and universities and make them available to all. And many people feel that's enough.

The point is, what do you think? It's not your job to come up with the final answer to this issue — but it's important that you come out with your opinion about it. And make your opinion known. In writing. To your Congressman, so he can weigh what you think when he votes on legislation.

We hope you'll write your Congressman on Hammermill Bond — world's best-known letterhead paper. But whether you write on Hammermill Bond or not . . . write. A paper-thin voice is a powerful persuader. Hammermill Paper Company, Erie, Pa., maker of 33 fine printing and business papers.

HAMMERMILL BOND.

Hammermill urges you to write your Congressman.

Figure 11-4   A company advertisement focuses on a social issue. Reproduced with permission of the Hammermill Paper Company.

controversy over what the role and functions of the Authority should be. Critics of the Authority cite its annual income of over $100 million and its liquid reserves of nearly $700 million. Critics argue that the Authority, through its own ventures, has seriously contributed to the city's "transportation mess," and therefore should become actively involved in solving the problems. The Authority's answer is that it is not in the mass transit business. It argues further that it has an obligation to its bondholders to avoid becoming involved in chronically insolvent mass transit.

1. In what ways is the Port Authority of New York and New Jersey operating in the manner of (a) a private business? (b) government? (c) a public-private organization?

2. Identify the publics to which the Port Authority of New York and New Jersey is responsible.

3. What are the responsibilities of the Port Authority of New York and New Jersey to the publics which it serves?

ISSUES OF GOVERNMENT REGULATION AND INFLUENCE

Americans have always had to balance their love of bigness and efficiency against their fear of power and their regard for individualism and competition.

Richard Hofstadter[1]

The job of this generation is not to abolish large-scale organization. It is to make it perform—for individual, community, and society alike.

Peter F. Drucker[2]

New York: December 27, 1993

The United States of America, Inc. (USA), the Solar System's largest multi-diverse conglomerate growth corporation, has announced plans to acquire European Common Nations, Ltd. (Europe), a large holding company that controls all of the land and manufacturing operation in what was once known as Western Europe. If the merger goes through, it will be the largest in history—far surpassing the merger two years ago between USA, Inc. and Canada, Ltd., in which USA bought Canada through an exchange of securities valued at 463 billion dollars.[3]

This quotation carries to extremes the possible ultimate end in merger activity, this end being control of the entire universe by a few unimaginably large and powerful organizations. And to project a bit further, the author goes on in the article to point out that the regulating agency, "the Interplanetary Trade Commission," had been ineffective in controlling the "oligopolistic tendencies of corporations." While the above example is fictitious, it does illustrate a phenomenon which is causing considerable concern both to government and to business.

This chapter is concerned with government influence on business decisions

[1] Richard Hofstadter, "What Happened to the Antitrust Movement?" in Earl F. Cheit (ed.), *The Business Establishment,* New York: John Wiley & Sons, Inc. 1964, p. 131.
[2] Peter F. Drucker, "The Concept of the Corporation," *Business and Society Review,* Autumn 1972, p. 17.
[3] Bernard J. Zahren, "Merger Madness," *The MBA,* January 1970, p. 54.

and business activity. The first part of the chapter will be concerned with direct statutory regulation, including the reasons for it and the effectiveness of it. The second part of the chapter will be concerned with more subtle indirect government pressures and influence on business.

REGULATORY RELATIONS

Economic profits are the result of utilizing productive resources in ways which produce more and better goods and services at increasingly lower costs. But unfortunately for society, greater profits can sometimes be made (at least in the short run) by producing inferior goods, by misleading or deceiving customers, by unwitting or unwise inattention to environmental factors, and by misusing business power. In order to control malpractices by business and ensure maximum social payouts, society has seen fit to impose controls and restrictions on a variety of business activities. Beginning with the Sherman Act, businessmen increasingly have been subjected to regulation and policing by a growing number of government agencies.

Most people, including businessmen themselves, agree that some regulation of business practice is desirable, but the amount and kind is often subject to debate. Partly because of a genuine recognition of public need and partly to avoid unrealistic regulatory action, businessmen often join public authorities in formulating regulation.

For example, business leaders sometimes appear before legislative committees that are drafting legislation which would directly affect business decision making and behavior. By making positive suggestions concerning how to make a new law or regulation more workable, businessmen often can get legislation they can live with.

A more complex cooperative approach to workable regulations is seen in the modification of the New York City building code. During the 1960s city government, building experts, builders, and trade unions all participated in developing a code which produced cost savings and innovations in building. Basically the code substituted performance requirements for those requiring specific materials, thus clearing the way for the city to deal better with urban problems such as low-cost housing.

It seems evident that regulation of business by all levels of government is here to stay. The trend has been toward more regulation, not less. The danger in this trend is that our pluralistic balance will be upset, thus rendering business less capable of efficiently performing its functions. In many areas businessmen feel that regulations already act as dampers on their ability to maintain high levels of economic performance. These criticisms are true to some degree, but the fact remains that society has felt it necessary to establish rules.

As the economy becomes more complex, regulating business activity also becomes more complicated. As technology increases, as markets expand, as economic and political relationships with foreign countries change, and as expectations of society are modified, rules governing business behavior which were once appropriate may no longer be adequate. The increasing complexity of the arena in which business must perform emphasizes the need for increased business involvement in regulatory processes. This means active participation by business at every opportunity in the formulation and modification of regulations. It means constructive contributions of the business point of view to the pluralistic process of rule setting rather than blind opposition to all regulation.

ANTITRUST POLICY
Background of Antitrust Policy

The avowed purpose of antitrust legislation has always been to preserve competition. To appreciate society's concern with bigness, one needs to examine the attitudes, economic philosophies, and emotional involvement surrounding the changes which took place during the closing years of the nineteenth century.

From colonial times until after the Civil War, America was largely a nation of farmers and small-town entrepreneurs. All in all, the American economic system fit fairly well the economic model of perfect competition. Most businessmen competed on reasonably even terms within small closed markets, and government stood weakly by, performing its assigned limited functions. Belief that perfect competition was right and natural became a national philosophy. Nearly every person grew up believing in the classical economic model, complete with its requirements of smallness, large numbers, and diffusion of power.

Social Concern over Business Concentration

After the Civil War, the economic system underwent such drastic and rapid change that most men of the times were ill-equipped either theoretically or emotionally to cope with the new environment. Looking at the social results of business mergers in the late 1800s, it is little wonder that men of the times forecast gloomy consequences if mergers and concentrations were not carefully controlled.

A major concern of society at the turn of the century was the question of where business concentration would lead if left unchecked. In light of experience, it seemed reasonable that unless the merger trend was stopped through exercise of government control, great corporations might continue to absorb one another until there existed one great syndicate of giant businesses which, if unchallenged, could control the whole country.

Another social concern that lead to antitrust legislation was the belief that monopoly hindered the progress of industry. Concentration, it was felt, always led to monopoly, and monopoly always inhibited technological progress.

And finally, society was concerned with ideas of consumer protection. It had been observed that when business firms combined to form a monopoly, the quality of products and services often deteriorated rapidly.

In retrospect, we can observe that these things did not happen. Even though mergers have continued in ever-increasing numbers, business has not become monolithic. There are more small businesses today than ever before. At the same time large size has enabled many firms to make positive contributions to consumer welfare through economies of scale. Additionally, technological advances have resulted from large expenditures of money on research and development. Small businesses rarely have financial resources to devote to major research and development projects.

Objectives of Antitrust

The objectives of antitrust legislation, at least as the policy was originally conceived, were threefold: (1) economic, (2) political, and (3) social. From the economic viewpoint, antitrust was an attempt to cling to the belief in the economic model of perfect competition. From the political viewpoint it stemmed from a reluctant choice to allocate to government more power over business. It seemed that the only way to check the powers of business was to increase the power of government. And from a social viewpoint antitrust was a result of a continuing belief in the Protestant ethic.

Contemporary public policy continues to reflect a lingering belief in the philosophy of perfect competition, and in the Protestant ethic. These lingering beliefs have resulted in antitrust policies which appear in many cases to be incompatible with the real world. Probably in no other area of regulation have businessmen encountered more confusion and frustration. The vagueness of the laws themselves and judicial inconsistencies in enforcement have left businessmen uncertain as to what they can do. It has become increasingly difficult for businessmen to conform to legal requirements and at the same time perform their economic functions as they perceive them. One observer has commented:[4]

> There can be no doubt of a need for a philosophical reappraisal of our attitudes and our legislation in the field of competition.
> It would seem that having accepted the economists' definition of perfect competition and finding it unattainable, we have lost all confidence in the ability of competition to do its work.

[4] Courtney C. Brown, "The Fading of an Ideology," in Robert W. Miller (ed.), *The Creative Interface*, Washington: The American University, 1968, p. 44.

Herein lies a social challenge to both business and government. Most businessmen agree that some form of regulation is needed to control unscrupulous business practices. The challenge is in reexamining where the public good lies and what kinds of regulation will contribute most to that public good. The problem seems to lie in trying to apply postulates left over from an earlier era to a dynamic period of rapid change—rather like driving a Model T Ford in the Indianapolis 500.

Effects of Antitrust Legislation

If, indeed, a major objective of antitrust legislation has been to limit size of business firms as a way of protecting competition, it has not been effective. Whatever else it may have done to preserve and promote competition, antitrust legislation has neither stopped mergers nor reduced the size of firms. For example, in 1911 the government split Rockefeller's Standard Oil Company into eleven separate companies. Today each of the eleven companies is larger than the original Standard Oil Company. Each has more invested capital, more employees, and more production than the parent had.

Mergers have occurred in waves, and each wave has been larger than the previous one. But, until recently, there has been little corresponding increase in attempts to curb business consolidation through exercising antitrust legislation. Furthermore, increases in numbers of mergers have occurred during periods of economic prosperity. All this suggests that society wants the economic benefits which result from large-size firms, but at the same time wants to guard against too much concentration of power by imposing restrictions and checks on business. This also suggests that government actions to enforce antitrust legislation or to "go easy" possibly may have reflected fluctuating pressures on government from other pluralistic groups seeking to restrain business.

From a social point of view the result of antitrust legislation has been to limit business consolidation to magnitudes which were socially acceptable at various times. From the businessman's point of view the result has been to crowd his life with uncertainties.

The biggest problem most businessmen have today in living within the antitrust laws is not so much that the laws regulate business. The real problems revolve around the ambiguity of the laws themselves and of government enforcement policies which result in confusion for the businessman. In the late 1960s one company president expressed the problem as follows:[5]

> I fail to understand the rationale of the federal government, particularly the Federal Trade Commission. On the one hand, if U.S. industry is to be attacked under

[5] Frank Peterson, "Planning the Premerger Pattern," in G. Scott Hutchison (ed.), *The Business of Acquisitions and Mergers,* New York: Presidents Publishing House, Inc., 1968, p. 3.

the guise of the Sherman Act, the FTC, and so on, wholly on the basis of bigness, then I think there is something illogically wrong. On the other hand, I completely agree and support the government in its contentions that any combinations which create restraint of trade, or develop trade practices which are unfavorable or unfair procedures, should be regulated. But to attack a merger movement or combination in the form of bigness and bigness alone is not, in my opinion, fair.

Nor has confusion lessened over time. In the early 1970s another corporate executive expressed business attitudes more succinctly: "This whole antitrust thing is so screwed up. . . . It's so fuzzy at the moment that you have to assume that you can't do anything. You don't know what you can do and what you can't do. . . . This situation certainly has to be clarified."[6]

The Businessman's Dilemma

At the center of businessmen's confusion are the dichotomies within anti-trust legislation. The Sherman Act is concerned with business performance. The law recites a long list of collusive dealings which are specifically prohibited. The Clayton Act, on the other hand, is concerned with business structure and size. Thus a company that is not engaged in any anticompetitive practices may be judged to be anticompetitive on the basis of size alone.

Most businessmen accept, in general, the prohibitions of the Sherman Act. From the viewpoint of managerial decision making, however, the most important antitrust development has been the tightening up of the prohibitions against corporate mergers and acquisitions. In 1950, the Celler-Kefauver amendment to section 7 of the Clayton Act made it clear that mergers would be illegal if they substantially lessened competition or created a monopoly. The rules which were laid down stated that (1) companies which are major competitors cannot merge under any circumstances; (2) companies cannot merge if, as a result, they would control 30 percent of the market; and (3) if one company is already a giant, it cannot acquire another, no matter how small the share of the market is.

Considerable controversy exists over whether or not antitrust laws, as they are currently being administered, really do strengthen competition. The Justice Department's policy of "grow from within, not by merger," has been attacked as lessening competition rather than strengthening it.

One argument is that the attitude of the Justice Department itself tends to lessen competition since it leaves smaller companies no way to grow and diversify in an industry which is dominated by giant corporations that originally became large through mergers and acquisitions. Thus, the Justice Department is really helping the giants by stopping mergers that would make others stronger.

---

[6] E. Mandell deWindt (chairman, Eaton Corporation), quoted in "The Views on Bigness Are Contradictory," *Business Week,* Aug. 7, 1971, p. 63.

Another argument is that American companies no longer compete solely with other American firms in small closed markets but are increasingly competing, both at home and abroad, with foreign businesses. Therefore, American firms that are already large need to be even larger if they are to compete successfully in the international arena with foreign firms of growing size. Foreign governments are giving both approval and encouragement to industrial combinations even though such combinations diminish domestic competition. There are numerous examples of foreign mergers, all designed to increase smaller foreign producers to the size of United States firms. The British combined five Scottish shipyards, and Germany combined fifty coal mines into one company. Japan, through consolidation of two steel companies, created the largest steel producer in the world. The French have combined the Peugeot and Renault automobile companies. The Dutch joined together two large chemical producers. And the Swiss, through combining drug-making firms, created a company that accounts for more than 7 percent of Switzerland's gross national product.

To add to the confusion, policies of government agencies other than those responsible for enforcing antitrust legislation seem to encourage companies to take the rapid path to expansion through merger.

One case resulted from the armed services' policy of evaluating companies who bid on government production contracts in terms of existing production facilities and financial strength indicated by working capital. Because it was strong in research engineering, one company was awarded a research and development contract. As a result of this contract, the company developed and designed a new piece of equipment which needed to be produced in volume. When the same company bid on the subsequent production contract, its bid was not accepted because it was not big enough.

Officials responsible for antitrust enforcement also face difficulties which in turn add to the confusion of businessmen. Officials sometimes seem to be considering the social as well as economic ramifications of their decisions. For example, government objections to a merger between a small electrical appliance maker and General Electric were later withdrawn. The apparent reason for blocking the merger was that General Electric is so large that acquiring even a small competitor would violate the Clayton Act. However, two senators, learning that plants of the small manufacturer in their states might shut down, thereby causing unemployment, asked officials to reconsider the decision. The decision was reversed and the merger approved, apparently on the theory that antitrust enforcement should consider other dimensions as well as competition.

Businessmen increasingly are making pleas for clarification and rewriting of antitrust laws. And enforcement agencies are responding to some degree. One observer commented:[7]

---

[7] Betty Bock, *Mergers and Markets: 7, An Economic Analysis of Developments in 1967-1968 under the Merger Act of 1950,* New York: National Industrial Conference Board, Inc., Studies in Business Economics, no. 105, p. 3.

> The major innovation during the 1967–68 period was the emergence of guidelines or formal statements by the enforcement agencies concerning their merger policies. . . . During the year, also, the Federal Trade Commission published summaries of its advisory opinions on proposed mergers where individual companies had requested an advance opinion.

It is doubtful that antitrust enforcement agencies will ever define simple right-and-wrong guidelines for business, and there is no assurance that business would be happier with a set formula which would preclude any flexibility. Enforcement agencies point out that a rigid formula would force them to move against combinations that really do spur competition. For example, a rigid formula would likely have prevented Honeywell from absorbing General Electric's computer business. Because of the specific circumstances, the Justice Department approved the combination of the third and fifth largest companies in a concentrated industry. Even this combination produced worldwide computer sales only one-seventh as large as those of IBM.

Private Antitrust Litigation

Perhaps even more important to domestic business than antitrust suits by government agencies has been the expanding trend of private antitrust litigation. Since 1890 companies that felt they had been damaged by unlawful anticompetitive practices of other companies have been allowed to bring suit in federal courts for damages equal to three times the amount of losses. However, until relatively recently such suits have not been popular. By 1914 only forty-six private suits had been brought and only four had been successful. By 1940 only thirteen private plaintiffs had won cases. In 1946 a Supreme Court decision gave juries more discretion in awarding damages, and since then the volume of private antitrust litigation has increased dramatically. In 1972 over 1,300 private suits were brought, compared with 96 filed by the Justice Department.

Until 1973 private suits brought under antitrust laws were civil suits asking for damages for alleged injuries resulting from anticompetitive practices. Such suits usually have depended upon and have followed closely successful criminal antitrust action by the government. For example, in 1963 following the electrical conspiracy cases, more than 1,700 suits were filed by electric utilities which charged that because of the price-fixing conspiracy, they were forced to overpay for electrical equipment.

But a more important development is that companies are bringing the kinds of antitrust suits that were once reserved for government. These suits go beyond the recovery of damages and seek to restrain alleged anticompetitive practices. For example, one large company sued another to stop leasing switchboard equipment and telephone lines at bargain prices. A large automobile manufacturer was

Antitrust Enforcement

If the Justice Department were the only enforcer, only limited action could be expected. But Arthur Cantor, a former aid to Dick McLaren, says: "Effective enforcement of antitrust laws depends on the willingness of those outside the Government to file suits. Whether Justice's enforcement is vigorous or lax makes little difference." His point is that federal agencies no longer have the resources to keep up.

The answer may well be: private lawyers and local antitrust. Antitrust divisions are being formed daily in state capitals where more than 40 antitrust laws that predate the Sherman Act have lain moldering as interesting relics of the farmer uprisings of the 1880s against the railroad combines. In addition, some businessmen now look on antitrust suits as a tool to use—cynically sometimes—in evening up the competitive odds.

From "Trust-Busting: Now Its a Game Everybody Can Play," *Forbes*, Oct. 1, 1973, p. 50–54. Reprinted with permission.

accused by a former dealer of fixing prices of local sales to automobile rental companies. A large fast-food franchiser was sued by a franchisee for allegedly tying insurance and purchases of supplies to the right to use the franchise name.

Even more important is the emerging trend of private suits which seek to alter the structure of firms by forcing divestitures. In two landmark cases decided in 1973 General Telephone and Electronics Corporation was ordered to divest itself of over $3.5 billion worth of properties it had acquired over the past twenty years, and Volkswagen of America was ordered to divest itself of its automobile air-conditioning business.

Like most other issues which affect the well-being of society, the issue of private antitrust litigation is subject to debate. Probably the most effective argument for encouraging private antitrust suits is that they may be the most effective way of policing the many comparatively insignificant local antitrust violations that government enforcement agencies do not see. Furthermore, policing becomes self-policing by business itself, thereby tending to discourage expansion of government agencies.

On the other hand, private antitrust cases that break new ground tend to generate inconsistancies in merger law. Furthermore, since many private antitrust cases are settled out of court they create no legal precedents to inhibit future violators or to provide guidelines for managerial decision making.

The Rise of Conglomerates

Most consolidations of business before 1950, and many that have occurred since, have been of the conventional forms of horizontal (one steel mill acquiring another) or vertical (a cement company acquiring a ready-mix concrete company) mergers. However, since 1950, the conglomerate form of merger between companies neither in the same market nor in a vertical relationship with one another has far surpassed other forms in popularity. In 1968 there were 4,462 mergers. Of the approximately 200 mergers in that year which involved companies with assets over $10 million, about 170 qualified as some form of conglomerate.

Because conglomerates combine different kinds of business rather than similar or related businesses, they are not easily brought within the control of current antitrust legislation. Nevertheless, the growth in business concentration is reawakening social fears of business power. The result is increased attention to conglomerates by both enforcement agencies and law makers.

In trying to make social evaluations of conglomerates, arguments for and against them are much the same as they have been since before the Sherman Act. The most common arguments against conglomerates are that they raise barriers to entry into an industry by smaller firms and that they discourage smaller firms from competing, but there is some evidence that activities of conglomerates have surprisingly little affect on the business scene.[8] A study of 348 companies acquired by nine large conglomerates showed no significant change in management or performance of the acquired companies. Furthermore, each acquired company wound up more often with a smaller share of total industry sales than with an increased share.

Society fears that concentration of power in one social institution will upset social equilibrium among pluralistic groups and destroy our pluralistic system. Society often looks with alarm at the growth of the business system and particularly the growth of individual firms, viewing this growth as being disproportionate to growth of other social institutions and thereby creating social disequilibrium. The business system and individual firms have grown. But so have government and individual government agencies, organized labor and individual unions, the educational system and individual universities, and other social institutions. Thus, it is doubtful whether the social system is more out of balance than it was.

Counterarguments stress the idea that national well-being depends on the best allocation and use of resources and that conglomerates and other large businesses can best perform this function. One business leader comments:[9]

> Everyone benefits from the takeover, including the public. It should be obvious that our national prosperity depends upon the maximum use of our existing resources and of our capital. National *policy* should direct funds into the hands of those who can and will invest them in a way to create the most productivity. If takeover accelerates this process and benefits stockholders, too, then who should protest?

[8] "The Conglomerates," *Business Week,* Jan. 6, 1973.
[9] Bruce D. Henderson, president, The Boston Consulting Group, Boston, Mass., in a letter "To Clients and Friends," n.d.

While most people are in favor of maximizing social well-being, just how conglomerates contribute to such well-being is not entirely clear to many. Those who support conglomerates contend that a number of advantages result from bigness. Conglomerates contend that they can provide benefits to their subsidiaries that the smaller companies cannot supply for themselves. One advantage is the ability of very large firms to supply capital and highly specialized management talents that might otherwise not be available to smaller firms. By providing these resources, conglomerates help other companies become more competitive. For example, Profexray, a small manufacturer of x-ray equipment, grew sevenfold after Litton Industries acquired it and made it competitive in its market. And, ITT helped Avis effectively challenge Hertz in the car rental field.[10]

Another answer is that congolomerates provide economic stability. Because of diversification, conglomerates can absorb economic setbacks in one area while moving ahead in others, thus smoothing out cyclical variations.

Conglomerates also contribute to social well-being through the ability to coordinate the activities of subordinates. While conglomerates are made up of firms from different industries, these firms often have complementary technology which can quickly and efficiently be directed toward solutions of economic and social problems.

Conglomerates also have the flexibility to capitalize on growth opportunities. Overall national economic growth depends, to a substantial degree, on recognizing and developing individual growth opportunities. Because of the very nature of conglomerates, they can move quickly in making decisions and committing capital to growth opportunities.

The conglomerate form of business is not uniquely American. Other countries have similar forms of business consolidation, and these provide some evidence that large business concentrations do contribute to economic strength and viability. Japan, for example, which ranks third in gross national product behind the United States and Russia, has a long history of successful business concentration. It also has a long history of cooperation between government and business. The huge pre–World War II *zaibatsu* holding companies were conglomerates, and although these holding companies were broken up by the occupation authorities, other more contemporary types of conglomerates have appeared in Japan along with horizontal and vertical mergers. For Japan, at least, economic concentrations of power have not been deterring forces in economic development. The exact opposite seems to be true.

The remarkable economic growth of Japan has been attributed to the close relationship between business and government in which the government attempts to identify objectives and priorities for the economy and to facilitate achievement of these goals. Business attempts to realize these objectives through industrial

[10] David N. Judelson, "The Role of the Conglomerate Corporation in Today's Economy," *Financial Executive,* September 1968, p. 21.

know-how and expertise.[11] The Japanese economic growth scheme has come to be known as "Japan Incorporated," and the total concept has been compared to a conglomerate.[12]

> Each major component of the conglomerate known as "Japan Incorporated," call it a corporate-division or industry, has considerable leeway, in fact direct operating responsibility to carry on its own business in the most efficient and profitable manner. Such units, and subdivisions of them, are free to compete with each other within broad limits.
>
> At the same time, the top management of the Japanese conglomerate is in a position to mobilize and deploy the resources of the entire combination. Top management coordinates the various component operations according to plan to make the conglomerate yield the maximum return for the Japanese nation. The conglomerate's managers continually seek to shift resources from mature to dynamic industries in order to advance the rate of economic growth.

By contrast, one observer viewing the American business scene commented:[13]

> This misconception [about conglomerates] is also indicative of a basic myopia on the part of both government and business regarding their mutual relationship. Their existing views of each other's roles appear to be quite obsolete. The government is exercising its very great power with rather limited insight and using assumptions that are no longer valid. Conversely, business on the whole is relying on largely outdated concepts and standards of measurement in managing its resources, and thus failing to optimize its performance—and hence its contribution to the common good.

GOVERNMENT INFLUENCE IN THE BUSINESS WORLD

In the previous section we have discussed business regulation through antitrust legislation. As we have seen, antitrust legislation is concerned with controlling the size and power of business. Businessmen also must live with a myriad of other regulatory laws which directly prescribe and limit day-by-day activity. Some of these will be discussed in later chapters. In addition to these laws which directly affect business activity, there are many laws which indirectly affect business.

As significant as these direct and indirect laws are to businessmen, perhaps equally significant is the influence government exerts on business through various roles it performs in the economy, such as the business role of customer. One

[11] Eugene J. Kaplan, *JAPAN: The Government-Business Relationship; A Guide for the American Businessman,* Washington: U.S. Government Printing Office, 1972, pp. 9–10.
[12] Ibid., p. 15.
[13] Henderson, op. cit., p. 2.

by-product of this role which has caused major concern is the military-industrial complex.

The Military-Industrial Complex

On January 17, 1961, in his farewell address to the nation President Dwight D. Eisenhower used a phrase which was to become one of the most quoted statements made by recent presidents. This phrase was a reference to "the military-industrial complex." He commented as follows:

> In the councils of Government we must guard against the acquisition of unwarranted influence, whether sought or unsought, by the military-industrial complex. The potential for the disastrous rise of misplaced power exists and will persist.
>
> We must never let the weight of this combination endanger our liberties or democratic processes. We should take nothing for granted. Only an alert and knowledgeable citizenry can compel the proper meshing of the huge industrial and military machinery of defense with our peaceful methods and goals, so that security and liberty may prosper together.

Interpreting the Military-Industrial Complex

In popular usage the military-industrial complex has developed two meanings. One meaning is that there is a group of high-technology companies of large economic size which work in close cooperation with the Department of Defense to design and produce military weapons. These firms depend primarily on military contracts for their sales. They have on their payrolls many retired military officers who help maintain close liaison with the Department of Defense; therefore, they constitute a closed power group bent on heavy military spending.

A second meaning is that the Defense Department through its massive military spending leads to business dependency reaching even to a small clothing store in a town near a military base. Similarly, the prosperity of communities depends on large military contracts awarded to business in their areas; hence military spending and location of military installations become political issues.[14] For one community, closing a naval base meant the direct loss of 41 percent of the jobs, 50 percent of the payrolls, 33 percent of the population, and 40 percent of the school children.[15] Indirectly the closing had substantial effects on local businesses such as transportation, real estate, and retailing. This whole economic-military relationship creates an unhealthy power bloc always pressing for more military

[14] For example, see the discussion of San Diego in Bill Sluis and George Grimsrud, "Defense-oriented City Strives to Ease Impact Of Pentagon Cutbacks," *Wall Street Journal* (Pacific Coast edition), Nov. 28, 1969, pp. 1, 15.
[15] "Panic in the Face of a Navy Exodus," *Business Week,* May 26, 1973, p. 70.

spending. President Eisenhower appeared to have this meaning in mind, because in his speech he commented, "The total influence—economic, political, even spiritual—is felt in every city, every statehouse, every office of the Federal Government."

Discussion of the military-industrial complex frequently becomes the proverbial can of worms, because it is intricately related to many emotional and social issues. It is a convenient whipping boy for those opposed to war, those opposing a particular war, isolationists opposed to foreign involvement, those objecting to weapons designed to harm others compared with surveillance equipment, those opposed to business profit of any type, and others. The military-industrial complex also suffers from cost overages and poor performance and is subject to political pressures, but there is no evidence that these characteristics are worse in defense than in other large government programs such as highway construction and social programs. Our discussion is primarily limited to the two stated definitions, since they most directly affect business.

Firms Which Are Primarily Defense-oriented

The first definition related to large firms which are primarily defense-oriented and work in close cooperation with the Department of Defense. Companies of this type do exist, but their number is small. The Department of Defense releases annual statistics on its 100 top contractors (including in 1967 two universities), and sales data are available for 82 of them. These data show that in 1967 during the war in Southeast Asia only 17 of the 82 firms received as much as 50 percent of their sales from defense contracts. Of the top 10 contractors only 4 had defense sales of 50 percent or more, and 2 had defense sales of only 5 percent or less.[16]

These data show that at least two-thirds of the top 100 defense contractors do not depend primarily on defense business. The remaining defense-oriented firms often do work closely with the Department of Defense, but they hardly constitute a large economic power bloc, compared with the combined power of all other businesses or even all other direct competitors for the defense budget. The power which they do possess arises more from their maintenance of a large pool of scientific manpower than any other reason. Because of their substantial resources, they are the ones to which the Defense Department is likely to turn for performance of large projects. This is as true among the universities as it is among businesses. The large, capable ones secure the prime contracts.

It can be argued that the firms with less than 50 percent of defense sales derive most of their profit from this part of their business; hence, they unduly profit

[16] A. E. Lieberman, "Updating Impressions of the Military-Industry Complex," *California Management Review*, Summer 1969, pp. 51–62. Although defense contractors also receive defense-related subcontracts from other firms, the contractors also subcontract some of their work, so these offsetting actions do not appear to alter the basic proportions discussed.

from defense business and bring social pressure for defense activity. In earlier decades there was considerable evidence to support charges of high defense profits, but tighter controls by the Department of Defense have changed this situation. Data for the 1960s show that defense profits were lower than profits on civilian business. The lower profit applied both to return on equity capital and to return on total capital invested. A 1971 study conducted by the government's General Accounting Office at the direction of Congress confirmed earlier data. Profits on defense work were lower than profits on commercial work when measured both on the basis of sales and investment.[17] If there is a profit-oriented military-industrial conspiracy, as is sometimes emotionally charged, "Conspirators should expect to be rewarded more favorably than that."[18]

Defense business is a boom-and-bust, high-and-low, unstable type of work which upsets employment and prevents long-range planning. This instability coupled with low profit is causing major defense contractors to diversify as fast as possible into civilian business so that military work will not dominate their business. In an advanced technological society, reasonably stable economic and social conditions are most conducive to profitability. They provide an environment which permits business to do the long-range planning for capital use, marketing, and pricing that is essential for profit success. For this reason the stock market tends to rise when there is news of peace and to decline when there are unsettling threats of war.

The dangers of power among defense-oriented contractors can best be evaluated in terms of proposed alternatives. One alternative is to reduce further the 17 identified companies among the top 100. This can be done, but it poses some risks because large military projects require giant firms with substantial pools of talent. Another approach is for the government to produce its own military materials. This was more frequently attempted in the past, for example, in government shipyards and arsenals, but it proved less efficient. In addition, this approach would *increase* military concentration and power, further reducing the pluralistic balance which now prevails.[19] In view of the alternatives, the most prudent course of action seems to be the present pluralistic system which uses different institutions while checking and controlling them carefully to assure that there are no undue profits or power.

Large Military Spending and Business Dependency

The second meaning of a military-industrial complex refers to the size and pervasiveness of military expenditures. Over half of these expenditures are direct business contracts, and even military wages find their way into the business system

---

[17] "The Profit Puzzle in Procurement," *Business Week,* Mar. 6, 1971, p. 44.
[18] Lieberman, op. cit., p. 59.
[19] One other alternative is to stop major defense activities entirely. This is a political decision for which it has been difficult to build popular support.

through local businesses where military personnel live. This viewpoint is directly related to ideas of pluralism. It is rooted in the philosophy that any large power bloc endangers pluralistic balance within the system. It may become so powerful that it is self-sustaining and not subject to adequate checks and balances. In times of changing social needs, it may divert to its own use resources which are sought for higher social priorities.

Arguments relating to the second definition concern pluralism, military-economic power, and social priorities. Those who discuss the dangers of the military-industrial complex in these terms do not imply conspiracy; "There is no more of a conspiracy here than in numerous other matters where legitimate lobbies influence public policy makers, or where conflicts of interest affect decisions of the legislative and executive arms of government."[20]

Economic effects of defense activities are definitely substantial; however, they do not portray a growing complex when compared with recent history. President Eisenhower made his speech in a relatively peaceful year, but military expenditures in that year consumed more of the federal tax dollar than they did in 1969, which was a period of undeclared war in Southeast Asia. In other words, other government spending increased more than defense spending; other priorities were winning the pluralistic battle for government funds. Similarly, although the defense budget was 10 percent of the gross national product in 1969, this was no higher than in a time of relative peace a decade earlier. Defense expenditures rose only in proportion to the gross national product. Furthermore, national defense purchases as a percentage of gross national product decreased from 7.1 percent in 1971 to 6.1 percent in 1973 even though the total defense budget increased.[21] Increases in the defense budget between 1973 and 1974 resulted from increases in wages and salaries of defense employees rather than from an expansion of defense activities.[22]

In view of the trends mentioned, what is the basis for public concern about the military-industrial complex? The reason is that the Defense Department controls a large portion of the federal budget, but is engaged in an activity of low priority with many persons; thus certain power groups use public pressures to chip away at its funds in order to get more resources to serve social needs which they consider of greater priority. They, too, are legitimate claimants on public funds to serve the priorities they think important. This is normal operation of a pluralistic system.

Barring unusual military developments, it appears that some other priorities will gain dominance. For example, by 1980 the Department of Transportation budget or the Housing and Urban Development budget may exceed the defense

[20] Jack Raymond, "Growing Threat of Our Military-Industrial Complex," *Harvard Business Review,* May–June 1968, p. 64. See also John Kenneth Galbraith, *How to Control the Military,* New York: New American Library of World Literature, Inc., 1969, pp. 26–41.

[21] *Defense Indicators,* Washington: U.S. Department of Commerce, May 1973, p. 14.

[22] *Michael E. Levy,* "The New Federal Budget," *The Conference Board Record,* New York: The Conference Board, March 1973, p. 9.

budget. At that time it will be appropriate to become concerned about the urban-industrial complex or the city-federal complex. In a pluralistic society we need to keep in mind President Eisenhower's admonition: "We should take nothing for granted."

Influence through Indirect Laws

Government, in addition to influencing allocation of resources and business activity through direct laws and through the military-industrial complex, exerts substantial influence through laws which affect business only indirectly. These laws do not directly impose specific activities on business, but make government support and assistance dependent upon certain conditions or actions which business must follow. Putting it another way, government sometimes achieves its desired results by threatening to withhold rewards or benefits unless certain conditions are met.

These benefits which can be given or withheld are usually in the form of monetary contributions, awarding of government contracts, licensing, or the like. Some of these kinds of legislation directly affect business, while others are directed toward states in the hopes that state government will require certain minimum standards of performance. For example, the Bacon-Davis Act prevents awarding government contracts for construction, alteration, or repair of public works to any firm that does not pay wage rates equal to those established by the Secretary of Labor. Similarly, the federal government may refuse to provide funds for highway construction unless vehicles using the highways comply with certain regulations. Another example is the refusal of the Federal Aviation Authority to license private aircraft which do not meet certain safety standards.

Indirect laws are justified in the same way other laws are—that is, in the interest of social well-being. Businessmen, on the other hand, sometimes look at them as somewhat backhanded ways of doing things which could not have been done by straightforward means. Oftentimes businessmen are so far removed from the source that they have little or no knowledge of the law until it is an accomplished fact. Or, because these laws are passed as riders on major laws, they are obscure to businessmen. Whatever the reason, businessmen often feel that they are subject to regulation about which they have had no *opportunity* to voice opinions.

Other Roles of Government

Today, government in one way or another is involved in virtually every phase of business life. In addition to its regulatory function, government relates to business in a variety of ways. It acts as a customer, as a competitor, as a supplier, as a partner, and as a financier. While each of these roles is important, only the roles of consumer and competitor will be discussed here.

With a $50-billion shopping list the federal government is America's largest customer, and as such has always depended upon business to furnish a variety of goods and services needed to accomplish its function. Government purchases an almost incomprehensible array of products. Disregarding military and defense spending, purchases range from paper clips to space capsules, and from adding machines to huge electric generators. Government also buys the skills of thousands of people who perform the tremendous variety of activities in which it engages.

Government purchases of goods and services along with procurement policies which guide government purchasing have a substantial impact on national economic health and social well-being. At the same time, government purchasing creates conflicting responsibilities for both government and business. One issue is the problem of captive suppliers. Government buys in such large quantities that it is sometimes easy for a firm to dispose of its entire output to the government. Similarly small firms are sometimes established for the sole purpose of providing a good or service to government, and thus they depend solely upon government contracts for survival. Small firms organized specifically to provide training for minorities or for hard-core unemployed are examples of such businesses, and there are many other types. On a larger scale, firms in the aerospace industry are examples of firms that become heavily dependent on government programs.

Heavy dependence by firms upon government purchases is usually a potentially dangerous situation, not only for the firms themselves, but for government as well. On the one hand, government cannot support programs or continue to purchase goods and services which are not needed. On the other hand, substantial withdrawal of government purchases from captive suppliers may cause business failures and accompanying undersirable economic adjustments.

There are other dangers of a broader nature inherent in selling to government. Government, in its role as a buyer, has had tremendous influence on business policies. Its purchasing power is sufficient to allow it to dictate terms of purchase, and as a result, management decision and control have been narrowed. So great has been the influence of government that many companies have found it necessary to modify policies in the areas of pricing, products, marketing, financing, and labor.

From a social point of view it seems desirable to encourage captive businesses to limit their dependence on government purchases to a reasonable proportion of total business. To accomplish this, these firms may find it necessary either to expand or to diversify, or both. In order to allow these firms to become economically and socially stable, government may find it necessary to reevaluate its stand on mergers and conglomerates.

Fundamentally the function of the government buyer is to purchase goods and services of the highest quality at the lowest price, but increasingly, government contracts have been used as powerful and convenient tools to put socioeconomic programs into force. There are a variety of laws, executive orders, and procurement regulations which direct government purchasing toward socioeconomic objectives. For example, the government must buy jewel bearings for time-keeping devices and precision instruments from a plant manned by Chippewa Indians. Minority business must receive a portion of prime contracts. All goods for the military, and at least one-half of foreign-aid goods must move in United States flag carriers. And contracts should be channeled into areas of high unemployment. While contracts that conform to these and other criteria do not always result in the highest quality at the lowest price, there is widespread feeling that the social benefits outweigh the economic costs to government. But at the same time conflicting objectives of government purchasing policies sometimes create confusion for both business and the government itself. For example, what happens when a minority enterprise in a healthy economic area and a nonminority enterprise located in an economically depressed area compete for the same contract? Similarly, how does the government decide to award contracts to large firms in areas of high unemployment or to small business? Few, if any, guidelines exist, and decisions are made by the agency concerned using its own best judgement.

Government also engages in a variety of activities that compete directly with private business. Businessmen feel (and so does much of society) that the government should not operate enterprises such as tin smelters, auto repair shops, paint production facilities, shipyards, or air and water transportation. Over the years government has, at one time or another, engaged in each of these activities. Experience has shown, however, that government operation of activities such as these has, in general, proved to be inefficient.

Government also competes with private business in a number of other ways. Through agencies such as the Small Business Administration, the Commodities Credit Corporation, and others, it loans money in competition with conventional lending agencies. Power produced by the Tennessee Valley Authority competes with privately produced power. And the Veterans Administration insures lives. In other areas, the government operates the largest single employment agency, competes with printers, makes false teeth, and provides a wide variety of consulting services which compete with private consulting firms.

In an attempt to help ease competitive pressures on private business, the Bureau of the Budget set out to revise the guidelines on when and how the government can provide products and services for its own use. While the order provides many conditions under which government may provide its own goods and services, it does spell out in detail a specific procedure that a federal agency must conform to in order to enter into any industrial or commercial activity.

SUMMARY

Since the Civil War society has been concerned with the increasing size of business firms and the economic and social power which accompanies size. In an attempt to control business growth and to limit business power, society enacted a series of laws to prohibit mergers. These laws have been relatively ineffective. The number of mergers has continued to increase over time. With the increasing popularity of corporate conglomerates, the size of firms continues to grow. The issue before society is how to achieve maximum social well-being. Postulates and assumptions which are at the base of antitrust legislation appear to be inappropriate to toady's dynamic pluralistic economy.

Government also attempts to control the activities of business through direct and indirect laws, as well as through influence. Of major concern is the military-industrial complex because the defense budget requires a relatively large proportion of the gross national product.

Important, too, is the influence government exerts through its various relations with business. Government acts as a consumer, a supplier, a competitor, and a financier, and in each of these roles has an effect on business decisions.

STUDY GUIDES FOR
INTERPRETATION OF THIS CHAPTER

1. Study recent antitrust cases brought by either the Justice Department or the Federal Trade Commission. To what extent, if any, do the cases reflect the economic philosophy of perfect competition?

2. Explain how private antitrust suits both reinforce and weaken existing antitrust legislation. Support your explanation with examples.

3. There is considerable argument today concerning the social desirability of conglomerates. Take a position either for or against conglomerates and compile a list of examples and reasons to support your arguments.

4. From newspapers or periodicals find estimates of the amounts of money that will be needed in the future to overcome social problems such as urban decay or pollution. How do these figures compare with current defense spending? Do you see in these figures a danger of a future urban-industrial complex or something similar?

5. Using your hometown as a model, list as many examples as you can of ways in which government (at all levels) influences business.

PROBLEM
The Green Acres Funeral Home

For several years Samuel J. Brown and his son operated the Green Acres Funeral Home in a Texas town of less than 8,000 persons. As part of its services, the funeral home operated the only ambulance service within a radius of 25 miles. In addition to attending to heart attack and accident victims and other emergencies, the ambulances were used routinely to move patients to and from rural communities where no hospitals existed to the hospitals and nursing homes in the cities. The service was licensed by the state.

The newest ambulance owned by Mr. Brown was fitted with the latest equipment, but the older vehicles had little or no special equipment. A few of the drivers and attendants were specially trained, but most were students from the local college. The specially trained personnel and the specially fitted ambulance were reserved for emergency calls.

The federal government passed legislation regarding standards for ambulance service. This legislation required that (1) ambulances must provide oxygen and resuscitation equipment and (2) the attendant to the patient must have passed advanced Red Cross instruction. The funeral home was informed by the Social Security Administration that unless its ambulance service met these requirements Medicare payments for transporting the elderly would be withheld. The federal government also notified the state that federal funds for highway construction would not be forthcoming unless all ambulances using public highways met the standards. The state passed legislation similar to federal legislation and notified Mr. Brown that unless all his vehicles met the standards, his license would not be renewed.

Because of the cost involved in meeting these requirements and the difficulty in maintaining a qualified work force, Mr. Brown discontinued the ambulance service; consequently, persons in this community and adjoining small towns had no ambulance service.

1. Identify and explain the business and social issues in this case.

2. Assume that the state legislation had not yet been passed. Further assume that you are the owner-manager of the Green Acres Funeral Home. Explain in detail what you would do upon learning of the proposed legislation.

CHAPTER

13 OWNERSHIP CLAIMS ON BUSINESS

Now that public expectations are exploding in all directions, we can no longer regard profit and service to society as separate and competing goals, even in the short run.

Henry Ford II[1]

As a practical matter, the doctrine of "enlightened self-interest" applies to the stockholders of a corporation as well as to management and other participants in the enterprise.

Committee for Economic Development[2]

During a series of regular meetings, the executive committee of a large American manufacturing firm was considering whether or not the company should attempt to penetrate a particular foreign market. Research indicated a rich potential, and all the executives agreed that the company had the technical competence and the marketing capabilities to make a successful market penetration. A new dimension was added to the question when it was learned that if the company were to be allowed to enter the new market, it would have to pay graft to a functionary of the foreign government concerned.

Some executives argued that the company should not pay graft under any conditions, even if it meant losing the market. Others argued that the risk of losing a highly profitable market jeopardized stockholders' interests and that paying graft was a necessary cost of doing business. Still others said that graft was an acceptable practice in the nation and that the business should not try to impose its American culture on the nation by refusing to pay graft.

Several years ago Peter Drucker in *The Practice of Management* demonstrated forcefully that the first duty of business is to survive.[3] And to survive, it must operate at a profit. Today business leaders are increasingly voicing

---

[1] Henry Ford II, "Business, the Environment and the Quality of Life" (speech delivered before The Harvard Business School Public Affairs Forum, Boston, Mass., Dec. 2, 1969), p. 6.

[2] *Social Responsibilities of Business Corporations,* New York: Committee for Economic Development, 1971, p. 29.

[3] Peter F. Drucker, *The Practice of Management,* New York: Harper & Brothers, 1954, p. 46.

this point of view. One prominent executive expressed his views on the subject this way:[4]

> The first duty of management is to so order its affairs that the corporation will survive. It then has a duty to encourage that the corporation grow and prosper for the benefit of its stockholder owners, its customers, its employees, its creditors and suppliers, its partner the government, and the general society in which the corporation operates.

There are few who question the legitimacy of profit in our modern economic system. But questions concerning how much profit and how those profits will be used are subjects not only of philosophical but of very real everyday concern to business. Indeed, these questions have encouraged modern business to reexamine objectives and methods of achieving those objectives.

One hundred or so years ago there was little question that business activity was conducted primarily for the benefit of the owner(s) or that the sole function of profit was to provide reward for entrepreneurial risk. In the Protestant ethic scheme of things, the more profit the better. Today, in our complex pluralistic society, business has become one of the major social institutions, and therefore, many groups make strong demands on business which tend to dilute profits. Each group, including stockholders (owners), feels that it has a vested interest in business firms, and each, in its own way, tries to maximize satisfactions of its demands.

Partly because of increased size of business and partly because of increased strengths of social groups, relationships between managers and owners have changed during the last century, and their views often conflict. Stockholders in widely held corporations, for the most part, perceive themselves as passive investors rather than co-owners of a business. Under these conditions, traditional control and decision making by owners breaks down and becomes unrealistic, thus placing on professional managers (who may or may not also be owners) the responsibility of making choices between alternative demands of claimant groups. And to make managers' jobs more complicated, they also must make decisions concerning present versus future demands of these same groups.

In this chapter we discuss conflicts between owners and managers occasioned by changing relationships between the two groups, legal responsibilities of management to stockholders, and finally the "management-trusteeship" concept of management responsibility to stockholders.

MANAGEMENT-OWNER RELATIONSHIPS

In every business there are two separate and distinct functions which must be performed if the business is to have life and survive. These have nothing to do

[4] James E. Robinson, chairman of the board, Indian Head, Inc., "The Search for Greater Board Effectiveness" (speech before the Conference Board, Nov. 18, 1971), p. 1.

with the traditional organizational functions of marketing, production, and finance. They are more basic than the organizational functions. They are the function of ownership and the function of management.

Every business must have a supply of money with which to acquire production resources in quantities necessary to achieve business objectives. Businesses are owned by those who provide the necessary capital. In the ultimate sense, then, the sole function of ownership is to provide capital. Owners expect to be rewarded through business profits. Management, on the other hand, is charged with the responsibility of operating the business and ensuring its survival. Questions of how a business should be operated, for whose benefit it is operated, and the purpose of a business in our society have often led to conflict between owners and managers because their points of view are different.

Conflict of Viewpoints

Separation of functions and conflict of viewpoints between ownership and management exist regardless of whether the business is organized as a single proprietorship, a partnership, a corporation, or a government business. Where owners and managers are the same person, as in a proprietorship, a partnership, or a small, closely held corporation, owner-managers play two roles which are in conflict with each other. But the very fact that owners and managers are the same person aids in resolving conflicts. In publicly held corporations conflict is more severe because owners and managers are two separate groups.

What are the responsibilities of managers to owners? Answers to this question depend on whether one takes the managers' viewpoint or the owners' viewpoint. Owners perceive management's responsibilities to be the operation of the business in a way that (1) provides the largest possible return on their investment and (2) causes the value of their ownership shares to appreciate. Both emphasize the concept of maximum profits. Both emphasize priority of ownership demands upon the firm.

There is an increasing tendency for managers to view their responsibilities as being primarily to the firm, rather than to owners. They perceive themselves to be responsible (1) for economic survival of the firm; (2) for perpetuating the firm through product innovation, management development, market expansion, and other means; and (3) for balancing the demands of all groups upon the firm in such a way that these demands do not hinder achievement of the firm's objectives. This viewpoint emphasizes optimization of profits within various constraints imposed by pluralistic groups. It emphasizes satisfactory rather than maximum profits. It emphasizes the idea of a socially profitable business and considers owners to be one group among many. Concerning their specific responsibilities to owners, managers today often express the belief that "what is good for the business is good for the owner."

The Functions of Profit

Profit performs at least four major functions. First of all, it provides a quantitative measurement of the effectiveness of business effort. Second, it provides a return on invested capital; it is the reward to owners for assuming the risks of the enterprise. Third, profit is a source of capital for innovation and expansion. And fourth, it provides for the costs of staying in business.

Management is vested with both legal and moral obligations to work toward the best interests of owners. Traditionally this has meant that management is obligated to work toward the largest possible economic return to owners consistent with the other functions of profit. For the most part, this concept has focused on short-run economic returns to owners. When conflict has arisen between owners and managers, it has arisen over questions of costs of doing business and "legitimate" expenditures of company funds. Company funds spent in the present were expected by owners to be fully recovered, thereby maximizing market values of ownership shares and financial rewards to owners. Today the focus has shifted away from maximizing economic returns to investors to maximizing security of individual firms, and indeed, the business system as a whole. Today businessmen tend to talk less about maximum profits and more about fair, adequate, and reasonable profits. Increasingly they are stressing a doctrine of enlightened self-interest which holds that it is in the best interests of business and all its constituent groups to promote public well-being in a positive way.

Profitability and Social Responsibility

The doctrine of enlightened self-interest requires a redefinition of stockholder interest. While businessmen continue to recognize their obligations to "make a dollar for the owner," they also recognize that business has broader responsibilities to develop the kind of society in which business can grow and prosper and that it is in the best long-range interest of stockholders to do so. The concept of *social profit* has been added to the requirement of *economic profit*. Therefore, according to the doctrine of enlightened self-interest, it is in the best interest of stockholders to use company funds for expenditures which will produce long-run social payouts even though short-run economic returns to stockholders may be diluted by so doing.

Arguments for enlightened self-interest are not complicated. First, business is an integral part of society and depends upon that society to provide resources, i.e., labor, capital, and customers. Expenditures which will promote a favorable environment in which these resources can prosper are not only justified but required. Thus a company that does business primarily in urban areas is justified in using company funds for improving central-city housing, education, recreation, and so forth. These expenditures help develop sources of qualified workers and customers. Similarly, expenditure of funds which focus on the future health and vitality of a firm and its future profits are also justified. For example:

> Two engineers who became dissatisfied with working for a large firm resigned and started their own company. The new company planned to develop and manufacture scientific breathing equipment which could be used in underwater work, in space exploration, and in hospitals. Partly in order to attract highly qualified personnel and partly to discourage unionization, the company established wage rates well above the union scale.
>
> Another illustration of business expenditures to improve the environment in which it operates is that of a large forest-products company that established a paper manufacturing mill outside a small town near the heart of a large forest area. After the mill was built, it was discovered that soil engineering work done on the problem of disposal of waste from manufacturing processes had been incomplete. There appeared to be a remote chance that waste from the plant could filter through the soil and contaminate the ground water, thus endangering domestic water supplies several miles away. Even though the chance of such contamination was slight, the company spent large sums of money to rebuild its waste disposal facilities.

The second argument for enlightened self-interest is negative. If business does not voluntarily accept responsibility for social issues, the result will be direct public pressure on business, government intervention in the business system, or both. Whether they like it or not, managers are required to consider in their everyday decisions forces which dilute short-run profits. Legal requirements on business operations, labor market pressures, the public visibility of business, and public expectations of business performance are some of the forces with which managers must be concerned when making decisions.

The issue of profitability versus social responsibility raises some interesting questions. One of the most interesting is the question of how managers balance the objective of short-run profit with the objective of social responsibility. Obviously the firm that does not have short-run profits cannot invest in solutions to social problems. Therefore managers must strike a balance in working toward these objectives. Henry Ford summed up the approach to achieving this balance as follows.[5]

> The company that sacrifices more and more short-run profit to keep up with constantly rising public expectations will soon find itself with no long run to worry about. On the other hand, the company that seeks to conserve its profit by minimizing its response to changing expectations will soon find itself in conflict with all the publics on which its profits depend.

One answer to finding this balance is that in many areas of social concern public pressure and governmental involvement often create profitable markets.

[5] Ford, loc. cit.

Demands for improvements in housing, manpower development, transportation, urban redevelopment, and other areas of social concern are opening new opportunities for business. Within these opportunities the pursuit of profit objectives and the pursuit of social objectives can be compatible and complementary. For example, demands for environmental improvement may open up large new markets for pollution abatement systems and for new manufacturing systems and technology. Similarly, demands for urban redevelopment offer opportunities for new concepts and designs of space use, new building materials and processes, and new ways of moving people and goods.

WHO ARE STOCKHOLDER-OWNERS?

Stockholders as a separate group are a relatively new development in American business. Prior to 1900, the majority of corporate securities in existence were held in large concentrations by only a few individuals. The objective of holding stock, for these people, was ownership and control. As nineteenth-century firms expanded into today's industrial giants, new issues of stock were dispersed over a wider range of buyers. Many old stock concentrations were broken up and spread over a greater number of people through inheritance or sale on the market. Furthermore, as new companies were founded and as they expanded, they sold new issues of stock, thereby increasing the numbers of people holding stock.

Individual Investors

After World War I, the public at large became significant holders of corporate stock. Today, over 32 million people have direct ownership in our great corporations.[6] That is, they own stock of one or more companies. People from practically every occupational group own stock. Professional people, farmers, teachers, workers at all organizational levels, merchants, public-service workers, and housewives represent a few groups that own stock.

As stock ownership became more diversified and as greater numbers of people held smaller amounts of stock, their reasons for holding stock changed. Few small shareholders today equate their ownership with corporate control. Rather, they view themselves as investors and are primarily concerned with returns on investment, not control. As corporations have matured and grown in size and wealth, there has been an increasing separation of management and ownership and the growth of a professional management group. Owners of large corporations (with the exception of those stockholders who are also corporate officers) do not make decisions. Rather, small stockholders, in their role as investors, depend upon professional managers to make corporate decisions. Stockholders, at least in the

[6] "Where, Oh Where, Has the Little Guy Gone?" *Financial World*, Feb. 28, 1973, p. 4.

large and socially powerful corporations, have been removed from decision-making roles and emerge as an external force exerting pressures on professional managers.

Institutional Investors

During the 1960s the growth of institutional investors was phenomenal. This means that ownership in large corporations is being expanded further. In addition to the more than 32 million people who have direct ownership in corporations, additional millions have indirect ownership through purchasing shares of institutions such as banks, savings and loan associations, pension funds, insurance companies, investment companies, university endowments, religious groups, and mutual funds.

Institutions have tens of millions of dollars invested in corporate stocks, and each year they increase their investments. By 1973 they owned 46 percent of the shares outstanding on the New York Stock Exchange, and they accounted for 66 percent of its trading volume in shares.[7]

What this means for professional managers is that ownership and control are becoming concentrated in large blocks external to the corporation. Historically, individual holdings of stock in any one company have been small, and the individual, *as an individual investor,* has had little inclination to interfere with the management of the firm. Recently, however, individuals—the historical capital investors—have become net sellers of corporate stock. During the decade from 1963 through 1972, they were net sellers in every year, resulting in net disinvestment of over $34 billion.[8] Ownership by large numbers of individuals is being replaced by ownership by a few large stockholders. And with purchases of large blocks of stock by institutional buyers comes potential power to influence corporate policies and financial health.

WHAT DO STOCKHOLDERS OWN?

It is commonly accepted that stockholders "own" the company in which they hold stock. But what do they really own? Do they own property? Do they own certain rights which are attached to private property? Or do they own merely pieces of paper whose value is determined in the stock markets?

Stockholders do not own property in the sense in which we usually think of property ownership. That is, they do not have title to company property, nor can they control its use in the same way that a single proprietor can control his property. Property is owned by the corporation, not by the stockholder, and

---

[7] "Are the Institutions Wrecking Wall Street?" *Business Week,* June 2, 1973, p. 58.
[8] Robert C. Klemkosky and David S. Scott Jr., "Withdrawal of the Individual Investor from the Equity Markets," *M.S.U. Business Topics,* Spring 1973, p. 9.

corporate management determines how corporate property will be used. Since stockholders do not own company property, they can control its use only to the extent that they can influence corporate policy and management decisions. Therefore, small stockholders who own only a few shares have little influence by themselves.

Because of the difficulties of making their voices heard, small stockholders more often than not view themselves as investors rather than owners and generally make little effort to influence actions of the business or its officers and directors. Generally they are concerned with how the company is run only to the extent that the value in the market of their ownership shares is affected. However, stockholders do have legal rights and government agencies to protect those rights. And recently, stockholders, in increasing numbers, have been exercising these rights.

LEGAL RIGHTS OF STOCKHOLDERS

While the law grants wide latitude of decision and action to corporate officers, it does not relieve them of their fiduciary responsibilities. However, the law does not define exactly what the corporate responsibilities should be nor to whom the corporation is ultimately accountable. Thus, relations between corporations and their stockholders sometimes become cloudy.

Specific rights of stockholders are established by law. Legally, stockholders can influence corporate policy through the voting mechanism or, if necessary, by challenging actions of corporate officers in the courts. Stockholders have the following legal rights (and these vary somewhat among states): Stockholders have the right to share in the profits of the enterprise *if dividends are declared by directors*. They have the right to receive annual reports of company earnings and company activities, and they have the right to inspect the corporate books. They have the right to elect directors and to hold those directors and the officers of the corporation responsible for their acts—by lawsuit if they want to go that far. Furthermore, they have the right to vote on mergers, consolidations, changes in the charter, and bylaws, and they have the right to bring other proposals before the stockholders. And finally, they have the right to dispose of ownership certificates.

OWNERSHIP, MANAGEMENT, AND CORPORATE POLICY

Stockholders have long been a docile lot, generally content not to interfere with management. Even though stockholders' rights are clearly spelled out by law, the rules under which these rights could be exercised generally have been so restrictive and burdensome that for all practical purposes small stockholders were powerless to act. Recently, however, small stockholders have discovered devices whereby they can make their voices heard. And they are being supported by government and by the courts. The results have been that relationships between stockholders and managements have changed in a number of ways.

Annual Reports and Stockholders' Meetings
(the Right to Hear and to Be Heard)

By law, stockholders have the right to know about the affairs of the corporations in which they hold ownership shares. Those who attend annual meetings learn about past performance and future goals through speeches made by corporate officers and other media such as the annual report. Those who do not attend meetings must depend primarily on annual reports.

Historically management has tended to provide stockholders with minimum information. Prompted by the Securities and Exchange Commission requirement that large companies must reveal in their reports to the SEC sales and pretax earnings for each product line that accounted for more than 10 percent of sales or pretax earnings, many companies are including in their annual reports more and better detailed information than ever before. A survey of sixty-five large corporations by the Financial Executives Institute found that 75 percent of the respondents favored sharing with stockholders information on product line or business segment profit.[9] At the same time they opposed sharing some other kinds of information —particularly financial figures on research and development—because of fears of competitive and/or government implications. Although the Securities and Exchange Commission requires that this information be filed with the commission, it does not require that the same information be included in annual reports. However, a compelling reason for management to do so is the fear of stockholder suits claiming that information not included in the annual report was material information and that they were injured by not having it. Such stockholder suits will be discussed in a later section of this chapter.

Because the subject of social responsibility is of growing concern to many companies and to many stockholders, annual reports often contain sections on performance and objectives in areas such as minority hiring, pollution control, land reclamation, urban renewal, and other areas of corporate citizenship.

Annual stockholders' meetings are held by law for the purpose of discussing corporate business, and to offer an opportunity to shareholders to approve or disapprove of management. Approval is generally expressed by reelecting incumbent directors and disapproval may be shown by replacing present directors with new ones. Where corporations are small and local in nature or where they are closely held, annual meetings work reasonably well. It is relatively easy to assemble a majority of stockholders, and corporate business is considered and acted upon personally by at least a majority of stockholders. But for the large, publicly held corporation with thousands of stockholders, annual meetings are not so satisfactory. The number and wide geographical dispersion of stockholders have altered the character of annual meetings. Typically, only a small portion of stockholders attend to vote in person. Nonattendees are often given the opportunity to vote by proxy, but more often than not proxy votes are insufficient to overcome

[9] "The Annual Report Becomes a Confession," *Business Week*, Apr. 21, 1973, p. 44.

Does the Shareholder Share Social Responsibility?

The capability of shareholders to act in this area [direct corporate effort toward socially acceptable actions] has been questioned because of their actual lack of control over and of power to influence either the board of directors or management. While according to legal theory the shareholder is the ultimate authority in a corporate enterprise, the reality is a permanent delegation of authority to a self-elected and self-perpetuating board of directors, and not infrequently delegation in turn to management. . . . Despite the charade which is acquiesced in by the vast number of shareholders, including institutions, the role of the annual meeting, especially the occasional proxy fight or even the threat of it, and the market place are in the last analysis the areas where management must be responsive to shareholders.

From Robert S. Potter, "The Investment Responsibilities of Boards Concerned about Human Welfare: A Response to the Threshold Objections of the Notion of Social Investment" in Charles W. Powers (ed.), *People/Profits: The Ethics of Investment*, New York: Council on Religious and International Affairs, 1972, p. 12. Reprinted with permission.

the votes of incumbents, thus, in many cases allowing the board to perpetuate itself if it chooses to do so and to continue with policy as it sees fit.

Even if they were so disposed, few small stockholders are equipped financially to initiate and wage a fight for control with existing management. To unseat present management requires gathering enough voting power by proxy to outvote the incumbents. In proxy fights, the odds for success are heavily weighted in favor of incumbent management. It is not easy to stir a group of apathetic stockholders to join the opposition. Lack of knowledge concerning issues typically leads small, uninterested stockholders to cast their lot on the side of management. Financially, too, present management has the upper hand. It may, and typically does, use both corporate personnel and corporate funds to gather proxies which it may vote in its own support. Financial competence necessary to overcome these odds does not lie with the small stockholder.

Historically, then, small stockholders have had little practical power to influence either corporate policy or who should manage the company. For all practical purposes they could only sell their shares if they became dissatisfied with company performance.

Shareholder Proposals

Beginning in the 1960s and gaining momentum in the 1970s, small stockholders found an effective way of making their voices heard in annual meetings. Historically it has been extremely difficult for a small stockholder to bring a proposal before an annual stockholder meeting. The right of a stockholder to attend annual meetings and vote is created under the *state laws* in which the company is incorporated. Under these laws, in order for a stockholder to submit a proposal to other stockholders for their consideration and action he must obtain a list of stockholders from the company and then send to each a statement of the proposal. This is an expensive and time-consuming process which few small stockholders are prepared to undertake.

Then in the late 1960s the Securities and Exchange Commission amended its rules and allowed small stockholders to place resolutions concerning social responsibility issues in corporate proxy statements. For example:

> During 1970, in what came to be called Campaign GM, a group named the Project on Corporate Responsibility asked General Motors to include resolutions on social issues in its annual proxy statement. GM refused and was subsequently required by the SEC to include proposals on adding to the board of directors representatives of consumers, environmental, and minority groups and to form a committee on corporate responsibility. The company went to considerable expense to oppose Campaign GM and, as a result, suffered a great deal of unfavorable publicity.

In one way Campaign GM failed. The resolutions were overwhelmingly defeated. Yet in another sense, it had positive results. It generated widespread discussion and considerable support from foundations, church groups, and universities. Public pressure resulting from Campaign GM led the company to appoint a black director. The company also formed a committee on public responsibility within the board of directors. But more than this, the SEC change of rules and Campaign GM opened the door to a reevaluation of the relationships between management and stockholders. One observer has commented that "recent events concerning shareholder proposals in companies subject to proxy rules must be rated as an important development in the relations between shareholders and managements of publicly held companies."[10]

While access to proxy statements has been largely confined to social issues, nevertheless some basic issues of management-owner relations have been raised. How much should stockholders vote on? What is the dividing line between stockholder rights and management prerogatives? Originally the SEC rules prohibited proposals which dealt with religious, political, or social issues. These rules were designed to protect management against harassment by nuisance proposals and from proposals by social reformers. The change of rules seems to reflect a spreading belief by society that stockholders should be allowed to vote on social as well as economic questions which are related to the business of the corporation.

Those who favor expanding proxy power of stockholders argue that this will force managements to become more responsible to social and environmental needs. At the same time it is hoped that shareholders will be forced to assess their own priorities. For example, would they rather have a less-polluted community

---

[10] John A. C. Hetherington, "Corporate Social Responsibility, Stockholders, and the Law," *Journal of Contemporary Business,* Winter 1973, p. 52.

with lower dividends and/or higher prices, or would they prefer a more-polluted community with higher dividends and/or lower prices? Those who favor expanding proxy power to stockholders argue that the door will not be opened to cranks and to harassment of management. Furthermore, it is argued, voluntary assumption of social responsibilities leads to good public relations. Perhaps most important of all is that management-controlled activities in the social areas broaden the scope of management decisions. On the other hand, even though stockholder resolutions are not binding, they tend to limit management's choice and threaten managerial discretion.

The Board of Directors

The legal responsibility of the board of directors in the United States is to see that the company is managed in the best interests of its stockholders. The board of directors is supposed to establish corporate objectives and develop broad policies. And the board is supposed to review management's actions to determine whether or not it is achieving objectives in a way which is in the best interests of stockholders. Traditionally the best interest of stockholders has been defined in economic terms.

There is a growing public concern, shared by some directors themselves, that boards of directors, as they have been constituted and as they have functioned in the past, are no longer meeting the requirements of a rapidly changing society. Critics demand that directors monitor more than just the economic performance of the companies they direct and question whether or not long-range stockholder interests are really being best served through primary concern with profit. They question whether or not corporations can survive if they do not place social performance at least alongside economic performance. A variety of suggestions have emerged to make boards of directors stronger and make them function better in terms of a changing concept of stockholder interest. Some suggestions have been to change the membership of boards, change the structure of boards, appoint smarter and better-informed directors, give boards more responsibility and then hold them more accountable for their actions, and finally perhaps do away with boards if they do not perform more effectively. We will discuss only two of these suggestions: proposals to change the membership of boards, and proposals to change their structure.

Membership

The proposal which has gained the most popularity among those pressing for corporate reform is that special interest or "public" directors should be appointed, thus changing the membership from its traditional makeup of businessmen. This proposal would include on boards of directors representatives from various constituent groups such as consumers, minorities, women, environmentalists, employees, and others. The objective of including public directors on boards is to broaden the corporate point of view and allow the public to participate significantly in corporate decision making.

There are several problems involved with special interest directors.[11] First is the lack of experience in America with special interest directors. German companies for some time have had employee representation required by law on their boards. And businesses in other European countries have been experimenting with employee directors. But it is questionable whether European models will work in the same way in the United States.

Second, there is a serious question about how effective special interest directors can be. Inclusion of such directors does not change the power structure of the board itself. If outside members are selected by the board itself there is a high probability that they will receive a harmonious reception and be included fully in board deliberations. On the other hand, outside directors who are imposed on a board may find themselves isolated from real deliberations no matter how competent they are. If important deliberations are conducted informally by small groups of directors and then acted upon routinely at board meetings, special interest directors are ineffective no matter how qualified.

A third problem with special interest representation on boards is assuring representation for all groups in society. And even if it were possible to accomplish representation by all groups, there is a serious danger that the efforts of the board might be diverted from its primary function of looking after stockholders' interests and become an arena for conflicting interest groups. Thus the interests of the corporation and stockholders might become subordinate to the interests of a special interest group.

A fourth problem and probably the most serious of all is the matter of director loyalty. Under law, directors owe their loyalty to the corporation and to stockholders. If directors represent special interest groups, to whom would they owe primary loyalty—to the corporation and stockholders or the groups they represent?

The last two problems do not mean that corporations should not have directors from minorities, or women, or employees, or other constituent groups, but these directors need to have other qualifications besides being a member of a group. There is a difference between being a member of a constituent group and being the representative of that group on a board of directors. While bringing a broader perspective to the board, public directors must be able to place the interests of their particular group in proper perspective of overall responsibility to the long-run health and survival of the corporation.

[11] For excellent discussions of boards of directors see Phillip I. Blumberg, "Who Belongs on Corporate Boards?" *Business and Society Review,* Spring 1973, and "The Board: It's Obsolete Unless Overhauled," *Business Week,* May 22, 1971, p. 50.

Structure

Another suggestion to make boards of directors more effective and responsive to social problems is to create a system of *dual* boards, that is, two boards rather than one with each performing distinct and well-defined functions. This system has been in effect in Germany for many years. Essentially the actions of companies are governed by two groups. The upper, or supervisory board, is made up of people from outside the company and employees. One of its functions is to elect (and remove when necessary) members of the lower, or management, board. Its second function is to receive reports from the management board and to supervise that board. The lower (management) board, which is made up of company executives, is charged with the day-to-day conduct of business.

This system has generally worked well in Germany, but has not always been successful. Critics contend that this system is subject to most of the shortcomings of the single-board system. Even though the top board is made up of outsiders and employees, and thus should bring a broad point of view to the corporation, its members often are superannuated executives from other firms, often cannot obtain from management the information they need, and do not meet frequently enough to be effective.

Stockholder Suits

Another development that affects corporate policy and actions and which has changed management-stockholder relations has been the broadening by the courts of rules under which injured stockholders could sue publicly held corporations, their officers, and their directors. Stockholder suits are not new. Such suits date back to the 1930s. But the rules under which stockholder suits could be brought were so restrictive that small stockholders were virtually precluded from bringing actions. Most states required a stockholder-plaintiff to own a substantial proportion of outstanding stock or be joined by others so that the combined holdings equaled the minimum required proportion before suits could be brought. In addition, the value of the combined stock had to meet rather high market value requirements. Few small stockholders could meet these tests. Moreover, outright fraud or dishonesty had to be proved against officers or directors. Furthermore, even if stockholder suits were successful, individual stockholders stood little chance of personal gains. Money recovered from officers or directors was recovered for the corporate treasury, not the individual. Thus the most individual stockholders could hope for was an unknown increase in dividends, and they were not assured of that.

Then in 1966 the Supreme Court changed the federal rules regarding class action procedures by broadening rule 10b-5, which is the fraud rule of the

Securities and Exchange Act of 1934. No longer is it necessary to prove that the corporation, through the acts of its officers and directors, was *dishonest*. In addition, rules concerning minimum requirements of stock holdings and market value have virtually been swept away, thus giving small stockholders access to the courts in case of alleged injury. And furthermore, under the revised 10b-5 rule stockholders may personally recover to the extent of their injuries. All that needs to be proved is *carelessness*. In increasing numbers, disgruntled stockholders are bringing suits in federal courts charging everything from false earnings reports to unfair merger terms.[12] For example:

> The chairman of the board of a large and prominent publicly held corporation instructed a stockbroker to revise downward his estimate for earnings for the company. Certain stockholders claim that the stockbroker told some favored clients about the downward revision before it became public knowledge. These clients sold at the same time the plaintiffs were purchasing stock in the company. By the time the revised earnings estimate became public knowledge the price of the stock had declined $20. Injured stockholders filed suit against the company to recover their losses contending that they were misled in regard to the earnings picture.

Another example illustrates the size of settlements that may face a business:[13]

> Minority shareholders in a company acquired by a leading mass merchandiser sued the company for omitting material information in its proxy statement on the merger. They have been awarded more than $12 million in claims.

Class action suits by minority stockholders appear *not* to be a passing trend. There is every indication that the trend will increase rather than decrease because there are a number of factors that favor stockholders rather than business. First is the relaxation by the courts of rules which previously made it financially burdensome or difficult for small stockholders to bring suit. A second factor that favors small stockholders is the broadening by the SEC of its disclosure rules. Rules requiring companies to file with the SEC more and broader information often provide stockholders with necessary information which they otherwise might not be able to obtain. A third factor is the willingness of an increasing number of lawyers to take class action cases on a contingency basis rather than on a flat fee basis. And finally, companies that are sued are often willing to settle for large sums. Because class action suits are extremely time-consuming and expensive, it is often cheaper to settle for large sums than to defend a case, even though the company may have a defensible case.

[12] "Sue, Sue, Sue: The Angry Stockholders," *Dun's,* August 1973, p. 25.
[13] Ibid., p. 26.

Insider Trading

A special category of management-stockholder relations which has attracted particular attention has arisen from "insider dealings." Insider dealing is the ability of corporate officers, directors, and other key people to profit from inside knowledge that has not yet become public. The precedent-setting case in the area of insider trading is the Texas Gulf Sulphur case.

The Texas Gulf Sulphur case dates back to 1965 when the SEC charged that a group of company directors, officers, and employees violated the disclosure section of the Securities and Exchange Act of 1934 by purchasing stock in the company while withholding information about a rich ore strike the company had made.

In 1963, test drillings by Texas Gulf Sulphur Company indicated a rich ore body near Timmins, Ontario. On April 12, 1964, the company attempted to play down rumors by describing the Timmins property as "a prospect." But four days later, a second press release called the Timmins property "a major discovery." In what the judge described as the first application of a "due diligence test," the first press release was found "to have been misleading to the reasonable investor using due care, and since the framers did not exercise due diligence in its issuance, TGS violated security laws."[14]

The insiders were directed by the court to pay into a special court-administered account all the profits they had made by trading on inside information. They were also ordered to repay profits made by outside people whom they had tipped. This account was used to settle stockholder suits brought by those who were led into selling their Texas Gulf Sulphur stock on the basis of the press release.

This case appears to say that corporate directors, officers, and key employees are insiders, and that they may not profit, or help others to profit, from knowledge about the company which is not public. It further seems to say that an outsider, if he is temporarily employed, becomes an insider. If these rulings are strictly enforced, it could mean that a corporate official or key employee, a legal counsel, a representative of an accounting firm, or a member of an outside firm doing contract work may be in jeopardy every time he discusses the company or releases information to the press.

The case appears to raise many difficult questions for businessmen. When can one buy or sell securities in his own company? How much information must he disclose to stockholders about the company's plans and outlook? Answers to these questions will probably not come easily, and the chances are that courts will become increasingly sympathetic with stockholders.

While this trend will no doubt have many effects on businesses and businessmen in the future, two phenomena are already apparent. First is the reluctance of highly qualified "outsiders" to serve as directors. Many feel that the

[14] For a review of the Texas Gulf Sulphur case and court remedies see "Texas Gulf Ruled to Lack Diligence in Minerals Case," *Wall Street Journal* (Midwest edition), Feb. 9, 1970, p. 1.

risks involved simply are not worth the return.[15] Second is the tremendous growth in liability insurance which insures corporate officers against personal loss from stockholder suits that allege carelessness (not dishonesty). Many major companies feel they cannot be without such protection for their officers, and the company generally pays all or a large portion of the premiums, thus reducing the amount of profit available to stockholders.

Institutional Influence

So far we have been discussing the influence of small stockholders on management, and only passing mention has been made of institutional stockholders. However, institutions have become an important force which business cannot ignore.

Institutional investors have now grown to such size that serious questions are being raised concerning their power and their responsibilities in exercising that power. The two main concerns are that these institutions (1) may exercise influence upon the corporations in which they hold substantial interests and (2) that as their holdings grow larger, they may no longer be able to sell their stock without endangering the interests of other stockholders or without having an adverse effect on the market generally.

Although institutional investors have had the power to influence corporate policies and actions, only rarely have they exercised their power to bring pressures on management. Traditionally institutional investors have emphasized their role *as investors* and have deemphasized their role of owners. As investors, institutions have been more concerned with returns on investment and appreciation of shares. Dissatisfaction with *performance of the shares* resulted in the sale of stock, not in participating in management decisions.

Recently, however, direct involvement in the affairs of corporations by institutional investors has increased and has had a direct influence on management decisions. Institutions have brought pressure to bear on management in a number of ways.

First is the threat of institutions voting large blocks of stock against management. While these threats have mostly been implied rather than direct, nevertheless they have been effective. The implied threats have largely taken the form of resolutions by institutions supporting activist stockholder proposals in areas of social responsibility or resolutions criticizing specific corporate policies or procedures. For example, Campaign GM brought forth several resolutions (although few actual votes) from universities and religious groups supporting minority stockholder proposals.

Second are direct pressures brought on management by institutions. While

---

[15] Lester B. Korn, "Why Would Anyone Want to Be a Corporate Director?" *Management Review,* February 1973, p. 15.

Trading by Insiders

Trading by insiders on the basis of nonpublic information injures no one —what causes injury or loss to outsiders is not what the insiders knew or did, rather, it is what they themselves did not know. It is their own lack of knowledge which exposes them to risk of loss or denies them an opportunity to make a profit. The purpose of imposing liability on insiders for trading on inside information is not to compensate outsiders for loss, rather, it is to discourage behavior which is considered unethical.

From John A. C. Hetherington, "Corporate Social Responsibility, Stockholders, and the Law," *Journal of Contemporary Business,* Winter 1973, p. 51. Reprinted with permission.

institutions traditionally preferred to dispose of holdings in a troubled company, public pressure sometimes forces them to interfere directly. For example:

A large British firm made thalidomide under license from a German firm between 1958 and 1961. (Thalidomide was the drug that was later proved to cause severe birth defects.) Subsequently, the firm got out of chemicals, but when deformed babies began to appear, a number of families began to sue the company. Although the firm denied responsibility, it awarded about $38,000 to each of sixty-two deformed children and later agreed to set up a trust to compensate the families. But some families objected to the terms of the trust and a prominent newspaper ran a series of articles on thalidomide and its effects, thus causing a wave of public indignation against the firm and public demands that the trust be increased. At this point three large institutional stockholders (two insurance companies and one bank) felt compelled to apply pressure on the company management to increase the terms of the settlement.

Third, some institutions refuse to invest in securities of firms that they judge not to be responsive to social problems. Types of institutions most likely to use social responsibility criteria in judging investment opportunities are religious organizations, foundations, and universities. *Business and Society Review* surveyed several such institutions to determine the extent to which social responsibility criteria had affected investment decisions.[16] The sample was small (six religious organizations, six foundations, and twelve universities). The researchers reached the conclusion that although the institutions were beginning to consider seriously social responsibility criteria, investment decisions in most of the organizations at that time were not significantly affected by them. Yet a year earlier a company that managed four mutual funds with assets over $3.5 billion polled its shareholders concerning their views on the relationship between corporate social

[16] "Who Uses Social Criteria in Institutional Investing?" *Business and Society Review,* Summer 1972, p. 95–98.

responsibility and investment policy.[17] Overwhelmingly, shareholders said corporate social responsibility should be a major criterion in investment decisions.

Church groups seem to be increasingly active in trying to influence corporate policies. An estimated $22 billion worth of securities puts them in a position to do so. The National Council of Churches, through research and publications prepared by its Corporate Information Center, attempts to keep its constituencies informed on company policies and actions. But more important, it attempts to persuade churches to use their leverage as shareholders to change corporate policies.

A fourth pressure which is sometimes brought to bear on businesses by institutions is the formation of special kinds of mutual funds that stress investment in socially responsible companies. These funds are based on the concept that there are many investors who are willing to forgo a small amount of profitability in return for socially responsible corporate activities. This is indirect pressure and affects businesses to the extent that such investment policies may make it more difficult for unresponsive corporations to raise money in the equity markets.

MANAGEMENT TRUSTEESHIP

Today, corporate directors and officers are generally considered to stand in a fiduciary relationship not only to stockholders but also to society as a whole. Courts seem to uphold this philosophy.

A basic case establishing this philosophy is *A. P. Smith Manufacturing Company v. Barlow.*[18] On July 21, 1951, the directors of A. P. Smith Manufacturing Company, wishing to exercise what they considered to be corporate public responsibility, donated $1,500 to Princeton University. Certain stockholders challenged management's right to dispose of corporate funds in this manner on the grounds that it was a misappropriation of corporate money and was, in fact, an *ultra vires* act. The stockholders contended that the directors of a corporation had no power to use corporate funds for any purpose other than those set forth in the corporate charter.

Through its president, the company argued that it considered the contribution to be a sound business investment. By contributing to educational institutions, it was argued, corporations were assuring a supply of properly trained people for future employment. It was further argued that the public expects corporations to support such institutions and that by doing so they gain goodwill in the community. Several highly respected business leaders supported this position by their testimony. The chairman of the board of Standard Oil testified that it was good

[17] "That Kind of Money Talks," *Business and Society Review,* Summer 1972, p. 98.
[18] 13 N.J. 145, 98 A.2d 481 (1953). Appeal to the New Jersey Supreme Court found in 26 N.J. Super. 106, 97 A.2d 186 (1953). Appeal to the United States Supreme Court found in 346 U.S. 861 (1953). A complete review of this case may be found in D. R. Forbush et al., *Management's Relationships with Its Publics,* Evanston, Ill.: Northwestern University Press, 1960.

business to accept "obligations of citizenship in the social community," and a former chairman of U.S. Steel commented that such expenditures were necessary for a company "in protecting the long range interests of stockholders, its employees, and its customers."

Both the trial court and the appellate court upheld the corporation and its directors and agreed that "anything that tends to promote with the public a company's good will is a reasonable measure toward the corporate objective of earning a profit." The United States Supreme Court dismissed the case for lack of a federal question.

The Trusteeship Concept

With the growth of large corporations has come growing support of the management-trusteeship concept. This view deemphasizes management's primary identification with ownership and emphasizes the social-responsibility concept. It recognizes that business, in modern society, has responsibilities to many pluralistic groups. It is a concept of plural trusteeship. Under this concept, ownership interest must take its place alongside vested interests of other social groups. Management, then, becomes an arbitrator in balancing conflicting interests of all groups.[19] In the final analysis, business is accountable to society, not to any one social group.

The trusteeship concept, however, is not universally accepted as being the correct approach to management-stockholder relations. Those opposed to the concept see it as establishing managers in authoritarian roles whereby they apportion shares of corporate income according to their own personal value systems. Shares are dictated on the basis of personal morals and ethics, rather than according to economic concepts of returns to factors of production. It is argued that acceptance of the trusteeship concept alters the nature and purpose of corporate enterprise and undermines the foundations of private property.

Even the most ardent proponents of management trusteeship would not contend that management has no responsibility to stockholders. On the contrary, it has very real and definable responsibilities. As Eells and Walton have stated, "It is one thing to say that the risk-bearing stockholder has little function; it is quite another to say that he deserves little respect."[20] It is generally conceded that management is obligated to preserve and protect the interests of stockholders—to operate the company in a way that does not waste corporate resources and thus endanger or threaten stockholder investment. Management decisions that result in large losses for the company always make management competence suspect, in the

---

[19] Adolph A. Berle, Jr., and Gardiner C. Means, *The Modern Corporation and Private Property,* New York: The Macmillan Company, 1932, p. 356.

[20] Richard Eells and Clarence C. Walton, *Conceptual Foundations of Business,* Homewood, Ill.: Richard D. Irwin, Inc., 1961, p. 151.

eyes of both stockholders and society in general. Ford Motor Company's debacle with their Edsel and General Dynamics' fiasco with the Convair 880 and 990 are cases in point. Unsound management practices endangered stockholders' interest as well as public interest in both cases.

The Edsel Case

Within the four years and seven months from the time the Edsel program was started until it was discontinued, Ford spent some $350 million on the new Edsel project.[21] Why was the venture a failure? It is difficult if not impossible to focus the blame at any one point. A combination of several factors is probably the real answer. Poor timing has been suggested as a major reason. The Edsel, a medium-priced, medium-sized car, was offered at the precise time that compact cars were becoming popular. Second, motivational research used to design the car did not provide the right kind of information. Third, the intense preintroduction advertising based upon suspense and mystery had the public so worked up that they expected a radical dream car. When the car proved to be fairly traditional, disappointment turned to resentment. Fourth, the car was introduced at the beginning of the 1957–1958 recession. Fifth, the design, while not wholly traditional, was not sufficiently different to motivate people to buy. Sixth, it has been suggested that the name Edsel conveyed the wrong image to the public. Last, heavy mechanical failure among the first cars along with considerable unfavorable press coverage destroyed public confidence.

While some of the above circumstances such as the 1957–1958 recession were difficult to forecast, others could have been avoided. In actual fact, the results were not as catastrophic for the company or its stockholders as might be imagined. Strength of the other Ford divisions allowed the corporation to absorb the huge losses. But potential dividends were lost, and market prices of stocks tumbled. Those stockholders who held their stock survived, but those who lost confidence and sold lost heavily.

The Convair Case

Even more severe were General Dynamics Corporation's losses through Convair Division's attempt to enter the market for commercial jet aircraft.[22] General Dynamics lost $490 million on its jet program. In effect it lost 90 percent of its assets on one venture. Again a number of managerial errors combined in an

---

[21] John Brooks, *The Fate of the Edsel and Other Business Adventures,* New York: Harper & Row, Publishers, Incorporated, 1963.
[22] Richard Austin Smith, "How a Great Corporation Got Out of Control," 2 parts, *Fortune,* January 1962, and February 1962.

exponential progression to result in the debacle. Poor cost analysis, unsound pricing, wrong forecasting of market needs and market potential, underestimating competition, and poor contract negotiation all contributed to the staggering losses. Death of a strong autocratic president who closely controlled the far-flung divisions left a gap in top management with no strong replacement. Lack of information and control at the corporate level occasioned by a highly decentralized organization let danger signals go unheeded. All these errors pointed General Dynamics squarely for the bankruptcy courts. Only putting strong controls into the hands of an executive committee of seven directors and imposition of severe financial restrictions by the banks has saved the corporation.

In retrospect, one senior vice president of the company summed up by saying: "It's a grave question in my mind as to whether General Dynamics had the right to risk this kind of money belonging to the stockholders for the potential profit you could get out of it. All management has to take a certain risk for big gains. But I don't think it's right to risk so much for so small a gain." [23]

NONPROFIT AND GOVERNMENT BUSINESS

So far in this chapter, we have discussed business in a narrow sense. We have limited our discussion to private enterprises, but there are many other kinds of businesses, and people invest in them in various ways.

Nonprofit businesses depend on resource inputs just as profit-oriented businesses do. People invest in nonprofit organizations in a variety of ways. They contribute time, talent, effort, financial support, and other inputs necessary for the business to function. Like investors in private enterprises, they depend on management to use these resource inputs wisely and to give the payoffs these investors seek. For example, the large symphony orchestra association or the large civic theater association is supported financially by contributions and ticket sales. Others invest time and talent. But the investors have little to say about how the resources are used. These decisions are made by a professional manager who is hired by the investors, and they depend on him to provide culture and a better community, which are their payoffs.

The same applies to many government activities. For example, national parks are purchased or developed with tax funds and hence are "owned" by citizens. But ownership does not carry control with it. Only in a remote way do citizens control the way national parks are run. They depend upon managers to run the parks for their benefit. And the "owners" pay fees for their use just as a nonowner (noncitizen) does. Or consider a municipally owned sewage disposal plant bought by citizen investment. Citizens, or investors, depend on professional managers to run the plant and, except through occasional elections, have little direct control.

[23] Ibid., February 1962, p. 187.

Ownership in nonprofit and government institutions is somewhat different from ownership in private enterprises. Owners do not own title to property. They do not even own certificates which they can sell in the market. Ownership in these institutions is really only an "investorship." Investors enjoy the right to use the benefits of their investment, but when they leave the area covered by the investment (for example, a city) they have no marketable shares to cash in.

In other words, the investor-manager separation prevails everywhere, not just in private enterprise, and the responsibility of managers to investors is the same whether we are talking about a private enterprise, a nonprofit enterprise, or a government enterprise. Managers are trustees for all the groups which make claims against the enterprise. Opera companies and national parks must bargain with labor, deal with suppliers, anticipate consumer demand, provide investor returns, and relate to other groups in much the same way as do other enterprises. And they must depend upon managers to fulfill these responsibilities.

SUMMARY

Conflicts sometimes arise between owners and managers because owners feel that businesses should be operated in a way that will provide maximum returns on invested capital. Managers, on the other hand, feel that they must balance the demands of owners with demands of other claimants, thus maximizing security and survival of the firm.

As stock ownership has become widely dispersed among large numbers of individuals, motives for owning stock have changed. Small stockholders see themselves only as investors. They have emerged as an absentee-owner group exerting pressures on a group of professional managers for social and economic payoffs.

With increased separation of management from ownership, an increased acceptance of the management-trusteeship concept has developed. Because results of business decisions are so widely felt, not only by stockholders but by other groups as well, management is increasingly considered to stand in a fiduciary relationship not only to stockholders but also to the rest of society. Increasingly there has been an acceptance of the philosophy "what is good for society is good for the stockholder." Increasingly management has come to view stockholders as one of several groups whose demands of the firm must all be properly balanced. Stockholders have the right to demand that management properly safeguard their investment in the enterprise, but so do other social groups.

STUDY GUIDES FOR INTERPRETATION OF THIS CHAPTER

1. From various sources at your command, gather all the facts you can about a stockholder suit and present the case to your class for discussion.

2. It has been observed that in modern society it is a mistake to think about pursuit of profit and pursuit of social values as separate and competing business goals. Develop two sets of arguments: one to support this statement, and one to repudiate it.

3. Does the management-trusteeship concept apply to nonprofit and government enterprises as well as to private enterprises? Select a nonprofit or government enterprise in your community and analyze it in terms of its responsibilities.

4. Find out all you can about institutional investors. What is your assessment of the power of these institutions to influence management decisions? Do you view this power as good or bad? Why? Do you think it necessary to regulate these institutions in any way? Why or why not? If you think it is desirable to regulate institutional investors, how should they be regulated?

5. Explain the doctrine of enlightened self-interest as it applies to stockholder interests. How can a company justify the concepts of social profit and economic profit at the same time?

PROBLEMS
The Blue Lake Chemical Company

The Blue Lake Chemical Company is located in a major Midwest city on one of the Great Lakes. The plant discharged some of its industrial waste into the city sewer system, which emptied into the lake. The company was charged by conservationists with contributing to the pollution of the lake and was asked to allocate $1 million to clean up its part of the problem. Analysis showed that only 6 percent of the pollutants were contributed by the chemical plant. The other 94 percent came from general use of the city sewer.

The question of whether or not to allocate the money was discussed in several meetings of the board of directors. In considering the question the following points were made:

1. Even if the company did spend $1 million, the largest part of the problem would still exist.

2. The public would not be able to see much improvement.

3. Expenditures of this sum would not increase future earnings.

4. Immediate earnings per share would be decreased, thus reducing the amount available to distribute to stockholders.

5. Failure to act would probably not result in widespread public reaction against the company.

6. People were becoming increasingly alarmed and aroused about the injury to swimming and fishing areas.

7. If pollution is to be stopped, someone has to take the lead.

1. If the board of directors decides *not* to allocate the money, how can the decision be justified?

2. If the board decides to allocate the money, how should the company proceed?

The Socially Significant Stock

One evening, a small group of young businessmen were discussing social problems and the relations of business to those problems. They agreed that because of its managerial and technical expertise, private enterprise should take the lead. They also agreed that maximum profits and maximum social good rarely go together. The question then became how can private enterprise make a maximum contribution to the solution of social problems and at the same time provide a satisfactory return to ownership.

A new kind of company was suggested, a company whose objectives would be the solution of social problems. But how could the company be financed? It was suggested that there were many people, particularly among the more affluent investors, who would invest in a company of this type. These people might be willing to trade off some economic gain for social gain and to accept a modest financial return if they could be assured of maximum social returns. The young businessmen reasoned that there are numbers of people who are willing to support financially a cause in which they believe, and used as an example to support their point the tremendous sale of low-yield war bonds during World War II.

1. Do you believe that a company of this type might be successful? Why?

2. What sort of product-service mix do you suggest for such a company? Be specific.

3. Do you believe that a company of this type could be financed in this way?

14
BUSINESS
AND ITS CUSTOMERS

Modern civilization is dependent for its existence absolutely upon the proper functioning of the industrial and business system.

Henry L. Gantt[1]

Consumers are turning more and more to their government for protection. They have to.

Bess Myerson Grant[2]

In a major Eastern city the formation of a new kind of profit-making corporation was announced. What distinguished this corporation from other corporations was its objectives. The stated primary objective of the firm was to sue companies "that have violated their public trust by polluting the environment or defrauding customers."[3]

In another city the fraud section of the district attorney's office filed a $4-million suit on behalf of customers against a company that distributes encyclopedias and other books door to door. Included in the suit were various officers and salesmen of the company. Charges of unfair and fraudulent business practices were lodged against the defendants, and the suit asked for civil penalties, punitive damages, and injunctions.

On a major highway an automobile broke away from the truck which was towing it and crashed into an oncoming car. Both occupants of the oncoming car were severely injured. In a suit against the automobile manufacturer, the injured parties claimed that the accident was the result of defective design of the front bumper tow bracket on the runaway car. The jury agreed, and the plaintiffs received a large monetary award.

[1] Henry L. Gantt, *Organizing for Work,* New York: Harcourt, Brace and Company, Inc., 1919, p. 3.
[2] Bess Myerson Grant, "Protecting the Consumer: An Interview with Bess Myerson Grant," *The MBA,* March 1970, p. 29.
[3] "The Anti-Corporation," *Newsweek,* Nov. 29, 1971, p. 93.

While the incidents mentioned above are not directly related to each other, they are all part of a growing movement in which consumers, sometimes with the help of government and sometimes without, are increasing their demands on business to improve quality and reliability of products and to make buying decisions easier. In this chapter we will discuss business and customer relationships and the ever-increasing responsibilities of business to interpret consumer wants, to provide dependable products, to help customers make intelligent choices of products, and to assume risks of product failure.

BUSINESS-CONSUMER RELATIONSHIPS

In the eighteenth and early nineteenth centuries the United States was primarily an agrarian nation with relatively simple needs and wants. The bulk of its population lived in rural areas. Those who lived on farms produced a substantial portion of the goods they consumed. Even many of those who lived in cities and towns produced domestically much of what they wore, ate, and used. Businesses were small for the most part. Merchants dealt mostly in either luxury goods or basic items which could not easily be produced at home. Manufacturers, likewise, concentrated their efforts on basic items which were difficult, if not impossible, to manufacture at home. Crude iron, gunpowder, and firearms, for example, found a ready market. Similarly, luxury items (for the times) such as china, silverware and pewter ware, and high-quality clothing found a market among the wealthy. And because technology was relatively unadvanced, most products were fairly easy to judge for quality. For the same reason, products were simple to use, and repairs were uncomplicated. For the most part, then, consumer reliance on business was limited.

As the nation became increasingly industrialized, as raw materials changed character and finished products became more complicated, and as urban concentration grew, consumer dependence on business also increased. New products appeared, and old products became more refined and more complex. And the United States, more and more, became a nation of specialists dependent in turn on other specialists for the assortment of goods and services necessary to live in an increasingly complex economy. Rather than citizens being rugged individualists, independent and capable of providing for their own needs, citizens today both individually and collectively are highly dependent upon others for their well-being. Typically, individuals no longer grow or preserve their own food, make their clothing, provide their own transportation, or make their own tools. Nor do they attempt to make or build the hundreds of other items that go into making life pleasant. Consumers today depend upon hundreds of businesses to satisfy their needs and wants. Consumer dependency is one side of a coin. The other side is business responsibility. Since citizens as consumers are dependent upon business to satisfy their needs, business must have responsibilities to consumers.

THE CONSUMER MISSION OF BUSINESS

The first quotation at the beginning of this chapter expresses the idea that business is a key subsystem in our modern society. Business can never be given unilateral responsibility for total well-being in our pluralistic society, but it does play a central role in a private enterprise economic system and is instrumental in shaping economic decisions.

Paul Samuelson points out that every society must answer three fundamental economic questions:[4]

1. What commodities shall be produced and in what quantities?
2. How shall goods be produced?
3. For whom shall goods be produced?

Business Decisions

In the free world, businessmen play a key role in answering the questions just mentioned. On the basis of their interpretation of consumer wants, they decide what commodities should be produced and in what quantities. And they bear the risk of wrong decisions. A decision to produce a radically different automobile model may be unprofitable for both the company and society if society rejects this type of model. On the other hand, a decision to produce low-cost, maintenance-free, simple-to-operate sewing machines may be profitable to both company and society if the product enables mothers who are at the poverty level to provide decent clothing for their children who might otherwise be kept out of school because of inadequate clothing.

Businessmen also decide how goods shall be produced. They decide how factors of production shall be combined and choose the best production process so that products and services may be produced at the lowest cost and thereby offered to consumers at the lowest price. Decisions concerning for whom goods will be produced are also made by businessmen. Decisions to produce high-quality and high-priced articles limit the number of consumers who can obtain the commodity. Businessmen, then, have a strong voice in determining the variety, quantity, and quality of goods and services that people depend upon for their comfort and well-being.

Consumers as Decision Makers

In a planned economy such as Russia's, answers to the basic economic questions of what commodities to produce, how they shall be produced, and for

[4] Paul A. Samuelson, *Economics,* 8th ed., New York: McGraw-Hill Book Company, 1970, p. 15–16.

whom they shall be produced are provided by a central planning agency. Russian businessmen are relieved of much responsibility to consumers. But businessmen in a free enterprise system are responsible to consumers, because in the long run it is the consumers themselves who provide most of the answers to the questions posed by Samuelson.

Businessmen in free enterprise economies have no place to turn for answers except to consumers, who hold a veto power over business decisions. Businessmen can determine how best to serve society by reviewing and predicting consumer behavior, that is, by noting what consumers buy or do not buy and by anticipating future consumer needs and wants. Consumer willingness to buy depends upon how well products and services satisfy these expectations. Satisfaction or dissatisfaction of consumer expectations, in turn, is readily translated into profits or losses. Consider, for example, Du Pont's experience with Corfam shoes.

Marketing studies indicated that by 1982 there would be a leather shortage and that about one-third of the shoes would have to be made from materials other than leather. Shoes made from Corfam were tested under representative conditions by representative users. Users were enthusiastic about the ease of care, and only about 8 percent complained of some discomfort compared with 24 percent of those wearing shoes made of other leather substitutes. However, after shoes made of Corfam were marketed in volume, other consumer dissatisfactions began to appear. The material did not feel, crease, or bend like leather. It did not take a permanent stretch like leather, and more consumers complained of discomfort than preliminary research had indicated. Also, technical problems of large-scale production which could not be solved at the time required product prices which could not compete favorably with leather. The combination of customer resistance to price and to the product itself spelled failure for Corfam shoes. After an investment of close to $100 million and several years of work DuPont discontinued the product.

Dissatisfied consumers behave in a variety of ways, some of which make it very difficult for businessmen to benefit from consumer judgments. The most common type of dissatisfied consumer behavior is the silent boycott. Consumers may silently refuse to purchase a product or service because they do not perceive a need for it. Other consumers who have purchased a product or service and have been dissatisfied may silently vow not to purchase that product or service again. Most businessmen prefer that customers make their dissatisfactions known. One restaurant operator commented: "If a customer is unhappy with his meal, we want to know about it immediately. We want to correct our mistakes and live up to his expectations, but we can't if we don't know about them." Sometimes consumers undergo strange transformations and become anticustomers,[5] telling everyone who will listen how bad the product is. Consider an extreme case.

[5] William G. Kaye, "Take in a New Partner—The Consumer," *Nation's Business*, February 1970, p. 54.

Ed Smith purchased a new model automobile from the Jones Automobile Agency. Unfortunately, it was one of the occasional automobiles which seemed to have an unending series of defects. Dissatisfied with the car and with the treatment received from the dealer, Ed Smith finally painted the car a bright yellow and parked it prominently in his front yard. Across the side of the car he had lettered in prominent black letters the following announcement: "THIS IS A LEMON. PURCHASED FROM THE JONES AUTOMOBILE AGENCY."

THE SYTEM CONCEPT OF BUSINESS

The business enterprise is a total system within itself and at the same time is a subsystem within the social suprastructure. Businessmen have not always looked at the business enterprise from a system point of view but have often tended to view various functional specialties within the firm as being largely independent of one another. Marketing and production were often viewed as separate functions which were only remotely related. In reality the specialized functions of production and marketing are both part of the same entrepreneurial function of satisfying consumer needs, and each depends upon the other. Both depend upon the consumer's assessment of product value. Therefore, both functions should start with the consumer.

A Problem of Definitions

One reason that it has been difficult for businessmen to view the business enterprise as an integrated system lies in traditional definitions of functional specialties. The definitions themselves tended to compartmentize each function and isolate it from other functions. According to most traditional business definitions, production was concerned only with the creation of form utility. Definitions of marketing assigned to the marketing function only the movement of goods and services from producer to consumer. A typical attitude was that the marketing department should sell whatever was produced in the plant. Marketing and sales were viewed as synonymous.

Today enlightened businessmen are shifting away from the production and/or marketing orientation and beginning to focus on overall responsibilities to consumers, as explained in the following quotation:[6]

> Effective marketing implies more than the satisfaction of customer expectations as related to product performance or appeal. Effective marketing means an ever more precise refinement of *all* organizational operations to conform to changing

[6] W. Thomas Anderson, Jr., Louis K. Sharpe, and Robert J. Boewadt, "The Environmental Role of Marketing," *MSU Business Topics,* Summer 1972, p. 69.

Consumer Orientation

Even the limited, unidimensional perspective of the consumer orientation does not free the marketer from his concern and responsibility over the broad spectrum of issues. Sooner or later he will undoubtedly be confronted with the disquieting groundswell of "consumerism" and the "consumer movement." It is important to recognize that this thrust of interest in consumer welfare extends well beyond simple dissatisfaction of customers with allegedly inferior products. It covers the entire question of the nation's poor, the minority groups, the elderly, and other disadvantaged citizens in terms of their ability to receive fair treatment in the marketplace.

From Leslie M. Dawson, "Marketing Science in the Age of Aquarius," *Journal of Marketing*, July 1971, p. 67. Reprinted with permission.

customer expectations for enterprise performance over time. The entire firm is evaluated through its products. The day is long past when firms could view their products as essentially autonomous from the firm itself.

Consumer Orientation

Another reason it has been difficult for businessmen to adopt a consumer orientation has been an idealogical conflict. The emphasis of pragmatism, social Darwinism, and the Protestant ethic on individualism contributed to a philosophy of producer sovereignty which embodied the idea that producers knew better than consumers what products and services would best satisfy consumer needs. This philosophy was also strengthened by a relatively limited supply of consumer products and fairly predictable consumer value systems and life-styles. It was relatively easy to dispose of products that provided reasonable consumer satisfactions, and therefore it was easy to separate production and selling into two unrelated functions.

As society moves from the industrial stage to the postindustrial stage, the philosophy of producer sovereignty becomes less and less workable and product decisions depend more and more on an expanded marketing function. The observation has been made that "only now, as marketing begins to assume responsibilities beyond skillful selling, do we realize the narrowness of most of its past efforts in the consumer field."[7]

Today's consumer is a product of the postindustrial stage of societal development. Consumers are more affluent, and their curve of expectations is rising sharply. Life-styles and value systems are changing rapidly. All this means that it is increasingly difficult for business to identify just who the customer is and exactly what customer expectations are. However, several consumer trends seem to be

[7] Richard H. Brien, Betsy D. Gelb, and William D. Trammell, "The Challenge to Marketing Dominance," *Business Horizons,* February 1972, p. 27.

evident. For example, age groups and income no longer correlate as they once did. Young people often are affluent enough to buy luxury products. Consumers are becoming more concerned with quality or the lack of it. Consumers shop more for price, quality, styling, and convenience than for particular brands. Finally, consumers are more unstable, buying things they do not really need but which complement their life-style.

The foregoing discussion suggests that if business is to fulfill its purpose in society, it needs to be sensitive and responsive to desires of those it claims to serve—that is, consumers. Strong customer orientation seems to be the key to success. In order for business to do a better job of relating to consumer expectations, Boyd and Levy made a suggestion some time ago that still seems appropriate today. They suggested that product decisions should be made in terms of *consumption systems,* that is, "the way a purchaser of a product performs the total task of whatever it is that he or she is trying to accomplish when using the product—not baking a cake, but preparing a meal."[8]

BUSINESS AS AN INSTRUMENT OF CHANGE

Because we live in a capitalistic economic system, we have grown used to change. Indeed, we have come to expect it, for capitalism itself is an evolutionary process. Competitive forces at work within our capitalistic economy center around finding better ways of performing the consumer mission of business, that is, providing more and better goods and services for consumers at lower prices. In short, we expect the economic system under which we live to provide a rising standard of living, and "the fundamental impulse that sets and keeps the capitalistic engine in motion comes from the new consumers' goods."[9]

Business as an Agent

As the agent of consumers, business has the responsibility of producing a never-ending flow of new and different goods and services, thereby contributing to increased consumer well-being. Consumers, then, have delegated to business certain responsibilities for their well-being, and increasing consumer well-being depends upon change. Business has always been an agent of social change. However, in today's dynamic social system it is increasingly difficult for business to fulfill its responsibilities for orderly change. It is not that business shirks these responsibilities. The problem is in the accelerated pace of change. The problem for

[8] Harper W. Boyd, Jr., and Sidney J. Levy, "New Dimension in Comsumer Analysis," *Harvard Business Review,* November–December 1963, p. 130.

[9] Joseph A. Schumpeter, *Capitalism, Socialism, and Democracy,* New York: Harper & Brothers, 1942, quoted in Edwin Mansfield (ed.), *Monopoly Power and Economic Performance,* New York: W. W. Norton & Company, Inc., 1964, p. 30.

business is in moving in the same direction and with the same speed as consumer expectations. No longer do consumers think of their standard of living only in terms of products. They think in terms of *all the things that go toward improving the quality of life*. They expect business to adjust quickly to rapidly changing life-styles, value systems, and consumer priorities and to provide goods and services consistent with these changes. Often change is so rapid that business cannot technologically and/or economically adapt products and services within the time frame expected by society, thus creating social dissatisfactions with the business system. In this age of instant potatoes, instant coffee, and instant credit, society has come to expect instant change from business—a phenomenon which business often finds difficult to accomplish. Nevertheless, it is often amazing that business has done as good a job as it has.

Responsibility for Innovation

How can business enterprises provide the kinds of goods and services demanded by consumers? How can business enterprises know what consumers want or need? The answer seems simple: Ask them. But in reality the answer is more complex. Consumers rarely know what kinds of products will best satisfy their needs. But they can and do define the need itself.

A few years ago women could not have told Du Pont that they wanted nylon stockings. But they could and did express their need for stockings which were as sheer as silk but which were more durable, held their shape better, and were easier to launder. Once the need was identified, a product could be developed that would satisfy the need.

Similarly, a few years ago not many home insurance buyers could define "comprehensive homeowners' policies" as we know them today, but they recognized the convenience of combining their insurable risks and dealing with just one company.

The companies that pioneered nylons and homeowners' policies were consumer-oriented. They were sensitive to the needs of the consumers *from the consumer point of view*. Examples of product innovation which have satisfactorily met consumer needs are numberless. Garbage disposals, television, electric garage doors, new techniques in vascular and heart surgery, computers, nuclear energy, new metal alloys, jet engines, plastics, and automobile and equipment leasing are a few examples of product research and innovation.

Innovation responsibilities go much further than just product research. These responsibilities today extend to broader questions of what society considers to be the quality of life and which products and services support that quality of life. As environmental problems become more severe, business may well find it necessary to accept increasing responsibility to provide an array of goods and services entirely different from that offered today.

In order better to exercise innovative responsibility, businessmen have learned to encourage and develop upward communications from consumers. They are beginning to listen to customer complaints and to encourage customer suggestions, and more research is being done to identify consumer needs. Only when consumer needs are understood can business properly exercise its innovative responsibility—its responsibility to be creative in the consumer interest.

THE CONSUMER MOVEMENT

Considerable difference of opinion exists concerning whether or not business has lived up to its social mandate of providing proper quantities of goods and services at the lowest price compatible with adequate quality. Many consumers feel that business has not lived up to its responsibilities, and the increasing number and size of organized consumer groups stand as testimony to this belief. The result has been the consumer movement, or consumerism.

The Anatomy of Consumerism

What is consumerism? Consumerism has been defined as "a social movement seeking to augment the rights and powers of buyers in relation to sellers."[10] It is basically a protest movement in which consumers are protesting against what they feel to be unfair use of business power.

Within a free enterprise economic system, sellers are presumed to have certain rights. Subject to considerations of consumer health and safety, sellers may offer for sale any product they wish in any size or style. They may even offer some dangerous products if warnings and controls are provided. They may price products any way they wish so long as pricing policies do not violate the Clayton Act. They may spend as much money as they choose on advertising to induce buyers to purchase, and they may use any message that is not misleading or dishonest. They may also use any buying incentive program that is not contrary to law.

Buyers also have traditional rights in a free enterprise economy. They have the right to buy or not buy as they choose. They also have the right to expect the product to be safe. And finally buyers have the right to expect the product to be what the seller tells them it will be.

At the heart of the consumer movement is the attempt to expand the traditional rights and powers of buyers and to make these rights and powers

[10] Philip Kotler, "What Consumerism Means for Marketers," *Harvard Business Review,* May–June 1972, p. 49.

Consumerism

Yet the misgivings of some businessmen have a certain justification. The New Consumerism comes in all shapes and intensities, and includes extreme zealots as well as sensible people. It sometimes seems dominated by activists to the point where it resembles a religious movement. Too often it is narrow, single-minded, and evangelical, selling its ideas with the same high pressure it abhors in commercial salesmen. Too often it lacks a sense of humor and the sense of proportion that goes with it (a lot of Americans these days seem to have no sense of humor), and so fails to distinguish between good and bad. Most important, its only cure for unfairness and deception seems to lie in the toils of government regulation.

From Gilbert Burck, "High-Pressure Consumerism at the Salesman's Door," *Fortune*, July 1972, p. 71. Reprinted with permission.

effective checks on the powers of business. Consumers are demanding four enforceable rights: the right to be fully and adequately informed; the right to have safe and dependable products; the right to make intelligent choices among products; and the right to be heard.

Reasons for the Consumer Movement

The basic reason for the growth in the consumer movement is that consumers feel there is an unfair use of business power because the power-responsibility relationship is out of balance. Consumer advocates claim that the balance of power lies with sellers and that business has failed to exercise responsibly the massive power it has. They claim that traditional buyers rights are not enough to maintain a power balance when consumers rarely have full information and when they are subjected to persuasive and sometimes conflicting advertising at every turn.

A key reason for the imbalance of power is that consumers today are more dependent on business for product quality than ever before. Because products are so complex, consumers have no way to judge at the time of purchase whether or not their quality is satisfactory. This was not so in the old days when a consumer bought a buggy whip or a plow.

A second reason for the imbalance of power also relates to product complexity. Complex products often require special handling or special use which is different from that to which consumers are accustomed. Instructions for use or care of the product are often complex and detailed to the extent that consumers cannot understand or cannot remember instructions.

A third reason for the imbalance of power revolves around packaging. Packaging often prevents consumers from adequately inspecting a product before purchase, thus forcing them to rely upon the written description on the package.

Consumers often complain that information on the package is so technical, complex, or vague that it is impossible for the average person to judge quality.

Finally, many products used routinely by today's consumer are not single products at all, but rather a combination of several different products assembled to perform a special function. Automobiles are an excellent example, and there are many more, such as sewing machines, lawn mowers, household appliances, and clothing. Many of the component parts of such products are invisible to consumers, who therefore cannot inspect them even if they had the technical competence to do so. Thus they must rely totally on producers for quality.

While dissatisfaction with product quality and reliability has been a major source of consumer frustration and thus has contributed to the growth of the consumer movement, dissatisfaction with services also has been a major contributing force. The following case is an illustration of the increasing number of stories about consumer frustrations.[11]

> Mrs. L. Hugh Hutchinson, wife of a retired Air Force colonel, ordered a self-cleaning oven for her new Atlanta town house. Workmen jammed the oven into a wall opening that had been cut for a smaller appliance, thereby bending the oven out of shape. They removed it and more carefully installed another that turned out to have a defective thermostat. A repairman pulled out the thermostat and broke it. He summoned a colleague, who arrived with a new thermostat that was 15 inches too short. The two procured yet another thermostat, spent an afternoon trying to install it, and after much hammering and knocking reduced the oven to what Mrs. Hutchinson calls "a basket case—literally. They carried it out in 14 pieces in a basket."

In earlier days people performed many more services for themselves than they do today. Because products were simpler they required less service and repair. When service or repair was necessary, less knowledge or skill was required. Also most people could not afford to hire someone else to perform services for them. Furthermore many people had basic skills and knowledge necessary to make simple repairs and perform uncomplicated services. Consequently, people tended to be relatively self-sufficient.

In today's world of complex products and specialized work, people are unable to provide services for themselves as they once could. Instead they rely on an expanding variety of businesses to provide services. Few people today can repair their own automobiles or home appliances nor do they want to prepare their own income tax returns or dispose of their own garbage. Thus, consumers have become dependent upon businesses that provide services in the same way that they have become dependent upon businesses that provide products. Consumers feel that because they are dependent upon business for services, business has the responsibility to provide quality services. They feel that failure to provide quality

[11] "America the Inefficient," Reprinted by permission from *Time. The Weekly News Magazine,* Copyright Time, Incorporated, 1970, Mar. 23, 1970, p. 73.

service is a misuse of business power just as is the failure to provide quality products.

We are not suggesting that the experience of Mrs. Hutchinson represents typical performance of American business. Far from it. There are thousands of businesses providing products and services which are far superior to any that have been offered in the past. The commissioner of the New York City Department of Consumer Affairs commented that "we have found that there are as many consumers who come to us with complaints which are irresponsible and without basis in documentation as there are fraudulent merchants."[12] The important point is that consumers are becoming more critical and are demanding more from business than ever before. It is also important to note that stories such as the experience of Mrs. Hutchinson are more and more frequently finding their way into print, thus making consumer dissatisfaction more visible.

In a broader sense, consumers are also becoming more knowledgeable and more aware of product safety and the effects of products and services on their individual and collective well-being. Led by men like Ralph Nader, society is increasing its demands on business for greater responsibility to consumers. And as social concern over the myriad of environmental problems grows, it is likely that demands for more responsibility to consumers will be directed toward both business and government.

Is Consumerism a Passing Fad?

There is considerable debate over whether consumerism is a temporary social phenomenon or a permanent social institution. Although the protest part of the consumer movement may disappear or reappear only occasionally, there are strong indications that the movement will endure. Philip Kotler suggests:[13]

> The ecology issue is here to stay and will continue to feel the consumer movement. The plight of the poor will continue to raise questions about whether the distribution system is performing efficiently in all sectors of the economy. There are more educated and more affluent consumers than ever before, and they are the mainstay of an effective social movement. The continuous outpouring of new products in the economy will continue to raise questions of health, safety, and planned obsolescence. Altogether, the issues that flamed the current consumer movement may be more profound and enduring than in the past.

There is also visible evidence of the permanency of the movement. Various "truth" laws, i.e., Truth in Lending, Truth in Packaging, and others, auto safety laws, clean-air and water acts, along with court decisions concerning product safety which have been favorable to consumers, all seem to indicate permanency.

[12] Grant, op. cit., p. 29.
[13] Kotler, op. cit., p. 52.

Similarly, the strengthening of the Federal Trade Commission and the federal Food and Drug Administration, along with the creation of the Environmental Protection Agency, also seems to indicate permanency.

Because of the increasing dependence on business by consumers there is little question that business responsibilities to consumers have also grown. The following sections of this chapter discuss some of the business responsibilities that have been emphasized by the consumer movement.

RESPONSIBILITY FOR PRODUCT INFORMATION

Understanding consumer needs and producing goods and services to satisfy those needs do not complete business's responsibility to consumers. Business has additional responsibilities to provide adequate and truthful information so that consumers can make intelligent buying decisions. For the most part this is accomplished through advertising and labeling.

Truth in Advertising

Consumers need a variety of information about products if they are to make intelligent buying decisions. Business can and does provide much of this information through advertising.

There has been, over the years, considerable controversy over both the economic justification and the legitimacy of advertising. It has been argued that advertising is economically undesirable because it serves no economic purpose. Further criticism also centers around truthfulness.

While criticisms of economic waste are still occasionally directed against advertising, they seem to occur less frequently and with less intensity than they did a few years ago. This may well reflect a more sophisticated understanding which accepts advertising as both socially and economically desirable.

More severe and persistent than questions of economic justification are criticisms of untruthfulness in advertising—misleading statements, half-truths, and failure to disclose full information about products. One nationwide survey among men and women of all ages, incomes, and backgrounds indicated "that 60% of those interviewed feel that recent criticism of advertising is totally justified. They also feel that less than half of all advertising is 'honest and informative.' "[14] Among other findings of the survey were that most respondents favored more regulation of advertising, that they regarded direct mail as the most unbelievable and misleading, and that they thought that ads are too repetitive.

In order to provide some standards against which to judge the propriety of

---

[14] Survey conducted by Warwick & Legler, Inc., and reported in "The Public Is Wary of Ads, Too," *Business Week,* Jan. 29, 1972, p. 69.

advertising claims, Congress in 1938 passed the Wheeler-Lee Act. The Wheeler-Lee Act empowers the Federal Trade Commission to prevent the use of false and misleading advertising of goods moving in interstate commerce. The law covers not only specific representations about products, but also the extent to which material facts are *not* revealed.

Responsibilities of business to provide full and truthful information seem clear. Consumers are fully dependent upon producers for product knowledge. Therefore, to fulfill adequately its responsibilities in its relations with customers, business needs to provide as much truthful information as possible. Consumers seek confidence that the product will be as represented and will do what is claimed for it.

Not all businessmen have seen fit to assume their responsibility for advertising accuracy. Nor is this situation peculiar to the present. Much advertising of a generation or two ago would be distasteful if repeated today. Consider some of the early advertising claims of one prominent company. In reviewing early U.S. Borax Company advertising, an observer commented:[15]

> There is little doubt as to how the sophisticated customer of today would react to the optimistic selling pitch of one of the company's first advertising booklets: 20 Mule Team Borax was recommended as an aid to digestion; to keep milk sweet; as a complexion aid (''Don't wash your face in ordinary lake water''); to remove dandruff; and for the bath (''Use half a pound of powdered borax to the ordinary family bath of twelve gallons of water''). . . . And as a final fillip, Borax, claimed the advertisement, was also ''excellent for washing carriages'' and useful in curing epilepsy and bunions.

While there are few advertisers today who could make such broad claims for their products, many current advertising practices are frowned upon. It is not so much the blatant untruths that cause the trouble as the half-truths and the subtle deceptions. Untruths are relatively easy to detect and control. Subtle misrepresentations and deceptions are much more difficult to control because they are subject to debate.

> For example, in a classic case the Federal Trade Commission charged that some photographs advertising a soup were misleading because the company and its advertising agency placed clear glass marbles in the soup to support vegetables and other solid ingredients. The Federal Trade Commission said the photographs exaggerated the amount of solid material actually present.

> The company responded that no extra food ingredients had been added, but since the solid ingredients tended to sink to the bottom they needed to be supported so they could be seen in a picture.

[15] Velma A. Adams, ''Why the Old Products Last,'' *Dun's Review and Modern Industry,* April 1965, p. 112.

What way do you suggest for fairly representing the amount of solids in a soup?

Responsible businessmen do not suggest that nothing should be done about misleading and deceitful advertising. They recognize that there are those who abuse the advertising media just as there are those who abuse other freedoms in a pluralistic system. Nor do responsible businessmen deny the need for some form of control to protect the public and maintain the usefulness of advertising. But most businessmen feel that the actions of the FTC are often unfair to business. They argue that the burden of proof is unilaterally on business because FTC claims are often not substantiated by fact, nor are they required to be. They argue that if business is required to substantiate its advertising claims, then the FTC should also substantiate its charges of wrongdoing. Further, businessmen argue, publicity released by the FTC concerning charges often inflicts an undue hardship on business, particularly if advertising claims are later proved to be correct. For example:

> A manufacturer of antifreeze used in automobile radiators advertised that its product not only protected against freezing but stopped small leaks in radiators. The company illustrated its product on television by punching small holes in a can containing the product and showing how, in a few seconds, the leak was sealed. The FTC charged that these illustrations were misleading, and the charges were publicized. Later the FTC withdrew its charges and admitted that the company's claims and the ads in question were not misleading.

Closely related to truth in advertising is the question of truth in labeling. Consumer advocates claim that the requirements of the 1966 Fair Packaging and Labeling Act are not enough and that additional legislation is required if consumers are to make meaningful price comparisons and economical buying decisions.

Two supplements to the 1966 law are commonly offered. One alternative is to equip all consumers with computational devices which, when given total price and weight, would yield the price per unit. This alternative is favored by retailers. They argue the devices are easy to use and inexpensive. Consumers are not convinced because the devices require more shopping time, and their use may not be easily learned by all consumers. A second alternative is for retailers to clearly mark the price per unit of net weight on each package. The second alternative is opposed by retailers because, they claim, they would have to increase their labor force which would result in higher prices for consumers.

There has been considerable controversy over whether indicating the price per unit really does help the consumer. Research indicates that it does. One study asked groups to pick the "most economical" item for several product groups using alternative methods. One method provided net weight and total price but also provided a computational device. An alternate method provided price per unit of net weight as well as net weight and total price. Results of the study "indicated that presenting the additional information of price per ounce of net weight produced a significant increase in accuracy of choices, while significantly reducing the time required to make such choices."[16]

RESPONSIBILITY FOR PRODUCT PERFORMANCE

Consumers have the right to expect products to perform in the way producers claim they will, and further, they have the right to expect products to be safe. In earlier days when products were simple and familiar to consumers it was reasonable to expect consumers to share the responsibility for product performance. Since products changed slowly, consumers were able to keep abreast of operating characteristics, quality, and purposes for which products could be used. If a product failed in use or if a user was injured, part of the responsibility lay with the user. Furthermore, most markets were small and closed, and consumers frequently dealt directly with producers, thereby making it possible to settle disputes over product failure on a face-to-face basis.

Product Liability Litigation

In today's complicated economy, consumer relationships with products they use and relationships with producers of those products are much more complicated and abstract. It is no longer reasonable to expect consumers to share the responsibilities for product performance as they once did. The burden of responsibility has been shifted to the producer. Although many businesses have attempted to assume much of the responsibility through money-back guarantees and other similar policies, society has felt that this is not enough and has demanded that business assume the major burden of responsibility. The result has been a strengthening of product liability laws and a softening of court attitudes toward consumer claims. Walls protecting producers from consumer lawsuits have crumbled, and there has been a dramatic increase in product liability suits. One corporate officer observed: "Today a poorly made product is no longer passed off with the remark, 'I got a lemon.' More likely the words are, 'I'll sue.' "[17]

Reasons for changes in product liability laws and for the increase in successful product liability lawsuits are much the same as the reasons for the growth of the consumer movement which were discussed in an earlier section of this chapter.[18] Changes in laws and court attitudes reflect society's sympathies with consumers'

[16] Robert D. Gatewood and Robert Perloff, "An Experimental Investigation of Three Methods of Providing Weight and Price Information to Consumers," *Journal of Applied Psychology*, February 1973, p. 81.

[17] H. D. Hulme, quoted in "They No Longer Say, 'I Got a Lemon'—Nowadays, They Say, 'I'll Sue,' " *Forbes*, Apr. 15, 1972, p. 55.

[18] Conrad Berenson, "The Product Liability Revolution," *Business Horizons*, October 1972, p. 71–72.

inability to cope with product complexities, their unfamiliarity with the product, and their lack of opportunity to inspect products because of the way they are packaged. Also, in today's long marketing channels consumers rarely have the opportunity to purchase directly from producers, even if they wanted to. Furthermore, the rapidity with which product improvements are made and the speed with which products are replaced in the marketplace make it virtually impossible for consumers to keep informed.

Magnitude of Litigation

For these and other reasons there has been a staggering increase in the number of product liability suits and in the size of judgments. The *Wall Street Journal* observed: "Products that don't work as they should, which now rival automobile accidents as the nation's No. 1 cause of litigation, were responsible for an estimated 500,000 court cases last year, compared with 100,000 five years ago, and many expect the annual total to reach one million by 1985."[19] The same report indicates that the percentage of awards to plaintiffs is also rising—from 49 percent in 1965 to 52 percent in 1972. Furthermore, even though no total statistics are available, it is evident that the size of individual awards to those injured by faulty products is increasing.

Traditionally consumers have had little legal recourse against producers of faulty products. The common legal defenses available to producers were the doctrine of privity of contract, warranties, and the doctrine of strict liability in tort. These defenses will be discussed in the following sections.

The Doctrine of Privity of Contract

The doctrine of privity of contract stressed direct contractual relationships and held that producers could avoid responsibility for product failure if a product was purchased from someone other than the producer himself. This meant that injured consumers could sue only the person from whom they purchased a defective product—not the producer. The dealer could then sue the wholesaler and so on up the chain of distribution. In the economy of the early 1800s this doctrine probably made a great deal of sense. But as the distance between user and producer widened and as products passed through longer and more complex channels of distribution, the strength of this defense has been dissipated through court decisions. The landmark decision was rendered in 1916.[20]

[19] Richard A. Shaffer, "More Customers Press Lawsuits against Firms Selling Faulty Products," *Wall Street Journal* (Midwest edition), Nov. 3, 1972, p. 1
[20] *MacPherson v. Buick Motor Company*, 217 N.Y. 382, 111 N.E. 1050 (Court of Appeals of New York, 1916).

Mr. MacPherson purchased a new Buick automobile from a local dealer. Shortly thereafter defective wooden spokes in a wheel collapsed, and Mr. MacPherson was injured as a result. He sued Buick. The company claimed that MacPherson had purchased the car from a dealer and not from Buick and therefore Buick had no obligation to him. The judge ruled that Buick had been negligent because the wheel had not been inspected before it was put on the car. He further ruled that Buick was responsible for defects resulting from negligence, regardless of how many middlemen were in between.

The philosophy of privity of contract has been expanded since the MacPherson decision. Today an injured consumer can sue any or all persons in the chain of distribution. In general the courts have reasoned that through advertising and labeling, manufacturers make a variety of representations about the product. The manufacturer intends and expects the product to be purchased and used in accordance with his representations of performance and assurances of quality. Therefore, when a consumer purchases the product and that product fails to live up to express or implied representations and thereby causes injury to the purchaser, that purchaser has the right to be reimbursed for the injury.

Warranties

Because buyers today are so heavily dependent upon producers' information in their buying decisions, problems of misleading information, fraudulent information, and implied safety of use, are receiving more attention than ever before. Heavy pressures from courts have emphasized business responsibility in the area of warranties. Recent decisions have stressed the point that since producers have done everything they can through advertising to convince consumers that their products are suitable and safe for a specific use, they must be liable for product performance.

There are two kinds of warranties—express and implied. When a seller offers a product for sale, he makes some claims for its characteristics. Claims that are explicitly stated by the seller are express warranties. Representations on a warranty card that the parts of a product will not fail within ninety days from the time of purchase are examples of express warranties. Not all express warranties are on the warranty card. Statements on labels, wrappers, packages and in advertising are also express warranties.

More troublesome for sellers is the question of implied warranties. Courts have held that simply by selling a product to a customer the seller implies that the product is fit for the ordinary use for which it is likely to be used. The landmark case in the area of implied warranty occurred in 1960.[21]

[21] *Henningsen v. Bloomfield Motors, Inc. and Chrysler Corporation*, 32 N.J. 358, 161 A.2d 69 (Supreme Court of New Jersey, 1960).

In this case Mr. Claus Henningsen purchased a new automobile which he and his wife drove around town for several days. Then, when driving out of town, the steering mechanism failed, and Mrs. Henningsen crashed into a highway sign and then into a brick wall. She sustained injuries and the car was a total loss. Mr. Henningsen went to court. The automobile company claimed that Mr. Henningsen had signed a disclaimer when he bought the car and this limited the liability of the company to replacement of defective parts. The court held that the company could not avoid its legal responsibility to make automobiles good enough to serve the purpose for which they were intended.

Doctrine of Strict Liability in Tort

A tort is a civil wrong that sometimes results in injury to a person. Within the last few years courts have increasingly taken the position that manufacturers are responsible for injuries resulting from use of their products. It is not necessary for consumers to prove either negligence or breach of warranty. Nor is contributory negligence an acceptable defense. If a product is judged to be inherently dangerous, manufacturers can be held liable for injuries caused from use of the product. And strict liability extends to all who were involved in the final product—suppliers, sellers, contractors, assemblers, and manufacturers of component parts. The concept of liability in tort has been summarized as follows: "The liability of the manufacturer does not stem from either contractual or promissory understanding; instead, *liability in tort arises from the fact that the courts are imposing a social responsibility on manufacturers and sellers.*"[22] The landmark case which opened the way for product liability suits under the concept of strict liability in torts occurred in 1963.[23]

Mr. Greenman, after reading promotional material and watching demonstrations of a Shopsmith combination power tool, expressed to his wife his desire to have one for his home workshop. She purchased one of the tools and gave it to him as a gift. Two years later he purchased a lathe attachment for the basic tool. While using the lathe attachment, the wooden block upon which he was working flew out of the machine and seriously injured him. He sued Yuba Power Products, the manufacturer, and he was able to prove certain screws in the machine were inadequate to hold the parts together. The California Supreme Court ruled that issues of negligence or breach of warranty were not relevant. The court held that "a manufacturer is strictly liable in tort when an article he places on the market, knowing it will be used without inspection, proves to have a defect that causes injury to a human being."

[22] Berenson, op. cit., p. 75.
[23] *Greenman v. Yuba Power Products, Inc.*, 59 Cal. 2d 57, 27 Cal. Reptr. 697, 377 P.2d 897 (Supreme Court of California, 1963).

Broadening Liability for Product Performance

Social philosophy, reflected in court decisions, is demanding that business assume an increasing burden of responsibility for products and services. One observer commented:[24]

> As things stand now in most of the states of the Union, anyone injured by a defective product can sue everyone connected with the product—the manufacturer, his suppliers, his distributors, the retailers. He can bring class actions on behalf of everyone who bought the product. All he need prove is that, for some reason, the product doesn't work the way a reasonable man—and perhaps even an unreasonable one—has a right to expect.

It seems clear that the responsibility of business for satisfactory product performance is well established. It also appears that the concept of product liability may be broadened in the future so that liability will be imposed on sellers —regardless of whether or not the product was defective. And as the courts become more liberal, it seems likely that product liability will be extended even further to include advertising agencies, public accounting firms, and others who stand in close relationship to sellers and upon whom consumers depend to make buying decisions.

Because many products are so complex, consumers also depend more heavily on producers to provide service in case of product failure. Few consumers today can repair their own refrigerator, washing machine, lawn mower, or automobile. As products become more complex and technical, producers have an increasing responsibility to provide parts and service. Manufacturers of farm machinery and automobiles have long recognized their responsibility in this area and have maintained marketwide service organizations and local inventories of parts.

Businesses are liberalizing their policies on repair of faulty products, cash refunds, and exchanges of unsatisfactory products. There is an increasing trend to formalize and strengthen warranties. Most electrical appliances now carry with them express warranties for one year. Not many years ago the usual warranty on a refrigerator was three months; now a five-year warranty is normal. The Federal Housing Authority requirement of a one-year guarantee by builders on houses to be sold under FHA mortgages has set a precedent for general contractors. Chrysler Corporation pioneered in the automotive field with liberalized guarantees. In the retail field, Sears, Roebuck led the way with their unconditional money-back

[24] "They No Longer Say, 'I Got a Lemon'—Nowadays, They Say, 'I'll Sue, '" *Forbes*, Apr. 15, 1972, p. 57.

guarantee. Much of Sears's success has been attributed to consumer confidence built in this way.

While many manufacturers cannot afford to maintain large service organizations, this does not relieve them of responsibility for service. Most reputable manufacturers have recognized this responsibility and have accepted it by maintaining stocks of parts, authorizing and training private service enterprises to service their products, and/or standing ready to repair items at their factories.

Responsibility for Self-Regulation

Under ideal conditions the business system would be a self-regulating system in regard to consumer responsibilities, particularly for product information and performance. Ideally, every firm should recognize its responsibilities to consumers and willingly exercise these responsibilities to its fullest ability. But this is a utopian approach which has little meaning in the real world. Because business behavior in the area of product information and performance revolves heavily around ethics, it is difficult to obtain general agreement on proper ethical behavior. There are differences of opinion between consumers and producers concerning what is proper behavior.

Earlier chapters of this book emphasized the idea that if a social institution does not serve society in a manner which provides suitable social payoffs, society will replace or modify that institution. Society, then, ultimately controls various institutions by setting standards of product information and performance. Business has little choice but to accept and conform to these standards. However, it does have two choices of how to conform. It may voluntarily regulate its own performance, or it may submit to forced regulation by society through legislation.

Business has not always taken the initiative in establishing high ethical performance standards for product safety and product information. This lack of leadership has encouraged minimum legal standards, such as those set by the Food, Drug, and Cosmetic Act and the Wheeler-Lee Act. On the other hand, much effort has been devoted by individual firms and by entire industries to encourage high ethical behavior.

Basically, there are three reasons why business tries to regulate and police its own activities. The first and most often proposed reason is to avoid government action. This reason reflects defensive thinking on the part of businessmen and focuses on minimum compliance with society's standards. It emphasizes legal performance boundaries beyond which business cannot go without interference. Review of relations between the Federal Trade Commission and the cigarette industry over the years suggests that efforts toward self-regulation on the part of the industry have been largely efforts to avoid restrictive legislation.

The second reason for self-regulation is to achieve status. In an attempt to "professionalize" an industry, businessmen sometimes submit themselves to self-administered policing under government procedures. For example, in many states contractors must be registered and licensed before they can operate. Contractors themselves often are quite active in establishing criteria for both registry and licensing and in formulating criteria for withdrawal of registry or license.

A third reason for self-regulation is a growing belief on the part of both industries and individual firms that "what is good for society is good for business." This belief is reflected in the authority given to some trade associations and in company codes of ethics. Rather than focusing on minimum performance, firms that hold this belief often choose to exceed society's standards.

CONSUMER BENEFITS VERSUS COST OF CONSUMER PROTECTION

In today's complex society consumers need help. But how much consumer protection is appropriate? How far should society go to ensure the consumer rights mentioned earlier in this chapter? Theoretically, society could devise and implement protective measures that would completely insulate consumers from all risk of wrong decisions. However, the fact that some protection is good does not mean that more protection is automatically better. There is the matter of the cost of providing consumer protection. Therefore, the question facing society is: Do the benefits of protecting consumers from business practices *and from themselves* justify the costs of providing that protection?

Economic Cost

One category of consumer protection cost is economic cost. Rising cost to sellers of product liability insurance, along with costs of defending charges of the FTC and other regulatory agencies, all result in higher product prices. Technological development costs as well as manufacturing costs of consumer protection devices, such as seat belts, pollution control devices, and built-in safety features of products used in the home, also increase consumer prices.

Another economic cost is the cost to taxpayers of developing and operating the government bureaucracy needed to formulate and administer consumer protection measures. For example, if consumer protection saves consumers $10 million but it costs $20 million to provide that protection, is the protection worthwhile?

Social Costs

Another category of consumer protection cost is social cost. One of the greatest potential social costs is the potential loss of individual freedom of choice. Loss of freedom is a serious social loss—perhaps even more serious than injury to some individuals. Should not the individual have the right to make an occasional mistake? Perhaps mistakes will help him learn to be more responsible. Overprotection, on the other hand, may make him dependent on the system, and thus he may lose his capacity to make decisions.

Another form of social cost concerns government. Proliferation and expansion of consumer protection agencies increases the size of government and thereby may upset the pluralistic balance.

Perhaps a less obvious but equally important social cost is that consumer protection tends to discourage innovation. Dangers of product liability suits and actions of regulatory agencies tend to inhibit the introduction of new products and services, thus depriving society of benefits which it might have had, or which it might have had sooner.

Opportunity Costs

A third category of consumer protection cost is opportunity cost, and these costs arise from the ordering of social priorities. Resources used for one purpose make them unavailable for other use. Disproportionate concern with consumer protection may divert attention and resources away from social problems which should have equal or perhaps greater priority.

SUMMARY

Consumers are beginning to emerge as a powerful pluralistic social institution. As the nation has become industrialized, as products have become more complex, and distances between consumer and producer have increased, consumers are forced to depend on producers more than ever before for product reliability and for truthful product information upon which to base purchasing decisions.

Business has not always responded well to consumers' needs and wants. As a result there has been an increasing amount of restrictive legislation. Courts, too, have become progressively more strict in requiring producers to assume responsibility for product failure. All in all the consumer movement poses a challenge for business: a challenge to become more consumer-oriented, and a challenge to "do better." On the other hand, society must realize that consumer protection is not free. However socially desirable consumerism may be, the costs should be weighed against the benefits.

STUDY GUIDES FOR INTERPRETATION OF THIS CHAPTER

1. Select two advertisements for consumer goods from newspapers, magazines, or television. Evaluate and compare them in terms of how well they provide reliable information which would help consumers make buying decisions.

2. How and to what extent can business depend on consumers to advise in production decisions? Do such activities add unnecessarily to costs?

3. Find out all you can about government consumer protection programs. Evaluate the following statement in terms of today's practices: The purpose of government consumer protection programs is "to help honest and conscientious businessmen by discouraging their dishonest and careless competitors."[25]

4. From interviews with insurance company representatives, lawyers, or other sources, find several examples of court cases concerning producer liability for product performance. What are the social issues involved, and to what extent do you or do you not agree with the decisions of the court? Why?

PROBLEMS
The New Rule

A federal government agency proposed rules that would require food stores to have available all advertised items and to sell them at advertised prices. The proposed rules came as a result of consumer complaints. The agency said that its investigators found considerable evidence that items advertised as "specials" in newspapers either were not available or had not been marked down to advertised prices.

The evidence was gathered as a result of two surveys made by the agency. One survey covered 137 stores operated by ten chains. The other survey covered 154 stores operated by nine different chains. The first survey showed that 11 percent of the items advertised as specials were not available in the 137 stores. The survey also revealed that substantially more "special" items were unavailable in low-income areas than in high-income areas.

About 9 percent of the advertised items were marked with prices higher than those advertised. And at the stores of several chains 10 percent or more of the items were mispriced.

The proposed rules would require any food retailer to have advertised specials readily available to customers in quantities sufficient to meet reasonably anticipated demands, and at or below the prices advertised. Under the proposed rules, companies cited by the agency for alleged violations would have the burden of proof that the rules were inapplicable to them or that the alleged violation did not occur.

The agency announced that it will have a hearing on the proposal and interested parties are invited to present their view.

1. You are a major official of a large grocery chain, and the president (your manager) has asked you to attend the hearing and present the company's

[25] President Richard M. Nixon, quoted in *Washington Report,* Washington, D.C., National Restaurant Association, Nov. 10, 1969, p. 2.

views. What stand will you take toward the proposal, and how will you present your case?

2. As a consumer make a cost/benefit analysis and explain whether you will support this proposal.

A Question of Uniqueness

The Federal Trade Commission brought a suit against a national baking firm asking that the firm be barred from making claims that its product is "special" unless it clearly describes the qualities that make it so and indicates that in other respects it is just like similar products.

The advertisement is a TV commercial which begins by asking the question: "How big do you want to be?" Children are then shown giving such answers as, "Big enough to see the parade," or "Big enough to surf." A child is shown on the screen progressing through various stages of growth while the announcer tells the audience that the child needs Wonder Bread during the Wonder Years—years one through twelve when a child grows to 90 percent of adult height. The announcer goes on to say that the product contains proteins, minerals, carbohydrates, and vitamins needed for growth.

The main argument about the ad revolves around the question of the extent to which it does or does not represent the product to be nutritionally unique. The FTC and the producer agree that the product is not unique. It is a standardized enriched bread meeting legal nutritional requirements. The FTC claims that the ad directly and by implication represents the product to be nutritionally outstanding. The producer claims it has the right to publicize certain qualities which the product shares with other similar products.

1. What are the basic issues involved?

2. Assume the role of either the FTC or the producer. Prepare as many arguments as you can to support your position on this question.

3. Assume that the FTC wins this case. What are the implications for manufacturers of products such as gasoline, sugar, and milk?

CHAPTER 15

BUSINESS, EMPLOYEES,
AND ORGANIZED LABOR

The computer may be to middle management what the assembly line is to the hourly worker.

Howard C. Carlson[1]

A [labor] *movement born as a voice of dissent has become a mainstay of the status quo in a period when even the staidest institutions . . . have felt obliged to take a critical look at all their most cherished precepts and scrap those made obsolete by changing technology and mores.*

A. H. Raskin[2]

After twenty-five years with a large manufacturing company Mr. Jones, a vice president, submitted his resignation. He announced that he was leaving his $100,000-a-year job for a small retail business and the presidency of a nonprofit, socially oriented organization because he wanted "to do something different."

In another city an upper-middle manager of a large, well-established company in the service sector spent a sleepless night wondering if he had made the right decision the previous day. He had resigned from the company for which he had worked for the past twenty years. At the same time he had completed arrangements to establish a one-man repair and service business in a small, somewhat isolated resort town.

In yet another city, workers walked off their jobs in a new automated assembly plant which was supposed to eliminate the hard work and drudgery of assembly lines and at the same time improve manufacturing efficiency. The workers and their union complained that the new plant accentuated monotony and "dehumanized" work.

While the above incidents are unrelated, they all illustrate a phenomenon which is growing in contemporary society. They all illustrate a widespread and growing discontent by employees at all levels. This chapter will discuss that discontent. We will examine reasons for deteriorating work satisfaction and

---

[1] Howard C. Carlson, quoted in "G.M. Zeroes in on Employee Discontent," *Business Week,* May 12, 1973, p. 141.
[2] A. H. Raskin, "The Labor Movement Must Start Moving," *Harvard Business Review,* January–February 1970, p. 110.

discuss possible solutions to the problems. We will also examine the relationships of business and organized labor.

EMPLOYEE DISSATISFACTION

Discontent with work is nothing new. It has been around as long as work itself. Workers who built the Pyramids staged a work stoppage over working conditions, and history is full of incidents of worker revolt. The theme of worker discontent in modern society seems equally evident. Factory workers who are sullen and bored on production lines, office workers who are equally bored, middle managers who view themselves as lost within giant corporations, and some top managers as well, who look upon themselves as lonely figures at the top—all are evidence of changing attitudes toward work and dissatisfaction with the work system itself. Many believe that worker dissatisfaction has caused the United States to lose its competitive advantage in world markets and is at the heart of consumer frustrations over shoddily made products and services that are offered with an air of arrogance.

Why should dissatisfaction with jobs be a critical issue in our modern society? Workers in general enjoy the highest pay ever. They work shorter hours than ever before. Much of the manual work has been eliminated or eased through technology. And working conditions are better than at any time in history. At the same time, however, increasing numbers of workers, at all levels, seem to be frustrated, alienated, and poorly motivated, all of which has led to high employee turnover, poor productivity, poor product quality, rebelliousness, drug problems, and even sabotage by workers. What kinds of responsible actions can business take to reduce these problems?

The Changing Work Force

Many young people who are entering today's work force are different from those who entered in the past. These differences are important because today's young workers are the establishment of tomorrow, and their beliefs, values, and expectations are becoming the norms of tomorrow, thus causing conflict with established systems of performing work. Furthermore, changing values and expectations of younger workers are often in direct conflict with established values of the companies that employ them and the unions that represent them.

Security is not uppermost in the value system of most younger workers today. Challenge is. Unlike the workers who grew up during the Great Depression and who were willing to take almost any job that provided security, today's young workers increasingly demand jobs that minimize routine activities and offer challenges to their abilities.

Closely related to the expectation of challenge is the demand for opportunity and reward. Today's young workers want opportunities for self-expression and individual performance, and when they perform in a way that they feel deserves a reward, they want the reward now. They are not content to wait for an annual salary review. Nor are they content with the traditional slow climb up the promotion ladder.

Younger workers also question the basis of authority which exists in traditional organizations. In most organizations authority is based on position, and younger workers often are unwilling to accept this criterion alone. Their criteria are more oriented toward expertise and performance of superiors along with personal integrity. Younger workers, too, expect to participate more in decisions which effect them and the work they perform. They are likely to question traditional ways of doing things and frequently are unwilling to accept "the way it has always been done."

Today's young workers are more mobile than ever before. Younger workers just entering the work force tend to be more mobile than those who are slightly older and who have begun to assume the responsibilities of a family, but this latter group is also more mobile than ever before. Company and union loyalty is not important. No longer do workers take pride in being the third or fourth generation to work for a company. Rather, today's young workers tend to be strong individualists who are willing to move on if they find jobs dissatisfying.

The Changing Success Ethic

While the foregoing discussion largely concerns younger workers who are entering business in entry-level jobs and searching for satisfactions at that level, there also is evidence that those in middle- and upper-level jobs are not always satisfied with the jobs they hold or the company for which they work.

At the heart of the matter there seems to be a changing notion about the kinds of rewards that should result from human effort. Concepts and measurements of success are changing. Under the Protestant ethic the traditional goal in life was wealth, and success was measured in terms of material accumulations. These no longer seem to be valid goals or measurements of success for large segments of society. One research study found that only 17 percent of the 2,821 businessmen surveyed believed that to most people success meant greater material rewards.[3] The research also indicated that 49 percent of those surveyed believed that success, for most people, is measured in terms of greater job satisfaction, and 34 percent believed that for most people success represents realization of noncareer goals.

That same research study revealed that within the preceding five years nearly 50 percent of the businessmen surveyed had either changed or seriously considered changing their line of work. And, more than one-third of all respondents to the survey believed that a career for themselves other than business would yield

[3] Dale Tarnowieski, *The Changing Success Ethic,* New York: American Management Association, 1973, p. 17.

greater personal satisfaction and reward. Among middle managers 44 percent believed that an alternate career would be more rewarding, and of this group 70 percent intended to make a change soon. Middle managers appeared to be much less satisfied with both career advancement and personal fulfillment than the group as a whole.

Another research study compared two groups of college graduates who went to work for one large company.[4] One group left the company within four years of employment. The other group was still with the company after four years. All the respondents had similar backgrounds and similar expectations about the job and the company before accepting employment. The job features that both groups considered to be most important when graduating from college were feelings of accomplishment, interesting work, opportunities to use abilities, opportunities to get ahead, and good pay. For those who left the company only one job feature——salary level—came close to meeting expectations.

Sources of Job Dissatisfaction

American workers in general today expect that working should bring greater rewards than just a pay check. The lack of those extras are the sources of worker dissatisfaction, and although the priorities in which these extras are ranked by various groups may differ, there seem to be some sources of dissatisfactions common to all groups. The preceding section indicated that major sources of job dissatisfaction for managers were lack of interesting work, lack of opportunities for advancement and for self-expression, and lack of personal fulfillment. Other research indicates that unchallenging or uninteresting work is the single most important cause of job dissatisfaction among workers in the lower-middle-income group.[5] Repetitive jobs that allow for little personal freedom and do not provide opportunities for decision making were the major cause of alienation. Other job-related sources of dissatisfaction were health and safety hazards, lack of fringe benefits, and insufficient income. Furthermore, many lower-middle-income workers feel that society today prizes work such as law, medicine, and science and neither appreciates nor respects those who produce goods and services.

Can Business Solve the Problem?

It seems evident that there is widespread worker dissatisfaction, which raises questions about the way much work is accomplished today. Since most of the work is done in the business sector, society looks to business for solutions to problems of

---

[4] Marvin D. Dunnette, Richard D. Arvey, and Paul A. Banas, "Why Do They Leave?" *Personnel,* May–June 1973, pp. 27–28 and 32–33.

[5] Jerome M. Rosow, "Productivity and the Blue-Collar Blues," *Personnel,* March–April 1971, p. 11.

worker discontent. Like many other problems in today's society, it is doubtful that business by itself can find a long-run solution. Rather, business will need the active participation and cooperation of both unions and government if it is to be successful.

Several approaches to overcoming worker alienation have been widely recommended. All have much to commend them, and each is being experimented with by major companies with varying degrees of success. Yet there is no certainty that any one alone will provide a workable long-run answer. What is more likely is that some combination of the suggestions will provide relief.

The approach that seems to offer the most potential is the reorganization of work. Workers themselves are seldom articulate about reforms, thereby increasing the difficulties of finding better ways to accomplish work, but many companies are trying. One suggestion has been to mechanize all repetitive and routine jobs. Technology is available to do so in many cases. But there are other considerations. Capital equipment costs are high. There is also no assurance that tending a machine will be less boring than present jobs unless the new job can be made to include some elements of personal freedom and challenges of decision making. A more productive approach seems to be the redesign of jobs so that workers can relate personal effort to tangible results. The American Telephone and Telegraph Company started a program in 1965 to discover what was wrong with jobs and to redesign those jobs along the lines of job enrichment. For example, consider the experience in one division of that company in compiling telephone directories.[6]

> As the process was originally laid out, it took twenty-one steps to complete the copy for a telephone book. The procedure was an assembly line type of operation in which the copy moved from clerk to clerk. Many of the steps required only verification of the previous clerk's work. When asked, the clerks said they could verify their own work, and the process was then cut from twenty-one to fourteen tasks. In the case of the thinner books, employees were asked if they would like to "own" their own book and perform *all* the necessary steps with no verification unless the employees themselves asked for it. In the case of larger books, an employee became responsible for one or more letters of the alphabet and performed all the steps required. After the jobs were redesigned, both turnover and number of errors diminished significantly.

Other companies are experimenting less successfully with job enlargement by giving a worker three or four job tasks instead of one. This approach has often met with worker complaints. They feel that they often have less rest time and that the job is no more interesting. Job rotation has also met with worker resistance. One worker explained that the work was no more interesting or challenging. The only difference was that he hurt in a different place each day.

[6] Robert N. Ford, "Job Enrichment Lessons from AT&T," *Harvard Business Review,* January–February 1973, pp. 97–98.

Job Enrichment

The enormous economic gains that sprang from the thinking of the scientific management school of the early 1900's—the time-and-motion study analysts, the creators of production lines—may have ended insofar as they depend on utilizing human beings more efficiently. Without discarding these older insights, we need to consider more recent evidence showing that the tasks themselves can be changed to give workers a feeling of accomplishment.

From Robert N. Ford, "Job Enrichment Lessons from AT&T," *Harvard Business Review*, January–February 1973, p. 96. Reprinted with permission.

Some union officials believe that there is little that can be done to make assembly line jobs meet worker expectations. Suggestions have been made that perhaps the only way is to raise wages sufficiently to compensate for the unpleasantness and to reduce hours so that workers can find satisfaction off the job.

Is Individual Challenge the Key?

Better opportunities for advancement potentially could contribute much to overcoming worker dissatisfaction, but if they are to contribute positively, opportunities must be genuine and highly visible to all employees. There must be opportunities for advancement at the lowest organizational levels as well as at the middle and higher levels. There must also be visible evidence that certain prescribed types of behavior *will* lead to advancement. Furthermore, advancement, particularly at the lower organizational levels, more often than not requires additional training for candidates, and this requirement imposes upon business and organized labor a responsibility to make a great variety of training opportunities available to employees.

More autonomy for individuals and greater dependence on individual judgment have been held to be keys in reducing worker dissatisfaction. Among other companies, Ford Motor Company is experimenting with allowing small groups of workers to make some job-related decisions. At the new Saab assembly plant in Sweden management is experimenting with letting workers in the engine assembly section determine how the routine tasks of assembling engines shall be organized. On the other hand, as the first quotation at the beginning of the chapter suggests, many clerical jobs and jobs of middle managers are being diluted through increasing use of computers and other mechanized systems which tend to reduce both individual autonomy and reliance on individual judgments.

Whatever may be the real sources of worker dissatisfaction and deterioration of job performance, major effort will be required not only from business but also from organized labor and government. All three social institutions are vitally involved. They are the major social institutions with the power and resources to shape the way work will be done in the future and to influence relations between employees and employers. If new social values which seem to be emerging become social norms, both business and institutional organizations will have to work toward organizational climates that accept and accommodate the new norms.

THE CHALLENGE OF CHANGE

Over recent years the American public has become increasingly aware of national industrial and economic problems. Something appears to be wrong with American industry, which has always been held out to the rest of the world as the model of productive efficiency. Consumers complain about product quality, worker discontent seems to have grown to proportions of major concern, American gains in productivity seem not to be keeping pace with gains in some other countries, and all these are wrapped in the persistent cloak of inflation. Industry blames organized labor and government interference for many of its problems. Labor, in turn, condemns business and government for not doing enough to improve the lot of workers. Government, while establishing ground rules, sometimes acting as referee, and occasionally overriding actions, tends to be reluctant to interfere in relations between business and labor.

Perhaps the basic solution of labor and management relations and their impact on social well-being lies in labor, management, and government each reevaluating its attitudes toward the others and toward society as a whole. Perhaps labor needs to rethink what its responsibilities and objectives ought to be in our rapidly changing society. Perhaps business, at the same time, needs to reevaluate its responsibilities to employees and to the national interest. Government, too, should seriously question whether its function should be primarily that of regulator, or whether its function needs to be focused on how to assist business and labor to perform their roles in society better. It seems clear that if America is to solve its problems of productive efficiency and maintain its position in world markets, organized labor and business will have to change their postures from those of adversaries to postures of cooperative problem solving. Government, at the same time, will need to change its posture from that of rule maker and policeman to the more positive posture of catalyst and enabling agent.

The Changing Composition of Organized Labor

An integral part of the philosophy of the American labor movement has always been that there is strength in numbers. Growth, then, is an important key to union success, but growth has been disappointing to labor leaders in recent years. After a spectacular growth between 1936 and 1944, membership continued to increase, but at a much more modest rate than before. By 1956, membership (excluding Canada) had reached 17.5 million. But between 1957 and 1961 labor lost over 1 million members. The loss has been recovered, and membership in 1973 stood at approximately 20 million with about 19 million members in the United States.

But a more discouraging fact for organized labor is that union membership has continued to decline as a proportion of the total labor force. Among workers in nonagricultural establishments, where most members are found and where organizing efforts are greatest, the proportion fell from 33.4 percent in 1955 to 27.4 percent in 1970.

There are two reasons why union growth has slowed, and both are important to business. First, expansion in employment has largely occurred in service-oriented occupations—not in the traditional manufacturing occupations which have been the stronghold for union membership. Over half of all workers in the United States are engaged in furnishing services of one kind or another, and labor force projections indicate that the proportion will increase. These occupations have been slow to respond to union organizing efforts; however, unionization among service workers is expanding.

Second, the increase in professional and semiprofessional workers has been greater than the increase in blue-collar workers. As a group, professional and semiprofessional workers have looked upon joining unions as being unprofessional behavior. However, there is an increasing trend among these groups toward organization for bargaining purposes, thus creating for business an added dimension to labor relations.

A Suburban Middle Class

Economic gains which have been won for union members over the years have brought an affluence which allowed many members to move to the suburbs. During the 1930s and 1940s union membership was much more homogeneous than it is today. Union leaders and membership shared the same background, and their interests centered around a commonality of wages, job security, and working conditions. Today the homogeneity is gone, and with it has gone the commonality of interest. Suburban living is not conducive to close ties with the union hall. Suburban living has produced for many union members a social, political, and cultural environment that is different from that of the "traditional worker neighborhood," where workers historically have lived. Thus, life in the suburbs has tended to substitute middle-class suburban values for the more traditional worker-class union values.

The shift in values of suburban union members has created conflicts with union leadership over unions' goals and policies. These very conflicts have made business relations with labor more complicated, because it is more difficult for business to predict the priority of bargaining issues.

Race, Age, and Sex

Not all union members have moved to the suburbs. Those who have are usually white and more affluent. Those who continue to live in industrial areas are the less-affluent white workers and members of minorities, thus creating divergent value systems between race and income groups in unions. These different values tend to create conflict on job issues.

At the same time, union membership is getting younger. Nearly one-half of union membership is under forty years old. Approximately one-third is under thirty-five. And about one-fourth is under thirty. The social and political values of younger workers are often quite different from those of older workers. Younger workers are more concerned with social issues and are impatient for change—now. The objectives of younger workers often differ markedly from those of older union members.

Women, too, are becoming a larger proportion of the work force. About 20 percent of all union members are women. In thirty unions the majority of the membership is female, yet few women hold either elective or appointive offices in unions. The drive for equality for women has caused internal problems for the unions themselves and has also complicated business's relationships with organized labor.

The differences in employee groups cause various conflicts. Younger workers want emphasis to be placed on more pay now. Older workers want better pensions and better fringe benefits. Blacks also talk about more pay and better advancement opportunities more quickly. Job security means different things to different groups. Older workers want tight seniority rules; younger workers view them as barriers. Younger workers also think unions should work toward social goals such as pollution control. Union leaders and older members think unions should stick to traditional objectives such as outlawing right-to-work laws and broadening picketing rights.

For business, the changing composition of union membership has created uncertainty, because it is often caught between the demands of younger workers and the more traditional bargaining demands of unions.

The Rebellious Rank and File

Impatient and dissatisfied with the performance of their unions, workers——particularly younger workers—increasingly are prone to reject union leadership and go their own way. Because of the diverse interests of various groups of union members, it is becoming more difficult for union leaders to put together a something-for-everyone program toward which to work. The something-for-everyone approach has complicated the collective bargaining process, because it has increased both the number and variety of issues over which business and unions must bargain. Furthermore, it often prolongs the bargaining period and increases the chances of a strike. For example, the three major issues that remained unresolved at the time a strike was called against Chrysler Corporation in 1973 were pension improvements, voluntary overtime, and plant safety.

The inability of unions to press uniformly for the interests of various groups has resulted in an increase in rejections by union members of agreements negotiated by their leaders. This same inability has also contributed to strikes which are unauthorized, and sometimes strongly opposed, by union leaders. These activities by members tend to complicate relationships between business and organized labor. Rejections of negotiated agreements and unauthorized strikes often put union leaders in the embarrassing position of having to support issues or actions which they believe to be inappropriate, thus diluting their credibility with management. Furthermore, such activities weaken the collective bargaining process and create uncertainty for business. It is one thing for business to have confidence that union leaders speak authoritatively for their members. It is quite another thing to wonder if negotiations are really final, or if union members will really abide by the terms of the collective agreement once it is signed.

Organizations of White-Collar and Professional Employees

Until recently organization of workers for purposes of collective bargaining was limited largely to blue-collar workers in the goods-producing sector of the economy. This is no longer true. With increasing frequency workers in the service industries, white-collar workers, professionals, managers, and even union organizers are organizing to press for their particular interests.[7] There is every reason to believe that this trend will accelerate.

Traditionally white-collar workers have identified with management and have therefore resisted unionization. Today there is a growing belief among these workers that they have lost contact with upper levels of management. They feel increasingly remote, isolated, and unable to communicate their needs and problems. And furthermore, there is a growing belief that upper levels of management are insensitive to their problems. For many, applications of technology to white-collar jobs have reduced job satisfactions. And finally, pay increases for white-collar workers have lagged behind those for blue-collar workers.

Professional employees are also becoming more receptive to organization. Cutbacks in aerospace activities, for example, demonstrated to engineers that they were subject to unemployment like everyone else and emphasized to that group the need for job security. A group of interns and resident doctors were successful in improving patient care as well as winning pay increases for themselves through

[7] For an excellent discussion of organization and bargaining among nonmanufacturing workers, see John T. Dunlop, "Major Issues in New Sector Bargaining," in Seymore L. Wolfbein (ed.), *Emerging Sectors of Collective Bargaining,* Morristown, N.J.: General Learning Corporation, 1971.

organized action. Teachers, too, in some cases have been able to improve the quality of education as well as increase economic and job-related benefits for themselves.

White-collar and professional employees' organizations have taken a variety of forms. Some have joined established labor organizations such as the AFL-CIO or the Teamsters. Others have developed independent professional organizations such as the Nurses Association and the American Association of University Professors, many of which are beginning to use union tactics and in many other ways to act like unions.

These trends mean that business will need to relate to organized groups of workers, both union and nonunion, on a variety of new fronts. These trends also mean new challenges for business on the productivity front. Technological change has increased productivity in production industries, and new technologies have enabled a constant or decreasing number of employees to produce more goods. On the whole, little has been done to apply new technology to service industries, although there are notable exceptions. Production of services, in general, remains labor intensive. As workers in the service industries press for higher wages, more fringe benefits, shorter hours, and so forth, business will be challenged to find ways to increase productivity in order to keep prices within reasonable bounds. This problem will be especially challenging where personal services are involved. Areas such as education, government, medicine, recreation, and lodging and restaurant businesses will be particularly hard pressed to respond to the challenge.

BUSINESS, LABOR, AND THE NATIONAL INTEREST

Seventy-five years ago business and government were major social institutions in America, and what they did or did not do contributed significantly to the well-being of society as a whole. While the activities of organized labor were often visible to the public—sometimes in dramatic ways—they had little effect on overall social well-being. Over the last seventy-five years this has changed. Organized labor has become a major social institution with great power, and today its policies and actions make a profound impact on the economic, social, and political climate of the nation. Precisely because of this power labor is increasingly falling into public disfavor. Large segments of society feel that the pluralistic balance has been destroyed. More frequently than ever before many of labor's efforts are being viewed as lacking in responsibility for the public interest.

Research conducted by the Opinion Research Corporation at the end of 1971 reflected the public mood.[8] These findings are summarized below, and it is interesting to note that union members themselves often shared the views of the general public.

[8] Research findings are summarized in "Trouble Plagues the House of Labor," *Business Week,* Oct. 28, 1972, p. 70.

71 percent oppose the continued growth of unions.

55 percent believe that unions have too much power and that this power should be curbed. (Among union members, 41 percent agree.)

68 percent think strikes hurt everybody too much. (61 percent of the unionists agree.)

59 percent blame costly union settlements for causing the United States to price itself out of world markets. (68 percent of the unionists agree.)

68 percent blame higher prices and living costs on unions. (57 percent of the unionists agree.)

62 percent believe unions should be subject to tighter government regulation.

65 percent say that government should intervene in strikes that hurt the public.

63 percent would bar strikes by firemen, 62 percent by policemen, 55 percent by teachers, and 54 percent by sanitation workers.

46 percent would bar food stamps and other forms of public assistance to those on strike.

65 percent rated the job union leaders are doing as "fair to poor." (59 percent of the unionists rated union leaders the same way.)

The loss of public confidence in organized labor as a major social institution reflects public concern over issues such as declining productivity, inflation, costly strikes, and union political activity. These topics will be discussed in this section.

Productivity

Annual rates of productivity increases have been steadily decreasing in the United States over the past years to the point where annual gains are now among the lowest of any major industrial nation. Productivity gains (or losses) vary from industry to industry and from employer to employer. One study showed that among the 1,093 companies responding, 65 percent said productivity had increased or at least had not deteriorated over the two years preceding the study.[9] Other businessmen give comparative examples of inferior current American productivity. One United States company built similar nuclear power plants in the United States and in Japan. The United States plant was constructed with over 5.4 million man-hours of labor, while the Japanese installation took fewer than 4.5 million. Businessmen who complain that worker output is less than it could or should be often link poor productivity to actions of organized labor. Practices

[9] Frank G. Gable, *Toward 100% Employment,* New York: American Management Association, 1973, pp. 8-9.

subjected to the heaviest criticisms are restrictive work rules and jurisdictional restrictions which prevent workers from performing as much work as they are capable of and which raise the costs of producing goods and services. Illustrations are numberless. In one plant only a union electrician can replace a burned-out light bulb. At an airline different people must unload baggage and freight even though both are carried in the same section of the airplane and require similar handling techniques. In New York it still takes thirteen separate crafts to install a bathroom in an apartment house or hotel, and all work stops if even the simplest job cannot be completed in proper sequence.

What can be done to increase productivity? Whatever is done, business cannot do it alone. Organized labor will have to include productivity gains as one of its major objectives, and government will have to participate directly and positively. A variety of approaches to productivity have been tried with varying degrees of success. Where these have not worked or worked only with minimal success, they have most often been introduced unilaterally by business. For example, increased capital investments and plant modernization are popular approaches to productivity improvement. But where plant modernization is undertaken without cooperation by unions, the unions tend to ask for and get provisions in labor contracts that tend to counterbalance productivity gains. Other approaches that have been used with varying degrees of success are engineering studies of processes, financial incentives, production efficiency studies, job enrichment, rearranged work hours, rearranged or increased number of shifts, and increased purchases of semifinished materials.

Perhaps the approach with the most potential is productivity bargaining. But because productivity bargaining is also an important part of the discussion about unions and inflation it will be postponed for a few paragraphs.

Inflation

Many people (including some economists) believe that inflation is the direct result of labor's aggressiveness in pushing continually for large increases in wages and fringe benefits. Historically America has prided itself on an industrial system which produced increases in productivity sufficient to pay for increases in worker's wages and decreases in consumers's prices. Because the annual rate of increase in productivity has declined, business finds it increasingly difficult to finance wage increases from this source. Rather, wage increases must often be covered by raising prices to consumers. Similarly, large pay raises won by major unions from large companies often become the pattern for smaller, less-affluent companies, thereby forcing upon them wage patterns which threaten their ability to stay in business. For example, in the electrical manufacturing division of an auto company workers who assembled electric refrigerators belonged to the United Auto Workers and received the same wages as workers in the automobile assembly plants. This put the manufacturer of refrigerators at a competitive cost disadvantage because employees of other refrigerator manufacturers were paid according to smaller wage patterns of electrical manufacturing generally.

Productivity bargaining may also be an answer to controlling inflation, because it relates pay increases to increases in productivity. Simply stated, productivity bargaining is an approach to collective bargaining which recognizes that cooperation between labor, management, and government is essential to identify and implement changes necessary to maintain and improve our economic and social position. Whatever changes are agreed upon must benefit both labor and business. Business must be prepared to grant something of value such as wage increases, fringe benefit improvement, and so forth. But business must demand something in return, and labor must be prepared to respond positively by modifying work practices or other labor actions that will lead to increased productivity. Thus both business and labor are winners in the bargaining process. So is society if part of the gains are passed on in the form of lower prices or improved products. Government, too, can participate directly by enabling business and labor to implement productivity improvements. Ways in which government can participate are through low-interest loans, tax credits, subsidized worker education and training, and similar devices.

Strikes

Traditionally the public has viewed strikes as being actions against big, vague corporate businesses. Because strike activity often occurred a long distance away and because large segments of the population were only minimally affected or not affected at all, strikes were not a major concern to many people. Today, however, strikes are a major concern because some strikes have widespread effects and others sometimes produce severe personal inconveniences. Strikes that cause garbage to pile up in the streets, schools to be closed, and shortages of goods have made strike activities and their effects highly visible. And increasing numbers of people view strikes as being contrary to the public interest. There is a growing conviction by all parties that strikes are too costly for everyone concerned and that there must be better ways of settling disputes and working out agreements. For business, strikes mean loss of production and income and potential loss of markets. A prolonged strike can quickly eat up union funds through strike benefits, cause severe economic hardships for union members, and sometimes result in elimination of jobs. And the public suffers inconvenience and often is deprived of goods and services.

Many labor leaders agree that while strikes are an effective weapon, they are a poor tool with which to preserve labor peace and to exercise responsibilities to society. Most responsible labor leaders are seeking acceptable substitutes for the strike. And business and labor have experimented with a number of alternatives.

One alternative solution that has had a high degree of success is simply to start contract negotiations earlier and work at them harder so that issues are resolved before the contract expires. Bargaining is viewed as a continuous process rather than a periodic confrontation. Under this philosophy there is smooth transition from one contract to the next with no work stoppage. For example:

> One large pharmaceutical manufacturer signed a three-year contract with its union-represented employees more than five months before the old contract expired. The reasons given by a company spokesman were to avoid having to pay for a costly strike and to enable the company to pass along savings in the form of a better contract for workers.

Another approach has been to negotiate a no-strike and a no-lockout agreement. For certain guarantees from business, labor agrees not to strike. For example:

> The Kaiser Steel-United Steelworkers plan, started in 1959, was a pioneer in assuring immunity to strikes. In an agreement between management and employees a set of mutually agreeable guarantees were worked out. Management guaranteed to match, without participating in negotiations, any gains that other unions won from "Big Steel." In return the union guaranteed not to strike.
>
> More recently building trades unions agreed with Procter and Gamble and Anheuser-Busch not to strike or otherwise interrupt work on proposed new industrial construction. Disturbed by the possibility that the new plants might be built in another location, St. Louis building trade unions pledged not to strike. The pledge bound the unions to work out peacefully, and before the contracts were let, all jurisdictional problems. It also bound them to handle preassembled equipment.

A more sophisticated version of the Kaiser Steel approach has been worked out between the major steel producers and United Steelworkers.[10] The difference lies in voluntary binding arbitration of issues not resolved by the time the contract expires. This agreement provides a basic wage increase and a cash bonus for workers in return for an agreement not to strike and to submit unresolved disputes to binding arbitration. The cash bonuses were the money that it would have cost the companies to shut down and to pay supplemental unemployment benefits in case of a strike.

Compulsory arbitration of all labor disputes has been suggested as a way to eliminate labor strife. This approach has been unacceptable to both business and unions. Both argue that compulsory arbitration at best often produces compromises which are unsatisfactory to both sides. At worst compulsory arbitration imposes the views of a third party upon the opponents which neither is ready to accept. Furthermore, it is argued, compulsory arbitration upsets the balance of pluralistic power.

[10] "Why USW Said 'Yes' to No Strike," *Business Week,* Apr. 7, 1973, p. 64.

A unique approach to eliminating public inconvenience and injury was tried several years ago in Miami.[11]

> In 1960 the Miami Transit Company and its bus drivers experimented in what may have been the first semi-strike. The city buses continued to run even though the drivers were on strike. The two parties agreed that:
>
> 1. The Public would receive free bus service.
> 2. The "striking" drivers were to receive no pay and were not to accept any tips.
> 3. The Miami Transit Company, the employer, would supply the fuel and maintenance required for the buses.

Under the agreement, the public was spared loss and inconvenience while the opposing parties to the dispute remained under heavy economic pressure to resolve their differences.

While strikes by large and powerful unions continue to generate public dissatisfaction with union actions, organized labor does appear to be changing its standards of conduct to reduce third-party injury and inconvenience and to reduce the tremendous social costs of strikes. Both labor and business seem to be working harder to eliminate or at least to minimize strikes. The 1973 United Auto Workers strike against Chrysler Corporation lasted only three days, which was the shortest strike in UAW history. The United Steelworkers and the steel industry have an agreement which will eliminate a strike in the future, and similar antistrike clauses have been working successfully for some locals of the Amalgamated Transit Workers, the International Printing Pressmen, and others. All this is promising evidence of greater cooperation between business and labor toward the objective of labor peace and national well-being.

Labor's Political Clout

Labor philosophy toward political action was well stated in an editorial which appeared in the August 1908 issue of the *American Federationist*.[12]

> We now call upon the workers of our common country to Stand faithfully by our Friends, Oppose and defeat our enemies, whether they be Candidates for President, For Congress or the other offices, whether Executive, legislative, or judicial.

[11] David B. McCalmont, "The Semi-Strike," *Industrial and Labor Relations Review*, January 1962, p. 191.

[12] Quoted in Mollie Ray Carroll, *Labor and Politics*, Boston: Houghton Mifflin Company, 1923, p. 173. (Capitalization is from quoted source.)

This philosophy stressed lobbying and the use of labor votes to tip the election balance in favor of friendly candidates. It also stressed avoidance of partisan politics.

Today labor is in a position to influence election results through contributions of money, organization, and votes to favored candidates. What is important is that labor is in politics *as labor* and therefore acts as a countervailing force to political action by business.

The Corrupt Practices Act (discussed earlier) applies to labor just as it does to business. The act prohibits contribution of dues money of union members to candidates for political office. But voluntary contributions by union members to the AFL-CIO Committee on Political Education (COPE) may be freely used for political purposes. In addition the law does not prohibit the use of dues money for educational purposes such as newspaper, radio, and television advertising directed toward public issues. Thus labor can indirectly back candidates who favor these same issues. In addition, the time and effort of full-time union officials may be devoted to political activity.

Every political campaign needs a large organization of campaign workers to organize and conduct meetings, to distribute campaign literature, to solicit and collect campaign contributions, to increase voter registration, and to ensure that people get to the polls and vote. Organized labor provides a massive pool of potential campaign workers. Thus a favored candidate has at his disposal a campaign organization that probusiness candidates are hard pressed to match.

Is there, in fact, such a phenomenon as a "labor vote"? There is little or no evidence that unions control a large bloc of votes that can be allocated to one party or one candidate. Union members, for the most part, continue to vote their own personal convictions at the polls. But at the same time, votes of union members do become important. Labor has traditionally favored the Democratic party and Democratic candidates. Unions can and do encourage more workers to vote—and to vote Democratic more often than not. Thus the number of union members voting or not voting may have an effect on which party or candidate gets the most votes.

It seems clear that a labor party will not appear on the American scene in the foreseeable future. It seems equally clear that labor is committed to a policy of organized political action. George Meany, president of the AFL-CIO, stated this policy well when he said:[13]

> The gains labor has made at the collective bargaining table are threatened in the legislative halls of Congress and the State Legislatures. To meet that challenge, effective political activity has of necessity become a vital part of effective trade unionism.

[13] George Meany, *How to Win: A Handbook for Political Education,* Washington, D.C.: AFL-CIO Committee on Political Education, undated, p. v.

This policy statement, like much collective bargaining activity, seems to be directed toward maintaining the status quo or applying pressures on business to do something. If labor is fully to live up to its position as a major social institution, it will need to revise its policy and mobilize its potential political power toward solutions of problems of a much broader social nature than union security, wages, and working conditions.

SUMMARY

Worker disatisfaction at all levels and among all types of employees has reached proportions of national concern. This dissatisfaction has caused declines in product quality, lower productivity, industrial sabotage, and other results. Business is now studying the composition and organization of work, and a variety of experiments are being made to understand and reduce worker dissatisfaction.

Labor, too, has an important stake in national well-being. Organized labor is now a powerful social institution and as such can no longer limit its actions to those of being an adversary of business. Together with business and government, labor must assume its new role with all the responsibility to society that is required of a major social institution. Through new approaches to responsible bargaining both labor and business are making positive progress toward solving problems of labor peace and related problems.

STUDY GUIDES FOR
INTERPRETATION OF THIS CHAPTER

1. To what extent is it necessary for business, organized labor, and government to cooperate to solve problems of worker dissatisfaction? Make a list of actions each can take to reduce or overcome worker dissatisfaction.

2. Consult local union leaders in your community to determine the extent of union involvement in finding solutions to community problems. Examples of problems might be school dropouts, poverty, slum clearance and rehabilitation of cities, and ecology issues.

3. From recent newspapers and magazines select and present to your study group an illustration of cooperative effort between business and labor to work out solutions to mutual problems.

4. Select for investigation one national labor organization. To what extent is that organization involved in political activity (a) locally, (b) statewide, and (c) nationally?

PROBLEM
The Semi-Strike[14]

The Universal Company had a history of moderately successful labor relations. Most contracts had been negotiated without work stoppages, but there had been some strikes. A few of the strikes had been long and costly for all concerned. As the time approached to sign a new contract, it became apparent that several basic issues could not be resolved and that a strike would result.

The following plan was suggested to the company and the union as an alternative to the traditional strike. It was proposed that production and sales be continued just as though no strike had been called. The plan called for "striking" workers to forgo one-half their normal wages. A group composed of representatives of management, labor, and the public would determine what the reduction in net earnings for the company would be if a regular strike were to be called, and the company would forgo one-half of this amount until the issues were settled and a new contract was signed.

The plan would be implemented as follows: At the end of each week the company would pay each worker one-half of what he would normally earn. The company would also write one check equal to one-half the wages of all workers. At the same time the company would write another check equal to one-half the profits that would have been lost if a strike had been in effect. Both of these checks would then be given to the local school board or the community fund or some other civic organization.

1. What advantages and disadvantages do you see for the different interest groups in this situation?

CHAPTER

16

THE INDIVIDUAL AND BUSINESS

At electric speeds, can private identity survive at all?

Marshall McLuhan[1]

It is our hypothesis that the incongruence between the individual and the organization can provide the basis for a continued challenge which, as it is fulfilled, will help man to enhance his own growth and to develop organizations that will be viable and effective.

Chris Argyris[2]

In this chapter we discuss the role of an individual as a *person* in his relationships with organizations. In this role he is a separate *human being* with inherent dignity, integrity, independence, and rights of privacy. Even though an individual is an employee within a company, he is still a person; and *in this role he is an outsider beyond the company gates.* He is a part of the environment of business. The focus of this chapter, therefore, is upon the individual as a human being and how this humanness affects his social transactions with business. Both business and the individual need ideological and operating guides to make their relationship effective. We discuss claims of the individual on the organization, the organization-man thesis, legitimacy of organizational influence, and rights of privacy. We conclude with a brief statement of individual responsibilities to the organization. Although we have used the conventional "he" or "his" in speaking of the individual, it is emphatically our intention to have the entire discussion apply equally to both men and women.

Consider the following situations and the questions that arise therefrom. In the first situation, is the repairman seeking to serve his personal interests in a way which conflicts with obligations that arise from social transactions he has made with his employer? In the second situation, is the organization improperly invading the privacy of four individuals?

[1] Marshall McLuhan quoted in "McLuhan Dissects the Executive," *Business Week,* June 24, 1972, p. 118.
[2] Chris Argyris, *Integrating the Individual and the Organization,* New York: John Wiley & Sons, Inc., 1964, p. 7. Entire quotation emphasized in original.

John Jones, one of seventeen television repairmen working for Mather Electronics, was called to a residence to repair a television set. He repaired the set and presented the bill, but he also did something else. He called the owner aside, gave him a business card bearing his name and home telephone number, and stated in a confidential tone, "Next time something goes wrong, call me at home. I'll come out in the evening and do the job for less than my company charges." In this manner, John earned added income that was nearly 50 percent of what his employer paid him.

During the same week the wholesale supplier of television parts to Mather Electronics gave each of its four shipping clerks their quarterly polygraph test to determine if they were handling orders honestly. Two years earlier the supplier had a 20 percent inventory loss in one year as a result of a theft conspiracy by all four shipping clerks. It replaced them with carefully screened clerks who agreed as a condition of employment to have a quarterly polygraph test restricted only to queries about on-the-job theft.

CLAIMS OF THE INDIVIDUAL ON THE ORGANIZATION

In order to understand the relationship of an individual person with an organization, it is necessary to examine in a general way what individuals expect from organizations. These generalizations normally apply whether the individual is a customer, neighbor in the community, stockholder, or some other person. As with most generalizations, there are exceptions.

Normally, an individual claims three basic payoffs or benefits in his social transaction with an organization. None of them can be provided in the absolute, but a measure of each is necessary to maintain a viable relationship. The more of each benefit that can be gained, other things being equal, the more successful the relationship will be for a person. The three claims are:

Improvement—the psychological purpose of an individual's relationship with an organization

Independence—the individual price required for cooperation

Justice—the social standard for relating to an organization

Improvement

Improvement is the basic reason a person chooses to relate to an organization. For his role investment he expects a payoff which brings him closer to his goals. If there is no payoff, he will cease his relationship if he is free to do so. Improvement is expressed in terms of the rewards he receives, such as opportunity, money, recognition, and personal development. Improvement has become a normal expectation of people in much of the world as they seek to improve both their standard of living and their quality of life.

All business claimants as individuals expect improvement from business. Owners want better returns. Customers want better prices and more quality. Community citizens expect a better community in which to live. For example, learning is increased through educational support and better books, health is improved through better drugs, and appearance is enhanced through better clothes. Business typically is expected to bring these kinds of benefits to society.

Independence

Independence is the basic demand that a person makes of any organization in return for his cooperation. He does not give all of himself. He reserves something for his own initiative, self-determination, and privacy. In interacting with the organization he insists on freedom of action. He seeks organizational practices which give him more independence. This is a part of his cultural heritage as well as his natural drive as a human being. This was the situation with the television repairman mentioned at the beginning of this chapter. He felt that his time off the job was his own, even if it placed him in competition with his employer. However, did he overstep the bounds of his social contract with his employer when he solicited business from his employer's customers on his employer's time?

Justice

Justice is the standard of treatment which a man expects from an organization in order to continue his relationship with it. Justice makes group life tolerable. It is based on fairness, reason, and prudence in organizational acts. It gives substance and meaning to human dignity because it protects the person in his dealings with the group. Justice means compliance with the spirit of a relationship as well as the letter of it. Justice is what holds an organization together in voluntary cooperation. If a man has a measure of independence plus improvement in the direction of his goals but suffers injustice, he will withdraw his cooperation and seek to place his role investments elsewhere.

The justice which a person typically seeks from organizations is known as *distributive justice*. It means that each person expects his rewards, when compared with rewards of others, to be in proportion to his inputs (social investments) in the situation. Education, for example, is considered to be a social investment. When a person uses it in his job, he expects appropriate rewards. In other instances seniority may be considered an investment. In general, if investments and rewards are not in agreement, people feel that the situation lacks justice. To them it is not fair. They express unhappiness, they complain, and they withhold their cooperation.

Justice is a social comparison with others; therefore, a change in what others receive can cause a person to feel injustice just as much as a change in what he receives. Assume that a business partner feels he has a satisfactory situation in a partnership. He then discovers when he examines yearly expense accounts that two other partners have been entertaining business clients more often and much more expensively than he has. If in his mind he can find no "rational" reason for the difference, he may feel that the situation is unjust, even though he did not feel so until this moment.

Justice has a historical basis. A person feels that there should be some relationship between what he has contributed in the past and received in the past, and what he is contributing and receiving now. A physician, for example, makes major internship investments with low financial rewards; therefore, he expects justice to provide him with quick financial rewards when he finally reaches his productive years. His is a delayed payoff in relation to investment. A different situation is that of a construction superintendent who has had high pay and status in the past and who expects the same on his present assignment, even though his contribution on this job is not quite as great as usual because the job is a small one. The just organization relates each person's investments to benefits, both in relation to history and in relation to the investments and benefits of others.

THE ORGANIZATION-MAN THESIS
The Basic Thesis

One threat to independence is the organization-man thesis. The underlying idea of the organization man is conformity by the individual to the organization in ways which reduce his independence. This contest between the person and the organization is as old as organized society. It assumes that people universally have drives for freedom and self-actualization, while the organization needs coordination and control to unify effort toward objectives. Modern interest in this struggle against conformity was stimulated by publication of *The Organization Man* by William H. Whyte, Jr., in 1956. The book quickly became a best seller. Whyte stated that a new social ethic had developed to rationalize the organization's demands for wholehearted dedication and loyalty. He wrote:[3]

> By social ethic I mean that contemporary body of thought that makes morally legitimate the pressures of society against the individual. Its major propositions are three: a belief in the group as the source of creativity; a belief in "belongingness" as the ultimate need of the individual; and a belief in the application of science to achieve the belongingness. . . . Essentially, it is a utopian faith. . . . It is quite reminiscent of the beliefs of utopian communities of the 1840s.

The social ethic according to Whyte is an ideology provided by intellectuals,

[3] William H. Whyte, Jr., *The Organization Man,* New York: Simon & Schuster, Inc., 1956, p. 7.

not by the organization. As a result of broad acceptance of this ideology, people are "imprisoned in brotherhood." They "belong" to the organization. They are the ones "who have left home, spiritually as well as physically, to take the vows of organization life"; however, the fault is not in the organization itself but "in our worship of it." We too easily conform to organizational norms.

Whyte perceived the individual as cared for and kept by organizations, and he strongly opposed personality testing, bureaucracy, and conformity. He even offered an appendix on "How to Cheat on Personality Tests." To Whyte, man's answer to the social ethic should be to fight the organization, but not self-destructively.

Whyte's organization-man thesis was supported by publication in the following year of Chris Argyris's *Personality and Organization,* which dealt particularly with psychological problems of work, such as alienation, frustration, and suppression of self-actualization.

The basic philosophy in Argyris's own words is as follows:[4]

> An analysis of the basic properties of relatively mature human beings and formal organization leads to the conclusion that there is an inherent incongruency between the self-actualization of the two. This basic incongruency creates a situation of conflict, frustration, and failure for the participants. . . .

When the ideas of the organization man are applied to the whole society, the result is a *beehive model* of society in which the total system perfects itself as the individual becomes steadily less significant.[5] Large organization overwhelms the individual until society becomes like a hive of bees in which there is little individuality. Even the queen bee is no exception, because she is a functional slave to the system like all the other bees.

Interpreting the Organization Man

There is an element of truth in the organization-man thesis. Individual and organizational goals are different, but this is only one side of the story. People and organizations have strong *mutual interests* in their relationship. People need organizations. Without organizations, many modern social goals would be impossible to accomplish. Organizations make available resources and opportunities which an individual operating alone could not have. They also satisfy many of his higher-order needs and provide psychological support for him. There is no ultimate conflict that either the individual or the organization must win. Both can gain.

The differences that exist between individual and organizational goals are

---

[4] Chris Argyris, *Personality and Organization: The Conflict between the System and the Individual,* New York: Harper & Brothers, 1957, p. 175.

[5] John W. Gardner, "Toward a Self-renewing Society," *Time,* Apr. 11, 1969, pp. 40–41.

not necessarily undesirable. An individual develops through challenge; consequently, some differences can be psychologically and socially healthful and creative. This is the manner in which democratic elections produce a more effective society. In other words, reasonable differences, constructively handled, can improve payouts for both the individual and the organization. But if differences are not handled constructively, organization-man conformity may develop.

Is Business a Special Source of Conformity?

The organization-man thesis is occasionally interpreted as an attack on business as a special cause of conformity compared with other organizations; however, there is little evidence that conformity is a hallmark of business culture. Business has no special problem, compared with the military, government, or even the slum street gang. The issue of the organization man is a universal one applying to all organizations and cultures. Whyte says: "This conflict is certainly not a peculiarly American development," and he adds with a flourish:[6]

> Blood brother to the business trainee off to join Du Pont is the seminary student who will end up in the church hierarchy, the doctor headed for the corporate clinic, the physics Ph.D. in a government laboratory, the intellectual on the foundation-sponsored team project, the engineering graduate in the huge drafting room at Lockheed, the young apprentice in a Wall Street law factory.

Limited research agrees with Whyte that business is not a special source of conformity. Perhaps it goes even further and suggests that business gives above-average emphasis to nonconformity. It is, for example, popularly considered that university professors are a prime example of a nonconforming group; therefore, they make a good group to compare with business executives. One study administered a psychological test on conformity to these two groups and found that the businessmen were no more conforming than the professors. The study did find a wide range of conformity among both businessmen and professors; so if one wanted to find examples of conformity in business he could find many.[7]

Another study examined whether the reward structure in business tended to support conformity.[8] Contrary to popular writing and opinion, the study found that those managers who scored lower in conformity were given higher ratings by their superiors.

[6] Whyte, op. cit., p. 3

[7] John B. Miner, "Conformity among University Professors and Business Executives," *Administrative Science Quarterly,* June 1962, pp. 96–109, reporting on forty-four executives and forty-one professors. The study found older persons less conforming; thus if a business had predominantly younger persons in it, it might have a higher conformity index.

[8] Edwin A. Fleishman and David R. Peters, "Interpersonal Values, Leadership Attitudes, and Managerial 'Success,' " *Personnel Psychology,* Summer 1962, pp. 127–143, covering thirty-nine managers in four soap manufacturing branches.

Considering the organization-man issue as a whole, it does not appear to be a special problem of business. To assure that individuals get maximum values from organizations which make minimum infringements on their freedoms is, however, an issue for genuine long-range social concern. These ideas are further developed in the next two sections. Primary emphasis is given to the employee because of his close relationship with the organization, but the ideas discussed apply in a general way to individuals in any relationship with an organization.

LEGITIMACY OF ORGANIZATIONAL INFLUENCE ON EMPLOYEES
To What Does One Conform?

The organization is one of many influences to which an individual conforms. Conformity implies a dependence on the norms of others without independent thinking. There are several different ways in which a person may be said to conform. First, there is a pseudo-conformity by which one conforms to the technology. That is, when the pot boils, take it off the fire; or when the batch in the furnace is ready, take it out. Some so-called conformity in industry is actually a response to the technology; but this is not true conformity because it does not involve the norms of others. Furthermore, this ''conformity'' is the same in or out of an organization.

Looking at genuine conformity to group norms at work, there are three groups to which one conforms. One of these is the organization itself. Another is the informal work group, and the last is the external community. It is evident that the last two represent conformity within the organization instead of conformity to the organization. The organization does not impose these last two norms; they are simply there because the organization operates in a social system rather than a vacuum. Excluding the two norms just mentioned, what is the extent and legitimacy of the organization's influence?

A Model for Legitimate Areas of Organizational Influence

Every organization develops certain policies and requirements for performance. If the organization and an individual define the boundaries of legitimate influence differently, then organizational conflict is likely to develop. This conflict can be sufficient to interfere with accomplishment of organizational purpose. If, for example, an employee believes that it is legitimate for management to control how much time he talks with his wife on the telephone while at work, he may dislike management interference with his freedom on this matter, but he is unlikely to develop serious conflict with management about it. If, however, he believes that talking with his wife on the telephone is his own private right, then this issue may become a center of conflict with management.

This same type of reasoning applies to any claimant with which the organization deals. As long as there is agreement on the legitimacy of influence among the parties, they should be satisfied with the power balance in their relationship.

Limited research shows that there is reasonable cultural agreement concerning areas where organizational influence on employees is considered legitimate. Studies have covered labor leaders, managers in management-development courses, university students in three areas of the nation, and managers in companies. The studies used the Schein-Ott legitimacy questionnaire which covers fifty-five areas of organizational influence ranging from highly job-related ones (such as employee working hours) to highly personal ones (such as the church an employee attends). The studies report general agreement on areas of legitimacy among all four groups, with high rank-order correlations for the fifty-five items ranging from .88 to .98. Managers gave somewhat more support to legitimacy than labor leaders, with students ranking in the middle; however, the important point is the general agreement among all groups. Items of high legitimacy were those which involved job performance and the work environment. Moderate legitimacy related to off-the-job conduct which might affect organizational interests, and low legitimacy concerned private acts and beliefs.[9]

Figure 16-1 presents a system of legitimacy which reflects both research and experience. The higher an item is in the system, the more probability there is that employees and the community will question management influence on that item. The system shows that routine coordinative requirements are most readily accepted. We are all acquainted with the traffic light, which does require a sort of conformity, but its purpose is to coordinate the free flow of traffic. The same reasoning applies to justify certain hours for a department store to be open, which in turn limits the choice sales clerks have for hours of work.

Substantive items relate more directly to job choices by management, such as the quality of work required. Legitimacy tends to become less accepted, however, as an act's connection with the job becomes more hazy. An example is the type of clothing worn to work. In some instances this is clearly job-connected for safety or public relations reasons, but in other instances it is unrelated to the job. As a further example, all groups surveyed showed low legitimacy concerning whether the employee wears a beard.

Off-the-Job Conduct

For off-the-job conduct, the organization can exert influence by means of educational programs, hobby groups, and communications, but what about its

[9] Edgar H. Schein and J. Steven Ott, "The Legitimacy of Organizational Influence," *American Journal of Sociology,* May 1962, pp. 682–689; and Keith Davis, "Attitudes toward the Legitimacy of Management Efforts to Influence Employees," *Academy of Management Journal,* June 1968, pp. 153–162.

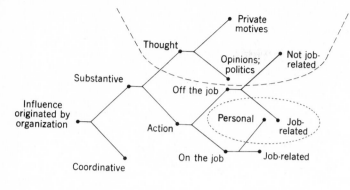

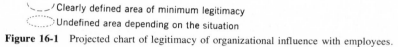

⌣⌣⌣ Clearly defined area of minimum legitimacy
⋯⋯ Undefined area depending on the situation

Figure 16-1 Projected chart of legitimacy of organizational influence with employees.

right to use disciplinary power to enforce its desires? We can begin with the premise that it cannot use its disciplinary power to regulate employee conduct off the job; however, the line of separation is difficult to draw. What about a petroleum employee living on a company pumping site and on twenty-four-hour call? But even when an employee has departed company property and is not on call, the boundaries of employer interest are still not fixed. Consider the angry employee who waited until his foreman stepped outside the company gate and then struck him several times in the presence of other employees. In cases of this type, arbitrators consistently uphold company disciplinary action because the action is job-related. In the United States at least, the organization's jurisdictional line is clearly functional, related to the total job system and not the property line.

One study of sixty-six arbitration awards found a number of ways in which off-the-job conduct could be involved in disciplinary action.[10] In addition to job-related fighting, conduct which damages organizational reputation or business interests is subject to discipline. This factor has been significant in public-service employment such as bus driving and news editing where employee reputation is likely to affect customer acceptance. In other instances, off-the-job conduct may show that the employee is unfit for his present responsibility. In one case a plant guard pulled a gun in an after-hours fight, and this action was held to indicate lack of judgment in the use of firearms.

[10] Arthur M. Sussman, "Work Disputes versus Private Life: An Analysis of Arbitration Cases," *ILR Research,* vol. 10, no. 1, pp. 3–12, Ithaca, N.Y., Cornell University, New York State School of Industrial and Labor Relations, 1964.

Trade Secrets

An area of both legal and ethical difficulty is the maintenance of a firm's trade secrets in a mobile society in which professional employees frequently move to a better job with another company. The basic issue with trade secrets is twofold. The organization certainly has a right to protect its trade secrets and other proprietary data which it may have spent much time and effort in developing. On the other hand, the individual is a free person who has rights to seek employment wherever he wishes and to try to make the best possible use of his abilities wherever he can do so. He is free of the master-servant relationship.

In serious cases a firm may go to court to protect its trade secrets. An example is an employee who steals and sells secret documents not ordinarily accessible to him. In normal relationships, however, the better approach is to develop procedures mutually agreeable to both parties. Some firms set up part-time consulting arrangements following employment, but these are available only if the employee does not work for a competitor during this period. Others provide stock options which the employee forfeits if he leaves the company. For example, do you consider the following option program to be a fair one?

An electronics company has a stock option plan available to key professional employees in exchange for their agreement that they would not "be directly or indirectly engaged in, . . . or have any material investment or any other material interest in, any business that is competitive with the business of the Company" for a period of one year after leaving the company. Exceptions were made in the case of merger and other special situations.

RIGHTS OF PRIVACY

Figure 16-1 shows that areas of least legitimacy are private thoughts, opinions, and motives. Privacy in this context refers to the individual's private person or psyche more than to his private (noncompany) activities. Employees, customers, and others believe that their religious, political, and social beliefs are part of their own inner self and should not be subject to snooping or analysis as a requirement for getting or keeping a job, although there are exceptions such as being employed by a church or political party. The same view applies to personal conversations and to certain personal locations such as company rest rooms and private homes. Exceptions are permitted grudgingly only when a job involvement is clearly proved, and burden of proof is on the company. For example, it might be appropriate to know that a bank teller is deeply in debt to his bookie or that an applicant for a national credit card has twice been convicted for stealing and using credit cards. On the other hand, does the credit card company really need to know the applicant's grandmother's maiden name and the kind of car he drives?

The Polygraph

The polygraph is one instrument whose legitimacy is often questioned, and some states regulate its use.[11] Science has determined that conscience usually causes physiological changes when a person tells a significant lie. Based on this information, the polygraph (lie detector) was developed. Business claims ample reasons for using the polygraph in special situations because its losses from pilferage are several billion dollars annually. Losses of this size have to be passed on to customers, along with the extra expense of protective efforts; so business claims it is in the public interest to use the polygraph in certain situations.

In decentralized retail operations, such as drive-in grocery stores, business states that polygraph tests permit it to abolish various audits and controls that would otherwise be oppressive. This arrangement gives the employee more freedom from surveillance and leaves him free to work in whatever manner is most productive to him. Similar reasoning applies to other positions of trust. For example, a jewelry chain uses the polygraph on job applicants and has found that between 10 and 15 percent of them fail the test.

Regardless of need for the polygraph, its intrusion upon the individual's psyche is evident. In addition, it is sometimes claimed that polygraph tests are improperly extended from theft investigation to marital life, political beliefs, and other nonjob subjects. Even when the polygraph is used only concerning theft, employees tend to resent it because they consider their conscience personal and they object to "being judged by a machine" over which they have no control. They especially object to having to prove themselves innocent, that is, take a test routinely even when no theft has been discovered or no evidence points to them as a thief. They object less to a specific test about a specific known theft of major proportions. In this situation they may welcome a test to take the pressure of suspicion off them.

Personality Tests

Another issue is the use and abuse of personality tests. Formerly personality tests were widely used, but they became less popular after the Civil Rights Act made illegal any use of tests that are not clearly related to job performance. People are able to accept tests of skill, but when their psyche is invaded by personal questions on personality tests, they are understandably rebellious. When one executive was asked in a test whether he was ever bothered with a feeling that someone was following him, he answered in derision: "No, I got rid of him before

[11] "Corporate Lie Detectors Come under Fire," *Business Week,* Jan. 13, 1973, pp. 88 and 90.

I came into the building to take the test!'' Some psychologists admit that personality testing invades privacy, but they contend that an employer has a large investment in an employee, which justifies invasion of privacy, but only for information directly bearing on job performance.[12]

Even if the psychologist handles his work perfectly, management is likely to require a report from him, and he has no control over how management may later misuse confidential data in his report. In one instance, for example, test files were available to any personnel clerk, and some clerks tended to pry into these files more than their jobs justified.

Another danger is that personality tests may produce a standardized work group because the tests overemphasize conformity and fitting into the group. The creative individualist is likely to fail because he *is* different; hence, a firm may test itself into conformity and stagnation. Furthermore, are we really testing what we want to know? Every man has primitive, uncivilized drives as far as can be determined. The crucial question is: How well does he handle them? With most normal people we learn this easily enough by observing their conduct, not by exploring their psyche.

An additional difficulty is that personality tests can be faked by an employee to give results that he thinks the employer desires, making their effective use even more difficult. The test result is then a fiction, rather than a genuine reflection of the employee's personality. Over the years several studies by social scientists have shown that a number of personality tests can be faked.

Taken as a whole, the history of personality tests in employment raises substantial questions of social responsibility. Both employers and psychologists need to reassess their use regularly to assure that they are being used in a socially responsible manner.

Encounter Groups and Sensitivity Training

Encounter group training, also called sensitivity training, is a group training method which may be rather routine, or it may employ intense, emotional group sessions which lay bare a person's psyche to the group. When it does so, it is an invasion of privacy; however, as with personality tests, the invasion is often justified because it is conducted by professional psychologists and is secondary to a more important purpose. In this instance the purpose is to improve sensitivity to the feelings of other people.

Some persons especially object if encounter group training is required rather than voluntary. Usually an employee is allowed to volunteer, but it is difficult to mark the fine line between genuine voluntary choice and coercive pressure to ''volunteer.'' If encounter group training becomes the route to special status and

---

[12] For a more detailed discussion of personality testing as an invasion of privacy, see Alan F. Westin, *Privacy and Freedom,* New York: Atheneum Publishers, 1967.

favors and if people who lack it are bypassed for promotion, they are being coerced to submit to what they perceive is an invasion of privacy.

An additional difficulty with encounter group training is that it may cause psychological casualties. That is, some persons may be psychologically damaged by the intense emotional encounters in the training. One study reported a casualty rate of nearly 10 percent when casualties were defined as enduring and significant negative outcomes caused by the training.[13] This magnitude of risk places major responsibilities on employers to use this type of training with caution. Certainly with a risk factor this high it should be clearly voluntary.

Medical Examinations

Even though medical examinations may invade privacy, the relationship of physician and patient is such a private and privileged one that medical tests of employees are usually permitted. In addition, the health and safety of the patient, as well as others, may be involved; so there is good cause for medical examinations. Normally a manager may require an employee to take a medical examination to determine either physical or emotional fitness to continue work. Some other situations, however, are more sticky. Should a package delivery firm, if it suspects a driver is under the influence of alcohol, be permitted to require a medical test to determine alcohol content in the blood? In this case both employee and public safety are involved; but some employees object to blood tests and others will say this is an invasion of their privacy. What other alternatives might be used to deal with this problem?

Treatment of Alcoholism and Drug Abuse

Related to medical examinations is the treatment of alcoholism and other drug abuses. These conditions present major medical and job problems; therefore employers need to develop responsible programs to deal with them without endangering rights of privacy. With regard to alcoholism, it is estimated that between 4 and 8 percent of employees are alcoholics and that they cost employers about $10 billion annually in absenteeism, poor work, and related costs. Contrary to popular opinion, alcoholics are found in about the same proportion in all types of industry, occupations, and job levels.[14]

Sometimes the job environment may contribute to an employee's alcoholism, but more often than not the employee's personal habits and problems are a major contributor to alcoholism. In some instances employees are well on the

---

[13] Morton A. Lieberman, Irvin D. Yalom, and Matthew B. Miles, *Encounter Groups: First Facts*, New York: Basic Books, Inc., 1973.
[14] "Business Dries Up Its Alcoholics," *Business Week*, Nov. 11, 1972, p. 168.

road to alcoholism even before they are hired. Regardless of the causes, an increasing number of firms are recognizing that they have responsibilities to help alcoholics break their habit. Their responsibilities arise from three reasons. One is that the firm and employee already have an ongoing social relationship on which they can build. A second is that any success with the employee will save both a valuable person for the company and a valuable citizen for society. A third reason is that the job appears to be the best environment for helping an alcoholic recover, because the preservation of his job helps him retain his self-image as a useful person in society.

Successful corporate programs treat alcoholism as an illness, focus on the job behavior caused by alcoholism, and provide both medical help and psychological support for the employee. The firm shows the alcoholic that it wants to help him and is willing to work with him over an extended period of time. A non-threatening, no-job-loss atmosphere is provided, however; there is always the implied threat that alcohol-induced behavior cannot be tolerated indefinitely. For example, if the employee refuses treatment after his problem is discussed, then the employer has little choice but to dismiss him if his incompetent behavior continues.

Following is the way that one company program operates. A supervisor notices that an employee has a record of tardiness and absenteeism, poor work, an exhausted appearance, and related symptoms which might indicate alcoholism or another serious problem. He discusses only the employee's job behavior with the employee, giving him a chance to correct himself. If correction is not forthcoming, the supervisor asks the employee to meet with him in the presence of a counselor. The supervisor presents his evidence of poor job behavior and then leaves the room so that the employee and counselor can discuss the situation privately.

In other instances medical examinations uncover alcoholism or an employee voluntarily asks for help. As soon as the problem is brought into the open, the treatment program is initiated in a supportive atmosphere. It may involve hospitalization to "dry out" the employee. Throughout the procedure the company is patient but firm. In one case, for example, a supervisor was allowed to refuse treatment for a year, although he was disciplined as a warning during that period. Finally he agreed to treatment, and the results were favorable.

Using the approach just described, the firm has achieved a recovery rate of over 50 percent.

Abuse of drugs other than alcohol, particularly hard drugs such as heroin, may cause severe problems for both employers and other employees. The seriousness of this problem is shown by a survey of ninety-five users of hard drugs, mostly

Selected Statements from a Company Policy on Alcoholism, Mental Health Problems, and Drug Abuse

Our company recognizes alcoholism, mental health problems, and drug abuse as illnesses that can be successfully treated. Our people who need help in these areas will be given the same consideration as those with other illnesses. It is our goal to help those who develop such problems by providing for consultation and treatment to prevent their conditions from progressing to a degree where they cannot work effectively. . . .

The decision by management to refer an individual for evaluation, diagnosis, or treatment will be based on evidence of continuing unsatisfactory job performance. Job security will not be jeopardized by such referral. Failure by the individual to accept evaluation or to follow through on professional advice will be considered in the same manner as any factor or illness that continues adversely to affect job performance.

Medical records of those with behavioral-medical disorders will be held confidential, as are all medical records.

From a policy statement of Employers Insurance of Wausau, Wausau, Wis. Reprinted with permission.

heroin, who were employed at the time they used drugs.[15] Ninety-one of them reported that they had been under the influence of drugs during working hours, and forty said that they had used drugs in the lavatory at work. Even more serious from the point of view of other employees, forty-eight of the drug users admitted that they had sold drugs to other employees, and sixty-eight specified other types of on-the-job criminal activity. For example, twenty-eight reported thefts of cash or checks from the employer and/or employees, and thirty-seven admitted stealing company property and selling it to support their drug habit. These statistics make it evident that the pattern of behavior of hard-drug users is a serious threat to an ongoing organization.

Company programs for treatment of drug abuse other than alcohol usually follow the same patterns as programs on alcoholism, except that hard-drug treatment may be more strictly controlled because of the hard-drug user's greater probability of criminal behavior on the job. Most organizations combine treatment of alcoholism, drug abuse, and related difficulties into one program for treatment of people with behavioral-medical problems. Normally the program focuses on both prevention and treatment.

Many firms are reluctant to employ former hard-drug users. Others recognize a social responsibility to provide jobs for persons who have recovered, and they are experimenting with carefully controlled employment programs. For example one firm employed recovered heroin addicts with the employment condi-

[15] Stephen J. Levy, "Drug Abuse in Business: Telling It Like It Is," *Personnel,* September–October 1972, pp. 8–14.

tion that they regularly provide urine specimens for analysis to determine that they had not returned to heroin or certain other hard drugs. Is this an unwarranted invasion of privacy, or is it justified because of the danger of criminal behavior if the employees return to hard drugs?

Surveillance Devices

Surveillance devices especially are used to observe shoplifting, which is estimated to cost business billions of dollars annually. A simple device is the curved mirror which is seen in some retail stores. Another is a camera mounted on a wall or ceiling. There are also more sophisticated electronic devices. Since the shopper is in a public place, these devices normally are not considered an invasion of privacy as long as they are used for the purposes intended and especially if their existence is indicated by a posted notice. Similar reasoning applies to secret surveillance of public places to provide evidence of illegal behavior. For example, in the following situation could the robber properly claim his privacy was invaded?

A statewide banking system installed hidden cameras which could be secretly activated during bank robberies. When the bank had pictures of the robbers in four unsolved robberies, it published close-ups of them in newspaper advertisements throughout the state. The next day one of the men pictured walked into a police station and gave himself up, saying that after seeing his picture in the paper he felt he could not hide any longer!

Hidden surveillance of private places, such as dressing rooms in a clothing store, employee locker rooms, and rest rooms, usually is considered an invasion of privacy. Exceptions sometimes are made in the case of a compelling public interest, such as detection of illegal behavior. People are even more sensitive about unknown electronic bugging of conversation. It almost always is considered an invasion of privacy.

Computer Data Banks and Confidential Records

The development of computers with massive capacity to store and recall information has caused people to be concerned about improper storage and release of personal information. Organizations need information about people in order to perform their functions, but rights of privacy must be judiciously balanced with the organization's right to know. Consider the case of confidential information kept by credit bureaus and firms extending credit to customers. When information such as annual income is supplied by an individual, the argument is that this is a voluntary act and that the information is functionally necessary in determining credit risk.

However, business needs to take great care to keep this information protected from improper use by others. In addition, if there is negative information that is significant enough to damage a person's credit rating, the individual insists upon his right to challenge the information. The Fair Credit Report Act of 1971 provided some protection along this line. It required credit agencies to tell persons refused credit the contents of their files. This is normal due process to protect an individual from being unfairly victimized by the system. It is an example of the basic human claim for justice mentioned earlier.

The most substantial study of computer data banks to date has been reassuring.[16] It reported that computer data banks generally are not collecting more information about the person than was done manually, and they are not collecting different information, although there has been a large increase in the number of persons covered. Nevertheless, more protection is needed because of potential dangers in these massive systems. The study recommends several public policies for better protection of the individual, including greater rights for an individual to examine his records and to challenge incorrect data, protection of confidentiality, and rules governing data sharing among organizations.

In 1973 Sweden became the first nation to pass a general law governing the use and privacy of data banks, both commercial and governmental. The law was spurred by several controversial incidents of release of data bank information. The law establishes a data inspection board which determines how each data bank may be used and what methods it may employ. An individual may petition the board to order corrections in his file and may sue for damages if misinformation harms him. The law prohibits certain types of data, such as religious and political affiliations, except that political parties and churches may computerize their membership lists. It is probable that the United States and other nations will follow with similar laws in due time.

Invasion of the Privacy of One's Home

It has been said that a man's home is his own private castle, and an area of increasing irritation at home is the large amount of unsolicited "junk mail" received from business. Computer tapes have made inexpensive the addressing of this kind of mail, so its quantity is increasing. An authority on privacy comments that "as long as I have the right to throw junk mail in the wastebasket, I think my liberty is pretty well protected."[17] Nevertheless, complaints persist on the basis

---

[16] Alan F. Westin and Michael A. Baker, *Organizational Databanks and Individual Privacy,* New York: Quadrangle Books: The New York Times Book Company, 1973.
[17] Alan F. Westin, quoted in "Squeezing Even More out of Tax Returns," *Business Week,* Dec. 6, 1969, p. 69.

that the recipient's private time is consumed in processing the unwanted mail to separate it from other mail.

There are also special situations where privacy is more directly threatened. For example, unsolicited obscene mail definitely may invade the psyche, shock the recipient, and cause emotional upset; therefore a federal law permits the recipient to file a form which requires the sender to remove the individual's name from his mailing list. According to this law, which was upheld unanimously by the Supreme Court in 1970, the obscenity of any piece of mail may be determined by the recipient. For example, a householder who was tired of junk mail objected to department store advertising on the basis that it showed girdles and lingerie. The Post Office Department agreed that the law allows an individual choice on this matter without relation to generally accepted community standards.

Judging Infringements on Privacy

There are many situational variations, some of which probably constitute infringements on privacy while others do not. Four tests may be applied to help determine the degree of privacy invasion. First, does the device invade the psyche, such as polygraphs and personality tests? Second, is the device unnecessarily secret? Companies are regularly using television cameras for various types of controls, but these are work observations that are not secret, so an employee has some opportunity to know whether he is being watched and, if he desires, to challenge the instrument. A third test is whether the activity or instrument serves a purpose which is predominantly in the public interest (such as observation of shoplifters), with any invasion of privacy being incidental and secondary. Fourth, is a private act or location being observed? According to the criterion, hidden cameras or microphones in locker rooms have been condemned.

Sometimes novel questions of privacy arise. Women employees in a major British company persuaded management to remove from their rest room a loudspeaker on the regular paging system. This was not a case of snooping. They simply claimed that they were shocked to hear a man's voice in their rest room, and they demanded privacy therefrom!

Indeed, privacy is a worldwide issue. As industrialization advances along with the technology of snooping, business must increasingly seek responsible behavior measured by criteria of the type we have been discussing.

RESPONSIBILITIES OF THE INDIVIDUAL
TO THE ORGANIZATION

The relationship of an individual to an organization is typically a mutual social transaction, and mutual responsibilities arise out of the relationship. This mutual relationship deteriorates if either party fails to act responsibly toward the needs of the other. An advanced civilization in which individuals have relative freedom is built upon responsible action by its individuals as well as by its organizations. For example, individual theft from the organization is just as irresponsible as organizational theft from the individual.

The polygraph provides a useful illustration of the mutual responsibilities of individuals and organizations in a complex system. There would be no use for the polygraph if it were not discovering breaches in conduct which the individual's *own conscience* recognizes. In fact, it is rarely used with groups such as professional accountants whose high standards of integrity and responsibility make it unnecessary. All individuals could destroy the usefulness of the polygraph by similar conduct. In other words, the roots of the polygraph problem lie in individual conduct and not in the device itself. We deal with only half the problem when we condemn the polygraph without also condemning the conduct which makes it useful. Theft was the original action which made a counteraction by the organization appropriate. This reasoning does not justify organizational use of the polygraph, but it does recognize from the point of view of the whole social system the mutual responsibility that exists for its use.

A word which comprehensively reflects the mutual responsibilities of individual and organization to each other is "integrity." The idea of integrity applies in two separate meanings of the word. First, each party in the social transaction needs to respect the *integrity* of the other, which means to accept the other's individuality and social function. Second, each party needs to *practice integrity* in its relationships with the other. Integrity in this context implies that each party acts in an open, responsible way, without deception and shallowness. If both parties respond with integrity, they will be able to develop greater benefits in relation to inputs, and society will be able to relax many social controls put upon them.

SUMMARY

The contest between man and his organizations is as old as history, and this condition challenges business to develop systems of accepted legitimacy which serve the needs of both. Three claims which the individual makes on business are improvement, independence, and justice.

The organization-man thesis, although it is sometimes overplayed, suggests vigilance to assure that organizations serve social needs with minimum intrusion on individual freedom and privacy. Some areas which raise issues of rights of privacy are the polygraph, personality tests, encounter group and sensitivity training, medical examinations, treatment of alcoholism and drug abuse, surveillance devices, computer data banks and confidential records, and unsolicited mail to one's residence.

The social transaction between the individual and the organization typically creates mutual responsibilities. When these are discharged with integrity, mutual benefits should predominate. In the final analysis, we do know that organizations can be used to free individuals as well as to confine them. For example, a physicist in a research laboratory is more free to do research than he would be working alone, because the organization provides him with equipment, supporting services, and other aids.

STUDY GUIDES FOR INTERPRETATION OF THIS CHAPTER

1. AB Sales, Inc., employs ten women at telephones all day long calling household numbers listed in the telephone directory to offer a sales pitch for a household appliance. Several persons have complained to the chamber of commerce that this is an invasion of their privacy. Give your own analysis concerning whether this is an invasion of privacy.

2. Mable Tyro, speaking for a group of sales clerks at Martin Department Store in an exclusive shopping center, says that women clerks should be permitted to wear slacks because it is sometimes drafty near doors and clerks have to stoop and bend to reach merchandise under counters. Store manager Mark Gomberg says that the requirement that women sales clerks wear dresses is necessary to provide the proper store image and sales climate. Comment.

3. Read literature on personality tests. Then *(a)* discuss specifically how they invade privacy, and *(b)* comment on whether a test of this type could be given without invading individual privacy.

4. *(a)* Examine union newspapers or booklets and comment on the manner in which they do, or do not, discuss responsibilities of the individual employee to the organization.
   (b) Use the same procedure with regard to consumer publications and their discussion of consumer responsibilities to the organization from which they make purchases.

PROBLEMS
The Forbidden Merger

August Bern was president and chief executive officer of a larger, merger-minded conglomerate in which he had an insignificant ownership interest. The firm had sales of over $100 million and was listed on the New York Stock Exchange. In this firm the chairman of the board of directors headed a committee of board members which initiated and appraised merger possibilities. This committee operated independently of the president until merger negotiations advanced to a serious stage. Recently a member of the merger committee mentioned in a board meeting that the committee was considering merger with a tobacco company. When the president heard this he said that he was a member of a religion which forbids use of tobacco and that he would not be associated with a firm which sold it. He threatened to resign if the merger was consummated.

1. Appraise the legitimacy of individual and organizational interests in this situation.

2. In the role of chairman of the board, what response would you make, if any?

The Smoking Ban

A representative of an antismoking group proposed to airlines that they ban all smoking on passenger flights. He acknowledged that they already ban smoking during takeoff and landing as a safety measure, but noted that they still allow each passenger to use "his own conflagration kit" during flight. He said that smoking could cause a flash fire under certain conditions; consequently, it is a safety hazard to all passengers and a psychological threat to those individuals who realize the fire danger from smoking.

1. In the role of president of a regional airline how would you respond when the letter making this request is brought to your attention?

The Holden Transit Company

Holden Transit Company provided bus service for a large metropolitan area with a population of over 2 million persons. It accepted advertising for "car cards" which were placed in display panels immediately above bus windows inside the bus. Advertising was also accepted for the outside of the bus. One advertiser approached the company with a request to furnish each bus with tape casettes which would announce advertising messages intermittently. The company accepted several installations on an experimental basis.

When the casettes were installed on the buses, large numbers of bus users protested that the announcements were an invasion of their privacy as passengers. When they were asked to explain why they objected to the voice announcements but not the car cards, they replied that they could choose whether to read the car cards but the voice announcements distracted them and interfered with what they were doing, such as reading, thinking, or talking to a friend. Some threatened legal action if the tapes were not removed.

1. Analyze this situation in terms of invasion of privacy. As company president, after thorough study of this situation, what action would you take and why?

PART 4

BUSINESS AND
THE COMMUNITY

CHAPTER

17

BUSINESS INVOLVEMENT IN COMMUNITY ACTIVITIES

Business leadership is more than leadership in business; it entails community responsibilities, often of a high order and expensive to a company.

Richard Eells[1]

Businessmen themselves must take a direct hand in helping solve the nation's social problems.

Frederick Kappel[2]

The community discussed in this chapter is an organization's area of local business influence. It often includes more than one political community, for political boundaries do not necessarily follow economic and social boundaries. A major company in a metropolitan area might have as its community the central city and nine satellite cities. Another company might be located in a rural area having three surrounding cities as its community. A public utility has a separate community for each of the local economic areas it serves. In all cases both company and community have a mutual dependence which is significant economically and socially. The following situations show how this mutual relationship is expressed in practice.

Residents in one city prepared to go before the city council to prohibit factory trucks from using streets in a nearby residential neighborhood as a regular thoroughfare. Plant officials responded by rerouting the trucks.

In another city during a coal strike the principal factory supplied two carloads of coal to the local hospital, even though the factory supply of coal was very short. During the same strike a factory manager in another city rejected a civic organization's plea for coal for a recreation hall. He silenced

---

[1] Richard Eells, "Beyond the Golden Rule," *Columbia Journal of World Business,* July–August 1967, p. 87.

[2] Frederick Kappel, quoted in *Community and Company,* Wilmington, Del.: E. I. du Pont de Nemours & Company, n.d., p. 3.

requests with the comment: "Which is more important, to assure work for several thousand men or to continue a recreation program?"

During a local recession in another city, a corporation found it necessary to lay off several hundred women assemblers. After consultation with local leaders, it made an exception to its regular policy of layoff by seniority. Women who proved they were the sole breadwinner in a family were not laid off, regardless of seniority.

Since this chapter is the introductory chapter in a part containing several chapters on business and the community, discussion will be limited to general business involvement with the community. Subsequent chapters will discuss specific areas of involvement such as urban issues and pollution. Following a general introduction covering community relations, this chapter will discuss three ways in which business affects the community. These are involvement of businessmen in civic affairs, business giving, and regular business practice in the community.

COMMUNITY RELATIONS

The involvement of business with the community is called *community relations* or *public affairs*. Two characteristics distinguish modern community relations from those 100 years ago. One is *urbanization*. Migration from rural areas to urban centers has changed community life and created new stresses for business and community. This is a worldwide trend, and there is no evidence that it will soon stop. Each census shows a greater proportion of population living in metropolitan areas (central city and suburbs). This trend intensifies a number of social problems, such as land use and pollution. It places a load upon land, air, utilities, and resources that they are hardly able to bear. In addition, people who move from a rural society to an urban community are often poorly equipped to adjust to it, and so they may fall prey to a variety of social ills.

The second characteristic is *greater system interdependence* of business and community. Urbanization is a partial cause of interdependence, but so is technology, for it requires communities to become much larger in order to maintain self-sufficiency. Ancient communities could be self-sufficient with a farm and a few artisans. But a modern industrial community needs a college nearby to support lifelong learning, recreational facilities, public utilities, specialized service facilities, urban transportation, capital sources, and a host of other services. Business depends on these services in greater variety than ever before. Just as a rocket can fail because of some tiny malfunction, so can a community experience difficulty because of indirect effects of some isolated event. There is no escaping general community interdependence today. Business cannot remain detached from the community.

Limited Resources Face Unlimited Community Needs

Business responsibilities in a community extend in a wide variety of directions from civil rights to support of community cultural activities. Almost any community has a multitude of social needs which require far more resources than are available. This situation *requires that choices be made with regard to priorities*. In some instances the community decides the priorities, but in many instances the business's management faces the hard choice of determining priorities for use of its limited resources. Further, in all cases, once management has decided to help serve a need, it must still decide how much of its resources can be applied to that need. This means that any action management takes will result in some dissatisfaction from those who get no help and those who do not get as much help as they want. It is impossible for business always "to do the right thing" and "come out smelling like a rose." There will always be dissatisfaction because limited resources are being applied to virtually unlimited social needs. In most instances the unmet needs are greater than the needs that are met; therefore dissatisfactions are likely to be greater than satisfactions. This is the nature of community relations.

The unlimited reach of community needs can be better understood by considering some of the main community responsibilities faced by a manufacturer in a major city. In the course of a year the following demands on company resources arose:

1. Assistance for handicapped and other disadvantaged persons
2. Support of air and water pollution control
3. Service responsibility for products sold to local consumers
4. Support of artistic and cultural activities
5. Employment and advancement for minorities and women
6. Assistance in urban planning and development
7. Support of local health care program
8. Donation of equipment to local school system
9. Support of local bond issues for public improvements
10. Aid to community hospital drive
11. Support of local program for recycling to conserve scarce resources and prevent pollution
12. Executive aid for local United Fund
13. Company participation in "get out the vote" campaign

Many of these demands consumed hours and days of employee time and thousands of dollars of company resources. Meanwhile the company had to meet its primary obligation of serving customers competitively throughout the world.

Small and Large Businesses Compared

Although large businesses usually have more public visibility in community relations, small businesses are vitally involved in setting general community standards. The conduct of appliance repair servicemen, used-car salesmen, and retail proprietors is a significant influence on the quality of life in a community, regardless of what United States Steel Corporation does at the national level. If these small businesses take advantage of their customers, oppose civic improvements, and let downtown go to seed, the community quality of life will deteriorate. If they take an opposite approach, the quality of life will improve regardless of what business giants decide to do nationally.

We can speak of the small businessmen as Lincoln spoke of the common people: "God must have loved them because he made so many of them." Approximately 95 percent of all business firms have fewer than twenty employees. In most communities there are so many small businessmen that diverse viewpoints may be expected. This fact sometimes stymies unified effort for civic improvement. It is difficult to get them all going in the same direction. But most of all, because they control individually their business practice, their personal ethics are much more involved than is the case with managers in large firms. The large organization makes decisions based on policy, but the small one usually decides according to the proprietor's personal views.

On the other hand, the large business has its negative aspects also. Though its business practice may be more consistent, its community interest is frequently more detached. There are two reasons for this detachment. First, the larger firm's sales area usually extends far beyond the community, even though its only office is in the community. In contrast, the small retail or service business depends on the community as its primary market.

Another reason that community detachment develops in large firms is that many of them have decentralized branches. The result is that the firms have an interest in many communities rather than one. Although they have many operational locations, they have only one headquarters where top management can be directly contacted for major support of community projects. Managers in the branches come and go as they move through the promotion ladder of the total organization. It is difficult for them to have the same interest in the community that a small retail proprietor has because their relationship to the community is different. Therefore, their decisions have to be based more on policy than on personal interest, and that policy is centrally determined, often without recognition of the peculiar needs of a certain community. This condition places heavy responsibilities on central headquarters to give local managers broad leeway to make community-related decisions. Even when these decisions seem to be exceeding the bounds of policy, there may be justifiable local reasons for them.

Headquarters policies emphasize branch economic performance, usually giving minimum attention to social performance. Branch managers act accordingly, often trying to squeeze out a few more dollars of economic performance while depleting human and community social assets. To avoid this unfortunate tendency, headquarters management has a responsibility to include in its branch appraisal process a social audit as well as an economic audit. Unless social measures are genuinely valued by headquarters, branch management will be tempted to give them little attention.

Community relations difficulties which branch managements face are shown in a survey of community leaders in three cities.[3] The community leaders were asked whether they thought branch managements were more interested or less interested in the community than local businesses. In each city the majority thought that branch managements were *less* interested in the community as follows:

Far Western city	95%
Eastern city	79%
Midwestern city	57%

However, the study did show that a branch plant could be recognized as an outstanding community citizen if its management was willing to make the effort. In one city, when community leaders were asked to identify businesses which were outstanding community citizens, one branch rated high, but two others rated low as follows:

Branch of a large automobile producer	64%
Branch of a heavy equipment manufacturer	14%
Branch of a large electrical equipment manufacturer	7%

This information suggests that branches operate under a community relations handicap compared with local businesses; therefore they probably have to make a greater effort than local businesses in order to be recognized as an outstanding community citizen.

The decentralized firm has special responsibilities for dealing with community rumor about its operations. Since some of its decisions are made in headquarters, the local operation is a natural subject for rumors, such as "leaving the community" or "won't help," every time a local problem arises.

Offsetting the personal detachment which branch executives may have is the fact that they do represent additional resources brought to a community from outside. They also can call upon headquarters for specialists to aid in civic planning. They can even call for economic support in special cases, beyond what a local business might be expected to contribute. They bring to communities a high quality of leadership which may be in short supply in depressed localities. Perhaps

[3] Opinion Research Corporation, *Community Relations* (Executive Summary), April 1966, pp. 6–7.

more important they bring a steady stream of new leaders with fresh ideas. The branch managers have broad experience and a viewpoint far beyond local provincialism. They can expand community horizons and help a community adjust to changing world conditions.

The net balance of these competing advantages and disadvantages appears to be favorable. Communities usually seek the help of branch executives and use them effectively. The possibility of transfer during a term of civic service is usually ignored. After all, small businessmen leave communities too.

The Pittsburgh Experience

An early example of business initiative in a major community development was the Pittsburgh Renaissance.[4] Located in a soft-coal area and having much heavy industry, Pittsburgh, Pennsylvania, had always been smoky and dirty. As early as 1840 Charles Dickens called it "hell with the lid off." Even in the 1940s lights sometimes had to be burned at midday because of the pall of smoke that obscured the city. The city came out of World War II with a bleak outlook. It had smoke, dirt, and few civic improvements. Urban blight had overcome its downtown Golden Triangle. Vigorous younger people were beginning to move elsewhere.

In this depressing situation, a group of business leaders formed the Allegheny Conference on Community Development to initiate a bold improvement program. Their first effort was smoke control because the smoke was destroying beauty and lowering morale in the community. In determining to control smoke, businessmen were in effect deciding to control *themselves* as well as homeowners with soft-coal heating systems. Working closely with local government, they overcame vigorous opposition from homeowners, politicians, and those within their own ranks. Through smoke control ordinances and voluntary effort, smoke was eventually reduced *90 percent,* long before federal and state clean-air standards were established.

With this victory the group tackled the Golden Triangle to convert it from a slum to a community showcase. One large improvement required nine major companies to sign twenty-year leases for space before ground could be broken. Since only the top executive in a firm could make this kind of decision, Pittsburgh was fortunate to have home offices of a number of major corporations. There was also opposition to the Golden Triangle project. Legal battles about some improvements were carried eventually to the United States Supreme Court. Finally, however, the Golden Triangle was rebuilt into a beautiful area. Although the primary objective of the Allegheny Conference was economic rejuvenation, cul-

[4] Edward C. Bursk, "Your Company and Your Community: The Lesson of Pittsburgh," in Dan H. Fenn, Jr. (ed.), *Business Responsibility in Action,* New York: McGraw-Hill Book Company, 1960, pp. 29–54.

tural improvements followed once the morale of the city was restored. The conclusion from the Pittsburgh experience is that business-government-citizen cooperation can restore blighted communities. In Pittsburgh the initiative came from business; in other cities initiative might arise elsewhere.

Community Responsibilities to Business

In the business-community relationship we cannot ignore the responsibility of community to business. If citizens, labor, and government abuse business or take advantage of it, then cooperation for improvement becomes more difficult. As stated by one businessman: "It's difficult to cooperate with a community which discriminates by taxing business property at one rate and other property at a cheaper rate." A retailer added: "Business should be friendly and courteous, but what about the customers? Some are so suspicious and irritable that no one likes to serve them." A manager of a used-car firm spoke up: "You should see the 'lemons' the customers trade to me without revealing defects. I could sue some of them for fraud, but what would that do to my business?" A grocery store proprietor added: "I accidentally caught one of my regular customers putting butter in a margarine box in order to cheat me of a few pennies."

The relationship of business with community is a social transaction which requires that both parties be open, honest, and fair with the other in order to achieve maximum effectiveness. Just as business is responsible, so are communities and their citizens responsible because they have social power affecting the business. The Iron Law of Responsibility applies to them as well as to business. In a socially effective society both business and community will act responsibly toward each other.

Following are a number of areas of community responsibility to business:

1. A cultural and educational environment which supports a balanced quality of life for employees

2. Adequate public services such as police and fire protection, and sewage, water, and electric services

3. A fair and open public press

4. Taxes which are equitable and do not discriminate for or against business

5. Open acceptance of business participation in community affairs

6. An adequate transportation system to business areas (for example, streets and public transportation)

7. Public officials, customers, and citizens who are fair and honest in their involvement with the organization

BUSINESSMEN IN CIVIC AFFAIRS

In a pluralistic society, the multiallegiant person has interests in many organizations. The businessman is no exception. Two of his allegiances are to his business and to his community. It is difficult to generalize about either allegiance because there are perhaps as many varieties as there are businessmen. Some businessmen were born and reared in their community. Others moved to their community when they graduated from college. Others may be transients merely seeking to make a "fast buck" and move on. Still others are young corporate experts more interested in their profession than in their community or company.

As with all pluralism, conflicts of allegiance sometimes develop. As a representative of the corporation, the businessman must be detached and objective about community demands. But as a family man and a member of social groups within the community, he is also intimately tied to community affairs.

Managers do not seem to shirk participation in civic affairs simply because conflict of allegiance may arise. Used to resolving conflict in organizational affairs, they feel at home in a similar civic environment. Nearly every museum board, development committee, or other civic group has business managers well represented among its members.

One survey of middle managers in a management-oriented professional group in a large city reported that *all of them* were involved in some community service work both during their regular working day and after working hours. The most involvement was in civic groups (such as a Rotary Club), service groups (such as Boy Scouts of America), and charitable groups. Moderate involvement was in cultural activities, and minimum involvement was in political-governmental activities.[5]

Reasons for Community Involvement of Managers

Many managers become involved in community service because their company encourages them to do so, but the research just mentioned suggests that managers also have strong personal drives to serve their community. As human beings they have the normal altruistic drives which most other people have. They also relate to their families, desiring the community to be a better place for them to live.

Perhaps a more complex reason for community service work is that its satisfactions are of a different psychological nature from those derived in employment. The reward is more immediate than the indirect feeling of service derived from productive work as an employee. Also the reward more directly relates to one's immediate neighbors, instead of an unknown and distant consumer public.

[5] Keith Davis and Frank H. Besnette, "Management's Obligation to Public Service Activities," *Advanced Management Journal,* April 1969, pp. 33–39.

Furthermore, in public service work, people give their time and talent without direct "cost" to the organization served. They receive "compensation" in the form of personal satisfactions, as all persons in public service must in order to be motivated to participate, but their compensation is of an intangible nature which does not require a major "give up" from the organization. Their "costless" reward means that they can feel they have unselfishly given, whereas in employment they know they are a direct cost to their employer and must render services at least equal to their cost in order for their employer to break even in the exchange. There is, therefore, a feeling of less risk of loss in public service work, that is, less chance that they will contribute less than their cost and thus create a net social loss. Their low-risk and high-reward relationship in public service work is undoubtedly one of the reasons many people are turning to it as an outlet for their excess time and energy.

Community Involvement Can Be Rewarding to Business

There is also the probability that community involvement will bring benefits to the business itself. There are, of course, the usual worries that active community participation will cause a business to lose customers when it is associated with a project which certain customers oppose. This does occur, but wise community leadership also can gain customers and goodwill. Limited research suggests that the key to community relations success is genuine *involvement*, as distinguished from more traditional approaches such as making charitable contributions and being a good employer. These more traditional activities are expected from any business; therefore the business which wants outstanding recognition will need to become directly involved in current issues such as pollution, education, transportation, and crime. The outstanding company makes a commitment to improving the quality of life in its community.

Opinion Research Corporation surveys show that both the general public and community leaders rate a company outstanding primarily because of its participation in local affairs. "Participation" means business leadership, expertise, and cooperation in solving problems, not passive financial aid. In two cities the main reasons for rating a company outstanding were as follows:

	Percent of Community Leaders (Eastern City)	Percent of General Public (Southern City)
Participation in local affairs	67	48
Financial contributions	41	23
Good employee relations	20	5

In both surveys "participation in local affairs" was mentioned more times than the next two reasons combined.[6]

Another study covering ninety-seven small businesses reported that those "organizations whose managers are actively involved in community affairs are also those that are most profitable for the owners." This correlation of community participation and profit was significant to the .01 degree of confidence.[7]

Community Power Structure

In their activities businessmen become part of the *community power structure*. Power is not in the man himself, but flows from the role he plays in the social system. It is dynamic and cannot be viewed apart from the community itself. If a businessman moves to another community, he is in a new system, and his power does not transfer. In fact, *within* the community the power structure varies with the problem being considered.

In a New York town having about 6,000 persons, five major community decisions were studied. Thirty-six leaders were involved, but twenty-two of them participated in only one of the five decisions. Only eight leaders were involved in two decisions; only four were involved in three decisions; only two were involved in four decisions; and no leader was involved in all five decisions. Businessmen's participation depended on the subject being considered. Flood control and the municipal building were determined by political leaders, and specialists determined the school bond issue. Decisions on the new hospital and new industry were dominated by businessmen.[8]

Evidence supports the general conclusion that there is no standard power structure in communities. Power varies depending on hundreds of factors, such as community history, degree of industrialization, and type of problem being considered. Businessmen do participate in the total power structure, but not necessarily in every major civic decision. Usually businessmen are influential, and they also may dominate decisions. On the other hand, one investigator concluded that

[6] Al Vogel, "Urban Crisis: New Focus for Community Relations," *Public Relations Journal,* September 1967, pp.12–13.

[7] Frank Friedlander and Hal Pickle, "Components of Effectiveness in Small Organizations," *Administrative Science Quarterly,* September 1968, pp. 289–304.

[8] Robert Presthus, *Men at the Top: A Study in Community Power,* Fair Lawn, N.J.: Oxford University Press, 1964, pp. 92–100. Somewhat similar results are reported in Endsley Terrence Jones, "The Businessman and the Small City Problems: What They're Doing, Not Doing, and Why," *Michigan Business Review,* November 1968, pp. 18–23.

politicians actually initiated policy choices and that businessmen merely rubber-stamped them after decisions were made.[9]

Of special interest is the manner in which labor leaders view the community activities of businessmen. A study of Lansing, Michigan, an industrial city, showed that labor leaders felt that businessmen dominated community decision making as a whole. However, when labor leaders named the ten persons they thought most influential in the community, they named only four businessmen. Only one of these, a newspaper publisher, was in the top five; therefore, the labor leaders' selections did not support their general conclusion of business domination. Others in the top five were the mayor, a Catholic bishop, the superintendent of public schools, and the president of the Labor Council. Labor leaders generally but not wholly supported the idea that businessmen are "interested, hard-working citizens who act openly and responsibly for the good of the community."[10]

Viewed as a whole, businessmen are men of power and status in the United States, but they are not an exclusive group dominating community decisions. They tend to be extroverted leaders willing to enter into affairs of the community, especially where business interests and expertise are involved. Effects have been both negative and positive. There has been interference and occasional autocratic control. On the other hand, communities have in this way gained the assistance of some of society's most competent leaders.

BUSINESS GIVING

Specific areas of giving, such as gifts to education and art, are discussed in the appropriate functional chapters. This section focuses on the general concept of business giving in the community. Since 1936 the federal government, through its income tax law, has encouraged corporate giving for educational, charitable, scientific, and religious purposes. Corporations are allowed to deduct contributions which do not exceed 5 percent of their taxable income.[11] If this deduction were not allowed, corporations would have to pay taxes and then give gifts from the residue of net income, thus requiring them to earn about $2 in order to have $1 to give away.

[9] Charles M. Bonjean and David M. Olson, "Community Leadership: Directions of Research," *Administrative Science Quarterly,* December 1964, pp. 278–300. This article provides an excellent summary of the literature. Comparative studies cited in the article show that two Mexican cities and one British city were less influenced by businessmen than were ten United States cities.
[10] William H. Form and Warren L. Sauer, "Labor and Community Influentials: A Comparative Study of Participation and Imagery," *Industrial and Labor Relations Review,* October 1963 pp. 18–19.
[11] Gifts given by business partnerships or proprietorships are governed by individual income tax laws.

Average corporate giving exceeds 1 percent of net income before taxes. A number of businesses, especially larger ones, have established foundations to handle their contributions. This approach permits them to administer their giving programs more uniformly and objectively. It also provides a central group which handles all requests. This procedure is usually not used for minor local contributions in order to avoid red tape and permit some local autonomy.

Reasons for Business Giving

There are several rationalizations to support business giving. Business giving is frequently justified as an *investment* that benefits the business in the long run by improving the community, its labor force, the climate for business, or other conditions affecting a particular business. A gift to a hospital building fund is rationalized in this way because it should create better health in the community. Gifts for education are viewed as improving the labor market or expanding the economy, thereby increasing a firm's potential market.

Another basis for giving gifts is to consider routine local ones as an *operating expense* of doing business. Gifts of this type are often thought to provide public relations or advertising returns and are treated like any other public relations expense. Examples are gifts of money to a local charity or souvenirs to visiting school students.

Both the investment and the expense philosophies are directly related to business objectives. Some of these gifts can be rationalized as supporting profit in the long run, if not in the short run. Others, such as general aid to education outside the plant community, have no direct connection with profit, but they are relevant indirectly because they affect the general economic and social climate of business.

A third philosophy assumes that a corporation is a citizen of the community as a person is, except that it has greater resources than most citizens. As a citizen it has a duty to support *philanthropy* without regard to its self-interest in the same way that a private person does. This philanthropic approach can open a Pandora's Box of giving. Unless it is governed by carefully formed policies, it may bind the corporation to support requests without careful screening simply because it has no policy reason to say "no." Since the corporation has money in the bank and philanthropy is one of the noblest qualities of civilized man, how can it refuse its needy brother? This kind of reasoning can lead to imprudent waste of funds in the trusteeship of management and thus be irresponsible action rather than a display of responsibility. As we have said before, businessmen are human and are likely to act that way. They do feel concern for their community and are partly motivated by philanthropic ideals.

Another assumption is that some corporate gifts take on the characteristics of *taxes*. Since it is the prevailing opinion that corporations should be good citizens, helpful neighbors, and human institutions, the community comes close to imposing some types of gift giving on the corporation as a kind of unofficial tax. The gifts are a cost of doing business. They are given to retain public approval for the business.

Regardless of whether gifts are viewed as an investment, an expense, a philanthropy, or a tax, most of their costs are probably passed on to consumers, because giving in the long run becomes a cost of doing business. If this view is valid, then the fifth reason is that business is acting partly as agent and *trustee* for the community, receiving funds and distributing them according to community needs. In its trusteeship role business responds to various pluralistic claims in its community, and one of these responses is gifts to claimants whose claims are perceived as either legitimate or so powerful that they threaten the business if not satisfied. Thus, both legitimacy of claim and power of claimants are considered when making a decision concerning corporate giving.

Policies for Giving

Any business which makes gifts needs a carefully thought-out policy for its actions. If a business lacks a carefully developed policy, there is danger that an aggressive minority of gift seekers will get most of the available funds, leaving an unbalanced company gift program and an unbalanced community.

Most firms concentrate their giving in selected areas in order to make an impact with a substantial gift, rather than spreading their resources thinly. Furthermore, there are several areas where businesses either do not give or exercise great care in giving. Law prohibits political contributions. Companies usually do not give to religious groups, because they believe religion is an individual choice for owners, employees, and others. They may, however, give to religious-oriented groups that serve all creeds, such as the Salvation Army, or to community projects with religious groups among their sponsors. Some firms avoid gifts to groups with limited membership such as veterans' organizations and fraternal societies. Others confine their giving to their market territory or the community where their facilities are located. Each firm's policies are different, based upon its own perceptions of needs and social responsibilities.

Leaves of Absence for Public Service

Related to giving is the idea of employee leaves of absence for community and other public service assignments. If the employee's salary is either partially or wholly continued during this period of public service, then this is a type of gift. In other cases the employee's leave is without pay, but even in this instance the business makes a sacrifice because it forgoes the employee's services and may suffer delay in some of the work with which the absent employee was involved.

Paid Leaves of Absence for Public Service

Three men with little else in common, David Evans, Robert S. Lee, and Louis C. Henderson, all do good deeds on company time. More formally, they participate in a leave-for-public-service program that enables IBM employees to take time off, usually with pay, to perform socially constructive tasks. Xerox Corp. recently announced a similar program, and a handful of other companies authorize such leaves on an *ad hoc* basis.

Probably the latest development in the growing corporate commitment to social action, the leave-for-service program stems naturally from the corporate conviction that a company's most valuable resource is its people. At IBM, nobody quite remembers when the program became official—only that it grew logically from IBM's philosophy of good citizenship. Executives recall that the first six-month and year-long leaves were granted during the 1960s, following a previous policy of granting days and half-days off for community work, and that Thomas J. Watson Jr., then chairman, urged local managers to give increased attention to leave applications in 1970.

From "Doing Good Works on Company Time," *Business Week,* May 13, 1972, p. 166. Used with permission of McGraw-Hill, Inc.

For many decades businesses granted short leaves for work on special community projects, such as the United Fund, for one month. This approach gave community projects valuable services that they could not otherwise secure on a short-term basis. Gradually longer leaves of six months or a year developed in special instances, and then in the 1960s a few firms such as International Business Machines began to develop official programs for public service leaves of absence. Policies were developed concerning types of projects suitable for leave, conditions for pay or no pay, length of leave, how the return to work will be handled, and related conditions.

The idea behind the ''giving'' of people rather than funds is that people are a business's most valuable resource, so it is giving something even more valuable than money when it allows its people to work on community and other public projects. Furthermore, both the business and the employees often feel that employees personally will grow in experience and understanding during their leaves; thus they may make better employees when they return to their jobs.

Following are two examples of public service leaves. One employee took a year's leave to work with a university to counsel high school graduates who were considering entering the university. He felt that his business experience could help him communicate to prospective students the relevance of education to the world of work. Another employee felt strong humanistic drives to serve people, so he took a leave to work with an orphanage.

In summary, business giving has become an integral part of modern society. In a pluralistic society, giving is an effective way to support other free institutions such as private education and local charity. Without this support, the local initiative and voluntary action which characterize communities might collapse. This situation would surely endanger pluralism and lead to concentrations of power which might in turn threaten free business institutions.

BUSINESS PRACTICES IN COMMUNITIES

Business practice has direct, significant effects on the community. These are not the effects of giving gifts or of volunteering time, but are the result of the way business conducts itself in the ordinary course of operations. Does business, for example, cause water and air pollution? Are its plants an aesthetic asset or a blight? Do its policies encourage unfair competition and business conflict?

Community Influence of Large Firms

It is evident that the day-to-day activities of many different firms help establish a climate of friendliness, distrust, or other characteristics in a community, but dominance by one or two large firms can have even greater effects. In this instance the success of a community is inevitably tied to that of its major business firm. When the business employs skilled and professional workers, the community has better-educated citizens, higher-quality homes and shopping centers, and a richer residential tax base. However, the situation is reversed when most of the employees are unskilled. In this case the social cleavage between management and workers, and between rich and poor in the community, may be more severe.

In a similar manner, if the business prospers economically, the community usually prospers, but the reverse can also occur. When Studebaker ceased making automobiles in South Bend, Indiana, that community was set back economically for years. The situation was recognized by management, which worked closely with the community to encourage other companies to move into the sprawling Studebaker plant in order to maintain employment. In the long run, the adjustment actually was desirable because South Bend became less dependent on one business.

Although dominant firms can hurt a community by leaving it or letting it deteriorate, these same firms can help in many ways. Their staff consultants and economic resources are especially helpful with community projects that are business-related, such as a downtown improvement study. Usually these efforts are justified under an investment philosophy because they promise long-run business benefits along with community improvement. Even in the days of rampant business individualism business investments of this type were made, such as in the following example.

In the early 1900s, Birmingham, Alabama, was menaced by serious health problems. Malaria, typhoid fever, and other diseases were prevalent because of unsanitary community conditions. This city was the site of a United States Steel subsidiary, Tennessee Coal and Iron Company, whose productivity was lowered by illness. Tennessee Coal and Iron organized a health department and hired a prominent specialist in the offending diseases from the Panama Canal Zone. In its first year of operation the health department spent $750,000 for draining swamps and improving sanitary facilities. This amount was thirty times the total health budget of the *entire state* of Alabama.[12]

Large business indirectly helps local communities by solving nationwide problems in which there is local involvement. Figure 17-1 shows the company announcement of an electronic breakthrough in controlling obscene telephone calls. This problem has caused much emotional suffering, invaded privacy of the home, and frustrated local citizen and police efforts to control it. Local and federal laws had failed to produce results, but a company research effort and equipment installation did get results. Furthermore, results were accomplished in a way which retained privacy of normal telephone conversations.

Easy-open beverage cans provide an example of group cooperation to deal with community problems caused by misuse of business by-products. Shortly after these cans were introduced, many communities discovered that the ring-pulls were being used as counterfeit coins in parking meters. Since parking meters could not be economically modified, municipalities appealed to can manufacturers, and the two groups worked together with parking meter manufacturers to design new ring pulls which would not work in parking meters.

Large Business in Small Communities

Whenever large companies operate in suburban communities or small towns, they play a substantial role in community life. Early in industrial history many of these communities became virtual company towns, with the employer owning retail stores, the water system, and other public services. Historians have presented the difficulties with this kind of community. Primarily pluralism does not develop, and control becomes monolithic. There is dissatisfaction of all parties involved, regardless of their good intentions. Modern companies face the same need for a complete community that their ancestors did, but they are taking a more sophisticated approach toward getting it. Usually they initiate long-range planning and coordinate it with public authorities, but they leave development to others. They own and control nothing in the community but their plant. Nevertheless, citizen concern about influence and dominance remains.

[12] Roger M. Blough, *Golden Anniversary,* New York: United States Steel Corporation, 1957, p. 14.

A warning to people who make obscene phone calls.

You're sick. Not clever, but sick.

Because the calls you make aren't jokes. They're crimes. By local law and now, by Federal law.

Congress has just recently passed a bill that can fine you and send you to prison for 6 months if you're caught and convicted.

And you will be. Because now the odds are on our side, not yours.

We can say that because as General Telephone--the second largest telephone operating company in the country—we know what's being done about you.

Although we don't have it throughout our entire system yet, today's special telephone equipment can not only trace back and identify your phone from the receiving party's end; it can also identify any number you call from your end.

And don't think you can beat it by keeping your call short, either.

Because it can also prevent you from disconnecting. As long as the party you call doesn't hang up, the line will remain open. No matter what you do.

And while they keep the line open, they can make another call. To us.

Then there's the work being done on the voice print—an electronic picture of the human voice.

If yours is taken, it's as good as getting your fingerprints. That's how distinctive your voice is. No matter how good you are at disguising it.

And if all that isn't enough to stop you, remember this the next time you get the urge to call:

We haven't told you everything.

General Telephone & Electronics

Figure 17-1 Company announcement of a useful device for protecting privacy of the home. (Source: *Life,* May 23, 1969, p. 24. Used with permission.)

In 1964, a giant paper firm which had a lumber mill in a town of less than 3,000 people decided to build an adjoining $35-million paper mill. The new mill added several hundred workers and changed the community in a number of ways. New community construction included a motel where visiting headquarters managers could stay, a shopping center, and a 200-lot real estate subdivision. Since paper mill work was new in the area, the company brought in twenty-five management men from company mills in the South. Other workers came from elsewhere; thus it became easier to buy regional foods such as okra and grits in stores. The community's mix of religious faiths changed, and new power alignments developed. The paper mill required a new group of skilled workers who earned more than lumber mill workers; therefore bickering arose about the lumber workers being ''poor second cousins.''

Most citizens agreed that the company brought new resources and leadership to the community, plus much more economic stability. However, there was uneasiness about the town's dependence on a company with headquarters far away in New York. Meanwhile company management carefully tried to avoid interfering in community affairs in order to prevent a charge of "company town" or company control. Some persons felt the firm should take a more active part in community affairs, but others preferred the existing situation.[13]

Self-policing by Community Business

In direct transactions with customers a fraudulent operator, "con man," or gyp may quickly harm the community image of business. There may also be honest misunderstandings about transactions in which mediation will help. One organization for meeting these needs is the local Better Business Bureau.

Better Business Bureaus are nonprofit, public-service organizations created by private business for self-regulation. There are Better Business Bureaus in most metropolitan areas of the United States. There are also Bureaus in Mexico, Canada, and other nations, indicating a gradual international expansion of self-regulation.

The unique and effective idea of Better Business Bureaus is that they reach customers directly, receiving their complaints and inquiries. There is no charge and no disclosure of names. This approach gives customers confidence that business genuinely seeks fair business practice and will aid customers in exposing rackets and gyps. The bureaus are well used, as shown by the fact that they receive several million inquiries annually. They investigate inquiries or complaints and make factual reports to the inquirer. They also bring any illegal action to the attention of law-enforcement groups. When an unfair or misleading practice is encountered, they try to discourage it, even using paid newspaper advertising to warn the public.

The Better Business Bureau approach to self-regulation does not stop all shady business practice, but it has been effective in discouraging practices of this type, and it should continue to expand internationally. It is one more step toward the maturity of business in working with the community.

SUMMARY

The community is an organization's area of local influence, rather than the political unit in which an organization is located. As a possessor of community social power, a business cannot remain aloof from its community responsibilities.

[13] William McAllister, "International Paper Co. Brings Wealth, Strains to Small Oregon Town," *Wall Street Journal*, Oct. 9, 1968, pp. 1, 19.

Small and large businesses, local and national, all affect their communities, but in different ways. Businessmen are an active group in the community power structure, but are not necessarily the leading power group. Businessmen primarily affect their community through active involvement in civic affairs, business gifts, and business practices in the community.

STUDY GUIDES FOR INTERPRETATION OF THIS CHAPTER

1. Consult library sources and discuss the role of business leaders in the community power structure.

2. Discuss from a stockholder's point of view the different philosophies for business giving. Then discuss from a community citizen's point of view.

3. One of the two accountants in your small business has asked for a two-hour lunch period once a week so that he can join and attend a Rotary Club. What would be your response and why?

4. Dustin Tower, a plumbing wholesaler in a town of 100,000 persons, claims that the community is giving all its efforts to attracting new large businesses headquartered elsewhere. He wants effort redirected to attract regional and small businesses "which would keep their profits here and would have more growth potential." He wants to organize a group to accomplish this objective. As a small businessman how would you respond to his idea?

5. Have you ever used a Better Business Bureau? Visit a Better Business Bureau in your community if one is available and draw conclusions about how effective it is.

PROBLEMS
Giving to the United Fund

The president of a large local firm employing thousands of workers had a major responsibility in the industrial division of the community's annual United Fund charity campaign. During the campaign he sent a memorandum to each employee through company mail. The letter pointed out that last year employees of a major competitor in town gave an average donation of $1 monthly, which was nearly twice as large as his firm's employees gave. He concluded his letter with the following statement:

> We never have, in this corporation, demanded a gift from any employee, and I hope we never shall. However, I personally shall be greatly disappointed if our

employees cannot afford an average gift of $1 per month to help alleviate some of the human suffering that exists in this community we all call home.

Upon receipt of the letter a number of employees complained that it was improper use of company power to coerce employee giving in order to make the company's community record look good.

1. Comment on the letter and the employee response mentioned.

2. As illustrated by this example, discuss the difficulties business has in trying to be socially responsible.

Bay Shore National Bank

In connection with the annual Community Services Fund (United Fund) drive in an East Coast city of over 500,000 population, the president of the city's second largest bank mailed the following letter to all employees.

BAY SHORE NATIONAL BANK

Dear Associate:

While each of us is faced with financial needs which sometimes make it difficult to stretch salary dollars as far as they are needed, it is nevertheless easy to look around and find many underprivileged and physically and mentally handicapped people who are far less fortunate.

As evidenced by our excellent support of past fund drives, members of our staff have always shared the view that each community is responsible to aid its own needy. In the long run, voluntary support proves less costly than reliance on government. The huge costs of increasing government welfare are soon felt in increased taxes.

Because of our good record of participation in the last campaign within the bank, we have not asked for new pledges for several years. Therefore, unless previous pledges were higher than suggested, those of us who have received pay increases in recent years are no longer giving the recommended fair share of one hour's pay per month. As a result, Bay Shore National Bank staff members are no longer high among the community leaders in average donations.

Enclosed is a new Community Services Fund deduction card, together with a salary conversion chart. To contribute the equivalent of just one hour per month to our community, please select the amount from the chart, enter this new amount on the card, and return the card to Personnel Services by November 9.

Please join me in helping this deserving cause.

Sincerely,

Jay Wrightman
President

Enclosures

1. Discuss the social issues raised by this case.

2. Compare this case with the preceding case, "Giving to the United Fund." Which was the better approach to employees? Was either one acceptable? Why or why not? Which best reflected the interests of all the pluralistic groups involved?

The Gentlemen's Agreement

In an Eastern state only one of its sixty-seven counties levied a property tax against industrial machinery. In order to place all counties on an equal footing for securing new industry, the state legislature in 1957 repealed the tax. To make the adjustment easier, the legislature reduced the tax 20 percent annually for the following five years. County and municipal officials said that public schools and other services would be disastrously affected because this tax provided about 50 percent of their revenue. They pleaded for help from major corporate taxpayers in the county. Finally corporate officials made a gentlemen's agreement that they would continue paying taxes on all existing machinery, but not new machinery, even though it was clearly understood that they were not legally liable for further taxes beyond five years on existing machinery. As stated by the president of one of the nation's top 100 firms, his company recognized "that the sudden withdrawal of these very large revenues would cause a financial crisis for the taxpayers, the councils, and school districts."

About a decade later, in 1967, a stockholder filed suit for $29 million against one of the companies and its directors alleging that they had illegally paid that amount in accordance with the gentlemen's agreement. A Chancery Court then issued an order seizing all shares of company stock held by sixteen directors named in the suit. If this case did succeed, many other companies would be subject to suits for tens of millions of dollars. The plants of a large number of these firms served national markets rather than local ones.[14]

1. Bypassing legal issues, thoroughly appraise in terms of social responsibility and pluralism the management decision represented by the gentlemen's agreement.

2. Discuss which philosophy of business giving probably dominated management thinking in this case.

3. Discuss the conflicts of different pluralistic groups represented in this incident.

---

[14] *Public Affairs Review,* Jan. 23, 1968, pp. 2–3.

CHAPTER

BUSINESS AND THE
URBAN COMMUNITY

*What is certain is that in the way we conceive of our cities, and
meet their challenges, we are determining for better or worse
the next chapter of man's adventure on this planet.*

August Heckscher[1]

*But many of us feel that business and businessmen, more than
any element outside of government itself, hold the key to solving
our great urban problems.*

Max M. Fisher[2]

Businessmen throughout the corporate community are becoming more and
more convinced that they should play a role in helping to solve the urban crisis
which includes physical problems of the cities as well as those concerning less-
advantaged citizens. Indeed, these two sets of problems go hand in hand, and it is
often difficult to tell where one stops and the other begins. Businesses increasingly
are being involved in broad problems which concern the very life and viability of
the cities in which they function, but urban problems are so complex that it is not
entirely clear how or to what extent business should become involved.

One businessman argued that business efforts should be confined to
one-time, short-term efforts directed exclusively toward the solution of a
specifically identified problem. Business should, for example, make a
one-time maximum effort to solve the ghetto problem.

Another businessman said that while business contributions to solving
city problems inevitably reduce profits in the short run, these same contributions will increase profits in the long run. Indeed, such contributions now
may ensure that there is a profit system in the future.

Still another businessman observed that being involved in urban prob-

---

[1] August Heckscher, "The City: Work of Art and Technology," in Brian J. L. Berry and Jack Meltzer
(eds.), *Goals for Urban America,* Englewood Cliffs, N.J.: Prentice-Hall, Inc., 1967, p. 21.
[2] Max M. Fisher, "Managing for Progress in the 70's: The Urban Crisis," *Transacta: Michigan State
University Business Alumni Magazine,* Winter 1970, p. 7.

lems was good for his company because it brought him in contact with people he might not otherwise meet and thereby gave him the opportunity to sell more of his company's product.

All of the above observations are probably correct *from the limited point of view* of those making them. The problem is that these men probably all perceived the proper role of business in urban affairs to be philanthropic. But business has much more to offer and much more to contribute than just money.

There are also those who believe that cities, as they exist today, should be torn down or abandoned. They argue that cities in their present form do not serve modern social needs and that it is doubtful whether they can be made to do so. Those who hold this point of view urge society to rethink the purposes of a city and then build new cities to accomplish these purposes. Under this philosophy business would be one segment of society contributing its expertise where appropriate.

Still others believe that the proper way to solve urban problems is to turn the whole thing over to business and let it define the problems, set objectives, and implement solutions. This would place the entire burden upon business, but it seems neither practical nor desirable to expect this much of business. One critic of business commented that[3] "satisfying social needs and making money are two distinct and often antagonistic undertakings"; and that businessmen should not play the dominant role in aid to the cities because "whatever other qualifications they may have, businessmen are not competent to design a new civilization"—and "have no democratic right to do so."

There is little question that cities today face serious problems and that the problems are of such magnitude that no one social institution working alone can hope to solve them. Like other complex social problems, problems of cities will most likely be solved by close cooperation among all the social institutions. Furthermore, it is doubtful whether cities can be saved by isolating problems and working on them independently. Each problem is related to others within the urban system, and relieving pressures in one subsystem may create severe and sometimes unexpected pressure in one or more other subsystems.

The Growth of Cities

The city is one of man's greatest achievements. It has now become one of his greatest challenges. One observer has commented that the American city today "is to a large extent ungovernable, uninhabitable, and unamiable."[4] But the city is not likely to disappear. Rather there is every indication that the city of tomorrow will

[3] Michael Harrington, *Toward a Democratic Left*, quoted in Robert C. Albrook, "Business Wrestles with Its Social Conscience," *Fortune,* August 1968, p. 90.
[4] Heckscher, op. cit., p. 14.

be larger and more complex even though it may be different in composition and perform different social functions than the city of yesterday.

Demographers estimate that by 1985 the United States will have a population of over 250 million persons.[5] Estimates also predict that by the year 2000 the United States will have a population of over 300 million. As population has grown, so have the cities and the areas immediately surrounding them. In 1970, about two-thirds of the population lived within Standard Metropolitan Statistical Areas (counties containing a central city of at least 50,000 population plus adjacent counties economically and socially linked with the central city), and the proportion is expected to increase. As more people move into Standard Metropolitan Areas and as the population increases naturally, these areas increase in size because most people move to suburban areas rather than to the central cities. Thus, as suburbs expand in areas where population is the most dense, something known as a megalopolis has developed—a continuous city development which is sometimes several hundred miles in length or width. Urban expansion has also taken place in less densely populated areas, but because there are no other large cities near these metropolitan areas they have developed independently of one another. In either case the result has been the same—dying central cities and increasing suburban problems. What has happened is that growth has occurred in concentric rings which encircle the city, leaving at the center an island which is isolated politically and culturally from the rest of the metropolitan area.

The Flight to the Suburbs

There has always been a tendency for the most affluent people to move to the outskirts of the city where they could enjoy less congestion, more private space, and cleaner surroundings. Increasing affluence in America has enabled the large middle class also to desert the congestion of the cities for the amenities of the suburbs. The rapid growth of population along with rising prosperity has created suburb after suburb, which has resulted in urban sprawl.

Business, too, has followed somewhat the same pattern. Anxious to escape the stultifying effects of city traffic, to enjoy lower taxes, or to move closer to adequate labor supplies, or for other reasons, many businesses have deserted the cities. Thus sometimes business has led and sometimes business has followed the exodus from the cities.

A national manufacturer of consumer goods had grown from a small company to one of the major corporations of America. Many of the component parts of its final product were purchased from other manufacturers. Other component parts were manufactured by the firm itself. The company had grown and prospered in a large Eastern city.

[5] *America's Next 30 Years: Business and the Future,* Washington: Chamber of Commerce of the United States.

The company was faced with a major decision concerning plant expansion and modernization. The complex of buildings which it occupied was old and needed major renovation. Additional space was also required, and the property surrounding the plant was extremely high priced.

The president had obtained an option for the company on a large piece of vacant property several miles outside the city and urged the board of directors to build a new plant on that property. He argued that:

1. The entire tract would cost little more than obtaining additional property at the present location.

2. Building a new plant would be no more expensive in the long run than modernizing existing facilities.

3. Taxes would be less on the new facilities.

4. Since the new property was close to two major highways, trucks could have easy and quick access to the plant, thus eliminating many difficulties now experienced in shipping and receiving by truck.

5. There would be little difficulty in obtaining a rail spur from the nearby railroad.

6. Many employees presently commuted from the suburbs. They could move to a small city near the new location. Or if they chose not to move, they could commute to the new location.

7. The new plant could be architecturally in keeping with the countryside, and the grounds could be well landscaped, thus adding to the beauty of the area and satisfaction of employees.

8. There was an ample supply of labor in the small communities near the new site.

How would you evaluate the president's arguments?

Results

Movement to suburbia has had two major results. First, movement of population away from cities has created an inner core whose major characteristics are different from anything we have experienced in the past. The central city has changed character—a busy and bustling thing by day, and an empty shell by night.

Second, suburbanization has created rings of "outer cities" around the central core. As these outer cities have grown and aged, they have begun to experience the same problems as the central core, that is, traffic congestion, air and water pollution, poverty, slums, crime, and physical deterioration.

The migration to the suburbs by business has lost momentum, but undoubtedly it will continue. Companies that are contemplating moves are sometimes finding that prospects are not as bright as they once were. Many have found that they have moved from an area of intense pressure to an area of mounting pressure.

They have merely moved their problems from one place to another. In many cases the very factors that encouraged moves to the suburbs are now sources of problems.[6]

Executive Isolation One problem with suburbs has been that executives of companies which move there sometimes feel "out of things," isolated, and trapped. They complain that they miss the excitement and stimulation of the city and that they no longer have the opportunity to associate with a wide variety of business leaders. They find it more difficult to keep abreast of, and in tune with, the rapidly changing dimensions of the business scene. Furthermore, many find that in order to transact business successfully, they must make frequent trips into the city, thus merely reversing the direction of their commuting rather than eliminating it.

Labor Supply The supply of labor has often been overestimated. Supplies which might have been adequate for the first company moving to a suburb often have changed quickly to severe shortages as other companies have moved in. For example, while many categories of labor have been affected, secretarial and clerical help has become critical for many suburban companies. The qualified clerical work force which exists in the city has, for one reason or another, been reluctant to follow business to the suburbs, and the supply in the suburbs has not been great enough to go around. Alternative sources have been housewives who return to the work force, young girls just out of school, and minority groups who live on the outskirts of the suburb. But these sources have proved inadequate. A large proportion of the younger girls still want to go to the city, and there are not enough married women in the suburbs returning to the labor market. Availability of clerical help was the key factor in the decision of one company *not* to move out of the city. Investigation revealed that if the company moved to the proposed location it would have virtually no clerical help at all. Rather than move to the suburbs, the company built a new headquarters building in the heart of the city.

Housing Costs and Taxes Lower taxes in the suburbs have been a major inducement for companies to move to the suburbs, and in the early days of the corporate migration lower tax rates were indeed an advantage. In many cases, this advantage has been lost, because as more business moved into a community, tax structures have changed. Businesses bring people, and people as well as the business itself demand increased services. More utilities are required; better and more streets must be built and maintained; schools must be expanded; police and fire protection must be expanded, and so forth.

Land values also increase, thereby raising the cost of housing, sometimes to the point where people who work in the suburbs can no longer afford to live there. Managers often complain that in order to find a place they can afford, they must

[6] Judson Goeding, "Roadblocks Ahead for the Great Corporate Move-out," *Fortune,* June 1972, pp. 78–83, 165–172.

commute thirty minutes to one hour each way. Lower-level employees are perhaps even worse off. Many potential employees, who might fill manufacturing jobs, are trapped within the inner city. Transportation is either unavailable or so expensive that employees cannot afford the cost of getting to and from the job.

Traffic Congestion   One thing that made company moves to suburbs attractive was the vision of escaping the traffic problems of cities. It was reasoned that employees and managers would no longer have to fight freeway traffic into and out of the city, and many parking problems would be overcome. But as more companies moved to suburbs, the traffic problem seems to be little better than it was in the city. This has become particularly true where several companies have moved to the same suburb. Since most employees still do not live where they work and must travel to and from their jobs, the freeways and the streets of the suburbs often become just as congested as the city from which the company moved.

Crime   Crime traditionally has been less of a problem in small towns than in large cities and, therefore, made suburbs attractive places to live and to do business. This is no longer true and many suburban areas are experiencing crime rates which are rising much faster than crime rates in cities.

Suburban Hostility   While companies are still moving to the suburbs, they are often finding it more difficult to do, for they are not always welcomed with open arms. Residents of suburbs often resent the prospect of increased services and taxes that a new influx of people would demand. And resistance has not always been passive. Residents sometimes tell companies they are not wanted, and sometimes they resort to legal action. For example, when one New York City–based electronics manufacturer let it be known that it intended to move its operations to a small town in Connecticut, the residents of the town changed zoning laws and otherwise put up so much opposition that the company stayed in the city.

THE FUNCTIONS OF A CITY

From a sociological viewpoint, cities have changed from places to work and live to places only to work during the day. City streets during the day are crowded with people and traffic snarls, and buildings teem with activity. At night those same streets and buildings are nearly deserted. Proportionately, few people live in cities *by choice*. Those who have "made it" move out, leaving behind those who have not. Those who remain in the cities are usually the most recent immigrants.[7] They are usually poor, have less education, and are unskilled.

At the same time, businesses that have remained in the cities or move to them

---

[7] For a discussion see Irving Kristol, "The Negro Today Is Like the Immigrant of Yesterday," in Nathan Glazer (ed.), *Cities in Trouble,* Chicago, Ill.: Quadrangle Books, Inc., 1970, pp. 139–157.

require many employees with rather high skills. Most people having the required skills live in the suburbs, thus creating a daytime commuting population that depends on the city for a great number of services, but they make little contribution to maintaining those services.

The urban crisis is not exclusively the fault of business, as some would like to believe. Rather, the crisis is a result of a number of socioeconomic factors. However, business has contributed (in most cases passively) to a number of urban problems, although at the same time it often tries to help solve these problems.

A substantial part of the urban problem lies in the fact that the functions of a city have changed.[8] Many functions which society once depended upon cities to provide have moved elsewhere, leaving only a limited number of functions to be performed by the inner city.

Most American cities developed around terminal points in the transfer of goods—particularly between rail and water. Docks and rail yards were needed along with labor to man these facilities. Manufacturing plants were built close by so that costs of moving raw materials were minimized. Much of this function has now been transferred to trucks whose terminals have been built far from the central city and to airports which are also far from the center of the city.

Manufacturing has also been moved to the suburbs. Electricity, natural gas, and technical improvements in processes have allowed manufacturing to move away from the central city. Suburban manufacturing plants can also take advantage of the flexibility of truck transportation, which can come to the door of the plant rather than having to transport products to docks or rail heads through heavy traffic.

Warehousing, which used to be a major function of cities, also has moved out of the city. Flexibility of trucks plus improvements in material handling make it more practical for business to use single-story, land-intensive warehouse facilities located somewhere other than in the central city. Wholesaling, like warehousing, has also moved out of the city in search of land to support single-story storage facilities.

The city used to be the retail center because that was where the people were. Most of those who could afford to trade at the retail stores of the central city have moved to the suburbs and most—but not all—of the large retail stores have followed.

The city also used to be the center for entertainment. With a few notable exceptions, this is no longer true. Large sports facilities are today usually not built in the central cities. Fine theaters and restaurants have followed their customers to the suburbs. And television has diminished the need for mass entertainment.

If all these functions which once made cities useful to society are no longer performed in the city, what is left? What functions that are now performed in the city make it useful? One function that remains and continues to make the central

[8] We have relied heavily in this discussion on Richard N. Farmer, "The Death of Cities—And What to Do about It," *MSU Business Topics*, Autumn 1971, pp. 11–18.

city useful is to provide a location for various business activities that require face-to-face contact—professional buying and selling, working on complex contracts, consulting, legal work, and other activities in which people like to see each other as they work. This explains why most construction in cities recently has been office buildings.

Governments, local, state, and federal, insist on remaining downtown and thus keep people in the city. Not only do they maintain large office complexes, but the presence of government offices also requires that a variety of support services remain nearby.

Perhaps more than anything else, cities provide housing for the poor. Cities are full of obsolete housing which has little use except to house the poor. And since most of the functions which might provide employment for the poor have moved out of the city, they continue to be trapped in the inner city.

But for those functions that remain, there is a need for small retailing and a variety of support services. The poor need retail stores; government workers and those who work in office buildings need restaurants and other types of services; and the companies themselves need a variety of support activities.

URBAN DETERIORATION

As many functions which once made cities viable organisms have disappered or moved elsewhere, cities have found themselves with problems of gigantic proportions. The social problems of deteriorating central cities are staggering. Some of these problems and the relation of business to them will be discussed in the following section.

Transportation

A major problem of cities is traffic congestion. People have become accustomed to high mobility and, therefore, demand freedom of movement within those areas. Because metropolitan areas are made up of numerous municipalities, many of which blend into each other, people often find that they live in one municipality, work in another, shop in a third, and carry on a variety of activities in others. The convenience, productivity, and incomes of people living in metropolitan areas depend upon systems for moving in and around the cities. Yet, cities have been unable to correct the inadequacies of their transportation systems.[9]

The two major problems of urban transportation are handling the rush of commuters to and from the city and providing the proper land use to accommodate needs of transportation systems. Most urban transportation facilities—rapid transit railways, public intracity transportation, and highways—are subject to maximum

[9] "The Agony of the Commuter," *Newsweek,* Jan. 18, 1971, pp. 44–49.

Should We Save Our Cities?

Two assumptions generally underlie discussions on urban problems. The first is that we should try to improve the condition of our cities. The second is that we are able to relieve the pressures and strains of urban life by applying technology. Such assumptions may actually be at the root of our difficulties.

We should pause to ask if we are addressing the causes of urban failure, or only the symptoms. Recent studies of the dynamics of social systems suggest that resources expended on symptoms usually do not produce enduring improvements. In fact, the results in the long run may be detrimental. In a complex social system, the consequence of an action may be to reduce one social stress at the expense of increasing another. Symptoms are thereby moved from point to point without net benefit.

From Jay W. Forrester, "Should We Save Our Cities?" *Business and Society Review*, Spring 1972, p. 57. Reprinted with permission.

use only during the peak hours at the beginning and the end of the workday. Operation of commuter railroads, for example, requires high concentrations of labor and capital that are largely idle twenty hours out of each twenty-four-hour working day. And during peak hours most freeway systems cannot adequately handle the volume of traffic which pours onto them. It appears that as long as it remains necessary to move large numbers of people, answers to transportation problems will not come easy.

The second problem is land use. Congestion is caused by too many vehicles competing for too little space. Most cities were not designed for the tremendous volume of motor vehicles in use today. The consequence is traffic snarls and slow movement which result in higher costs of deliveries, additional expense of operating vehicles, and inconvenience and frustration for the people who must work in the cities. It is virtually impossible, in most cases, to increase road space in the cities. Also, valuable space must be set aside for parking, train tracks, and the like. Often this space could and should be put to more productive use.

Business contributes to the problems of traffic congestion just by being there. Traffic problems are created by people going to and from work and by going about the tasks of conducting business. It is not suggested that all business should desert the cities. But a question does arise—should businesses move into already congested areas, thus bringing even more people to add to congestion?

A major United States business announced that it planned to move its corporate headquarters to a large Eastern city. The company boasted that several hundred people would be employed in the new headquarters. It was well aware of the congestion and transit problems that existed.

Yet, moving into areas that are presently less congested does not always provide satisfactory answers to company relocation. Some businesses feel that the need to be close to other businesses of similar nature or to be close to adequate support services is the overriding factor in decisions about company locations.

A by-product of motorized traffic is the intensification of air pollution which has become a major concern in most cities. It is estimated, for example, that approximately 40 percent of the air pollution in New York City is caused by automobile exhaust. Much of this contribution to air pollution is generated from business-oriented traffic. While the automobile and petroleum industries are under strong pressure to produce pollution-free engines and fuels, it remains to be seen how effective these efforts are in solving pollution problems.

Physical Deterioration

Physical deterioration of the inner cities is a function both of business and of the social movement of people. Many types of businesses no longer need to be in the inner city and have moved out, leaving buildings that no longer have a useful purpose. Similarly, as the more affluent people have moved to suburbia, much housing has been taken over by the poor who cannot afford to maintain dwellings themselves. Caught between high taxes and low rents, landlords often cannot afford to maintain property, thus causing a blighted area. Sometimes inner-city property simply will not generate sufficient income to pay taxes, in which case landlords often abandon buildings. Unattended buildings soon become uninhabitable, thus creating areas of crumbling buildings which eventually must be torn down.

There is vast economic waste in abandoning property in the city and building in the suburbs. But such write-offs are often prudent investment decisions because many older buildings and land which is isolated from commercial activity no longer lend themselves to profitable use. Right or wrong, investment tends to go "where the action is." Since most of the business action that remains in the city is performed in offices, most new investment in cities has gone into office buildings which are concentrated in a tiny proportion of total city area. Thus, the large areas surrounding this island have deteriorated owing to lack of new investment.

Government, too, sometimes causes urban blight and decay by its actions or proposed actions. Proposed highway or transit systems may cause shifts in population, changes in land use, and decreases in property values. For example:[10]

> The highway department in one state announced the location of a new 3-mile stretch of highway to be built through a residential neighborhood. After ten years the highway had never been built. But as leases expired, tenants of property in the highway path and in neighborhoods adjacent to the proposed path moved out and could not be replaced. Landlords could not meet taxes nor could they maintain the houses. Some buildings were abandoned and rapidly decayed.

[10] "Specter of an Unbuilt Road," *Business Week,* May 2, 1970, p. 104.

Crime—A Business Challenge

Every citizen, particularly those in leadership positions, must lend full support to necessary reforms if the explosive growth in crimes of all kinds is to be halted and reversed. This is doubly true of businessmen, who have unusual community influence and whose enterprises are the primary targets of lawlessness—through internal thefts, shoplifting, vandalism, and the depredations of organized crime.

Regrettably, the business community has hesitated to use the machinery of public law enforcement in its own defense. Firms often rely upon security bonds and theft insurance to protect against loss, not concerning themselves with ultimate justice. Prosecution of employees who embezzle or pilfer has seemed more trouble than it is worth. Time taken by employees to testify in court against offenders is grudgingly allowed. And fear of retaliation inhibits business collaboration in suppression of the syndicates. It must be conceded that some businessmen have a general philosophy that the fewer their contacts with government, for whatever purpose, the better. But silence is a form of complicity. Civic responsibility coincides with the necessities of self-defense.

From *Reducing Crime and Assuring Justice,* New York: Committee for Economic Development, June 1972, p. 62. Reprinted with permission.

Loss of businesses and affluent residents to suburbs has decreased tax revenues to central cities, thus making it increasingly difficult for cities to provide services. Inadequate garbage removal and treatment facilities, chuckholes and broken paving, and increasing crime are all evidence of deterioration of cities.

Crime in the Cities

Another evidence of urban deterioration is reflected in rising rates of crimes of violence, crimes against property, and white-collar crime. The FBI's *Uniform Crime Reports* indicate that serious crimes doubled between 1965 and 1971.[11] The highest crime rates have always occurred in poor neighborhoods. Today this remains true. Crime in the city is five to ten times what it is in rural areas.[12] But because poor neighborhoods are now immediately adjacent to city business districts, even these areas are subject to a high incidence of crime. Furthermore, mobility provided by the automobile has diffused the incidence of crime over a greater part of the metropolitan area so that even suburbs which once were safe are no longer immune.

Organized crime extracts billions of dollars each year in truck hijacking, theft, and extortion. Such costs, along with those from shoplifting and theft by employees must be passed on to customers and investors. Perhaps even more

[11] *Reducing Crime and Assuring Justice,* New York: Committee for Economic Development, June 1972, p. 10.
[12] Ibid., p. 11.

important is organized crime's involvement within legitimate businesses. There appears to be increasing evidence of organized crime's infiltration into business. Legitimate business sometimes offers opportunities to organized crime for investment of surplus funds. On other occasions legitimate business offers fronts for illegitimate activities. And sometimes illegal gambling is established through company employees. In addition, businessmen are often forced to pay graft or protection money, and they sometimes become directly involved in business dealings with members of the underworld. But from both a social and business viewpoint the biggest difficulty seems to be apathy within the business community concerning the problem of organized crime. Where organized crime has made penetrations, it appears that business must share at least a part of the blame.[13]

THE NEW URBAN CENTER

It is generally accepted that city ills stem from the inabilities of cities to adjust to changing political, social, and economic requirements. Political boundaries which fragment governmental effectiveness, social mobility of higher-income groups, and economic entrapment of less-advantaged citizens have all contributed to the urban crisis.

If the problems of urban America are to be solved, it will take a great deal of thinking about what a city is and what its purposes should be. There are many who believe that traditional approaches to city planning and development are obsolete in our modern social system and that trying to rebuild cities in the traditional patterns will not solve the problems. One observer has warned that "as the world becomes urbanized, the city must be organized on new principles, but ultimately the choice is not merely between different kinds of cities, but different concepts of man."[14] And reasoning along the same lines, Peter Drucker has observed:[15]

> One reason for the misery and disorganization of megalopolis is that it has outgrown what we still consider modern technologies. . . .
> To organize megalopolis we need a new perception. . . . The lack of such a perception makes all efforts at "city planning" futile.

Planners and critics alike seem to agree on certain requirements. To be healthy, viable, and strong, a city must have two basic ingredients—density and variety. It must have a variety of buildings for different uses and a variety of people performing a variety of functions.

Two solutions suggest themselves. The first is to build entirely new cities

[13] Stanley Penn, "Mafia Inroads: Business Shares Blame," *Wall Street Journal* (Midwest edition), Jan. 27, 1970, p. 18.
[14] Heckscher, op. cit. p. 10.
[15] Peter F. Drucker, *The Age of Discontinuity: Guidelines to Our Changing Society,* New York: Harper & Row, Publishers, Incorporated, 1969, p. 33, 35.

based on concepts and technology never before used in city planning. The second is to work with metropolitan areas that presently exist, creating new centers and new individuality as one moves outward and at the same time rebuilding the dying central cores according to some master plan which takes into account all the variables and the relationships between these variables.

In either case solutions are likely to require cooperation between the major social institutions to a degree which has seldom been achieved. Government's role will need to be largely that of setting objectives, planning, and financing. The role of business will need to be that of providing government with tested planning techniques, such as systems analysis, and of applying technical expertise and capability to urban problems. Labor's contribution must come from accepting and even initiating new ways to organize and perform work.

The Dilemma of Government

Unfortunately, many government efforts have been of questionable value because they have been organized on a vertical basis, with little or no communication or coordination between various agencies. Work has been organized on a project basis and assigned to various government agencies which operate as semiautonomous units. The result too often has been that government agencies work at cross purposes. For example:

One agency may be building roads to bring more cars into the city, while another agency is developing mass transit systems to keep them out.

Recently the Federal Aviation Agency awarded money for modernization of a city airport while at the same time the Civil Aeronautics Board was denying certification of the only commercial flights into the city served by the airport.

Similarly, one government agency may be trying to persuade business to use more minority subcontractors in an area, while another agency is planning to reduce the number of prime contracts in the same area.

Uncoordinated efforts such as those just mentioned can lead only to divergent and often conflicting objectives and to fragmented efforts which waste resources. Furthermore, such actions by government often leave businessmen frustrated and uncertain and sometime discourage investment which might make positive inroads into city problems.

Business Efforts Also Are Often Isolated

Business efforts, too, have sometimes suffered from fragmentation. Businesses often have tried on an individual basis to contribute positively and actively to solutions of urban problems. While there have been many successful efforts by business, others have failed. Where failure has occurred, there often has been a breach of the rule of functionalism. Government often has tried to "do" rather than to set objectives for city rejuvenation and then to provide support for other social institutions than can perform better. At the same time business sometimes has tried unilaterally to assume the function of setting overall objectives for urban improvement and has proceeded in ways it felt best. This also violates the rule of functionalism, because business is only one of many institutions that should have a voice in setting community objectives.

Rebuilding Downtown

Unlike the slum areas and the ghettos, the central business district of most American cities has not suffered from neglect. On the contrary, over the past twenty-five years, business has been busy transforming the business district into a collection of shining office buildings. But even by day, cities have become forbidding and inhospitable places. In New York a committee of executives reported that the pleasures disappearing from Manhattan were diversity, coherence, grandeur, style, and humanness.[16] And these criticisms apply equally to most other American cities.

Through extensive planning which emphasizes a systems approach, planners are trying to control development, so that the central business district will again become a friendly, human, cohesive whole. Some of the ingredients seem to be open spaces devoted to fountains, small plots of grass, trees, outdoor sitting areas, arcades, a variety of attractive stores, outdoor cafes (weather permitting), theaters, few automobiles, and people living in the city.

There is little question that all these things and more will be necessary to revitalize the central business district. The key to success will be the correct balance of components. Based on computer simulation models, one expert[17] suggests that the key to economic and social health of cities lies in the balance between jobs and housing. For most cities this would mean emphasis on professional and managerial jobs and on premium housing that would be attractive to people holding these kinds of jobs. This means finding ways to encourage people to move back to cities to live. And in addition to the correct balance between jobs and housing, all of the supplementary services that together make up the "good life" must be provided in the correct balance.

Obviously, American cities cannot be rebuilt overnight. The rebuilding must occur a bit at a time. But most cities are formulating long-range plans which attempt to relate, coordinate, and control rebuilding efforts. Most rebuilding and modernization in central business districts is being accomplished through coopera-

[16] Quoted in Walter McQuade, "Downtown Is Looking Up," *Fortune,* February 1970, p. 133.
[17] Jay W. Forrester, *Urban Dynamics,* Cambridge, Mass.: The M.I.T. Press, 1969; reviewed in "A Daring Look at City Ills," *Business Week,* June 14, 1969, pp. 142–146.

tive efforts of federal government, city government, and private capital. Much city redevelopment that has taken place has occurred under government-controlled urban renewal plans in which the key is the city's right to condemn land and write down the cost with the aid of federal funds and to have private capital build and operate the facilities.

Not all businessmen are convinced that government money or extensive government cooperation is necessary to rebuild cities. Many believe that it is the responsibility of business leaders to take the initiative in planning and building well-balanced improvements in the central business district. Some have emphasized developing sites just outside the central core.[18]

Philadelphia's Franklin Town, Washington's Georgetown riverfront, Houston's Houston Center, and Kansas City's Crown Center are all examples of business involvement in urban redevelopment. Kansas City's Crown Center is typical.[19]

Over a period of fifteen years one business leader acquired nearly 100 acres of rundown neighborhoods adjacent to the main downtown area of Kansas City. Redevelopment of the area is well underway. When it is completed, the Center will contain over 1 million square feet of office space, a 750-room hotel, two motor inns, several movie theaters, a legitimate theater, specialized shops, underground parking for 7,000 cars, and 2,400 residential apartments.

There is one danger, however, with independent developments such as the one mentioned above, and that is the danger that these projects may be difficult to integrate into a comprehensive pattern of development. Especially careful planning will be needed to ensure compatibility with overall redevelopment of a city.

The Traffic Problem

From both technological and social points of view, the movement of people may be the most difficult problem facing the cities. Cities have always been built around the need to transport merchandise and people—that is, a need for a central marketplace and a need for people to make the marketplace function. Continued belief in this need to transport both commodities and people to a central gathering place has produced the congestion problems of which we are all aware.

Technologically we have most of the know-how to eliminate the need for central gatherings and the excessive movement of goods and people. The new technology emphasizes the need to transport information and knowledge, not

[18] "Business Goes After Urban Renewal with Profit in Mind," *Industry Week* July 12, 1971, pp. 9–11.
[19] "Lifting the Face of Kansas City," *Business Week,* May 20, 1972, p. 96.

people and things. With the electronic communication techniques available today, there are few technical reasons for an executive to be in face-to-face contact with subordinates, customers, secretaries, or associates. Technically, people could shop, go to theaters, and visit friends without ever leaving their own home.

But from a social point of view we are not yet ready to surrender our mobility and flexibility to communication media. We are basically social animals, and the urge for social contact is strong. The need to move people for social, if not for business, reasons will remain. Therefore, the challenge will be to find new ways of moving people that will preserve the flexibility provided by private automobiles and at the same time eliminate or reduce our dependence upon the automobile. Rapid transit systems as they are being developed will undoubtedly provide part of the answer, but a complete answer will need to go far beyond the limits of contemporary public transportation systems.

THE NEW-CITY CONCEPT

There are strong feelings that efforts to rebuild our cities, no matter how great, will not be enough to cope with problems caused by rapidly expanding population. If growing population is expected to be absorbed into already existing cities, the result will likely be further urban sprawl and intensification of already existing problems, such as smog and traffic congestion. To avoid urban paralysis, many believe it will be necessary to build completely new towns.

Many new towns already have been built. Sun City and Lake Havasu in Arizona are successful examples, and there are many others. Dozens more new towns are in the planning and development stages throughout the country. Many of the schemes for building new towns consist of some form of partnership between business and government. Both federal and state governments are joining with business to make possible new urban developments. Technically there will be little problem in building a new town; all the technology that is needed is already available, and, indeed, there are single companies large enough and sufficiently diversified to build an entire city. The major problems are in financing and the developmental costs. Few, if any, companies can commit the needed amounts of capital for the long period of development. To overcome financial problems, the federal government, through the Department of Housing and Urban Development, is guaranteeing long-term loans for the purpose of new-city development. Loans of up to sixty years, along with deferred-payment provisions, relieve developers of the heavy debt-service burden until the town becomes established and starts to pay off. It also has been suggested that private corporations be allowed to sell tax-free bonds to finance construction of public facilities such as schools, parks, and playgrounds.

Undoubtedly the new-city concept, as it is being developed, will do much to overcome urban problems, particularly if the factors vital to the city are well planned and well balanced. There are some, however, who view the new cities (particularly those located close to existing cities) as being at best only a temporary solution to urban problems. There is a conviction on the part of some that we will need to look for entirely new places and new ways to build cities. There are many unique possibilities. Cities which float on the ocean or on our rivers have been suggested. Subterranean cities have been a practical reality for centuries, and technology for building cities on the ocean floor is not far off. Similarly, it seems likely that research will soon provide answers which will make it possible to build cities in space.

SUMMARY

Whatever direction urban development takes, one thing is certain. As population continues to increase, urbanization will also increase; and urban problems will increase rather than decrease. Business can and must play an active role in improving the urban quality of life. Business is the principal social institution capable of providing the managerial and technical skills needed to implement plans for the city. But business cannot play the leading role in areas such as goals and social priorities. Solution to urban problems will require coordination among all major institutions in a magnitude and to a degree never before achieved in our social system.

STUDY GUIDES FOR INTERPRETATION OF THIS CHAPTER

1. Explain how functions of today's city differ from functions of a city twenty-five or thirty years ago.

2. Assume that you are the president of a manufacturing company and that you are considering moving your company from its present city location to the suburbs. Discuss advantages and disadvantages of this type of move *(a)* from your company's point of view, and *(b)* from the metropolitan community's point of view.

3. Write your representative in Congress and ask for information about existing and proposed federal government activity in planning and management of urban land use. Then discuss the roles that government and business play in planning and management of land use.

4. How can business best contribute to the solution of urban deterioration?

PROBLEM
The City Planning Commission

Mr. Brown, a prominent business leader in a large city, was asked to serve as a member of the city planning commission. Mr. Brown's city was experiencing most of the urban problems faced by other cities. Among these problems were movement of more affluent residents to suburbs, movement of business out of the city, loss of tax revenue, increasing costs of municipal services, urban deterioration, slum crowding, increase in crime, and traffic congestion.

At his first meeting, Mr. Brown listened to a fellow commissioner urge adoption of a program which he felt would do much to relieve the city's problems. The more important suggestions contained in the program were:

1. Tear down 5 percent of the inner city's already scarce low-income housing and replace it with luxury and semiluxury apartments, thus attracting back to the city those who can afford to pay taxes to support necessary city services.

2. Clear away an equal volume of aging business properties. Require that any office structure built to replace an old business property reserve at least all street level and mezzanine space for retail uses including retail stores, theaters, movies, restaurants.

3. Spurn programs for housing, job training and other outside help that would tend to keep low-income people within the city.

4. Spurn government financial aid such as urban development and depend entirely upon private investment to do the job of rebuilding.

In many ways these recommendations seemed attractive to Mr. Brown particularly since they seemed to offer both challenges and opportunities to business. At the same time, he had the uneasy feeling that many other social dimensions of the city's problems were being overlooked and that business alone could not and should not attempt to solve the whole problem by itself.

1. What issues of social responsibility of business are raised by the proposal?

2. In what ways would or would not the proposal solve the city's problems? Assuming that the program did solve the city's problems, in what ways do you see other social problems being compounded?

CHAPTER 19

BUSINESS, MINORITIES,
AND LESS-ADVANTAGED PERSONS

We have not yet seen what man can make of man.

B. F. Skinner[1]

*Equality . . . reflects the desire of individuals to emulate the
good life as exemplified by others, to catch up, to improve, to
excel, to realize more fully their potential, to develop and express
themselves, to contribute, to count (and to be counted) as
responsible actors in their time.*

Max Ways[2]

In late 1973 a judge in a Midwestern city found a large producer and
distributor of electricity guilty of discriminatory practices in hiring and promoting
employees. The decision followed a 1971 class action suit filed by a group seeking
better opportunities for blacks at the company. The government joined in the
lawsuit under provisions of the 1964 Civil Rights Act. Plaintiffs were awarded $5
million in damages to unknown persons—those who may have wanted to work for
the company, but did not apply because of the company's reputation. The company was ordered to place the money in the court, which will screen persons who
consider themselves victims of the hiring system before awarding funds.

In the same city, Rollie Jackson, along with several other young men,
climbed out of the company-owned Volkswagen bus that had stopped before the
employment office door of a large manufacturing firm. Rollie and the others had
been recruited from the ghetto. All had been classified as hard-core unemployed.
Rollie was black. He was twenty-five years old, had dropped out of school during
the sixth grade, had been in trouble with the law several times, and had been
sentenced to juvenile correction institutions and prison four times. He had never
held a job for more than two months and had not been employed for the last two
years. After a brief training period he was placed "on his own." The first three
mornings he was between one and three hours late for work. The fourth day he did

---

[1] B. F. Skinner, *Beyond Freedom and Dignity,* New York: Alfred A. Knopf, Inc., 1971, p. 215.
[2] Max Ways, "Equality: A Steep and Endless Stair," *Fortune,* March 1972, p. 80.

not show up at all. Personnel representatives found him and persuaded him to return to the job. After several weeks of similar behavior, but with more personal attention from his supervisor, he learned "how to work" and became a steady and valuable employee.

Both of the above examples demonstrate business involvement in problems of less-advantaged citizens. Both concern problems of hiring and training workers from minority groups. While business involvement with hiring and training hard-core unemployed who are members of ethnic minority groups is increasing, so is its involvement with problems of other groups of less-advantaged persons who find themselves at a disadvantage in the world of business, and these groups are included in the following discussions. Even though the discussions in this chapter focus on ethnic minorities to a large extent, other groups of less-advantaged persons experience many of the same difficulties and frustrations that ethnic minorities do. Women, for example, even though they make up the majority of the population, feel they do not have the same advantages as men. Members of ethnic groups who are otherwise qualified often find themselves underemployed. Older workers often feel they are discriminated against because of age. And spokesmen for the mentally retarded contend that business has a responsibility to this group which it often fails to consider.

REASONS FOR BUSINESS INVOLVEMENT

Business involvement with problems of less-advantaged citizens is steadily increasing and for good reasons. One reason is that the pool of labor on which business has always depended is drying up. There is no longer a sufficient supply of ready and willing workers who can perform or be trained to perform all the jobs required in the social and economic system. To fill the expanding number of jobs, business must turn to the large pools of workers that have been largely overlooked in the past.

The second reason that business involvement in problems of less-advantaged citizens is increasing is that from a social as well as a business viewpoint, it is to the advantage of business to do so. Business thrives best in a healthy community, and it is in the self-interest of business to help reduce dependency, crime, disease, poverty, and the waste of human resources.

Another reason for involvement is that business is responding to public expectations. As a leading social institution, business is expected to commit its power, wealth, and expertise to solutions of social problems. It is responding to this social mandate through expansion of minority hiring, by providing technical advice and monetary help to minority business, by attacking slum problems, and through other means.

A further reason for business involvement is negative. It stems from a feeling that if business does not exert leadership in finding solutions to problems of less-advantaged people, government may impose more stringent demands than now exist. And new demands might be more difficult to meet than the ones that now exist.

A final reason is that many business leaders feel that becoming genuinely involved is the right thing to do. They believe that business has an ethical obligation to give equal opportunity to all persons.

It is evident that a variety of factors have combined to encourage business concern and action with less-advantaged persons. Spurred by civil rights legislation in 1964, business has become involved, and progress has been made. Although not as much has been accomplished as some critics would like, business has made substantial inroads into problems, and these business actions will be the subject of this chapter.

During the 1960s many American cities were torn by racial strife. Riots destroyed large sections of some cities where property losses ran into millions of dollars. During the same period militant leaders of numerous organizations were making their voices heard. These social disorders were largely the result of racial frustration with a system which denied equal opportunity on the basis of ethnic membership. Virtually every social institution came under attack. Ethnic groups began to demand and press actively for equal educational opportunities, equal housing opportunities, equal opportunities to participate in governmental processes, and especially, equal opportunities for responsible and meaningful jobs. Other groups such as churches added their voices of discontent to the turmoil.

Not all culturally disadvantaged persons are members of ethnic groups although ethnic minorities have received more attention and publicity than many others because of civil rights legislation. Women, for example, historically have been culturally stereotyped into certain types of jobs. Poor rural whites have often experienced cultural disadvantages. And many who live in city ghettos are disadvantaged whites. These and other groups of less-advantaged persons should be included in discussions of the culturally disadvantaged along with minority groups.

The social unrest of the 1960s focused attention of social institutions on the plight of large numbers of people who were denied opportunities because of economic, educational, and social disadvantage. Along with other institutions, business was forced to rethink its policies on hiring, training, and promotion. One businessman summed up the situation as follows.[3]

> But there is such a thing as being wrong for the right reasons. Hiring the most qualified man is a good philosophy—so long as you give everybody the opportunity to be qualified. That simply has not been possible for many Negroes. I think it is just plain wrong not to correct that situation now. . . . The hard-core unemployed of city ghettos, who have been routinely screened out in the past, are now to be deliberately screened in.

[3] Leo Beebe, quoted in Morton Adelbert, "Industrial Training of the Hard-Core Unemployed," *Personnel,* November–December 1969, p. 24.

In a way these less-advantaged persons had been programmed out of society. Social and economic progress had passed them by. Historically, it is not difficult to understand why businessmen were not more conscious of and sensitive to the problems of the less-advantaged and why they did not respond faster and more positively. It is not that businessmen were callous or unkind, nor were they unintelligent. Rather, in the rush of economic and social change, business became so isolated from the problems of the less-advantaged that it was difficult to understand what the problems actually were. For the most part, business leaders lived in comfortable white neighborhoods and had never seen a ghetto, and they rarely associated closely with a black or a Mexican American. Nor until relatively recently have they discussed these problems with articulate members of minority groups. However, once the problem was defined, once the facets of the problem became clear, once the challenge was clearly posed, business has responded. There are several separate but closely related dimensions to the problems of employment opportunities for the less-advantaged—employing the hard-core unemployed, employing those with acceptable skills, and mobility upward into managerial ranks. Each of these, along with problems of minority business enterprise, will be discussed in the following sections.

THE BUSINESS ROLE UNDER CIVIL RIGHTS LEGISLATION

Few would disagree with a social objective of achieving equal opportunity for all Americans. And indeed, equal opportunity became a firm national objective during the 1960s. In few other instances has the concept of functionalism been so clearly applied to a major social problem. Clearly the role of government was to establish objectives, formulate policies, and provide support which would enable business and other social institutions to achieve the objectives. It was equally clear that actual achievement of objectives lay not with government but with other social institutions that controlled opportunities for equality. Business, government, labor, and various nonprofit organizations controlled job opportunities; school systems controlled educational opportunities; city councils and other municipal agencies controlled housing opportunities, and so on. Since this book is about business, emphasis in our discussion will be on equal opportunity for jobs, although business can and does affect opportunities for the less-advantaged in other areas such as housing.

In its efforts to end discrimination in employment, government has relied on two major programs. One program was established by title VII of the Civil Rights Act of 1964, which forbids discrimination on the basis of race, color, religion, sex, or national origin. The act also established the Equal Employment Opportunity Commission (EEOC), which, since 1972, has had the power to sue to bring about compliance. The other major federal program concerns businesses that contract with government and the special obligations imposed on them. This program originated under President Roosevelt in 1941, when, by executive order, he outlawed racial discrimination by defense contractors. Subsequent executive orders by other Presidents have broadened the coverage until now it affects every division of every company with a government contract of $10,000 or more. About 250,000 companies employing about one-third of the United States labor force are covered by the executive orders.[4] Compliance with these executive orders is the responsibility of the Department of Labor and is accomplished through the Office of Federal Contract Compliance (OFCC).

Thus, federal legislation has imposed upon business responsibilities to eliminate discrimination and equalize employment opportunities for all regardless of sex, race, religion, color, or national origin. It has imposed upon business a requirement for "affirmative action," that is, setting goals to eliminate discrimination and timetables for achieving those goals. Companies have responded in several ways. Some companies have adapted a posture of *passive nondiscrimination,* under which all decisions about hiring and promotion are made without regard to race or sex. This posture focuses on the present and future and does not consider the past. It does little to overcome past discrimination which leaves many potential employees unaware of present opportunities. Another approach to ending discrimination is *affirmative action.* Under this approach companies make every effort to ensure that employment opportunities are highly visible and to seek minorities for employment. While this approach enlarges the number of applicants, hiring and promotion decisions most often are made on the basis of qualifications for the job. A third approach is *affirmative action combined with preferential hiring,* which not only tries to expand the number of people from whom to choose, but also gives preference to women and minority groups in hiring and promotion. A fourth approach is to *establish hard quotas.* Unlike affirmative action with preferential hiring, which does not establish any particular numbers of disadvantaged who must be hired and/or promoted, hard quotas establish specific numbers or proportions which must be hired.

The Question of Employment Quotas

Two major questions concerning hiring of the less-advantaged have become troublesome for businessmen. One question is: Whatever became of merit? The second question is: Which posture toward employing the less-advantaged does government really want us to take? Each question is related to the other. Most government officials interpret civil rights legislation to mean nondiscrimination with affirmative action. However, in spite of the wording of the law there are many people in the United States today who favor preferential hiring and/or hard quotas, and they argue persuasively at times. One argument for establishing minority hiring quotas is that past discrimination against minorities and women entitles them to hiring and promotion advantages now.

[4] Daniel Seligman, "How Equal Opportunity Turned into Employment Quotas," *Fortune,* March 1973, p. 162.

A second argument admits that in an ideal world the only just method for hiring and promotion would be merit. However, in the real world of today, the criteria that make up merit are systematically denied to large portions of the population. Merit, as the word is generally defined, cannot be attained unless all have equal educational opportunities and equal opportunities to be hired. Merit cannot be attained unless cultural bias is removed from qualifying tests for employment.

Another argument for quotas is that traditionally hiring and promotion decisions are not made on the basis of objective and proven methods for assessing an applicant's qualifications. Hiring decisions of many employers are made on subjective and unproven criteria; thus racial and sexist stereotypes are created which exclude minorities and women regardless of their actual qualifications.

Yet another argument is that while progress has been made, discrimination still exists. For continued progress, minimum standards must be set, and when a minimum standard has been set, this is the same as setting a quota. Conversely, if no standards are set, there is not likely to be any more progress.

A Case against Minority Employment Quotas

On the other side of the coin are the arguments opposing the establishment of hard quotas for minority hiring. One argument is simply that quotas are illegal. Civil rights legislation clearly forbids discrimination on the basis of membership in a group.

A second argument against quotas is that they promote hiring of less-qualified persons over those who are better qualified. A person should progress in life on ability, not appearance. In spite of the language of the law, quotas force employers to focus on color or sex rather than upon how well a person is qualified for the job.

Another argument against quotas is that they cause reverse discrimination. Quotas encourage discrimination in favor of minority groups, and it is impossible to discriminate *for* one group without discriminating *against* one or more other groups. Thus, the very nature of quotas produces discrimination against nonminority groups. Discrimination against some should not be remedied in our society by discriminating against others. A corollary to this argument is the question: If it is proper to establish quotas for blacks and women, why not do the same for Armenians, Orientals, and all the other groups who might be thought of as minority groups? And what about employees who because of religious beliefs do not work on Saturday or Sunday?

Another argument is that quotas are demeaning and paternalistic. The practice of hiring less-qualified minority-group members to meet a quota is likely to put a stamp of "less-qualified" on all members of that group. There is likely to be a question of the real abilities of all regardless of how well qualified individuals may be. This question is likely to be asked by white job applicants, customers, and the minority-group member himself.

A further argument is that quotas sometimes are construed as maximums rather than minimums, thus limiting opportunities for minorities. Quotas are sometimes viewed as ceilings above which minority proportions should not or need not go, rather than floors upon which greater opportunities for minorities should be built. However, when quotas are used, ceilings need to be applied, because if a quota for one group is exceeded, then it enroaches on some other minority's quota or the majority's quota.

Who Are the Hard-Core Unemployed?

Discrimination, lack of education, and lack of industrial experience have created a large group of people who are known as the hard-core unemployed. They are poor, and they are unemployed. They find it difficult to qualify for most jobs and have given up the idea that "the system" can offer them any opportunities. The National Alliance of Businessmen has developed a profile of the hard-core unemployed, and while the profile may not fit all people who are classified as hard-core, those who are so classified meet most of the criteria. According to the NAB definition, a person classified as hard-core unemployed has never received intensive skill training and has been unemployed for at least eighteen months. His parents were unskilled. He has seen a physician only once in his life and needs eyeglasses and dental work. He is married with three children. He has no transportation. He has a sixth-grade education, a tested third-grade reading level, and a tested fourth-grade level in mathematics. He has had some contact with the law and has spent at least thirty days in jail.[5]

The term "hard-core unemployed" is often equated with the term "ethnic minority," thus implying that all hard-core unemployed are members of ethnic minority groups. Many of the hard-core unemployed are members of ethnic minority groups, and their plight has been emphasized by civil rights legislation and by publicity. However, there are also large numbers of hard-core unemployed who are white. For example, there are many white former farm workers now living in city slums who have no skills to offer a modern industrial society. Furthermore, there are large numbers of whites living in city ghettos who, for a variety of reasons, simply have never had the chance to obtain employable skills. There are also those who are classified as hard-core because of limited mental or motor ability.

The Challenge of Providing Jobs

Persons who have the characteristics outlined above are almost certainly prohibited from qualifying for meaningful employment, because they do not meet

[5] Lawrence A. Johnson, *Employing the Hard-Core Unemployed*, New York: American Management Association, 1969, pp. 31–33.

traditional hiring criteria which have been established by business and they have no skills to offer employers. Thus they have remained trapped in ghettos of the cities or isolated in rural areas with few options open to them for maintaining life and decency. As a result there has developed a large group of people who have been chronically unemployed and who have been viewed by business as unemployable.

In 1967 when Clifford Alexander accepted the chairmanship of the Equal Employment Opportunity Commission, he commented that jobs were at the heart of three-quarters of the ghetto problems.[6] Also during the 1960s dozens of new organizations were added to those that were already established and pressing for greater opportunities for less-advantaged persons.[7] Society's challenge to business was loud and clear—rethink hiring practices and change those practices in whatever ways are necessary to provide equal opportunities for high-paying and responsible jobs to all persons. While progress in hiring minorities perhaps has not been as fast or as great as some social critics would like, business has risen to the challenge and has made remarkable progress in a short time. Perhaps one of the most effective programs to bring the hard-core unemployed into the work force has been the one established by the National Alliance of Businessmen (NAB). This program has consisted of a partnership effort between business and government to attack the social problem. The NAB *Employers Digest* describes the program as follows: "Its implementation combines government resources with business know-how. Its goal is to find permanent jobs for the hard-core poor in the nation's largest cities and summer employment for in-school youth from the inner city."[8]

Aside from the challenges to society in general which have been raised by the social mandate of equal employment opportunity, many hard challenges have been posed to business. In a variety of ways these challenges have forced business to rethink "the way things have always been done." What, for example, are the responsibilities of business in recruiting, hiring, and training hard-core unemployed? These subjects will be discussed in the next sections.

Recruiting

For many people the search for a job is not difficult. They know how to locate job opportunities; they know how to go to the company employment office to apply; they know how to fill out forms; and they expect to be hired if no one else is better qualified. For the most part the hard-core unemployed do not have this knowledge, and for a variety of reasons they simply do not apply for jobs.

First, experience has taught the hard-core unemployed that because of their lack of marketable skills, low education levels, police records, and a history of

---

[6] "Jobs Are the Heart of the Problem—An Interview with Clifford Alexander," *The MBA*, February 1971, p. 7.
[7] A partial list of organizations may be found in Robert S. Benson and Harold Wolman (eds.), *Counterbudget*, New York: Praeger Publishers, 1971, pp. xxvii and xxix.
[8] *Employers Digest*, Washington: National Alliance of Businessmen, n.d., p. 2.

rejection because of discrimination, the chances of obtaining a meaningful job are very remote. Second, when they do apply, they are often frustrated by complex application blanks and other forms they are required to fill out. Third, and perhaps more subtle, is that the decor of the personnel office and the formality of personnel often so intimidate hard-core applicants that they walk out or refuse to enter. Finally, most jobs are located long distances from where the hard-core live, thus requiring a long trip by public transportation to the employment office. Often the person is broke and cannot make the trip; or if he does have the money, he is reluctant to spend it on a venture he expects to result in failure.

The message for business has been that if the hard-core unemployed will not come to you, then you better find ways of going to them. The challenge is to find better ways to reach them. One life insurance executive assistant advised: "Take a card table under your arm and your own folding chair. Go into the black barber shops of the ghettos. Set up your own employment office right there. Since you can't be in all the shops, enlist the barbers as your recruiters."[9]

Not all businesses can or want to "take a card table to the barber shop." Most have preferred to work actively through various government and/or community agencies, depending on the agencies to do the actual recruiting; however, most major companies also have developed some off-premises hiring arrangements.

Hiring Practices

Locating hard-core unemployed who want to work and convincing them that jobs are really available to them is only the first step. Many preemployment screening and selection devices used by business have come under close scrutiny by the EEOC in recent years, because the devices themselves often discriminate against the hard-core unemployed and against minority groups in general. One example is the use of arrest records. The EEOC and the courts have held that, in general, the use of arrest records to disqualify persons from employment is discriminatory because blacks have been more commonly arrested than whites. Consider the case of John Smith.[10]

John Smith was convicted of assault and robbery. When he was released from prison, the one thing he wanted to do was "go straight." But this was not easy. He tried construction work without success because with his record he could not get into the union. He could not sing with a group as he once had done because he could not get a cabaret license to sing where alcoholic beverages were served. And he could not even practice the trade he had learned in prison—barbering. The state would not issue barber licenses to those with prison records.

[9] Johnson, op. cit. p. 55.
[10] Richard Shaffer, "Erasing the Past," *Wall Street Journal* (Midwest edition), Nov. 13, 1973, p. 1.

Hints for Testing and Hiring Hard-Core Unemployed

Companies involved in the employment of the hard-core, having faced the problems of testing, offer some hints that may be helpful to others:

1. Know specifically what equipment or tools the employee will be required to use, the level of arithmetic he must know, the type of writing he will have to do, the kind of instructions he will have to understand, and the types of problems he will face.

2. Make sure the tests are valid for the job and relate to the applicant's ability to learn the desired function. The tests should attempt to measure ability to learn a job not to do the job without training.

3. The screening, interviewing, and testing of hard-core applicants should be conducted if at all possible by personnel knowledgeable in intergroup relations.

4. Make sure tests are not screening out those applicants (particularly minority group members) who are capable of performing effectively on the job but whose cultural or economic backgrounds handicap them in taking the tests.

5. Use testing as only one indicator among others in the hiring decision.

6. Remember that motivation may be even more important than test scores in indicating successful job performance.

From Lawrence A. Johnson, *Employing the Hard-Core Unemployed*, New York: American Management Association, Inc., 1969, pp. 87–88. Reprinted with permission.

Other hiring practices that tend to discriminate against the less-advantaged are the formal requirements of many preemployment forms and the use of tests as screening devices. Hiring the hard-core unemployed simply does not fit traditional hiring patterns. A person from the ranks of the hard-core unemployed, for example, may not be able to complete successfully an application blank. First of all, because of reading ability, he may not understand the questions. And second, he may not know or be able to recall much traditional information such as social security number, date of last employment, previous employment, or salary on last job. For these reasons some employers have simplified application blanks for the hard-core unemployed. Others have chosen not to simplify forms but rather have a trained personnel person help the applicant fill out the form to the extent that information is available.

Another hiring practice that has caused serious problems in hiring hard-core unemployed is the practice of using tests as screening devices. The whole area of preemployment testing, and especially psychological testing, has come under critical scrutiny. There is little argument that testing is a valuable instrument in predicting success of job applicants and in identifying training needs. The real problem lies with the tests themselves and questions of validity and reliability. So far as the EEOC is concerned, the burden of proof is on users of tests to prove that the tests measure traits or abilities that are truly critical to successful job performance.

One problem is that many tests are culturally biased—that is, tests which may be valid for one ethnic group may not be valid for other ethnic groups. Because the hard-core unemployed are usually culturally disadvantaged, they are often ill equipped to take tests. Low levels of education may make it very difficult to read and understand questions or to write satisfactory answers. Furthermore, they may have a psychological block against taking tests because from experience they have learned to fear all tests that determine whether or not a person gets a job.

Another problem is that tests used by employers sometimes eliminate all but those who are overqualified for a job. That is, standards of performance required by the tests are often much higher than standards of performance actually required by the job. Thus, many who could perform the job if given the opportunity are needlessly eliminated.

Training

What are the responsibilities of business to train the hard-core unemployed? Should business-conducted training programs go beyond the usual in-house orientation and on-the-job training? If so, how far? Should business be expected to assume responsibilities for education and training that normally occur in the school and family? The main reason why the hard-core unemployed remain unemployed is that the educational and training process has somehow passed them by. In our society, we expect that people will in the normal course of growing up receive education in academic and social skills through the schools and the family, and will therefore be prepared to enter the world of work at a reasonable age. For many of the hard-core unemployed, this process has broken down or simply has not occurred. This means that if a member of the hard-core unemployed group is to become a productive member of the work force, he must somehow be helped to recover lost ground. Experience has shown that offering a job is not enough. In order to perform their jobs properly, some hard-core unemployed will need training in one or more areas such as face-to-face communication, speaking, listening, reading, writing, simple arithmetic, job-related vocabulary, customer relations, and other basic social and business-related skills such as promptness and personal reliability.

Business has accepted the challenge of training hard-core unemployed, and while some programs have not succeeded, many have. And, as business learns from experience how to develop and implement hard-core training, the rate of success is increasing. Most successful programs seem to contain two key elements, feedback and flexibility. *Feedback* means that counselors or supervisors listen periodically to employees' personal problems. This enables the employer to get a better idea of what he should or should not be emphasizing in the program. *Flexibility* means the willingness to change and adapt the training program to the trainees' needs. This includes the willingness to include social skills within the training program and to relax discipline where appropriate. For example, one company found it appropriate to relax standards concerning lateness when it found that bus service in several areas where trainees lived was very irregular. Perhaps a third key to successful programs is a clear understanding by trainees that they are expected to meet standards of behavior and progress (even though these standards may be different from those of regular hires) and that if they do not meet these standards, they will be dismissed.

EMPLOYING THE UNDEREMPLOYED

Not all those who have been discriminated against in employment opportunities are hard-core unemployed. Indeed many have been capable, well-trained individuals who have not been able to find jobs consistent with their skills and capabilities because of stereotyped social attitudes concerning race or sex. Discrimination has resulted not so much from unilateral business practice as from business decisions and practices which have been shaped and encouraged by attitudes of society as a whole. Business practices have been a mirror of overall social attitudes. On the other hand, business, for the most part, is where job opportunities are. Therefore, because business is a major social institution, it faces the challenge created by changing social attitudes—attitudes which demand that those who have been discriminated against in the past now be assured that they can compete for jobs solely on merits of their talents and abilities.

Significant strides have been made in bringing minority groups, especially blacks, into business at all levels. Passage of civil rights legislation and subsequent government efforts to enforce the laws triggered a rush to hire minorities. But minorities continue to insist that while business has made a good start, it has much further to go. They complain that blacks and other minorities still are not being given equal opportunities because they are, for the most part, kept out of the main managerial stream that leads to promotion. Many blacks, they argue, were brought in merely to demonstrate compliance with the law, even though there may not have been a specific job which could utilize his talents. A second argument is that minority managers have been most often assigned to special staff jobs dealing with minority-group problems—jobs such as urban affairs, community relations, recruitment of minority employees, and special minority markets. These arguments seem to be substantiated to some degree. At least there are few minority persons in high-level executive positions in major companies. To demonstrate this point, one black executive reported his experience in the Harvard Business School's advanced management program.[11]

> There were guys in the class from about 125 U.S. corporations, and they didn't want to believe that blacks weren't making great progress in major companies.

[11] Ernest Holsendolph, "Black Executives in a Nearly All-White World," *Fortune*, September 1972, p. 142.

But when the three blacks in the class asked them what blacks their companies had in meaningful jobs, they had to say none. Each thought his company was probably an exception.

Business argues that there are very few minority persons who are really qualified at this time to assume high-level positions of responsibility. Because of historical cultural isolation from the world of big business, people from minority groups often have not had parents, relatives, or close friends who could help them understand and relate to the corporate world. Furthermore, business argues, there is no such thing as an instant corporate president. Movement through the ranks, which provides experience and maturity required by top jobs, takes time. Most minority persons have not had time to make that climb.

What most members of minority groups want is an opportunity to move into the promotion stream and be allowed to succeed or fail on the basis of their performance in the same way that nonminority persons are allowed to succeed or fail. The challenge to business is to make *genuine* promotional opportunities open to all.

SUPPORT OF MINORITY ENTERPRISE

The social objective of equal opportunity is not limited to opportunities for meaningful jobs. In a larger sense the objective means opportunities for all forms of economic and social equality. This includes opportunities for business ownership. And increasing minority ownership of business (especially black ownership) has become one subobjective of the civil rights movement. This is more difficult than providing meaningful job opportunities, because black people historically have been denied or otherwise have been unable to obtain the ingredients which are essential to business success.

Historically, black people have not become business owners in any significant numbers. There are notable exceptions, of course, but for the most part black ownership has been limited to small, marginal, and poorly run businesses located in ghetto areas and serving limited ghetto markets. There have been a number of reasons why this has been so.[12] First, there has been a lack of personal identification with business accompanied by a lack of knowledge and understanding of the business system. Second, social prejudices have severely limited opportunities for successful business ventures outside the ghetto. A third reason has been the inability to obtain adequate financial resources. And finally there is a very real absence of managerial know-how.

Efforts to help black persons and other minority group members to overcome

[12] For a discussion of problems of black ownership of business see Abraham S. Venable, *Building Black Business: An Analysis and a Plan,* New York: Earl G. Graves Publishing Co., Inc., 1972, especially pp. 24–33.

Building Minority Business

Creating a successful business is one of the most difficult things that anyone ever sets out to do. But, like Abe Venable, I believe that the growth of a successful business community is an essential part of the development of the entire black community. Minorities must become more involved in business, for until we have the full participation of all minorities—and I'm thinking about Chicanos and Puerto Ricans and Indians and Orientals and others as well as black people—this will never be a truly strong nation. As long as there are people trapped in the cellar, America will not be a happy house. I hope that "Building Black Business" will help us reach that goal of full involvement for all of America's people.

From Jackie Robinson, in Foreword to Abraham S. Venable, *Building Black Business: An Analysis and a Plan*, New York: Earl G. Graves Publishing Co., Inc., 1972, p. v. Reprinted with permission.

the barriers to business ownership have become a national challenge. As with other social problems, business cannot supply the entire solution. But business and government together, each performing functions that it can do best, can go far in eliminating the obstacles. And, although many mistakes have been made by all concerned, substantial progress has been achieved.

Identification with Business

At the base of the problem of developing minority-owned business is the lack of identification with business by black people. Less than 1 percent of United States business is owned by black people.[13] Little accumulation of business knowledge or business heritage exists among black people of the ghetto. Therefore, practically every black person starts from scratch when he enters the business world. Young blacks have not been attracted to business because historically they have been assigned only minimal jobs regardless of their education and training. Few were encouraged by their parents to enter the business world for the same reason. It, therefore, seems evident that business should encourage young people to obtain training in business. At the same time opportunities for older blacks to obtain instruction in business methods and techniques must be made available. The educational system, particularly two-year colleges, four-year colleges, and universities, seems to be the most viable delivery system to disseminate business training. But education is costly, and until recently there were few black colleges that offered programs in business administration. Similarly, there were few black students in business programs in traditionally white colleges. To strengthen business programs in black colleges, business has helped with money and, in some cases, with personnel who are released to teach.

[13] *Business and the Development of Ghetto Enterprise*, New York: The Conference Board, 1971, p. 3.

Business has also helped through minority scholarship programs. A few universities have developed programs which are designed specifically for small businessmen from minority groups. An excellent example is the Small Business Guidance and Development Center at Howard University in Washington, D.C.[14]

The center started with a problem clinic for black members of the construction industry in which participants could discuss common problems and obtain guidance to help solve the problems. A successful format was established early: small groups of not more than fifteen; a conference format with no speakers; special guests who offer professional guidance when asked; subjects selected in advance by the businessmen themselves; and highlights distributed to each member. From this beginning other clinics have been developed to discuss problems of black businessmen in other industries. All have been successful. They are valuable to the participants because they supply a mixture of formal academic information and informal practical experience.

Availability of Capital

It requires money to start a new business or to expand one that already exists. Two kinds of capital are needed—equity capital and debt capital. Until recently there has not been much of either kind available to black businessmen, because black businesses have in general proved to be poor investment and credit risks. Especially difficult has been the problem of equity capital. Both government and business have tried to respond to this need. Perhaps the most serious attempts by government to help provide equity capital have come through the Small Business Administration and its licensed Minority Enterprise Small Business Investment Companies (MESBICS). These are investment companies that are financed by large businesses and pledged to help minority businesses by supplying equity capital. The MESBICS have been only moderately successful because of limited funds.

Business also has made major contributions to the problem of supplying equity and debt funds in other ways. The American banking industry has substantially increased its participation in government loans. The American Banking Association instituted a $1-billion investment program to increase loans to minority businessmen. And the commercial banking industry established an investment company to provide equity capital to minority businesses. Perhaps even more important has been individual company participation by establishing plants or subsidiary businesses in disadvantaged areas and then selling the companies to minority investors. One of the oldest of this type of venture is the Watts Manufacturing Corporation.

[14] Venable, op. cit., pp. 80–86.

The Watts Manufacturing Corporation was originally founded and owned by Aerojet-General Corporation but was staffed entirely by local black management. Later the company was sold to the Chase Manhattan Bank, which in turn loaned the employees' trust enough money to buy 80 percent of the company.

Since the Watts Manufacturing Company was established, other major companies have helped to establish or strengthen many minority businesses.[15]

Location in Less-advantaged Areas

Many business efforts have combined the objective of helping minority businessmen with the objective of creating more jobs for the less-advantaged. Thus many new plants and new businesses have been established in or close to ghetto areas. For the company such locations provide a supply of labor, although many employees may require special training because they are hard-core unemployed. For the residents of the area the new business is a source of jobs that they might otherwise find difficult to obtain. Furthermore, ownership in a successful business gives a sense of community pride.

Managerial Know-how

Minority managerial talent has been the scarcest commodity in every program to develop minority business, and it is perhaps the most critical ingredient. Where attempts to launch a minority business or turn over a business to minority persons have failed, the failure, in most cases, has resulted from inadequate management. Business can provide money and other capital equipment on relatively short notice, but it cannot provide enough competent minority managers if only a few exist. Furthermore, many competent minority managers have chosen to stay within the ranks of existing business or to work for other nonbusiness organizations such as foundations or public agencies, rather than go into business for themselves or work for minority-owned enterprises.

To help solve this problem, business needs to train more minority managers. There are several approaches. One approach has been to staff company-owned ghetto plants or enterprises with experienced white managers at the top and minority managers in every other managerial job, thus providing training and experience for top-management positions. A second approach is to provide special managerial training for minorities within the parent company with full realization that these people will probably not stay with the company but will move on. Such a program might be strengthened if government training subsidies now offered for

[15] *Business and the Development of Ghetto Enterprise*, pp. 89–101.

hard-core training were extended to management training. A third approach is through trade associations. Associations such as the Menswear Retail Association, the National Association of Manufacturers, and the Institute of Certified Public Accountants are only a few of the national trade associations that have pledged no-cost management and technical assistance to minority businessmen.

SUMMARY

Since the passage of civil rights legislation in the early 1960s, business has become increasingly involved in problems of less-advantaged persons for a variety of reasons. One reason, of course, is the legal requirement to do so. Other reasons are to expand the labor force and to promote an economically and socially healthy community. Furthermore, because business is one leading institution in our pluralistic social system, society has challenged business to apply its resources to the problems of less-advantaged persons.

Business cannot do the job alone. But with cooperative efforts of government and other social institutions, business has made progress. Programs to recruit, hire, and train hard-core unemployed who previously have been considered unemployable have been established. Substantial progress has been made in clearing away barriers to upgrading the underemployed. And substantial effort has been made to encourage and develop minority business enterprise.

STUDY GUIDES FOR
INTERPRETATION OF THIS CHAPTER

1. Why have businessmen become involved in problems of less-advantaged persons?

2. Review the literature and report on one successful and one unsuccessful company program for training hard-core unemployed. Describe the reasons for success or failure.

3. Research and report on a minority business founded or sponsored by a major company. Describe the reasons for success or failure.

4. Business has been asked to increase the number of minority-group employees at all levels. One approach is to establish quotas of minority-group employees to be hired within a given period of time. Discuss the arguments for and against this approach. Do you have a different approach? If so, what? Give your reasons.

PROBLEM

The Acme Metal Products Company

The Acme Metal Products Company helped two young minority-group men start a metal-stamping business in a ghetto area of Acme's headquarters city. The project looked favorable. The product was similar to those manufactured by Acme, and therefore it would be relatively easy to provide technical assistance. Furthermore, the production operations would lend themselves to a less-advantaged work force, and there were substantial numbers of hard-core unemployed in the immediate area of the new plant. The two young men came from middle-management positions in other manufacturing firms. Acme agreed to provide some managerial assistance, to contact prospective customers, and to furnish raw materials at attractive prices until the new company could establish sources of supply.

Within a year the new company was in financial difficulty. Expected sales volume was not reached, operating costs were very high, and personnel turnover was high. Additional financing did not overcome the problems, and the company declared bankruptcy approximately two years after it opened its doors.

In retrospect, Acme concluded that the project was premature. The project's managers believed that the support given by Acme was inadequate. Acme also charged federal agencies with failure to follow through on promised contracts and further charged other businesses with lack of support and token orders.

1. What are the issues in this case?

2. In what ways do you think the project might have been premature?

3. Why do you think the expected sales volume was not reached?

4. Give as many possible explanations as you can for high labor turnover.

CHAPTER

20

THE INTERFACE BETWEEN BUSINESS AND HIGHER EDUCATION

In short, what is needed is a marriage between learning and leadership.

L. F. Urwick[1]

Roy Dow graduated from community college and went to work in the office of the Borden Insurance Company. At the time he was barely nineteen years of age. In a year he married and three years later had a young son. Dow was an intelligent and ambitious employee. He worked hard and tried to learn all that he could about the insurance business. On two occasions he was able to attend a company training program on technical aspects of insurance. He also read a few books on the subject. He was so successful in his self-development that six years after employment he was promoted to supervisor of a clerical section. Although he was an effective supervisor, he gradually began to recognize the limits of his technical and intellectual training. It became evident to him that he would be better qualified for further promotion if he had more education. At this point he became interested in what the local university could do for him. He wondered if it had recognized its responsibilities to people in situations similar to his. Was it prepared to help him in his quest for lifelong learning in order to grow as a person and as an employee? Likewise did his company recognize its responsibilities to help him grow? Did it have policies and programs which supported continuing education for him?

Dow's situation is an indication of the changing interface between business and education. Since business employs the majority of university graduates and draws its leadership from them, the relationship of the university campus to business is a significant factor in business viability; hence it is the focus of this

---

[1] L. F. Urwick, "Learning and Leadership," *Columbia Journal of World Business,* July–August 1969, p. 73.

chapter. First, we discuss how a knowledge-oriented society affects the interface of business and higher education. Then we examine the various ways in which business and universities work together and the university climate for business. Discussion in this chapter is limited to education beyond high school.

BUSINESS AND EDUCATION IN A KNOWLEDGE-ORIENTED SOCIETY

The close and relevant interface of business and higher education is a new development. Centuries and even mere decades ago each had a somewhat hands-off attitude toward the other. A relatively small intellectual elite maintained their seclusion in ivied university halls, educating a few selected students to become intellectual and social leaders of their nation. Education was not for the masses who labored in factories, fields, and stores. University educators had little interest in business, and businessmen had little interest in educators. Each lived in a different world. Many educators showed an elitist disdain for businessmen who were perceived as less nobly motivated than educators. Most businessmen admitted that the disdain was mutual, since the men in the ivory tower had little that was practical to offer business.

The separation of business and education gradually waned as higher education expanded in accordance with democratic ideals of equal opportunity, but the real breakthrough came with the rapid trend toward a knowledge-oriented society.

A Knowledge Society

A *knowledge society* may be defined in two ways. One definition is that knowledge society exists when more than half the gross national product is provided by the knowledge industries. There are the organizations which produce and distribute ideas and information rather than goods and services. Examples of knowledge industries are newspaper publishing, television, education, book publishing, telephone communication, and data processing.

Perhaps the second definition is more relevant from the point of view of an employer. It is that a knowledge society exists when more than half the labor force is employed in knowledge-based occupations rather than manual occupations. Knowledge-based occupations are most of the professional, managerial, and technical occupations as defined by the census.

It is estimated that according to both these definitions the United States will become a knowledge society sometime in the 1970s.[2] Under these conditions knowledge rather than manual skill becomes the principal means of serving human

[2] Peter F. Drucker, *The Age of Discontinuity: Guidelines to Our Changing Society,* New York: Harper & Row, Publishers, Incorporated, 1969, pp. 263–264.

needs. Therefore, the society which wishes to serve human needs and to advance civilization *requires* a large proportion of educated, knowledge-oriented citizens. No longer can it afford the luxury of a small and isolated intellectual elite. Knowledge must be widespread, because it is the foundation of most of society's occupations. In economic terms, knowledge becomes the chief factor in production; however, it is important to realize that the idea of a knowledge society is more than a narrow business or economic concept. It applies to the entire social system.

Just as it is almost impossible to run a productive large business without a computer, it is also nearly impossible to provide advanced hospital care without an elaborate collection of complex electronic and chemical apparatus. The country doctor of two generations ago would not know what to do with this equipment. Moreover, most of the equipment is operated and maintained by a broad array of new knowledge workers who usually are not physicians. Though these knowledge employees may work with their hands, they are applying knowledge derived from education, instead of a skill learned by a tradesman's apprenticeship. Their work is more intellectual than it is manual.

Effects of a Knowledge Society

The United States probably will be the world's first knowledge society, so there is no history from which to predict what will happen, but certain trends seem rather apparent. We will discuss those which relate to business and education.

One effect, and perhaps the principal one, is *to require a close and active interface between business and education.* Each institution develops new responsibilities to work closer with the other. Since business is committed to fulfilling certain areas of human need, it requires large numbers of knowledge workers to function effectively. It secures these from educational institutions; hence, it becomes more dependent on them to prepare knowledge workers capable of making useful social contributions through the institution of business. There is also a need for business to work closely with knowledge-oriented faculty for research, consulting, and continuing education of business's knowledge employees. This faculty-business relationship is distinctly new.

A second effect of the knowledge society is to require the individual to engage in lifelong learning and the university to provide continuing educational programs for this lifelong learning. People need to continue learning in order to keep up with the increase of knowledge in their occupations. The employee is in a constant race with job obsolescence. For example, when accounting procedures change from accounting machines to computer accounting, major relearning may be required of the accountant. In other instances knowledge developments may make an occupation obsolescent, requiring a person to learn a second or even a third occupation during his lifetime. Both business and the university stand in the forefront in introducing knowledge changes into society, and both bear responsibilities to make the transition run smoothly by providing lifelong learning opportunities for people.

A third effect of the knowledge society is to give business additional responsibilities for improving the quality of its employee motivation. Intellectual work requires a different kind of motivation than manual work. Normally a person can be persuaded by the use of authority to dig a ditch. Usually the threat of penalty is enough to get results. However, it takes more sophisticated motivation to lead a person to do research or write creative advertising copy. Intellectual work requires internal motivation and a more positive motivational environment. If employers of knowledge workers fail to provide this type of environment, their employees will work less effectively. Both the business and the employee will be losers in this relationship.

A fourth effect of the knowledge society is to place additional responsibilities on the university to expand its offerings in the new applied-knowledge disciplines such as engineering, education, nursing, business, and computer technology. These disciplines are needed to prepare people to serve social needs by means of the new knowledge occupations. A century ago the educational environment was dominated by liberal arts and a few peripheral areas such as law. Since that time most university growth has been in the new applied-knowledge areas because this kind of ability is needed by the social system. In turn, businesses and other institutions are directing their interests more toward the new knowledge disciplines because they want individuals who can process ideas within these frameworks. The result has been a broadening and realignment of curricula in universities.

A survey of chief executives of *Fortune*'s top 500 companies shows the degree to which liberal arts now shares with applied-knowledge-oriented disciplines the responsibility for developing business leadership in a knowledge society. The executives were asked: "If you had the opportunity again to prepare yourself for the position you now hold, or if you were advising your son who aspires to a role of leadership in management, how would you rate the educational preparations listed below?"

Only 28 percent of respondents rated four years of liberal arts as good or excellent, and five or more years of liberal arts fared even worse. On the other hand, both of the following programs were rated good or excellent by 94 percent: (1) four years of liberal arts combined with two years of business, and (2) four years of engineering combined with two years of business. Clearly over three times as many executives opted for some applied knowledge in preference to straight liberal arts.[3]

---

[3] James W. Kelley, "Management Grades the Graduate Business School," *Personnel*, September—October 1969, pp. 16–26.

A fifth effect of the knowledge society is to increase the confusion and insecurity of some students. Such a large number of learning and occupational choices are available to students that some of them become distracted and bewildered. Additionally, students are locked into a long educational cycle which keeps them from full-time employment until sometime after biological adulthood, and so some of them become frustrated. Also new knowledge has opened up new hopes for solutions to some of the world's major social ills, but the route to solution is hazy and progress is slow. In effect, present learning has created a better understanding of the problems than of how to solve them. The psychological dissonance between what is and what ought to be is so great that some students drift into insecurity and alienation. These conditions place heavy responsibilities on both education and business to make their work relevant to the real world.

A sixth effect is that the knowledge society has imposed heavier responsibilities on business, education, and youth (as well as other institutions and groups) to manage change successfully. As knowledge expands, its normal effect is social change. Consider, for example, the effects of only one technological development on one of the groups mentioned. This is the effect of television on youth.

For the youth of the 1960s and 1970s, television collapsed both space and time. It brought the world right into their living rooms so that distant events could be known and seen, thus collapsing the parochial walls of home and community which bound youth in earlier generations. It also collapsed time by showing these events as they happened. There is a difference between seeing something as it occurs and reading about it later in a newspaper or history book. Under these conditions the face and ideas of a spokesman for a pluralistic group 2,000 miles away often became better known than the face and ideas of the local mayor. Young people were socially conditioned for change and for having it now. Why not now? If society could bring instant news, why not instant social action? The inevitable result was a weakening of parental, religious, and community restraints, plus impatience with the normal pace of change of traditional institutions such as business.

Business, education, youth, and other groups in society have key, cooperative roles to play in improving the quality of life in a knowledge society, but in order to achieve their potential, they need to emphasize their mutual goals and responsibilities instead of their differences and rights. Optimum social progress depends on the components of a pluralistic society agreeing on social priorities, because all problems cannot be solved at once. Next it will be necessary for these groups to marshal resources to deal effectively with the priorities they have selected. Then they need to educate themselves regarding how new knowledge can help them solve their problems. Finally, they need to show the patience and cooperation that is necessary to work within the complex organizational systems that a knowledge society requires. The complexity of knowledge and interests does not permit individualized solutions to major social problems.

Without a doubt, the knowledge society has introduced ideas and practices which will affect the long-run life-style of civilization. The knowledge society frees modern youth to move out of the restricted environment of the primitive tribe or the small town, but this freedom and mobility also impose on youth a heavy burden of choice. Young persons have many occupations, many locations, many types of institutions, and many life-styles from which to choose. Thus, there is forced upon them a responsibility for deciding what they want to become and how they want to live. In essence, more than ever before, they have to decide how they will apply their abilities to help their fellowman. They have freedom, choice, mobility—and responsibility.

BUSINESS RELATIONSHIPS WITH UNIVERSITIES
Encouragement of Continuing Education

Business in a knowledge society needs educated employees. Employees as persons want to keep growing and increasing their opportunities, but education takes employee time as well as money. The result is that business and employees join together to encourage continuing employee education and to share the costs. Companies have a variety of plans. Some pay tuition and book costs. Others pay only tuition, rationalizing that books become personal property of the student. Occasionally firms pay just part of tuition, expecting the student to share economic costs. Some give released time from work to attend a course at a nearby college, while others emphasize off-duty education. Regardless of the rules, the key point is that most large firms strongly support continuing education for employees because they recognize its significance in a knowledge society.

Examples are plentiful regarding how company support of continuing education helps employees grow. In one instance a skilled tradesman studied languages and showed special ability for learning them. He learned seven languages and now interprets foreign correspondence and contracts for the company. In another case a woman engineer secured a law degree which merited substantial increases in pay because of her improved usefulness to the firm. Another example is a night custodian who studied personnel work and eventually became a personnel administrator.

Two-year community colleges are an area of special interest because they have both academic and vocational courses. Employees can attend these colleges either to upgrade specific vocational skills or to prepare for a degree program in a senior college. These colleges are often available near residential neighborhoods or downtown business areas, so that travel time and costs are reduced compared with those of senior colleges and universities.

Excerpt from a Statement of Objectives of an In-Company Seminar for Developing Members of Higher Management

The focus of the Seminar Program makes it possible to accomplish the objectives in the short span of four weeks. It is *not* intended that *subject matter* be emphasized during this period. The purpose of the Seminar is to broaden—to expose executives of clearly established strengths to the subtleties and problems of the chief executive in the effective management of the enterprise as a whole. It will also endeavor to stimulate participants to formulate, initiate, and implement policies dealing with the responsibilities of industry toward society.

Question: Comment on the usefulness of this type of development for helping top managers become more socially aware and more able to manage corporate social action.

One approach used by community colleges and some universities is the work-study program. Normally two students occupy one job, and they rotate between their job and their school. During part of the year the first one works while the second one goes to school. During the next part of the year the second one gets his work experience while the first one goes to school. Another variation is for one to work in the morning and one in the afternoon while both go to school on a limited basis. Either way, the student gets experience while attending school. Work experience helps make his education more relevant, possibly improves his motivation, gives him a sense of fulfillment as he performs work, and provides experience that should help in job placement upon graduation. Further, the work provides income to help cover expenses of his education. The main disadvantage is that work-study usually requires a longer-than-normal period before the degree is secured.

An approach which can be used by a large company or group of companies is to establish its own management development facility and then bring university instructors to the facility to help its own staff teach in-company programs.

The Motorola Executive Institute at Oracle, Arizona, is designed to serve worldwide management development needs of Motorola, Inc. The institute seeks both to broaden the executive for his management duties and to inspire him to continue to study and learn. The idea is to make generalists out of specialists, to widen their horizons about business involvement w. the external world, to examine the responsibilities of business to society, and to develop better balanced insights and attitudes. The objectives can be summarized as balanced personal and professional growth for the manager.

Managers study in a relaxed environment away from the daily pressures of their jobs. The institute faculty is made up of leading experts from around the world who come to the institute for a few days to discuss their ideas. This gives the institute a faculty that any single university would find impossible to assemble. Instead of traditional lectures, there is widespread student involvement in the program aided by advanced learning resources such as video tape, projection equipment, and time-sharing computer terminals.

Television Education

Many major universities provide educational television courses, and this type of education gradually will expand. It brings education into the home or business classroom, but one limitation is that a student cannot engage in direct discussion with his instructor. Advanced electronic systems overcome this limitation, and some firms with substantial educational needs are using these.

In the Dallas–Fort Worth industrial area a number of companies have established a microwave television network which brings graduate courses from nearby universities directly into electronic classrooms in their plants. The classrooms have television screens which show the instructor, and each desk has a telephone which a student can pick up for direct voice connection with the instructor. This system permits questions and back-and-forth discussion even though it is not face-to-face. The company-university system carries engineering, science, and business courses, and students may register for credit toward a degree.

This complex system is expensive, but firms which use it believe it is more economical and practical than sending students to a distant campus or bringing faculty to the plant. It also allows students to use top-quality courses from several universities rather than just one, in accordance with each student's needs.[4]

Management Development Programs and Conferences

Annually thousands of managers temporarily abandon their jobs and families in order to attend live-in executive programs at major universities. In addition there are thousands of special university conferences and short courses heavily attended by business specialists of all types. Most of these courses are not restricted to businessmen; thus they give business people an opportunity to share ideas with representatives of other pluralistic institutions. The magnitude of this continuing education movement is illustrated by the enrollment figures in a metropolitan college of business. Although its regular student enrollment was large, each year it had a larger number of participants in programs sponsored by its Center for Executive Development.

[4] "Bringing Graduate School to the Plant," *Business Week*, Jan. 10, 1970, pp. 64–65.

The underlying concept of all of the programs discussed is that business people in a knowledge society need continuing renewal and upgrading in order to retain their personal effectiveness and keep business viable. The ancient statement that "old dogs cannot be taught new tricks" has been turned to state that "old dogs keep young by learning new tricks." Even more, "there are some tricks that only old dogs can learn," because they are able to interpret theory in terms of experience.

The training institute of an international drug company illustrates the variety of university-business interface required in a knowledge society. While one of the authors discussed management with executives in one conference room, across the hall in another room there was a company symposium on genetic factors involved in the conception of twins. The symposium was directed by a panel of renowned scientists from universities in several nations. The company was studying drugs related to fertility and birth control, and apparently it believed the large cost of this private symposium was worthwhile for its scientists working on the project.

Other Relationships

Faculty consulting with business has proved an effective instrument for mutual benefit of faculty, students, and business. The faculty members learn more about the realities of business, which should improve their teaching and research. The students benefit from better teachers who can more realistically interpret business to them. Finally, the business which initiated the relationship expects to gain from the faculty members' aid and advice.

A partial reversal of this relationship is the executive-in-residence program of some universities. In this instance leading business executives are brought to a business school for a week or more in order to exchange ideas on a face-to-face, give-and-take basis with students. They are in a sense consultants to the students, giving them direct interaction with "real, live executives," not retired ones or ones who come to make a public relations speech and then hasten away. The experience is rewarding to students, faculty, and executives. Each learns more about the other. In the words of one executive in residence, his revelation was that "businessmen are likely to be appallingly ignorant of what business students want and need to know before they can perform any satisfactory service."[5]

Another way in which business and the university interpret their needs to each other is through school of business advisory committees. Functions of an advisory committee include comments about the relevance of proposed curricula, aid in fund drives, cooperation with field research programs, and contact with faculty and students.

[5] James E. Patrick, "Bridging the Student-Business Gap: The Role of the Executive-in-Residence," *Business Horizons,* April 1969, p. 59.

The knowledge society has caused a major expansion of business recruiting on campus. During the economic depression of the 1930s graduates had to seek their own jobs, and they felt lucky to get one. Now business recruiters along with recruiters from other institutions seek the graduate, and competition is keen for qualified persons. Recognizing their responsibility in this interface, colleges and universities have established substantial facilities for recruitment on their campuses.

Business Gifts to Higher Education

About 0.4 percent of corporate income before taxes is given to support higher education. Since public gifts of corporations total about 1 percent of income before taxes, this means that higher education receives a large share (two-fifths) of corporate gifts. This proportion of giving to education shows that business has a serious interest in upgrading the education of citizens and potential employees. Gifts include scholarships, research grants, capital grants for buildings, endowed professorships, and outright grants for general expenses. (Educational payments for present employees are recorded separately as a fringe-benefit cost.)

Figure 20-1 shows that from 1950 to 1960, as the trend toward a knowledge society became evident to business, the proportion of gifts to higher education more than tripled. Since that time the proportion has remained relatively stable. The claims of other social needs such as urban problems and the less-advantaged became so important in the 1960s that business was unable to give a larger proportion to higher education. It appears likely that this proportion will stabilize around 0.40 percent or even decline as other social claims are made on business.

Different Gift Practices

A greater proportion of large businesses than small businesses give to higher education. Perhaps one reason is that larger businesses tend to employ more specialized college graduates. Another is that small businessmen usually have no established policies of gift giving. Since there are not many planned campaigns by those needing educational gifts, small businessmen simply forget to give. Since local charity drives usually bring a knock at the door, there is more direct motivation to give in these circumstances. Small businessmen could benefit from planned giving according to policy just as much as larger businesses do. Otherwise the ''squeaky wheel'' gets the gifts.

Companies which are large enough to give substantial sums usually establish carefully developed policies, just as they would for any other expenditure. Some of them give to both private and tax-supported institutions because they hire employees from both and feel that both have similar objectives. Other companies, while not prohibiting gifts to tax-supported institutions, give priority to private

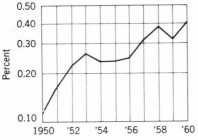

Figure 20-1   Percentage of corporate profits before taxes contributed to higher education. (Adapted from *Business Week,* Apr. 3, 1965, p. 132. Data from Council for Financial Aid to Education, Inc., and U.S. Department of Commerce.)

ones. They do so because the private institution depends on private society for nearly all its income, while tax-supported institutions can call upon government taxing power over the whole society, including the corporation. Further, aid to private institutions keeps that sector of education viable in the face of encroachments from tax-supported higher education. Thus, private aid further supports pluralism in society.

Business aid to education is typically justified under the investment philosophy of giving. It is considered to be an investment in educated citizens (some employed by business), in advancing technology which business uses, and in a better public climate for business. All these objectives can be demonstrably related to business's long-range well-being.

It seems certain that business aid to education will continue. It is founded on basic values of pluralism. First, there is support by one institution (business) for another institution (education) which provides it with useful services. Second, both business and education have a mutual interest in a free society (free business decisions on the one hand and free inquiry on the other). Third, regarding private educational institutions, there is the further point that one private institution wishes to help another keep viable in order to balance pluralistic interests better, especially to offset greater government control of education. Wherever businesses have examined policy implications of business giving to education, they have supported it. They are not, however, opposing tax-supported education. They recognize that the entire educational job is beyond their capacity, but they do wish to play a role in it to confirm their pluralistic interest therein.

THE UNIVERSITY CLIMATE FOR BUSINESS

In a pluralistic knowledge society which depends on the effective functioning of many institutions, society needs to ask the question: Are universities educating students with a sound understanding of business's role as a social institution serving human needs? If students graduate without understanding business but have to live with it for the remainder of their lives, they may become less-effective citizens, in the same way that a citizen may be less effective if he does not understand another major social institution such as government or education. In addition, business could become less effective if universities direct students away from business, drying up its proportionate share of potential leaders.

Business in the University Curriculum

With the financial aid of James Wharton, the first academic business school was established in 1881 as the Wharton School of Commerce and Finance at the University of Pennsylvania. By the 1950s there were over 500 collegiate business schools in the United States, and graduate schools of business were well established in major universities. In the United States business was a popular subject. In other nations business schools developed more slowly, but interest quickened in the 1950s as nations began to see business schools as a means of providing leaders to make better use of limited resources.

As business schools gradually proved themselves in the university community, their curriculum gained academic stature, particularly graduate business education and the M.B.A. degree. However, some academic areas with a longer and richer heritage still look on business as a newcomer of dubious reputation. Though business is a major social institution, educators in areas such as science, liberal arts, fine arts, and education are reluctant to have their students take even one business course before graduation. Even in 1970 the majority of college graduates entered the world of work (and voting citizenship) without a course in business.

Student Attitudes toward Business

In long-run terms, during the last century student attitudes toward business seemed to improve gradually as business gained academic respectability, but there have been cyclical swings based upon economic and social conditions. The 1960s provided a major downward swing as student idealism and unrest grew. Studies of student attitudes report that during the 1960s attitudes became more negative toward authority figures, assuming managerial roles in large organizations, and accepting administrative responsibility.[6]

Further insight into student attitudes is obtained from a survey at the Sloan School of Management, Massachusetts Institute of Technology. Students, faculty, and executives in a Sloan executive program were given a

[6] John B. Miner, "Changes in Student Attitudes toward Bureaucratic Role Prescriptions during the 1960s," *Administrative Science Quarterly,* September 1971, pp. 351–364.

survey which included the following statement: "Corporations have a definite obligation to be actively involved in community affairs." Only about 54 percent of both students and faculty agreed with this statement, but *84 percent* of executives agreed with it. Even though this was a school of *management,* not liberal or fine arts, a substantial portion of students and faculty still apparently held the classical economic doctrine that business has no *obligation* (this is the word used in the survey) in community affairs. However, the executives—the men with experience—saw an obligation. For other questions concerning "business in society" students and faculty maintained their joint disagreement with business executives, and the executive viewpoint was consistently more oriented toward social responsibility. Somehow the university people did not see business in society in the broad way that executives saw it.[7]

Influence of Faculty and Curricula on Students

Figure 20-2 shows the influence of faculty and curricula on student attitudes concerning how well business meets its responsibilities to society. The research covers 581 students at Michigan State University. Students in all curricula start as freshmen with approximately the same attitudes. Engineering and education majors retain their beginning attitudes for their entire undergraduate program, which suggests that the instruction they receive is approximately neutral toward business. Business students gain about four points between their freshman and senior years. This improved attitude should be expected since business is their chosen field of study. Arts and letters (liberal arts) students, on the other hand, suffer a strong drop of about *ten points* between their freshman and senior years. Their attitude toward business shifts from favorable to unfavorable beginning with their junior year. Their fast decline, in the absence of decline by others, suggests that there is something in their specific program which increases their dissonance with business. At the graduate level all other student attitudes decline (perhaps representing a more questioning point of view), while arts and letters students increase slightly (perhaps representing broader insights).

The pattern of difference between business and liberal arts is maintained for all four other areas of the survey: economic attitude, ethical norms of business, status of business careers, and worth and quality of collegiate-level business education. In each instance attitudes of liberal arts students toward business move from a favorable freshman attitude to an unfavorable one in their senior year. (No other group is unfavorable toward business in its senior year, except education majors regarding ethical norms of business.)

When the same survey form was given to university graduates working in business, it showed that experience tempered their collegiate differences. After

[7] Edgar H. Schein, "Attitude Change during Management Education," *Administrative Science Quarterly,* March 1967, pp. 601–628. This article also reports substantial differences among faculty subgroups such as marketing, organization, and finance.

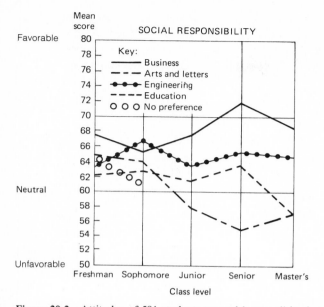

Figure 20-2 Attitudes of 581 students toward how well business meets its social responsibilities, classified by student's academic major. (From Leslie M. Dawson, "Campus Attitudes toward Business," *MSU Business Topics,* Summer 1969, p. 40. Reprinted by permission of the publisher, the Bureau of Business and Economic Research, Division of Research, Graduate School of Business Administration, Michigan State University.)

two years of business experience, attitudes of all groups toward social responsibility were about the same, and all were favorable. (Education majors were excluded because not enough were in business.)[8]

In general, the evidence indicates that business in the long run is gaining academic status, but the total university climate discourages many students from wanting to enter business. Many academic attitudes toward business represent traditional classical economic doctrines, rather than modern corporate business in a pluralistic social system.

SUMMARY

A knowledge society requires an active and close interface between business and education. It gives students a bewildering number of occupational choices and alternatives for solving social problems, thereby increasing student alienation and

[8] Leslie M. Dawson, "Campus Attitudes toward Business," *MSU Business Topics,* Summer 1969, pp. 36–46. There are also substantial differences in attitudes of entering freshmen concerning status of business careers and worth of business education, with business majors highest and arts and letters majors lowest in each instance. Another study confirms this entrance difference regarding status of business occupations. See Andre L. Delbecq and James Vigen, "Prestige Ratings of Business and Other Occupations," *Personnel Journal,* February 1970, pp. 111–116.

doubts about business as a career. Although business education gradually has gained academic stature, the general university climate has not strongly encouraged business as a career. Nevertheless, business and higher education tend to work cooperatively because of their interdependent needs and mutual interest in a free society.

STUDY GUIDES FOR INTERPRETATION OF THIS CHAPTER

1. Following a collegiate speech by the president of a large chemical firm, a student directed the following question to the president: "You businessmen could solve the world's hunger problem if you would release your secret patents to the people; why don't you do it?" As president, how would you respond?

2. In the same discussion another student commented, "Business does not care enough about higher education. I have read that business gives only 0.39 percent of its profit for this purpose." As president, how would you respond?

3. Another student asked, "Why are profits necessary? Our state university does not have to make a profit each year to be successful." As president, how would you answer?

4. Discuss the effects of the knowledge society on the business-education interface.

5. What business actions do you propose to get more university students interested in business as a career?

PROBLEMS
The Fabian Company

Management of the Fabian Company, a drug manufacturer, has decided that it wishes to give four student scholarships in support of university education. Among the alternatives it has considered are the following:

1. Give scholarships to children of employees, allocating them on the basis of need, a competitive screening process, or a chance drawing.

2. Give scholarships to students who live in the plant community and who wish to study any field allied with medicine.

3. Give money to the local university to grant to any student taking any field allied with medicine. The university would select scholarship recipients based upon other criteria which it determined.

4. Give money to the community high school system with the specification that scholarships be given to deserving disadvantaged students who probably could not otherwise go to college.

1. Appraise in pluralistic terms each of the alternatives considered. Then offer your own best scholarship proposal to the management, giving a full explanation of why your proposal is superior.

The Weapons Manufacturer

During a recruiting trip a recruiter for a chemical manaufacturer talked before a senior class in chemistry, explaining the many advantages of working for his company. During the discussion period one of the seniors stated, ''Why should I want to work for your company? It produces chemicals for rockets used by the United States military, and I abhor war.'' The recruiter knew that the statement was true, because 2 percent of the company's sales were to the federal government. Some of these products had military uses, while the remainder were used in other governmental functions.

1. As the company's recruiter, how would you respond to the statement made?

2. What are the social responsibility issues raised by the student's statement?

21

BUSINESS INVOLVEMENT WITH CULTURAL AFFAIRS AND COMMUNICATION MEDIA

The basis for the new power is information, not money or force.

Peter B. Clark[1]

Every day we print a partial, incomplete version of certain selected things we have learned, some of them inevitably erroneous, all of them inevitably distorted by the need to abridge and by the force of our own preconceptions and prejudices.

David S. Broder[2]

The story is told that businessman-philanthropist Andrew Carnegie grew weary of being called upon each year to make a gift to cover the large deficit of a community symphony orchestra. Finally he refused to pay the deficit again. With his strong work ethic he felt that the fund committee should invest some of its own efforts by going to other wealthy people in the community. In order to encourage the fund committee to try this approach, he said: "If you raise half the money from other donors, then I will donate the remaining half."

A week later the committee returned and informed him that the other half had been raised. Mr. Carnegie was very pleased and wrote his check for the balance. As he handed his check to the committee, he inquired, "Would you mind telling me where you got this amount of money so quickly?"

"Not at all," the fund chairman replied with a grin. "We got it from Mrs. Carnegie!"

Business has always had some involvement in cultural affairs and communication because of its wealth, power, and commercial trading, but during the last ten to twenty years it appears that this involvement has increased. Both business and society are recognizing the system relationship which business has to all elements of a pluralistic culture. Business and culture are tied together in many ways. Business is a major supporter of community cultural projects, and it is probably the

---

[1] Peter B. Clark, "The Reporter and the Power Structure," *Editor & Publisher,* Dec. 7, 1968, p. 10.
[2] David S. Broder (Pulitzer Prize–winning journalist), "Time for Modesty from the Press," *Shreveport Times,* May 12, 1973, p. 6-A.

largest employer of performing artists and of journalists in communication media such as radio, moving pictures, records and tapes, television, and newspapers. It also provides the advertising revenue which maintains most of our free newspapers, magazines, radio stations, and television stations. From another point of view, business health and growth depend on a balanced society which includes widespread cultural activities and open communication.

In this chapter we discuss business's increasing role as a participant in the cultural life of society, as exemplified in gifts for cultural projects and business's beautification of its own properties. We also discuss the role and responsibilities of business as the chief operator of mass communication media in society.

BUSINESS PARTICIPATION IN CULTURAL AFFAIRS
Support of Cultural Activities

A growing area of business giving is community cultural activities. Throughout the centuries, art has been heavily dependent on some form of patronage for support. Pharaohs, noblemen, the church, and the state have all provided patronage because the market could not be depended on to support culture to the extent sought by societal leaders. Traditionally in Europe, deficits are made up by state subsidies. In the United States wealthy persons have supported culture; but with greater tax restrictions on accumulation of wealth, this source has declined, requiring a broader base of support. Cultural organizations have sought support from business and, in small amounts, from today's more numerous middle class. Over 5 percent of the business gift dollar now goes for cultural activities, and the list of business donors to operas, art shows, symphonies, and ballets is gradually expanding.

Business justifies its gifts in terms of a better quality of life in the community. In turn, this quality of life improves recruiting and retention of employees. It also improves satisfaction of employees with their community, provides a better place for their children to grow up, and encourages each employee's own cultural growth. The system effects continue in many directions in the same way that a stone cast into water extends its ripples to the limits of a lake. If, for example, the firm sells its products locally, a community with a better cultural life should have improved chances for growth, thus providing more customers. Further, culture should attract a better quality of citizen, thus improving the quality of the labor pool from which the firm recruits. Cultural opportunities also may challenge youth in the community, raise their achievement drives, and provide favorable outlets for their energies, thereby reducing tendencies toward delinquency. In turn, less crime and delinquency may reduce the tax burden. When a systems view such as this is taken, it can be argued that an investment in community culture tends to improve the entire social system.

Limitations on Business Giving

There are, however, limitations on business giving. One point is that business needs to exercise caution that it does not overcommit itself to cultural activities alone, because there are many alternative social needs for business funds, such as education and the less-advantaged. A second point is that business support depends upon genuine community participation in the long run. Business may be the primary initiator of a project, but strong community support is needed to keep a project going and to carry its intended effects into the community.

The Minnesota Theater Company performs in a very stylish playhouse built primarily with business funds, although school children and others gave to the project. Its performances have received high ratings from critics. During a period of seven years it has received normal gifts, plus $400,000 through a federal school program and a grant of $870,000 from the Ford Foundation (the Andrew Carnegie of modern times!). In spite of these advantages, it had a record deficit of about $365,000 in its seventh year. Community interest and attendance declined, and the theater was not yet able to pay its own way. The theater company asked businessmen for gifts to make up the annual deficit.[3] (If you were a community businessman, how would you respond?)

Another point is that, although business may occasionally support a risky venture in art just as it does in commerce, generally it should be sure that any project has sound management and financial planning. Art projects often need business talents such as management and marketing expertise more than they need business money. If business intends to support a project, then it also has some responsibility to insist that management should be sound. For example, if financial planning is inadequate, then business may find itself saddled with requests for substantial additonal funds which it feels it cannot afford, but which it feels it must give in order to salvage the cultural investment it has already made.

The Spanish Pavilion was a key attraction of the New York World's Fair in 1964; therefore, it was reasoned that the pavilion should be an equally important attraction in dressing up the St. Louis, Missouri, waterfront. The Spanish government donated it to St. Louis, and a public foundation was set up to operate it. Estimated costs of bringing it to St. Louis and setting it up were $3 million, but actual costs were about $6 million.

St. Louis businessmen originally contributed nearly $2 million of the funds. When costs began to rise far above estimates, the mayor appealed to businessmen for more help. According to one business leader, "The same

[3] William Glover, "Can Community Theater Live without Subsidy?" *The State Journal* (Lansing, Mich.), Dec. 21, 1969, p. E-17.

companies contributed reluctantly the second time, despite the fact we didn't think it was a very sensible project. The only reason we went along was that we felt the mayor had gotten himself into a mess and needed help.''

When the pavilion opened, the anticipated visitors failed to show up and the pavilion had an average monthly deficit of $35,000 for the first seven months. At that point the mortgage holder filed a lawsuit, and cultural leaders came to business asking for more gifts to help bail them out of their financial morass.[4] (If you were a businessman in this situation, what would you do?)

A final point is that business giving should not be so total that it makes individual artists dependent upon business support. Art needs to be an expression of a free spirit. Both the artist and the businessman have a mutual interest in maintaining independence and a climate of freedom in which each can make his own type of social contribution.

Cultural Affairs in the Individual Business

Concurrently with their gifts for cultural activities, businessmen have discovered art as a means of creating a desirable in-company environment for employees and customers. Banks were among the first to move art from the museum to the office. Many banks and other offices today are, indeed, places of beauty with tastefully presented art collections that might even arouse envy in a museum director. One bank, for example, developed a purchase award of $1,500 for the first prize in a local art show, and in this manner it gradually acquired an outstanding art collection for its offices.

It is popularly thought that businessmen are less interested in art and cultural affairs than the typical citizen, but this seems mostly to be a myth created by people who perceive businessmen in terms of the theoretical model of economic man. Businessmen throughout history have shown a strong interest in art, beauty, and cultural affairs. They developed great collections of art which they gave to public museums, gave land for public parks, supported symphonies, and created libraries (for example, Carnegie libraries).

An example of the cultural interest of one businessman at the beginning of the twentieth century is the magnificeant Huntington Library in the Los Angeles area. It was formerly the home of Henry E. Huntington, a Western railway executive and community developer. Huntington spent many years assembling a choice art collection and an outstanding library which is especially rich in early English and American editions. The house itself is a work of art, and the grounds are beautifully landscaped with plants

---

[4] ''The Mayor's Tilt with the Windmills,'' *Business Week,* Jan. 31, 1970, p. 105.

from around the world. In 1922 Huntington gave this entire collection and estate to the American public and included an $8-million trust fund to support and expand it.

Beauty in Business Building Design

From ancient times to the present, attention has been given to beauty in the design of many public buildings, but this idea did not carry into the design of factories in the Industrial Revolution. Generally, factories and many other business buildings have focused strictly on utilitarian function. The result was not just an absence of beauty, but a genuinely distasteful ugliness, sometimes called the Nineteenth Century Ugly school of factory design. As a result, in recent decades many manufacturers have encountered zoning opposition when they tried to move into a community. The potential factory's neighbors had images of factory blight and lowered home values. They wanted the factory's economic contribution, but not its social by-products.

In response to pressures from a pluralistic society and their own expanded view of their factories' effects, businessmen began giving more attention to combining beauty with utility in business buildings. Many factory sites today are genuine industrial parks, often more attractive than their surrounding neighborhoods. The effect is to upgrade, rather than to blight, the neighborhood.

The cost of a factory "beauty treatment" is usually 1 to 10 percent of factory cost, but firms which have tried it usually report that it is worth the cost. These firms expected a better public image from beautification, but some additional effects were less expected. Improvements reported are higher labor productivity, decreased absenteeism, lower turnover of good employees, and improved recruiting. In addition, some firms report a heightened spirit of mutual interest, creativity, and job satisfaction. Employees seem to feel better and work better in aesthetically pleasant surroundings.

A cement plant in the bleak Mojave Desert, for example, maintains that employee absenteeism and turnover became significantly lower after it landscaped its plant. The plant site is landscaped with $150,000 of plum, olive, elm, and peach trees, and it has colorful year-round gardens of flowers. The result was so impressive that the company set aside a larger amount for landscaping a new plant in another location.

An unusual case is that of a steel-strapping plant which built on 60 landscaped acres in a rich suburb of $50,000 to $80,000 homes. In the beginning the plant's neighbors opposed it, but once they saw its parklike landscaping, they considered it an asset to their neighborhood. The plant was so good-looking that its wealthy neighbors asked it to expand into an adjoining tract to prevent a real estate developer from building lower-priced homes on it. They felt that the lower-priced homes would depreciate their neighborhood more than the factory![5]

Costs of Securing Aesthetic Beauty

Costs of beautifying a building site may be considered a nominal capital investment which can be recovered because of the benefits mentioned, but there are other beautification costs which are more substantial. They also create major questions of public policy concerning who should pay for them. Overhead electric utility lines are certainly unsightly in metropolitan areas, but they are also expensive to place underground.

In a metropolitan area an electric utility company faced the choice of building a new high-voltage line overhead for $15 million or placing it underground for $160 million. This difference is substantial and would affect consumer cost of electric power. Who should pay this cost? Should it be the people who live near the line and would directly benefit from its being underground? Should it be all customers served by this line? (In this case, they are at the end of the line; so those along the route would pay nothing.) Should it be all persons in the metropolitan area served by the line? Should it be all persons served by the utility in the state? Should it be government at the local, state, or national level? These answers do not come easily.

Furthermore, any rate increase required by the underground line will have to be approved by the public utility commission. This problem, therefore, is a matter of politics and public policy, as well as a socioeconomic decision for the firm However, since the transmission line will exist for many years, the company must look ahead and develop a strategy that will be publicly acceptable for twenty years. It would be an economic and social waste to build an overhead line now and then in a few years be required by public pressure to place it underground.

Perhaps a rational strategy in this instance is to place low-voltage neighborhood lines underground as quickly as possible, because these affect more people and an acceptable technology is already available. Since underground high-voltage lines are very costly and affect the neighborhoods of fewer people, perhaps the placement of these lines underground may need to await a technological breakthrough or a more affluent society which can afford the cost. In the short run, society probably has more desirable alternatives for use of its limited capital and labor. (If you were the utility executives, what strategy would you decide? Or, as a citizen, what strategy would you desire?)

[5] Steven M. Lovelady, "A Thing of Beauty . . . Handsome Factories Yield Unexpected Joys," *Wall Street Journal* (Pacific Coast edition), Dec. 1, 1965, p. 1.

A costly strategy already decided is found at the Henderson mine of American Metal Climax, Inc., in the Colorado wilderness. Mine tailings (ore waste) normally are stored in ponds near the mine, but the mine in this instance is near a major highway. For this reason the mine spent $25 million to tunnel more than 9 miles through a mountain so that it can deposit its tailings out of view in a relatively inaccessible area. This arrangement increased the cost of the mine nearly 15 percent, and there will be continuing operating costs to transport the tailings to this area. However, since the mine is a long-run investment, a preconstruction strategy was required which it is hoped will meet aesthetic and conservation requirements for several decades.

In addition, the company designed and colored buildings to blend with the landscape in order to improve the usual drab appearance of mines. It also built access roads which preserve as many trees as possible.[6]

It seems certain that the interface of business and cultural affairs will increase in future years. The systems model of business and society makes it clear to businessmen that the aesthetic and cultural quality of society does have an effect on the quality of business practice. For these new conditions business needs to develop strategies which will be consistent with future expectations of society. Business needs to lead, rather than reluctantly back into the future.

BUSINESS AND MASS COMMUNICATION MEDIA

In the philosophy of democracy, a free society depends on open communication. This means that in the free world a large proportion of mass communication media, such as books, newspapers, motion pictures, radio, and television, are operated by independent business organizations, most of them operating on a profit-making basis. In each of these areas the state performs a regulatory role and produces some output itself, but the dominant operation is typically by free business (with the probable exception of television).

Business's operation of communication media places upon it a heavy burden of responsibility. It must assure a high quality of output, else the quality of society itself may deteriorate. It must assure reasonable saturation of its market so that all citizens are informed and have a chance to develop their potential. It must maintain an open system (free speech), but at the same time it must assure that the most outspoken groups do not dominate because this becomes *de facto* restriction of the openness of the system. Not only must it tell the truth, but it must tell the *whole truth* to assure that citizens have a balanced view of reality as it exists—and of

[6] "The War That Business Must Win," *Business Week*, Nov. 1, 1969, p. 71.

future aspirations of both the common people and society's most capable idealists. The power of business is great in mass communication; therefore, in accordance with the Iron Law of Responsibility the responsibility of business is also large. It takes great institutions and noble business leaders to bear these substantial responsibilities, especially during a fast-changing age of discontinuity.

The subject of free mass communication and business's role in it is worthy of many books. In this chapter we briefly discuss certain key issues in the business-society interface. In discussing these issues we shall apply the criteria just mentioned: quality of output, reasonable saturation of market, open system with balanced representation of different views, the whole truth, and the Iron Law of Responsibility.

Freedom with Responsibility

Freedom of the press and other mass communications is not an end in itself but is a means to an end of a free society. Obviously mass communication is not set up simply for the profit of business. Business's social role is to provide the people a valuable service which helps maintain their freedoms. Since this service has deep ethical and political significance, business has special obligations to assure that it performs this service responsibly. Irresponsible abuse of free communication would threaten the foundations on which a free society is built. This philosophy is aptly phrased in a section of the constitution of the state of Connecticut written in 1818. It provides freedom of speech and press but states that all citizens are "responsible for the abuse of that liberty."[7]

In a similar manner free communication does not exist just for the pleasure and profit of communication professionals such as journalists and authors. They, like business, are the servants of the people. They have a deep ethical obligation to society to provide communication which meets the criteria mentioned earlier. Since they are the ones who actually produce the service which business sells, they have a responsibility to provide quality of output, balanced representation of views, and the whole truth. If journalists engage in irresponsible abuse of free communication, they—like business—will threaten the foundations on which a free society is built.

It is evident from this discussion that freedom of mass communication also implies some responsibility for the abuse of that liberty. The Iron Law of Responsibility applies equally to journalistic "producers" of communication and to business "sellers" of it. As a matter of fact, both journalists and businessmen have a mutual interest in developing open, responsible mass communication, because both know that their own freedoms depend on maintenance of a free society.

[7] Richard L. Tobin, " 'Responsible for the Abuse of That Liberty,' " *Saturday Review,* Jan. 13, 1968, p. 107.

Who Controls Mass Communication?

Business's role in mass communication can be better understood by examining the centers of control of mass communication. At first glance, the answer may appear obvious. It can be said that, since business owns and controls the economic assets of communication such as printing presses and broadcasting studios, it must certainly control mass communication. However, ownership of assets in our complex, pluralistic society does not mean complete control of how these assets are used. In the highly interdependent structure of mass communication, many groups in addition to business owners and managers apply their control and influence.

Government, for example, controls the limits of communication through its court decisions on obscenity and on mergers which lead to monopoly of the press. It controls other communication media through administrative agencies such as the Federal Communications Commission. At the local level it exercises control through censorship boards and local laws.

The consumer also controls mass communication. He decides which books and magazines to purchase. He chooses which moving pictures to attend, and he is the one who turns the dial on his television set to select the program he desires. However, certain communication media such as newspapers, motion pictures, and television offer only a limited number of outlets; so he can choose only from the alternatives offered him. If both local newspapers are conservative or if both are liberal, then his choice is limited. Similarly, if all three motion picture theaters in his neighborhood are showing X-rated films, he cannot take his children to the neighborhood theater; but he may go elsewhere or choose another form of entertainment.

In addition, advertisers exert control on media which depend on advertising for their support. If a television producer cannot find an advertiser to support a specific program which he desires to produce, he may have to give up his project regardless of how worthy he thinks it is.

Similarly, various partisan groups control communication media by means of their information inputs into the system. Normally they issue information releases which are favorable to their points of view. In other cases they bring social pressures on newsmen to present their points of view, or they plan meetings or protests in terms of attracting news coverage.

Another major control group is composed of those who write and edit mass communications, as will be discussed in the next section.

The purpose of this discussion of control is to show that although business owns communication assets, it is only *one of many influences* on the content of mass communication. What is evident here is the normal operation of a pluralistic society in which many semiautonomous groups are influencing the quality and content of communication. Pluralism helps keep the system free of monopoly and open to different points of view. It encourages development of different types of media and different types of output. In this manner it helps achieve the free society which is the ultimate objective of free and responsible mass communication.

Keeping in mind the basic ideas which have been discussed, we will examine selected situations in which business encountered difficulty in its operation of mass communication media.

The Crisis in News Coverage

A normal model of pluralism assumes that social equilibrium is maintained by balanced influences of many interest groups. If one group gains excessive power which primarily serves only its interests or values, social disequilibrium develops, and quality of output tends to diminish. Further, in order to restore a balance considered more "just" or "right" by the parties involved, countervailing pressures will develop. This is the situation which developed with news coverage in the late 1960s. The public began to feel that they were not getting the whole story, that news coverage was negative in tone, and that it consistently followed an ideological bias. (These objections applied to *news* only; bias on the editorial page was generally accepted as part of a free press.) Some of the public blamed business (the managers of news media) for this condition, but most of them centered their dissatisfaction on reporters and television newscasters. These men play a key role in the powerful technostructure of modern mass communication.

For decades, news has typically emphasized disaster, violence, and problems. In the heritage of journalism, these conditions make news. However, the public reaction was caused by two additional factors. First, many persons felt that news coverage was dominated by journalists with a common ideological viewpoint; consequently, news tended to carry a uniform ideological bias. The situation was interpreted by a representative of a national broadcasting company as follows: "Men of like mind are in the news. It's provincial. The blue- and white-collar people who are in revolt now do have cause for complaint against us. We've ignored their point of view. It's bad."[8]

In the judgment of one newspaperman, journalists were sometimes offering subtle moral judgments and presenting biases agreeable with their own ideologies. They generally offered a philosophy of humanistic idealism compared with the typical reader's philosophy of realism. The result was a basic incongruence between the news as presented by one group and understood by the other, leading to a decline in news credibility.[9]

[8] Fred Freed, quoted in Edith Efron, "The 'Silent Majority' Comes into Focus," *TV Guide,* Sept. 27, 1969, p. 7.
[9] Peter B. Clark, "Newspaper Credibility: What Needs to Be Done?" *Michigan Business Review,* January 1973, pp. 1–6.

In a few instances there was contrived or faked news. Nine alleged television examples were presented before a congressional committee, and later spokesmen for the networks involved reported that the employees causing the incidents had been disciplined. For example, in a presentation on pollution, preserved fish specimens from other sources were scattered on the beach to give an appearance of pollution damage. In another sequence a high school demonstration was staged.[10]

A second cause of dissatisfaction was that some persons believed that careless journalism was contributing to public problems. It was felt that some journalists were underqualified. They lacked enough technical knowledge in some news areas to present their stories adequately. They often did not understand the larger system effects of their subject. Consider the following example of inadequate news.

The U.S. Department of Labor released annual figures of per capita income and employee wages for each of the fifty states. The figures reported that a certain state had per capita income below the national average. Under the news heading "State Income Below Average," a reporter in that state built a two-column article criticizing business for being a low-wage employer and not caring about worker economic needs. He reported an interview with the state director of the AFL-CIO who condemned business for economic exploitation of workers. He also interviewed two workers who reported dissatisfaction with their income. No economist or busiessman was interviewed.

As a matter of fact, if the reporter had examined the Department of Labor report more fully, he would have seen that manufacturing wages, construction wages, and other major wage classifications in the state were substantially *above* the national average. Had he consulted an economist he could have learned that per capita income is affected by many variables such as number of children in families and income from sources other than wages. In this particular state, even though wages were above the national average, per capita income was below average, in particular because of a high proportion of large families with wife and children not working and a low proportion of very rich persons receiving income from nonwage sources.

This example suggests that a considerable part of the bias attributed to journalists may result from shoddy research and inadequate knowledge of the subject being reported.

The public's fundamental conclusion concerning news problems was that journalism had exceeded the bounds of justice, balance, and representativeness.

[10] "Explain News Fakes, Two Networks Asked," New York Times Service, *Arizona Republic*, Oct. 6, 1972, p. 17.

The National News Council's Area of Activity

The National News Council is designed to serve both the public and the news media. Its "ombudsman" role includes investigating complaints brought by the public and the news media and issuing reports on matters affecting the press. The Council will have no coercive power, relying instead on the cooperation of the news media in making known its findings.

The national news suppliers with which the Council will initially be concerned are the Associated Press, United Press International, Los Angeles Times/ Washington Post News Service, New York Times News Service, *Newsweek Time, The Christian Science Monitor, The Wall Street Journal,* and the network news programming of the American Broadcasting Company, Columbia Broadcasting System, National Broadcasting Company, and public television and radio.

From a press release of the National News Council, May 8, 1973, p. 3.

Question: Comment on the appropriateness of ombudsman activities such as those of the National News Council.

Excessive power had drifted into the hands of a small elite which was unduly influencing public thought patterns. In pluralistic terms, journalists had acquired power which they were not using responsibly. As a result, public confidence in the press declined. The Harris poll reported that from 1966 to 1972 those who had a great deal of respect for the press declined from 29 to 18 percent. Those with hardly any respect increased from 17 to 26 percent.[11] There was some improvement in attitudes following press success in disclosing the Watergate affair, but then press overkill in the situation raised further public dissatisfactions.

A Rise of Countervailing Power

The widespread news credibility gap caused a gradual buildup of counter-vailing power, as might be expected in pluralism. Countervailing pressures developed toward both journalists and business as the employer of journalists. Pressures came from a variety of sources such as public personalities, journalism teachers, comedians joking on the subject, advertisers, and community action groups. For example, under the leadership of a Stanford University professor of communication, two experimental community press councils were established in the West. Their purpose was to review the fairness of press coverage in their community.

At the national level a task force report of the nonprofit Twentieth Century Fund recommended in 1972 the establishment of a nonpartisan, private national council to examine news problems. Based on this report, a fifteen-member

[11] Speech by Louis Harris to American Newspaper Publishers Association, New York City, Apr. 25, 1972.

National News Council became operative in 1973 supported by eight nonprofit foundations. The council's role was determined after studying press councils in other nations, notably the British Press Council, and local press councils in the United States. It is to investigate and report on both (1) questions of news credibility and (2) threats to freedom of the press. The council focuses on national suppliers of news, leaving local news problems to be examined by community press councils if the public desires. The council relies only on publicity to give force to its findings. It has no enforcement powers.[12]

The chief criticism of business in the news credibility crisis is that it could have acted more responsibly to keep the crisis from getting out of hand. As an employer of journalists, it could have encouraged more self-development and broadening of background, challenged careless or biased news reporting, and given assignments more suited to each journalist's capabilities. There is no suggestion that business managers tell journalists how to write the news. Professional independence of journalism is essential to a free society, but independence does not relieve journalists of responsibility for the abuse of their liberty. Nor does it relieve business of its obligation to operate mass communication responsibly.

The Fairness Doctrine in Federal Regulation of Broadcasting

The issue of fair news coverage is related to the *fairness doctrine* of the Federal Communications Commission in its regulation of the radio and television industry. This doctrine applies across the board to all broadcasts, rather than to news alone. Essentially the doctrine states that stations have a public obligation to air both sides of important public issues and to allow free time for persons or groups to reply if their "honesty, character or integrity" is challenged on the air. The Commission has applied this doctrine to political candidates, public controversy presented in an unbalanced way, attacks on individuals, and even cigaret commercials. For example, if an editorial favors a political candidate, opposing candidates must be given free and equal time to reply. As another example, until radio and TV cigaret commercials were banned by law in 1971, the Commission applied the fairness doctrine to them, requiring that stations which carried these commercials had an equal duty to inform listeners of the health hazards of smoking.

In an effort to improve television responsibility and forestall application of the fairness doctrine to advertising of nonprescription medications, the National Association of Broadcasters in 1973 adopted sweeping new

---

[12] *A Free and Responsive Press,* New York: The Twentieth Century Fund, 1972, and news releases of the National News Council.

rules for drug advertising. The chairman of the Television Code Review Board stated that the new rules "demonstrated again that voluntary, self-regulation machinery can protect the public interest by dealing effectively with difficult issues."[13] One of the new rules prohibited personal endorsements of drugs by authority figures or celebrities. Another prevented drug advertising in or adjacent to programs designed primarily for children. Further, children cannot be used in presentations of medications intended for adults. Also on-camera talking of pills or capsules is prohibited.

Broadcasters have opposed the fairness doctrine on the grounds of interference with rights of free speech, added broadcasting costs, and the fact that the doctrine may tend to suppress discussion of controversial issues or personalities. In June, 1969, however, the U.S. Supreme Court in the Red Lion Broadcasting Company case in a rare unanimous decision sweepingly upheld the Federal Communications Commission's constitutional and statutory right to apply the fairness doctrine.

Why does the fairness doctrine apply to broadcasting, but not to other mass communications such as newspapers and magazines? The reason is that broadcasting is a restricted marketplace, while printing provides a fairly free marketplace. For technological reasons, there are only a limited number of broadcast channels available, and this fact requires the Commission to choose among applicants who promise to meet public interest, convenience, and necessity. The granting of a broadcasting license, therefore, imposes on the licensee a responsibility to serve the public interest fairly. In the words of the Supreme Court a licensee has no right "to monopolize a radio frequency to the exclusion of his fellow citizens. It is the right of the viewers and listeners, not the right of the broadcasters, which is paramount."[14]

In the case of printed media a variety of options are available to the public, and so the normal workings of pluralism in a free society should assure a reasonably open presentation of different points of view. This concept does not deny that on some occasions ideas will be suppressed and bias will predominate; but viewed as a whole, open communication will tend to prevail. Thus, the *Chicago Tribune, Time,* and *Playboy* can go their merry ways without cautiously having to balance points of view among their contents.

[13] "Strict Rules for Drug Ads Unveiled by TV Leaders," Associated Press news release, *Arizona Republic,* Feb. 23, 1973, p. 24.
[14] *Red Lion Broadcasting Co. v. Federal Communications Commission,* 395 U.S. 367, June 9, 1969; and "Radio, TV Stations Have to Air Both Sides, Justices Decide in Upholding FCC Doctrine," *Wall Street Journal* (Pacific Coast edition), June 10 1969, p. 4. Looking toward the future, television violence is receiving increased attention. It may be further regulated either by the industry itself or by government guides such as the fairness doctrine.

Motion Picture Self-Regulation by Means of a Rating System

Another area of business difficulty in mass communication is motion pictures which have undesirable qualities for some of the population, particularly young persons. Motion pictures serve a broad audience ranging from young children to mature adults. In order to serve that audience, pictures of different maturity regarding sex and violence are produced. The maturity level, however, is not easily identified by the title of a movie, so children and others might attend movies which were unsuitable for them. The result was a growing disenchantment with motion pictures by a substantial portion of the public. Various citizen rating groups arose and community censorship increased, threatening chaos in the industry.

Recognizing its responsibility, the motion picture industry moved toward self-regulation. Since it had no power to prevent filming of any picture which met the minimum standards of the U.S. Supreme Court, it established in 1968 a rating system to designate the maturity level of films produced by its members.

The following rating system is used. "G" films are recommended for general audiences of all ages. "PG" films have unrestricted admission, but they are mature films for which parental guidance is advised. "R" films are restricted-admission films which do not admit persons under sixteen unless accompanied by a parent or adult guardian. They are clearly adult films. "X" films do not admit anyone under age sixteen. Their adult content may be offensive to some adults. In some states the age limit for both "R" and "X" films is higher by law.

Communication Trends

Mankind has gone through four information revolutions, and a fifth one appears to be developing. A critical issue is whether business will be able to absorb this new revolution effectively, or whether it will default to government or some other organization. The first revolution was the development of language by which people could codify their ideas and communicate with each other both by speaking and writing. Business played only a minor role in this development. The second revolution was the development of printing, which allowed for more open communication with more people. It also provided better storage and transmission of ideas for future generations. Business did play a major role in bringing printing to its full fruition and in encouraging an open system of printed communication.

The third information revolution was the development of mass media, especially radio and television. Again, business adjusted to this new revolution and played a major role in its development. The fourth information revolution was development of the computer as a primary instrument for storing and processing information. It has introduced new ways of life, and business has successfully played a major role in this activity.

The potential fifth information revolution is the introduction of massive information utilities which will store and process information for multiple uses by the whole community. A student may use the utility for programmed learning, a housewife may use it to make and pay for purchases from her home, and a citizen may use it for voting. As in the past, will business again be able to absorb this information revolution and use it responsibly? Will it be able to provide open communication with due regard for confidential information and personal privacy? Can it serve the whole society? Time will tell, but the opportunity is there.

SUMMARY

Business interface with cultural affairs is increasing. There are, however, limitations of business involvement in cultural affairs, because there are many alternative needs for business's efforts. Community cultural affairs are most likely to be successful when they have strong community support, rather than business dominance. Business's proper role is secondary; both the artist and the community need to retain their independence.

Free mass communication is a necessary means for achieving the social goal of a free society; consequently, business's operation of communication media places upon it a heavy burden of social responsibility. Business needs to provide a high quality of output, reasonable saturation of its market, open and balanced communication, and the whole truth. These responsibilities have proved difficult to meet in an age of discontinuity, as business works with independent journalists and strong pluralistic pressures.

STUDY GUIDES FOR INTERPRETATION OF THIS CHAPTER

1. The River City Fine Arts Association has proposed to the local chamber of commerce that businessmen build and support a community playhouse in order to upgrade community cultural life. As chamber of commerce president, how would you respond?

2. Discuss how large a percentage surcharge you would permit on your electric utility bill in order to pay for placing high-voltage trunk lines (not neighborhood lines) underground.

3. Choose a two-column news items from *The New York Times* or other major newspaper and critically appriase it for journalistic bias.

4. What is the publisher's responsibility when biased news journalism is supplied by a journalist?

5. In response to a citizen complaint about biased news coverage of a certain event, a television executive commented, "Your complaint is not relevant. Our journalists are all qualified professionals and men of good intentions." Appraise this statement.

6. The United Sates Constitution, Amendments, Article 1, reads in part as follows: "Congress shall make no law . . . abridging the freedom of speech or of the press. . . ." Discuss in terms of this provision of the Constitution: (*a*) the fairness doctrine of the FCC and (*b*) proposals for local national independent centers to evaluate news presentations.

PROBLEMS
The Building Design Review Board

An attractive suburban community strongly emphasized beauty in new building construction. The city established a design review board to approve building designs and specify changes required for the total attractiveness of each building and building site.

In this city a nationwide retailer proposed to build a department store, garden shop, and auto service center on a major commercial street near a residential area. The design review board approved the plan including the following conditions:

1. Buildings shall cover not more than 25 percent of the land, and the site shall be landscaped throughout, including landscaping 10 feet deep along all street frontages. Interior boundaries shall be marked with a 6-foot wall properly landscaped.

2. All outside sales, service, and loading areas shall be screened from public streets.

3. No signs shall be on the side of the building facing residences, and any lights located there shall be directed away from residential areas.

4. No windows shall be above the ground level floor.

Residents in the neighborhood protested that these requirements were inadequate, requiring reconsideration by the board. The board then added the following additional conditions:

1. The building shall be located at least 100 feet from residential property. This change placed the building nearer the front of the lot, requiring substantial customer parking at the rear of the store.

2. Fences shall be 8 feet tall, with landscaping having an initial height of 12 feet.

3. Any open sales area shall be screened on all sides by a decorative masonry wall 8 feet high.

4. The automobile entrance doors of the auto service building shall be screened from the street by walls and/or landscaping.

5. Unpaved areas reserved for future buildings shall be turfed or otherwise treated attractively.

The retailer protested that major customer parking at the rear of the store was unworkable. Several builders and businessmen protested that the new requirements would drive this needed retail store out of the city into a nearby suburban city. The local newspaper editorialized, "Stop the harassment that will paralyze business in our city. We need to shop here as well as live here."

1. What are the social responsibility issues raised by this problem?

2. A homeowner commented, "The protests of other businessmen not directly involved in this dispute are an unreasonable interference with our rights." Appraise this comment and prepare a reply to it.

The Pornographic Film

Warren Wilson has been in the theater business for thirty-three years, most of the time working for a national film distributor and theater operator. He is now sixty years old and regional manager for this firm. The four theaters which he supervises in the town where he lives are top-quality theaters. A month ago when he reviewed his booking list he learned that an unrated foreign film had been booked into one of his theaters. He viewed the film, which had already been banned by censorship boards in several cities, and judged it to be base pornography not suited to the quality theaters which he managed. He agreed in principle with Supreme Court rulings allowing controversial films to be shown to adults, but he felt that managers should have the right to apply common sense and make local interpretations of appropriateness. At that time X-rated films were showing in two of the four theaters he managed.

Wilson protested the film's bookings to higher management, giving his reasons, and two weeks later he was notified the film had been dropped from his booking list. Then, only a few days before the opening date originally scheduled for the film, he received a telephone call from the parent company which owned the national firm for which he worked. The top official who called him said the owner of the film would file a lawsuit for damages if the film was not shown, so it would have to be shown. Wilson objected, but the official said the film would be shown.

1. In the role of Wilson analyze the situation and determine what course of action you will take. What alternatives are available to him?

2. What social responsibility issues are raised by this problem?

The Television Code

A part of the Preamble of the Television Code of the National Association of Broadcasters reads as follows:

> Television and all who participate in it are jointly accountable to the American public for respect for the special needs of children, for community responsibility, for the advancement of education and culture, for the acceptability of the program materials chosen, for decency and decorum in production, and for propriety in advertising. This responsibility cannot be discharged by any given group of programs, but can be discharged only through the highest standards of respect for the American home, applied to every moment of every program presented by television.

1. Note the clear focus on the *home* in this Preamble. Discuss the reasons for this focus and its implications for the content of television programs compared with the content of motion pictures prepared for showing in commercial movie theaters.

ECOLOGY AND
BUSINESS RESPONSIBILITY

*All this talk about ecology: What the world needs is grass to lie on
and people who will help keep it clean.*

**A Sign Posted on a Lawn in the
Honolulu, Hawaii, Zoo**

*An activist is the guy that cleans up the river, not the guy that
concludes it's dirty.*

H. Ross Perot[1]

There are a number of imaginative ways of dealing with the ecological crisis. A solar energy specialist has proposed a 25-square-mile solar energy cell operating in earth orbit.[2] It would produce more power than is used by the entire New York City area. The power would be beamed by microwave to a 36-square-mile field on the earth. Wires spread over the field would collect the waves, convert them to electricity, and feed the electricity into the existing power grid. The wires and microwaves would make the field unsafe for housing, but it would be suitable for farming.

This unique plan is feasible with existing technology, and it would avoid all present forms of pollution from power generation (However, would the microwaves create a new form of pollution or some unforeseen ecological imbalance?) At any rate, it is a creative approach. Its originator points out that, contrary to the argument that space funds could be better spent on earth problems, he is perceiving that ''space technology might save life on earth,'' because of the superior capacity of space to generate pollution-free energy.

Outer space may eventually solve some of civilization's problems, but meanwhile back on earth there are a host of ecological issues that must be faced,

---

[1] H. Ross Perot, quoted in Christopher S. Wren, ''Ross Perot: Billionaire Patriot,'' *Look,* Mar. 24, 1970, p. 32.
[2] ''How to Get Sun Power for New York,'' *Business Week,* May 9, 1970, p. 128.

because the earth is a relatively closed ecosystem. *Ecology* is concerned with the relationships of living things and their environments. It provides a framework by which we can see that all living things are related to other living things, and they are all likewise related to their physical environment. Thus, a dry season may reduce vegetation, which affects the population of rabbits, thereby affecting the population of wolves. Likewise, the amounts and kinds of air pollution in an area may affect the health of orange trees—and of people.

Ecology and environmental quality are of interest to all people. It appears that quality of environment will be in the 1970s and 1980s a genuinely populist movement, appealing to people regardless of political views, religious beliefs, ages, or income levels. Probably pictures of earth from space did more than anything else to convince people that the earth is a tiny planet covered with a thin sheet of life-giving air and orbiting in hostile nothingness. If so, then this idea alone was perhaps worth the cost of all space exploration, because it may have saved mankind from extinction by irreversible pollution.

There is little doubt that mankind is facing an ecological crisis of various proportions around the world. It is easy to paint a bleak picture of man's senseless struggle against nature—a struggle which he cannot win. However, we believe that the systems concept of ecology requires man to think beyond the bleakness of defeat toward how mankind may apply his intellect to use the system for improvement. This is what man has done historically. He has improved through harnessing natural forces, such as water power, improving on nature as in hybrid seeds, and developing a technology which enables him to live in houses instead of in caves. It is significant that in the Chinese language the ideograph for "crisis" consists of two symbols: *danger* and *opportunity*. We believe this symbol represents the true propositions of the ecological crisis.

Most readers of this book are already knowledgeable about ecology and pollution, so this chapter will focus on business in an ecological system, a historical perspective of pollution, and economic issues in ecology. The following chapter will discuss general approaches toward pollution control, government regulation, and control of different types of pollution.

BUSINESS IN AN ECOLOGICAL SYSTEM
Complexity of an Ecosystem

An ecosystem is a total ecological community, both living and nonliving. The key point about an ecosystem is its immense complexity and interrelatedness. Mankind is just now coming to understand that each act he takes is intricately tied to many other events in the chain of life of an ecosystem. Since these intricacies have not been understood by experts, businessmen likewise often have not realized the effects of their actions. This lack of understanding means that even the best of intentions may have unforeseen and undesirable results.

For example, Egypt sought for years to build its great Aswan Dam on the Nile River because it was seen as a benefit in countless ways for Egyptians who needed flood protection, a more stable water supply, and irrigation for parched desert farmlands. Predictions indicated that the entire lower Nile Valley would be a better life area because of the dam. Further, protective measures were taken to overcome negative effects of the dam. Valuable animal life was saved from areas to be covered by the lake, and important archeological specimens were either protected or removed.

Now that the dam has been built, unforeseen negative effects on the ecosystem are being discovered.[3] The stabilized water flow prevents buildup of silt dunes at the end of the delta as the Nile enters the sea. These dunes formerly kept the sea away from rich delta farmlands, but now sea erosion is overcoming these dunes and flooding 1 million acres of farmland with salt water.

An additional problem is the spread of water hyacinths which evaporate large amounts of water in the lake above the dam. It appears that the lake may lose by evaporation about as much water as it was supposed to send down the Nile for irrigation. Of course, the hyacinths could be poisoned, but this would mean poisoning the lake.

Another danger predicted by an eminent zoologist is that a disease-carrying snail may spread through 500 miles of new irrigation canals below the dam. Peasants using the canals may catch the painful and normally incurable disease it carries.

Thus, we must ask, was the ecological system of the Nile improved or deteriorated by the Aswan Dam? The answer hinges on whether the possible negative effects can be overcome by man's ingenuity.

Now let us look at two projects more directly involving business. Both had unforeseen outcomes. One was favorable and the other was unfavorable.

Oil and gas drilling expanded rapidly in the Gulf of Mexico beginning about 1957.[4] One predicted negative effect was damage to marine life by oil spills, so controls were established to minimize damage. There have been oil spills, some receiving much publicity, but damage has been relatively minor. Meanwhile, an unforeseen effect has been produced by the thousands of docks, platforms, and pipes. These structures provide a better place for lower forms of sea life to attach themselves than the silt-laden sea bottom in this area. In a sense, the structures operate like a coral reef. Through supporting lower sea life, they attract and support larger quantities of

[3] David Perlman, "America the Beautiful?" *Look,* Nov. 4, 1969, p. 25.
[4] Ruth Sheldon Knowles, "Oceans of Resources—and Questions," *Wall Street Journal* (Pacific Coast edition), Sept. 30, 1969, pp. 22.

desirable fish. Consequently, since oil expansion began, the commercial fish catch has doubled in this area, while it has declined as a whole in all other United States fishing areas. The Department of Interior gives credit for this increasing catch to the increase in these undersea structures.

Meanwhile, in the scenic Santa Barbara Channel of California the effects of oil drilling were worse than expected because of oil leakages from geologic faults in the sea bed. And lower sea life did not need the underwater oil structures, because it already had an adequate supply of rock formations to which it could attach itself. As a result, President Nixon asked Congress to cancel offshore leases in the area and create a 198,000-acre marine sanctuary in their place. Again, the evidence is clear that each ecosystem presents complex *individualized* factors, many of them beyond man's present capacity to foresee.

Social Trade-offs

Man's actions in an ecological system usually involve social trade-offs. These social trade-offs are of two types. First, there is the *priority* choice. All things cannot be done at once. If man allocates his time and resources to, let us say, reducing air pollution, then he has less time and resources for reducing water pollution, improving education, or recreational travel. Just how much, for example, are we willing to give up to achieve a cleaner world? Will we give up individual automobiles and accept public transportation? Will we give up our right to leaf burning in autumn, to smoking, or to backyard barbecues? Will we pay for the new municipal sewage system and the new street- and park-cleaning labor force?

The international Organization for Economic Cooperation and Development estimates that among the developed nations approximately 4 percent of gross national product is required merely to hold the line against more pollution.[5] That is tens of billions of dollars *annually* in the United States. More important, many times that much will be required to make inroads into pollution existing from past causes. Is this a more important priority than poverty reduction, education, housing, or crime control? If it is, what pollution problems should be dealt with first? Should we tackle the easier problems with greater net returns or the harder ones that are more serious? Should you have to pay for cleaning up water pollution in New York or Colorado, if you do not live there? The choices are numberless.

A second kind of trade-off is what some have chosen to call the *gross national by-product* in order to contrast it with the gross national product (GNP). The idea of a gross national by-product implies that any major action which mankind takes for its benefit may also offer some negative results in the total ecosystem. For example, if a mine is opened in a rural area, it brings truck traffic, night work, the probability of air, water, and solid-waste pollution, perhaps an

[5] "The Rhetoric of Ecology," *Life,* Mar. 6, 1970, p. 36.

earth-jarring dynamite blast at noon each day, and a host of other changes that some persons will judge to be negative.

Many of the conditions mentioned can be controlled by allocating enough time and money to them, but there is no doubt that major business or social actions tend to produce some gross national by-product. Man's choice is to make sure that, considering the system as a whole, he takes one of the alternatives with the greatest net benefits. We believe it is idealistic to insist that the one "best" choice be taken because there are too many intangibles and unpredictable future events in most social choices. Mankind acts wisely when it chooses one of the better alternatives on the basis of careful research of the whole ecosystem and cautious prediction of the unknown.

Public Visibility

From the viewpoint of business, a notable quality of ecology is the public visibility of some dysfunctions within the ecosystem. It is easy to see a coal mining scar on a green hill, the ugliness of a factory yard, and street trash in a downtown commercial district. A person can smell the stench of paper mills, untreated sewage, and dead fish from water pollution. These situations make humorous jokes, as shown in Figure 22-1, but they are also quite serious in their effect on business's image if there is any way that the public can connect the visible pollution with business.

In general, business is more visible in its pollution than other institutions and thus more vulnerable to public criticism. It is easier to see the black or yellow smoke coming from a factory smokestack than the wastes from thousands of home oil furnaces which actually may be polluting the air more than the factory. The same reasoning applies to mostly invisible pollutants coming from hundreds of thousands of automobiles in a large city. It took a great amount of scientific research to identify automobile exhaust (aided by photochemical action from

FUNNY BUSINESS   *By Roger Bollen*

Figure 22-1 The seriousness of pollution is sometimes communicated through humor. (Source: *State Journal,* Lansing, Mich., Dec. 8, 1969. Reprinted by permission of NEA.)

Ecological Problems Are Complex

BAYTOWN, Texas—Clyde Floyd's gracious waterfront home boasts a large lot, a picturesque view of the Gulf of Mexico and amenities befitting an expensive structure.

But it harbors some peculiarities, too. The boat dock is four feet under water, the driveway periodically submerges and egrets bob for softwater crabs on what was once 5,000 square feet of luxuriant lawn.

Mr. Floyd's home, along with much of his neighborhood in the Houston suburb, is sinking, additional evidence of man's inhumanity to man. Specifically, it has declined nine feet in 30 years and is sinking five inches annually, mainly because of compression of the earth below as water supplies are pumped out for human needs.

From William M. Bulkeley, "Clyde Floyd of Texas Has a Headache, & His Home Is Feeling Low," *Wall Street Journal* (Pacific Coast edition), Jan. 12, 1973, p. 1. Reprinted with permission of *The Wall Street Journal.* © 1973 Dow Jones & Company, Inc. All rights reserved.

sunlight) as the primary source of Los Angeles smog. The major publicity was required to convince the people that the research was accurate. "The factories and refineries must be causing our smog," the people insisted. And, of course, they were partly right; the public visibility was there. However, by 1969, with normal regulation, combined industrial-residential-commercial sources caused only about 10 percent of air pollution in Los Angeles County. The rest came from motor vehicles, even though some emission controls were already required on vehicles.

A HISTORICAL PERSPECTIVE OF POLLUTION

Pollution needs to be seen in its historical perspective in order for it to be understood with a balanced view. It is not something new to the twentieth century. People have dumped their trash into the soil and water since the beginning of civilization. Archaeological excavations show the trash of several civilizations (not generations) dumped one on top of the other. Smoke from man's fires has polluted the air since the Stone Age. Citizens of early Rome complained that soot from fires dirtied their clothes, and London was described in 1660 as covered with "clouds of smoke and sulphur."[6]

[6] M. A. Wright, *The Business of Business: Private Enterprise and Public Affairs,* New York: McGraw-Hill Book Company, 1967, p. 27. London endured these "clouds of smoke" for 300 years until the Clean Air Act was passed in 1956. Under the law government authorities could set up tight standards for emission of dark smoke. Since much of the smoke came from home heating, householders were given subsidies of up to 70 percent to pay for conversion of heating equipment to take smokeless fuel. A report released after thirteen years of experience with the law showed that it was immensely effective. For an annual per capita cost of 36 cents the average Londoner received 50 percent more winter sunshine, and visibility was increased from 1.4 miles to 4 miles. Respiratory diseases also declined, indicating the complex ecology of the community. See "London Sees the Light, Thanks to Its Clean-Air Law," *Washington Post,* Mar. 17, 1970, p. A3.

Natural Pollution

Nature, as well as man, also pollutes the air. Dust storms toss dirt and debris into the air, natural forest fires cast a pall of smoke over mountain valleys, and lightning creates certain chemical compounds. The pollution from volcanoes is phenomenal and puts modern pollution clearly in perspective. The director of the United States Geological Survey states that only three eruptions in the last 150 years—Krakatoa in Java in 1883, Mt. Katmai in Alaska in 1912, and Hekla in Iceland in 1947—*have produced more air pollution than mankind in all of history.* From these three eruptions, "More particulate matter in the form of dust and ash, and more combined gases were ejected into the atmosphere than from all of mankind's activity."[7]

Perhaps the most uncomfortable and irritating of all natural pollutants, as many persons with allergies can testify, is the pollen released every day by trillions of plants. This pollution causes great human suffering.

Although pollution has existed since the early history of man, it was usually of minor significance. Only a few serious problems developed, such as polluted drinking water near metropolitan areas, destruction from volcanic eruptions, and allergies. Since 1700, however, three additional causes have arisen which have fundamentally altered the seriousness of pollution. They have upset the delicate balance of nature which allowed people to live comfortably in their environment. They are the Industrial Revolution, a higher standard of living, and the population explosion.

The Industrial Revolution

A primary cause of air and water pollution has been the Industrial Revolution. Its factories spread first across Britain and then the rest of the world, with smokestacks belching contaminants into the air. Industry requires energy, much of which is secured from incomplete combustion which releases pollutants of various types. The complex chemical processes of industry produce undesirable by-products and wastes that pollute land, water, and air. Its mechanical processes often create dust, grime, and unsightly refuse. More recently, the Agricultural Revolution as an adjunct of the Industrial Revolution has produced overkill with pesticides, odors, refuse from cattle feeding "factories," and other unpleasant conditions.

The International Council for the Exploration of the Sea reports that the Baltic Sea is becoming polluted from agricultural pesticides and fertiliz-

[7] "Geologist Says Nature Equals Man as Despoiler of Earth," United Press International news release, *Arizona Republic,* June 8, 1970, p. 14.

ers, industrial wastes, and sewage.[8] Phosphate concentrations, which are especially hazardous to sea life, are three times higher than fifteen years ago. Mercury pollution is so high that there is a ban on fish caught in some areas of the sea. DDT concentration in seals is ten times that of nearby North Sea seals and scientists fear that reproductive ability of some fish species is being reduced.

A Higher Standard of Living

Industrialization has raised the standard of living enormously. As people consume more their consumption tends to create more wastes. The more elegant their tastes for food become, the more garbage and other refuse they produce. The more they buy, the more paper and packaging are required, most of which become refuse. When they buy a car to replace a horse and buggy, they travel more and the engine they use leaves more airborne pollution. As they travel, they leave a trail of debris such as cans, bottles, and wrappers.

Every rise in the standard of living means a related rise in pollutants produced by individual persons. Further, as their consumption increases, their economic demand requires an increase in industrial production with its related pollutants. For example, solid wastes discarded in the United States are nearly a ton a year per capita.

Since people have been improving their standard of living for centuries, it is proper to ask why pollution has suddenly become a major problem. The answer lies partly in the concept of *compound growth,* meaning that growth in each subsequent year is built on a larger base so that the same *rate* of growth produces a larger *amount* of growth each year. It works the same way as compound interest. Assume that the growth rate is 5 percent annually. Many years ago when the gross national product of the United States was only $1 billion, a growth rate of 5 percent produced an increase of only $50 million. Using the same growth rate when the gross national product reaches $1 trillion, the increase was $50 *billion.* The difference in *amount* of growth in the two years is $49.95 billion, even though the growth rate is the same. This is the result of compounding. It is a fact that the real economic output of the United States grew about as much from 1950 to 1970 as it did in the three centuries from the time the Pilgrims landed in 1620 until 1950! And pollution tended to increase at somewhat the same pace. Meanwhile the earth's capacity to recycle wastes remained substantially unchanged. The result is that normal and moderate increases in standard of living in the last few decades have created an ecological crisis.

Imagine for a moment that the entire population of the world could secure the present standard of living in the United States. There would then be some 3

[8] "Pollution Threat to Baltic Sea," London Times News Service, *Arizona Republic,* Mar. 6, 1970, p. 19.

billion automobiles and countless other sources spewing their pollutants into the atmosphere. Probably the ecosystem could not stand the strain. This suggests that the idea of a continually rising standard of living raises some major long-run issues for civilization; however, there is an additional complicating factor. That is the *compound growth* of population.

The Population Explosion

The ultimate time bomb in pollution is a speedup in population growth.[9] This has happened mostly during the last 200 years as a result of economic and medical progress which allowed people to live longer. Every additional person adds pollutants to land, air, and water, although the amount of these vital natural resources remains the same. The result is more intensive pollution of these existing resources, unless mankind takes steps to reduce pollution. In the year 1900 in the United States, for example, about 3 million square miles accommodated less than 80 million people. By 1970, this area, and the air and water that go with it, had to accommodate over 200 million persons. It should, therefore, not be surprising that the environment is becoming more polluted.

It is estimated that world population is doubling every thirty-five years. If existing rates continue, the 1970 population of over 3 billion will be over 6 billion by the year 2000, as shown in Figure 22-2. If this rate continues for a few hundred years, the earth will be covered with people with standing room only. This is obviously an impossible situation, so eventual pollution control must rest on a base of realistic population control. Some progress is being made; by 1973 the United States had reached a birth rate of approximately zero population growth.

A WORLDWIDE PROBLEM
All Nations Are Affected

Pollution is a global problem. In Russia the Volga River boatmen are complaining that chemical plants are discharging wastes which kill sturgeon and endanger Russia's caviar supply, and Russia's Caspian Sea is threatened with becoming a dead sea because it is absorbing so many pollutants. The Russian people are complaining about strip mining, air pollution, and other ecological damage. The problem is so serious that the Russian government has launched a substantial corrective program.

In Europe the Rhine River is badly polluted in spite of efforts to clean it. The Rhine begins relatively pollution-free in Switzerland, but by the time it reaches the sea it has been estimated to carry 10 tons of mercury and 80 tons of arsenic a month,

[9] Paul R. Ehrlich, *The Population Bomb,* New York: Ballantine Books, Inc., 1968, presents in detail problems of population growth.

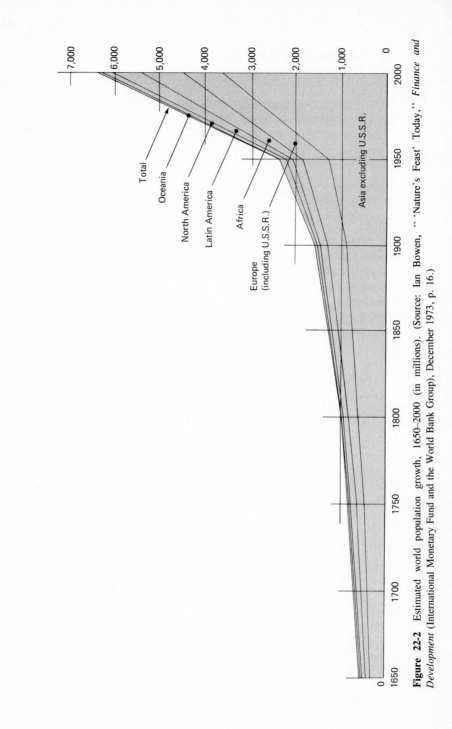

Figure 22-2 Estimated world population growth, 1650–2000 (in millions). (Source: Ian Bowen, " 'Nature's Feast' Today," *Finance and Development* (International Monetary Fund and the World Bank Group), December 1973, p. 16.)

along with city sewage and other pollutants. Air pollution is severe in metropolitan and industrial centers, and it is carried over most of Europe by air currents. Italian paintings and monuments are being eroded by pollution. Governments are taking action by establishing pollution control laws and boards.

The town of Sudbury, Ontario, Canada, has had the dubious honor of being one of the world's dirtiest cities. Within a 25-mile radius there is practically no vegetation, and dust-puffing smokestacks have created a reddish-brown pall over the area. Slag dumps from mineral smelting line the highway. In the summer when atmospheric conditions are right, large amounts of sulfur dioxide and other pollutants have been forced to the ground, killing plants and affecting people. Improvements are gradually being made to relieve the pollution.

Japan may be the world's most polluted industrial nation. Its high population density and large base of heavy industry have contributed to the problem. Rivers are filled with both chemical wastes and debris, and the air in many areas is severely polluted. The Japanese government has initiated a major program to reduce pollution, and courts have strongly supported a clean environment. Two decisions are especially significant. First, the courts have held that defendants are not free from liability for pollution damage just because they have met government minimum standards. Second, companies are required to exert reasonable care to prevent pollution regardless of its effect on commercial profit.[10]

In less-developed nations runaway population and urban crowding are causing polluted land, polluted water, and the stench of waste and filth. It is clear that pollution is a worldwide problem facing all nations. Each nation is a source of pollutants, and also it may be affected by pollutants which originate in other nations and are transported by waterways and air currents. For example, one nation may be down the river from another nation, or two nations may share a river as their national boundary.

The existence of pollution in all types of nations and cultures clearly shows that pollution is not a result of any single economic or political system. All systems have pollution problems. Neither is pollution a result of any one social culture. Whatever the way of life of the people, problems of pollution arise. Rather, pollution is primarily caused by the three conditions mentioned earlier: the Industrial Revolution, a higher standard of living, and the population explosion.

International Cooperation

If pollution is a worldwide problem, then international cooperation is required to control it. A historic first step was taken by the United Nations Confer-

[10] "Decision on Yokkaichi City Pollution," *Japan Labor Bulletin,* September 1972, p. 2.

ence on the Human Environment in 1972. Over 1,000 delegates representing ninety nations attended. The conference sought to establish basic principles and guidelines for controlling pollution. It attempted to establish ecological cooperation among both developed and less-developed nations. Going beyond routine attempts for control of pollution, the conference initiated discussion about how the people of the world might reorder their priorities to enhance the quality of life and live in better harmony with their environment. As a result of the conference ninety-one nations later in the year signed a sea-waste pact to control sea dumping of pollutants. Dumping of some wastes is totally prohibited, while other wastes may be dumped when a permit is granted. The pact was hailed as a historic step toward control of global pollution.

In addition to continuing United Nations actions, some nations are cooperating regionally in pollution control. For example, because of substantial pollution in the Mediterranean Sea, fourteen nations in the Mediterranean basin held a World International Conference for the Protection of the Mediterranean in 1973. The conference sought to devise plans for reducing the many wastes that are poured into the Mediterranean from the surrounding land. In addition, the European Economic Community nations are cooperating on pollution control. The Community has formed a commission to develop minimum standards and controls for the entire membership of the EEC.

ECONOMICS AND ECOLOGY

A reasonable question is: Why have people polluted the earth? One reason is that until recently people did not realize the ecological seriousness of polluting actions. But now that they do know, why do they still pollute? A key reason is that the *economics* of the situation has made it cheaper to pollute than not to pollute.[11] Before examining this phenomenon as it affects business, let us first consider it as it applies to an individual citizen. Consider the case of persons who toss their beverage cans from their car onto a roadside. You can preach to them about ecology and social priorities, but one of the major reasons they throw their cans away is that it is cheaper for them to do so than other alternatives. Their behavior is partly guided by the economics of the situation. Economics is a major common denominator for applying society's values to the daily working of the social system, and in this case it is essentially no economic cost to them to toss cans away. It would cost them time and money to take the cans to a recycling depot. It would also cost them time and inconvenience to take the cans home and put them in their garbage.

[11] For a more extensive discussion of economics and ecology see Frank C. Emerson (ed.), *The Economics of Environmental Problems*, Ann Arbor, Mich.: University of Michigan, Graduate School of Business Administration, 1973.

The Economic Theory of Pollution

Economists generally explain the pollution problem as originating from a discrepancy between social and private costs of production. Since product prices take into account the cost of resources to the manufacturer, but not necessarily the full costs to society, we may be receiving too many or too few of some goods and services and they may be produced by socially undesirable methods. For example, consider a municipal sewage plant that only partially treats effluents before releasing them into a lake that is used for fishing. If the amount of untreated sewage is so great as to reduce the fishing productivity of the lake, society will pay a lower cost for faulty municipal sewage treatment and a higher price for fish than otherwise would be the case. This inequality between social and private costs is termed a spillover or externality. In the case just described, the sewage plant results in an external diseconomy since its operation means increased costs for other sectors of society. The plant is using a common property resource to the detriment of other users and or potential users. In addition to a reduction in fish catch, the sewage may make the lake unfit for swimming, boating, and for use as a water supply source. Proper sewage treatment to give the lake additional uses may be relatively inexpensive, but management has little incentive to implement pollution reduction measures since there is no direct benefit from its doing so.

From David L. Scott and Charles R. Britton, "Standards and Effluent Charges for Pollution Abatement," *Arizona Business Bulletin,* November 1972, pp. 15-16. Reprinted with permission.

It is evident that the economics of this situation encourages pollution. If the economics could be changed to discourage pollution, then people would tend to pollute less. For example, if they had to pay a deposit of 20 cents on each can until they returned it to a store or a recycling depot, then they would have an economic reason not to pollute. If they did toss cans away, others would have economic motivation to clean the cans from the roadside in order to claim the deposit. In this manner the roadside would be kept free of cans because the economics of the situation encouraged it. It would not be necessary to employ large police forces to patrol the road to catch polluters, because the economics of the situation would encourage voluntary ecological action by individuals. Essentially this same framework applies to business.

Economic Free Goods

The environment has been mostly an economic *free good* for a businessman to use as he wished. This reasoning especially applies to air and water, two of society's main areas of pollution. They have been considered part of a *public common* available to all persons. They have been an economic externality which the business did not need to incorporate into its internal cost system. The steel-maker could use oxygen from the air for his blast furnace without paying society a penny for it, and he could also use the air as a common dumping ground for his wastes. Similarly he could draw water from the river and discharge his wastes into it without paying for this service. Society placed no economic value on these public commons. They were free goods. In this manner both the businessman and his customers avoided paying costs for degradation of the common, and these costs were transferred to society as social costs. This was not a serious problem as long as the load on the common was light, but when it became heavy, society found itself with burdensome costs that it did not care to bear. Examples of these costs are fish kill, expenses of purifying water for drinking, and eye irritation from air pollutants.

Essentially the economic situation in which business has operated is one in which it is costless to degrade the environment and expensive to stop degrading it, because the businessman has to pay for installing and operating the pollution control equipment. This gives those who continue degrading the environment an economic advantage over those who attempt to reduce degradation. It is an Alice-in-Wonderland situation in which socially undesirable acts are encouraged and socially desirable acts are penalized. What is needed is *to revise the economic cost system to make a polluting activity less rewarding than a nonpolluting activity*. This can be accomplished by such means as economic incentives, regulations and fines for noncompliance, and effluent charges and taxes, all of which will be discussed in the next chapter.

The cost system can be readily revised if society chooses to do so. *Society originally established the cost system; thus society can change it*. The main difficulty will be getting political agreement among different pluralistic interest groups and working out details.

Who Should Pay the Costs?

How shall the economic costs of cleaning the environment be allocated? This is a complex issue that involves both ethics and economics. It is reasonable to argue that those who cause environmental degradation should pay for cleaning it. Another party can argue with equal reason that those who benefit from environmental improvement should pay for it. Perhaps the most justifiable approach is to require customers to pay for pollution control costs, because in this manner they are required to pay the social costs of producing the products they use, and it has been unfair for them to pass these costs on to others in the past. The philosophy is that *a fair consumer price for a product is one which includes all costs of production without degrading the environment*. Eventually in the normal working of a social system most costs are passed on to the ultimate customer by an increase in product price and to the taxpayer through the tax system. But which customers and which taxpayers should be required to pay? There are many alternatives.

Furthermore, those who appear to pay the costs may not be paying all the costs in the economic sense of having less wealth. Consider the following example. Assume that the citizens of Massachusetts want cleaner air and vote to require power plants to use low-sulfur coal which costs more. They agree to pay higher prices for their electricity; hence it appears that they are paying the entire economic cost of the environmental improvement. However, some of the ultimate costs of clean air in Massachusetts may be borne by miners of high-sulfur coal in Pennsylvania who lose their jobs, but they neither caused the pollution nor will benefit directly from it. In turn, miners of low-sulfur coal in a Western state will benefit along with the railroad which hauls the coal, and so on. The economic effects are a complex web of interdependence.

This analysis suggests that if society gets into a debate about who should pay the costs of pollution control, it poses unanswerable questions which will surely delay action. Control of pollution should be free of the millstone of distribution of wealth. Let the wealth distribution issue be settled through other public action as it has been in the past. The most direct and workable approach for pollution control is to have those emitting pollution to pay for stopping it to the extent technically and socially reasonable, letting the costs flow through the system where they may. Exceptions should be made only when certain effects will be significantly against public policy. Government's role in this situation is to provide the goals, standards, monitoring systems, bureaucracy, and incentives necessary to achieve a clean environment with deliberate speed.

Effects on International Balance of Payments

One economic issue that arises with environmental improvement is its effect on the improving nation's international balance of payments, because costs that would not otherwise exist are added to the system. A business pays not only the capital costs of pollution control equipment but also operating costs. It also finds that pollution abatement costs of others have increased costs of materials and supplies. For example, the price paid for electricity is higher, and its higher cost is incorporated into products purchased from others. Since the business's costs are higher, its competitiveness in international markets is reduced, unless producers in other nations face similar costs. Since some nations do not require similar environmental costs, their producers will have a competitive advantage over producers from an environmentally oriented nation, assuming that all other relevant factors remain the same *(ceteris paribus)*. The result is that a producer in an environmentally oriented nation sells less internationally, which unfavorably affects his nation's international balance of payments. If the balance is already in a poor condition, this development could have serious results.

There are many mitigating factors in the relationships just described; therefore the balance-of-payments effect of pollution abatement in the United States is thought not to be a serious problem. However, difficulties could develop for certain industries. The businesses that especially might be affected are those offering products of standard quality that are produced in other nations, such as steel, copper, and chemicals. If any developments of this type threatened the national interest, the government could use subsidies or tariffs to equalize the competitive situation.

Cost/Benefit Analysis

Cost/benefit analysis needs to be applied to environmental improvement just as much as to other social issues. The process is the same as discussed in an earlier chapter. *Social costs* and *opportunity costs* must be considered along with traditional *economic costs*. Some environmental improvements may be beneficial, but they may not be beneficial enough to justify action *when all costs are considered*. Fundamentally, business seeks a social result in which benefits of all types are greater than costs of all types, as expressed by the formula $B > C$. The relation of benefits and costs is shown by the equation $B - C = G$, where B is benefits, C is costs, and G is the net gain to society. The higher the gain (G), the more socially effective a business is.

Selected costs of environmental improvement are as follows. Customers will have to pay higher prices because some of the costs of pollution control have been added. In addition, taxpayers will pay additional taxes to support such items as regulatory bureaucracies and incentives. There will also be *displacement costs* as marginal firms are put out of business by pollution control costs. Some firms and communities will be hit hard.

For example, the town of San Juan Bautista, California, has a history dating back to 1797, when it was founded as a mission settlement. In early days it was a substantial trading center, but in recent decades the population of slightly over 1,000 has been supported by a cement plant. There are no other industries nearby. When air pollution regulations were applied, the sixty-year-old cement plant was forced to close because it was too outmoded to be renovated. This action severely damaged the town's economy.

Another cost will be loss of business and personal freedoms. Business will not be able to take certain actions that it formerly took. Similarly, consumers will not be able to buy some products that were formerly available but are now considered undesirable. For example, throwaway bottles may be prohibited because they are considered a threat to the environment. The consumer then does not have the freedom to buy them and throw them away as he once could.

EFFECTS OF ENVIRONMENTAL IMPROVEMENT ON BUSINESS

When the full system effects of environmental improvement are considered, it is evident that business will be significantly affected. One certain result is that business will face more regulations from all levels of government. Involvement of government is necessary in order to establish priorities and goals and to maintain coordination toward them. A second result, caused partly by the first one, is that business will have increased costs and liabilities for environmental improvement. Air and water, which formerly were part of the public common and were relatively free resources to be used as business wished, now will be part of the internal cost system of business.

A third effect is that the business decision-making environment will become much more nebulous and difficult. Environmental problems are complex, and the participation of many pluralistic interest groups in the decision matrix will make decisions even more difficult. New decision tools and organizational units will need to be brought to the situation. New values and ways of thinking also will be involved. For example, new ecological management units will become a major influence in policy making and in operating decisions. Ecological influences will be felt in all functions and at all levels of the organization.

A fourth effect is that business will need to adjust its procedures, organizational units, and life-style in order to improve both its social inputs and outputs. Business intelligence particularly needs to become more sensitive to inputs beyond economic ones. Business's economic competence has been without peer, but sensitivity to social values has been weak.

A fifth effect is that business will find it necessary to do much more system thinking and global thinking than formerly. Businessmen cannot confine themselves strictly to economic issues, leaving ecological externalities to be considered by others. The whole ecological system and social system must be considered in a global and system way. System thinking will cause a redefinition of the traditional economic concept of profit maximization. System thinking will also require more extensive long-term planning in order to incorporate environmental complexities into business actions. For example, environmental issues often become a major factor in plant location. The day is past when a community is willing to degrade its environment in order to improve its economic base.

Business Responsibility for the Environment

The remarks in this chapter may be incorporated into a set of social responsibilities which business faces with regard to the environment. As society's major economic institution for production, it cannot ignore its responsibility for ecology. The social responsibilities of business for ecology include the following:

1. To reduce pollution to the extent that is socially and technically reasonable.

2. To design future facilities and activities for ecological harmony. Included is the obligation for innovation to create better ways to live in harmony with the environment.

3. To develop thorough ecological inputs from the social system and to respond thoughtfully to them.

In this situation society has reciprocal responsibility toward business. Society's responsibility is to work supportively and reasonably with business to accomplish the social mission of a clean environment. This is not a time for accusations, emotionality, or panic.

For example, in 1970 and 1971, public anxiety developed concerning possible damage to health from mercury poisoning. There was a scare about mercury in tuna and swordfish, and it was feared that heavy concentrations of mercury in air and water were in the ecological food chain. Commentators and scientists joined in accusing business and warning about the hazards of increased mercury in the environment. The public became alarmed, and the Food and Drug Administration took quick action by banning sales of certain fish catches.

A team of researchers sought to determine scientifically the historical trend in mercury contamination. They examined preserved human tissue dating back to 1913 and found "an extraordinary decline in mercury content" in human tissue since 1913. There was strong evidence that mercury contamination of the environment was decreasing and "presented no health hazard." The reason for the decline was believed to be a reduction in the use of coal for heating, because coal emits mercury when it is burned.[12]

SUMMARY

Ecology is concerned with the relationships of living things and their environments. As a contributor to pollution, business is involved in society's ecological crisis. Pollution has become serious because of compound growth of the Industrial Revolution, a higher standard of living, and a population explosion.

[12] Stuart Auerbach, "Mercury Not a Threat Now, Survey Finds," *Washington Post* news release in *Los Angeles Times,* Oct. 13, 1971, part II, p. 8. This study related to the general environment and not individual situations where mercury emissions were causing localized problems.

Pollution is found in all types of economic and political systems. It is not limited to one nation or social culture; therefore nations are working regionally and through the United Nations to reduce pollution.

The traditional operation of economics has tended to provide air and water as free goods to business. This system rewards degradation of the environment and penalizes businesses that seek to clean up the environment. To correct this situation, economic incentives, effluent standards, and effluent charges will be applied. Cost/benefit analysis will be used to guide decisions. Some of the effects on business will be more regulation, increased costs, more complex decisions, improved social inputs and outputs, and more system and global thinking.

STUDY GUIDES FOR INTERPRETATION OF THIS CHAPTER

1. Early New England towns had a public common usually near the center of town where people could have meetings and graze their horse or cow. The use of the common was free to all; however, as the load on the common became too heavy, its use was restricted. For example, a person would probably draw the police if he tried to graze his cow on Boston Common today. Compare the use of the New England common with current controversies about the use of air and water as a public common.

2. From current news events find examples of the complexity of the ecosystem and discuss them with your group.

3. Explain how compound growth has worked to make pollution a recent major issue.

4. Explain how economic systems work to reward those who degrade the environment and to penalize those who try to improve the environment.

5. Apply cost/benefit analysis to an ecological proposal of your own choosing, carefully listing both costs and benefits.

6. A group of militant environmentalists has proposed to the board which governs the city-owned convention center that the board deny use of any of the center's facilities to any business or business group which "contributes to ecological imbalance" of the world. The group has specifically mentioned mines, agribusiness groups, chemical firms, automobile firms, and petroleum firms. You are chairman of the governing board and vice president of a local chemical plant producing industrial chemicals. How would you respond?

PROBLEM

The Republic of Nauru[13]

The Republic of Nauru is situated on a small island of 5,263 acres in Polynesia near the equator. It is 2,600 miles southwest of Hawaii. The republic has a population of 3,304 persons. These people may be the richest in the world, and they are getting richer every day. Investment income and annual phosphate mining royalties paid to the government by the Nauru Phosphate Company, in which the British have an interest, amount to over $6,000 annually *for each Nauruan.*

Few Nauruans work because their affluence does not require labor to support their needs. The phosphate mines are worked by Polynesians from other islands. The government, except for top positions, is run by employed civil servants mostly from Australia. They are paid such high salaries by the Nauruans that the Australian government is considering a special tax on their incomes. Most other work on the island is performed by Chinese.

There is enough phosphate on the island to last another twenty-five to forty years at the present rate of mining. If mining were stopped immediately, annual investment income for every Nauruan would be $1,200 for life. Nauru has no other significant source of income, although its colorful postage stamps are popular with philatelists. There is one beach area with possibilities for tourist development. There is no port; only open sea anchorage is available. Air transportation to the island is provided by Fiji Airlines once a week and Air Micronesia every two weeks. In order for planes to land, the phosphate mining operation is shut down the day before the plane is due. If it did not shut down, clouds of dust from the mining operation would obscure the runway and prevent the plane from landing.

1. Discuss ecological problems and decisions which Nauruans will face during the next ten years. How is business involved?

2. What kinds of ecological problems will Nauruans face during the next ten to forty years? How is business involved? Discuss.

3. Compare the Nauruan's problems with the problems of all people on planet Earth.

[13] Birch Storm, "South Sea Republic of Nauru Emerges," *Honolulu Advertiser,* Dec. 8, 1969, pp. D-4, D-5. The republic's name and facts in this case are not disguised.

CHAPTER 23

CONTROLLING POLLUTION

We have discovered that we cannot throw anything away.

An ecologist

We have met the enemy and we are it.

Attributed to "Pogo" comic strip

A large power plant was built in a scenic area of the West, and since it was planned after the United States became concerned about the environment, substantial effort was made for environmental harmony. Archaeological surveys of the area were made before construction. The plant's architecture was designed to be aesthetically pleasing and blend with the environment. Measures were taken to ensure adequate noise suppression, and elaborate dust control equipment was installed to control coal dust. Hot precipitators were selected to remove fly ash from the smokestack with an efficiency of 99.5 percent, and the latest sulfur dioxide removal equipment was selected. Stack monitoring devices were installed, and nine air quality stations were established in the surrounding area to monitor air quality. The cooling system uses giant cooling towers and returns no water to the river from which it is taken. These are substantial efforts for environmental protection, but they also have substantial economic costs. Out of a total cost of approximately $800 million for the project, environmental costs were $190 million of this amount, *nearly one-fourth of the project's total cost.*

With regard to pollution it is evident that people are a principal cause of it. As stated in one of the quotations introducing this chapter, "We have met the enemy and we are it." Now we must pay the costs of environmental improvement. This chapter continues an examination of business and ecology by discussing general approaches toward control of pollution, government regulation, and control of different types of pollution.

APPROACHES TOWARD POLLUTION CONTROL

Although there are exceptions, *pollution basically arises when society's wastes begin to impair the quality of environment for living things*. Thus carbon dioxide is not normally considered a pollutant when people exhale it, because it is recycled by nature and does not impair the quality of life. Jet aircraft noise is waste from energy use, and when it is loud enough to interfere with the qualify of life, it is considered noise pollution. Natural contaminants which impair the quality of life, such as smoke and ash from a volcano, also may be called pollution.

As one of the authors approached Honolulu on a commercial flight, the pilot announced that the airplane was tenth in the "stack" awaiting landing because the airport was under ground-controlled landing conditions. The view below as one looked out the window was a deep black like a dark rainstorm viewed from above. No land was visible. Finally we moved through the blanket of black to an easy landing. Only then did we learn that the city was blanketed with "vog" (volcanic fog). A volcano on another island had a minor eruption the day before, and unusual winds had blown the suspended ash to this spot and held it there. The condition was strictly temporary and unusual. The next morning there was no trace of it; and the ash wherever it had blown, would soon be carried to the ocean in rain squalls.

A few weeks later one of the authors approached St. Louis, and the pilot made a similar announcement. The air below was a brownish black, and again no land was visible. As he descended through the brown blanket his eyes began to burn, and he knew he was in smog. On the ground the newspaper reported that this was the third day of a smog alert, and no relief was in sight for two more days.

Whether the pollution is water, air, solid waste, noise, or something else, some of it is transitory like the Honolulu vog and will soon be solved by normal ecological processes. Other pollution is man-made and tends to be more permanent or to recur frequently, unless man does something about it. Almost without exception, a preventive approach is better than a remedial approach.[1]

Pluralism in Action

Efforts toward pollution control provide an excellent example of pluralism in action, showing both its faults and strengths. There are duplicated efforts, confusion, and slow responses; but there are also wise countervailing powers, an array of

---

[1] For a more extensive discussion of pollution and pollution control, see Stahrl Edmunds and John Letey, *Environmental Administration,* New York: McGraw-Hill Book Company, 1973.

different talents and approaches, and the creativity and enthusiasm that come from active participation. Among those involved are different branches of government, professional groups such as architects, labor, business groups with different interests, conservationists, and neighborhood groups. Several approaches toward pollution control used by these groups and others will be discussed in the following paragraphs.

The Search for Technological Breakthroughs

Perhaps the most exciting approach to pollution control is the search for technological breakthroughs which turn potential pollutants into harmless or desirable by-products. As population increases and standards of living rise, man's need for power for his machines and equipment increases so dramatically that an energy crisis is developing as supplies of fossil fuels are depleted. For example, it is predicted that the entire world will use as much energy in the years from 1970 to 2000 as it did from the beginning of civilization to 1970. It is evident that sources other than fossil fuels eventually must be developed in order to prevent an energy shortage. Further, a difficulty with present use of fossil fuels is that they cause polluting by-products such as fly ash, gases, and heat. Atomic fission once was seen as the solution to most of these problems, but its by-products of thermal pollution and radiation have not been solved. Atomic fusion avoids the radiation hazard, but a workable technology seems some distance away.

The exciting ultimate source of nonpolluting energy is the sun. Its energy is enormous. For example, it is said that the sun energy falling on Lake Erie on an average day would supply the daily energy needs of the United States if the energy could be harnessed.

A University of Arizona professor has proposed solar farms consisting of solar panels covering the Arizona-California desert where there is unused land and sunshine most of the year.[2] A solar farm of 5,000 square miles (slightly over 70 miles square) could supply over 1 million megawatts of electricity, which would meet the power demands of the United States for the next 100 years. Molten salt tanks would store heat for cloudy days and night periods. The molten salt would provide heat for producing electricity in conventional ways. He believes technology exists for this kind of project, but capital costs are high and would increase the cost of electricity somewhat. The process is essentially nonpolluting.

The solar farms may be combined with another idea to use hydrogen as a carrier of energy. Hydrogen is essentially pollution-free. Its waste is water vapor which is recyclable. Further, it would be relatively simple to convert

[2] Robert L. Thomas, "New Process Could Produce Electricity, Water from Sun," *Arizona Republic,* Oct. 1, 1972, sec. L, p. 1.

vehicles, homes, and factories to use hydrogen instead of fossil fuels. Experimental hydrogen vehicles already exist. In this plan the solar power plant would produce electricity to be used by a plant to produce hydrogen from water. Then the hydrogen would be transported to the point of use by conventional vehicles and pipelines. Thus it may happen that the remote Arizona-California desert someday will supply most of the nation's energy needs including automobile fuel.

The point of this discussion is that significant technological breakthroughs are needed in order to enhance the environment. The breakthroughs may be nonconventional and develop in places where we are not looking for them. Business has a major role to play in this process because it is the principal institution by which technology is translated into useful application for society. Business innovation is expected by society.

Voluntary Business Response

Another approach to pollution control is voluntary business action to prevent pollution or remove it. Hundreds of millions of dollars annually are being invested in this way. It can be argued quite properly that business action is not wholly "voluntary," because business is responding to countervailing pressures. This is correct in many cases. Business typically recognizes pollution control as one more cost of doing business in a modern environment. As stated by one businessman, "We used to consider mostly minimum capital and maximum efficiency in our plant design, but now we have a third ingredient, pollution costs." *Capital costs* for environmental protection may be as high as 25 percent for a power plant and 10 to 15 percent for paper mills and chemical plants, but for many plants they are a more reasonable 1 to 10 percent. It is estimated that *operating costs* for effective environmental protection of the whole nation will average 1 to 5 percent of gross national product; however, costs will vary greatly among individual businesses. An example of the complexities and costs of pollution control is the experience of Mobil Oil Company with its Ferndale refinery.[3]

> To combat air pollution Mobil engineers designed many refinery units in a way that minimized emission of mist, sulfur dioxide, petroleum vapor and other chemical compounds. A special incinerator was installed to convert smelly compounds to less objectionable materials. A smokeless flare and blow-down system was provided to insure that all hydrocarbon releases were properly burned. Oil storage tanks with floating roofs were selected to minimize evaporation losses. These and more design innovations put a tight clamp on air and plant pollution.
>
> Control of water pollution turned out to be an even tougher nut to crack. . . .
>
> The men who designed Ferndale planned six separate sewer systems to handle different types of waste. Expensive—but effective. These systems separately ac-

[3] "Ferndale Refinery: Profile of a Good Neighbor," *Mobil World,* February 1965, p. 7.

commodate oil process waste, sanitary waste, phenolic process waste, normal storm drainage, emergency storm drainage and ship's ballast discharge.

"We even have educated 'bugs' to help us decontaminate the first three types of waste water" [said a process engineer].

Ferndale's bugs are fussy. Once they get accustomed to a certain concentration of phenol, they die or quit eating if served up a different diet of phenol. The waste water that goes into their tanks is, therefore, carefully controlled, and a reserve supply of sludge is always maintained just in case the main floc overeats. . . . When they're through, phenol in the water is nil.

A different type of business response is to improve a product's desirability for customers by designing improved pollution control into it, such as producing a less-polluting automobile engine or manufacturing process. However, even when the product is more desirable, if it costs more, it may have difficulty gaining acceptance until this cost is worked into the whole social structure.

Air compressors at construction sites are unpleasantly noisy, and people agree that quieter ones should be used. Ingersoll-Rand designed a quiet "Whisperized" air compressor, partly to meet requests of New York City for this type.[4] Contractors agree that the quiet compressor is a substantial improvement, but it costs 25 percent more. Unless quiet compressors are specified in construction contracts, contractors using quiet compressors are at a disadvantage in bidding on contracts, because a quiet compressor does no more work than a noisy one. The result is that broad acceptance of the product eventually will depend on city noise ordinances and the government's willingness to specify this type of product in its own contracts. Even after the product was available, the City of New York continued to order more of the noisy compressors.

A direct business approach is to design and market pollution control equipment and services. This is a standard business practice in existence for decades, and a few companies earn most of their income from this type of operation.

Countervailing Powers among Businesses

Like most other groups, businessmen do not have uniform attitudes toward the environment. Different types of business want different conditions in the environment; consequently, powerful countervailing pressures arise within business itself. For example, commercial fishermen filed a damage suit against certain chemical companies for polluting Lake Erie with mercury compounds. The fishermen wanted to make profit from their fish catches, and the chemical com-

---

[4] "The Trade-offs for a Better Environment," *Business Week,* Apr. 11, 1970, p. 66.

panies wanted an economical dumping ground for their wastes. These two goals finally came into conflict, and so the fishermen instituted countervailing pressures through the legal system. In another instance, a large chemical plant wanted to build near an area that real estate developers believed was prime residential land, and so the latter used publicity to build enough opposition to block the necessary zoning permit for the plant.

Since most of these cases involve pressures rather than legal rights, the outcome can go either way. However, with society's strong interest in pollution control, the business group which takes action against a polluter or potential polluter has a powerful ally in the form of public opinion. Therefore, the antipollution group is the typical winner, and this is encouraging an occasional business to take action against its polluting neighbor. The general conclusion is that if the public will give strong support, some business groups with antipollution interests may prevail upon other businesses to reduce their pollution beyond the minimum required by law.

Conservationists

Strong allies in any drive for a cleaner earth are the conservationists, such as fishermen, campers, boating enthusiasts, and nature lovers in general. The largest and most influential of these, and one of the most militant, is the Sierra Club. It has worked to save redwood forests and block the building of dams in the Grand Canyon of the Colorado River. It has lobbied against the supersonic transport (SST), because of possible noise pollution and ecological damage from its supersonic shock waves. The club also has initiated legal actions to prevent construction of a pulp mill in Alaska, to stop a mining company from dumping taconite tailings into Lake Superior, to prevent a six-lane expressway along the banks of the Hudson River, and to stop construction of a ski resort in California.

A major difficulty with conservation groups is their singular interest in almost a pure, pristine, back-to-nature environment. Through legal actions they may bring long delays in projects which, on balance, are needed social improvements. These kinds of delays have already prevented necessary power plant construction, leading to power brownouts in various parts of the United States.

ROLE OF GOVERNMENT

Government cannot watch all of us to determine whether we toss our candy wrappers into the gutter, but certainly it has a major role in pollution control. In terms of functional analysis, it has strong capabilities for setting priorities, general policies, and minimum standards for environmental quality. It also can provide economic incentives to encourage businesses, communities, and regions to reduce pollution, and it can offer just legal and administrative systems for resolving disputes about pollution.

Often businessmen favor government standards because they realize that a cleaner environment can be accomplished only by joint action of all firms. If only one firm acts to reduce pollution, the environmental improvement may not be evident, and the remaining pollution will continue to give even the nonpolluting firm a poor public image. Further, the nonpolluting firm will have a competitive disadvantage because of the cost of its control equipment. Clearly this is a situation requiring government standards.

Regulation is needed by various levels of government. For example, air moves freely. Regulation in the corporate limits of one city will not stop pollution; therefore, the national government found it necessary to establish standards for air quality. Eventually, international standards may be established. On the other hand, since each region's air pollution problem is different, national minimum standards should not preempt the authority of states, regions, or communities to set more stringent standards within the bounds of reason to meet local needs.

Administrative Controls

In 1970 a three-man Council on Environmental Quality was established by law within the executive office of the President. The law is similar to the one creating the Council of Economic Advisers in 1946. The 1970 law declares that it is the policy of the United States to use all practicable means to maintain conditions of productive harmony between man and nature and to fulfill the social, economic, and other requirements of the people. The principal duties of the Council are (1) to assist and advise the President in preparation of an annual report on environmental quality, (2) to develop and recommend national policies which promote environmental quality, (3) to accumulate data for continuing analysis of trends in the national environment, and (4) to interpret and apply certain environmental acts of Congress.

As various environmental laws are passed by Congress, an administrative bureaucracy is established to interpret and apply them, such as the Environmental Protection Agency (EPA). Generally an act of Congress states only broad, general guidelines for control. Someone must interpret and apply these guidelines, and that task usually falls upon an administrative bureaucracy. In the American system it is this administrative group which actually applies the law and determines whether it will be a success or failure.

Ways of Applying Government Controls

Government will apply pollution controls in a variety of ways, because the situation is too complex for just one approach to work. In order to cover different pollutants, kinds of pollution sources, economic conditions, and technological features, government will need to use its full arsenal of "social motivators" for environmental improvement. Following are the principal approaches that may be used.

1. Legislative standards enforceable in courts of law

2. Administrative boards which may set standards enforceable in courts of law

3. Zoning and other regulations which require new construction or new products to meet certain pollution standards (such as waste discharge of new plants or exhaust emissions of new automobiles)

4. Tax incentives for pollution control equipment (such as faster depreciation or tax credits)

5. Matching grants or subsidies for installation and operation of pollution control equipment

6. Monitoring, research, and investigative bodies which make reports, recommend legislation, and use the pressures of publicity (such as the Council on Environmental Quality)

7. Denial of government contracts and other privileges to violators (or perhaps granting privileges to nonpolluters, similar to veterans' preference in government employment)

8. Research grants for development of new control methods, and demonstration grants to test them in service

9. Effluent charges for pollution emissions (such as a certain number of dollars for each ton of noxious fumes from a smokestack or each gallon of a chemical waste dumped into a river)

The regulatory approaches which appear to be used most often are incentives, environmental standards, and effluent charges. These will be discussed in more detail.

Incentives for Environmental Improvement

The government may offer various types of incentives to those firms which reduce pollution. Sometimes these incentives work toward standards that may eventually be required. At other times they work for any improvement. For example, the government may decide to purchase only from those firms that meet certain pollution standards, or it may offer matching grants to those that install pollution control equipment.

The major advantage of incentives is that they encourage voluntary improvement without the stigma of governmental force. They allow different indus-

Society Needs to Control the Cause of Pollution, Not Its Symptoms

The cause of pollution problems is simple: polluting activities which impose costs on society do not bear these costs. This basic cause has produced many symptoms: nobody bothers to make control technology available or to use what is available; consumers make little effort to consume less pollution-intensive goods and services. Most public policies have concentrated on trying to eliminate the symptoms by supporting technological development, trying to force the use of control devices, encouraging or coercing consumers to consume differently. As with all policies which attack only the obvious symptoms while leaving the basic causes unchanged, these policies have had and will continue to have disappointing results. If we want to solve pollution problems we must design policies which eliminate the cause of pollution problems, i.e., which make pollution about as expensive to those who produce it as it is to those who suffer it.

From Larry E. Ruff, "Who Should Pay the Pollution Bill?" in George A. Steiner (ed.), *Selected Major Issues in Business' Role in Modern Society*, Los Angeles: University of California, Graduate School of Management, 1973, p. 191.

tries and businesses to proceed at the pace which is best for their individual situation. Further, some business may be encouraged by incentives to go beyond the minimum standards of compliance that a regulation would have been able to achieve. The main disadvantage of incentives is that what is voluntary may not be accomplished at all.

A unique incentive is a government agency for waste treatment. For example, the Texas legislature established the public Gulf Coast Waste Disposal Authority for treatment of industrial wastes.[5] Five companies originally chose to use the project, paying a proportionate fee for treatment of their wastes. The incentive is the saving in waste disposal, usually from 10 to 25 percent. Savings result from a variety of reasons. Being a public agency, the plant pays no property taxes, and it secures its capital at a lower rate of interest. It also secures economies of scale from its large size. Perhaps the most unusual advantage is that some of the chemical wastes from different plants help to neutralize each other, such as acidic waste coming from one plant and alkaline waste from another.

Environmental Standards

Another type of pollution control is environmental standards. These standards are established by legislative action and applied by administrative agencies and courts. One type of standard is an *effluent standard*. For example, the law may

[5] "A Water Treatment Plant That Cuts Clean-up Costs," *Business Week*, Mar. 3, 1973, p. 45.

specify that the permissible release of fly ash from a smokestack is 1 percent of the ash available. Then each business is required to install fly-ash control equipment that removes at least 99 percent of the fly ash. Even more effective equipment could be used, but it would not be required by law.

A second type of standard is an *environmental quality standard*. In this instance the specified environment is permitted to have only a certain amount or proportion of pollution, such as a certain proportion of sulfur dioxide in the air. Polluting sources are required to control their effluent to maintain the standard. This approach has been applied against mineral smelters for control of sulfur dioxide in isolated locations. This means that when weather conditions are such that the air is quiet and not dispersing pollutants, the smelter may be required to reduce its emissions. Then when weather is more favorable, more emissions may be released, because they are more widely dispersed and the air standard is maintained. Environmentalists strongly object to this approach because it appears to encourage pollution up to the limits permissible.

An advantage of environmental standards is that they are enforceable in the courts; therefore, there is greater assurance that their requirements will be met than through the use of incentives which are voluntary. Further, they are usually across-the-board standards applicable to all, and so general compliance in society is assured. A disadvantage is that in order to apply the standard to all businesses fairly, the lawmakers may so water down the standard and fill it with exceptions that it is not effective. A further disadvantage is that the law is only as good as the administrative agency enforcing it. A number of sound laws have been weakened by poor administration. Another disadvantage is that across-the-board standards may cause inequity and suffering because each business faces a different pollution control problem. Older, less efficient plants especially face problems because it is costly to renovate them, and a new nonpolluting plant may not be justified because of capital costs or market conditions.

When environmental standards were applied in a Western state, two paper mills in one city announced within a period of two weeks that they were closing. Both mills blamed the environmental standards for their actions. One mill had been in the town eighty years, and its old equipment was not suitable for renovation. It employed 750 workers with a payroll of $6 million annually. The other mill employed over 300 workers. The loss of more than 1,000 jobs was a blow to the community. Even though society may have been better off because of this action, there was human suffering locally.

Effluent Charges

Another type of pollution control is establishment of *effluent charges*. Each business pays fees for the quantity of undesirable waste that it releases, and the fee varies with the amount of waste released. The result is, "The more you pollute, the more you pay.'' For example, one type of effluent charge is a fee for the amount of biological oxygen demand (BOD) which effluents place on waterways. Biological oxygen demand is a major cause of water deterioration; thus it is a common denominator that can be applied to many wastes.

Effluent charges are based on the proposition that market mechanisms are a better form of control than extensive standards with the large enforcement bureaucracy which they require. Sufficiently high charges must be put on pollution to discourage its release. Then each firm is allowed to work out its own least-cost relationship for waste release or abatement according to its own special set of circumstances.

A favorable feature of effluent charges is that they place the cost burden of pollution directly on the polluter. The social costs associated with pollution are internalized within the firm's accounting system. No longer are these costs an economic externality to the firm. Another feature is that because costs are internalized in the firm, it is encouraged to do more than meet minimum standards. Each firm can go as far as economically feasible, perhaps even to zero pollution, because there is a continuing economic incentive to lower pollution amounts further. On the other hand, when environmental standards are used, the polluter's motivation tends to be different. Once pollution standards are met, there is no incentive for additional reductions.

Another favorable feature of effluent charges is that they allow each firm to have different levels of pollution according to its own best least-cost combination, thus achieving efficient performance. An additional feature of some importance is that the charges provide substantial government funds for cleaning up the environment. It is also thought that effluent charges are easy to administer and can be implemented more quickly than standards which often require lengthy court proceedings for enforcement. For the reasons given, environmental groups which once uniformly opposed effluent charges now tend to support them.

The principal disadvantage of effluent charges is expressed by critics as ''a license to pollute.'' It does not seem consistent with environmental philosophy to allow people to pollute even when they pay a charge for doing so. Further, some critics fear that charges will be so low that present polluters will continue. Another disadvantage is that for some types of pollutants it may be difficult to compute charges, and so this approach may not be effective.

TYPES OF POLLUTION AND THEIR CONTROL
Water Pollution

Clean water historically has been a substantial concern of citizens of the United States as shown by the Federal Refuse Act of 1899. The law allowed fines of $2,500 for each day or incident of discharging wastes into a navigable stream without a permit from the Corps of Engineers. An interesting part of the law is that it granted the reporting individual a bounty of one-half the fine. If the government failed to prosecute, the citizen could sue the violator in the name of the United States and collect the bounty. Perhaps if this law had been better known to citizens and enforced by government, water pollution would not have become the problem that it has.

Water pollution in the United States is mostly caused by municipal, industrial, and farm wastes. It is controlled by the Federal Water Pollution Control Act of 1972 (Clean Water Act). The law requires all parties that discharge wastes into any waterway to apply for a permit. In this application they must state the amount and nature of their pollutants. Permits may be granted subject to certain deadlines in the law, as shown in Figure 23-1. By July 1, 1977, each company is required to apply the "best practicable" control technology in its pollution abatement. "Best practicable" has been defined as the level of control achieved by the least-polluting plants in a given industry. By July 1, 1983, companies are required to install the "best available" control technology, which means that the most-advanced waste control system should become the standard for all plants in an industry.

The Clean Water Act calls for "zero discharge" of pollutants by 1985, although this is a goal rather than an enforceable standard. Based upon experience with the law, Congress will reconsider this goal at a later date. Zero discharge appears to be technologically feasible in most instances, but the costs may be prohibitive and an unwise use of social resources as long as other pressing needs exist. A major purpose of the zero discharge goal is to encourage firms to move to closed-loop water control systems which recycle waste water. In a closed-loop system firms are required to treat their water only to the extent necessary for their own production processes.

Once pollution is reduced, waterways tend to renew themselves through natural processes. In Oregon a state Department of Environmental Quality sought to restore the Willamette River, which was reputed to be the most polluted river in the Pacific Northwest.[6] Strict enforcement of state laws with public support achieved a 90 percent reduction in pollution in five

Date	Control Technology Required
July 1, 1977	Best practicable
July 1, 1983	Best available
1985	Zero discharge

Fig. 23-1 Timetable for Deadlines, Clean Water Act of 1972.

[6] James E. Bylin, "Rescue of a River," *Wall Street Journal* (Pacific Coast edition), Oct. 25, 1972, pp. 1 and 14.

years. The improvement allowed swimming again and permitted spawning of salmon for the first time in many decades. Cost of the improvement was $150 million for municipal sewage facilities and $50 million for industries.

Air Pollution

Air pollution in most parts of the United States is primarily caused by automobiles, but in a few areas industry is the major cause. Of all forms of pollution it is the one which reaches the most people and has caused the most political ferment. Air pollution is regulated by the National Air Quality Standards Act of 1970 (Clean Air Act). The law requires the Environmental Protection Agency to set nationwide air quality standards for ten major pollutants. Then states translate the federal standards into local standards subject to general supervision of the EPA. Violators are subject to fines of $25,000 daily and/or a year in jail. The law also requires new factories to use the latest pollution control technology. In most instances the technology for zero discharge into the air does not exist in the manner it does for water wastes.

Automobile emissions are controlled by the Clean Air Act requiring manufacturers to reduce exhaust emissions for hydrocarbons, carbon monoxide, and nitrogen oxides.

Solid Waste Pollution

Solid wastes are more of a state and local problem, because they do not normally move in interstate commerce; however, the federal government plays some role in solid waste control through the Solid Wastes Act. In its industrial processes, business produces solid wastes such as mine tailings, but its primary role in solid wastes is as a producer of material goods which are later discarded by the user. Critics have charged that the design of packaging does not consider its effect on ecology. For example, glass is not biodegradable. When it is used as a throwaway container, it becomes a long-run blight on the environment. Should government require business to use only returnable bottles, and should it control the price of the deposit on the bottles to assure their return for recycling? Business argues that costs would increase and people would be inconvenienced. Critics argue that recycling products of this type reduces environmental deterioration. Further, city garbage has so many throwaways that it has been called urban ore. Critics have challenged business either to develop ways "to mine" this ore profitably or to reduce drastically container throwaways. Waste paper is biodegradable, but there are nevertheless benefits from recycling it because each reused ton of paper saves cutting more than fifteen trees.

458 BUSINESS AND THE COMMUNITY

Solid Waste Control Is a Management Problem

Solid waste management differs greatly from air pollution and water pollution control. Solid waste disposal involves the *management* of moving, placing, and processing waste, rather than disposing, although the latter term is commonly used in referring to waste. When an air pollution control officer enforces an air pollution requirement against industry, it is likely that the industry will convert the air pollutant into a solid waste. The same is true of the water polluters—to meet pollution regulations, the wastes that are dispersed in water become solid waste. This means that environmental protection and improvement creates a problem for solid waste management of staggering magnitude. For every American, one ton of solid waste is produced annually—or about 200 million tons for the nation each year. (These figures exclude agricultural and mining wastes, which far exceed all other solid waste in quantity.) At a cost of about thirty dollars per ton, including all the costs of storage, transportation, processing, and disposal, we've got a six billion dollar industry. It's the third most expensive public service after schools and highways.

From Frank R. Bowerman, "Managing Solid Waste Disposal," *California Management Review,* Spring 1972, p. 104. Reprinted with permission.

Noise Pollution

Business is a major cause of noise pollution. There is increasing evidence that loud noise is detrimental to people. For example, one study suggests that there may be a positive association between loud sound exposure and illness.[7] Another study found that men who worked in noisy conditions were more aggressive and distrustful than similar employees who worked in quieter circumstances. They had more problems with their supervisors, and they appeared to carry their attitudes home, because they had more than twice as many family problems.[8] Another study found that children living in residences exposed to louder street noises for as long as four years had lower reading achievement.[9] There is also evidence of decline in auditory discrimination, lower tolerance of frustration, and other difficulties.

Because of the dangers of noise pollution, the Federal Occupational Safety and Health Act of 1970 regulates it for manufacturers in interstate commerce. The law requires that the loudest continuous noise to which an employee may be exposed for an entire workday is 90 decibels. Fines may be as high as $1,000 each

[7] Paul Cameron, Donald Robertson, and Jeffrey Zaks, "Sound Pollution, Noise Pollution, and Health: Community Parameters," *Journal of Applied Psychology,* February 1972, pp. 67–74.
[8] Theodore Berland, "Bbrrreeeeeeuuuuuuaaaaaaggghhhh! Clatter, Rattle, Whirr . . . Boom!" *Smithsonian,* July 1972, p. 17.
[9] David C. Glass, Sheldon Cohen, and Jerome E. Singer, "Urban Din Fogs the Brain," *Psychology Today,* May 1973, pp. 94–99.

day. The government also controls aircraft noise through Federal Aviation Administration regulations.

BASIC IDEAS ABOUT ENVIRONMENTAL IMPROVEMENT

In concluding these two chapters on environmental improvement, it may be helpful to review some of the more fundamental ideas developed.

1. *Quality of life.* People insist on a higher environmental quality of life. This idea affirms the right of human habitation and comfort as ranking above material needs and industrial processes. Perhaps this kind of demand is a luxury arising from an affluent society, but in any case the United States and some other nations now have affluence.

2. *Ecology.* Mankind's activities need to be kept in harmony with nature in order not to threaten the long-run existence of the human race.

3. *Complexity.* Ecological problems exist in a complex system. There is no easy solution. There is no economical solution. Since there are many unknowns in the situation, a variety of approaches and the best of man's creative talents are required. Research needs to precede action whenever possible, as the following incident illustrates.[10]

Kaneohe Bay is an ocean jewel nestled against green hills on Hawaii's windward coast. It is surrounded by small boat docks and the town of Kaneohe. Concern gradually arose among citizens that the bay was becoming polluted by wastes from boats and homes, along with commercial and residential sewage released into the bay after processing. When most of the clams in the bay suddenly died, the people became alarmed, and a government-financed ecological study of the bay was initiated.

With the aid of $90,000, twenty-three scientists, and one year of research, the study concluded that ecological conditions of the bay were in "exact balance." That is, organic matter (including sewage) going into the bay was consumed as fast as it entered; hence, the organic matter was needed to supply the large amount of sea life in the bay. The only spot where the water did not meet the state's stringent water standards was directly over the main sewer outfall. (Since large population increases could upset the existing ecological balance, periodic future studies were recommended.)

Then what killed the clams? Research disclosed that they were

[10] Claude Burgett, "Water Pollution Study Finds Kaneohe Bay in 'Exact Balance,' " *Honolulu Star-Bulletin,* July 19, 1969, pp. 1, A-7.

killed by a prolonged rainstorm which flooded the bay with so much fresh water that clams could not survive in the less-saline water. Human wastes had nothing to do with their death.

4. *Social costs*. Air and water are no longer free public goods. The user now must pay for his effect on them. A fair price to the consumer for a product is one which includes all costs of production without degrading the environment.

5. *Mutual cooperation*. Environmental problems are so large that they require the cooperation of all segments of a pluralistic society. The task requires the resources and expertise of the entire society.

6. *International cooperation*. Since ecological difficulties are worldwide, international cooperation regionally and within the United Nations is required.

7. *Cost/benefit analysis*. For effective environmental decisions, cost/benefit analysis is required.

8. *Government's role*. Government has the substantial role of determining priorities, policies, and standards for pollution control.

SUMMARY

Pollution basically arises when society's wastes begin to impair the quality of the environment for living things. Technological breakthroughs, government regulation, and other approaches are being applied to reduce it. The role of government is primarily that of setting priorities, policies, and standards. The regulatory approaches used most often are incentives, environmental standards, and effluent charges. The Environmental Protection Agency is the chief regulatory arm of government. Pollution of water and air, solid waste pollution, and noise pollution are the main areas regulated. Society expects a better quality of life, and business has a responsibility to help satisfy this need.

STUDY GUIDES FOR INTERPRETATION OF THIS CHAPTER

1. Study news releases concerning actions of the Environmental Protection Agency. Then give your interpretation of the Agency's effectiveness.

2. Study information about noise pollution, including its possible effects on health and human comfort, and report your conclusions.

3. Discuss the advantages and disadvantages of effluent charges for pollution control compared with incentives and environmental standards.

4.   Discuss current enforcement of the Clean Air Act.

5.   Develop arguments for and against prohibiting businessmen from marketing throwaway glass containers.

PROBLEMS
"They Can't Put Us Out of Business"

The manager of a metalworking firm in a city of 50,000 persons has defied pressures by various groups to stop his factory's minor pollution of a river which runs through the town. His firm is complying with all existing pollution control laws. He commented, "Pollution control is money down the drain, because it adds nothing to the product. All you get is a little local goodwill, and we sell our products nationally. They know they can't put us out of business, because we employ 1,500 people in this plant."

Investigation shows that available control equipment will cost $50,000 for installation and $15,000 annually for operating expenses.

1.   You are president of one of three other major employers in the town, and you believe that you have considerable influence with the manager of the metal-working firm. Your firm releases no pollutants into the river. Pollutants from your firm's smokestacks are moderately controlled, but better equipment appears to be available. Your firm's products are sold nationally and are not in competition with those of the metalworking firm. What would you do, if anything?

2.   Assume you are a banker who is president of the local chamber of commerce. The metalworking firm has its account in your bank. What would you do, if anything, in your role as president of the chamber of commerce?

The Mount Ida Minerals Company

The state board of health in a Western state, after a public hearing, issued regulations for sulfur dioxide emissions from mineral smelters. The regulations were considerably more stringent than federal air standards, because of strong public pressures for clean air in this scenic state. Following release of the regulations, the president of Mount Ida Minerals Company announced that the firm's antiquated East Mountain smelter could not meet the new regulations and asked for a hearing. The firm operated another smelter in the state and had plants throughout the world. In the hearing the general manager of the smelter testified that costs of meeting state standards would be $75 million but that federal standards could be met for $12 million. If the smelter were required to meet state standards, it could not do so economically and would have to close. About 2,000 workers would be put out of jobs, because the company was not expanding in other locations and could not absorb most of them. Perhaps 1,000 could be absorbed in three years when a smelter opened at a new mine 300 miles away in another state.

The general manager said that the smelter could operate indefinitely under federal standards, probably for several decades until the ore was exhausted. He requested that in any case the smelter be given a conditional permit to operate for three more years until the new smelter in another state was opened. He also argued strongly for an extension of time beyond the three-year period, and to support his argument, he presented a picture of severe hardship in the small smelter community if the smelter were required to close. He said that the firm would comply with federal standards but should be exempted by a "grandfather clause" from more stringent regulations because they were not economically justified.

When the board of health consulted with scientists, their expert opinion was that it would be economically unfeasible to operate the smelter under the more stringent state regulations. A public debate developed in which a number of prominent citizens in the state published a newspaper advertisement supporting the company.

1. Analyze the interests of different pluralistic groups in this controversy.

2. You are president of a major manufacturing firm in the state. Business associates have asked you to sign an advertisement supporting the company. What would you do? If you did agree to sign, would you allow your company name to be used in the advertisement?

3. As president of a firm which operates a competitive smelter in the state which is complying with the stringent state regulations, what would you do, if anything?

PART 5

BUSINESS IN AN INTERNATIONAL WORLD

THE SOCIAL RESPONSE OF MULTINATIONAL BUSINESS

> *Essentially, then, the multinational corporation may be viewed as a powerful engine for diffusing the benefits of superior management and technology across national boundaries. . . .*
>
> **Emile Benoit**[1]

> *The idea is gaining acceptance that multinational industry is perhaps a more stabilizing factor than government in international relations.*
>
> **Daniel Parker**[2]

Nations of the world as a matter of national policy are seeking to improve their social and economic development. Multinational business has a significant and perhaps leading role in achieving these social goals. The people have needs. Business has the know-how and resources to meet these needs and perhaps to improve international cooperation at the same time.

Some years ago a soft drink bottler entered a nation which was just beginning its development.[3] At that time the society was quite poor and almost wholly agrarian. Even bottles and wooden bottle cases had to be imported, but the company quickly started working with nationals of this country who were community leaders to develop local supplies and services related to its business. To secure a bottle-making facility, it helped these nationals organize a company, gave them a large order, helped them construct their plant, and advanced working capital to them. This glass-making facility now employs hundreds of people, and the nation's glass container needs are served wholly by domestic ownership and management.

The bottler translated its truck maintenance manuals into the local language and taught a local truck operator how to maintain its trucks, which

[1] Emile Benoit, "The Attack on the Multinationals," *Columbia Journal of World Business,* November–December 1972, p. 22.

[2] Daniel Parker, "To Improve the Conditions of Life for Everyone Everywhere," *Columbia Journal of World Business,* July–August 1968, p. 22.

[3] J. Paul Austin, "The Management of Abundance," *Advanced Management Journal,* January 1968, pp. 9–10.

at the same time helped him extend the life of his own equipment. His facility has now grown into a large automotive body works and maintenance business.

Other citizens were encouraged to make wooden crates for bottles and metal coolers for keeping drinks iced. Each later became a large factory owned and managed by citizens of the country. In this manner the multinational bottler helped others serve human needs while it fulfilled its own goals of providing low-cost soft drinks for masses of people.

Based upon universal needs for development and the rising aspirations of people, modern business relationships have become worldwide. Expansion beyond national boundaries is much more than a step across a geographical line. It is also a step into different social, educational, political, and economic environments. Supply lines are lengthened, and control becomes more difficult. It is hard enough to run a business in one language and one culture, but when there are two, three, four, five—or seventy—languages and cultures, difficulties are compounded. Complex businesses of this type push men's organizational skills to their limits. The best of men's intellectual capacities and goodwill is called upon in order to make those organizations workable.

In the next two chapters we shall explore the international environment as it affects business, and vice versa. In the current chapter we discuss the nature of multinational business and the responses it is making to international needs. Then we discuss some of the major environmental constraints on business and relate them to a Law of Persistent Underdevelopment.

MULTINATIONAL ENTERPRISE

The people of the world are organized into communities and nations, each in its own way according to its resources and cultural heritage. There are similarities among nations, but there are also significant differences which define the boundaries of business practice in each nation. Some nations have a customer-oriented economy, while others have a centrally planned economy, and there are various shades of practice in between. Some are economically developed, but others are just now developing. Some are political dictatorships; others are more democratic. Some are socially advanced, while others have minimum literacy and social development. And in each case the managerial conditions of work are different because of different expectations from participants.

Development of Multinational Enterprise

In an attempt to meet worldwide social needs, the traditional international business is changing into multinational enterprise. The traditional "international business'' has been a predominantly national company which also operates in a limited way in a few other nations, such as having a mine, processing plant, or shipping office in another nation. This type of company viewed only one nation as its major area of operations, and it looked to that nation to provide its capital, markets, and even legal system for security and justice. It was *ethnocentric* in the sense that its standards were based upon its home nation's customs, markets, and laws.

The traditional international business is now becoming outmoded because developments in areas such as technology and communication have created an interconnected, worldwide social system. There are worldwide capital and market needs, and an ever-increasing flow of tourists and others among nations. People today are less inclined to accept the restrictive economic and export policies of self-centered nations. As a consequence, the world's largest businesses need to operate multinationally with their full line of services in order to remain viable.

This more modern type of international business is typically known as *multinational enterprise* because it is truly multinational in its markets, sources of managers, communication flow, and other activities. Since it centers upon the world as its area of operations, it is *geocentric* in its outlook, as shown in Figure 24-1. This figure can be interpreted as showing the headquarters orientation of a firm as it moves from traditional ethnocentricism to polycentric attitudes and eventually to a multinational, geocentric outlook. The ethnocentric attitude is represented by the statement, ''These managerial practices work in our nation; therefore, they are also best for your nation.'' It says, ''We will supply the leadership and management, but we can use the foreign nationals to do the more routine work.''

The multinational, geocentric attitude, on the other hand, recognizes that practices must be adapted to different cultures, but it still maintains worldwide identity and policies for the firm. It develops leadership among all nationals and truly seeks to use the best people for all jobs regardless of their country of origin.

Forms of Multinational Enterprise

Different forms of multinational enterprise are being explored in order to achieve better adjustment to the variety of business conditions in other nations. Since nations do feel concern about direct foreign investment, some firms are adopting a policy which shares ownership with host countries. The firms establish joint ventures or other arrangements which have substantial local ownership, even more than 50 percent. Then the business is looked upon not as an intruder but as a part of the host country's business system.

A variation is to acquire overseas subsidiaries in exchange for stock in the central corporation. Nationals then become multinational *owners,* reaping dividend benefits based upon the whole business's success internationally. This approach is rather different from that of having nationals share ownership in the

Organization Design	Ethnocentric	Polycentric	Geocentric
Complexity of organization	Complex in home country; simple in subsidiaries	Varied and independent	Increasingly complex and interdependent
Authority; decision making	High in head-quarters	Relatively low in headquarters	Aim for a collaborative approach between headquarters and subsidiaries
Evaluation and control	Home standards applied for persons and performance	Determined locally	Find standards which are universal and local
Rewards and punishments; incentives	High in head-quarters; low in subsidiaries	Wide variation; can be high or low rewards for subsidiary performance	International and local executives rewarded for reaching local and worldwide objectives
Communication; information flow	High volume to subsidiaries: orders, commands, advice	Little to and from head-quarters. Little between subsidiaries	Both ways and between subsidiaries. Heads of subsidiaries part of management team
Identification	Nationality of owner	Nationality of host country	Truly international company but identifying with national interests
Perpetuation (recruiting, staffing, development)	Recruit and develop people of home country for key positions everywhere in the world	Develop people of local nationality for key positions in their own country	Develop best men everywhere in the world for key positions everywhere in the world

Figure 24-1 Three types of headquarters orientation toward subsidiaries in an international enterprise. From Howard V. Perlmutter, "The Tortuous Evolution of the Multinational Corporation," *Columbia Journal of World Business*, January–February 1969, p. 12. Used with permission.

success of the subsidiary alone. A subsidiary could fail or be manipulated by the persons who control it, but multinational stock ownership brings to owners the full security of the whole company. It is likely that multinational ownership of businesses will continue to grow.

The multinational enterprise which comes closer to an ideal form is one with truly diversified ownership, management, markets, and operations, without domination of any of the four features by one nation. Its managers look at the world as an operating unit, and they are capable of managing in more than one culture. Nestlé International (Nestlé Alimentana S.A.) is an example of a firm that has

Multinational Firms Are Major World Forces

A random selection of facts about world trade:

- Of the 120 largest industrial corporations in Belgium, 48 are controlled partly or wholly from abroad. And it is forecast that in a few years one of every five Belgian manufacturing workers will work for a foreign—and probably American —company.

- German corporations now have more capital invested in South Carolina than anywhere else in the world except Germany. (The investment is in chemical and textile plants.)

- Some 90% of Europe's production of microcircuits is controlled by American companies.

- Switzerland's largest corporation, Nestle Alimentana S.A., does 98% of its business outside Switzerland.

- If a corporation's sales were to be equated with a nation's output of goods and services, then 51 of the world's 100 biggest money powers would be international corporations and only 49 would be countries.

From Charles N. Stabler, "Multinational Firms Now Dominate Much of World's Production," *Wall Street Journal* (Pacific Coast edition), Apr. 18, 1973, p. 1. Reprinted with permission of *The Wall Street Journal.* © 1973 Dow Jones & Company, Inc. All rights reserved.

become multinational. It sells in most nations and manufactures in many. In addition, its managers and shareholders are from many nations.

Supranational Enterprise

Perhaps a further development will be the *supranational enterprise*. It is a worldwide enterprise charted by a substantially nonpolitical international body such as the International Monetary Fund or the World Bank. It operates as a private business without direct national obligations. Its function is international business service, and it remains viable only by performing that service adequately for nations which permit its entry. With its integrative view, it should be able to draw the economic world closer together. It could serve all nations without being especially attached to any one of them. Because of its independence of any nation and its universal outlook, it is also called the extranational enterprise, the "geocorp," and the "cosmocorp." Somewhat related supranational organizations outside the business area are the International Red Cross, religious bodies, and scientific associations.

This kind of organization may sound ideal, but it does have limitations. It is still an outsider to any nation, and it probably will be dominated by people from certain nations compared with others. It will be essentially sovereign unto itself with little direct control by persons other than its management cadre and its board of governors. Would it really be more responsible and responsive to human needs than modern forms of multinational enterprise?

THE RESPONSE OF MULTINATIONAL BUSINESS TO HUMAN NEEDS
Benefits Brought by Multinational Companies

Multinational firms can bring a number of benefits that improve the quality of life for a host nation, particularly a less-developed nation. Two of the most significant benefits are access to worldwide markets so that the host nation may produce for a larger market, and broader access to capital which may be in short supply in the host nation. They also help transfer advanced technology among nations so that all can share in the latest technology. This benefit is especially useful when a multinational firm transfers advanced technology to a less-developed nation. The multinational firm also can introduce economies of scale in research and development as well as other functions. In this manner ideas and techniques that otherwise would not be available can be used by a small branch in a host nation.

One significant benefit that frequently occurs is to encourage development of more locally owned progressive businesses. Usually when a firm moves into a host nation, particularly a less-developed one, it requires a large number of supplies and services that are not economically feasible to import, so local business is encouraged to provide them. Some multinational firms go even further and have a conscious policy of encouraging local business development.

Sears, Roebuck and Company is an example of a multinational firm which actively encourages development of local suppliers. Sears's program has been especially successful in Latin America, leading to the establishment and growth of hundreds of companies. In the beginning, Sears could purchase within a nation only a small percentage of the merchandise it sold there, but after a few years in Latin American nations, such as Mexico and Brazil, over 90 percent of its merchandise was produced within the nation.

With regard to benefits for labor, a multinational firm provides additional jobs for employment of any surplus labor which a nation has. It also provides additional training for labor, and in the case of less-developed nations it tends to upgrade skills of the host nation's labor force.

Normally a multinational firm provides wider access to high-quality managerial talent that tends to be scarce in many nations of the world. It can bring managers from various parts of the world in order to provide effective leadership for a local branch. Incoming managers bring in fresh ideas and techniques so that the host nation's capabilities are broadened. Further, multinational businesses have been world leaders in developing a better quality of management because they need it for their complex operations. One of the most successful multinational management development programs is IMEDE (the Institut pour l'Etude des Methodes de Direction de l'Entreprise) in Lausanne, Switzerland. It is a Swiss foundation established in 1957 by Nestlé International in cooperation with the University of Lausanne, and its purpose is to develop top-level multinational managers.

A similar program is the European Center for Permanent Education. Convinced of a need to develop multinational executive teams that can work in a wide variety of international cultures, several large European enterprises joined to form the European Center for Permanent Education (Centre European d'Education Permanente, called CEDEP) in Fontainebleau, France, in 1971. Managers from a variety of nations with different social and economic conditions are brought together for mutual study of management practices under different environmental conditions. This joint study among different nationals helps weld together a truly multinational management cadre for each firm and perhaps at the same time helps build better international relationships.

Another possible benefit of multinational firms is that they may provide consumers with better access to products. They can do this by introducing a new product such as a television set not formerly available, or by improving availability of a product such as a type of automobile that had been scarce because of import difficulties. If a multinational firm is able to improve efficiency in a host nation, this condition often leads to lower-cost products for local consumers. If a multinational firm makes products for export, this tends to contribute favorably to the international balance of payments in the host nation. In any case a multinational firm provides taxes and other resources for public improvements, although this benefit may be offset by the additional load that the firm places on public services such as police protection and public roads.

One further benefit of multinational business is its encouragement of world economic unity which may, in turn, lead to social and political integration and encourage world harmony. People have tended to look to governments, religious bodies, and philosophers for improvement in world cooperation. Are they overlooking another strong ally—business? Multinational business thinks globally. Its effectiveness depends on rational cooperation and the honoring of agreements. It requires stable political systems in order to perform its long-range planning. Since this is its pattern of life, it may spread, by its own example, ideals of mutual cooperation and constitutional government throughout the world. One international business analyst comments: "Finally, the multinational corporation is the only institution so far—and the only one visible on the horizon—that creates a genuine economic community transcending national lines and yet respectful of national sovereignties and local cultures.''[4]

For a long time many philosophers and international analysts overlooked the potential of business in building worldwide cooperation. Business was either ignored or viewed as an exploiter which led to conflict. Certainly this view has been accurate on numerous occasions; however, world conditions change, and so do business practices. Perhaps now the situation is different. Hans B. Thorelli comments: ''Whatever it does, the cosmopolitan corporation should be mindful of the fact that it represents a more successful instance of international cooperation and a closer approach to global thinking than we have thus encountered among governments. It is the torchbearer of One World.''[5]

Difficulties Brought by Multinational Companies

As is the case with many activities, there are potentially disadvantageous by-products that may accompany the benefits brought to host nations by multinational firms. One significant political difficulty is that the host government may feel some loss of national sovereignty since it is not able to control all that a multinational company does. In fact it is sometimes said that a large multinational company negotiates with a host government more like another sovereign state instead of a resident business in the state. Is it perhaps a developing type of sovereign state whose interests and powers are independent of nation states?

In any case the host nation may experience some loss of control over its own economy. The multinational firm's actions are guided partly by worldwide needs rather than internal needs of the host nation; thus some actions may not be consistent with what is desired by the host nation. For example, dislocations may occur in the host nation's international balance of payments, particularly when a multinational company imports materials or transfers funds.

With regard to rates of pay for labor, even when multinational firms pay the going rates or above, the fact that they pay higher wages in other nations leads the host nation to a nagging feeling that its labor is being exploited. The standard of comparison always seems to be the highest price paid for labor. Further, firms in a host nation often resent the additional competition brought by an outsider. If higher wages are paid, they object because they may then be forced to pay higher wages for the labor they employ.

In general, it is difficult to allay the fears of citizens and politicians in a host nation. They know that a multinational firm is deriving some benefit from its activities, so they feel exploited because they cannot rationalize that the activities may be of mutual benefit to *both* the company and the host nation.

[4] Peter F. Drucker, *The Age of Discontinuity: Guidelines to Our Changing Society,* New York: Harper & Row, Publishers, Incorporated, 1968, p. 97.
[5] Hans B. Thorelli, ''The Multi-national Corporation as a Change Agent,'' in Richard N. Farmer, *International Management,* Belmont Calif.: Dickenson Publishing Company, Inc., 1968, p. 73.

People in the home country of a multinational firm also may object to some of its activities. They see jobs being created in another nation, so they complain that the firm is harming the economy by "exporting jobs." This is a common complaint of United States labor, although economic evidence does not strongly support this point of view.[6] Citizens in the home country also may be less tolerant of the host nation's culture. For example, they may claim that the multinational firm's operations in a host nation having a dictatorship are supporting dictatorship, or that operations where there is racial discrimination are supporting that practice. The multinational firm argues that it must fit into the customs of a host nation in the same way it does in its home country, and also that it can help accomplish social improvements better by staying in a nation than by leaving it.

Multinational firms do cause some dislocations in nations of the world because they are agents of change, but on balance their advantages seem to outweigh substantially their disadvantages.[7] The multinationals appear to be the prime hope for less-developed nations to upgrade their quality of life rapidly. It will be necessary, however, for multinational firms to adapt their operations to their host nation's exercise of sovereignty. Their activities need to be consistent with the host's long-range development plans, which means that the multinational firm may need to sacrifice some desired short-run activities in order to fit long-run patterns.

THE ENVIRONMENT FOR MULTINATIONAL BUSINESS

Having discussed the social role and response of multinational business in world development, let us examine some of the environmental constraints that restrict business's social response, especially in the developing nations. We will examine this environment by discussing some of its major social, educational, political and economic aspects. Although we discuss these items separately, it should be understood that all of them are bound together in a complex social system.

Social Environment

The most evident and widespread factor in the social environment is the variation in culture among peoples. It makes each operating situation unique,

---

[6] For discussion of both sides of this issue, see articles in *Columbia Journal of World Business,* Spring 1973, pp. 13–32.

[7] For additional discussion, see Benoit, op. cit., pp. 15–22; Donald A. Fink, "The Role of the Multinational Corporation in the Economic Development Process," *MSU Business Topics,* Autumn 1972, pp. 58–62; and Sanford Rose, "Multinational Corporations in a Tough World," *Fortune,* August 1973, pp. 52ff.

creating both opportunities and problems; and it is discussed throughout the next two chapters. Two other significant social factors follow.

Social Overhead Costs   Social overhead costs are public and private investments which are necessary to prepare the environment for effective operation of a new business unit. When a business moves into a developing area, it normally finds that support facilities such as schools, hospitals, roads, and public utilities either are not available or are in such short supply that efficient operation of the business is prevented. A productive business system cannot simply be grafted onto the emaciated body of a poorly developed society. The whole system must be upgraded, and this action takes substantial social overhead costs as well as additional start-up time.

> When Indonesia's Gresnik cement plant was built, for example, a village had to be constructed to house imported scientists and administrators and also local skilled workers.[8] Schools and recreation facilities were built, police and fire protection established, and a bus system started for transporting workers. Ocean dock and oil storage facilities were acquired, a diesel power station constructed, a bag factory built, and railroad equipment added. The cost of these social overhead items was nearly $15 million. This sum was approximately the amount by which the cost of the Gresnik plant exceeded the cost of a similar plant in the United States.

Public Visibility   Not only must a multinational business live up to different standards in each country, but it also must be prepared to meet these standards with more perfection than national businesses are expected to do. As an interloper from afar, its public visibility is greater than that of local businesses. Nationalism, love of one's own people, and desire to protect national business make local citizens more sensitive to the effects of a foreign business. They know that its whole loyalty—or even its primary loyalty—is not to their economy and their people. They are quick to condemn its indiscretions and hesitant and faint in their praise of its benefits.

Of equal importance is the tendency of critics, when they observe an indiscretion of a foreign business, to generalize therefrom to condemn all businesses from that same country. Native businesses are not subject to this kind of generalization.

> A country in Asia serves as an example. When one of its national businesses acts in a way considered contrary to the national interest, it is merely regarded as a bad citizen. But when a German subsidiary misbe-

[8] Leonard A. Doyle, "Some Problems of State Enterprises in Underdeveloped Nations," *California Management Review*, Fall 1963, p. 27. See also Leonard A. Doyle, *Intereconomy Comparisons: A Case Study*, Berkeley, Calif.: University of California Press, 1965.

haves according to those same standards, its record is used to condemn the whole group of German businesses in that country. Managers who make decisions in this climate of public visibility must actually pay more attention to local standards and national objectives than purely local businesses need to do.

Insight into all these variations of social conduct is difficult for even the best-qualified businessman. He needs to be broad in his thinking and highly sensitive to political and social trends. If he comes from outside the host country, he cannot by himself sense all the fine points that should bear on his decisions; therefore, he depends on the counsel of local associates who are loyal and communicative. If they understand that above-average behavior is required because the business is a foreign one, they can be quite helpful in counseling toward responsible decisions. Unless they do see the situation broadly, they may for reasons of national pride be hesitant to help a multinational business conduct itself better than local businesses do.

Educational Environment

The educational environment is usually a major handicap in upgrading developing nations.

Scarcity of Qualified Human Resources   An evident characteristic of developing nations is the scarcity of human resources qualified to serve social and economic needs in an advanced society. There are major shortages of managers, scientists, and technicians, and these deficiencies limit business's ability to employ local labor productively.

In the absence of sufficient human resources, people with needed abilities are temporarily imported, while vast training programs prepare local workers. In fact, the lending of trained people to a nation may be of more lasting benefit than the lending of capital because of the *multiplier effect* by which these people develop a cadre of qualified nationals, who then become the nucleus for developing more nationals in an ever-widening arc of self-development.

Underdeveloped Educational Facilities   The shortage of qualified human resources would be less serious if excellent educational facilities were available to prepare people quickly; however, these facilities normally are also inadequate. There are shortages of schools and equipment for them. In turn, there are not enough qualified teachers to supply an expanded educational system; thus either existing universities must be expanded or new ones established to train teachers. All education is tied together in a system relationship, requiring a nation to start at the beginning of the sequence in order to be successful. Economic and social growth are difficult until human resources have been developed.

**Environmental Constraints Cause Problems
for Multinational Management**

U.S. operating patterns and procedures generally must be altered to take account of the local socioeconomic setting of developing nations. Local skills, values, attitudes, and legal and political traditions are not geared to management practices that have been developed in an entirely different environment and under a different system of values. As a consequence, local environmental factors often constrain or limit the effective transfer and application of elements of U.S. management know-how in developing countries.

These environmental constraints pose problems for multinational management. Multinational management must allow foreign subsidiaries enough flexibility to adjust their management practices to the local environment. At the same time, if a subsidiary is allowed too much autonomy, communication and other critical links needed to bind each operating unit into a worldwide network may be destroyed.

From Barry Richman and Melvyn Copen, "Management Techniques in the Developing Nations," *Columbia Journal of World Business,* Summer 1973, p. 50. Reprinted with permission.

Political Environment

The social and political environment are closely related. The political system influences attitudes of citizens, and the citizens concurrently have a substantial influence on the kinds of political leaders and policies which exist.

Nationalistic Drives   As has been mentioned, many people have strong nationalistic attitudes. They want their nation and their economic system for themselves without substantial interference by foreign nationals. In Burma, for example, a visiting professor presented a case problem where there was conflict between a British shipmaster and a Burmese crew. Expecting a human relations discussion, the professor was surprised when his class focused on how to train Burmese to take over from the British master so that they would not have to deal with him.

Government Controls   When a multinational firm does enter another nation, it often is subject to a variety of special controls, licenses, foreign exchange rules, and sanctions supplied by government. These are complicated by the fact that the government itself is sometimes unstable, inconsistent, and bureaucratic, though well-meaning. Decisions are made on a political basis with little thought given to business needs. The state normally plays a major role in central planning in both developing and developed nations.

In most nations there is also heavier government involvement in social welfare than exists in the United States. This affects a foreign business in a number of ways. Fringe-benefit costs as a proportion of wages will be high, running as much as 50 percent of wage costs. Layoffs of employees may be restricted and made expensive. And taxes are likely to be high to support government welfare payments.

Joint Ownership with Government   In many nations, particularly with regard to basic industries, the government will insist on being a partial owner in a foreign business which it admits. In other cases it is a full competitor, owning and operating a business selling the same type of product. The market may be allocated with a certain portion going to the state and another portion to the foreign business. The general conclusion is that in nearly all countries outside the United States, the government is more involved in business than is the case in this country. Businessmen in these nations have to be actively interested in government affairs in order to operate successfully. Sometimes they must give political considerations priority over economic and technical values when they make decisions.

A complex example of joint government ownership and control is the Scandinavian Airlines System (SAS).[9] One airline each from Sweden, Norway, and Denmark have joined together under the symbol SAS. They share operations, flight equipment, and ground facilities, even though each airplane is owned separately by only one of the three airlines. To further complicate the situation, each of the three member airlines is owned 50 percent by its respective national government and 50 percent by private business. Net proceeds of operations are divided according to a negotiated ratio. This complex arrangement allows three smaller airlines to operate as one large international airline.

The various types of government involvement in business may be summarized as follows:

1. Government ownership of an industry; other firms not allowed
2. Government ownership of a firm in an industry having private firms in competition with government
3. The arrangement described in item 2, with the market allocated
4. Partial government ownership of a private foreign firm
5. Government economic planning with sanctions applied to private industry to assure compliance
6. Routine government licensing and control only

Expropriation as a Special Political Risk   When a government nationalizes or expropriates the business of a foreign company, it assumes ownership and control of the property. The government may or may not pay for what it takes. One study

[9]Donald M. Barrett, "Multi-flag Airlines: A New Breed in World Business," *Columbia Journal of World Business,* March–April 1969, p. 9.

identified at least 187 United States companies which had experienced an expropriation since World War I, and it reported that only a minority of them received any compensation for asset losses. United States assets expropriated by Cuba in 1959–1960 amounted to nearly $1.5 billion.[10] Assets of companies from industrialized nations other than the United States have been similarly expropriated at various times.

The risk of expropriation is a strong deterrent to investment in nations which have a history of expropriation, have an unstable government, or have hostile attitudes toward private industry; consequently, many less-developed nations fail to get needed capital because there are no international assurances protecting against expropriation without compensation. The United Nations or some other international organization could make a substantial contribution to world economic stability and free flow of capital into less-developed nations if it could develop some reliable plan for controlling expropriation.

When expropriation does occur, an equal or greater loser tends to be the expropriating nation itself. It can only expropriate the property. It cannot expropriate managerial skills, technical know-how, international markets, and the many other benefits which a multinational business offers a developing nation. The multinational business is needed in most cases because, through its multiplier effect on local people and businesses, it becomes an effective medium for spreading management skills, capital, technology, and market opportunities worldwide. Many nations are voluntarily recognizing the benefits of multinational enterprise and are entering into joint ownership agreements rather than taking the self-centered and risky route of expropriation.

Economic Environment

Business is so thoroughly involved in the economic life of a nation that it would take an entire book to discuss the international economic environment of business. There are high interest rates, capital shortages, unstable economic systems, and restrictions on repatriation of profits; however, inflation is the one item selected for discussion because of its widespread social influence and its severity in many nations which most need development. A high level of inflation creates so much instability and social unrest that it restricts business's capacity to respond to human needs.

In the United States, which has had mild inflation for decades, the value of the dollar was cut more than half in the generation from 1940 to 1965, but in other parts of the world currency has been cut to one-hundredth or even *one-thousandth* of its value since 1940, as reflected by cost-of-living indexes. What used to cost one unit of currency now costs 1,000 or more. In terms of dollar currency, an ice-cream cone that originally cost 20 cents would now cost 20,000 cents, or $200!

[10] Franklin R. Root, "The Expropriation Experience of American Companies," *Business Horizons,* April 1968, pp. 69–74.

The extreme of inflation is represented by Indonesia, which in the 1960s had the highest rate of inflation in the world. In one decade its inflation rate was an incredible 160,000 percent.''

With high inflationary conditions, such matters as inventory policy, sales policy, and cash discounts are guided substantially by the state of inflation. Interest rates run as high as 5 percent monthly, which is 60 percent yearly; yet borrowing can be economical if the inflation rate runs higher, such as 8 percent monthly, permitting the debt to be repaid with cheaper money. An entire year's profit can be wiped out by a currency devaluation or some other development external to the firm. Typical ''good management'' through long-range planning is very difficult, and even regular operations become unsettled.

Just as business operations are unsettled, so is the worker's economic life. He must spend quickly lest his money lose its value. Savings payable in fixed currency units become meaningless because they lose their value; hence, he seldom plans for his own security, as workers do in the United States. He develops more dependence and more anxiety, and he becomes more politically volatile.

As a worker's money income increases, his aspirations naturally rise; however, since there is inflation, his standard of living does not significantly rise. The result is increasing unrest. This condition can be stated as a formula $(A - S) + I = U$, where A is the worker's aspirations, S is his standard of living, I is his insecurity, and U is his level of unrest. This means that as the difference between aspirations and standard of living increases, unrest also increases. When this is added to the unrest caused by insecurity in the system, the result is a general measure of social unrest. Inflation contributes significantly to this condition.

Since inflation weakens confidence in money, it often causes capital to flee from the inflated country to one with a more stable currency. This condition increases capital shortages and further limits business growth. In summary, high inflation tends to perpetuate underdevelopment and a low growth rate because it creates substantial economic and social dislocations which interfere with business efforts to develop productivity.

The Farmer-Richman Model of Environmental Constraints

Farmer and Richman have developed a model for comparing environmental constraints on business efficiency in different nations.[12] They reason that efficiency is substantially affected by constraints imposed by the external environment. That is, if the external environment does not permit and encourage internal efficiency, it will not be forthcoming. Constraints are grouped into four classes

[11] Robert Keatley, "Model Bureaucrat," *Wall Street Journal* (Pacific Coast edition), Oct. 4, 1968, p. 1.

[12] Richard N. Farmer and Barry M. Richman, "A Model for Research in Comparative Management," *California Management Review*, Winter 1964, pp. 55–68; and Richard N. Farmer and Barry M. Richman, *Comparative Management and Economic Progress*, Homewood, Ill.: Richard D. Irwin, Inc., 1965.

which are approximately the same as those we have discussed: sociological, educational, legal-political, and economic. Each class is divided into weighted subclasses which are rated for each nation to determine that nation's total constraints. A high constraint score indicates that external constraints are giving high support to efficient business.

Sociological constraints will serve as an example. Their maximum weight is 100 points out of 500. The subclasses and maximum weights are as follows: view of managers as an elite group, 10; view of scientific method, 40; view of wealth, 10; view of rational risk taking, 10; view of achievement, 20; and class flexibility, 10. The sum of constraint scores is the constraint index, which reflects society's support of business productivity. This type of analysis helps pinpoint reasons why a nation is low in efficiency, because a low score on a particular constraint shows that it needs improvement in order to have a gain in productivity.

The Law of Persistent Underdevelopment

The many constraints on productive enterprise in developing nations lead to the general conclusion that an underdeveloped nation's cultural foundation for productivity often is as underdeveloped as its economy is. Cultural factors operate in an interacting system to suppress both social and economic growth. The nation becomes locked into a self-perpetuating cycle of low development, and it has difficulty breaking out of this imprisoning cycle without outside help or unusual effort of its own. We call this system relationship the *Law of Persistent Underdevelopment*. It is not a "law" in the sense that it forever condemns a nation to underdevelopment. Rather, it is a law in the sense that it is self-perpetuating unless some *new force* is added to break a nation out of its grasp. It gives notice to nations that intentional, determined effort is necessary to initiate a cycle of development. The Law of Persistent Underdevelopment simply states that an underdeveloped social system is locked into self-perpetuating low development until new social forces can be introduced to break the cultural chains which bind it.

The key cultural and economic components of the Law of Persistent Underdevelopment are shown in Figure 24-2. Cultural factors, represented by the larger circle, and economic factors, represented by the smaller circle, operate in tandem to perpetuate underdevelopment. As shown by the larger circle, in the beginning an underdeveloped culture leads to low educational attainment, which causes an inadequate supply of management, resulting in ineffective leadership, which perpetuates the underdeveloped culture. In the economic sphere a similar perpetuating chain exists. The scarcity of capital causes low efficiency, which leads to low return on investment, causing low savings, which perpetuates the scarcity of capital.

A country which is caught in these self-perpetuating tandem chains requires large economic and cultural inputs to generate a takeoff force which will break the

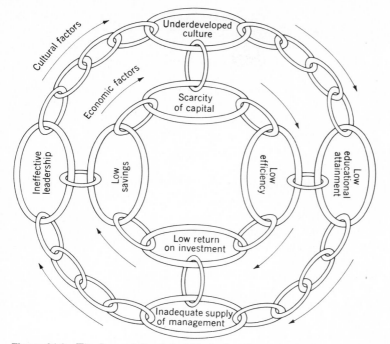

Figure 24-2 The Law of Persistent Underdevelopment: Tandem cultural and economic chains perpetuate underdevelopment.

circle and head it toward a more advanced social condition. Business managers are a key factor in this takeoff force because they provide leadership to overcome inefficiency and cultural lag. By making a society productive enough to reward those who qualify themselves, management motivates citizens to upgrade their skills and education. Without advancement opportunities provided by successful business, citizen educational lethargy persists. People seek education as a result of self-motivation, not because of public exhortation to become educated.

SUMMARY

As a result of worldwide needs for economic and social development, major businesses are moving rapidly into multinational operations. Ethnocentric ways of looking at the world are being discarded for more global, geocentric attitudes. Major social responses that multinational business is making include upgrading social and economic systems, helping develop local business, participating in international management groups which seek to improve world development, and building world cooperation and peace.

In its multinational operations business is required to work with a variety of environmental constraints in different nations. Major social, educational, political, and economic constraints were discussed, along with the Farmer-Richman model for evaluating them. In many nations the combined conditions are so severe that they tend to bind a nation in perpetual poverty according to a Law of Persistent Underdevelopment.

STUDY GUIDES FOR INTERPRETATION OF THIS CHAPTER

1. The United States automobile manufacturer of which you are international vice president owns the plant of a long-established automobile manufacturer in England. Recently, as you spoke at a civic association meeting in a city near the plant, a member of the audience challenged you as follows: "Your ownership of our plant means foreign control of one of this region's largest employers. In case of a real crisis in the industry, we will see that you hold the whip and we are the slaves." How would you respond?

2. Discuss the social effects of high inflation on business environment in a developing nation.

3. Explain how the Law of Persistent Underdevelopment may operate to lock a nation into low development.

4. You are general manager of a genuinely multinational company operating in an African nation. Eight hundred and seventy of the nine hundred employees are black. The other thirty employees are North Americans, Asians, and Europeans. They are mostly in professional and managerial occupations. The African nation's minister of labor has contacted you, saying that it is the government's "urgent request" that the nonblack work force be reduced to ten persons within six months. How would you respond?

5. Survey three persons from other nations and learn their attitude toward a business from an advanced nation which is operating in their country.

PROBLEMS
Hartman Chemical Corporation

Hartman Chemical Corporation is a major multinational company which produces chemicals and petroleum products. Its products are sold in many parts of the world. An individual stockholder owning 3,000 shares of stock out of 34 million company shares has proposed the following stockholder resolution for the annual stockholders meeting. The company printed the proposal in the official notice of the annual meeting.

Whereas the nation of South Africa has social and political domination by a white minority, it is, therefore, not a democratic society and it engages in racial discrimination.

Therefore, be it resolved that the Hartman Chemical Corporation shall not conduct business in the nation and shall disband its existing facilities in South Africa within the next two years.

In South Africa the corporation has a raw material and chemical processing plant employing 1,275 persons. Over 1,000 employees are black, but none of them are in managerial positions, and only a few are in skilled jobs.

In response to the stockholder proposal, the president of the corporation made the following statement:

Frankly, we had hoped the South African question would have been settled by now, but it has not been. Our basic policy is to obey the laws of our host country, while doing our best to improve conditions for our employees. We cannot solve those problems overnight, but we are convinced that nothing will be gained by our withdrawal from these areas, and much is to be gained by our staying.

We clearly pay above the going wages in the area, and all workers receive equal pay for equal work regardless of color. Hartman Chemical Corporation is hastening the day of racial equality in South Africa, but our task is not easy. In our efforts to break down barriers to equality, labor unions offer as much resistance as the government does. Skilled labor unions have balked at our efforts to move blacks into skilled trades through apprenticeship training.

The president also referred to an independent survey of nonwhite residents in the city where the firm's plant was located. The survey reported that over 90 percent of those interviewed had positive attitudes toward the company and that 96 percent wanted the company to remain in the community, primarily because they felt it had a favorable effect on wages and employment practices.

1. Develop arguments both for and against the stockholder proposal.

2. Discuss the different interests of various pluralistic groups in this situation.

3. What is the social responsibility of Hartman Chemical Corporation in this situation? In the role of another stockholder, how would you vote?

Bankruptcy for the Subsidiary

Flagstaff Company, a major electronics manufacturer operating primarily in the United States, owned a subsidiary in a poorly developed city in Southern Europe. Ownership developed gradually during a period of twelve years through purchase of a locally owned company using some of the Flagstaff Company's technological know-how. The original plant grew until it employed over 1,000 workers by the time Flagstaff assumed complete ownership. During the twelve years the plant had rarely been profitable; so when Flagstaff bought full ownership, it dispatched a management team to bring up the plant's profitability. During the following year the plant's losses were greater than ever.

To improve the situation management decided to close its most unprofitable operation, laying off 275 workers. As a result of the layoffs, there was heavy labor strife. There were two or three wildcat strikes a week, which further reduced productivity; management threatened to close the plant unless the strikes stopped. Because the strikes continued, management closed the plant a few weeks later. To the surprise of management, the mayor of the city, using an obscure law, physically seized the plant and locked out management, supposedly to prevent the company from liquidating its assets. (There was also some evidence he used the seizure as leverage to try to force management to reopen the plant.) Shortly thereafter the subsidiary filed for bankruptcy.

One major issue is that the subsidiary owes banks in the nation about $6 million in unsecured loans which were made without any bank request that the loans be guaranteed by the parent company in the United States.

1. Identify and explain any apparent errors in judgment made by parent-company management in operating this subsidiary.

2. Does the parent company have a responsibility to pay the unsecured loans? What are the implications of (*a*) paying the loans or (*b*) not paying them?

CHAPTER

BUSINESS ENCOURAGEMENT
OF INTERNATIONAL DEVELOPMENT

*The multinational corporations will be the pivot upon which the
creation of employment in the Third World rests.*

André Van Dam[1]

*It can be said without too much oversimplication that there are
no underdeveloped countries. There are only undermanaged
ones.*

Peter F. Drucker[2]

Consider the following prediction made in the 1960s.[3]

If present trends continue, it seems likely that famine will reach serious
proportions in India, Pakistan and China in the 1970's, followed by Indonesia, Iran,
Turkey, Egypt and several other countries within a few years, and then followed by
most of the other countries of Asia, Africa and Latin America by 1980. Such a famine
will be of massive proportions affecting hundreds of millions, possible even billions,
of persons. If this happens, as appears very probable, it will be the most colossal
catastrophe in history. . . . This is the Malthusian Doctrine finally coming true after
170 years.

The prediction begins with an "if," so birth control and other developments
may prevent the occurrence of all these predictions. Nevertheless, a rapidly
expanding world population does create an urgent need for nations of the world to
make productive use of their resources. As a major change agent for productivity,
business has substantial responsibilities for international development.

Even if population could be controlled, the aspirations of people around the

[1] André Van Dam, "The World's Work: Who Needs It Most?" *Columbia Journal of World Business,* September–October 1971, p. 30.

[2] Peter F. Drucker, "Management's New Role," *Harvard Business Review,* November–December 1969, p. 54. Italics in original.

[3] Raymond Ewell (ed.), *Population Bulletin,* quoted in *Columbia Journal of World Business,* January–February 1967, p. 89.

world have risen dramatically. Generally speaking, impatient society does not wish to wait for slow, generation-by-generation improvement, like the drip-drip of a cavern stream forming a stalagmite. In its concern for others and for "progress," society is in a hurry—perhaps too much so for its own good. Nevertheless, it wants progress now. It is depending on business to introduce quickly and effectively many of the changes it wants.

Business is only one of many organizations serving human needs internationally. In fact, the various institutions serving international development provide an excellent example of pluralism in action. All of them are bound together in a complex system relationship. These organizations include private business, labor unions, venture capital organizations, foundations, religious groups, universities, local governments, and foreign governments. Essentially, each institution is following the idea of functionalism, performing its special functions to contribute to the mutual objective of international development.

In this chapter we discuss the way in which business encourages cultural changes toward more productive patterns of life. After some introductory observations, discussion will be in terms of integrating social systems, introducing change, developing productivity, and motivation in a less-developed environment.

SOME GENERAL OBSERVATIONS

Business is a major change agent in relatively developed nations as well as developing ones. Its influence in developed nations is illustrated by two forceful books on the challenges of development in Europe and Japan.

"The American Challenge"

In 1967 in Paris Jean-Jacques Servan-Schreiber published *Le Défi américain (The American Challenge),* which discussed the successful "invasion" of Europe by productive United States business.[4] Although written as a popular book rather than an academic analysis, it is full of valuable cultural insights about business practice. It quickly became a best seller, being translated into English in 1968. Servan-Schreiber maintained that United States business learned how to use the opportunities afforded by the European Common Market better than European business did. The result was that most European companies, when faced with the need to strengthen their competitive position, preferred to join with American multinational companies rather than other European firms. He concluded that the success of United States business resulted primarily from its productive management culture and extensive education of knowledge workers. Europe could meet

[4] J.-J. Servan-Schreiber, *Le Défi américain,* Paris: Editions Denoel, 1967. See also J.-J. Servan-Schreiber, *The American Challenge,* New York: Avon Books, 1969, and other editions of the book.

this challenge of business "colonization" only by adopting this management culture and abandoning its elite concept of education for a few intellectuals.

The thesis of *The American Challenge* has itself been challenged in many ways. It has some truth and some exaggeration. Nevertheless, it presents many interesting differences among business practices in developed nations.

> The possibilities for increases in productivity in Europe are illustrated by one report.[5] Through better management practices, many European factories routinely have increased productivity 20 to 30 percent. One electrical components firm doubled its output in three years without increasing its labor force. Another firm increased productivity of casters 400 percent, and another increased typewriter productivity 770 percent!

"The Japanese Challenge"

In 1969, Haakan Hedberg published *Den Japanska Utmaningen (The Japanese Challenge)* in Stockholm. This book presents the thesis that in the late 1980s Japan will have the largest per capita income of any nation, thus becoming the affluent society's first "economic superpower."[6] The Japanese are moving toward this position through close business-government cooperation, superior long-range planning, large investment programs, and loyal semipaternalistic cooperation. They also have strongly favorable attitudes toward productivity. One study, for example, reported that considerably more Japanese managers have strong values favoring high productivity than American managers.[7]

> In the Matsushita Electric Industrial Company, workers can receive medical care in a company hospital, be married in a company chapel, purchase a home with company financing, and vacation at company resorts. As explained by the company's founder, "I have impressed on the employees that each must perform his task or the system breaks down. Each man is taught that he is managing the company through his own work, and that with this work he is doing something for society."[8] The success of this philosophy is reflected in the company's growth in worldwide markets and profitability. In addition, in only one year the company's 55,000 workers submitted 420,000 ideas through the employee suggestion program.

---

[5] James H. Duncan, "Old and New Productivity Techniques Start Closing Gaps," *Columbia Journal of World Business,* January–February 1969, pp. 69–70.

[6] Haakan Hedberg, *Den Japanska Utmaningen,* Stockholm: Albert Bonner Publishing Company, 1969.

[7] George W. England and Raymond Lee, "Organizational Goals and Expected Behavior among American, Japanese and Korean Managers—A Comparative Study," *Academy of Management Journal,* December 1971, pp. 425–428.

[8] "Japan's Remarkable Industrial Machine," *Business Week,* Mar. 7, 1970, p. 64.

In its rise toward advanced industrialization, Japanese business has been able to retain much of its old culture and still be competitively productive. Japanese workers are hired virtually for life, and managerial promotions are often based on seniority. However, most of the technological improvements of modern business have been introduced into this cultural context. What Japanese business loses in production rationality, it seems to gain back in employee stability and loyalty. Culture is used to reinforce productivity rather than to interfere with it. Meanwhile, the culture is gradually adapting to industrialization. At Matsushita Company, for example, a manager who operates an unprofitable facility may not hold his job just because he has seniority. But neither is he fired, as is often the case in the United States. Rather, he is moved to a less demanding job, often with a large bonus for "past contributions."

The Convergence Hypothesis of Industrialization

The experiences of both Europe and Japan[9] provide support for the *convergence hypothesis* of industrialization, and trends in less-developed nations are additionally supportive. The convergence hypothesis holds that as societies industrialize they are inevitably pulled toward similarity. There are factors inherent in industrialization, such as rationality, responsibility, and long-range planning, which in effect require some degree of cultural accommodation. They make convergence *necessary* if industrialization is to be successful.

An example of convergence theory is the trend toward trained career or professional management. As nations industrialize, they tend to emphasize professional management regardless of earlier practices, because competent, qualified professional management proves necessary for effective use of socioeconomic resources.

The convergence hypothesis illustrates the significant effects of environmental constraints on productivity, as discussed in the Farmer-Richman model in the preceding chapter. The environment is a key input into an industrial system; therefore, it must gradually adapt in order to allow industrialization to advance effectively. Since business is a principal change agent for industrialization, it constitutes a strong pressure for more education, social development, dependable law, rational cooperation, and other conditions of industrialization. Improvement in these environmental inputs is necessary for continued growth in outputs of goods and services, both material and cultural.

This input-output relationship of environment and productivity in the social system has been proved countless times when technologically advanced businesses enter developing countries. A well-equipped plant is not enough. The

[9] Bernard Karsh and Robert E. Cole, "Industrialization and the Convergence Hypothesis: Some Aspects of Contemporary Japan," *Journal of Social Issues*, vol. 24, no. 4, 1968, pp. 45–64.

society needs to adapt in terms of education, health, respect for contracts and obligations, view of quality, and so on.

The following experience of one of the authors emphasizes the relationship of environment and productivity in a developing country.[10] Visiting that country's modern rayon plant, he noticed that sheets of cellulose (the main raw material) were made in Canada, 9,000 miles away. He asked why this was so because he knew that this developing nation had vast forest reserves and some cellulose plants. The reply was, "We have the proper equipment, but we haven't been able to operate it well enough to make the high quality of cellulose needed for the rayon plant."

Since less-developed nations typically provide the greatest lack of convergence and, therefore, the most difficult environment for industrial change, the remainder of this chapter will focus primarily on conditions which arise when a firm from a more advanced nation enters a developing nation.

INTEGRATING DIFFERENT SOCIAL SYSTEMS
Understanding Social Systems

The overriding factor in all international business is that it operates within different social systems. Th amount of difference between any two systems may be called *cultural distance,* and in many situations this distance is substantial. As concisely stated by a citizen of an Asian country, "We are two days and 200 years distant from Washington."[11] Whatever the amount of cultural distance, it does affect the responses of all persons to business. Imported managers naturally tend to be ethnocentric and to judge conditions in a new country according to standards of their homeland. Although this way of perceiving conditions is very human, it will thwart understanding and productivity. In order to perform effectively, an expatriate manager will need cultural empathy for local conditions. Having this empathy, then he needs to be adaptable enough to integrate the communities of interest of the two (or more) cultures involved. But cultural adaptation is not easy.

When a manager enters a developing nation to install advanced technological equipment and get it operating, his role is that of a *cultural catalyst* to accelerate change in the developing nation. He will need to make adjustments in the leadership techniques he employed in the advanced economy from which he came. Also, local employees in this new installation will find that they can no longer follow the ways of their less-productive culture. In other words, both the manager

---

[10] Both authors of this book have participated in development programs in other nations.
[11] Jose de Cubas, "Let's Call 'Time,' " *Columbia Journal of World Business,* November–December 1967, p. 7.

Responsibilities for Employing Local Management

While the trade-offs between costs and benefits of using expatriate managers are important considerations, well-publicized statements of international staffing policy, such as Unilever's, appear to have another rationale. Concern with images and politics, rather than with managerial efficiency, seems to have dominated the nationality problem; and the attention paid to it appears to have stemmed from managers' discomfort in confronting the political question, "who commands?" Behind the policy of "as many local managers as possible" lies an intuitive assumption on the part of many international executives that people prefer to be governed by "one of their own" even if he in turn must respond to orders from far away. A local boss seems to symbolize a certain independence, however vestigial. Moreover, it is often assumed that control by a foreign firm is more willingly accepted when a national "member of the family" holds a place in its central management. It may be that IBM is "more acceptable" in France because some Frenchmen take a certain pride in the fact that the head of IBM world trade is a compatriot.

From Lawrence G. Franko, "Who Manages Multinational Enterprises?" *Columbia Journal of World Business,* Summer 1973, p. 31. Reprinted with permission.

and the employees need to change. A fusion of cultures is required in which both parties adjust to the new situation of seeking greater productivity.

Culture Shock

A manager or technician who enters another nation may suffer *culture shock* and be unable to perform effectively. His surroundings appear to be behavioral chaos. He becomes disoriented and retreats into isolation or wants to return home on the next airplane. But a different culture is not behavioral chaos; it is a systematic structure of behavior patterns, probably as systematic as the culture in the manager's home country. It can be understood if the manager has a receptive attitude. But there *are* differences, and these differences strain a person, regardless of his adaptability.[12]

One study, for example, reports that United States managers in joint ventures with Japanese in Japan suffer considerable culture shock.[13] Another study reports that European managers in the United States endure a discomforting and lengthy process of adjustment.[14] In spite of one's preparation it is difficult to move from one culture to another without experiencing adjustment difficulties.

[12] For a major study of different managerial values see Mason Haire, Edwin E. Ghiselli, and Lyman W. Porter, *Managerial Thinking: An International Study,* New York: John Wiley & Sons, Inc., 1966. See also David A. Heenan, "The Corporate Expatriate: Assignment to Ambiguity," *Columbia Journal of World Business,* May–June 1970, pp. 49–54.

[13] M.Y. Yoshino, "Administrative Attitudes and Relationships in a Foreign Culture," *MSU Business Topics,* Winter 1968, pp. 59–66.

[14] James Leontiades, "The Uprooted European Manager in America," *European Business,* Winter 1973, pp. 62–73.

Managers and technicians who have the ability to operate effectively in more than one culture are truly *transcultural* employees. They are low in ethnocentrism and adapt readily to different environments without culture shock. Usually they can communicate in more than one language. They are a vital asset to multinational business.

Organizational Design to Accommodate a Culture

There is a natural tendency for firms operating in advanced nations to want to install advanced business and production systems in a developing nation. The host nation readily agrees because it wants "the latest and best equipment." Though this kind of policy sounds like a desirable one, it is often a mistake. A simpler system may get better results because the advanced system is beyond the capacity of local managers and workers.

In one nation a smaller, slower paper-making machine produced at a lower unit cost than a modern, high-speed machine. Reasons were that the slower machine could employ less-skilled labor, breakdowns could be more easily repaired by nationals, and when breakdowns did occur they were less wasteful of time and material. For example, paper breakage on the high-speed machine wasted paper at the rate of nearly a mile a minute until it could be rethreaded through the rolls of the machine, and the threading process required more skill. When the machine itself had major breakdowns, it often lay idle for days while specialists from other nations were brought in to make repairs.

The significance of equipment breakdowns is illustrated by the experience of three factories producing similar products and with comparable technology.[15] The factory in the United States had breakdown time of less than 1 percent. In India, on the other hand, the subsidiary plant of a United States firm had a breakdown rate of about 7 percent, while a comparable native Indian plant had a rate of 15 to 20 percent. With breakdown differences of this magnitude it is evident that simpler equipment could result in greater net productivity if it could be kept operating more of the time.

The same kinds of comments which apply to factory machines also apply to office systems, accounting controls, and other components of an advanced business system. The system can be too difficult for effective operation by the supply of labor available. Figure 25-1 shows the potential mismatch between an advanced firm's labor needs and the available labor pool in a developing nation. At the top there is often a surplus of available high-level people, as represented by area *a* in the chart. They are the educated elite in the society. Even though these people are

[15] Barry M. Richman, "Empirical Testing of a Comparative and International Management Research Model," in *Academy of Management Proceedings* (1967 Meeting), Bowling Green, Ohio: Academy of Management, 1968, p. 47.

educated in subjects such as law and political science, rather than needed disciplines such as engineering and business, many eventually can be developed to meet company needs. Meanwhile, top-level specialists can be brought to the nation to fill in the manpower gaps.

As one approaches the middle of the organization, large shortages appear, as represented by area *b*. The nation usually has a small middle class, and there are major shortages of technicians, middle managers, and skilled workers. This shortage is substantial and is the principal reason why simpler organizational systems may be more productive in the beginning. To overcome this shortage, large social overhead investments in training and education are required. As the labor force is upgraded, then organizational processes can be upgraded also, eventually approaching the system design and productivity achieved in an advanced nation.

Area *c* on the chart represents a large group which is unsuitable for employment. Some are illiterate, others lack social adaptability to rigorous work, and others are in poor health. This group typically needs the aid of government programs directed toward improving the whole social system. Business can cooperate with government in these programs.

INTRODUCING CHANGE
The Social Nature of Change

Whether the changes required are large or small, the work culture of a nation tends to change slowly, and in so doing, it gives stability and security to society. This is an advantage. However, there is an offsetting disadvantage; this very stability makes changes more difficult to initiate. As we have learned from both experience and research, change is a social problem as well as a technological one. The technological part of change is usually solvable by the logics of science, but the social part is more dependent on the uncertainties of human nature.

A point of major significance is that top management or lower management

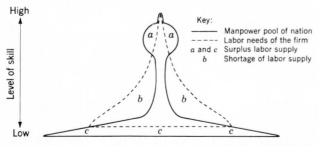

Figure 25-1 Comparison of a developing nation's available manpower pool and the labor needs of an advanced business entering the nation. (Adapted from Richard N. Farmer, "Organizational Transfer and Class Structure," *Academy of Management Journal,* September 1966, figs. 2 and 3, pp. 209 and 211.)

may block change. It is a mistake to consider that only technicians and workers are culturebound by tradition.

A United States consulting group, for example, made a detailed productivity study of a French shoe factory.[16] In presenting their report to the factory owner they showed how certain changes would increase both his income and that of his employees. He shrugged his shoulders and rejected the report because it would require him to make changes he could not socially accept. His family had owned the factory for three generations. If he installed new machinery, it would cause unpleasant stress on faithful older employees who had worked for his family all their lives. He also might have to work harder, and his wife would object to his longer hours. Why risk this much when he already had a pleasant life and sufficient income for his needs? (If you were "in his shoes," how would you respond?)

In another French firm the president accepted a consultant's changes, but his associates and middle managers blocked it.[17] After making a methods study in one small section of the plant, the consultant was able to increase productivity by 60 percent. The president was impressed, but his other managers finally persuaded him not to extend the study to the remainder of the plant.

Even changes designed for employee or customer service, rather than the company's benefit, will fail unless they integrate with the customs of the people affected. For example, a United States bank had a successful branch in the principal town of a small Polynesian island. Management sought to improve customer service by installing a drive-in window. Customers failed to use the window, and it was finally abandoned. Investigation revealed that "going to the bank" had become a mark of status and a major social event in the community. Customers wanted to be seen by others at the bank and have an opportunity for social visiting. The bank had become the social center of the community somewhat in the manner of the general store or post office in rural America years ago. If customers used the drive-in window, they denied themselves these social amenities, so they declined to use it!

Encouraging Support for Change

Since management initiates most changes, it has the primary responsibility for handling them in such a way that there will be satisfactory adjustment. Although management initiates change, employees control the final decision to

[16] Donald C. Stone, "Bridging Cultural Barriers in International Management," *S.A.M. Advanced Management Journal,* January 1969, p. 57.
[17] Duncan, op. cit., p. 71.

accept it or reject it, and they are the ones who actually accomplish it. Under these conditions, employee support becomes vital.

Most people in less-developed countries are not accustomed to the rigid demands of an industrial system. They are not prepared for the rigorous timing and discipline, precise division of labor, rational forms of action, and impersonal styles of supervision and control that prevail in advanced work systems. And they cannot be so prepared by a speech or two and a few haphazard instructions. Long-run environmental forces are required to establish cultural changes of this magnitude.

Using Community Forces   Even experienced multinational firms often overlook the power which community forces have in influencing the acceptance of changes *within* the firm. When certain changes are essential for productivity, it is desirable to enlist the support and participation of all possible community status groups, such as government leaders, unions, church dignitaries, mayors, universities, prominent social clubs, and others. This action helps each worker understand that people he respects are supporting this particular improvement. A business is one part of a community system; so the more support it can get from that system, the better are its chances for success.

Using Group Forces within the Firm   Although most changes probably are introduced by management authority and staff persuasion, internal group forces are more effective when it is possible to use them. This process uses participation and group discussion to help people understand the need for change and to apply their own ideas to make change more workable on the job.

Beginning at the Top   Since we already have discussed how top managers can block effective change, it is evident that their support is vital to a new project. In developed nations there is often substantial decentralization of authority; so a project may succeed in spite of some opposition from the top manager. On the other hand, the management structure in most developing nations is authoritarian. If the top management does not approve, the project will probably gain little support at lower levels.

One highly successful development project in the Cauca Valley of Colombia combined all three approaches which have just been discussed.[18] This was a community development project, rather than one by an individual firm, but it was spearheaded by businessmen. This program focused on the "movers and shapers," who were the few people at the top of the human resource pyramid in the community. These people were at policy-making

[18] Described to one of the authors by Professor Roderick F. O'Connor of Georgia Institute of Technology, and reported in Roderick F. O'Connor, "This Revolution Starts at the Top," *Columbia Journal of World Business*, Fall 1966, pp. 39–46.

levels, had proven competence, and already had some desire to improve their society. They had both the capability and the power to make productive changes if their energies could be focused on this goal. They primarily used group discussions to develop long-run plans for improvement, aided by a local university and an outside consultant. The improvements initiated by these people brought a dramatic upsurge in development of the Cauca Valley. Further, by means of the multiplier effect, the developmental spirit of these people spread to others in the valley.

Unlearning Old Habits and Reinforcing New Ones   Productive change requires the unlearning of old habits, instead of simply adding new habits on top of the old ones. Take the situation of local supervisors who are taught by an overseas management new ways of leading employees. What sometimes happens is that they retain most of their old approaches also, so that now they have a strange mixture of newer, positive practices which are substantially offset by holdover practices from their old habit patterns. As a consequence, there is little net benefit from the new practices. If they do not believe substantially in these new practices, they tend gradually to return to their old ways of doing things because these ways are more secure. Even when they do believe in the new practices they may become frustrated because their old habits (and those of their manager) interfere. This condition means that any changes which are introduced require regular social and economic reinforcement to keep them going until they become firmly established as new habit patterns.

DEVELOPING PRODUCTIVITY
The Social Goals of Work

There are essentially three ways of perceiving the goals of one's efforts in a social system. Usually a single goal dominates, and when it does, it substantially determines how people use resources within their society.

One goal is to *work competitively to redistribute* power, income, property, or some other desired resource in the society. This means that a person is trying to get from others some of what they have, or trying to keep them from getting more. This goal is usually selfish, though it can be an effort to get more for someone else with whom one does not personally identify (i.e., not one's group, class, or craft). A typical example is workers in a developing nation who assume that there is a static pool of economic resources and the only way they can get more for themselves is to take from others. In popular terms, they try to take a larger slice of a static economic pie. Their main efforts are diverted away from trying to increase wealth and toward utopian equilitarian schemes which promise to redistribute it. Wealth could, of course, be more easily redistributed *as it is increased,* but the dominant worker attitude is simply getting a larger slice of a static pie.

A second goal is to *work more of the time* in order to have more of what one wants. For example, a person may work longer hours or may decrease absenteeism. He may also put his wife and children to work, thus increasing the wealth of his family.

A third goal is to *work more productively*. Productivity is an input-output relationship which implies a larger value of outputs in relation to inputs. It provides for more effective use of resources, whatever their amount. It is normally the most rewarding of the three choices from the point of view of the whole society.

All three goals may be pursued at the same time. Workers may be more productive through increasing their skill, but also work longer hours and through their union seek to raise wages at a rate greater than productivity gains. The important point is that the view which predominates will color strongly these attitudes toward work and the society in which they live.

Social emphasis in most of the developed nations is upon the third goal, with moderate additional emphasis on the first goal in order to achieve a better balance of income and power among people. In less-developed nations the first goal often dominates, with minor emphasis on the second and rare attention to the third. The result is that these nations are working below their capacity and have an urgent need for business systems which emphasize productivity.

Building the Idea of Productivity

With few exceptions, a society is poor not because it lacks resources, but because it is unable to organize and use its resources productively. This means that *productivity* is the central idea which the people of a nation need to absorb in order to develop the spirit to rise above poverty and inefficiency. Without a devotion to productivity, new capital inputs are dissipated. Without a belief in productivity, more education merely increases the demand for wasteful personal aides, attendants, and helpers. Without productivity, achievement drives merely increase competition for resources that are not growing. These drives cause the achievers to step harder on their neighbors' shoulders as they climb to the top, and since national resources are not expanding, whatever one gains is at the expense of the other.

It often comes as a surprise to uninitiated observers to discover that the majority of workers in a developing nation do not really understand the idea of productivity or identify with it in their work. This lack of understanding even extends to managers who have difficulty interpreting the difference between achieving "more production" and "more productivity." Production is only more in quantity, but productivity is an input-output improvement. Consider, for example, the employer who hires 10 percent more workers in order to secure a 5 percent increase in output. This is an increase in production but a decline in productivity.

Although societies typically have emphasized economic values in their efforts for productivity, all types of inputs and outputs may be considered in a productivity model. Thus, productivity can apply to social inputs and outputs just as much as it does to economic ones. The point is that productivity is an all-encompassing idea for effective use of resources. Society chooses whether it will value economic or social inputs and outputs more highly in the input-output model.

One influence on productivity is the existence of *counterproductive factors* in a nation. Counterproductive factors are those that harm productivity instead of merely failing to contribute to it. For example, one of the authors observed in an Asian nation that university students are taught not to do production work because it is beneath the dignity of an educated person. The university system emphasizes law, theoretical economics, and political science; and most graduates seek work in the government bureaucracy. Most of the nation's talented manpower is tied up in government, and so business and other applied areas do not have an adequate pool of talent for improving productivity. The result is that the whole nation is the loser.

A more complex system example of a counterproductive factor is government policy which funnels capital into urban housing and grandiose public buildings, giving an impression of wealth and comfort in the city. In turn, unskilled country people crowd into the city to "share the wealth," leading to urban unemployment, displaced persons, and rising crime. Crowded shantytowns and slums develop near the city, overtaxing the capacity of government to provide public utilities such as water, sanitation, and roads. Meanwhile the supply of needed farm labor declines. The result is less productive employment of labor and increasing social unrest.

MOTIVATION IN A LESS-DEVELOPED ENVIRONMENT

In multinational management the most important idea regarding motivation is to apply it *in terms of the environment of the people involved* rather than in terms of an advanced industrial economy. Most companies desire to hire native supervisors, and there is little use trying to motivate workers until these supervisors can be trained and motivated. What is effective motivation in one environment may not be in another.

In a South American factory, for example, accidents were high. The six native superintendents were not following management's instructions for accident prevention. They seemed agreeable, but somehow failed to sell accident prevention throughout the organization. The overseas top management of the company then tried a high-powered safety publicity program of the type used in its own home plants. This was of no avail. Finally, a wise manager found an effective solution. Paper mâché heads of the six superintendents were molded and colored, the idea being that each week these heads would be arranged on a "totem pole" at the front gate in the order of the weekly safety rank of each man's department. No superintendent wanted to see himself as low man on the safety totem pole, so the accident problem was quickly corrected. In this case, management used existing cultural values of the country in order to accomplish the desired result of better safety.

Less-advanced Need Structures

Most workers in less-developed nations are correspondingly less advanced in their need structures. Modern psychology reports that new human needs take priority whenever former needs are reasonably satisfied. In other words, people are motivated more by what they are seeking than by what they already have. Human needs are generally recognized to be in some order, with physiological and security needs preceding social and ego needs. In less-developed countries, most employees are still seeking basic physiological and security needs. Hence, some of the more sophisticated and elaborate motivational devices of modern industrial management may not be appropriate in these countries. The needs of workers may be more simply reached by direct motivation. In many countries, workers have lived in economic systems in which there was little direct connection between their work performance and the amount of their rewards. Therefore, they require management to show them simple, direct evidence that if they work more effectively, they will receive more. In other words, work must be interpreted in terms of their immediate needs, rather than waiting for indirect results through a complex economic or social system. Accordingly, action which would be inappropriate in an advanced country may be workable in a less-developed country, as illustrated by the following events.

In South America, an international petroleum company employed about twenty local workers in an oil-well perforation team managed by an overseas executive. In spite of management efforts, each perforation job averaged nine days. Since a similar job with similar equipment was done in the United States in 1½ days, management reasoned that—even considering the more primitive operating conditions in South America—the job could surely be done in six days or less. Since the job did require genuine teamwork and since the men worked in isolated locations less subject to direct supervision, management decided on a drastic step to break the cultural pattern. It offered nine days' pay for each job, regardless of the actual number of days worked. This dramatic economic incentive proved sufficient to alter long-standing cultural habits.

The employees' attitudes gradually changed. Within four years, they had reduced perforation time to 1½ days, the same as in other efficient countries. Team members readily offered suggestions to improve teamwork and adapt technology to the special conditions of that area. On two occasions, the team encouraged transfer of men who would not change their habits and were thus holding back the team.

Motivation May Be More Difficult in a Different Culture

Another reason why international U.S. companies have difficulty implementing effective incentive programs across national and cultural boundaries is that they do not recognize important environmental differences which affect such programs. As a result, they often fail to structure incentives—or base pay, for that matter—to account for the fact that various foreign industries, functions, and professions have different status and pay levels from those of their counterparts in the United States.

In the United Kingdom, for example, the *average* pay structure of financial firms is higher than that of industrial companies, but the reverse is true in the United States. A Delft engineer in Holland has completed roughly the same amount of studies as a Ph.D. in the United States, while a diploma engineer in Germany is addressed as "Herr Doktor" and has much greater status than a Ph.D. in the United States.

From Milton L. Rock and C. Ian Sym-Smith, "Incentives for Foreign Nationals," *Harvard Business Review,* March–April 1973, p. 34. Reprinted with permission.

To restate the basic point we are making, managerial practices from an advanced country cannot be transferred directly. They need to be adapted to the particular cultural practices, level of development, and employee need structure which a host country has. In effect, neither the advanced nation's nor the host nation's traditional practices are used. Instead, a third—and situationally better—set of practices is developed which integrates the most workable ideas from both sets of traditional practices.

The Achievement Motive

Research by David C. McClelland discloses that emphasis on the *achievement motive* in a nation has an important influence on the drives of its people.[19] The achievement motive is present in everyone, but some people are consistently more oriented toward achievement than others. The achievement motive is a basic general attitude toward life, rather than a narrowly defined psychological need. It apparently can be stimulated by a nation's culture, for there are great differences in it among nations. McClelland found that the achievement motive is stronger in economically advanced countries and "growth" countries. As further evidence of cultural support of achievement, even children's books in the achievement-motivated countries give more emphasis to this drive, compared with books in nations low in achievement motivation.

People with strong achievement motives make accomplishment an end in itself, leaving in a secondary role the profit from accomplishment. They take

[19] David C. McClelland, *The Achieving Society,* Princeton, N.J.: D. Van Nostrand Company, Inc., 1961.

moderate risks, rather than high or low ones, because they feel responsible for their decisions. They are realistic. They plan carefully and persist toward goals. Above all, they work productively.

The achievement motive may be contrasted with competence, affiliation, and power motives.[20] These appear to be significant distinctions everywhere in the world. The achievement motive is more likely to develop the entrepreneur, innovator, and responsible leader. The achievers choose the best people to help them regardless of personal dislikes, while persons with affiliation motives choose their friends. Achievers work harder when they have feedback about progress, whereas affiliators work best when they are complimented for their attitude and cooperation.

Perhaps the main point to be drawn from studies of motives is that there will be a different mix of them in different cultures. If international managers wish to motivate local workers, they need to learn the motive most emphasized in the local culture and try to use it constructively. Then they need to try to interpret how motives vary among their people. For example, in South America the affiliation motives might be expected. Submanagers could be expected to hire, purchase supplies from, and otherwise bestow favors on their brothers, in-laws, cousins, and personal friends. However, a sample of 100 persons in the plant might be distributed by cultural motivation as follows: achievement, eleven; competence, thirteen; power, twenty-seven; and affiliation, forty-nine. If achievers can be identified and developed, they are likely to be responsible, innovating managers. The ultimate goal is to have many nationals managing operations as quickly as possible—and even moving to management positions in other countries, which would create a truly multinational work force for business.

SUMMARY

The nations of the world have urgent needs to make more productive use of their resources. Business is a major change agent and cultural catalyst in serving these needs. When an international business enters another culture, it is usually most effective when each culture adapts somewhat to the other. This idea especially applies when an advanced business enters a developing nation, but it also applies when both nations are advanced. The idea is reflected in the convergence hypothesis which holds that cultures tend to become more similar as they industrialize.

Multinational managers need transcultural capabilities in order to perform effectively without culture shock. Successfully managed businesses have the capacity to integrate social systems within a business context, introduce change, improve productivity, and motivate employees in a less-developed environment.

[20] Saul W. Gellerman, *Motivation and Productivity*, New York: American Management Association, 1963.

STUDY GUIDES FOR
INTERPRETATION OF THIS CHAPTER

1. Marfa Electronics, a multinational firm, is planning to build an assembly plant on a hill overlooking an Asian city with about 100,000 population. Local contacts have advised that many persons might refuse to work there because they believe the hill is haunted by evil spirits. The contacts have suggested that the city's leading mystic be employed to hold a public ceremony to drive the evil spirits away before construction is started. They report that the mystic's price, including decorations and refreshments, will probably be $5,000. As chief of the construction mission what would you do?

2. Read two articles or news items regarding international business and report whether they in any way support or refute the convergence hypothesis.

3. Choose another country, study its culture from books or personal contacts, and prepare a presentation telling a United States automobile manufacturer how his company's business practices should be amended for the new branch it is starting in the country.

4. With the aid of the most recent information available, appraise the accuracy of J.-J. Servan-Schreiber's predictions in *The American Challenge*.

5. From the point of view of an advanced business entering a developing nation, discuss the significance of the chart comparing a developing nation's man-power pool with the labor needs of an advanced business. What major plans and policies does the chart indicate you should make?

PROBLEMS
Human or Mechanical Power?

A. A multinational firm took 49 percent ownership in a joint venture with an Asian nation to manufacture a consumer durable good. One stated purpose in the venture agreement was that the multinational firm would provide its know-how to make the plant productive. The plant was to be located in a metropolitan center with substantial manufacturing. In planning for operations the multinational firm proposed using five mechanical forklift trucks to transport goods to and from production areas and in the warehouse. The government representative objected and proposed human labor with hand trucks. He gave the following reasons for his objections: (1) added capital costs, (2) difficulty of getting parts for the trucks and technicians to repair them, (3) difficulty of training qualified operators, and (4) unemployment in the city which made it politically essential for the plant to provide as many jobs as possible.

B. A multinational food producer took 49 percent ownership in a joint venture with a South American nation to process and can vegetables in a remote mountain region. One stated purpose in the venture agreement was that the multinational firm would provide its know-how to make the plant more productive than the typical local food processor in the nation. In planning for operations the multinational firm proposed five electric typewriters for office work. The government representative objected and proposed manual typewriters because (1) they tended to have fewer breakdowns and so required less maintenance, (2) they could be maintained by less-skilled technicians, available in a city 40 miles distant, and (3) electric service was unreliable; so the machines and their operators might be idled at times when they were needed.

1. In each instance, as the top local manager of the joint venture, how would you respond?

The Paper Mill in Brazil

Olin Corporation presented a two-page advertisement in *Business Week*. One page showed a picture of Karl Marx. The other page read as follows (reprinted with permission of Olin Corporation):

> *If Africa, Asia and South America go communist, don't blame him.*
> Karl Marx is not responsible for famines in Asia or epidemics in Africa. It's not his fault that the average South American earns 75¢ a day.
> All he did was predict the consequences.
> That a population living in misery will turn to communism as a way out. Unless something is done to alleviate these conditions.
> But the countries themselves don't have the economic resources to make these changes. The U.N. doesn't. Even the United States doesn't.
> They need the help of world industry. Particularly U.S. industry.
> Industry is in an ideal position to do this. It can deal directly with the people of a country. It can change their lives in a way no government can.
> A small case in point: in 1958, Olinkraft, a subsidiary of Olin, bought a paper mill in Igaras, a small town in the remote interior of Brazil.
> Igaras was the kind of town on which communism thrives—a declining mill, no doctors, shoeless children, men working an 84-hour week, etc.
> It wasn't hard to increase the production of the mill eight-fold, to lower hours and raise wages, to reforest the woodlands—but that wasn't enough.
> We hired a doctor, nurses, teachers; expanded the school; built a dispensary, a clubhouse; provided free medical and dental care (and medicines at cost to non-employees); financed housing loans and helped set up a cooperative store.
> And then the people joined in. They rebuilt their own homes, paid for their own teachers, built and operated their own store and, in effect, revitalized the whole town.
> But the people weren't the only ones to benefit. Olinkraft did well enough from the mill to start an extensive expansion program.

Igaras, of course, is only one town. But Olin is only one company. Imagine this kind of success multiplied by tens of thousands of companies and towns all over Africa, Asia and South America.

The deeds of industry may well be as important as the gospel of democracy.

1. Appraise this advertisement in terms of the multiplier effect, paternalism, the Law of Persistent Underdevelopment, the trusteeship role of management, equitable rewards to pluralistic investment groups, convergence hypothesis, social overhead costs, role of management as a change agent and productivity catalyst, and other applicable ideas discussed in this book.

CHAPTER 26

LOOKING TOWARD THE FUTURE

Progress doesn't happen; it must be made to happen.

Charles B. Thornton[1]

It just may be that by the social audit we may develop an acceptable method to institutionalize in business desirable and evolutionary reforms which will make business stronger and more able to serve the social purpose.

George A. Steiner[2]

New conditions bring new issues. Certainly a major issue of modern times is the relation of organizations to society, as has been discussed throughout this book. The central issue is how to meet the needs of the organization (business, in this instance) along with the needs of its individual participants and of society in general.

In short, the issue is how to keep organizations viable along with man and his whole society. If we emphasize organization viability alone, society may become an organized monstrosity with human puppets dangling from its organizational strings. If we emphasize individual viability alone, we deny man the cornucopia of benefits that derive from organized activity. And if we emphasize only society as a whole, we deny man the individuality and freedom with which nature ordained him, and we reduce both organizations and men to servitude under the "plan." The only satisfactory answer is a balance which harmonizes all interests. The modern social balance is called pluralism. It is dynamic, not static, evolving into new forms that probably eventually will give it a new name also.

In this chapter we shall take a broad look at how the issues we have discussed are moving toward a more responsible business society in the future. We shall discuss how new relationships are evolving between business and society and how

[1] Charles B. Thornton, "The Challenge to Business Management," *The Deltasig* (Delta Sigma Pi), November 1969, p. 21.

[2] George A. Steiner, "The Social Audit," speech before Western Division, Academy of Management, Yosemite Village, Calif., April 1972, p. 11.

the social audit is a useful instrument to evaluate these relationships. Society is coming to understand the importance of business for achieving a better quality of life around the world, and the concept of a socially profitable business is emerging.

BUSINESS AND SOCIETY
Business in a Pluralistic Social System

The modern business is a social system in itself, but it is also part of a larger social system represented by society in general. Clearly there is a reciprocal relationship between business and this larger society. Society does affect business through religion, law, custom, and a host of other influences. But business is not a mute servant; it speaks with a voice of leadership in the affairs of society. It is a change agent influencing society in many ways. It is an important voice in a pluralism of many voices.

The society which created business could, of course, destroy its independence. Business is continually on trial before the high court of public opinion, but, in a free society at least, it is permitted to testify in its own defense by showing how its actions contribute to the general welfare. Except for the dark days of the Great Depression of the 1930s, business testimony has been effective. The public has little doubt about business's net contribution. The issue is not whether business should be stripped of power, but rather how its power and drive can be channeled into greater contributions. As explained by Taylor:[3]

> A pluralist society is obliged to proceed always on a principle of counterpoise: it discovers its equilibrium, not by eliminating oppositions, but by using them, by making them party to a larger design which exhibits the public dimension of every private act. . . .
>
> We do not solve the problem of governing the modern corporation by extinguishing its independence. We solve the problem by defining the limits within which its independence is admissible and beyond which its independence is an encroachment on the public interest.

We believe that the next few decades will be an era of pluralistic society. The idea of pluralism will tend to be used more and more to explain institutional conduct and analyze its consequences. As stated by one observer, "The trend has been toward a decidedly pluralistic pattern in which it is recognized that the existence of numerous decision centers throughout the social structure of the nation vitalizes the economy and is essential for the protection of basic liberties."[4] The idea of pluralism focuses on the social needs of many groups, the interfaces

---

[3] John F. A. Taylor, "Is the Corporation above the Law?" *Harvard Business Review,* March–April 1965, p. 130.

[4] Richard Eells, "Beyond the Golden Rule," *Columbia Journal of World Business,* July–August 1967, p. 83.

among them, and the system relationships that evolve from these interfaces. It increases the need to look upon conditions in terms of a whole.

The Socially Profitable Business

In earlier chapters we have referred to the socially profitable business. In this kind of business various types of social investments are received from many claimants. Management, acting particularly as trustee along with its other managerial roles, takes these investments and tries to develop payouts to claimants that are greater than their investments. The payouts cover all types of claimant expectations, including social and psychological rewards such as community improvement, personal growth, and social interaction.

When social and psychological goals become a part of the organization's basic system of objectives, rather than some thorn which must be tolerated to get the economic job done, then we have the foundation for a truly socially profitable business. Just as it is with economic profit, some businesses will do better than others, but the key point is that social profitability becomes part of the firm's basic objectives. Social goals are no longer a peripheral, nonbusiness item. When business accepts this expanded view of the social system, it will be released from its "economic ghetto" to play a larger part in the affairs of mankind than ever before.

Society's expectations of business are increasing dramatically—perhaps excessively. Not only does society expect business to take material goods and produce something better, but it also wants business to take employees and make them better. Society expects that a business which enters a community will make it better. In whatever business undertakes, the expectation is leadership toward improvement in the quality of life, rather than simply satisfaction of minimum standards of conduct. This high expectation places heavy responsibility on business to act in a socially profitable way.

To the extent that business fails to seek social profitability in accordance with human expectations, the Iron Law of Responsibility stands in the background to remind business of the urgency of its task. This law promises that a group which has power and fails to use it responsibly will eventually find its power slipping away to other groups which are ready to use it more responsibly. A number of years ago Berle stated clearly the alternatives available to business:[5]

> The choice of corporate managements is not whether so great a power shall cease to exist; they can merely determine whether they will serve as the nuclei of its organization or pass it over to someone else, probably the modern state. The present current of thinking and insistence that private rather than governmental decisions are soundest for the community are clearly forcing the largest corporations toward a greater rather than a lesser acceptance of the responsibility that goes with power.

[5] Adolf A. Berle, Jr., *The 20th Century Capitalist Revolution,* New York: Harcourt, Brace & World, Inc., 1954, pp. 172–173.

Where Is the Golden Mean?

Two answers are going to be wrong. It is going to be wrong to say that business does not and should not do anything but maximize profits. That is nonsense. It is also going to be wrong to say that business should forget all about the profit motive and the invaluable profit measure and simply settle down to do social good. Somewhere in between these wrong answers, accountants, lawyers, businessmen, and communicators are going to have a pretty interesting twenty years, at least, wrestling with the problem.

From Max Ways, in *Business Leadership in Social Change*, New York: The Conference Board, Inc., 1971, p. 66. Copyright 1971 by The Conference Board.

The world of business is no longer just a technological and economic world—and probably it never was. Now, for sure, it is a social world also.

Social Profitability Includes Economic Profitability

Economic profit is basic to business success. Business deals with economic inputs, and if these resources are dissipated, the organization lacks the capacity to continue its services. Economic outputs need to exceed inputs, or else there is no reason for economic investors to allocate resources to the business. These economic facts of life are as true for publicly owned business as they are for private business. If the public invests its resources in a state enterprise, it expects a favorable return therefrom just as a private investor does. Therefore, when we speak of social objectives for business performance, we think of economic objectives as one part of this whole framework. We need businesses which are both economically and socially productive.

The business which achieves both objectives is the one which will be immensely stronger and better accepted by society. Looking at the situation this way, we see that the idea of social performance is in a sense a broadening of the profit idea to include social outputs as well as economic ones. Society seeks both social and economic returns from its business institutions, and it expects profitable outputs of each in relation to inputs.

Business's difficult task is to balance economic outputs with social outputs in accordance with the priorities of each social system in which it operates. This task exposes business to the risk that its economic productivity will decline as it gives more of its energies to social outputs. Nevertheless, in a world of rising social expectations, both outputs are required from business.

In order to perform their new socioeconomic role effectively, business leaders need to develop value systems that recognize responsibilities to claimants other than stockholders. There is strong evidence that many managers already have this kind of value system.

A study of over fifty regional and national firms known to have social action programs showed that managers ranked responsibility to society a close second to traditional stockholder responsibility.[6] The weighted values for rankings of four groups covered in the survey were as follows:

Stockholders	237
Society	195
Employees	170
Management	125

Furthermore, the managers showed a strong value commitment to their social action programs. When asked how they would respond to stockholder objections to a social action program, 90 percent said they would not abandon the program. Similarly, 95 percent would not abandon the program when faced with union objections. Clearly their commitment was to broader social responsibilities.

There is no doubt that business serves society's economic needs, but the businessmen in the survey are saying that business also is obligated to serve some social needs. One analyst explains the situation in the following manner.[7]

> It is no longer sufficient to tell either stockholders or society that the enterprise shows a profit. The socially responsible corporation now must be able to demonstrate to both its stockholders and the public that it has measured costs and benefits for its policies, not only for the organization but also for the society in which it operates.

On the other hand, although managers accept the general ideal of social responsibility to the whole society, this idea often has not worked its way into day-to-day operating judgments of organizational performance. An illustration is a survey of 163 top-executive members of the Presidents Association.[8] Members were asked to rank ten items in response to the question, "How do you measure the effectiveness of any business?" One of the ten selections was "Enlightened social consciousness," and only *3 percent* of the respondents ranked this item in the top five measures of effectiveness. Instead they favored such items as growth in earnings and efficient planning. When judgments were made about operating effectiveness, social consciousness seemed to be far down the value scale, even though a general idea of social responsibility is accepted.

The traditional business arguments for economic efficiency are unlikely to

---

[6] Fred Luthans and Richard M. Hodgetts, "Government and Business: Partners in Social Action," *Labor Law Journal,* December 1969, pp. 763–770.

[7] David Novick, "Cost-Benefit Analysis and Social Responsibility," *Business Horizons,* October 1973, p. 72.

[8] "The Country's Most Effective Companies," *Organizational Dynamics,* Autumn 1972, pp. 60–66; and Merrill E. Douglass, "How Do You Measure the Effectiveness of a Business?" *Organizational Dynamics,* Autumn 1973, pp. 47–50.

be sufficient in the long run for two reasons. One reason is that traditional efficiency existed only from a narrow point of view and was partly a fiction when considered from the whole social system, because "efficient" firms merely transferred many costs to society. For example, an efficient firm discharges untreated wastes into a stream, thereby increasing the costs of a downstream municipal water installation. These costs properly belong to the business's products, but they have not been charged there. Similarly, odors from a paper mill may have prevented a householder from fully enjoying his backyard patio. In the eyes of the public the costs of odor prevention should have been added to product costs rather than being passed on to the community. There is a strong feeling that products should as nearly as possible carry the full costs of their production, rather than a portion of those costs being passed to the community.

A second reason is that people's tastes have changed precisely because of their economic affluence provided by business efficiency. Now that people have a minimum economic base from which to operate, they have become more concerned with social values. They insist that since business is a major institution in the social system, it should be concerned with social payouts along with its economic payouts. In effect, they are asking business to enlarge its mission to both social and economic values. They are not asking business to stop its economic contribution and turn only to social contributions, because that would be a folly which would lead to an economically destitute society. What they want is a socially profitable business bringing both economic and social benefits.

The foregoing comments suggest that business can maintain and reinforce its legitimacy in the social system only to the degree that it maintains its relevance to the needs of the people who make up the social system. Those needs are changing, and so business must change its activities in order to restore relevancy and remain viable. Business should learn to handle social change in the same manner that it has met technological change. In this area it has acted aggressively and successfully with few failures. It can do likewise with the social change that confronts it.

During this period of change, however, action needs to be tempered by moderation and caution. With all the clamor for social action, there is a danger that emotional voices will force business into areas where it has little competence and cannot deliver what is expected by society. Business cannot be all things to all people. It merely shares with other institutions a responsibility for social performance.

Further, whatever progress is made toward improved social performance, society needs to recognize that new problems often arise from the once-heralded solutions to old problems. A problem solution is not solely positive; it also may create negative side effects. For example, through better health maintenance, society extended human life spans. The result was a devastating population bomb that had to be controlled. In the real world, for nearly all gains there are concurrent losses to be reckoned with. Progress is always a cost/benefit analysis. The challenge is to keep the benefits above the costs.

Determining Areas of Social Performance

When a firm tries to determine the most appropriate areas for major social performance efforts, the following criteria may be helpful. First, business needs to respond in terms of social priorities. All needs cannot be met at once; therefore priorities must be determined. Government has a key role in setting priorities so that business can know where to act. For example, court decisions and the Civil Rights Act of 1964 gave priority to equal employment opportunity, and government then served as moderator helping a variety of social institutions carry out this priority.

A second criterion is the degree of connection between a social performance area and regular business activities. When business activities are directly affecting some social area, society expects business to perform these economic activities in socially constructive ways. For example, if business makes automobiles and they pollute the air, then it has some responsibility for social performance in areas of air pollution. Similarly, if business affects the economic life of its plant community, then it has certain obligations to assure that its social effects are constructive. Society insists that business handle constructively all social costs of its economic activities.

A third criterion is that business primarily should work in its areas of competence. If business lacks competence to work in a social area or cannot satisfactorily acquire this competence, then its social involvement might cause more problems than it corrects. Particularly when society is experimenting with untried areas of social performance where even the experts are not sure what to do, it would be folly to demand aggressive social programs by business.

Finally, demands for business social performance should not be of the types which destroy business's economic performance. A gain of social performance at the expense of economic performance would merely be trading one problem for another; thus it would not provide much net gain for society. This point is perhaps the one most emphasized by businessmen in their discussions of social issues. They believe that they have a significant economic mission to perform and have done it well, and they want to assure that this particular aspect of the quality of life of the whole social system is protected. They argue that there is no net social gain if society singlemindedly pursues social performance while destroying economic performance. It is not necessary for all the foregoing criteria to apply in each instance. The only requirement is that the criteria exist in sufficient combination in each instance to provide compelling reasons for giving attention to social performance.

THE SOCIAL AUDIT
Definition

In any discussion of social performance a key question is how social performance will be evaluated, and one important aid to this evaluation is the *social audit.* [9] It moved into prominence very quickly in the 1970s. A social audit is a systematic study and evaluation of an organization's social performance, as distinguished from its economic performance. It is concerned with possible influences on the social quality of life instead of the economic quality of life. The social audit leads to a *social performance report* or social audit report for management and perhaps outsiders also.

In this definition the term ''social performance'' refers to any organizational activities that affect the general welfare of society. The idea of social performance emphasizes total needs of the whole community and the whole society. It is a systemwide view. It tends to focus on general humanistic values while reducing traditional economic and technical values to subsystems within the larger social system. It is concerned with the human meaning of events.

The evaluation of social performance is not a wholly new idea. For many years organizations have been making judgments about how their activities affect society, but these judgments typically have been spur-of-the-moment, intuitive affairs. The idea of a *systematic study and evaluation* of organizational social performance is relatively new, because only recently has society given major emphasis to social values. The social audit for business originally was proposed by Howard R. Bowen in 1953 in a brief discussion in his book *Social Responsibilities of the Businessman.*

Features of a Social Audit

Areas for social audit include any activity which has a significant social impact, such as activities affecting environmental quality and equal employment opportunity. An extensive list of these areas was presented in Chapter 1.

Normally, a social audit can determine only what an organization *is doing* in social areas, not the amount of social good that results from these activities. It is a process audit rather than an audit of results. Social results are so nebulous that they are difficult to measure, and generally accepted social norms are almost nonexistent. There are a variety of opinions about what is ''good'' and what is ''bad,'' and even when there is agreement about the desirability of a result, there are different measures of how much good is accomplished.

Social results are also difficult to audit because most of them occur outside an organization, and so a firm has no way to secure data from these outside sources. Even when data are available, causes are so complex that a firm has no way to know how much of the results its actions caused. For example, violent crimes decreased 4 percent in an urban ghetto where a firm had a minority

---

[9] A more extensive discussion of the social audit may be found in Raymond A. Bauer and Dan H. Fenn, Jr., *The Corporate Social Audit,* New York: The Russell Sage Foundation, 1972.

[10] Howard R. Bowen, *Social Responsibilities of the Businessman,* New York: Harper & Brothers, 1953, pp. 155–156. Bowen's proposal received reinforcement from Blum in a major article; see Fred H. Blum, ''Social Audit of the Enterprise,'' *Harvard Business Review,* March–April 1958, pp. 77–86.

The Absence of Social Norms Limits
Usefulness of Social Audits

If there is a single obvious technical flaw in the audits that have been attempted, it is the relative absence of norms whereby to judge performance. Granted, many norms are hard to come by; what, for example, would be a good norm against which to judge a company's performance with minority suppliers or community relations? Circumstances vary so much from company to company that it may be a long time before we can come up with any criteria for judgment beyond "honest efforts."

From Raymond A. Bauer, "The Corporate Social Audit: Where Does It Stand Today?" *Personnel*, July–August 1973, pp. 16–17. Copyright 1973 by AMACOM, a division of American Management Association.

employment program. How much of the benefit, if any, was caused by this program? Even though results cannot be proved, an audit of what is being done still is considered desirable because it shows the amount of effort that a business is making in areas deemed beneficial to society. Further, if effort can be determined, then informed judgments can be made about potential results.

Social audits can be made by internal specialists, outside consultants, or a combination of the two. The internal auditor has the advantage of familiarity with the business, but his judgments might be influenced by company loyalties. An outside consultant has the advantage of an outsider's view, but he lacks familiarity with organizational activities, so he may overlook significant data. In any case, if audit information is to be released to the public, the outside auditor has more credibility.

A significant issue is whether the audit, or any portion of it, is to be made public by means of a social performance report. The philosophy of an open system suggests that the public interest is best served by public reporting; however, the present state of the art with social audits is so imprecise that public disclosure might do more harm than good. Imprecise data and informed judgments are helpful for internal decision making, but they probably are not concrete enough to satisfy the public. Further, there are so many differences of opinion that almost anyone could find reasons for criticizing a firm's performance, and dissident groups could expand some detail far beyond its importance. The result could be that social conflict would increase and firms would withdraw from social programs in order to avoid reporting on them, thus defeating the original purposes of social reporting. Bowen's original proposal was that a social audit should be made by *outside* consultants for *inside* use only, and that it should be made only every five years.

Because of the problems involved, progress toward public disclosure of social audits will be slow. It seems wise to proceed with caution, but the eventual direction seems certain to be toward more social reporting. An occasional firm already has made extensive disclosures when it thinks these disclosures will contribute to public understanding of an important issue. One corporation, for example, released detailed statistical and descriptive material about its employment practices in South Africa, where racial discrimination in employment exists. It believed that its own practices were a sound alternative to activist proposals, and it wanted to replace rhetoric with facts in this public debate.

Use of Quantitative Data

Social audits use both quantitative and qualitative data. The pressures to use a quantitative approach are strong because of its respectability and apparent objectivity. Quantitative data are precise and convincing, but in the area of social philosophy and human values it is misleading to report only in quantitative terms. They can communicate only a part of the total situation, only a part of the whole truth. Both qualitative and quantitative data are essential. Normally a firm uses as much quantitative data as possible, provided it communicates accurately, and then supplements it with qualitative data. Examples of useful quantitative data are proportions of minorities employed and costs of a pollution abatement program.

An example of the *misuse* of quantitative data is a public project in Britain which would require demolition of a historic twelfth-century Norman church. A cost/benefit analysis of the proposed project calculated that the loss from demolition of the church would be only the face value of the fire insurance policy on the church. No consideration was given to the historic social value of the church.

In spite of the difficulties with quantification, the lure of objective figures remains, particularly dollar figures in the form of traditional accounting statements. For example, one firm made a genuine effort to conduct a social audit which it reported in dollar terms in its annual report.[11] A "social income statement" attempted to portray social income that the firm provided for society, and in this context payments for benefits such as employee tuition reimbursement represented social income. Social costs were represented by such items as projected effects of layoffs and employee discharges. The difference betwen social income and social costs represented the net social income that the firm provided for society. There was also a related "social balance sheet" which reported cumulative debits and credits.

While the foregoing approach is useful, its weakness is that it is limited to economic terms and may overlook the social meaning of activities. Purely dollar presentations appear to present only part of the whole picture of a firm's social performance.

[11] Raymond A. Bauer, "The Corporate Social Audit: Where Does It Stand Today?" *Personnel,* July–August 1973, pp. 8–18; and Raymond A. Bauer and Dan H. Fenn, Jr., "What *Is* a Corporate Social Audit?" *Harvard Business Review,* January–February 1973, pp. 37–48. A related approach is the proposal for a socioeconomic operating statement in David F. Linowes, *Strategies for Survival,* New York: AMACOM, 1973, pp. 169–178.

The most progress in assigning dollar values to social data has been made with *human resource accounting* in employee relations.[12] Human resource accounting attempts to account for changes in the quality of a firm's human organization. Its purpose is to enable management to know whether its actions are increasing or decreasing the quality of human resources and approximately by what amount. For example, investments in training are treated as a long-run improvement in the quality of the work force.

Benefits of a Social Audit

Essentially an organization conducts a social audit because it exists in a social world and in order to live effectively in that world it needs social data to guide its actions. Within that broad context, what does an organization expect from a social audit? What benefits does an audit provide? Certainly one benefit is that it supplies data for comparison with policies and standards so that management can determine how well the organization is living up to its objectives. Many firms have established affirmative action programs, ecology programs, and similar activities, and they need to evaluate the progress made with these programs. Just as a spaceship in flight must know where it is in order to correct its flight and reach its objective, a business must know where it is in relation to its objectives. An organization can also make comparisons over a period of time to determine how fast it is moving toward its social objectives.

Related to the first benefit is the fact that a social audit encourages greater concern for social performance throughout the organization. It has been shown that subordinate managers and employees tend to give their attention to activities where reports are required and evaluations made by higher management. In the process of preparing reports and responding to evaluations, employees become more aware of social data and the social implications of their actions, and corporate social objectives are more strongly reinforced in all areas of the organization.

A third benefit of the social audit is to provide data for comparing effectiveness of different types of programs. In one branch plant, for example, a firm may emphasize counseling in the employment of hard-core unemployed persons, while in another branch it emphasizes an elaborate training program. An examination of the problems and progress made in each of these programs will give management useful inputs for establishing better programs.

A fourth benefit is the provision of cost data on social programs so that management can relate the data to budgets, available resources, company objectives, and projected benefits of programs. If a business is going to devote significant amounts of its resources to social programs, then it needs some evidence of what those programs cost. Direct costs such as a gift are easy to compute, but indirect costs are more difficult. Should managers keep records of their time so that

[12] Rensis Likert and David G. Bowers, "Improving the Accuracy of P/L Reports by Estimating the Change in Dollar Value of the Human Organization," *Michigan Business Review*, March 1973, pp. 15–24.

appropriate portions of their salaries can be charged to social programs? Shall a firm compute its opportunity costs for alternative uses of resources and charge those costs to social programs?

>An example is a bank that had a loan program for minority businesses. These loans were made at a lower interest rate than regular business loans, and the bank could have employed all its funds in regular loans. In addition the default rate for minority loans was higher than for regular loans, so a higher proportion of the average loan was lost by default. Available time studies on loans also showed that the processing time for minority loans was considerably longer because of such factors as additional business counseling. In order to determine extra costs of the minority loan program, the bank subtracted the minority loan yield from the regular loan yield to determine opportunity costs and then added the extra administrative costs of the loans.

A fifth benefit of a social audit is that it provides information for effective response to external claimants that make demands on the organization. News reporters, minority groups, and a variety of others want to know what a business is doing in areas of their special interest, and a business needs to respond as effectively as possible. The social audit shows a business where it is vulnerable to public pressures and where its strengths lie.

The foregoing benefits indicate that essentially an organization conducts a social audit to provide managers with information inputs about their firm's current state of social performance so that better decisions may be made. Managers are key decision makers in an organization, and the quality of their decisions is related to the quality and amount of information inputs they receive prior to their decisions. For balanced decisions in a social world they need dependable social inputs along with other inputs. This improvement in business decision making eventually should lead to improved benefits for society. From society's point of view rather than the firm's point of view, this is the ultimate benefit of a social audit. In the process, however, the firm also benefits because it increases its social viability.

Operation of Audit Programs

The social audit is such a new concept that there are very few guidelines for making it, and there is no standard procedure that will compare with the rather definite standards that exist for accounting audits. Most firms are at the beginning of the learning curve with social audits. They are starting to experiment with them, but they have only limited results. When firms do begin audit procedures, they tend to find that the process is more complex than originally contemplated. Everything is related to everything else. The following company experience illustrates operation of an audit program.[13]

[13] Barry Richman, "New Paths to Corporate Social Responsibility," *California Management Review*, Spring 1973, pp. 23–24.

The board of directors determined that a social responsibility committee should be appointed by the board chairman to make a social audit for the firm. The committee consisted of two company officers and one public member. It found very few audit guidelines and had to develop its own program with the counsel of persons both inside and outside the company. Early in the program the committee recognized that the audit needed to be more comprehensive than anticipated and that social effects of company operations were more extensive than expected.

Eventually six areas for audit were developed as follows: social importance of regular activities, consumerism, community service, environment, equal employment, and fixing responsibility within the firm for social performance. Audit programs were developed for each area, and both qualitative and quantitative data were sought. The entire process helped management translate vague ideas about social performance into hard realities.

Limited experience indicates that a social audit is a more massive undertaking than firms expect. Although some social data are available in existing records, much needed information is nonexistent and new procedures are required for measuring and reporting it.

When one considers the many difficulties involved in social auditing, such as credibility, identification of cause and effect, complexity, quantification, measurement, and absence of norms, it is evident that business faces a major task. Firms find that they need to move slowly. In the beginning most of them select only a few areas for audit, rather than trying to conduct a complete audit of all operations. Progress toward social auditing and reporting is being made, but it will be slow evolution not instant change. Even modest programs will give managers and the public useful information that they have not had earlier.

THE CHALLENGE TO BUSINESS LEADERSHIP

It is an age of discontinuity. There is a youth revolution, a moral revolution, an educational revolution, a technological revolution, a minority group revolution, and so on. The pressures for change come endlessly from all directions.

With so many changes coming, business leadership in the next generation will be an increasingly difficult task, requiring intensely prepared managers. The task is enormous, and so it is dangerous to expect miracles in a decade. But the challenges are exciting. The opportunities are substantial. The new emphasis on quality of life opens a whole new planet for development in the business universe. No one claims that in the physical universe the task of reaching the planet Mars is easy, but it is exciting. The same excitement applies to the new planet of social outcomes which business is seeking. The payoff may be far greater than that derived from reaching and developing Mars. Consider, for example, the influence of one businessman on the Renaissance.[14]

> One would like to have a record of the thinking of the great Italian banker, Cosimo de' Medici, in the mid-fifteenth century. His bank and his business had come to dominate Florence. He ran the little country, though he assumed no political title. He subsidized art and artists, and supported queer penniless refugees from Byzantium who insisted on copying and translating Greek classics. Did he realize he was laying one of the foundation piers for the Italian Renaissance, one of the greatest efflorescences of human spirit in the Christian era? He was a reflective man, and he may have speculated on the subject. There are some marked similarities between his situation and that of American business firms five hundred years later.

There are indeed some similarities between the fifteenth and the twentieth centuries. Business today is coming to an era of social response to create a better quality of life. Business is pushed by world events, so it really has no choice concerning whether to step into this era or not. The social results can be just as exciting and as beneficial as those of the Renaissance—or even more so. This is business's great challenge.

SUMMARY

A socially profitable business is one which provides society both economic and social net gains in relation to inputs (costs). Society expects business to give increased attention to its social profitability. One reason is that the economic success of business frees people from economic bondage so that they may turn their attention to social performance. In determining the most appropriate areas for social performance efforts, the following criteria may be helpful: performance particularly needs to be in areas of social priority, where regular business activities affect society, where business has competence, and in ways which maintain economic performance along with social performance.

A social audit is a systematic study and evaluation of an organization's social performance, as distinguished from its economic performance. It is essential for a firm's internal decision making and for external social reporting. It mostly reports what an organization is doing, rather than the difficult-to-measure social good that results from these activities. An audit is expressed in both quantitative and qualitative terms. Benefits of an audit include data for comparison with standards, increased concern for social performance, comparison of different types of programs, cost/benefit comparisons, and data for external social reporting.

[14] Berle, op. cit., pp. 176–177.

STUDY GUIDES FOR INTERPRETATION OF THIS CHAPTER

1. By means of additional reading and thinking about the material in this book, prepare to discuss the nature of the social opportunities that businessmen appear to be facing around the world.

2. Is the idea of a socially profitable business a useful concept (*a*) for businessmen and (*b*) for persons appraising business actions?

3. Discuss the benefits that a social audit may provide.

4. You are on the staff of an international fast-food franchise chain that is planning a social audit, and you have been asked to present a plan for the audit. Present your plan stating what areas you will evaluate and what criteria and standards you will use in the evaluation.

5. Discuss arguments for and against stockholders electing an independent Committee for Corporate Responsibility to audit and report on a company's social performance in the same way that an accounting firm audits and reports on the company's financial performance.

PROBLEMS
The Feedback System

Martin Sober is a bright young M.B.A. from a prestigious graduate school. He is now one of five executive assistants on the staff of the executive vice president of a national manufacturer of home appliances. Since assuming this position six months ago, he has regularly insisted that the company establish (*a*) a better system of feedback about the social effects of its actions and (*b*) "better mechanisms for receiving inputs about forthcoming social problems which may affect the company's operations." This morning the executive vice president called Sober into his office and asked him to prepare within the next two weeks a five-page report proposing realistic and specific ways to accomplish the two items he had mentioned. The vice president implied that Sober might be assigned to implement some of his proposals if they were accepted.

1. In the role of Sober, prepare the report.

The Dangerous Drug

Margarita Pharmaceutical Products manufactures a prescription drug which is the only known effective treatment for a debilitating, lingering, and eventually fatal illness which primarily affects older persons. The drug produces marked improvement for four of five users, so it is popular with both physicians and patients. However, the drug has discomforting side effects in three of five users, and these effects are severe in one of five users. Several deaths have been attributed to use of the drug. The drug is approved by the federal government for prescription use; however, it probably would not have been approved if other less dangerous drugs were available to treat this disease.

This morning the president of Margarita opened the newspaper and read that in a public speech a Congressman from another state had attributed seventeen deaths to the drug during the last year. He called the drug "an atrocity on mankind" and an example of the "collusion between federal enforcement officials and drug company exploiters."

The president believed the stated number of deaths was reasonably accurate. He estimated that about 400,000 victims of the disease used the drug in the United States. He was convinced that, on balance, the drug was beneficial and desperately needed. His research scientists said they could find no way to reduce side effects of the drug, and this view was confirmed by several research physicians working with the disease in medical centers. However, the president was concerned that adverse publicity for the company would harm sales of its other products. About 40 percent of its products were nonprescription consumer drugs.

1. As president, what alternatives are available to you and what are the advantages and disadvantages involved?

2. What are the claimant groups in this situation and what investments in this situation give rise to their claims?

3. As president, what would you do, if anything?

Proposal of Japan Committee for Economic Development

On March 18, 1973, Keizai Doyukai (Japan Committee for Economic Development) issued a statement on the responsibility of business to society. It stressed the need for changed behavior on the part of business and called for business to act more in concurrence with societal expectations. The statement set forth five principles as guidelines for business conduct as follows:[15]

1. Firms must act creatively and efficiently to supply goods and services of a good and safe quality to fulfill societal expectations. Firms must provide an adequate income and a safe and pleasant work place for their employees while also serving the interests of stockholders.

2. Firms must act positively to solve the more urgent problems of society. At the present these include pollution and the effective use of resources. Enterprises should take the initiative in this area before legal regulations are enforced.

[15] "The Social Responsibility of the Enterprise: Some Proposals by Keizai Doyukai (I)," *Japan Labor Bulletin,* November 1973, p. 7.

Employers' organizations at the industry level should act to formulate guidelines for enterprise behavior and seek to implement such guidelines as seem necessary.

3. Firms must define their goals so as to incorporate a social perspective with an eye on the long-term welfare of the firm even though the resulting goals may not necessarily enhance the firm's short-term profits. These goals should be made public and then implemented. In particular, firms should engage their resources to help realize a welfare society by improving the environment, assisting urban and local community development, and contributing to manpower development.

4. Firms must seek to promote fair inter-enterprise competition by supporting further liberalization of trade and capital, and the establishment of new enterprises. Such competition is key to improve enterprise conduct. Firms should make sincere efforts to accept constructive criticism from outside social groups formed by consumers and citizens in the local community.

5. In relation to the foregoing, firms must engage in an active dialogue with society Firms need to see the enterprise as one of several constituents going to make up the social fabric. They should provide information on enterprise activities in so far as they influence the broader society, and thereby build mutual trust with members of the broader society.

1. Assuming that business will endeavor to follow these guidelines, are they adequate to achieve a responsible business-society relationship in Japan? If they are not adequate, indicate what other guidelines are necessary and prepare them.

2. Discuss the strengths and weaknesses of the guidelines for the purpose of improving responsible action by business.

3. Would these guidelines be appropriate for business in the United States? Discuss.

CASES

Cases provide a useful medium for testing and applying some of the ideas in this textbook. They bring reality to abstract ideas about business, society, and environment. The cases have a decision-making emphasis in the sense that they end at a point which leaves some participant with a decision to make. One question often is, "Do I have a further problem?" If that question is answered in the affirmative, then further decisions must be made and analysis undertaken regarding what problems exist, why they are problems, what claimants are involved, what the contents and validities of their claims are, what alternatives exist within the constraints of the situation, and, finally, what action should be taken and what its implications are. This is the reality faced by all persons in operating situations. There is no escaping it.

All case names and certain case details are disguised except for the Denver and Rio Grande Western Railroad Company, Silverton Branch, and the Lockheed Aircraft Corporation.

These cases are not presented as either good business practice or poor business practice. Perhaps each case incorporates some of both. All persons must make these judgments for themselves.

CASE 1

THE DENVER AND RIO GRANDE WESTERN RAILROAD COMPANY, SILVERTON BRANCH,[1] PART A

On December 21, 1959, the Denver and Rio Grande Western Railroad Company,[2] a common carrier by railroad subject to Part 1 of the Interstate Commerce Act, filed an application under section 1(18) of the act for a certificate of public convenience and necessity permitting the abandonment of that portion of its narrow-gauge line known as the Silverton Branch. Protests against the abandonment were filed by several city chambers of commerce, the county commissioners of two counties, the Colorado Public Utilities Commission, the Colorado State Mineral Resources Board, various railway labor organizations, the San Juan Wool Growers' and Cattlemen's Associations, and a number of ranchers and businessmen from the area.

The Silverton Branch of applicant's system is a narrow-gauge line that extends between Durango and Silverton, two towns in the rugged mountainous area of southwest Colorado. The Silverton Branch was constructed by applicant in 1881 and 1882 for the purpose of transporting ore and concentrates from many rich mines in the Silverton area to the smelter in Durango and also for the purpose of transporting passengers and freight between the two towns and intermediate points. Prior to completion of the Silverton Branch, freight could be transported only by pack animal or freight wagons.

Over the years, mining operations in the Silverton district have gradually

---

[1] Adapted from the report and order recommended by the hearing examiner in interstate commerce, Finance Docket No. 20943. The true company name is used in this case.
[2] Hereinafter referred to as "applicant."

declined, and the demand for freight service to carry ore and concentrate to the smelter at Durango, and supplies and other freight to Silverton, has slowly decreased. In 1924, the railroad stopped operating separate freight and passenger trains and instituted a daily (except Sunday) mixed-traffic service.[3] The amount of service was gradually reduced over the years, although the railroad continued to offer year-round service. From March 1949, to September 1953, the year-round service consisted of one mixed train per week. However, beginning in 1951, triweekly round-trip mixed-train service was started in the summer. This service was designed primarily to accommodate tourists and sightseeing passengers who wished to ride on an antique, picturesque narrow-gauge train, pulled by an old-time steam locomotive through the beautiful Colorado mountains. In 1953, the railroad stopped providing any year-round scheduled service, confining its scheduled trips to the tourist season of June 1 to September 15.

The line is subject to maintenance problems characteristic of narrow-gauge lines located in the mountains. It is difficult to maintain and operate, particularly during the winter and spring months. Heavy snows block the tracks, snow and rock slides often occur, and flooding (particularly from fast and heavy thawing in the spring) causes washouts of tracks.

Applicant estimated that the cost of rehabilitating the line so that it would be suitable for year-round operation would total $447,400. Although the track between Durango and Hermosa (a distance of 11 miles) is low and subject to flooding, no damage from floods had been experienced in recent years. A number of culverts along the line need replacing, and some portions of the roadbed require ditching. Much of the existing lightweight rail needs replacing, and because of age, bridges need to be reinforced and strengthened.

Although no regular year-round service has been provided over the line in recent years, maintenance work has been on an accelerated basis for the past several years. This has resulted in a general upgrading of the bridge structures and in the restoration of the track to a level entirely satisfactory for the restricted use that has been made of it.

Applicant admits that without any increase in its regular maintenance program, the line could be adequately maintained to afford service during the summer and that the extensive rehabilitation work outlined would be necessary only if year-round service were rendered.

Each summer since 1951, the combination sightseeing and freight service has been provided from early June to the end of September. At the commencement of each summer season, triweekly service is provided. During the peak of the tourist season, it is increased to daily service and is then reduced to the triweekly basis toward the end of the season. The train, normally consisting of a coal-burning locomotive, ten passenger cars, and two freight cars, departs from Durango at 9:15 A.M. and arrives at Silverton at 12:40 P.M. After a two-hour lunch period, the train makes the return run to Durango, arriving there at 6:00 P.M. Although the train

---

[3] A mixed train is one which carries both freight and passengers.

normally accommodates a total of 385 passengers, including some standees, occasionally additional standees are permitted, thus increasing the passenger maximum to 485. Such freight as may be available for movement is also handled on the trains.

Since applicant's line is narrow-gauge from Silverton to Alamosa, any freight moving between points on the branch and standard-gauge-line points must be transloaded into the larger cars at Alamosa. While freight has continued to move over the branch in this manner, the volume thereof has been greatly reduced in recent years.

Prior to 1952[4] (when all passenger service over the narrow-gauge lines, other than that provided on the Silverton Branch, was discontinued), applicant rendered passenger service over the entire narrow-gauge line to Alamosa, where passengers transferred to and from trains operating on applicant's standard-gauge line. Through such service, some interstate passengers were handled, and some were moved to and from points on the Silverton Branch. Since the discontinuance of passenger service between Durango and Alamosa, only intrastate passenger service has been provided over the Silverton Branch. Applicant no longer holds itself out to provide interstate service over the line, and no arrangements exist for the through movement of interstate passengers wishing to travel over the branch line. Tickets for transportation over the line are offered for sale at Durango only.

Although no regular service is provided after the close of the summer season, applicant does claim to hold itself out to transport freight over the line whenever a shipper has ten or more carloads to be transported at one time. Under an arrangement with its wholly owned subsidiary, Rio Grande Motor Way, Inc., less-than-carload freight moving on applicant's line to or from points on the branch line is transported by the motor carrier. Applicant asserts that this provides an adequate substitute for rail service during periods when no regular rail service is provided over the line.

Applicant has published no schedules since 1953 covering any of the services rendered over the line, and it has obtained no authority from any regulatory body authorizing any temporary suspension of service over it. Also, no adjustments have been made in its intrastate and interstate tariffs, placing any limitation on the traffic that would be transported or establishing a minimum on the volume of shipments that would be handled.

Over the years, mining operations in the area gradually declined, and in 1938 the smelter at Durango closed. After this closure the decline in freight traffic moving over the line became more pronounced. Finally, applicant concluded that the slight demand for service that existed did not justify the expenditures involved in attempting to keep the line in operation on a year-round basis, and in 1953 it abandoned any attempt to provide any regular service over the line, except during the summer months, and established the arbitrary minimum carload requirement

[4] After 1952 the Silverton Branch became the last regularly scheduled narrow-gauge line in the United States.

previously mentioned. Applicant made no attempt, however, to create any embargo on traffic but merely notified shippers in the area and posted notices in the stations at Durango and Silverton of the minimum rule it had established.

The number of round-trip passengers transported over the line has increased substantially from year to year during each of the past four years, increasing from approximately 25,000 in 1957 to more than 35,000 in 1960. During the same period, passenger revenues increased from almost $86,000 to over $163,000. In most instances the train was filled to capacity each trip, and at times the demand exceeded the space available. During the summer of 1960 there were at least 2,500 persons, representing three times that number of prospective passengers (families), who were unable to obtain tickets to ride the trains because of the heavy demand.

The amount of freight transported over the line in recent years has not been substantial. In 1957 there were 277 tons of freight handled, and the revenue therefrom amounted to $1,997. In 1958 there were 371 tons of freight handled, and the revenue was $2,410. In 1959 the revenue from 444 tons of freight amounted to $5,499.

For the first nine months of 1960, the total branch-line revenue amounted to $168,216, the branch-line expenses were $76,605, and the net branch-line operating revenue was $91,611. The net revenue to the system for freight handled over the branch line amounted to $2,704, and the net return to the system from branch-line operations amounted to $94,315.

From time to time, applicant has, by license or agreement, permitted individuals to use the tracks. People having property located at points on or near the tracks have been allowed to operate small motorized vehicles over the tracks for limited purposes. Applicant considers that the agreements are a matter of private contract between it and the individuals concerned and that they are without significance insofar as the issues involved in the instant proceeding are concerned.

With respect to passenger service, applicant asserts that the line provides no service whatever to that segment of the public residing in the area and that the motor-bus service provided to and from points along its line is more than adequate to meet the needs of the public traveling to and from the area. It alleges that the only use to be made of the line in the transportation of passengers is as a mere tourist attraction, appealing to those seeking the novel and unique experience of riding on a narrow-gauge railroad but having no relation to what is considered public convenience and necessity. It admits that the potential for the continuation of this type of patronage is good; that, by leaving off the freight cars presently handled, one or two more coaches could be utilized, thus adding considerably to the revenue earned by the line; and that it reasonably may be expected that the summertime tourist service would continue to be profitable if continued. Applicant considers the service rendered the tourist trade to be a special service for the pleasure of the passengers, rather than a necessity, which it, as a common carrier, has no obligation to provide. It alleges that inasmuch as the public no longer needs the service, public convenience and necessity do not require continuance of the passenger train operation.

If, however, it is concluded that the passenger service should be continued, applicant then requests that consideration be given to the fact it has entered into an agreement with a newly formed corporation, the Durango-Silverton Railroad Company,[5] whereby said company would purchase the branch line, if abandonment were authorized, and would undertake to render intrastate passenger service to the tourist trade over the line. Applicant recognizes that the charter of the new corporation does not authorize the performance of any freight operations or authorize the corporation to operate in interstate commerce; applicant also recognizes that the abandonment of the line is not authorized. Applicant admits that the sole purpose of the instant application is to free it from the obligation presently imposed upon it as a common carrier to serve the line, and it asserts that it is willing to lose all the net revenue now accruing to the system from the branch line in order to be relieved of all its responsibilities toward the line.

Protestants assert that applicant had no right to limit its service in the manner described without first obtaining appropriate authority from the Interstate Commerce Commission and the Colorado Public Utilities Commission, and they contend that applicant's act in so limiting its service was, in legal effect, an actual abandonment of the line without authority. They argue that applicant, having committed an illegal act, cannot now rely on it in any way to establish justification for the abandonment but, instead, must rely on the situation as it now exists, which, they assert, shows the line to be profitable and necessary in the movement of both freight and passenger traffic. They contend that no burden is imposed upon interstate commerce by the line and that the best interests of applicant will be served by requiring operations to be continued.

In brief, applicant concedes that operation of the line as it is presently conducted, and if rehabilitation is not required for year-round service, is not a burden on interstate commerce.

Highway 550 is approximately parallel to the railroad between Durango and Silverton. It is a paved, all-weather highway and is one of the principal north-south highways in western Colorado.

Rio Grande Motor Way provides daily (except Saturday and Sunday) common-carrier service by motor vehicle, transporting general commodities, with certain exceptions, in interstate and intrastate commerce between Durango and Silverton as a part of its through truck service over Highway 550 and other highways between Durango, Silverton, Ridgeway, Montrose, and Grand Junction, Colorado, and other points. Continental Trailways Bus System operates one bus schedule daily in each direction between Durango and Silverton over Highway 550 as part of its scheduled interstate service.

Occasionally truck and bus operations are interrupted because of weather

[5] A group of local businessmen who organized a corporation for the purpose of purchasing the Silverton Branch (if abandonment was authorized) and operating it as a tourist attraction.

conditions on the highway between Durango and Silverton. These interruptions, however, occur rarely and usually do not continue for more than one day at a time. Although most of the populated areas between Durango and Silverton are provided transportation service over Highway 550, between those towns there are portions of the canyon area that are not served by any motor carrier.

As mining operations in the Silverton area declined and as other means of transportation became available the need for freight service over the branch line declined. By 1953 all mining operations in the Silverton area had terminated, and those mines which had formerly transported their ore from another mining district to Silverton for movement over the branch to Durango had begun transporting their concentrates by truck to a smelter at Leadville or to applicant's standard-gauge railhead at Montrose. Except for one 40-ton car of zinc ore transported in 1957, no ore or concentrates moved over the branch from 1953 to 1959. In 1960, there was renewed interest in mining operations at certain points along the branch, especially in the Silverton area, and one mining company became actively engaged in performing the preliminary work incident to placing one or more mines into production. This company does not intend, however, to utilize the branch line for the transportation of its ore and concentrates, but will transport its shipments by truck to applicant's railhead at Montrose.

There are other companies and individuals who own mining claims along the branch and who desire to institute production operations. The record does not indicate, however, when production at any of these claims may be expected to commence.

Although numerous shipments of livestock used to be transported over the branch line, such movements have now practically ceased. In former years applicant provided convenient service for shippers of livestock and furnished adequate loading and unloading facilities for such movements. When the service was no longer convenient and when the needs of the shippers and the loading and unloading facilities on the branch either were eliminated or, because of lack of repairs, became unusable, most of the livestock shippers found it necessary to use other means of moving their livestock to and from the feeding ranges in the area served by the branch.

In 1957, the only shipments of livestock were three carloads of cattle that moved between points on the branch and other points on applicant's system. In 1958, the livestock shipments consisted of fifteen carloads of sheep that moved to or from points on the branch. In 1959, the only livestock transported over the line consisted of two carloads of cattle and calves. No livestock was handled over the line in the period during 1960 when operations were performed.

Applicant takes the position that the transportation needs of the area are adequately served by the truck and bus service presently available therein and that, in view of the insubstantial use being made of the branch line, there no longer is any need for its continued operation.

A total of twenty-five witnesses appeared in opposition to applicant's proposal. With respect to the passenger service provided over the line, the executive director of the Colorado State Advertising and Publicity Department described the numerous activities of the state in publicizing the branch line throughout the United States and the favorable results flowing therefrom. He stressed the economic benefits accruing to the communities involved and to the state from the large number of tourists who came to Durango each year to ride the train and enjoy the scenic beauty of the area. The branch line has now become one of the most important tourist attractions in Colorado. Not only does the state of Colorado consider that the interests of the tourists are served by the operation of the train, but it also considers the continued operation of the service to be of extreme importance to the welfare of all residents of southwestern Colorado.

Applicant's passenger traffic manager, who was one of the officers of the Colorado Visitors' Bureau, testified, pursuant to subpoena, that it is the policy of the bureau to encourage tourists to visit various attractions in Colorado, including the narrow-gauge line here considered, and that the bureau's efforts had been very successful. He expressed the view that, to the extent that tourists come to Durango to ride on the train, the needs of the public were thereby served.

The Chambers of Commerce of Durango and Silverton and officials and businessmen in Silverton consider the passenger service provided over the branch to be essential to the economic well-being of these towns and of the surrounding communities. Several business establishments in Silverton are dependent almost entirely upon the trade from the tourists riding the trains, and all businesses in the town also derive substantial benefits therefrom.

Protestants contend that by virtue of the very substantial demand that exists for passenger service over the line, it must be concluded that its continuance is required by public convenience and necessity.

With respect to the freight service provided over the line, protestants refer to the fact that there are certain areas on the line which are not accessible by motor vehicle and which can be served only by the branch line. They also point to certain mines and mining properties along the line which are not now producing ore but which the owners are endeavoring to place in production. They assert that the value of these properties would be reduced by the elimination of the only transportation services available.

At present there are approximately 47 million board feet of commercial timber in the Elk Park area of the national forest available for cutting, and the branch line affords the only means available for transporting a large portion of that timber out of the area. The United States Forest Service, however, has not authorized cutting that timber or indicated that such authorization may be given.

Protestants refer to the fact that Rio Grande Motor Way is not authorized to transport all types of freight between Durango and Silverton and that it is not physically possible for it to serve certain points in the canyon area that are served by the branch line. They therefore assert that this establishes that the needs of the communities involved and of the public can be adequately served only by the continuance of the freight service provided by applicant.

Several sheep raisers testified to a need for freight service in the movement of sheep to and from the summer range areas in the national forest near Silverton. Because of a lack of convenient service and adequate loading and unloading facilities on the line, most of the sheep raisers in the area have not utilized applicant's service for the movement of their sheep for a number of years. Instead, they have utilized truck service or have "trailed" their sheep to and from the summer ranges. Trailing involves walking the sheep along the highway through the national forest to the range areas. Each spring the sheep are moved into the national forest near Silverton, and they are then moved out in the early fall. Approximately six days are consumed in trailing the sheep between Durango and Silverton.

Sheep do not readily adapt to travel by motor truck, and for that reason the sheep raisers prefer not to utilize that means of moving their sheep. Furthermore, the truck service that is provided in the area not only is expensive but, many times, is not available when required. As a result, most of the sheep are trailed to and from the summer ranges.

Apparently applicant's freight service from Durango to other points on its lines is utilized by some of the sheep raisers in moving their sheep to market. If adequate and convenient service were provided over the branch and if applicant would provide proper loading and unloading facilities at points along the line, rail service would again be utilized by the sheep raisers opposing abandonment of the line.

The United States forest ranger for the area involved, who appeared under subpoena, testified that consideration is now being given to the imposition of a ban on the trailing of sheep through the national forest to the summer ranges but that no decision had been reached on the matter. If such a ban were imposed, the sheep would be moved either by truck or over applicant's line.

With respect to use of applicant's service for the transportation of livestock, it should be noted that applicant has the obligation of providing service and facilities adequate to meet the needs of the public. If it is found herein that the public convenience and necessity require the continuance of freight service over the line, applicant, of course, would be required to provide service and facilities adequate to meet the needs of the aforementioned shippers of livestock, and any failure on its part to provide such service might, of course, justify appropriate action to obtain the service required.

Certain operators of coal mines in the Durango area opposed the abandonment of the line on the grounds that the service was required for the movement of coal to Silverton. Although some coal is transported over the line each year, the witnesses conceded that truck service is available for the transportation of coal from the mines direct to customers in the Silverton area. One motor carrier at Silverton who was engaged in the delivery of coal from the rail siding in Silverton to consumers in the area testified, however, that he would abandon his motor-truck service if abandonment of the line was authorized.

DISCUSSION QUESTIONS

1. List the business claimants in this situation and explain the social investment each claimant perceives. What are the payoffs or benefits each claimant seeks?

2. What obligations does the railroad have to the communities it serves?

3. Do the communities involved have any responsibilities to the railroad? If so, what? If not, why not?

CASE 2

THE DENVER AND RIO GRANDE
WESTERN RAILROAD COMPANY,
SILVERTON BRANCH,
PART B

In the early spring of 1961 a decision was handed down from the Interstate Commerce Commission denying the request of the Denver and Rio Grande Western Railroad Company to abandon that portion of its narrow-gauge line from Durango to Silverton, Colorado, known as the Silverton Branch.

Throughout the hearings the railroad had emphasized that it was primarily in the business of transportation and moving freight and that it had neither the capability nor the desire to be in the tourist or sightseeing business. Nevertheless, the 1961 decision of the Interstate Commerce Commission placed the railroad squarely in the tourist business and left it with no other alternative than to continue operating the Silverton Branch as a tourist attraction. At that time a decision was made by the board of directors to develop the tourist potential of the Silverton Branch to its maximum by offering to the public the fullest and most comprehensive tourist facilities possible. The overall plan consisted of two major parts. One part of the plan was concerned with upgrading and expanding train service. The other major part of the plan was to develop ancillary services normally desired by tourists, and to make the area surrounding the Durango train depot into an amusement and entertainment center.

To accomplish the second part of the plan, the railroad began immediately to acquire land around the depot in Durango which could provide ancillary tourist services such as hotels, restaurants, shops, and amusement.

Like many small towns which were founded in the final quarter of the last century, Durango had grown away from the railroad depot leaving the depot, roundhouse, railyards, repair shops, and other railroad activities at the extreme end of Main Avenue. In 1961 property on Main Avenue near the old depot had deteriorated badly, and the area had become a sort of skid row consisting of run-down rooming houses, cheap bars, makeshift warehouses, and junky stores. Tourists who desired to ride the train were often subjected to a variety of inconveniences and indignities. Parking was totally inadequate, thus forcing tourists to walk long distances to reach the depot and to move through an area of dilapidated buildings which was largely populated with loiterers, panhandlers, winos, peddlers, handbill passers, and sometimes even train ticket speculators.

A real estate broker from Denver was sent to Durango by the railroad to acquire the property on lower Main Avenue. He secured purchase options on all property on both sides of 1½ blocks of Main Avenue adjacent to the depot. When the railroad exercised these options at a cost of over $800,000, it acquired the land and buildings which were to be developed into an area called Rio Grande Land. Shortly thereafter the job of director of Rio Grande Land was created. Mr. Alexis McKinney was hired for that job, and revitalization of the area began.

The first step was to clean up the area and alleviate the parking problem. Five of the Main Avenue buildings that had deteriorated beyond rapair were demolished and cleared away. A portion of the railroad yards across the tracks from the depot and one block from Main Avenue was converted to a large paved parking lot. Construction of the parking lot cleared an area that had previously been an unsightly expanse of junk heaps, decrepit equipment, and weeds. The parking lot provided adequate and convenient parking facilities in the city, cleaned up an eyesore, and made money for the railroad.

With the basic cleaning up of the area completed, the job of developing Rio Grande Land began in earnest. The central idea was to maintain as nearly as possible the atmosphere, architecture, and interior decor of the Victorian era of the late 1800s. The depot itself was repaired and repainted, and the area that had once been the freight office was converted to a pleasant and comfortable waiting room for passengers. A small third-rate hotel was transformed into a small thirty-four-room motor hotel which was plush and modern inside and decorously restored outside. A large building adjacent to, but separated from, the depot by a wide expanse of lawn and shrubs was converted into a plushly appointed gay nineties restaurant. Other buildings with fronts appropriate to the architectural scheme of the late 1800s were repaired and repainted. False fronts were added to other buildings. The cost to the railroad of clearing old buildings was approximately $500,000. Another $750,000 was spent on remodeling and parking.

Silverton also received attention from the railroad although not to the extent that Durango did. The Silverton depot is some distance from the center of the old mining town, which meant that passengers had to walk several blocks over unpaved streets to reach the restaurants and the shopping area. In 1961 the railroad extended the tracks from the depot to midtown. When a second train was added in

1963, a parallel set of tracks was built into the town so that both trains delivered passengers directly to the center of activity.

Concurrently with the development of Rio Grande Land efforts were started to increase and improve train service. Obviously the number of people who could ride the train depended upon the amount of equipment the railroad could put into service. As the demand for seats increased, the railroad quickly found itself handicapped by a lack of serviceable rolling stock. Many of the old wooden cars (which had been built in the 1880s) had become unserviceable over the years and had been sold or scrapped. Most of the smaller locomotives used in the early days of the railroad had also worn out and had been replaced. In 1961 the railroad owned only eight railworthy narrow-gauge passenger cars and three small 470 series K-28 engines. There were twelve heavier locomotives (six 480s and six 490s) but these were considered too large for the bridges and clearances on the Silverton run.

The rolling stock that was left was quickly refurbished, and the cars were repainted the bright orange-yellow which became known as Rio Grande Gold. In 1963 eight new steel coaches were manufactured in the Rio Grande Railroad shops in Denver. These were almost exact replicas of the old 1880 wooden cars. Between 1963 and 1965 six gondola passenger cars were added. The gondolas were made from standard-gauge freight cars which were converted to open-sided narrow-gauge gondolas with seats running longitudinally. They were covered with metal boxcar roofs painted with aluminum paint. Thus, by 1965 the rolling stock of the Silverton Branch consisted of three locomotives and twenty-one coaches (one very old car had to be decommissioned). In addition, there are three private cars available for charter—one swanky business car owned by the railroad and two plush 1880 private cars which are privately owned but leased by the railroad for charter to special parties.

As the daily demand for seats increased, more cars were added to the train each day. Figure 1 shows the number of passengers riding the Silverton Branch of the Denver and Rio Grande Western for selected years. By 1963 demand had exceeded the capacity of the one train hauled by a single locomotive. Maximum load for the small 470 series locomotive is eleven loaded coaches. For a number of safety reasons it was impractical to make the train a doubleheader (two engines). The obvious answer was to run two trains, and since 1963 two trains daily have made the round trip from Durango to Silverton one hour apart during most of the season.

Over the years the railroad made little effort to advertise and promote the Silverton trip nationally. By 1963 the mountainous area of southwestern Colorado was already becoming a popular tourist area. During the summer months the railroad was hard pressed to provide seats for all who wanted to ride the train. In addition, tourist accommodations were often inadequate to serve the number of people coming into the area. The railroad reasoned that it would not be performing properly its responsibilities to the community by encouraging more tourists to come into the area.

Year	Number of Passengers	Year	Number of Passengers
1961	37,711	1967	79,917
1962	37,855	1968	85,860
1963	49,962	1969	97,010
1964	65,187	1970	91,937
1965	71,057	1971	102,952
1966	77,959	1972	105,626

Figure 1 The number of passengers for selected years who rode the Silverton Branch of the Denver and Rio Grande Western Railroad.

In 1970 the event that everyone had feared occurred. Cloudbursts in early September caused severe flooding in the mountain canyon through which the train tracks ran. As a result bridges were weakened and miles of track were washed out, thus requiring train service to be discontinued for the remaining month of the season. Initial estimates of the costs of repairing the tracks were well above $1 million, and there was serious speculation concerning whether the railroad could repair the tracks at all. The washout had a profound impact on both Durango and Silverton. The loss of one month's train operation demonstrated the extent to which the economy of the area depended on the operation of the train. Delegates from both communities offered to assist the railroad in any way possible to restore service.

Fortunately the roadmaster for the railroad in Durango was a veteran of mountain narrow-gauge operations, and with the most dedicated work he and his crews rebuilt the railroad in far less time and at far lower cost than had been estimated. Working into the late winter and beginning work in the very early spring, the crews had the tracks ready for use on Memorial Day of 1971. The final cost was approximately $250,000.

Shortly after the flood the president of the Denver and Rio Grande Western announced in a speech before the Durango Chamber of Commerce that the railroad wanted to sell the Silverton Branch. He indicated that Rio Grande Land (excluding the properties necessary for operating the railroad) would also be for sale. He emphasized that the railroad would not sell to just anyone, but to someone who they were sure had enough money and enough commitment to both communities to ensure continuance of the Silverton Branch as a tourist attraction. He emphasized that as part of the deal the railroad stood ready to provide its repair and service facilities at cost and to offer operating advice. He also emphasized that any sale would be contingent upon the approval and endorsement of the communities. He admitted that the Silverton Branch had been profitable, but pointed out that the business of the Denver and Rio Grande Western was primarily moving freight, and that it was ill equipped to be in the tourist business. He also pointed out that any sale of the Silverton Branch (the right-of-way and rolling stock) would require another hearing before the Interstate Commerce Commission, and he asked for public support in the event such a hearing was held. He suggested that if the conditions of the sale mentioned above were met, the Interstate Commerce Commission would undoubtedly approve.

Since the president's speech there have been numerous inquiries, but only three or four potential buyers seemed to have sufficient capital and community commitment to qualify as an acceptable buyer. For one reason or another each failed to qualify fully. However, in the spring of 1973 Rio Grande Land was sold for approximately $750,000.

DISCUSSION QUESTIONS

1. In what ways have the actions of the railroad between 1961 and 1973 been socially responsible? In what ways have they been socially irresponsible?

2. Is the list of business claimants the same in 1973 as it was in 1958? What are the payoffs and benefits each claimant seeks?

3. What responsibilities do the two communities have to the railroad?

4. If you were a small businessman in either Durango or Silverton would you support the sale of the Silverton Branch to a qualified purchaser? Define your criteria for a qualified purchaser. How can these criteria be measured?

CASE 3

BENEFICIAL BUILDERS

Beneficial Builders is a major subdivision home builder in southern California. During the last fifteen years it has developed seven large subdivisions in the Los Angeles area. Its policy is to buy large tracts of land on the edges of suburbs and build good-quality, low-cost homes for working families. In order to keep costs low, Beneficial Builders uses only a few house plans in each subdivision, enabling it to precut lumber and subassemble walls, door frames, windows, cabinets, and other house parts in its shops. There are several variations of the front, or "elevation," of the houses, so that the streets are not identical in their appearance

A shopping center and 800 homes had been planned for the Hills East subdivision, located in high foothills 50 miles east of Los Angeles. Over 700 homes had been built and sold when the heavy fall rains started. After the ground had been thoroughly soaked, an unprecedented 12-inch rainfall occurred on Monday night in the foothills just above the subdivision. A stream which drained these foothills ran through the center of Hills East. In planning this subdivision, Beneficial Builders recognized that heavy thunderstorms did occur in the area, so it widened and straightened the stream bed according to a plan approved by county engineers.

The rain sent torrents of water down the steep stream bed at an estimated 30 miles an hour. It appeared that the stream bed was adequate until the fast, high water uprooted a giant eucalyptus tree on the edge of the stream and carried it ⅓ mile to a highway bridge. The tree lodged against the bridge and held fast, soon collecting other debris until it blocked an estimated 60 percent of the streamflow. The lake created behind the bridge soon flooded a few homes, and even worse, it caused a major streamflow over a low spot in the highway 100 yards from the bridge. This overflow could not return to the stream bed, so it continued down a street for several blocks, horizontal to the stream but one block away.

Soon there was a torrent of raging water 3 to 5 feet deep in this overflow route. Homeowners were awakened suddenly about 5:30 A.M. by the sound of water running through their houses and cars crashing against carports and house walls. Water rose above 3 feet in over twenty-five houses, and occupants had to flee to roofs or to a second story if they had one. Walls and doors were torn away, but no house was swept from its foundation. Two persons were swept away by the current and drowned.

In a few hours the flood subsided, leaving a jumble of automobiles, uprooted trees, furniture, and house parts. Forty houses and thirty-five automobiles had damages estimated at $300,000. National Guard, civil defense, armed services, and city police helped restore order and provided trucks to haul away debris. Light showers continued, but the stream was back in its bed, and no further flooding was predicted. All utilities including water were disrupted, and none of the damaged homes could be occupied.

Glen Abel, president of Beneficial Builders, heard of the flood early in the morning and drove directly to his subdivision. He talked with public officials on the scene and with dazed and shocked residents. Although some were understandably bitter, there was no evidence that they thought the flood had been caused by poor design of the subdivision. Their homes had received the same heavy rains that hit the foothills, so they knew the rainfall was torrential. A flood victim described his experience to Mr. Abel as follows: "When I woke up, the water was leaking through the walls at the joints. We all started picking things off the floor so they wouldn't get wet, and then there was a crash as the water broke a plate-glass window and an outside door.

"The furniture started to float on top of the water, and big pieces like our dresser fell over. I knew then that we had to get out, but I didn't know how or where to go.

"I started to the boys' room, but before I got there the bedroom wall gave way and they came floating right by me out into the yard, both in their beds. I started after them, sort of swimming. Finally I reached one of the boys, still on his bed, and I handed him up to my neighbor on the roof of his house. I just handed him up; the water was so high, I didn't stand on a ladder or anything. Somebody else reached my other boy and put him on a roof.

"My house is still standing and the roof is good, but most of the walls are gone. I really don't know how it all happened, because you couldn't see anything in the dark."

Abel checked with city street engineers at the bridge, and they reported that the stream bed had proved large enough to hold the flood and that there was no overflow except that caused by the blocked bridge. On the basis of these discussions and all other evidence he had, Abel concluded that the subdivision drainage design was sound and that his firm had no liability for the damages.[1]

Although no company liability was evident, Abel was nevertheless distressed by suffering caused by the flood. He felt sure that the homeowners had no insurance protection against floods; hence many home buyers faced the loss of all their savings or might be forced into personal bankruptcy. He knew that these wage-earning residents, most with young families, were not financially prepared to cope with losses this large.

From a business point of view, Abel recognized that even though the Hills East subdivision was nearly sold out, any remaining sales would be handicapped by publicity about the flood. He reasoned that many persons would not be able to repair their homes, which would leave eyesores of wrecked buildings until mortgage settlements were made. He expected that various types of lawsuits and legal entanglements would develop among homeowners, automobile insurers, real estate mortgagors, chattel mortgagors (furniture and appliances), repairmen, finance companies, and others.

While on the scene Abel checked with city engineers and determined that they would work with civil defense and National Guard truckers to clear all debris and return furniture to homes. The city would rebuild streets. Abel also worked with officers of the Hills East Community Improvement Association to arrange for flood victims to live temporarily with neighbors. The improvement association was a voluntary community group encouraged by Beneficial Builders when the first home buyers moved to Hills East.

Later that afternoon Abel returned to his downtown office serveral miles from Hills East in order to discuss with his associates what might be done for the flood victims. They considered asking the state governor for state flood aid, but delayed for two reasons. First, they felt that government aid should be requested only when all private and public self-help, such as the American Red Cross, was insufficient. Second, government aid would probably require much red tape and delay, and action was needed now.

They were discussing what direct action Beneficial Builders might take, when Arch Smith, the union business agent for Beneficial workers, arrived and asked whether the union might help. He said that he had talked informally with several union leaders and could guarantee 200 volunteer carpenters and other selected skilled workers all day Saturday and Sunday to repair all structural damage to houses, if someone would supply materials, equipment, and supervision.

After extended discussion, Beneficial executives and Smith decided they

---

[1] Weeks later a special engineering report requested by the city council and made by city engineers concluded that the flood was an "act of God" and that no negligence was evident.

would take direct action to repair all flood damage with donated labor and materials, provided Apex Lumber Company would donate lumber and building materials. Apex was considered the key to this plan, for lumber was the main building material needed. If Apex agreed, Abel and Smith believed that all lesser services would "fall in line." Apex was one of the largest building suppliers in the West, and it had been the principal supplier of Beneficial Builders since Beneficial Builders was organized.

If Apex accepted, the following plan would be used. All services would be donated. All homes would be restored to approximately their original condition, except for furniture and household supplies. A newspaper release would announce that the restoration was a joint effort of businesses, unions, and community agencies. Appeals for help would be made privately through existing groups; there would be no public appeal playing upon emotions and possibly leading to disorganized action. Unions would provide sufficient skilled labor for ten hours daily on Saturday and Sunday (an estimated 200 men) and the following weekend if necessary. Beneficial Builders would provide supervision, shop services, and construction equipment (worth an estimated $20,000 wholesale). Apex would provide all building materials (worth an estimated $30,000 wholesale). Community agencies would be asked to supply unskilled labor (about 100 men). Other groups employed by Beneficial Builders to construct its subdivisions would be asked to donate services, such as plumbing and electrical work, appliance repair, landscaping, and painting. All services except painting would be donated for the forthcoming weekend so that homes would be livable on Monday. Painting would be donated the following two weekends. The Red Cross or some other service agency would be asked to provide food and coffee for all volunteer labor.

Abel and Smith were convinced that 95 percent of the repairs could be made in one weekend because of the fortuitous circumstance that Beneficial's shops had completed cutting and assembling all components for the last fifty houses in the Hills East subdivision on the Friday before the flood. These components provided a ready-made inventory matching most of the houses destroyed. In the few instances where necessary items were not assembled, Abel promised to work his shops overtime to assure that all needed precut materials and subassemblies would be delivered to the carport of each home by 6:00 P.M. Friday. This procedure probably would delay by ten days the completion of the remaining fifty houses because new lumber would have to be cut and assembled. Some persons who had bought one of these fifty houses might be inconvenienced or have added expenses if they had already promised to vacate their present residence and move to Hills East on a certain date, believing that their home would be available at that time.

By the time Abel and Smith completed their plans, it was 7:30 P.M. They telephoned Abe Silver, southern California manager of Apex Lumber, at his home near Los Angeles. When he learned the purpose of their call, he agreed to an appointment in his home at 9:00 P.M. that evening.

At 9:03 P.M. Abel and Smith rang the doorbell of Silver's palatial home.

DISCUSSION QUESTIONS

1. If you were Abel, what presentation would make to Silver? If you were Smith, what would you do? Role-play the 9:00 P.M. meeting of Abel, Smith, and Silver.

2. What are the different investment groups in this situation, and what are the investments and payoff expectations of each?

3. Discuss this case in terms of business values, viability, and public visibility.

4. Discuss this case in terms of the Iron Law of Responsibility.

5. What are the possible risks and rewards of social involvement by Apex Lumber in this situation?

RODO CATTLE COMPANY

The Rodo Cattle Company is located in the metropolitan suburbs of Pleasantville, a city of over 600,000 people in a Western state. The primary business of the Rodo Company is operation of cattle feedlots for fattening cattle for slaughter. Although cattle feedlots have been used for centuries, commercial development of feedlots as a large business operation is fairly new. The Rodo Company is a specialized business of this type. Its cattle pens cover 80 acres and will feed at one time over 25,000 cattle worth several million dollars.

Rodo Company's feedlots are organized into separate pens of about 1 acre each, and modern, laborsaving methods are used throughout its facility. The pens are ringed with concrete feed bunks and water troughs. Feed is mixed from truckload batches in the company's feed mill at the feedlot. Mixed feed flows by gravity to other trucks, which distribute it to the feed bunks. The entire acreage is covered by an overhead water sprinkler system that reduces the amount of manure dust in the dry afternoons; this helps prevent cattle tuberculosis and other lung diseases. The sprinkler system also reduces the drift of dust from the feedlots to neighboring residential properties; however, the lots cannot be kept wet enough to prevent all dust, so there are many complaints from neighbors, as will be discussed later. If too much water is used in dust treatment, muddy conditions develop which increase both neighborhood odor and cattle diseases.

The company regularly sprays its pens to control flies. Its monthly expenditure for insecticide exceeds $300, and both the county health officer and neighbors agree that flies are effectively controlled. Manure in the pens is mechanically handled. After it has accumulated in a pen for several months, it is scraped up by a bulldozer and mechanically loaded into trucks which take it to the edge of the property, where it is stacked in large, flat piles 30 feet high. Portions of this manure are occasionally sold to a processor who pulverizes and bags it for sale to home gardeners and farmers. The supply of manure is much greater than the demand for it, so Rodo Company has an inventory of thousands of tons, which is increasing by hundreds of tons annually. The general manager and principal owner of the company, Mr. Jesse Rodo, is not sure what to do with this growing inventory because he is running out of storage space.

The Rodo Company was established sixteen years ago on 120 acres purchased especially for feedlot operation. In the beginning there were pens for only 500 cattle, but its facilities expanded rapidly as the idea of custom feeding became popular with local farmers and business investors. At the time the feedlot was established there were three other feedlots nearby, so the property was already recognized as a stockyard area. The land was rocky and uneven, was located near a river bottom, and was unfit for residential housing. The property was 6 miles from downtown Pleasantville, and the nearest residential developments were 1½ miles away on either side. Pleasantville was toward the west, and a suburban town was toward the southeast.

The other three feedlots in Rodo Company's area have also expanded, until this area now has pens for nearly 100,000 cattle. Meanwhile, the Pleasantville metropolitan area has also grown, pushing residential suburbs closer to the stockyard area. One new residential area is within 500 feet of the edge of Rodo's property, and homeowners are complaining loudly about feedlot dust and odors. In fact, the whole stockyard area is surrounded on three sides by residential and commercial developments less than ½ mile away. The municipal stadium is only 1 mile away, and several fine motels are on the highway about the same distance. The city auditorium, the site of operas and other gala events, is slightly over 2 miles away. On winter evenings when the air settles, an intense odor from the stockyard area sometimes reaches the auditorium at about the time programs begin. This one fact has caused strong protests from several influential Pleasantville people.

The odors and dust produced by a feedlot operation are much different from those of the common farm barnyard. Because of heavy use of the ground (several hundred cattle on 1 acre), the type of odor is much more putrid, and it exists in a stronger concentration than it does on the farm. The foul odor causes nausea and illness in sensitive people. And if the pens are not properly sprayed with water when the cattle are milling about in late afternoon before bedding down for the night, clouds of unpleasant dust, similar to those which arise behind an automobile moving along a dusty road at sundown, cover the neighborhood.

This combination of factors has placed a large segment of the community in conflict with feedlot operators. Residents of the suburbs southeast of the Rodo feedlot have organized a Fresh-Air Committee, whose purpose is to encourage community action to control air pollution. Committee members include many influential citizens of the suburbs. The group holds public meetings, and officers regularly attend city council meetings to offer proposals for feedlot regulation and city prosecution under nuisance laws, since three of the four feedlots now are within the city limits of the suburb. The group is also developing proposed city ordinances for control of feedlot pollution. The group has employed a photographer and a scientist to gather evidence of feedlot pollution, and members are outspoken against the odor and dust derived from feedlots. The committee had proposed that since the cattle feeders cannot or will not do anything about the offensive nature of the feedlots, they should move to a rural area zoned especially for long-run cattle feeding. A local journalist reported the proposal as follows:

> That hero of Western lore, the cattleman, could be headed for a reservation just like his predecessor, the Indian, if a group of unhappy citizens has its way.
>
> The reservation proposal is the brainchild of the Fresh-Air Committee and is aimed specifically at cattle-feeding operations in urban areas.
>
> They propose that statewide zoning be initiated by the legislature to provide a permanent area where cattle and dairy operators can work free from encroachment by residential areas. This zone would be buffered with a 5-mile ring of orchards to protect people against the cows, and vice versa.
>
> The Fresh-Air Committee is only one of many groups troubled by the scent of "Corral No. 5" and the dust rising every evening from the community's cattle-feeding operations.
>
> The list of complainants is long. It includes hotel and motel operators, airport authorities, city officials, doctors, health officials, homeowners, and tourists. The airport manager commented: "During the height of the tourist season, the airport receives the full 'benefits' of the stockyards. People get off the plane, and they want to get right back on."

In addition, a few months ago residents of some of the worst fallout areas filed lawsuits against all four cattle companies, alleging that they were maintaining a public nuisance. Some eighty citizens filed suits asking for damages totaling $859,040. The suits allege that stockyard dust settles in homes even when they are closed, requiring more frequent cleaning than in other areas of the community. They complain that use of patios and yards is denied on many evenings, that extra money must be spent for air conditioning and filters to keep odors and dust out of homes, and that home prices have depreciated more than normal. They allege that odor and dust have become worse since they moved into their homes because more cattle are being fed and larger piles of manure are accumulating. Some also allege nausea and bronchial difficulties caused by the nuisances. One of the complainants, speaking to a reporter, warned persons interested in buying a home in the area not to close the sale in the daytime. "All the people around here bought their houses during the daytime, when the dust and odor do not settle so badly," the complainant said. "The real estate people either evade the subject or ignore it when they're selling a house."

The lawyer who represented most of the complainants in their lawsuits made the following comment to a reporter: "We don't mind the stockyards, but we do mind the dust and odor. The basic legal question as I see it is the right of habitation or the right of agriculture. I believe that human habitation is superior to that of livestock."

Meanwhile, the Citizens' Council for Beautification of Pleasantville was taking an interest in the feedlot problem. The council is a civic committee appointed by the mayor to coordinate work of all voluntary groups seeking to make the metropolitan area a more beautiful, cultured, and pleasant place to live. The council was particularly concerned because feedlots caused a large blighted area on the edge of town, several distinguished visitors had inquired about the odor when alighting at the airport, several cultural events at the city auditorium and other locations had been made unpleasant by stockyard odor, and a number of residents had complained. In fact, some businesses on the highway were so affected by the feedlots that their managers were writing letters to anyone who would heed them. Some dispatched letters to their United States senators and representatives. They also complained to the county health officer, but at one of the council meetings he told the group that his office had investigated the feedlots and was convinced that neither their dust nor their odor constituted a health hazard to citizens.

Jesse Rodo became embroiled in the feedlot controversy in two ways. First, as owner and manager of Rodo Cattle Company, he was the object of lawsuits (which included both the corporation and its manager in each complaint), and he was under pressure to move his feedlot or take corrective action, which would be expensive. Second, he was at this time serving a three-year term as president of the Cattle Feeders' Association, which was the trade association of the feedlot operators. The association was working hard to offset unfavorable publicity which feedlots were receiving.

Several years ago, when complaints first started to develop, the Cattle Feeders' Association took the position that the feedlot operators were there first; hence, anyone who built a home or business in the area did so at his own peril. As one operator stated: "An age-old concept in common law is 'Let the buyer beware.' It is the buyer's legal duty to be aware of environmental conditions which might affect his home or business prior to investing in it. The feedlots should not be blamed because people insist on moving closer to them."

This argument reduced complaints and probably would have worked for the long run, except that the feedlots continued to expand their facilities and pile their refuse. The result was that people who originally built in an odor-free and dust-free neighborhood soon found that these nuisances were reaching their neighborhood also. Then, when the Fresh-Air Committee entered the controversy, its officials reported legal opinion that prior occupancy of the area did not give feedlots an easement to inflict obnoxious dust and odor on adjoining property. In other words, adjoining property owners had just as much right to use their property freely as the feedlot owners had to use theirs.

At about this time Rodo became president of the association, and he persuaded members to hire a public relations firm to improve the feedlot's public image. The firm recommended emphasis on the economic benefits of feedlots to the state. This approach gained support of operators outside the Pleasantville area because some of them were beginning to receive complaints from their neighbors also; however, nearly half the state's feedlots were in the Pleasantville area. The public relations firm prepared news releases for mailing to all papers in the state at least once a month extolling the economic virtues of feedlots. Releases reported that during the last year nearly $150 million worth of cattle were sold out of feedlots in the state. In terms of dollar value this was the second largest agricultural product in the state. Fresh-Air Committee officials countered this argument by reporting that tourism brought $400 million to the state and that urban feedlots were driving away tourists.

Another publicity release explained that the feedlot industry provided employment for over 1,000 persons and had invested over $40 million in land and equipment. Rodo and the public relations firm also persuaded leading feedlot operators to prepare speeches and seek speaking invitations to luncheon clubs and other meetings.

The number of complaints did not diminish, so association officials persuaded a number of the worst offenders to experiment with spraying a masking agent (offsetting perfume) in their lots daily. In most cases the cattle odor and masking odor seemed to combine to produce a third odor as obnoxious as the original one. In fact, the new odor aroused additional complainants not aroused by the original odor.

As a result of the failures mentioned, the Fresh-Air Committee continued to gain strength and worked with the city council of the suburb where Rodo Company's pens were located to develop a stringent ordinance regulating feedlots. The ordinance required operators to remove all organic refuse at least once a week and to haul it outside the city limits entirely. The feedlot operators felt that compliance with this ordinance would be expensive and unduly restrictive; therefore, they proposed a program of self-regulation to the city council. They offered to use masking agents and sprinkler systems and to remove refuse twice a year. The council "took the proposal under advisement" and continued with its plans for an ordinance.

The council's action caused feedlot operators throughout the state to become concerned that each city might set up its own special ordinance for feedlots. Differences in ordinances might cause cost variations which would upset competitive conditions. Feeding costs now were about equal throughout the state, but a local ordinance might increase costs in one city, driving a feedlot's customers to another lot and eventually driving the feedlot from the city. One influential operator proposed that the association go to the state legislature, which was then in session, and request a law requiring nuisance regulation by the state livestock sanitary board. Since the board consisted mostly of cattlemen, this approach would put them in the position of regulating themselves; therefore, regulations could be kept reasonable. Another operator said he would move his feedlot from the state if the state law was passed.

Rodo decided to call a statewide meeting of the entire association membership to decide what the next move should be. He knew that a strong plea would be made for the law requiring regulation by the livestock sanitary board. He also knew that association members were looking to him for leadership, but he was not sure what to propose next. He was further confused by the situation with his own company. He owned land elsewhere in the state and was about ready to move his feedlot from the Pleasantville area; however, whenever he hinted to other operators that a move might occur, they strongly objected. They said that all feedlot operators must "stick together and not retreat at this time." They felt that if one feedlot left, it would be an "admission of guilt" and would make it necessary for the other lots to move in a short time.

DISCUSSION QUESTIONS

1. In Rodo's role as president of the Cattle Feeders' Association, prepare his speech to the association recommending a particular course of action. Give reasons for the action chosen.

2. In Rodo's role as general manager and principal owner of Rodo Cattle Company, appraise the question of whether you should move your feedlot in the near future. What issues are key ones in making your decision?

3. Discuss the ecological aspects of this case.

4. Discuss the different investment groups in this situation and the countervailing powers, if any, which each sought to apply.

CASE 5

LOCKHEED
AIRCRAFT CORPORATION

Lockheed Aircraft Corporation was established in 1932 with the assets of the Lockheed Division of the bankrupt Detroit Aircraft Corporation. It gradually became a leading producer of aircraft and related products and services. Although successful civilian aircraft were produced, the firm became primarily a supplier of military aircraft and defense equipment. Successful aircraft included the F-80 and U-2, and the military transport planes C-130,C-141, and C-5A. By the 1960s the firm was the leading defense supplier in a number of different years. Company production generally was on target with regard to both schedules and costs.

In the 1960s, when some 90 percent of Lockheed's business was with the government, the company made plans to diversify into more nongovernment lines of business in order to avoid a number of insecurities connected with government contracts. For example, the flow of government contracts was erratic, they were for large amounts involving high risk, and profit margins tended to be low and subject to a variety of controls. The company sought the supersonic transport (SST) program but did not get it. Immediately thereafter in January, 1967, it moved most of its SST team into a wide-bodied transport project which eventually became the L-1011 commercial trijet aircraft program. Marketing studies at that time showed a requirement for probably 1,000 to 1,375 trijets, based on projections of passenger-seat-miles needed in the free world, as shown in Figure 1.

Since Lockheed estimated its breakeven point for the L-1011 at between 250 and 300 aircraft, it moved forward rapidly with its plans in order to try to attain leadership in this wide-bodied trijet market. Only one other company was planning

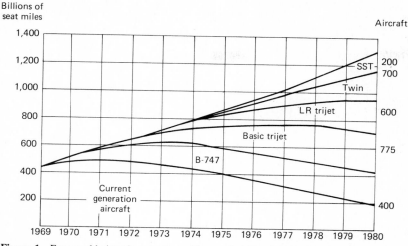

Figure 1 Free world aircraft projections. (Source: Lockheed Aircraft Corporation.)

a competitive plane at this time. It was the DC-10 planned by McDonnell Douglas Corporation.

Meanwhile Lockheed had a number of large military programs which placed a heavy drain on its cash flow; therefore in 1967 it sold $125 million of 4¼ percent convertible subordinated debentures due in 1992, with no sinking-fund requirements until 1978. Following the sale all bank loans were liquidated.

In February 1968, American Airlines placed a conditional order with McDonnell Douglas for a number of DC-10s, but this was not enough to place the airplane in production. In March, Lockheed received orders for 144 L-1011 Tristars valued at over $2 billion and immediately launched production of the airplane. The orders received were fifty from Eastern Airlines, fourty-four from Trans World Airlines, and fifty from Air Holdings, Ltd., for resale outside the United States. A few days later Delta Airlines ordered twenty-four Tristars. In April, McDonnell Douglas received additional orders and began production of its DC-10

Engines are a key component of a jet plane, and Lockheed and its customers had available for evaluation three engines, the General Electric CF-6, Pratt & Whitney JT9D, and Rolls-Royce RB211 to be produced in Britain. The RB211 was selected on the basis of several advanced design features. McDonnell Douglas and its customers selected the General Electric engine.

The production of a commercial jet aircraft of the size of the wide-bodied jets requires a massive amount of planning, tooling, and work in process. At any one time a number of planes are in various stages of completion, each costing tens of millions of dollars. In connection with its L-1011 program and its government contracts Lockheed computed its cash flow and determined that it would need $400 million of interim financing. In May 1969, it established an unsecured credit agreement with twenty-four banks for revolving credit of $400 million. The repayment pattern was based on the estimated cash flow from the completion of programs in process at the time.

Later in 1969 and 1970 a number of cost overruns and problems developed with regard to four major government programs, the C-5A transport, the AH-56A Cheyenne helicopter, the SRAM missile propulsion system, and ship construction. All the programs except ship construction were under a fixed-price total package procurement procedure that was later determined unworkable by the Defense Department and abandoned for subsequent new programs. One problem was frequent changes in specifications in order to incorporate the latest developments into the equipment. Disputes with the government regarding these projects led to delayed payments and huge losses. The largest losses were $200 million on the C-5A and over $100 million on the Cheyenne helicopter. Applicable losses in 1970 produced a net loss of $86 million for the year and reduced corporate net worth to $235 million, as shown in Figures 2 and 3, further weakening the company's borrowing capacity.

	Year Ended December 27, 1970	Year Ended December 28, 1969
Sales	$2,535,603,000	$2,074,639,000
2,074,639,000		
Interest and other income	12,377,000	7,592,000
	2,547,980,000	2,082,231,000
Costs and expenses, including provision for losses on Department of Defense contracts of $190,000,000 in 1970 and $150,000,000 in 1969	2,675,721,000	2,145,895,000
Interest expense	32,261,000	13,158,000
	2,707,982,000	2,159,053,000
Loss before federal income tax	160,002,000	76,822,000
Credit for federal income tax:		
Refund of prior years' tax due to loss carrybacks	—	114,300,000
Provision for deffered tax	—	(70,120,000)
Reduction of deferred tax	73,720,000	
Net credit	73,720,000	44,180,000
Loss for the year	$ 86,282,000	$ 32,642,000
Loss per share of capital stock	$7.60	$2.90

Figure 2 Lockheed consolidated earnings, 1970, compared with 1969. (Source: Lockheed Annual Report, 1970.)

Assets

	December 27, 1970	December 28, 1969
Current Assets:		
Cash	$ 40,207,000	$ 52,062,000
Short term commercial paper and U.S. Treasury bills	39,290,000	—
Accounts receivable—U.S. Government	137,505,000	195,598,000
Other accounts receivable	41,582,000	49,177,000
Anticipated refund of federal income tax	—	114,300,000
Inventories	693,920,000	500,417,000
Prepaid expenses	19,407,000	15,343,000
Total current assets	971,911,000	926,897,000
Investments, at lower of cost or estimated realizable value	4,184,000	4,277,000
Property, Plant and Equipment: (Note 5):		
Cost	662,924,000	608,806,000
Less accumulated depreciation and amortization	319,478,000	270,957,000
	343,446,000	337,849,000
Deferred Charges	3,088,000	2,421,000
	$1,322,629,000	$1,271,444,000

Liabilities and Stockholders' Equity

	December 27, 1970	December 28, 1969
Current liabilities:		
Accounts payable	$ 244,815,000	$ 278,539,000
Salaries and wages	77,027,000	77,961,000
Federal income tax		
Current	1,400,000	1,849,000
Deferred	31,733,000	106,625,000
Other taxes	19,462,000	20,965,000
Customers' advances in excess of related costs	29,230,000	14,431,000
Retirement plan contribution	66,379,000	74,886,000
Other liabilities	33,449,000	38,897,000
Total current liabilities	503,495,000	614,153,000
Long-term debt	584,375,000	336,250,000
Stockholder's equity:		
Capital stock, $1 par value: 20,000,000 shares authorized (1,724,137 shares reserved for conversion of debentures and 743,278 shares authorized for stock options)		
Issued at $1 per share	11,359,000	11,359,000
Additional capital	79,025,000	79,025,000
Retained earnings	144,375,000	230,657,000
Total stockholders' equity	234,759,000	321,041,000
	$1,322,629,000	$1,271,444,000

Figure 3 Lockheed consolidated balance sheet, 1970, compared with 1969. (Source: Lockheed Annual Report, 1970.)

The company began negotiating a new line of $600 million credit with its bankers and was only a few days from signing an agreement when it received a major and unexpected blow. On February 4, 1971, Rolls-Royce, Ltd., the engine supplier, announced bankruptcy because it was unable to meet costs for continuing development of the RB211 engine. Regardless of the outcome, this event delayed completion of L-1011s and further increased the cash flow requirements of Lockheed. Although Lockheed received advance payments of about $200 million on its L-1011 orders, the balance of about $2 billion would not be paid until aircraft were delivered.

At this point Lockheed and its customers were forced to reconsider the engine selection for the L-1011. An engine change was determined to increase costs by $150 million and the customers still preferred the RB211 for technical reasons; therefore negotiations were made with Rolls-Royce to continue production with financial support from the British government. Finally in May 1971, a conditional agreement was signed to continue production provided Lockheed could increase its borrowings to cover its cash flow needs. The banks declined to grant additional credit unless two conditions were met: (1) loan guarnatees from the United States government for any credit over $400 million; and (2) additional financial support from L-1011 customers. Lockheed determined it would need additional loans in the amount of $250 million, making a total of $650 million credit. If the government loan guarantee were not received, Lockheed and its creditors agreed that it probably would be forced into bankruptcy.

It was determined that the United States government could guarantee $250 million of the loan only by an act of Congress, and so Lockheed and other interested parties began working for this action, and eventually an appropriate bill was introduced. The bill provided for a guarantee of $250 million in bank loans. This was simply government backing for bank loans; no government money would be required unless the company defaulted. The arrangement was similar to government FHA guarantees on home loans, except that home loans are guaranteed for the entire amount of the loan and receive an interest rate concession.

In support of its position Lockheed argued that it was in the interest of the United States government and its people to provide the loan. If Lockheed went bankrupt, government contracts would be jeopardized, and any that could be completed by a successor company would be at higher prices. It was generally conceded that no company would continue production of the L-1011, so McDonnell Douglas would be left with a monopoly in this important segment of the market. In addition the airline business would be severely dislocated. Failure to deliver the airplane would mean a loss of $75 million in deposits by Eastern Airlines, with similar losses by other L-1011 customers. Since L-1011 customers could not hope to secure DC-10s until much later than other airlines, their competitive situation would be weakened and airline bankruptcy could occur.

Lockheed further argued that parts suppliers would lose the huge investments they had made in the L-1011, that 60,000 persons would become unemployed, and that 56,000 stockholders would lose their savings. In addition the government would lose $500 million in projected company income taxes, and its international balance of payments would be affected adversely because fifty or more aircraft sales outside the United States would not be completed. It also pointed out that there were government loan guarantees under existing programs for $190 million to finance overseas sales of DC-10s, and so a guarantee to Lockheed in these special circumstances would not be unfair competition.

Opponents of the loan argued that it would be a reward for past mismanagement by the firm and that it would set a precedent for other mismanaged firms to come to the United States for financial aid. No previous loans of this type had ever been guaranteed by the government; therefore it was argued that this was an area into which the federal government should not move. In fact, if it did act, it would be establishing an unhealthy dependency relationship between business and government that would upset free competition. Action of this type would be a threat to the free enterprise system. If government acted in this situation, where could the line be drawn with other companies? Further, it was argued that government had better alternative uses for its resources and that this was an unfair obligation to place on the already overburdened taxpayer. In addition, the government guarantee might give Lockheed an unfair advantage over its competitor, McDonnell Douglas.

DISCUSSION QUESTIONS

1. What are the business-society issues raised in this case? Comment on the role of business in society, the way in which the free enterprise system operates for business and for society, the business-government relationship, and similar issues as they relate to this case.

2. Do you see any special obligation arising for government because Lockheed is the largest defense contractor and the prime contractor on several significant government programs?

3. Discuss the various claimant groups in this situation and the social investment each claimant perceives. What are the benefits each claimant expects? Include in your discussion congressional representatives from locations of Lockheed plants, antiwar groups, the federal Internal Revenue Service, employees, suppliers, owners, other airlines, Lockheed competitors, airline passengers, the British government, Lockheed customers, and others.

4. Does government have a social responsibility to business or to Lockheed in this case? Does Lockheed have a social responsibility to government in this case? Discuss.

5. As an informed citizen how would you want your representative in Congress to vote on the proposed Lockheed legislation?

DOME CORPORATION

Dome Corporation is a large international manufacturer of electronics equipment. Its home office is based in the United States, where most of its employees and sales are located. The firm employs over 50,000 workers and operates in twenty locations in the United States. It maintains a typical health insurance program for its employees and their families, paying for hospitalization and other medical costs. The health insurance program costs $13 million annually.

Health insurance costs have been climbing, and therefore the health program coordinator in the personnel office recently made a study of employee health care costs in the twenty cities in the United States where the company operates. The study disclosed an interesting fact. Among the twenty cities the one with the highest hospital charges was St. Louis, which also happened to be the city where the firm has more employees than in any other location. Because of the number of employees and the high charges, this city appeared to be a major cause of the increase in rates during the last three years. Looking into the matter further, the corporation examined cost-of-living and other data to determine the general level of prices within the city, and the data showed that costs were slightly below the national average. For example, the U.S. Department of Labor cost-of-living index for the city was 123 compared with an index of 127 for the average city in the United States. The company was unable to find any general community reason for the high cost of hospital charges in that city.

Further investigation disclosed that the hospital charges of the nonprofit Mercy Hospital Service in St. Louis were $10 to $20 a day higher than charges of other hospitals in the area. Mercy Hospital Service is a medical conglomerate which operates four hospitals in the metropolitan area and four satellite hospitals in small towns in distant areas of the state. Analysis disclosed that most of Dome Corporation's employees used the four Mercy hospitals because they were convenient to where employees lived; thus this fact further contributed to Dome's costs. The four hospitals had about half the hospital bed capacity in the metropolitan area.

When the company executive committee in its weekly meeting reviewed the health insurance cost analysis, it decided to discuss costs with Mercy Health Service in order to determine if cost reductions could be made. The assistant to the chairman of the board and several functional specialists met with Mercy officials on September 5 and 25. They asked for data justifying the high costs and discussed possible cost reductions. Mercy Health Service officials were routinely responsive to the suggestions of the Dome group.

Using the data supplied by Mercy plus data from other sources, Dome made an extensive study of Mercy's cost structure and on December 19 made twenty-three recommendations for cost reduction to the Mercy Board of Directors. The following comments were included in the foreword to the recommendations:

> The recommendations in this report are not intended to be critical of the many fine professional, technical and skilled people who serve Mercy Health Service. These recommendations are constructively critical of Mercy management's use of its capital and human resources. . . .
>
> We want the best of health care for our people at fair and reasonable rates. Hospital management can tell what is needed. Dome can tell how to do it economically. Implementation of these recommendations will save $5 million a year or more in Mercy expenses and will make Mercy rate increases unnecessary during the next two years.

Members of the Mercy board were courteous but only mildly responsive to Dome's report. At about this time, as required by statute, Mercy Health Service requested from the Comprehensive Health Planning Council a rate increase for one of its hospitals. Dome officials concluded that the health service was not giving sufficient attention to its cost-reduction recommendations, so the company argued against the increase before the health planning council. Discussion became somewhat heated, with the company pushing its recommendations strongly and the health service defending itself. The company claimed that it was speaking in the interests of all citizens in the community who used Mercy Health Service.

Dome officials felt that the issue was so important that it had a responsibility to bring its position to the attention of the public, and so it took two-page advertisements in all the metropolitan newspapers to present a condensed version of its recommendations to the Mercy Board of Directors. It also published the same advertisement in its employee newspaper for the St. Louis area. The heading of the advertisement read, "Dome Recommends a $5 Million Reduction in Mercy Expenses." Following are some of the recommendations with their supporting data. All the following material is abbreviated from the more extensive presentation in the advertisement.

Recommendation 1. Mercy should merge its open-heart surgery facility with Central Hospital's because both facilities are smaller than necessary for efficient use. This recommendation had been made 18 months earlier by a medical study group. Estimated saving is $670,000 annually.

Recommendation 2. All four satellite hospitals have fewer than 100 beds, and they have little chance for growth. All are losing money. Hospital Associates, a study group, reports, "A 100-bed hospital is too small to be efficiently operated." The hospitals should be closed or their full losses subsidized by their communities, instead of having Mercy's St. Louis patients support these hospitals as they are now doing. Estimated saving is around $500,000 annually.

Recommendation 3. Parma Hospital should be closed and patient activities moved to Northside Hospital, both part of Mercy Hospital Service. Parma Hospital has only sixty-two beds, and it was only 56 percent occupied during the last year. Northside is a successful, larger hospital and has adequate vacant bed space. Both hospitals serve the same community area.

Recommendation 4. Mercy should sell or lease its very lavish $500,000-headquarters building and use hospital space or lease more modest offices. Dome argued that "The size and elegance of its board room surpasses many board rooms of large industrial corporations in America." It mentioned that recently a national medical journal had called the lavishly decorated headquarters a "Taj Mahal."

Recommendation 5. Mercy should cancel its plans to build additional hospital beds as long as it has an excess of vacant beds. The capital and operating costs of Mercy's vacant space are becoming excessive.

Recommendation 6. Mercy should reduce its staff by 15 percent because its employment is above regional averages. Mercy's largest hospital has 3.31 employees per bed, but Hospital Administration Service's figures for similar hospitals in the region show an average of 2.65 employees per bed. In terms of employees per patient day, Mercy has 3.82, but the regional average for similar hospitals is 3.26.

Recommendation 7. Some clinical laboratories and pathology in the four metropolitan hospitals should be centralized for efficiencies and lower costs.

Recommendation 8. Mercy purchasing department needs more modern purchasing methods to reduce costs.

Recommendation 9. Mercy pharmacy costs can be reduced by better inventory control and purchasing methods.

Recommendation 10. Mercy food service for patients and employees should be organized as a profit center in each hospital.

Recommendation 11. The large public relations staff of six persons is more than needed for a hospital of this size, and it does not make a direct contribution to patient care. It should be reduced to two persons.

Recommendation 12. Except for the president's automobile, Mercy should stop providing free automobiles for its executives. Mercy has leased about twenty luxury Oldsmobile cars for its managers. It also pays all gas, oil, and maintenance costs. A University of Chicago study reports that only 24 percent of hospitals surveyed furnish a car even to the top hospital administrator. Rarely do they furnish automobiles to lesser managers.

In addition, Dome Corporation offered eleven other recommendations with similar forthrightness.

The report concluded with the following statement:

> Dome will be glad to make available at no cost to Mercy, on a consulting basis and at Mercy's request, Dome executives who are specialists in purchasing, food services, industrial engineering, construction and maintenance, supervisory training, personnel, accounting, compensation, and other fields in which Mercy would be interested. Dome would also be pleased to conduct a seminar under the auspices of the University of Wisconsin Motivation Studies Center for employee group incentive plans, at no cost to the hospital.

The publication of these recommendations provoked intense public interest in the issue. There was wide discussion of the recommendations and also a variety of opinions about the correctness of the company's actions. Some persons, particularly those concerned about the high cost of medical service, felt that Dome's actions were "a great public service" and "evidence of a socially responsible attitude." Some said that Mercy should welcome Dome's financial and managerial expertise. Others felt that the company was interfering where it did not belong. Some even felt there was a personal conflict between officials of the two organizations probably as a result of some alleged wrong in the past. In any case, the interest of the "man on the street" was captured. Medical costs became a topic of community debate. They were a genuine concern to citizens.

DISCUSSION QUESTIONS

1. Were Dome Corporation's actions evidence of socially responsible behavior? Explain.

2. Identify and discuss the different pluralistic interest groups in this case.

3. Assuming that the corporation was taking a socially responsible action, were the methods that it used responsible and appropriate?

4. Can a business participate actively in community issues without making some enemies? Discuss.

5. What do you think of Dome's proposal to lend executives to Mercy Health Service? Is this a socially responsible act or an unreasonable interference in internal affairs of the health service? Should business generally provide this kind of assistance for nonprofit public services? Discuss.

WAGNER CHEMICAL COMPANY

The Wagner Chemical Company was founded by Charles E. Wagner. Mr. Wagner, president and general manager, graduated from college summa cum laude in chemistry. He later received his Ph.D. in chemistry from one of the country's outstanding universities.

He began his career with Du Pont as a research chemist working on applied research, where his achievements were recognized as outstanding. However, his desire was to perform pure rather than applied research. Subsequently, he left Du Pont, and with the aid of money borrowed from his father, started what is now the Wagner Chemical Company. Because of his spirit of adventure, creativity, and fresh approach to complicated industrial chemical problems, his company soon became successful. Creativity became the watchword of Wagner Chemical and still remains today as one of the company's major objectives. Some outstanding discoveries in the fields of synthetics, drugs, vitamins, pesticides, insecticides, and fertilizers were patented and contributed heavily to the early success of the enterprise.

Present Situation

The company is presently engaged in research and manufacture of a highly diversified line of products for home and industry. It ranks among the top fifteen chemical and drug companies, with an annual gross income in excess of $250 million. Mr. Wagner has always surrounded himself with competent and respected businessmen and hired the finest chemical minds available. His director of research is John Gordon, a respected chemist, who is well known throughout the world for his knowledge, ability, and creativity.

Competition in the chemical industry is extremely severe, and the heart of any leading company is in its research department. Finding and developing new products is essential, and to accomplish this, Wagner Chemical is constantly engaged in both pure and applied research.

Heavy emphasis on research in the chemical industries causes rapid change and product obsolescence. In order to survive and prosper in this highly competitive industry, firms find it necessary to allocate a much higher percentage of gross sales to research than most other manufacturing industries.

Wagner's Philosophies

Mr. Wagner and Mr. Gordon share the philosophy that no expense restrictions should be put on the scientists who are engaged in pure research. The budget for this activity is generous, and some scientists are performing revolutionary experiments without regard for any ultimate financial return.

Relatively low earnings of the company reflect the large sums spent on research. However, since leading stockholders lack unity and organization, no restrictions have been placed on research expenditures. The board of directors, in conjunction with Wagner, also contribute a reasonable percentage of the earnings to hospitals, community service centers, universities, the Red Cross, and other charities.

In justifying large research expenditures at the last annual meeting, Mr. Wagner expressed the belief that: "In my judgment, contributions and research are in the stockholders' best interest because they help retain public goodwill." He further pointed out that these expenditures are encouraged by tax laws, sustained by the courts and legislatures, and endorsed by the public.

The Research Department

The research department has been a major department since the corporation was founded. Mr. Wagner has always inspired his scientists and chemists to be creative and has been financially generous in order to obtain the best personnel available.

Mr. Gordon has proved to be an ideal man to head the research department. During his association with Wagner Chemical, Gordon has discovered and improved a vast number of new products and has written numerous papers for the Manufacturing Chemists Association. Under his direction, the company has greatly diversified its product line and has steadily improved its image in the industry. Among the new and diversified products which Wagner Chemical has been actively working on are pesticides and insecticides.

Pesticides and insecticides and their use have recently attracted wide public attention. Growing public concern over the harm which these products do to human beings, fish, and wildlife has been accentuated by a number of best-selling books on the subject. In addition, the Department of Agriculture, the Food and Drug Administration, the U.S. Wildlife Bureau, and the Surgeon General have been reviewing the effects of these poisons. Several conclusions have been drawn from their studies. It is generally agreed that poisons do accumulate on the food people eat and that people, plants, and animals may be damaged by this accumulation; however, the long-range effects of pesticides are not known. On the positive side, it is further agreed that the yield of crops is higher, that the quality of the harvested product is better, and that insect control is necessary for human health.

Mr. Wagner's Problem

Mr. Wagner is a rational businessman. He is aware of the dangers of pesticides, and he is also aware that agricultural producers need them and that cities need weed and insect control.

The Department of Agriculture and the Food and Drug Administration have set standards concerning the maximum amount of poison allowable on food, and producers of pesticides must conform to these standards. These government agencies have been satisfied with the results obtained with the use of some insecticides, but admit that they are not certain what long-range effects they may have. The Surgeon General has also voiced concern over the unknown harmful side effects of the use of these poisons.

U.S. Wildlife Bureau scientists have been studying the birth rate, death rate, fertility, and other changes in species of birds and other wildlife. They have found changes, but they cannot be certain of their causes or of how extensive the changes really are. There is also growing concern over water pollution due to pesticides and the harm it causes to fish and animals.

Mr. Wagner has had several meetings with his competitors, heads of government agencies, and personnel in his research department. He has authorized additional funds for research to be used to eliminate or reduce the harmful effects his products have.

There are other dimensions to the problem. Certain insects become immune to insecticides, and this increases the need for stronger poisons or new products. The cost of research is already high in the industry, and stockholders want higher dividends and less research expenditure.

Mr. Gordon has made speeches and written papers saying that the problem has been blown out of proportion by popular literature and that insecticides and pesticides produced by Wagner Chemical conform to government and company standards. He adds that to discontinue their use would endanger the health of the nation and cause a food shortage. He further contends that the real cause of harm to wildlife is misuse of the products and use of them too close to water and game reserves.

Mr. Wagner has evaluated his problem and finds that over one-third of his company's income is derived from insecticide and pesticide sales. He is convinced that his products conform to government standards, but he does not want to be responsible for the death of wildlife, pollution of streams, or possible damage to human beings.

He must also face pressures from stockholders to reduce research expenditures, from competition to keep costs down in order to get his share of the market, and from the public to make his products safe for general use. He cannot ignore these pressures.

Any research into the long-range effects upon plant and animal life is an extensive, formidable undertaking, and there is little chance of obtaining conclusive answers. He knows that competition would take over if he discontinued producing insecticides and pesticides. He feels that he is filling a need by producing them. Mr. Wagner wonders what he should do.

DISCUSSION QUESTIONS

1. Discuss the ecological aspects of this case.

2. Is Wagner Chemical Company responsible for damage to fish and wildlife by its chemicals? If not, who is?

3. To what extent should Mr. Wagner feel responsible for effects on human beings of his company's pesticides and insecticides?

4. Evaluate the arguments Mr. Wagner has been using in his speeches.

CASE 8

THE SAGA OF
CHRYSLER'S "CLEAN"
FOUNDRY[1]

In 1964, Chrysler Corporation, ignoring the advice of its own engineers and outside consultants, announced plans for the construction of a new foundry within a residential area on the east side of Detroit. The claims were extravagant. The one most frequently heard was that the plant would be pollution-free. It would have to be—rarely had a major foundry been planned so close to private homes.

Some people took the claim at face value. In May, 1967, *Factory Magazine* named it one of its "Top Ten Plants of the Year," citing specifically the lengths management had gone to to protect the environment around the plant.

What the editors of *Factory* overlooked was that less than 30 days after the plant had gone into limited debugging operations in October of 1966, occupants of the small, orderly homes immediately across Huber Avenue, on which the foundry is located, began filing complaints against it.

By the time the awards issue of *Factory* appeared, more than two dozen residents of the Huber community were threatening court action. Today, six years after start-up, Chrysler is still mired in lawsuits over the Huber foundry. Its attorneys like to think the end of litigation will come this fall. But attorneys for the residents like to think they are just getting started.

How did it happen that a so-called "clean" foundry was ever sited next to a residential community? And what ever became of the equipment that was meant to make that foundry "clean"?

[1]James Wargo, "The Saga of Chrysler's 'Clean' Foundry." Reprinted from *The MBA,* October 1972, by permission. Copyright © by MBA Communications, Inc., 1972.

The answers are really lessons. Chrysler has learned them at a cost of millions. Others can benefit from Chrysler's bad dream and save themselves the same amount or more.

According to Chrysler's official press release, the Huber Avenue location was selected because the company already owned the land, the site was adjacent to two other Chrysler production facilities, skilled labor was plentiful, and there were excellent rail connections to other Chrysler plants within a 30-mile radius.

Deal with Detroit

Jerome Cavanagh, at that time mayor of Detroit, tells it a different way. According to his version, he learned towards the end of his first term that Chrysler was planning to abandon an antiquated foundry on the east side and relocate production in an Ohio suburb.

At that time Detroit hadn't seen any new heavy industry for 11 years, and many other existing plants were cutting back or closing down. The relocating of Chrysler's foundry would idle another 2,500 Detroit workers.

Cavanagh soon learned that Chrysler's main objection to any site in Michigan was a special state tax on jigs, dies, tools and fixtures. He felt he had enough political clout with the state legislature to suspend the tax. Would Chrysler, he inquired through channels, build in Detroit if he could get the tax lifted?

No, came the reply, if the tax were removed Chrysler would probably build in nearby Warren, Michigan. Cavanagh applied personal pressure on Chrysler executives, and they relented. The Detroit bloc in the legislature succeeded in getting the tax lifted and Chrysler soon dropped plans for an Ohio foundry.

Designing a Clean Foundry

Actually Chrysler had reservations about the site other than the taxes. Across the street from what became the main entrance to the foundry was a neighborhood of lower middle class whites, primarily of central European ethnic origin. While they were good neighbors to a nearby Plymouth assembly plant, was it possible they could get to know and love a foundry as well?

Chrysler engineers said no. Chrysler consultants said no. Common sense said no. But Cavanagh said he had a man, Mort Sterling, in the city's air pollution control bureau who would sit in on planning sessions to guide Chrysler in equipping the foundry with those systems which would best protect the residents. Every pollution control system adopted had Sterling's stamp of approval.

In early spring of 1967, the Huber foundry went to work producing engine blocks, heads, flywheels, brakedisks and crankshafts. Casting operations were fed by two enclosed, water-cooled cupolas, each 108 inches in diameter and rated at 50 tons per hour, along with five 100-ton holding furnaces.

High-noise areas were protected by extensive sound-deadening devices. An exhaust system, aided by 33 dust collectors, was to have provided a complete in-plant change of air every eight minutes without discharging dust to the neighborhood.

Outwardly Clean

The outside of the plant, fronting Huber Avenue, was designed windowless, but is clean-cut and attractive. To this day it can pass as a long, but not unattractive suburban office structure, set 16 feet in from the sidewalk and fronted with a carefully manicured, treed lawn.

Unfortunately, with the exception of the trees, hardly anything that was designed to make the plant a good neighbor functioned as planned. Chrysler engineers think they know why, and their reason is a good one.

Their theory: the plant was too advanced. Many of the environmental systems were simply not designed to work that close to a residential community. And because environmental concerns were not commanding as much attention in 1964 as they are today, some of the systems purchased were, in effect, ordered out of catalogues—Chrysler was the first to buy them. When these systems malfunctioned, the suppliers were at as much of a loss to explain what was wrong as were Chrysler personnel. As for the neighbors, they really didn't give a damn. They were going to court. At least 328 of them are still there.

Raw Smoke and Dust

The first things to go wrong were two massive 105-inch fans installed to pull gas through the dust collectors. Within days of their first usage they began vibrating. Welds at the base of the blades would break, causing noise that was annoying as far as several blocks away. To kill the noise the fans were shut off. Since Chrysler was depending on the foundry for vital parts, operations continued while raw smoke and dust billowed out to settle over the neighbors.

After each failure there would be a meeting with the supplier ending with the same conclusion—that the welds had been faulty. In 14 months five replacement fans were ordered. Soon after installation, the breakdown process would begin again. In addition, the fans were turned on and off so often that the motors wore out. Bigger, more costly motors were ordered.

After the fifth fan failure it was determined by an outside consultant that the welds had been okay all along—but that the fan housing was poorly designed. It was of such a shape that it compressed the air before releasing it. The constant pulsing set up a rocking motion in the blades which in turn caused them to wobble and break. More than a year and a half after the first blade broke a new housing design abetted by tapered blades was put into operation, solving the problem.

But other problems, sometimes more easily solved, continued to plague the pollution control equipment for another two years. Each time one of the failures occurred, antipollution equipment would be shut down and billowing smoke would again blanket the neighborhood. The last cupola breakdown occurred in June, 1970, four years after the plant opened.

The Mysterious Hum

While the worst noise problem was fixed in 1968, grumblings continued about a hum. For months Chrysler officials dismissed these as crank complaints because they could hear nothing. The complaints continued, however, so Chrysler put some engineers on the job of figuring out why. They came back with nothing, yet residents continued to complain of a humming noise.

Eventually Chrysler hired an accoustician who went from house to house interviewing complainants. An inquisitive man with an open mind, he was willing to consider all factors. After several months he determined that those complaining found the hum most annoying at night. Checking their bedrooms he found that most measured 12 feet in width, or close to it. His ruling . . . the sound-deadening chamber above the new fans with their tapered blades was emitting a pure tone with a 12-foot wavelength. Anyone within two miles trying to sleep in a 12-foot-wide bedroom was being slowly driven off the scope.

Thinking the solution was within grasp, Chrysler broke into the sound deadening chamber to install different baffles only to find that the original baffles, glass fiber wrapped with mylar, had deteriorated from the surges of heat experienced with each fan breakdown.

Space-Age Solution

No longer sure that the heat surges were containable, Chrysler searched for a new means of wrapping the baffles. Normal suppliers could offer nothing able to tolerate the 600°F blasts. But an article on space-age technology led Chrysler to Du Pont which had developed a plastic that could take up to 750°F. Du Pont was willing to sell Chrysler as much as it wanted, but mentioned as an afterthought that no means of sealing the stuff existed. Chrysler people went into their labs, devised their own sealing method, and then encased the newly wrapped, newly designed baffles in stainless steel boxes. It worked. Lapsed time: about a year.

Concurrently, other Chrysler engineers were working to correct a flaw in Huber's auxiliary dust-collection system. Originally all 33 collectors were interconnected. When a single one broke down, the option was either to shut down the entire foundry or to keep working while dust poured out into the neighborhood. The obvious solution—and one which could have been avoided in the initial plant design—was to sectionalize the system so that malfunctioning units could be bypassed. In carrying this out it was discovered that butterfly valves originally designed to permit manual adjustment of dust flow had worn out because of the frequent adjustments needed.

The butterfly valves were replaced with pinch valves in late 1968. Limited failures of small groups of collectors continue to be experienced, sometimes as frequently as once every six or eight weeks, but they have been mild in comparison with the original ones and Chrysler, although not necessarily the neighbors, regards the problem as solved.

The Rotten Egg Smell

Some 18 months after the plant went into operation, residents began complaining of noxious odors. The rotten egg smell. Like everything else, it got worse. Chrysler checked each venting point under different conditions to trace the source of the foul air. Again a team of consultants was brought in. After several months they could only reduce the possible source to four auxiliary stacks over the core room.

For a while it was assumed that one of the vegetable by-products used in the core process was the cause, but months of experimentation got them nowhere. Finally, unable to isolate and stop the specific odor, Chrysler gave in and ordered an activated charcoal system for the vents instead. It went into operation in July of this year with Chrysler officials crossing their fingers. The system, very expensive for a plant the size of the Huber foundry, is even more costly to operate. Moreover, it was ordered without knowing the precise problem it was meant to correct.

The attorney for the majority of the complaining neighbors confided to a reporter that some of his clients admitted the odor problem had abated since the new equipment was installed. But the admission came a week before the activated charcoal system was put into operation!

While Chrysler's engineers and consultants were working to solve each problem that came up, the residents were complaining and suing. Top Chrysler executives were frequently confronted by the residents, by Mort Sterling (who in time was made head of the Wayne county air pollution control office into which his old office was incorporated), city councilmen, and a now-new mayor . . . all wanting to know what Chrysler was doing about the problem at Huber.

With each such visit or contact, Chrysler spokesmen tried to simplify the involved and frustrating work being conducted to resolve each main cause of complaint. The language was so complex, however, that the only thing a complainant would get out of it was, "We're doing everything we can"—an answer that rang increasingly hollow.

Monetary Settlements

When the fan weld problem was at its peak, Chrysler engaged Ottawa Appraisal Services to assess damages on neighborhood cars and houses. Many people were paid for their damages and a goodly number got sore as hell because they didn't get anything.

It was at this point that the neighbors began pooling their grievances and formulating a class action suit that is still sputtering today. The first person they went to was, of course, Mort Sterling. the people's recourse for air pollution problems. This is the same Mort Sterling who sat in on the planning of the foundry, who understood the complex nature of each breakdown, and the long road to each solution. His problem boiled down to one of keeping the citizens happy without unfairly penalizing a company that was doing all it could to solve problems for which it wasn't solely responsible in the first place. After all, Chrysler originally wanted to build in Ohio.

Mort Sterling's Solution

In October of 1971 Sterling found his out. He sued Chrysler under the Michigan Environmental Protection Act, scant hours after the law went into effect. This is a revolutionary law. It permits anyone to sue anyone else they regard as damaging the environment. An almost identical version has been proposed in Washington by Michigan Senator Phillip Hart. Under the Michigan law only civil action can be brought. You can get a polluter to stop, but you can't get him fined.

Sterling said he sued Chrysler to "get in writing (Chrysler's) oral agreement to shut down whenever equipment breakdowns occurred." Chrysler had been doing this for several months prior to Sterling's action. According to others, however, Sterling felt that by using the new Michigan law he could placate those demanding not sympathy but action and at the same time not increase the pressure on an already overburdened Chrysler.

Harried Chrysler officials were reluctant to view Sterling's motives so simply, and company attorneys took great pains in preparing and arguing any agreement they would consent to. They waited too long. According to a member of Sterling's staff, "We were within two paragraphs of an agreement" when the Huber 328 jumped in with both feet, properly entering the case as intervenors.

They had one goal in mind: to force into the court's decree an admission from Chrysler that it had wrongfully polluted the neighborhood. With this admission on the books, it would be child's play to get Chrysler to pay the claimed damages to health and property in a suit the 328 had already filed in another court.

Consent Decree Signed

After intervenors had blocked the signing of the settlement for more than a month, Chrysler attorneys appeared at a hearing and moved that the admittance of the intervenors to the case be reconsidered. Sterling rose and uttered token opposition, following which the judge granted the Chrysler motion and the settlement was signed.

The settlement established a binding policy for cupola shutdown and outlined an extensive maintenance program. Both Sterling and Chrysler attorneys agreed off the record that the entire program was in effect even before Sterling had sued under the environmental protection law.

The settlement was signed in October of last year. The Huber 328 continued their case. In June of this year it went to a jury, which found Chrysler to be culpable for all damages traceable to its plant emissions up to June, 1970.

That would seem to settle the case. Unfortunately there is a rather large discrepancy between what the plaintiff thinks the jury said and what Chrysler attorneys feel was decided.

The attorney for the plaintiffs thinks the decision included damage to health and he is prepared to argue each case independently, each one taking a week or more. Over at Chrysler, the jury's ruling is regarded as relating solely to property damages, and they delight in noting that a sizable number of the Huber 328 didn't reside there until after June, 1970.

It's a difference that a court must resolve, and it's one of those things that can drag on and on . . . as the Huber Foundry case has already done for almost eight years.

Racial Overtones

The local press in Detroit, which has never once reported that Chrysler originally opposed building in the city, handles the Huber affair as a straight environmental story. Chrysler has dirtied the air and corroded houses and cars——and the people want payment.

Just as Chrysler's $3 million struggle to make a "clean" plant clean is ignored so do some nuances in the plantiffs' motivation go uncommented upon. The residents were assumed to be motivated solely by a desire for a pollution-free neighborhood until the spring of last year, when the Federal Housing Administration announced it would cease guaranteeing loans on homes in the Huber area because of industrial pollution. The ban was subsequently limited to Huber Avenue and the street behind it. Other homes in the area, the revised FHA ruling said, would be eligible for loan guarantee provided the buyer signed a release stating awareness of industrial pollution in the area. With that development, protests against the foundry took on a new stridency.

The FHA release did not specify the foundry. There is ample evidence that other plants in the area contribute substantially to the neighborhood's periodic blanket of dust. Umbrage from the residents, however, was vented solely at the foundry.

The FHA, by its ruling, denied to the residents of the Huber area their one hope of selling their homes for anywhere near the value they themselves put on them. Being in an area long zoned for heavy industry, their homes are now among the least desirable in the eyes of any prospective buyer.

The children of the ethnic groups are moving to the suburbs, leaving only the poor to buy their old places with the aid of federal housing subsidies. Since January of this year, eight welfare recipients buying homes in the Huber area have defaulted and abandoned their homes, leaving them destined for demolition by the government. It is for the old timers in the Huber area the end of the neighborhood, the end of an era; and, since the foundry was the last thing to arrive on the scene before they noticed the change was irreversible, they are placing the blame solely on Chrysler.

Thus it is understandable why the counsel for the plaintiffs confides off the record that as soon as he finishes collecting for health damages he intends to launch action to get Chrysler or the government to buy all the homes in the area and then tear them down to create a buffer zone.

How far he gets remains to be seen. He himself admits that several of his clients have lost interest, moved out, and that there is no way for his client base to grow.

One top Chrysler executive, when asked what advice he would give to anyone searching for a site for a foundry, replied, "I'd tell him to get in his car and drive, and drive, and drive."

There is scarcely a city in the United States that is not mourning the fact that business and industry are fleeing to the suburbs. In each one of these cities is a mayor or a chamber of commerce breathing into the ear of the captains of local industry, trying to get them to expand, or at least to remain, in town.

Chrysler bowed to just such pressure in 1964 and has been up to its ears in litigation ever since. There is no doubt a solution to the problems of both the Detroits and the Chryslers. But, as has been learned from the Huber Avenue experience, these solutions must be proceeded toward very, very carefully.

DISCUSSION QUESTIONS

1. What are the issues involved? As a member of Chrysler management, how would you solve each one?

2.   Three main groups were involved in this case: Chrysler officials, public officials, and the people living near the foundry. In what ways did each group act responsibly and irresponsibly?

3.   To what extent could the problems encountered by Chrysler have been avoided by moving to either of the alternative locations originally considered by the company? Explain.

A REPORT ON OPERATIONS OF AN AFFILIATE AND A SUBSIDIARY OF TEXACO, INC., IN THE REPUBLIC OF SOUTH AFRICA[1]

The accompanying report has been prepared by Texaco Inc. ("Texaco") in response to inquiries received from institutions holding Texaco stock, requesting information concerning Texaco's interests in the Republic of South Africa. Certain of these requests have come from church groups in the United States, including the World Division of the Board of Global Ministries of the United Methodist Church, beneficial owner of a substantial number of shares of Texaco stock.

Texaco believes that it has an obligation to keep its stockholders informed concerning important matters affecting Company interests. It has, therefore, assembled the requested data relating to its affiliated and subsidiary companies which operate in South Africa. These are: Caltex Oil (S.A.) (Pty.) Limited ("Caltex Oil"), 50% owned, which conducts refining and marketing operations; and Regent Petroleum South Africa Ltd., 100% owned, which surrendered a half interest in one offshore sublease in South Africa acquired for programs of exploration and production of petroleum, but continues to hold a half interest in another such offshore sublease. Since Caltex Oil alone has employees within the Republic of South Africa, the report is largely concerned with its operations.

In providing this information, Texaco wishes to draw attention to several factors which it believes should be carefully weighed in any consideration of Caltex Oil's operations in the Republic of South Africa.

[1] Reproduced in full from an insert in *The Texaco Star*, vol. 60, no. 2, 1973. Copyright 1973. Reproduced with permission of Texaco, Inc.

An appraisal of Caltex Oil's operations in South Africa will show that its activities there have improved the economic and social conditions of its non-white employees. Such an appraisal, however, may indicate that the political conditions affecting Caltex Oil's non-white employes have not been affected in any material way. In Texaco's view, there are compelling reasons why an American-owned corporation cannot and should not engage in activities of a political nature, and why it would be improper for Caltex Oil to engage in political activity in South Africa in an attempt to influence change in its racial laws.

In the United States, the restriction prohibiting political activity by corporations is mandated by law. Over the years, it has been evident that the people of the United States uphold the principle of the non-political role of corporations; the Congress and state legislatures have elaborated this principle in a varied series of laws, and our courts have affirmed it in case after case. All of these laws and court decisions, backed by public opinion, have combined to make it clear that American corporations should aim their operations at the economic and commercial spheres and not the political.

We strongly feel that corporations should serve strictly commercial purposes and that it would contravene their role in society to be used as instruments for political activity.

Since its founding in 1902, Texaco has made every effort to avoid involvement in political activities. Affiliates and subsidiaries of Texaco operating outside the Unites Stated have followed the same principle.

The most cogent statement of this long-standing policy was published back in 1958 in the Company's magazine, *The Texaco Star,* in an article written by Augustus C. Long, who was Chairman and Chief Executive Officer of the Company at that time. "Texaco," Mr. Long wrote, "has played a leading role in international oil. We have made our investments on a long-range basis, and with full knowledge of the costs and risks that are involved. In our relations with foreign governments, we have found that our best protection lies in living up fully to our obligations, concentrating on the oil business, and staying out of politics. At the same time, we have done everything possible to make a maximum contribution to the welfare and progress of the countries in which we have worked. We have prospered under this policy, and we intend to continue living by it."

The reasons for keeping corporations out of politics are well known to managers in the 135 countries and territories where the Company's subsidiaries and affiliates are engaged in business. If these companies were to engage in politics, it is highly probable that many of their respective governments would cause them to cease operations within their borders.

While a corporation such as Caltex Oil, which is registered to do business in South Africa, must abide by the laws of the country in which it operates, this does not, however, imply agreement with such laws.

The system known as "apartheid" in South Africa is a political matter subject only to political decision by the people of the Republic of South Africa. It has aroused the concern of other nations, and has come under close and continuing study by the United Nations. The United States Government is also concerned with this question as a matter of foreign policy. Under the laws of the United States, only the government may conduct its foreign policy, and it is specifically contrary to the law for any individual American citizen or corporation to attempt to carry out such activity.

A publication issued by the National Council of Churches has questioned the ethical and moral validity of investments by American corporations in South Africa, contending that such investments have the effect of "strengthening the existing regime." The publication said:

> Corporations would like the public to believe that progressive employment policies and greater investments are the starting point and key to change in South Africa. However, the issue in South Africa is not one of 'material well-being' which greater investment might bring, if indeed there were a direct and substantial benefit accruing to the oppressed majority. The issue is rather the right of African, Asian and Colored people to self-determination.

In reply to this position, Texaco offers the following points for consideration by its stockholders:

1. If self-determination is the issue in South Africa, then this is entirely a political matter in which no American-owned company incorporated in South Africa, such as Caltex Oil, can properly take a part.

2. Since self-determination in South Africa is a political issue, the proper channel for representations to the Government of South Africa by Americans concerned with this issue is the United States Government. Through its Embassy in South Africa and its Representative at the United Nations, the United States Government is in a position to make known the views of its citizens.

3. The material well-being of its employes in South Africa is the primary area which Caltex Oil can properly affect through its operations. The record clearly shows that Caltex Oil is making steady improvement in the well-being of all of its employes in South Africa, both white and non-white; in fact, the Caltex Oil wages rank among the highest in that country. In addition, the Caltex Oil record shows that the company is making every effort to treat non-white employes in a manner equal to that accorded all other employes.

A proposal of some U.S. citizens concerned with South Africa is that American corporations operating in South Africa withdraw entirely from that country. Texaco believes such a withdrawal would be harmful to the people of South Africa as well as to the interests of Texaco stockholders. Texaco also believes that such action would produce an effect opposite to that sought by those seeking to improve the lot of non-whites in South Africa.

Such action would endanger the jobs of the hundreds of non-whites employed by Caltex Oil. If American companies were to withdraw from South Africa, they would quickly be replaced by local companies or by companies based in other industrialized nations of the world. The economic and social advances presently being achieved by non-white employes might well be interrupted by any such change.

In addition, withdrawal of American investments from South Africa would constitute economic sanction. The use of economic coercion of this type is regarded as an extremely serious matter in international relations and is of direct concern to corporations whose operations are affected by such sanctions. Nations that invoke economic sanctions usually take this action after diplomatic efforts have failed to produce a desired result; the invoking nations believe they are seeking a method of achieving their ends short of armed conflict, and may consider economic measures to be an acceptable peaceful means. In most cases, however, economic sanctions immediately heighten rather than reduce international tensions and encourage the very conditions that often lead to extremism and conflict. Moreover, the history of such sanctions indicates that they rarely if ever achieve the purposes for which they were designed. Instead, they set new and unexpected forces in motion and frequently accelerate the trends they were intended to deter. Economic sanctions are therefore a dubious method for bringing about peaceful social and political changes in any country.

Both in its own operations, and in those conducted by affiliated and subsidiary companies, Texaco continues to believe it can perform its most useful function by concentrating on its business, by complying with local laws, by living up to its obligations, and by staying out of politics. In its 71-year history, Texaco and its subsidiary and affiliated companies have helped the economic advancement of peoples throughout the world by providing for the supplies of energy essential to improving standards of life. Texaco has constantly sought to provide its employes with fair salaries, decent working conditions, and generous benefits. By adhering to its business goals and principles, it has contributed to the growth of international trade, which has enhanced the prosperity and peaceful prospects of nations around the globe.

As shown in the accompanying report, Caltex Oil has functioned in a creditable manner in the Republic of South Africa. It has demonstrated that it can bring and is bringing improvements to the lives of both white and non-white employes. Caltex Oil should be given due credit for these past accomplishments, and should be encouraged by the stockholders of Texaco to continue its good work in the years ahead.

THE REPORT
I. History

Caltex Oil (S.A.) (Pty.) Limited ("Caltex Oil") is incorporated under the laws of the Republic of South Africa and conducts petroleum refining and marketing operations in that country. Texaco Inc. ("Texaco") and Standard Oil Company of California each hold a 50% interest in Caltex Oil, whose history dates back to 1911. In that year, a subsidiary of The Texas Company (as Texaco was then known) began marketing kerosine, gasoline, and lubricants in what was then the Union of South Africa. In 1936, Standard Oil Company of California acquired a 50% interest in the Texaco subsidiary operating in South Africa and the Caltex name was given to such company. Caltex Oil began operation of a refinery at Milnerton, near Cape Town, in 1966 and today this plant, with 50,000-barrel-a-day capacity, supplies a full range of petroleum products in the Republic. The total Caltex Oil investment in South Africa is approximately $100 million in marketing and refining operations.

Until recently a second company, Regent Petroleum South Africa Ltd. ("Regent"), 100% Texaco-owned, held a half interest in a sublease covering 3,526,000 acres offshore South Africa for the exploration and production of petroleum. Chevron Oil Company of South Africa ("Chevron"), a subsidiary of Standard Oil Company of California, held the other 50% interest in the sublease. An exploratory well on which drilling was commenced in December, 1972, resulted in a dry hole; subsequently, the Regent and Chevron interests in this sublease were relinquished in April, 1973.

All work on the sublease was conducted by independent service contractors, and neither Chevron nor Regent had employes in South Africa for the venture. Investments by the two owner companies totaled approximately $5,000,000, and $40,000 was paid to the Government of South Africa in acreage rentals.

In addition, the same two companies each hold a half interest in an offshore sublease covering approximately 7,000,000 acres in South African territorial waters. Seismic work is presently being conducted by an independent service contractor.

Since most of the questions raised with respect to Texaco's interests in South Africa do not apply to this exploration venture, the following information refers only to the activities of Caltex Oil.

The operations of Caltex Oil in South Africa have been profitable, but Caltex Oil does not publish its annual earnings; its figures are, however, reflected in the consolidated financial statements of its owner companies. The profits of Caltex Oil are considered to be competitive and proprietary information.

Caltex Oil is a substantial taxpayer in South Africa, and to the extent that such taxes were used by the Government of South Africa to finance its national health, educational, and other social programs, Caltex Oil indirectly contributes to the support of such programs.

During 62 years of activity in South Africa by itself and predecessor companies, Caltex Oil has employed people representing all of the major racial groups in South Africa—Africans, Asians, Coloreds, and Whites. In 1962, the number of Caltex Oil employes totaled 2,400, comprising 776 Africans, 7 Asians, 259 Coloreds, and 1,358 Whites. In 1972, the total number of such employes was 1,830, made up of 394 Africans, 24 Asians, 189 Coloreds, and 1,223 Whites. The

Average Monthly Wage (in U.S. Dollars)

Salary Class	Typical Positions	Africans 1962	Africans 1972	Asians 1962	Asians 1972	Colored 1962	Colored 1972	Whites 1962	Whites 1972
1B	Cleaner, General Laborer, Watchman, Messenger	63	115	—	129	67	118	—	—
1A	Aircraft Refueling Assistant, Boiler Attendant, Bunkering Assistant	74	132	—	—	79	151	—	—
1	Chauffeur, Clerical Assistant, Forklift Operator, Handyman	85	155	90	165	87	174	95	—
2	Gauger, Printing Operator, Package Driver, Senior Clerical Assistant, Checker, Loader, Asphalt Plant Operator	—	184	—	—	—	204	—	—
3	Senior Printing Operator, Junior Clerk, Stores Assistant, Laboratory Tester, Trainee Operator, Stenographer	—	—	—	212	—	240	136	215
4	Printing Foreman, Operator, Fieldman, Sr. Stenographer	—	—	—	255	—	254	166	268
5	Truck Operator, Laboratory Technician, Clerk, Secretary, Guard	—	227	—	258	—	274	201	333
6	Laboratory Technician, Mechanic, Senior Clerk, Programmer Trainee	—	—	—	—	—	357	240	419
7	Draftsman, Accountant, Programmer, Sales Representative	—	—	—	512	—	472	292	507
8 and above	Supervisory and Middle, Senior, and Top Management positions								

Note: 1. The above 1972 wages include a pro rata of one month's pay as Christmas bonus.
Note: 2. The conversion rate used for the above and all other salary amounts is 1 Rand = U.S. $1.325.

Table A Wages by functional job descriptions comparing African, Asian, Colored, and White workers.

Salary Class	1962				1972			
	Africans	Asians	Colored	Whites	Africans	Asians	Colored	Whites
1B	481	0	160	0	156	1	38	0
1A	275	0	89	0	142	0	48	0
1	14	3	6	14	49	1	50	0
2	6	4	4	17	5	0	15	0
3	0	0	0	88	0	6	19	13
4	0	0	0	380	0	3	9	28
5	0	0	0	141	42	11	8	274
6	0	0	0	246	0	0	1	323
7	0	0	0	248	0	2	1	173
8 and above	0	0	0	224	0	0	0	412
Totals	776	7	259	1358	394	24	189	1223

Table B   Number of employes by ethnic groups.

reduction in total numbers over this 11-year span occurred as part of a worldwide reduction in total Caltex employes during the 1965-68 period. This reduction was caused by increased productivity and by automation of the type which occurred earlier in the United States.

The 1972 and 1962 wages for the types of jobs held by the employes of different racial groups employed by Caltex Oil are described in Table A. The numbers of employes occupying the various categories of jobs are given in Table B. From these tables, it is evident that, in general, non-white employes are occupying positions requiring relatively less education, training, skill, and experience. However, as indicated in the tables and in the subsequent description of Caltex Oil training programs, the non-whites are steadily advancing to higher jobs.

Caltex Oil makes substantial contributions to a number of South African charitable, educational, health, and community organizations; such donations rose from a total of $47,900 in 1963 to $127,400 in 1972. Such contributions were intended to assist all major racial groups, directly or indirectly (see Table C).

II. Relations with Workers

As a company incorporated in South Africa, Caltex Oil is required to observe the laws of the Republic of South Africa. However, the Company has consistently gone beyond the minimum standards set by law, i.e., in terms of higher salaries and more generous benefits, as well as in opportunities for training and advancement. There are no trade unions or work committees among the employes of Caltex Oil in South Africa; however, Caltex Oil does not oppose the establishment of unions or work committees. Any grievances which arise are handled through normal supervisory levels and can be appealed to higher levels of the Company.

Over the past 11 years there has been a steady improvement in the salary rates, employe benefits, and promotions for all groups of Caltex Oil employes —Africans, Asians, Coloreds, and Whites.

Organization	1963	1972
Major Community Donations*		
South Africa Foundation	$ 7,000	$ 7,000
South African Wildlife Foundation	—	7,000
South African Road Federation	1,400	1,400
South African National Tuberculosis Association	1.400	1,400
National Veld Trust	1,400	1,400
1820 British Settlers Monument Trust	1,400	1,400
South African Road Research Council	2,100	2,100
Cape Town Community Chest	1,400	1,800
Boys' Town	—	1,400
Schools and Universities**		
University grants, equally to 11 universities	10,000	43,300
Post Graduate Scholarship—School of Business Administration		
Bursaries	—	1,400
University of Zululand	600	2,800
University of Fort Hare	600	2,800
University of Turfloop, in the Transvaal	300	2,800
Natal University for Indians	900	2,800
University of Western Cape	900	2,800
Wilderness Leadership School (Training in Conservation for		
Service in National Game Reserve)	—	1,800
Minor National Donations	5,000	15,800
Provides for minor national charities in amounts ranging from $700 to $50		
Minor Charities in Branch Areas	5,000	15,000
Various small amounts disbursed to worthy causes by Branch Managers		
Farm Planning and Farm Management	8,500	11,200
Provides for 4 seminars of 15 conferees each, covering travel expenses of conferees to and from their homes, accommodations, and the production of materials required for each seminar		
Totals	**$46,500**	**$127,400**

*See Footnotes C-1.
**See Footnotes C-2.

Footnotes C-1

South African Wildlife Foundation—Formed in 1968, the Foundation promotes the conservation of wildlife, and is affiliated with the World Wildlife Fund. It is sponsored mainly by business organizations and private citizens. It also contributes to support of a Chair of Wildlife Management at Pretoria University.

South Africa Foundation—Independent, nonprofit, nonpolitical organization sponsored by private industry to promote understanding by overseas business concerns having interests in South Africa of constructive efforts to solve social and industrial problems in the country. It frequently sponsors visits to South Africa by prominent overseas figures.

South African Road Federation—Supports research and development in highway engineering and route planning.

South African National Tuberculosis Association—Organized in 1947, the Association consists entirely of voluntary workers who establish and staff their own treatment centers. The South African Government subsidizes more than 85% of the budget.

National Veld Trust—A nonprofit organization formed in 1942 which depends principally on public support. Promotes conservation through combatting soil erosion.

1820 British Settlers Monument Trust—Set up to finance the erection of a suitable monument to commemorate landing of the British settlers near Port Elizabeth in 1820. Monument will consist of a library, museum, and conference center, and will be erected at Grahamstown.

South African Road Research Council—Concerns itself with various aspects of highway construction, such as environmental impact, roadbed construction, and surfacing materials.

Cape Town Community Chest—Provides for the needs of underprivileged families at the social welfare level. It is Coloreds principally who benefit from the proceeds of this fund.

Boys' Town—Institution situated in the Transvaal, near the Natal border, which works to rehabilitate white schoolboys with criminal records. It was established in 1958 as a registered welfare organization. It is also registered as a private school, but depends on welfare funds for operations. Cost per resident is R680 ($865) per year.

Footnotes C-2
Universities Receiving Equal Caltex Oil Grants

Cape Town	(Mainly Whites, some Coloreds)
Stellenbosch	(Whites only)
Grahamstown	(Whites only)
University of South Africa	(All races)
Port Elizabeth	(Whites only
Orange Free State	(Whites only)
Natal	(Indians only)
Pretoria	(Afrikaans, Whites only)
Potschefstroom	(Whites only)
Witwatersrand	(Mainly Whites, some Coloreds)
Rand Afrikaans	(Whites only)

Bursaries

University of Zululand	(Blacks only)
University of Fort Hare	(Blacks only)
University of Turfloop	(Blacks only)
Natal University for Indians	(Indians only)
University of Western Cape	(Cape Coloreds only)

Table C   Caltex Oil (S.A.) (Pty.) Limited contributions in and for the Republic of South Africa.

A comparison of salary ranges between 1962 and 1972 shows that the salary ranges for Caltex Oil's non-white employes have steadily advanced in relation to salary ranges for white employes of Caltex Oil. Today the salary ranges in all job classifications are the same for both white and non-white employes (see Table D).

For example, in 1962 the salary range for non-whites in one job category was $80 minimum and $103 maximum per month, while the salary range for whites in the same job classification was $114 minimum and $172 maximum. Today there is a single salary range for this job classification which applies equally to both white and non-white employes; the monthly minimum is $152 and the maximum is $226.

The length of the work week for employes of Caltex Oil is the same for white and non-white employes. Office employes in the Cape Town headquarters offices, for example, work 36¼ hours a week, Monday through Friday. Most refinery employes, white and non-white, work a scheduled 40-hour week.

Salary Class	White Salary Ranges January 1, 1962		Non-White Salary Ranges January 1, 1962	
	Minimum	Maximum	Minimum	Maximum
1	—	—	57	80
2	—	—	69	92
3	114	172	80	103
4	140	209	—	—
5	170	254	—	—
6	201	305	—	—
7	244	371	—	—
8	292	437	—	—
9	352	529	—	—
10	419	623	—	—
11	498	742	—	—

	Salary Ranges—All Employes—Whites and Non-Whites* May 1, 1972		
1B	113	169	Relates to positions in Salary Class 1 as of 1/1/62
1A	130	197	Relates to positions in Salary Class 2 as of 1/1/62
1	152	226	Relates to positions in Salary Class 3 as of 1/1/62
2	177	262	
3	205	305	
4	244	366	
5	295	438	
6	352	524	
7	416	632	
8	503	754	
9	596	897	
10	711	1069	
11	854	1285	

*Salary ranges for May 1, 1972, include a pro rata of an extra month's pay given to all employes each year as a Christmas bonus. Truck operators and clerks in Class 5 have a special range extending from minimum Class 4 to maximum Pay Class 5.

Table D   Salary ranges in job classifications. The conversion rate used is 1 Rand = U.S. $1.325.

As for benefit plans. Caltex Oil has long provided numerous benefits to its employes in pensions, health care, vacations, sick leave, accident insurance, subsidized cafeterias, and other forms of assistance. While there were some differences in these plans as between white and non-white employes in 1962, the benefits of such plans are now identical (see Table E). For example, both white and non-white employes are eligible for three weeks' annual paid vacation upon joining Caltex Oil, four weeks' annual vacation after 10 years of service, and five weeks' annual vacation after 20 years of service. Also, all employes, white and non-white, after five years of service are eligible for the Caltex Home Ownership Plan, whereby Caltex Oil guarantees up to 100% of home mortgage loans. A full comparison of the benefit plans since 1962 is contained in the table [pages 581–583].

In its training and promotions programs, Caltex Oil has been active in providing opportunities for both white and non-white employes to better their positions in the company. A list of the number of promotions earned each year since 1962 is contained in Table F. Not indicated in this list, however, is the

Whites			Non-Whites		
Plan	Purpose of Plan	Changes to Plan	Plan	Purpose of Plan	Changes to Plan
Contributory Pension Plan	To provide benefits for employes of the company on their retirement through age or ill health, and for their dependents.	*January 1, 1962*—Career Salary Plan with Life Assurance Benefit. Improved in 1964, 1968, 1969, and 1971.	Non-contributory Pension Plan	To provide a pension and a lump sum retirement or death benefit allowance.	*January 1, 1962*—Career Salary Plan with credit for service prior to January 1, 1961, at 1¼% annual wage as of date installation plus 1½% aggregate wage for all service after December 31, 1960, with lump sum retirement allowance. Increased in 1968 and 1970.

May 1, 1972—Rules amended to include all employes (whites and non-whites) on same basis in Contributory Pension Plan.

Whites			Non-Whites		
Ill-Health Retirement	To make a special provision for retirement in cases of serious ill health.	*January 1, 1962*—Payment after termination of service of 12 months' salary over 48 months, employe provided with death benefit coverage equivalent to two years' salary for four-year period, employe contributions to Pension Plan returned. *April 1, 1964*—Disability Pension provided in accordance with Pension Plan if employe has completed 15 years of pensionable service. *August 1, 1971*—Disability Pension provided after completion 10 years' pensionable service.	Ill-Health Retirement	To make a special provision for retirement in cases of serious ill health.	*January 1, 1962*—Non-contributory Pension Plan provided maximum benefit of 12 months' salary for employes under 50 years of age, if 50 years of age and over received early retirement. Discontinued Pension. *May 1, 1972*—Cash payment and Disability Pension provided according to Pension Plan—same benefits as are applicable to white employes.
Recognition of Long Service	To standardize procedures for the marking of long-service achievements.	*January 1, 1962, to date*—Service award emblems presented every 5 years, gold watch at 30 years.	Same	Same	*January 1, 1962, to date*—Same program as applicable to white employes.

	Whites		Non-Whites		
Plan	Purpose of Plan	Changes to Plan	Plan	Purpose of Plan	Changes to Plan
Vacation Leave	Provides for vacation leave with full pay.	*January 1, 1962*—Under 10 years' service or less than age 30—three weeks' vacation. Over 10 years' service—four weeks' vacation. *April 1, 1966*—As above plus—on completion 20 years' service—five weeks' vacation.	Same	Same	*January 1, 1962*—All employes—three weeks' vacation. *October 1, 1968*—As above plus—on completion 20 years' service—four weeks' vacation. *January 1, 1973*—Same program as applicable to white employes.
Sick Leave	To make provision for sick leave.	*January 1, 1962*—Government wage determination of one day per month with maximum of 24 days in each two years of service, improved in 1964 and 1968. *January 1, 1973*—Twenty-four days for each completed 24 months' service, noncumulative.	Same	Same	*January 1, 1962*—Same as for whites. *January 1, 1973*—Same as for whites.
Medical Aid Plan	To provide insurance against the cost of medical treatment in the case of illness or injury.	*January 1, 1962, to date*—Subsidised Plan providing reimbursement of costs in accordance preferential medical aid tariff as follows: Surgical 100% Medical or Dental Hospital 80% Medicine 50% Employe pays monthly premium based on number of dependents: Single employe $ 4 per month Married + 5 dependents $11 per month	Same	Same	*January 1, 1962, to date*—Same as for whites; however, provincial hospitals supply all services at low cost in accordance with salary earned. Example: Charge for visit to outpatient department 27¢ for employe with monthly salary of $106.
Medical Policy	To provide pre-employment and periodic medical examinations. Special periodic examinations are carried out in cases where the employe's duties may be of a hazardous nature.	*January 1, 1962, to date*—Pre-employment periodic and special examinations provided to all employes.	Same	Same	*January 1, 1962, to date*—Same as for whites.

Travel Accident Insurance Plan	To provide special insurance against accident while the employe is traveling on company business.	*January 1, 1962, to date*—Company provides Travel Accident insurance for employe traveling outside city of assignment by air or sea on company business.	Same	Same	*January 1, 1962, to date*—Same as for whites.
Home Ownership Plan	Facilitates borrowing of part or all of a down payment on a home.	*January 1, 1965*—Eligibility to participate requires minimum of 5 years' pensionable service. Company guarantees loan to make up 100% mortgage. *May 1, 1971*—Qualifying pensionable service one to 5 years.	Same	Same	*May 1, 1971, to date*—Same as for whites. *May 1, 1971, to date*—Same as for whites.
Transfer Expense and Transfer Reimbursement Policies	To provide reimbursement for the costs involved when an employe is transferred.	*January 1, 1962, to date*—Reimbursement of all relocation cost when transferred by company.	Same	Same	*January 1, 1962, to date*—Same as for whites.
Educational Assistance Plan for Employes	To cover the full cost incurred by employes who successfully complete approved study courses on their own time.	*April 1, 1966, to date*—Reimbursement of costs incurred by employe for approved study costs.	Same	Same	*April 1, 1966, to date*—Same as for whites.

Table F: Fringe benefits since 1962.

	Whites	Non-Whites
1962	23	14
1963	47	24
1964	64	28
1965	51	31
1966	80	32
1967	69	11
1968	83	26
1969	185	54
1970	167	10
1971	124	29
1972	123	58

Table F Annual promotions.

progressive action taken by Caltex Oil to open to non-white employes certain jobs such as gasoline transport truck drivers and refinery operators.

In a highly industrialized country such as the United States, the position of truck driver in the oil industry carries with it considerable responsibility, both financial and operational; the driver handles company funds, performs accounting functions, and must be a skilled and responsible driver, as indicated by the average wage rates for this position in the U.S. Similarly, in South Africa, the truck driver for an oil company holds a position of considerable responsibility and prestige with his fellow workers. In the case of the refinery operators, there is a requirement for technological knowledge and aptitude which gives this position considerable prestige and makes promotions to it also highly desirable.

As evidence of such progress, 12 non-whites in 1969 occupied positions in Caltex Oil which under applicable law had been previously reserved only for whites; in 1972 a total of 98 non-whites occupied such positions.

Caltex Oil seeks to encourage all employes to further their own advancement by offering opportunities for technical training and education both on and off the job. These programs are open to all employes, regardless of race. At the Caltex Oil refinery, there are training programs for jobs in the laboratories, tank farm operation, product blending and shipping, processing operations, and warehousing control. Today, as one result, the staff of the refinery laboratory consists of 2 white and 16 non-white employes. In the marketing organization, there are training programs for sales representatives, truck operators, clerks, and supervisors.

The progress in the training programs of all types has resulted in more balance between participants of the different racial groups. In 1972, there were 221 white and 50 non-white trainees. In 1973, there will be approximately 170 white and 93 non-white participants; the latter figure includes 14 employes who will be trained for skilled positions as refinery process operators.

Further to help employes in their own careers, Caltex Oil also reimburses 100% of the tuition and examination fees for technical and academic courses completed by all employes.

While Caltex Oil provides personnel counseling to individual employes of all races, it provides legal assistance only with respect to actions wherein company interests or property are involved.

The employes of Caltex Oil are predominantly South African, with only 15 United States and 4 United Kingdom expatriates employed out of a total of 1,830. Caltex Oil does not engage in any international recruiting or hiring for its operations in South Africa, and has no present business plans to invest in the Bantu areas.

III. Relations with the Government of South Africa

Caltex Oil (S.A.) (Pty.) Limited, as a South African company, must comply with the laws of the land in which it is incorporated. While Caltex Oil as a nonpolitical private corporation does not engage in political action to persuade the government of South Africa to modify the laws applicable to its citizens, Caltex Oil has been active in assisting its African, Asian, and Colored employes in dealing with the problems that can arise as a result of complicated racial laws.

Although the Official Secrets Act of the Republic of South Africa prohibits Caltex Oil from disclosing information relating to products or services sold to the South African Government, following is a list of South African laws which directly affect Caltex Oil in its employment practices:

1. The Factories Act of 1941
2. The Physical Planning and Resources Act of 1967
3. The Bantu Labour Settlement of Disputes Act
4. The Group Areas Act No. 36 of 1966
5. The Bantu Labour Act No. 67 of 1964
6. The Bantu Urban Areas Consolidation Act No. 25 of 1945
7. The Wage Act of 1956
8. The Unemployment Insurance Act
9. The Workmen's Compensation Act
10. Liquid Fuel and Oil Trade Wage Determination Under the Act of 1956
11. Bantu Services Levy and Transport Services Act
12. Registration of Employment Act
13. Transport Services for Colored Persons and Indians Act of 1972
14. The Shops and Offices Act of 1964
15. The Workmen's Wage Protection Act No. 40 of 1956
16. The Apprenticeship Act No. 37 of 1944
17. The Training of Artisans Act of 1951

*   *   *

In summary, Texaco believes that the record of Caltex Oil in its treatment of all of its South African employes shows that, while complying with South African laws, the company has made considerable progress in the fields of salaries, training, job assignments, and benefit plans.

DISCUSSION QUESTIONS

1. Is Texaco acting socially responsible in this situation? Discuss in what ways it may be doing so and in what ways it may not be doing so.

2. What actions, if any, do you propose that the company should take to be more socially responsible? Discuss, dealing in specifics rather than generalities, and being realistic in terms of the situation in which the company finds itself.

3. Should Texaco leave South Africa? What would be the benefits and disadvantages to Texaco and to South Africa? What other social investment groups are involved and how would they be affected?

4. Do you recommend political activity in South Africa by the company on racial issues? Specifically what kinds of actions do you recommend, if any? Discuss.

NAME INDEX

SUBJECT INDEX